Inside Distributed COM

Guy Eddon
Henry Eddon

PUBLISHED BY
Microsoft Press
A Division of Microsoft Corporation
One Microsoft Way
Redmond, Washington 98052-6399

Library of Congress Cataloging-in-Publication Data
Eddon, Guy, 1974-
    Inside Distributed COM / Guy Eddon, Henry Eddon.
      p.   cm.
    Includes bibliographical references and index.
    ISBN 1-57231-849-X. -- ISBN 1-57231-849-X
    1. Electronic data processing--Distributed processing.
   2. Application software--Development.   I. Eddon, Henry, 1945-   .
   II. Title.
   QA76.9.D5E33   1998
   005.2'76--dc21   98-12108
                                                  CIP

Printed and bound in the United States of America.

2 3 4 5 6 7 8 9 QMQM 3 2 1 0 9 8

Distributed to the book trade in Canada by Macmillan of Canada, a division of Canada Publishing Corporation.

A CIP catalogue record for this book is available from the British Library.

Microsoft Press books are available through booksellers and distributors worldwide. For further information about international editions, contact your local Microsoft Corporation office. Or contact Microsoft Press International directly at fax (425) 936-7329. Visit our Web site at mspress.microsoft.com.

Acquisitions Editor: Eric Stroo
Project Editor: Patricia N. Wagner
Technical Editor: Robert Lyon

To Gali and Maya

CONTENTS

PART III REMOTING ARCHITECTURE 287

CHAPTER TEN

The Interface Definition Language   373

CHAPTER ELEVEN

Security   399

Foreword

Well, it's been over a decade since I started writing applications for Microsoft Windows. Back then, it was easy for someone to say they really understood Windows and all of its subsystems. Each of these subsystems exposed only a few hundred functions: in Windows 2.11, Kernel had 283, User had 141, and GDI had 213, for a grand total of 637 functions. How hard could it be to understand what these few functions did?

Over the past 10 years, Microsoft has greatly extended these modules and has added numerous subsystems to Windows: telephony, remote access, print spoolers, 3-D graphics, Internet access, security, registry, services, multimedia, networking, and so on. It is now impossible for any individual to fully understand the entire operating system. For this reason, I advise developers to pick certain components of the system, study them, learn them, and become specialists in them. This is not to say that you should ignore other parts of the system—I have specialized in Kernel and User, but I have also dabbled in GDI, networking, and lots of other areas.

At Microsoft, different teams develop each of these subsystems and each team develops its own "philosophy." For example, I know that the registry functions all start with a *Reg* prefix and return an error code. But I also know that most Kernel functions have no special prefix and return *FALSE* if they fail; in these cases, I have to call *GetLastError* to see the reason for the failure. This inconsistent behavior among subsystems is one of the reasons Windows programming has had a reputation for being difficult to learn. Many developers refer to this inconsistency as "job security."

It should be obvious to everyone that Microsoft is firmly committed to Windows for the present and the foreseeable future. Microsoft wants the entire world (and probably beyond) to adopt Windows. To achieve this end, Microsoft needs a plan that allows new subsystems to be added to the system without steepening the developer's learning curve too much. In other words, there must be consistency in using the various subsystems (or components). One of the major technologies that addresses this need is Microsoft's Component Object Model (COM).

Microsoft exposes any new technology by implementing each new subsystem as a COM object. You can easily see this design when you use directory services (Active Directory Services Interface), transaction services (Microsoft Transaction Server), graphics (DirectX), shell extensions, controls (ActiveX controls), data (OLE DB), scripting (ActiveX scripting), and on and on. COM is now *the* way to interact with these subsystems. In fact, in an effort to reduce the Windows learning curve for new developers, Microsoft is going back to older subsystems and reexposing those systems as COM objects. The result of this reworking should be more evident by the year 2000.

For now, it is imperative that Windows developers understand the core infrastructure of COM. This understanding will enable you to easily take advantage of these new subsystems as well as make it easier for you to expose your own subsystems. Distributed computing is a massive undertaking requiring that many difficult problems be addressed, such as data transfer, incompatible computer architectures, disparate network architectures, timing issues, and so on. Fortunately, Microsoft has teams of developers working to solve these problems and make things easier for the rest of us. Microsoft Windows NT 4.0 shipped with the first release of Microsoft's solution: the Distributed Component Object Model (DCOM).

Clearly, this technology is in its infancy and much work remains to be done, but Microsoft is just as committed to DCOM as it is to Windows itself. With Microsoft firmly behind DCOM, there is no doubt that it will be the best way to interact with subsystems, not only on a single machine but also on any computer anywhere in the world (and possibly beyond). *Inside Distributed COM* can be our guidebook. Let's keep our fingers crossed and hope that it is translated into Martian.

Jeffrey Richter

Preface

In this book, we make two assumptions—you are interested in learning about the Component Object Model (COM), and you are already familiar with a modern programming language such as C++, Microsoft Visual Basic, or Java. One of the central tenets of COM is the concept of language independence, and we have structured *Inside Distributed COM* in support of that idea. Although COM-based components can be built in a wide variety of development environments, we focus on the most popular trio: C++, Visual Basic, and Java. With this approach, we definitely part ways with the prevailing practice among the COM cognoscenti, for whom only C++ will do. Visual Basic and Java developers will learn a lot from this book, even though these languages hide a large part of the COM infrastructure. In many cases, we present examples in C++ and then show how components written in higher-level languages can tie into the same functionality. However, you must understand the fundamentals of C++ in order to utilize many of the sample programs.

When we were writing this book, we debated whether the C++ examples should use MFC (Microsoft Foundation Classes) or ATL (Active Template Library). We eventually decided to use neither, the logic being that even though class and template libraries will come and go, COM is here to stay. Also, a class library can hide some of the important details of COM. Once you understand the fundamental infrastructure and richness of COM, using a class library will not be difficult to acquire. Thus, we do not assume that you know OLE, ActiveX, ATL, MFC, the Win32 API, or any one of a myriad of other related technologies. Although proficiency in these areas (especially some knowledge of the Win32 API) might prove useful to you during the learning process, it is not a prerequisite.

Before you proceed with us on this journey, we would like to get something off our chests—this is a COM book. Distributed COM (DCOM) fulfills the promise of location transparency that has been part of COM since its very beginning. Throughout most of this book, we refer simply to COM. The occasional references to DCOM occur when we discuss the remoting features of COM specifically.

As we were preparing material, we were reminded of that really old joke in which a patient in a dentist's chair is afraid to open his mouth. The patient asks the dentist if the work can be done through his nose. The dentist replies that yes, it can, it just takes longer that way. When you program distributed components with COM, you will find that there are many ways to accomplish the same goal; some are just easier than others. For example, there is an easy way to build a type library and a difficult one. There is an easy way to marshal interface pointers and a difficult one. There is an easy way to implement Automation and, you guessed it, a difficult one. In short, if you take the time to learn the rules and idioms of COM, we think you'll find it quite easy. Otherwise, you can still do the same thing—it will just take longer. Sure, you will find some messy parts here and there, but on the whole, we think you will find COM a flexible and pragmatic platform on which to base the development of distributed component-based systems.

Remember the Sojourner rover roaming the surface of Mars during the summer of 1997? It ran on an 8-bit Intel 80C85 processor containing only 6500 transistors (compared with 5.5 million transistors in the Pentium sitting on your desk). It had a radio modem capable of 9600 BPS and was powered by solar energy and nonrechargeable lithium D-cell batteries. It was a feat of modern engineering achieved with the most basic components. In a less dramatic way, COM is like that—it consists of a fundamental set of ideas giving rise to some amazingly powerful systems.

Thanks to Eric Stroo, our acquisitions editor, for guiding yet another book to a successful conclusion. Patricia Wagner, the project editor, Jennifer Harris, the manuscript editor, Robert Lyon and Jean Ross, the technical editors, and copy editor/proofreader Richard Carey deserve our profound gratitude for making our prose more concise and correct. Thanks also go to compositor Paul Vautier for making this look like an actual book and artist Michael Victor for the illustrations. Mark Ryland, Charlie Kindel, Mary Kirtland, and Saji Abraham of Microsoft Corporation supported us throughout this project by answering many questions. (We hope that this small token of gratitude will earn us some brownie points for future questions.) Mike Nelson deserves special mention for taking the time to answer questions about the COM security model and for providing us with late-breaking information on the DCOM specification. Thanks to Eric Maffei, Joanne Steinhart, Joe Flanigen, and the rest of the MSJ gang. (Hey, do we get a column now?) Thanks to David Barkley for the good company and thoughtful insights into what people really want to learn. And thanks to the people at Learning Tree International, who have provided so many opportunities for growth over the last several years.

Positive comments on the book (and slight errors found) may be sent to the e-mail address below. Even though we can't guarantee a response to every question, we certainly try to reply—especially when we know the answer! We are occasionally available for short term consulting assignments; in the subject field of your message, please put the words "High-priced consulting."

Guy Eddon
Henry Eddon
IUnknown, NJ
guyeddon@msn.com

PART I

FUNDAMENTAL PROGRAMMING ARCHITECTURE

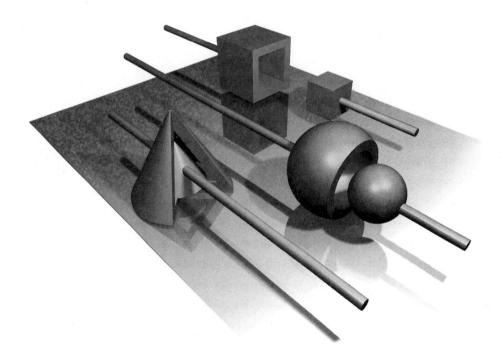

CHAPTER ONE

The Road to Distributed COM

As is the case with most Microsoft technologies, DCOM was not invented overnight by a caffeine-crazed developer. Instead, DCOM is the coalescence of two separate paths of technological evolution, as shown in Figure 1-1. To better understand the underpinnings of DCOM, you need to begin with the technologies from which DCOM evolved.

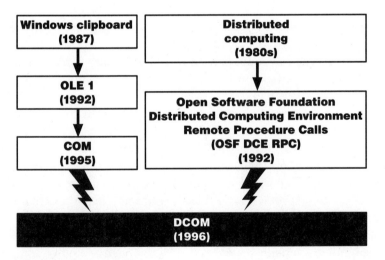

Figure 1-1.
The evolution of DCOM.

From OLE to DCOM

Microsoft's MS-DOS operating system was developed for a very limited computer (by today's standards) and therefore was designed to run only one application at a time. As Intel advanced with the more powerful CPUs, such as the 80286 and 80386, Microsoft began to envision the limitless possibilities of running multiple applications concurrently. Then, with the advent of the cooperatively multitasking Microsoft Windows environment, Microsoft realized that users wanted to exchange data among various applications. The clipboard and Dynamic Data Exchange (DDE) initiatives were two of the first interprocess communication facilities incorporated into Windows. DDE was a message-passing service designed for use by developers to incorporate data exchange facilities into their applications. However, DDE was a rather complex protocol for developers to follow, and consequently few applications aside from Microsoft Excel implemented it successfully.

The clipboard provided users with a primitive but easily understood paradigm of cut, copy, and paste operations. The clipboard could be used in the creation of compound documents. The term *compound document* refers to a document containing different types of content—for example, a user's word processing document might contain text, bitmaps, charts, and sound clips. Imagine that you had wanted to create the 1992 annual report for your company using one of the first versions of Microsoft Word for Windows. First you would probably have written the text describing the state of the company and the progress made over the prior year. Then you might have loaded Excel to create a spreadsheet with specific figures on your company's performance. Last you would have selected some cells in the spreadsheet, copied them to the clipboard, and pasted them into your Word document. Without the clipboard service, you might have had to print your Word document and Excel spreadsheet separately and then literally cut and paste them using scissors and glue.

The fact that the clipboard service was both easy to implement from the developer's perspective and easy for the user to control made it an immediate hit with most applications. This popularity continues even in today's Windows applications. Nevertheless, the shortcomings of the clipboard quickly became apparent. The basic problem with the clipboard as a means of creating compound documents was the lack of intelligence involved in the data transfer. For example, after you had created your company's annual report using the clipboard, you might suddenly have discovered the need to update some of the figures in the Excel spreadsheet. This editing required that you once more select, copy, and paste the new figures into your Word document. The original concept of object linking and embedding (OLE) grew out of an effort by Microsoft's applications division to address this problem.

OLE was first released with Microsoft Windows 3.1 in 1992. The idea of OLE 1 was to provide an improved mechanism for dealing with compound documents. For example, these smart compound documents could either embed the Excel spreadsheet data in or link it with the Word document. Now whenever linked figures were updated in the spreadsheet, the new data automatically found its way to the Word document. Also, it was possible to open and edit the linked or embedded figure in Excel by double-clicking it in Word. This capability was a great boon to users, although few understood how it operated. In fact, DDE was used internally by OLE 1 as the interprocess communication protocol. OLE 1 contained some very interesting ideas, foremost of which was the concept that compound document objects supported by different applications could work together in the creation of a "superdocument." The OLE designers continued to broaden and refine their ideas until at some point they began to view compound document objects as software components—small, self-contained software objects that could be plugged into an application, thereby extending its functionality.

With the release of OLE 2 in 1993, the linking and embedding capabilities of OLE were further refined and the linking and embedding facilities were extended with *in-place activation*. In-place activation, sometimes called *visual editing*, allows one application to take on the appearance of another, enabling the user to edit all of the data contained in a compound document without leaving the context of a single window. Although most developers did not realize it at that time or for a long while after, the architecture of OLE 2 was built around the revolutionary idea of component-based software. In the long run, this has proved to be by far the most important contribution of OLE 2. Over the years, OLE has faded into the background while COM has taken center stage. With the release of Microsoft Windows NT 4.0 in 1996, COM gained the functionality necessary to invoke components that were running on remote computers connected via a network. This first release of DCOM was followed by the DCOM add-on for Microsoft Windows 95, released in early 1997. For the time being, DCOM embodies the glorious conclusion of a long evolution of ideas that began with OLE.

How DCOM Evolved from RPC

DCOM also had its beginnings eons earlier in the 1980s. In those bucolic times, simply connecting several computers together over a local area network was a major achievement. For the personal computer takeover to come to fruition, there needed to be a distributed support system analogous to that of a centralized operating system. However, this approach was not going anywhere unless industry groups cooperated on the creation of standards. In the world of mainframe computers, standards were a nonissue; software was written for specific hardware and IBM's computers were not expected to talk to other company's computers.

In the late 1980s, attempts were made by various industry groups to get enough companies to define standards and then agree to abide by them. One of the groups, the Open Software Foundation (OSF), became an industrywide consortium with a mandate for the definition of standards in a broad spectrum of areas. The members of the OSF decided to address the issue of distributed computing. Out of this effort grew the specifications for the Distributed Computing Environment (DCE). The overall goal of DCE was to provide an environment for creating distributed systems. To this end, DCE began collecting a comprehensive and integrated set of tools and services to support the creation of distributed applications, in a manner analogous to the support offered by the operating system in a centralized environment.

One outcome of the Open Software Foundation (OSF) Distributed Computing Environment (DCE) was a specification for communicating between computers. This specification, known as Remote Procedure Calls (RPCs), allows applications on different computers to communicate. DCOM uses RPCs for its intercomputer communication and thus indicates how DCOM evolved from RPC.

Parallel Processing

For as long as personal computers have existed, one of the most important goals of the industry has been to provide increasingly powerful hardware for CPU-hungry software. Over the years, companies such as Intel have upgraded their processors from 8 to 16 to 32 bits and have increased their clock speed from 4.77 to over 300 megahertz (MHz). Under development are 64-bit processors that will run at clock speeds higher than 300 MHz. Yet the cost of developing a new processor is so prohibitive that only the largest of corporations can afford the expense. And we might someday run into the law of diminishing returns, making the expense of development outweigh the possible improvements.

Aside from building more powerful CPUs, many other ways have been suggested for improving overall processing speed. Foremost among these initiatives has been the concept of *parallel processing*. Parallel processing holds that in an ideal environment, if one CPU can do x amount of work in a certain amount of time, 10 CPUs can do $10x$ work in the same time. Parallel processing can be implemented in two major ways: *symmetric multiprocessing (SMP)* and *distributed computing*. Distributed computing will be discussed in the next section. SMP is a design in which several (or several hundred) CPUs are placed inside a single computer. As a prerequisite, SMP requires that the host operating system support multithreading. In this way, different threads can be scheduled to run on different CPUs concurrently. Implementing SMP requires special software support. Windows NT, for example, was one of the first operating systems capable of running on a personal computer to support SMP. Current versions of Windows NT can quite flexibly support 1 to 32 processors.

Advantages of Distributed Computing

For our purposes, we will define distributed computing as a system in which computers are interconnected for the purpose of sharing CPU power and appear to the users as a single computer. The definition is rather vague when it comes to the exact manner by which the computers are interconnected. For example, if you wanted to print a document on the color printer located down the hall from your office, you could copy the file to a floppy disk, walk to the computer connected to the color printer, insert the disk, and print the document. Is this an example of distributed computing? In theory, the exact manner by which computers are interconnected is irrelevant. Perhaps the more important issue is the throughput provided by the information conduit. A distributed system connected by a 100-megabits-per-second, Ethernet-based local area network (LAN) will yield very different performance from a system connected by a 28,800-bits-per-second modem.

Before proceeding to expand on this definition, let's explore a realistic, albeit hypothetical, distributed system. A large bank has branch offices all over the world. The bank used to have a mainframe-based computing center at its world headquarters, and all branch offices used terminals connected to that mainframe. (So far, we have an example of a centralized system with all account and customer information stored in one place.) The bank then decided to retire the mainframe computer and replace it with a distributed system. Each branch office now has a master computer that stores local accounts and handles local transactions. In addition, each computer is connected with all the other branch computers via a global area network (GAN). If transactions can be performed without regard to where the customer actually is or where the customer's account data is actually stored, and if the users cannot tell the difference between the new system and the centralized mainframe-based system it replaced, we have an example of a successful distributed system.

Economics

What would cause the bank to replace the centralized system with a distributed system? The cost of doing business is the chief factor driving the industrywide push toward distributed systems. It can be much more economical for an organization to purchase and administer hundreds or even thousands of PCs than to purchase and maintain a single mainframe computer. But price alone is not the answer. A well-designed distributed system can also yield better performance for the same amount of money spent. In other words, the price/performance ratio tends to work in favor of the distributed solution.

Performance

Another factor that might influence the bank's decision away from a centralized system is the realization that the overall processing power of a distributed system could outperform any mainframe. Current technology makes it quite possible to build a network of 5,000 Intel Pentium-based PCs, each running at about 200 million instructions per second (MIPS), yielding a total performance of 1,000,000 MIPS. A single CPU producing that kind of performance would need to execute one instruction every 10^{-12} second. Even assuming that electricity could travel at the speed of light (300,000 kilometers per second), only a distance of 0.3 millimeter would be covered in 10^{-12} second. To build a CPU with that sort of performance in a 0.3-millimeter cube would truly be a feat of modern engineering, but the CPU would generate so much heat that it would spontaneously combust.

Reliability

Reliability is both a major concern and a goal of any distributed system. The complex nature of such systems has in some cases led to reliability problems in hastily implemented distributed systems. However, a well-designed distributed system can realize much higher overall reliability than a comparable centralized system. For example, if we conclude that a particular centralized system has a failure rate of only 2 percent, we can expect users to experience 2 percent system downtime. During that downtime, all work grinds to a halt.

In a distributed system, we might evaluate each node as having a 5 percent failure rate. The difference in failure rates can be attributed to the fact that most mainframe computers are kept in specially cooled and dust-free rooms with an around-the-clock team of trained operators, whereas PCs are often locked in a closet and forgotten. Ideally, if 5 percent of the machines are down at any one moment, that translates into only a 5 percent degradation of total system performance—not total system failure. For mission-critical applications, such as control of nuclear reactors or spaceship navigation systems, in which reliability and redundancy are of predominant consideration, a distributed system can introduce an extra degree of reliability.

In the following formula, P is the probability of occurrence for the two unrelated events A and B:

$$P(A \cap B) = PA \times PB$$

The more general case is shown here:

$$P_{c,n} = c^n \times 10^{-2n}$$

$P_{c,n}$ is the probability that if there are n related events and each one has a c percent probability of failure, all events will fail simultaneously. Thus, even with a 5 percent rate of failure per node, users of a system with 100 nodes will experience only a 20^{-100} percent chance of any downtime whatsoever. This case is rather extreme since it is highly unlikely that 100 out of 100 computers would fail simultaneously. Let's use the logic shown above to evaluate the risk of several computers failing at the same time.

Figure 1-2 shows the likelihood of simultaneous failure for between 1 and 5 computers out of a total of 10.

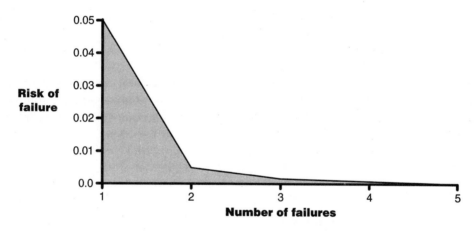

Figure 1-2.
Risk of multiple simultaneous failures in a system of ten nodes.

Incremental Growth

The ease with which a distributed system can be upgraded is a major advantage. At best, upgrading a centralized system requires that the system be taken off line, upgraded, and restarted. At worst, it requires that the old mainframe be carted out and a new one installed in its place. Either way, the upgrading process requires that the entire system go off line for an extended period, wreaking havoc in the company's day-to-day operations. For this reason, companies often purchase as much mainframe capacity up front as they can afford, hoping that it will be enough to meet demand for a long time to come.

Distributed systems, on the other hand, do not need to be taken off line for upgrade or maintenance work. Several servers may be taken off line at one time or additional servers may be added, all without unduly inconveniencing users or jeopardizing the company's main business. Capacity planning can also be done in a more sane and logical manner, as there is little incentive to purchase extra processing power in advance of need.

Architecture

All the good reasons for building a distributed system notwithstanding, some applications inherently require a distributed architecture. The two basic categories of distributed applications are:

- Distributed applications built to share data
- Distributed applications built to share CPU power

An application such as Microsoft NetMeeting, which allows users to chat, draw figures, speak, and see video of one another in real time over the Internet, is an example of a distributed application that focuses on sharing data. Multiple-player games that allow users to connect with and play against each other are also an example of the data-sharing model. The second type of application attempts to harness the CPU power of multiple computers in order to perform quicker computations or data processing. Future versions of Microsoft SQL Server are under development that will break down a user's query into several parts, sending each component to a different server for processing.

Building Distributed Systems

Building a distributed application is not an easy task. In almost all cases, it is more difficult than designing an equivalent centralized system. In theory, distributed systems can be custom-built on top of practically any operating system that offers networking functionality. Realistically, the following services are generally required of the operating system in order to build a robust distributed system:

- Networking
- Multithreading
- Security

Even with these services, developing a distributed system is a daunting task. When you are working with a low-level network protocol, you must be prepared to deal with the many issues that arise in a network application—for example, the errors that might occur if the network connection is terminated abruptly. And if you want one server to be able to service multiple users simultaneously, you need to build in multithreading support so that the server spawns a new thread to deal with each client that connects. Security also becomes a major factor in the design and development of any distributed system. For example, how do you ensure that the clients that connect are really who they claim to be, how do you limit their access to certain services, and how do you enable an administrator to audit the system?

COM Background

Software development processes have not really changed that much over the years. Most software development efforts are beleaguered by cost and time overruns, and the results are often bug-ridden and unmaintainable. Over the years, a number of different paradigms and methodologies, from flowchart creation to object orientation, have been offered and sometimes accepted for varying lengths of time as a panacea for the problems inherent in software development. Over time, all of these purported solutions have failed to meet expectations, and no reliable substitute has been found for the success achieved by small groups of individuals, working on one project at a time. This is not to say that flowcharts are unhelpful or that object-oriented designs are flawed, but simply that they do not reduce software development to a formula or recipe that guarantees results. Perhaps these paradigms have been oversold, or perhaps the users of these methodologies have expected too much. The time has come to realize that software development is inherently difficult and fraught with many problems that have no single solution.

Object-Oriented Programming

Object-oriented programming is one of the more recent paradigms to enjoy a long and somewhat favorable reception by the software industry. This acceptance is reflected in the popularity of object-oriented programming languages such as Ada, Smalltalk, Java, and C++. Each of these languages carries the object-oriented flag at varying heights, depending on the original areas of expertise of their designers, the problems they set out to solve, and the limitations with which they had to contend. C++, for example, takes a pragmatic view of object-oriented programming, although this can be traced mostly to

11

its roots in C and its stringent compatibility requirements with that language. And although Visual Basic is not fully object-oriented, object-oriented ideas have permeated its design and it continues to evolve toward a more complete object-oriented language.

In a nutshell, rather than writing a program in a procedural and organized manner intended to mimic the logic of a computer, the goal of object-oriented programming techniques is to make programming easier and more effective by writing software that deals with the way individuals think in the real world. Object-oriented programming methods recognize that most software attempts to model, or "virtualize," things (objects) that we work with every day. Rather than reducing these objects to a procedural set of steps necessary to accomplish a task, object-oriented programming languages allow developers to better express the existence of objects directly in the code. It is hoped that this will lead to more expressive code that will be easier to develop and less costly to maintain.

In most object-oriented programming languages, an important distinction must be made between the concepts of an *object* and a *class*. A class is a template that defines its members. An object is an instance of that class and can actually do things. This relationship is perhaps better illustrated with the following example. Compare a cookie cutter and a cookie. A cookie cutter is like a template (class) that defines various attributes of cookies, such as shape and size. A cookie, on the other hand, is analogous to an object, since the cookie is created based on the cookie cutter. (Although cookies don't really do much except taste good.)

The object-oriented paradigm expounds three major ideas that are necessary for an object-oriented programming language to support:

- **Encapsulation**—The hiding of an object's implementation details
- **Inheritance**—The ability to reuse existing objects in the creation of new, more specialized objects
- **Polymorphism**—The ability of code to exhibit multiple behaviors depending on the object being used

These ideas are developed in the sections that follow.

Encapsulation

Encapsulation specifies that your code should be combined with related data in order to define an object. This connection between code and data does not exist in most standard procedural languages such as C, in which code is written in modules of functions that operate on data. This combination of code and data is called the *implementation.* The implementation is considered to be private to the object, which means that the object's internal implementation is really nobody's business but its own, a sort of "black box." The object also exposes a public interface through which the data can be accessed; this interface constitutes the contract between the object and its users. The idea behind this type of design is that it allows the internal implementation of an object to be modified, improved, and expanded, so long as the public interface exposed by the object is not compromised.

Properly done, encapsulation imposes a slight performance penalty on software due to the extra layer of the public interface. For efficiency, it is sometimes necessary to allow certain users of an object to bypass this public interface and access your private implementation directly. In these cases, it is appropriate to specify these special users as *friends,* thereby giving them access. If abused, the friend concept ruins the whole idea of encapsulation, so use it only when necessary. When you encounter a case in which you are considering making one object a friend of another, reconsider the design to see whether there is a better way to structure your code. When used appropriately, however, the friend concept provides an escape hatch from the constraints of encapsulation.

NOTE: If you later modify the internal implementation of an object, only the friends of that object will need to modify their code.

Inheritance

Code reuse is the Holy Grail of object-oriented programming. If you consider the time and effort expended developing and debugging code that has been written countless times before, you will recognize code reuse as a very tantalizing promise being made to companies by the proponents of object-oriented technologies. Inheritance is a means of achieving code reusability within an application by creating an object that inherits functionality from another object. You should use inheritance techniques when you have an existing class that has the basic functionality you need but does not behave exactly as you might want. The new class will be a superset of the base class, allowing you to reuse the functionality available in the base class and at the same time to add new functionality, thus enabling code reuse. Using inheritance techniques, however, almost always requires that you have access to the source code of the base class. Often developers will want to simply copy the code of a base class member function into an override function in the derived class and then modify it slightly—a technique that is nearly impossible without source code.

When to Use Inheritance

As a general guideline, inheritance techniques should be used whenever you can recognize an "is a" relationship among the classes in your project. For example, consider the case of attempting to define classes for a package shipping company. The basic class might be determined to be a package, since that is the main object with which the company works. However, over time it is likely that the company will introduce new services in addition to basic package shipping. For instance, the company might begin to ship more specialized packages, like next-day-air packages and second-day-air packages.

An object-oriented design would enable the company's software to adapt more flexibly as new services were introduced. You might create classes for many of these objects by inheriting functionality from the base *Package* class. Then you would modify and add the necessary functionality to better define what makes these specialized packages unique. In some cases, an "is a" relationship between classes is easy to recognize. A next-day-air package "is a" type of package, but a specialized type at that. This brings us to another way of thinking about inheritance: inheritance can be viewed as a type of specialization. Use inheritance when you want to refine an existing class, bringing into sharp relief the specific attributes that define the new class as unique.

Recognizing and defining the classes for a particular project is not always as easy as in the package shipping company example. Sometimes it is quite difficult to assess the main object with which the business is concerned. In fact, object-oriented analysis and design (OOA&D) has been developed to help people deal with these problems. Prior experience should have taught us that drawing hierarchy charts and object diagrams does not create useful, bug-free software. Inheritance, however, can help to better structure a program. Once you identify the objects you'll be working with in a project and then define the relationships between those objects, inheritance will be one tool you'll be able to use to better express relationships and algorithms in code.

The ability to inherit functionality from existing classes has given rise to application frameworks and class libraries such as the Microsoft Foundation Class (MFC) library, used in conjunction with Visual C++ to develop Windows applications. These class libraries provide much of the default code needed to create a standard Windows-based application. The class libraries will then allow you to create classes that inherit this default functionality. This technique makes it easy to begin writing Windows-based applications since most of the common drudgery has been done for you. All you need to do is add your own customizing code and possibly override default code in the base classes to create your own application—the "just add water and mix" approach to Windows programming.

Another feature available in some object-oriented languages such as C++ is *multiple inheritance.* Multiple inheritance allows developers to inherit code from two or more base classes at a time. For example, imagine that you have a *TextEdit* class that provides text editing capabilities and a *Window* class that provides a windowing system. If you want to create one class that has a text editor in a window, you could use multiple inheritance. In theory, this sounds great, but in reality, things don't always turn out quite so rosy. If by unlucky coincidence both the *TextEdit* and *Window* classes themselves were originally built by inheriting from some other class—for instance, a *Display* class—you would now have two sets of identical data members colliding in the new multiple inheritance class. While C++ provides a workaround for this problem in the form of virtual base classes, you could legitimately question the maintainability of such complicated designs. (As an interesting aside, the Java programming language avoids such problems by not supporting multiple class inheritance, but it gets around this limitation by supporting multiple inheritance from interfaces that have no data members and therefore will not have duplicate data members colliding.)

Polymorphism

In cases in which you use inheritance, you will find that many of the classes in your inheritance hierarchy will implement identical methods, each overriding its base class implementation. Polymorphism is a potential benefit possible only in inheritance trees where the "is a" relationship reigns. By allowing you to write relatively general code for the base class that then works properly with more specialized derived objects, polymorphism permits code to adapt to a wide variety of situations that might not have been initially planned for. Imagine that you have written a *Vehicle* class containing a *Go* method. Sometime later in the life of the project, you add an *Airplane* and a *Car* class, both of which inherit from *Vehicle.* In the *Airplane* class, you override the *Go* method with a function that causes the plane to fly, and in the *Car* class, you override the *Go* method with a function that causes the car to drive. Polymorphism says that if you call the *Go* method on a *Vehicle* object that is actually an *Airplane* object, the *Airplane* object's *Go* method is called, causing the plane to fly, whereas a *Car* object's *Go* method would cause it to drive.

As a more realistic example, let's consider the package shipping company again. (See the sidebar "When to Use Inheritance.") The generic *Package* class will probably have a *Ship* method that knows how to ship the package. The *NextDayAir* and all other package types will also have *Ship* methods of their own. Each package type will require a special *Ship* method that takes into account when the package needs to arrive, how it will be shipped (air or ground), special precautions (insured packages), and so on. Now suppose you have a general process in your application—say, running on a computer at a shipping counter—that ships packages. You want this process to deal with any type of package that comes along, including package types that don't currently exist. The process knows about the generic package type, but you would like to keep it nonspecific—you would rather it knew nothing detailed about any derived package types. Nevertheless, when the process invokes the *Ship* method on whatever package it has on hand, you want it to do so using that specific package's *Ship* method.

This ability to take on many shapes is polymorphism. You can code for a basic type of object, but at run time you might in fact be working with something derived from it. It's as if you are sending a generic message to an object that then has the ability to interpret the message in the context of what the object is capable of doing. One thing to keep in mind when you are using polymorphism is the overhead imposed by this type of late binding. Because the compiler does not know at development time what object type will be used, it must delay making the decision of which function to call until run time (late binding), which imposes a varying performance penalty, depending on the nature of the programming language's implementation. Nevertheless, the ability to write relatively general code that can then work correctly with specialized types of objects is a clear benefit of polymorphism.

Code Sharing and Reuse

Object-oriented programming became as popular as it did due largely to its promise of allowing developers to share code among entirely different projects. As mentioned, the redevelopment of similar code and algorithms occurs all the time, resulting in an incredible waste of time, effort, and money. While code sharing and reuse is considered to be a primary benefit of a well-implemented object-oriented design, the percentage of code actually being shared is still small. Until recently, even applications in suites such as Microsoft Office each had different code to implement standard features such as toolbars, status bars, and spell checkers. In Windows 95 and Windows NT, many of these standard graphical user interface (GUI) controls have been built into the operating system, allowing all applications to share them. If you think about it, an operating system is a great (but not tremendously flexible) example of code reuse.

Code reuse seems to be one of those things that everyone sort of assumed would happen spontaneously. This turned out to be a lot of wishful thinking, since code reuse needs to be planned for and its implications carefully thought through. If you write some code and then give it to friends so that they can use it, is that code reuse? What about code libraries that programmers link to their applications? While these are examples of code reuse, each has its problems. If you give your code to your friends and they don't like some aspects of it, they might go into your source code and make modifications. This tinkering is not in keeping with the idea of code reuse. Modifying someone else's source code is like breaking a figurine in a china store—the hapless browser becomes the proud new owner. If something doesn't work after someone changes your code, you are not obliged to support the code anymore. In addition, when you later update your own code and then make available the new version, your friend will have to go through it and integrate his or her own changes anew. The code is then manifestly not reusable. If you purchase a class library and you don't like the way it works, that's too bad unless you also buy the source code so that you can alter it, and that brings you back to the previous problem. To better understand code reuse, a more solid definition is needed: true code reusability is the ability to use code written in a general enough manner for reuse in your software to build something larger, while still being able to customize the way the code works and what it does.

Another problem with most types of code reuse is that they normally require the original developers of the software and the person who wants to reuse the code to be working in the same programming language. If a class library is written in C++, for example, it is basically impossible to reuse that code in an application written in any language other than C++. By the same token, a Java class can be used only in a Java program. So although you often get more software reuse using an object-oriented programming language than you would get if you didn't, there are still limitations.

How then can we apply what everyone agrees to be the great idea of code sharing and reuse to practical, real-life programming? While object-oriented programming has long been advanced as a solution to the problems at hand, it has yet to reach its full potential. Before COM, no standard framework existed through which software objects created by different vendors could interact with one another in the same address space, much less across address spaces or network and machine boundaries. According to the COM specification, the major result of the object-oriented programming school has been the production of "islands of objects" that can't talk to one another in a meaningful way across the sea of application boundaries.

Three Faces of COM

What is COM then? When we sat down to answer this question, we came up with the following (all correct) answers:

■ COM is a specification.

■ COM is a philosophy of modern software development.

■ COM is a binary standard for building software components.

The following sections discuss these three aspects of COM in detail.

COM as a Specification

COM is a specification. By this, we mean that COM is a document that can be printed and read. Our copy of the COM specification is stained with blood, sweat, and tears. The complete COM specification can be downloaded from Microsoft's Web site (http://www.microsoft.com/com) and is included on the companion CD. (For the sake of completeness, we should mention that COM is not only a specification, it also consists of some system code implemented by Microsoft.)

COM as a Philosophy

COM is a way of thinking about modern software development. The COM specification describes a world in which applications are built from components. Most software projects are still designed around the idea of producing a behemoth, encompassing all the features a user might ever want. The trouble with this model of software development is that applications become more fragile as they grow. It is difficult to have a complete understanding of an application containing 100,000 lines of code, and all but impossible with 1,000,000 lines. Even a small modification in an application that size requires extensive retesting of the entire system. Often what appears to be an innocuous modification in one section of code does damage in many other locations.

But the days of the monolithic application are over. The dinosaurs are extinct, and in the brave new COM world, developers create compact, well-defined components that work together. These components can then be re-used in many environments on both the client and the server. For example, a particular business component can be used in a desktop application as well as by a Web application running in Microsoft Internet Information Server or by a back-end server running Microsoft Transaction Server. Building a system based on interoperable components doesn't mean that the user can't have an icon on the desktop to launch the application. As an example, let's examine the architecture of Microsoft Internet Explorer. The shell is a simple ActiveX document host, and the actual parsing and rendering of HTML is done by an ActiveX document component loaded whenever the user navigates to a Web site. If that Web site contains an ActiveX control component, the control is downloaded and installed. This COM-based architecture keeps every part of the shell focused on a specific job. Different teams using different programming languages can develop components, and so long as everyone plays by COM's rules, they will work together seamlessly.

COM as a Binary Standard

COM is the name of the specification for Microsoft's basic object technology that defines what it means to be a COM object and how a COM object is called. COM's role is that of the "glue" between components, enabling unrelated software objects to connect and interact in meaningful ways. To put it succinctly, COM is a binary standard for integration between components.

To better explain the reason for COM's existence, let's begin by reviewing some of the challenges faced by the software industry that led Microsoft to develop COM. As everyone knows, the continuous evolution of computer hardware and software has brought an ever-increasing number of sophisticated applications to users' desktops and networks. With such complex software has come a commensurate number of problems for developers and users alike, as discussed in the COM specification:

- Modern software applications are large and complex—they are time-consuming to develop, difficult and costly to maintain, and risky to extend with additional functionality.

- Applications continue to be developed in a monolithic style—they come prepackaged with a range of static features, none of which can be added, removed, upgraded independently, or replaced with alternatives.

- Applications do not lend themselves to integration—neither the data nor the functionality of one program is readily available to another program.

- Programming models reflect the provider's upbringing—they vary widely depending on whether the service is coming from a provider in the same address space, in another address space on the same machine, in another machine running across the network, or in the operating system.

Will COM fix all this? As the nature of the difficulties described here suggests, no one piece of software can single-handedly solve all these problems. But as you'll see in the following sections, software built on a COM architecture can better meet these challenges.

Componentware

The COM specification proposes a system in which application developers create reusable software components. The breakdown of a project into its logical components is the essence of object-oriented analysis and design. That's also the basis for *componentware,* which is software composed of building blocks. A component is a reusable piece of software in binary form (as opposed to source code) that can be plugged into other components from other vendors with relatively little effort. These reusable software components present their functionality through a defined set of interfaces—a crucial concept in COM. We are not talking about user interfaces here, but rather the programmatic kind of interfaces that enable one piece of software to talk to another. For example, the Win32 API is an interface to the functionality of the Windows operating system. With COM, not only operating systems can make an interface available (sometimes called publishing, or exposing, an interface) but so can software components built by us ordinary folk. An interface is actually a very simple thing, a defined set of functions that are grouped together under one name. For now, this will be our working definition of an interface.

Components created using COM can fall into a variety of categories, including visual components, such as buttons or list boxes, and functional components, such as ones that add printing or spell checking capability. For example, a spell checker component from one vendor could be plugged into several word processing programs from different vendors. This capability could hold many advantages for the end user. You might love the word processor produced by company A but hate the spell checker it comes with. So you can buy the spell checker you like from company B, which specializes in spell checkers. This capability allows different software developers to specialize in what they do best. A good analogy is found in the automobile industry. Many car manufacturers buy individual car parts, such as engines and transmissions, from various manufacturers and then assemble cars from all these components. The key point is that the pieces can be used as they are—they don't need to be recompiled, you don't need the source code, and you aren't restricted to one programming language. The term for this process is *binary reuse,* because it is based on binary interfaces rather than on reuse at the source code level. While the software components must adhere to the agreed upon interface, their internal implementation is completely autonomous. For this reason, the components can be built using procedural languages as well as object-oriented languages, although the latter provide many advantages in the component software world.

COM is an object-based programming model whose main goal is to promote *interoperability*. Interoperability is one of those buzzwords in the computer field that means different things to different people. COM supports interoperability by defining mechanisms that enable components to work together. The designers of COM tried their best to give a fresh look to the process of software development. When they recognized areas in which software seemed to be forced together unnaturally, COM's designers tried to break things up into components. Let's use the example of controls. In the good old days of Windows-based programming, if you needed a new widget for your application, you wrote it. If a toolbar was needed in your program, you would simply write the toolbar code directly into the main part of the application. This example has two inherent problems: First, your goal is not to create a cool toolbar but a great application that has a toolbar. Second, now that you have consumed many precious hours developing a toolbar, perhaps somebody else in your company would like to use that toolbar in his or her project. How is that possible if the toolbar code is sprinkled throughout your program, responding to *WM_CREATE, WM_PAINT,* and *WM_LBUTTONDOWN* messages?

COM's designers would take this case, in which you can easily spot software being grouped together unnaturally, and say that we should turn the toolbar into a component. The problem is how the toolbar component and our application should interact—the whole issue of interoperability. This is where COM comes in. COM would define the interface between the component and the application using the component. As long as both sides followed the interface, interoperability would result. In the toolbar example, the application developers could now concentrate on the software and simply purchase the toolbar component from some other developer who specializes in making great toolbars, thus saving development, debugging, and maintenance time. (Of course, this solution will deprive you of the opportunity to create a toolbar on company time, but that is a different issue altogether.)

While this type of architecture has many obvious advantages, developers are often concerned (and rightly so) with the overhead involved in separating software into components. There is no doubt that an architecture built on the idea of components imposes overhead. COM attempts to minimize this overhead by staying out of the components' way as much as possible. For example, COM is heavily involved in helping components connect, but once the connection is established, COM drops out of the picture. COM serves to connect a client and server, but once that connection is established, the client and object can communicate directly, without suffering added overhead. It is also important to realize that COM is not a prescribed way to structure an application. Rather it is a specification that makes the programming, use, and independent evolution of binary objects possible.

Object-oriented programming concepts used in conjunction with COM allow developers to build flexible and powerful objects that can easily be reused by other developers. One important principle of object-oriented programming, discussed earlier, is encapsulation. Remember encapsulation specifies that the implementation of an object is of concern only to the object itself and is hidden from the users of the object. The users of an object have access only to the object's interface. Developers who use prebuilt objects in their projects are interested only in the "contract"—the promised behavior that the object supports. COM formalizes the notion of a contract between an object and a client. Each object declares what it is capable of by implementing certain interfaces. Such a contract is the basis for interoperability.

COM Interfaces

As stated in the COM specification, COM defines a completely standardized means for creating components and for controlling the communication between these components and their clients. Unlike traditional programming environments, these mechanisms are independent of the applications that use the components and the programming languages used to create the objects themselves. COM therefore defines a binary interoperability standard rather than a language-based standard. With COM, applications interact with each other and with the system, through collections of function calls known as *interfaces*. In COM, an interface is a strongly typed contract between a software component and a client that provides a relatively small but useful set of semantically related operations. It is an articulation of an expected behavior and expected responsibilities, and it gives programmers and designers a concrete entity to use when referring to the component. Although not a strict requirement of the model, interfaces should be factored in such a way that they can be reused in a variety of contexts.

The use of COM interfaces is instrumental in creating adaptable component software. COM provides for the functionality in applications to evolve over time. One of the major problems with previous attempts at component-based software was the issue of *versioning*. Versioning of software components can be problematic when a component relies on some other code that is modified.

This was a common problem with dynamic-link libraries (DLLs) in Windows—a program that depended on a particular DLL might fail if it encountered a newer or older version of the DLL than it was expecting. Similar problems face component software. Over time, as the developers of a component make changes to it and modify its interface, the applications dependent on that component will be affected.

COM addresses this problem by dictating that COM-based components are never permitted to change their interface. For this reason, you should be very careful when designing a component's interface. After a product is released, the interface may not be changed; the only thing that can be done at that stage is to publish a new interface. Client applications aware of this new interface can take advantage of it, while older applications will work with the updated software through the old interface.

The ability of a single object to support multiple interfaces simultaneously is an important feature of COM. This feature allows an object to introduce new interfaces that support added functionality in successive versions of the object, while at the same time retaining complete binary compatibility with applications that depend on those objects. In other words, revising an object by adding new or even unrelated functionality will not require recompilation on the part of any existing client. Because COM allows objects to have multiple interfaces, an object can express a number of interface "versions" simultaneously.

The rule that COM interfaces are never changed might raise some questions. For example, we have said that instead of updating an existing interface, a new interface needs to be created. Suppose the time has come to update your great *ICool* interface. What is to be done? For starters, you might create a new interface named *ICoolEx* that contains the desired modifications. But what happens when it comes time to update *ICoolEx*? Would you name the new interface *ICoolExEx*? To avoid this confusion, it is better to use numbers to version interfaces—in our example, *ICool2* would then be followed by *ICool3*.

But when you design *ICool2*, do you now have to implement the code twice for *ICool*, once for the old *ICool*, and once for the new *ICool2*? Not necessarily, as COM allows objects to have a single internal implementation of the common capabilities exposed through two or more similar interfaces, such as successive versions of an interface. Immutable interfaces combined with the ability of an object to support multiple interfaces effectively solve the problem of versioning.

With all this talk of calling interfaces, you might be wondering exactly how to call a COM-based component. Well, every COM object must support at least one interface: *IUnknown*. When a client initially gains access to an object, that client will receive at minimum an *IUnknown* interface pointer (the most fundamental interface), through which it can only control the lifetime of the object and invoke *QueryInterface*. *QueryInterface* is the basic function in COM through which one piece of software determines what interfaces are supported by a component. In other words, this is a type of high-level handshaking in which the client can determine whether the component supports a particular capability. If a word processor encounters a component it wants to use as a spell checker, it might ask the component via *QueryInterface* whether it supports a predefined spell checker interface. If the answer is yes, *QueryInterface* will return a pointer to the requested interface, through which the word processor can now call any of the functions contained within that interface.

When working with in-process components, COM interfaces enable fast and simple interactions. Once a client establishes a connection to an object via *IUnknown* and *QueryInterface*, calls to that object's interface functions are simply indirect function calls through pointers. As a result, the overhead of interacting with an in-process COM object is negligible—basically identical to calling a DLL function. Interfaces do not define any implementations, meaning that interfaces do not contain code. An object can be said to implement an interface only when that object implements each and every member function. Through the *QueryInterface* method of the *IUnknown* interface, the interfaces implemented by a COM object are exposed to outside clients. Every interface has an identification number known as a globally unique identifier (GUID) that eliminates any chance of collision that could occur with human-readable names. (A GUID looks like this: *{13198125-998D-11CE-D41203C10000}*.) Component developers assign a GUID to each interface and must consciously support that interface—confusion and conflict among interfaces do not happen by accident.

Types of Components

Components come in one of three flavors—in-process, local, or remote—depending on the structure of the code module and its relationship to the client process that will be using it.

In-Process

In-process servers are loaded into the client's process space because they are implemented as DLLs. As you may know, DLLs are code libraries that are loaded at run time (dynamically) by the operating system on behalf of programs that want to call functions in the DLLs. DLLs are always loaded into the address space of the calling process. This is important because in Windows 95 and Windows NT each program (process) is loaded into its own private 32-bit address space for security and stability. Since it is not normally possible to access memory locations beyond this private address space, DLLs need to be loaded in-process. The Windows operating system is itself implemented in numerous DLLs, the most famous of which are User (the user interface), Kernel, and GDI (Graphics Device Interface).

The main advantage of in-process servers is their speed. Since the objects are loaded in-process, no context switching is necessary to access their services, as is the case with DLLs. The only potential disadvantage to in-process servers is that since an in-process server is in fact a DLL and not a complete application executable (EXE), it can be used only in the context of a calling program and cannot be run as a stand-alone application. ActiveX controls are implemented as in-process servers.

Local

A local server runs in a separate process on the same machine as the client. This type of server is an EXE of its own, thus qualifying as a separate process. Local servers are significantly slower to access than in-process servers because the operating system must switch between processes and copy any data that needs to be transferred between the client and the server applications. The one advantage of local servers is that since they are EXE files, they can be run as stand-alone applications by the user without an external client. An application such as Microsoft Internet Explorer is an example of a local server. You can run Internet Explorer to surf the net, or you can call Internet Explorer's objects from another application, such as Visual Basic.

Remote

A last type of component process is a remote server that runs on a separate machine connected via a network. Remote servers therefore always run in another process. This functionality can be implemented using Distributed COM (DCOM). The beauty of DCOM is that it does not require any special programming to enable this functionality. Without this network support for communication, programmers face the daunting task of writing their own specialized code for each component and network protocol that needs to be supported.

Visual Basic developers might have heard of Remote Automation, a precursor of DCOM that was included with Visual Basic 4.0 Enterprise Edition. Remote Automation allows OLE Automation servers to be called across the network in a manner similar to DCOM. Visual Basic 5.0 now supports both Remote Automation and DCOM, but Remote Automation is no longer recommended unless you have 16-bit clients.

As mentioned, DCOM supports distributed objects—that is, it allows application developers to split a single application into a number of different component objects, each of which can run on a different computer. DCOM works by using a proxy to intercept an interface call to an object and then issuing a Remote Procedure Call (RPC) to the "real" instance of the object that is running in another process on another machine. A key point is that the client makes this call exactly as it would for an in-process object and that DCOM performs the interprocess and cross-network function calls transparently. Remember that although there is, of course, a great deal more overhead in issuing an RPC, no special code is required. Since DCOM provides network transparency, these applications do not appear to be located on different machines. In properly implemented systems, the entire network can appear to be one large computer with enormous processing power and capability.

A major goal of COM is to insulate the developer using a component from the differences between in-process, local, and remote servers. It is apparent that very different mechanisms are used to call code in a remote server on another computer than need to be used to load an in-process DLL. COM's aim, however, is to hide those differences from users of an object so that all these types of servers appear identical. Obviously, depending on the type of component employed, there will be differences in operating speed.

The COM Library

It should be clear by now that COM is not just a paper specification. COM also involves some system-level code—that is, some implementation of its own. The COM implementation is contained in the *COM library*. This implementation is provided through a DLL that includes the following elements as described in the COM specification:

- A small number of fundamental API functions that facilitate the creation of COM applications, for clients and servers. For clients, COM supplies basic object instantiation functions; for servers, COM supplies the facilities to expose the servers' objects.

- Implementation locator services that enable COM to determine from a class identifier which server implements that class and where the server is located.

- Transparent remote procedure calls when an object is running in a local or a remote server.

- A standard mechanism to allow an application to control how memory is allocated within its process.

COM as a Foundation

It is important to realize that COM is simply an underlying architecture built on the concept of binary standard interfaces that enable various software components to interact intelligently. The basic elements of COM that we have been considering up to now form the foundation on which the rest of COM and ActiveX technologies are built. COM itself provides more than just the fundamental object creation and management facilities described previously. It also builds an infrastructure of three other core operating system components: *persistent storage, monikers,* and *uniform data transfer,* as described in the COM specification.

Persistent Storage

Persistent storage is defined by a set of interfaces and an implementation of those interfaces that create structured storage, otherwise known as a "file system within a file." Information in a file is structured in a hierarchical fashion of storages (similar to directories) and streams (similar to files), which enables sharing storage between processes, incremental access to information, transactioning support, and the ability for any code in the system to browse the elements of information in the file. In addition, COM defines standard "persistent storage" interfaces implemented by objects that support the ability to save their state to permanent (persistent) storage devices, such that the state of the objects can be restored at a later time.

Monikers

Monikers embody the ability to give a specific instantiation of an object a particular name in order to enable a client to reconnect to that exact same object instance with the same state (not just another object of the same class) at a later time. This feature also includes the ability to assign a name to some sort of operation, such as a query, that could be executed repeatedly using only that name to refer to the operation. This level of indirection allows changes to happen behind the name without requiring any changes to the client code that uses that particular name. Since all monikers are polymorphic, any client that uses a moniker can use any moniker.

Uniform Data Transfer

Uniform data transfer refers to standard interfaces through which data is exchanged between a client and an object and through which a client can ask an object to send notifications (call event functions in the client) in case of a data change. The uniform data transfer standards include powerful structures used to describe data formats as well as the storage mediums on which the data is exchanged.

ActiveX on COM

Microsoft's ActiveX technology supersedes what used to be known as OLE. ActiveX is a collection of additional higher-level technologies that build on COM and its infrastructure. All the features of ActiveX are implemented by means of specific interfaces on different objects and defined sequences of operation both in clients and in servers. Their relationships and dependencies on the lower-level infrastructure of COM are shown in Figure 1-3 on the following page.

ActiveX has three important areas of functionality: Automation, ActiveX documents, and ActiveX objects. Automation (formerly called OLE Automation) is the ability to create "programmable" applications that can be driven externally from a script running in another application to automate common end user tasks. Automation enables cross-application macro programming.

ActiveX documents provide the ability to embed information in a central document, encouraging a more document-centric user interface. OLE introduced in-place activation (or visual editing), a user interface improvement to embedding whereby the end user can work on information from different applications in the context of the compound document, without having to switch to other windows. ActiveX documents support a new feature that allows an application to open a document window within another application. Internet Explorer, for example, allows applications that support the necessary ActiveX document interfaces to open documents within its windows.

The ActiveX Controls (formerly known as OLE Controls) specification defines the interfaces that must be implemented by a component in order to qualify as an ActiveX control that can be used in Visual Basic and other environments such as Internet Explorer. The ActiveX Controls specification also defines the interfaces necessary to create a control container such as Visual Basic itself.

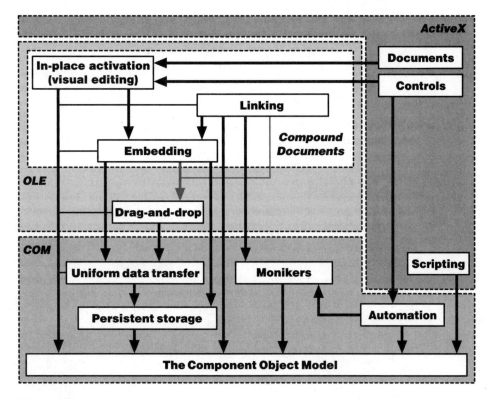

Figure 1-3
Relationships between ActiveX, OLE, and COM.

"The Road to Distributed COM" has discussed how early versions of Windows provided operating system support for the composition of compound documents, first in the form of the clipboard and later as OLE. The first version of OLE was built using the DDE protocol; OLE 2.0 introduced the radical idea of a component-based architecture. DCOM is the result of merging two lines of software evolution: OLE to COM to DCOM on the one hand, and distributed processing to RPC to DCOM on the other. Distributed processing is gaining importance as more companies replace centralized, mainframe-based systems. In this chapter, we have explored the fundamental reasons for this industry trend and the advantages that it offers. Distributed processing also brings with it certain difficulties that technologies such as RPC and DCOM are specifically designed to address.

IUnknown and *IClassFactory*

This chapter focuses on the fundamentals of COM programming: defining custom interfaces in the Interface Definition Language (IDL) and then implementing the interfaces using any programming language you desire. The example constructed and developed in this chapter culminates in a complete in-process component and a matching client. Creating this sample component requires an in-depth understanding of the two most primitive COM interfaces: *00000000-0000-0000-C000-000000000046* and *00000001-0000-0000-C000-000000000046*, otherwise known as *IUnknown* and *IClassFactory*. In this chapter, we blaze a trail from these fundamentals to a full-fledged component. Along the way, we'll encounter IDL, the starting point for programming COM.

> **DEFINITION:** An *interface* in COM is a set of semantically related methods.

Let's begin by defining a custom interface, *ISum*, that our in-process component will implement. Interfaces defined by Microsoft, such as *IUnknown* and *IClassFactory*, are called *standard interfaces*; interfaces that you define are known as *custom interfaces*. In this chapter, the C++ declaration of the *ISum* interface is defined as follows:

```
class ISum : public IUnknown
{
public:
    virtual HRESULT __stdcall Sum(int x, int y, int* retval)=0;
}
```

As you can see, here the class *ISum* has only one public member function, *Sum*, which is declared as a pure virtual function. The *virtual* keyword indicates that the member function can be redefined in a derived class. When you refer to a derived class using a pointer of the type of the base class, a call to one of the base class's virtual functions will execute the derived class's version of that function. This property is called *polymorphism*, or the ability of an object to exhibit multiple behaviors. The C++ compiler inserts the address of each virtual function into a special table called a *virtual function table,* or *v-table* (sometimes abbreviated as vtbl). This binary structure is used to implement polymorphism in C++; it also forms the basis of COM interfaces. At run time, every COM interface actually exists in memory as a v-table, as demonstrated by the following equation:

COM interface = C++ virtual function table

The *pure* attribute of our *Sum* function is specified by placing *=0* at the end of the function declaration. Using the *pure* attribute tells the compiler that no implementation for this function is provided. A class containing one or more pure virtual functions is known as an *abstract base class.* An abstract base class cannot be instantiated because at least some part of it is undefined; it can be used as a base class only when you are declaring other classes that will derive from it and implement its methods. Normally, an abstract base class is used to enforce a certain protocol of methods. For example, *IUnknown* is defined in C++ as an abstract base class, which ensures that all its methods must be implemented before any classes deriving from it can be instantiated.

The *Sum* method in this interface is also declared as __*stdcall,* which in the bygone days of traditional Windows programming was known as the *Pascal calling convention.* The Pascal calling convention specifies that parameters are pushed onto the stack from left to right and that the called function pops its own arguments from the stack before returning. These days, __*stdcall* is used to call Win32 API functions and COM interfaces. Somewhat surprisingly, __*stdcall* still works just like the Pascal calling convention. The *Sum* function takes two integer arguments and returns their sum. Well, to be exact, the function's return value is an *HRESULT* value indicating the success or failure of the call. The actual summation is returned as the function's third parameter, a pointer to an integer. Most interface methods return *HRESULT* values and provide their return values as pointer arguments. All COM errors are handled in the form of a 32-bit *HRESULT* value beginning with *0x8000xxxx.* To interpret *HRESULT* values, you can either consult the winerror.h system header file or call the Win32 API function *FormatMessage,* which provides a string explaining the error value. *HRESULT*s and richer error handling mechanisms are discussed in Chapter 5, "Automation and Component Categories."

Last notice that *ISum* publicly inherits the *IUnknown* interface. As we know, all COM objects must implement the *IUnknown* interface, so any object that implements the *ISum* interface will have to implement *IUnknown* as well. The following equation clarifies the relationship between a C++ object and a COM object:

C++ object + *IUnknown* = COM object

From this examination of *ISum*, you can see that a COM interface is simply a contract, requiring all implementations of an interface to adhere to the defined specifications. A COM interface does not contain any code. A *COM class* is a named implementation of one or more interfaces. In C++ programming, a COM class is usually implemented as a C++ class, although the two are not synonymous. In Microsoft Visual Basic, for example, a COM class is implemented as a Visual Basic class module. One or more COM classes are contained in a *component*. A component is a sort of housing for COM classes and can be built as either a DLL or an EXE.

The Interface Definition Language

One of the most important aspects of COM is its language independence. A COM component can be written in any language and then seamlessly called from any other language. In the previous section, we defined the *ISum* interface using C++ code. In Java, the same *ISum* interface would look like this:

```
public interface ISum extends com.ms.com.IUnknown
{
    public abstract int Sum(int x, int y);
}
```

And in Visual Basic, *ISum* would look like this:

```
VERSION 1.0 CLASS
BEGIN
  MultiUse = -1  'True
END
Attribute VB_Name = "ISum"
Attribute VB_Exposed = True
Attribute VB_Creatable = True
Public Function Sum(x As Long, y As Long) As Long

End Function
```

These three language-based definitions expose the fallacy of our assumptions. How can we claim to have a language-independent architecture and then define a single interface differently in every programming language? This would lead to chaos, since a single interface could have multiple correct definitions. The answer to this problem lies in IDL. We introduce IDL here, but for more details on IDL, see Chapter 10, "The Interface Definition Language."

The Open Software Foundation (OSF) originally developed IDL for the Remote Procedure Call (RPC) package for its Distributed Computing Environment (DCE). There IDL helps RPC programmers to ensure that both the client and server sides of a project adhere to the same interface. It is important to realize that IDL is not a programming language, it is a language used only to define interfaces. For this reason, Microsoft decided to adopt IDL for use in defining COM interfaces. By standardizing on one special language for defining interfaces, we do away with the confusion generated by having multiple languages define the same interface differently. The implementation of an interface defined in IDL can still be coded in any language you want.

> **NOTE:** IDL plays an important role in the development of COM objects, but it is not part of COM. IDL is simply a tool used to help programmers define interfaces.

Today all COM programming should begin in IDL. The interface definition for *ISum* written in IDL is shown in Listing 2-1.

component.idl

```
import "unknwn.idl";

[ object, uuid(10000001-0000-0000-0000-000000000001) ]
interface ISum : IUnknown
{
    HRESULT Sum([in] int x, [in] int y, [out, retval] int* retval);
};
```

Listing 2-1.
The IDL file for the ISum *interface.*

The IDL file quickly betrays its C language roots. A cursory examination reveals a construct rather like a header file, providing forward declarations for functions. Several aspects of this interface definition immediately attract attention. First, the definition begins with the *object* attribute, a Microsoft extension to IDL that is used to identify a COM interface. Any interface definition not beginning with the *object* attribute describes an RPC interface, and not a COM interface. After the *object* attribute comes the *universally unique identifier (UUID)* assigned to the interface that distinguishes it from all other interfaces. A UUID is a 128-bit number represented in hexadecimal, guaranteed to be unique across space and time. Two different developers might define an interface named *ISum,* but so long as both interfaces have different UUIDs, no confusion will result. The *ISum* interface as defined in the IDL file derives from *IUnknown,* the root of all COM objects. The interface definition of *IUnknown* itself is imported from the unknwn.idl file, where it is defined as follows:

```
[
  local,
  object,
  uuid(00000000-0000-0000-C000-000000000046),
  pointer_default(unique)
]

interface IUnknown
{
    typedef [unique] IUnknown *LPUNKNOWN;

    HRESULT QueryInterface(
        [in] REFIID riid,
        [out, iid_is(riid)] void** ppvObject);
    ULONG AddRef();
    ULONG Release();
}
```

Globally Unique Identifiers

A UUID is equivalent to a *globally unique identifier (GUID),* the term more commonly used in COM. Normally, GUIDs are created using the guidgen.exe utility. Alternatively, a GUID can be generated at run time by calling the *CoCreateGuid* function. This method is used by Visual Basic to dynamically generate the GUIDs applied to components.

You might wonder why a simple 32-bit value couldn't have been used to identify interfaces. After all, a 32-bit value gives us 2^{32}, or 4,294,967,296, possible unique identifiers. However, the issue is not so much the total number of possible interfaces but how that space is divided in order to guarantee uniqueness. Witness the problems encountered with Internet Protocol (IP) addresses that also use 32-bit identifiers. There are not yet more than 4 billion computers connected to the Internet (maybe next year), but a lot of the addresses are wasted due to the allocation method.

The 128-bit interface identifier used by COM gives us the theoretical possibility of creating approximately 340,282,366,920,900,000,-000,000,000,000,000,000 unique interfaces. That's enough to create one trillion new interfaces every second for the next 10,782,897,-524,560,000,000 years. (The sun is expected to last only another 4.5 billion years, after which COM will no doubt lose some of its universal appeal.) In reality, the algorithm used to generate GUIDs limits the total number to significantly fewer unique interfaces, but still plenty for the foreseeable future.

Notice in the *ISum* interface definition that each argument of the *Sum* method is preceded by a directional attribute, *[in]* or *[out]*. Since the interface defines the communication between a client and a component, which may end up running on separate machines, the interface definition specifies the direction in which each parameter needs to travel. In this case, the first two parameters of the *Sum* function need to be passed only to the component; they do not need to be passed back to the client because their value will not have changed. The third parameter is flagged with the *[out, retval]* attributes, indicating that the parameter is a return value and thus needs only to be passed back from the component to the client. Some languages such as Visual Basic and Java that insulate the developer from the returned *HRESULT* value will transparently make the *[out, retval]* parameter appear to be the value returned by the function. Note that the *[in]* attribute is not required because it is applied to a parameter by default when no directional parameter attribute is specified.

Once an interface has been defined in IDL, the Microsoft IDL (midl.exe) compiler can be used to translate the interface into several C language source files. For the time being, we will focus on the *idlname*.h header file and the *idlname*_i.c source file generated by the MIDL compiler, where *idlname* is a placeholder for the name of the IDL file. The header file contains a C++ version of the interfaces defined in IDL. For example, after compiling the *ISum* interface definition discussed above, the MIDL compiler generated a header file named component.h that includes the following code:

```
interface DECLSPEC_UUID("10000001-0000-0000-0000-000000000001")
ISum : public IUnknown
{
public:
    virtual HRESULT STDMETHODCALLTYPE Sum(
        /* [in] */ int x,
        /* [in] */ int y,
        /* [retval][out] */ int __RPC_FAR *retval) = 0;
};
```

This code looks a lot like the C++ interface definition presented earlier in this chapter; the only difference is in the use of the *interface* rather than the *class* keyword and the addition of the UUID definition. In objbase.h, the keyword *interface* is defined simply as a *struct*. In C++, a structure is the same as a class except that its members are public by default. The keyword *STDMETHOD-CALLTYPE* is defined as *__stdcall*. In rpcndr.h, *DECLSPEC_UUID(x)* is a macro defined as *__declspec (uuid(x))*. This Microsoft extension to C++ enables you to attach a GUID directly to a class or structure.

The *idlname*_i.c source file generated by MIDL contains the actual definitions for the GUIDs defined in the IDL file, as shown here in component_i.c:

```
// {10000001-0000-0000-0000-000000000001}
const IID IID_ISum =
{0x10000001,0x0000,0x0000,{0x00,0x00,0x00,0x00,0x00,0x00,0x00,0x01}};
```

After discussing the problems involved in defining interfaces in a specific programming language, we learned how IDL can be used to define interfaces in a manner independent of any individual programming language. And now we have used MIDL to generate C/C++ code, bringing us back to a language-dependent interface definition, the point at which we began. If MIDL could generate VB and Java code in addition to C++ code, language-specific interface definitions generated from IDL code would be acceptable. However, you would be wrong to assume that MIDL contains some magic command-line parameter to generate anything other than C/C++ code. To avoid having to update MIDL's code generation engine for every new language that comes along, Microsoft decided that a more extensible mechanism was needed. The solution is for MIDL to generate interface definitions in a single, universal format that all languages, including Visual Basic, Java, and C++ (arguably a broad range of languages with quite different goals), can understand. While you ponder the possibilities, let's turn to the client project.

The Component's Client

Now that we have defined the *ISum* interface in IDL, let's write the code needed to create a client application that uses this interface, assuming for the time being that we already have an implementation of the *ISum* interface. For starters, we'll create the client and the component in C++, since this affords the greatest understanding of the underlying COM mechanisms. In Chapter 3, "Type Libraries and Language Integration," we'll branch out into Visual Basic and Java, in which the same principles apply but details are often hidden from view.

The *CoInitialize* Function

All COM applications begin with a call to *CoInitialize*. This function initializes the COM library and must be called before you can use any other COM services except the *CoGetMalloc* function and memory allocation calls. Alternatively, you could use *OleInitialize*. *OleInitialize* calls *CoInitialize* internally, but this technique should be used only when an application specifically intends to use the compound document features of OLE. The only parameter accepted by *CoInitialize* is *NULL*, as shown in the following code fragment:

```
HRESULT hr = CoInitialize(NULL);
if(FAILED(hr))
    cout << "CoInitialize failed." << endl;
```

In early versions of OLE, applications could replace the default memory allocator by passing the address of a custom allocator object to *CoInitialize*. COM does not currently support applications replacing this allocator, and if the parameter is anything but *NULL*, *CoInitialize* returns an *E_INVALIDARG* error. Notice also that all COM function names are prefixed with *Co*, indicating that they are part of the COM API.

The *CoCreateInstance* Function

After initializing the COM library using *CoInitialize*, the client needs a way to instantiate the desired COM class containing an implementation of *ISum*. The *CoCreateInstance* call is the standard way to do this, as shown here, and can be thought of as the COM equivalent of C++'s *new* operator:

```
// {10000002-0000-0000-0000-000000000001}
const CLSID CLSID_InsideDCOM =
{0x10000002,0x0000,0x0000,{0x00,0x00,0x00,0x00,0x00,0x00,0x00,0x01}};

hr = CoCreateInstance(CLSID_InsideDCOM, NULL, CLSCTX_INPROC_SERVER,
    IID_IUnknown, (void**)&pUnknown);
if(FAILED(hr))
    cout << "CoCreateInstance failed." << endl;
```

The first parameter to *CoCreateInstance* is a *class identifier (CLSID)*. A CLSID is a GUID that is associated with the COM class we want to instantiate. *CoCreateInstance* uses this CLSID to search for a match in the HKEY_CLASSES_ROOT-\CLSID section of the registry in order to locate the desired component. HKEY_CLASSES_ROOT\CLSID is undoubtedly the most fundamental COM-related key in the registry. *CoCreateInstance* fails if no match is found. Assuming that an entry for the CLSID is located, the various subkeys provide COM with information about the component.

DEFINITION: An instance of a COM class is called a *COM object.*

As you may know, a component can contain multiple objects. A component that supports multiple objects needs to register a unique CLSID for each supported class of objects. *CoCreateInstance* must be called once for each object you want to create. If some of the objects coexist in the same component, that's all right with COM. In the registry, each object is listed by its CLSID, and the entry contains information specifying the component containing that object. Figure 2-1 shows two calls to *CoCreateInstance* for two different objects that turn out to be housed in the same component. Using an object's CLSID, *CoCreateInstance* looks in the registry for the component; in this case, both *Object1* and *Object2* exist in component.dll.

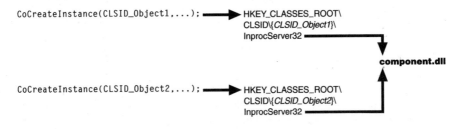

Figure 2-1.
Two COM classes that live in the same component.

The second parameter to *CoCreateInstance* is used to specify whether we are creating this object as part of an aggregate object. Aggregation is covered in the section "Aggregation" later in this chapter. Since this example does not use aggregation, we pass *NULL* for this parameter.

The third parameter of *CoCreateInstance* enables you to specify the class context in which the component will run. COM provides support for building three types of components: in-process, local, and remote. Sometimes a particular component may be implemented in several flavors—for example, a component may be available as an in-process version and as a local and remote version. In such cases, you can select the version that best meets your needs. The class contexts *CLSCTX_INPROC_SERVER, CLSCTX_INPROC_HANDLER, CLSCTX_LOCAL_SERVER,* and *CLSCTX_REMOTE_SERVER* are defined. (*CLSCTX_REMOTE_SERVER* is used with *CoCreateInstanceEx,* which is covered in Chapter 8, "DLL Surrogates and Executable Components.") If you aren't particular about the component type, specify *CLSCTX_SERVER* to retrieve the first available in-process, local, or remote component, in that order.

The *CLSCTX_INPROC_HANDLER* class context is a special type of in-process component that runs in the client process and implements client-side structures of this class, while instances of the actual class are accessed remotely. In our client project example, we will access an in-process component and therefore will specify the *CLSCTX_INPROC_SERVER* class context.

The following table shows the subkeys of HKEY_CLASSES_ROOT\ CLSID\{*YourCLSID*} that identify the different component types available for a particular COM class.

Subkey	Description
InprocHandler32	Full path to a 32-bit DLL component handler.
InprocServer32	Full path to a 32-bit DLL component; specifies the threading mode.
LocalServer32	Full path to a 32-bit local EXE component.
AppID	Information for remote components is stored in the HKEY_CLASSES_ROOT\AppID\{*YourAppID*} section of the registry.

When you instantiate a component using *CoCreateInstance*, the fourth parameter enables you to specify the interface identifier (IID—also equivalent to a GUID) of the desired interface. A pointer to this interface will be returned in the fifth parameter. In this case, we are looking for *ISum*, so we could pass the *IID_ISum* value to *CoCreateInstance*. However, convention dictates that an application should normally get a pointer to the *IUnknown* interface first and then use the *QueryInterface* call to locate the other interfaces. Never ones to disregard convention, we pass *IID_IUnknown*.

The *IUnknown* Interface Methods

Assuming that all has gone well, a pointer to the *IUnknown* interface of the requested COM object is returned in the fifth parameter of *CoCreateInstance*. The name *IUnknown* highlights the fact that at this stage the true capabilities of the object are unknown. With this pointer, we can call any of the three *IUnknown* methods: *QueryInterface*, *AddRef*, and *Release*. The *AddRef* and *Release* methods are designed to perform reference counting for each interface. Reference counting is used to determine when an object can be freed from memory.

For every interface pointer, *AddRef* must be called prior to calling any other methods, and *Release* must be called when you have finished using the interface pointer. To make things more efficient, COM specification dictates that *AddRef* is automatically called before *CoCreateInstance* returns. For this reason, the client can skip the call to *AddRef* and proceed directly to the most interesting *IUnknown* method: *QueryInterface*.

The *QueryInterface* Method

Every COM object is guaranteed to support the *IUnknown* interface, a pointer to which can be provided by *CoCreateInstance*. Aside from this rule, however, there are no guarantees. The purpose of *QueryInterface* is to determine what other interfaces an object supports. We like to call this the "discovery phase" of the relationship between the client and the COM object, since the client calls *QueryInterface* to discover the capabilities of a particular object. In the following code, the *QueryInterface* method is used to determine whether an object supports the *ISum* interface:

```
hr = pUnknown->QueryInterface(IID_ISum, (void**)&pSum);
if(FAILED(hr))
    cout << "IID_ISum not supported." << endl;
```

The first parameter to *QueryInterface* is the IID of the interface being queried for. Recall that the *IID_ISum* value is declared in the component_i.c file generated by MIDL. Assuming that the object supports the desired interface, a pointer to that interface is returned in the second parameter of *QueryInterface*. Convention dictates that *AddRef* has already been called on any interface pointer returned by *QueryInterface*.

The *AddRef* and *Release* Methods

Once we have a pointer to the desired interface, we no longer need the *IUnknown* pointer that was originally returned by *CoCreateInstance*. Accordingly, the *IUnknown::Release* method can be called to decrement the interface's reference counter, as shown here:

```
m_cRef = pUnknown->Release();
cout << "pUnknown->Release() reference count = " << m_cRef << endl;
```

The value returned by the *Release* method is the interface's reference counter. This value is for debugging purposes only and should not be used to make a determination as to the internal state of an object.

Note that calling *Release* on an interface pointer does not necessarily destroy the object providing the implementation. *Release* simply decrements the reference counter for the interface. If the interface's reference count falls to *0* and no other interfaces of this object are in use, the object is freed from memory. In the preceding code, we are releasing the *IUnknown* pointer; however, the object is not yet destroyed because the *ISum* pointer just returned by *QueryInterface* has incremented the object's reference count via an automatic call to *AddRef*.

Since we don't have to worry about calling *AddRef* on the *ISum* pointer, we are now ready to call the *Sum* method, as shown in the following code fragment. This, after all, is the point of the entire sample project.

```
int sum;
hr = pSum->Sum(2, 3, &sum);
if(SUCCEEDED(hr))
    cout << "Sum(2, 3) = " << sum << endl;
```

In this example, it is important to emphasize that we don't need to call *AddRef* because it has already been called on interface pointers returned by *CoCreateInstance* and *QueryInterface*. Nevertheless, *AddRef* must be explicitly called whenever an interface pointer is aliased, as shown here:

```
IUnknown* pUnknown;
ISum* pSumOne;
ISum* pSumTwo;

// QueryInterface calls AddRef on pSumOne.
pUnknown->QueryInterface(IID_ISum, (void**)&pSumOne);

// Release IUnknown; we don't need it anymore.
pUnknown->Release();

// Copy a pointer.
pSumTwo = pSumOne;

// This requires an explicit AddRef.
pSumTwo->AddRef();

pSumOne->DoSomethingUseful();
pSumTwo->DoSomethingMoreUseful();

// Now we've finished; call Release.
pSumTwo->Release();
pSumOne->Release();
```

Here the interface pointer *pSumOne* was copied to *pSumTwo*. This aliasing results in two interface pointers, and therefore *AddRef* must be called in order to increment the reference counter. In some cases, if you are certain that the reference count will remain above *0*, thus ensuring that the object is not freed, the extra *AddRef* and *Release* calls can be optimized away, as shown here:

```
// QueryInterface calls AddRef on pSumOne.
pUnknown->QueryInterface(IID_ISum, (void**)&pSumOne);

// Release IUnknown; we don't need it anymore.
pUnknown->Release();

// Copy a pointer.
pSumTwo = pSumOne;

// Don't need this. Reference count is sure to be at least 1.
// pSumTwo->AddRef();

pSumOne->DoSomethingUseful();
pSumTwo->DoSomethingMoreUseful();

// Matching AddRef commented out.
// pSumTwo->Release()

// Now we've finished; call Release.
pSumOne->Release();
```

Note that in more complex code, it is often difficult to correctly remove the unnecessary *AddRef* and *Release* calls. In addition, such code becomes very fragile if someone modifies it without being aware of the reference counting assumptions made by the original developer. And in most cases, the performance improvement that can be achieved by optimizing *AddRef* and *Release* calls is not significant. As we shall see in Chapter 12, "The Network Protocol," the proxy caches *AddRef* and *Release* calls when you are accessing remote objects using DCOM so that each client call does not necessarily result in an RPC. All in all, *AddRef* and *Release* optimizations have been oversold.

The *CoUninitialize* Function

With the main job of the interface completed, we need to perform some cleanup duties. *IUnknown::Release* must be called because we have finished with the *ISum* pointer. Note that this is the last open pointer to the object, and therefore the reference counter will be decremented to *0* and actually initiate the destruction of the COM object. Last *CoUninitialize* is called to close the COM library, freeing any resources that it maintains and forcing all RPC connections to close, as shown here:

```
CoUninitialize();
```

The *CoInitialize* and *CoUninitialize* calls must be balanced—if there are multiple calls to the *CoInitialize* function, there must be the same number of calls to *CoUninitialize*. Only the *CoUninitialize* call corresponding to the *CoInitialize* call that initialized the library can close it.

The V-Table Situation

Figure 2-2 shows the mechanism through which a client program holding an interface pointer is able to call methods in a component.

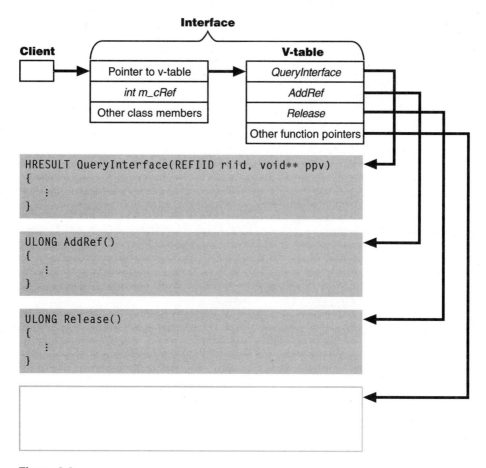

Figure 2-2.
Diagram showing that an interface pointer is really a pointer to a pointer to a v-table containing function pointers.

Here you can see that for every C++ class containing virtual functions, the language automatically creates a v-table structure containing pointers to all the class's virtual functions, including those that are declared in a base class. Note that a v-table is built on a per-class basis, not for each instance of the class. A pointer to the v-table itself is stored as the first member in the object's memory structure, followed by the other members of the class. What we refer to as an *interface pointer* is actually a pointer to a pointer to a table of function pointers (a rather inconvenient way to describe the mechanism through which a client calls an object). C++ helps us forget about the extra level of indirection by implicitly converting *pUnknown->pVtbl->AddRef()* to *pUnknown->AddRef()*.

The indirection provided by a v-table can be compared with the software interrupts used by MS-DOS. An MS-DOS application requests service from the operating system by setting parameter values in various registers and then issuing software interrupt 21h. MS-DOS provides a pointer to an interrupt handler installed at vector 21h in the interrupt table and therefore responds to the application's request. MS-DOS installs a pointer to an interrupt handler at vector 21h in the interrupt table and, through it, responds to the application's request. Although v-tables are based on direct function calls rather than on software, they provide a similar, well-known entry point for accessing an arbitrary service.

It is also important to realize that the function pointers in the v-table are stored in the order of declaration—that is, the first method declared in the IDL definition corresponds to the first function pointer in the v-table for that class. The v-table order of virtual functions that are declared in a base class and implemented in a derived class is determined by the order of the functions in the base class. Therefore, you cannot mess up a standard interface such as *IUnknown* simply by declaring its methods in the wrong order: the order of the *IUnknown* methods in your class's v-table is determined by their order in the header file (unknwn.h) where *IUnknown* is declared.

When multiple inheritance is used to implement several interfaces in one class, the compiler concatenates the v-tables of the various interfaces. The order in which their entries appear in the v-table is determined by the order in which the interfaces are inherited.

Building the Client Project

To build the client project, first compile the IDL file shown earlier in this chapter at the command line using the MIDL compiler. Use the following command:

```
C:\Program Files\DevStudio\VC\bin>midl component.idl
```

Then create a Win32 console application project in Visual C++ containing the client.cpp file and the component_i.c file generated by MIDL. The complete client.cpp code is shown in Listing 2-2. Last build the project.

client.cpp

```
#include <iostream.h>
#include "component.h" // Generated by MIDL

// {10000002-0000-0000-0000-000000000001}
const CLSID CLSID_InsideDCOM =
{0x10000002,0x0000,0x0000,{0x00,0x00,0x00,0x00,0x00,0x00,0x00,0x01}};

void main()
{
    IUnknown* pUnknown;
    ISum* pSum;

    HRESULT hr = CoInitialize(NULL);
    if(FAILED(hr))
        cout << "CoInitialize failed." << endl;

    hr = CoCreateInstance(CLSID_InsideDCOM, NULL, CLSCTX_INPROC_SERVER,
        IID_IUnknown, (void**)&pUnknown);
    if(FAILED(hr))
        cout << "CoCreateInstance failed." << endl;

    hr = pUnknown->QueryInterface(IID_ISum, (void**)&pSum);
    if(FAILED(hr))
        cout << "IID_ISum not supported." << endl;

    pUnknown->Release();

    int sum;
    hr = pSum->Sum(2, 3, &sum);
    if(SUCCEEDED(hr))
        cout << "Client: Calling Sum(2, 3) = " << sum << endl;

    pSum->Release();

    CoUninitialize();
}
```

Listing 2-2.
The complete client code.

The Problems with *QueryInterface*

In the C++ header file, unknwn.h, the *IUnknown::QueryInterface* method is declared as follows:

```
virtual HRESULT __stdcall QueryInterface(REFIID riid,
    void** ppvObject)=0;
```

This declaration is the source of much consternation and many bugs in COM programming. Figure 2-3 shows how the *QueryInterface* mechanism works when used correctly. Notice that COM objects are drawn with standard and custom interface "lollipops" extending from the left side of the object, whereas *IUnknown* is drawn separately on top of the object because all objects support this interface.

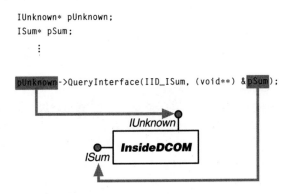

```
IUnknown* pUnknown;
ISum* pSum;
    ⋮

pUnknown->QueryInterface(IID_ISum, (void**) &pSum);
```

Figure 2-3.
Querying an object for its ISum *interface pointer.*

Since *QueryInterface* must be able to query for any interface (*IUnknown, ISum, IYouNameIt*), the second parameter is declared as a pointer to a pointer to pretty much anything (*void***). This very flexible declaration allows a programmer to do pretty much anything, including making pretty much any kind of mistake. Examine the following code to see whether you can find the insidious bug that the C++ compiler cannot:

```
hr = pUnknown->QueryInterface(IID_ISum, (void**)pSum);
```

The problem here is that the address-of (&) operator is missing before *pSum*. The compiler, blinded by the explicit *void*** cast, assumes that we know what we are doing and stuffs the retrieved pointer into any invalid location pointed to by *pSum*. The result is an immediate crash.

The Component

Let's review the *ISum* interface definition we are attempting to implement as a COM class:

```
[ object, uuid(10000001-0000-0000-0000-000000000001) ]
interface ISum : IUnknown
{
    HRESULT Sum([in] int x, [in] int y, [out, retval] int* retval);
}
```

Another Good One to Tell Your Friends About

```
ISum* pSum;
hr = pUnknown->QueryInterface(IID_IUnknown, (void**)&pSum);
int sum;
pSum->Sum(2, 3, &sum); // Uh-oh!
```

What's wrong with this code? Well, the *QueryInterface* call requests the *IUnknown* interface (*IID_IUnknown*), but it stores the pointer in *pSum*. *pSum* is a pointer to an interface of type *ISum*, not *IUnknown*, but the compiler thinks this is all right because *pSum* is explicitly cast to *void***. Since *pSum* is a pointer to an interface of type *ISum*, the compiler doesn't have any problem calling the *Sum* function. Of course, in this case *pSum* is only a pointer to *IUnknown* and might spontaneously combust when the *Sum* function is called. (Actually, this code will run without complaint in this case since our implementation of *ISum* inherits from *IUnknown* and does not define additional member functions. However, the slightest change to the *ISum* v-table would make this code deadly.)

In the interest of world peace and to make *QueryInterface* safer, we present *TypeSafeQI*:

```
#define TypeSafeQI(Interface, ppObject) \
    QueryInterface(IID_##Interface, \
    (void**)(static_cast<Interface**>(ppObject)))
```

TypeSafeQI is a macro that replaces and internally calls *QueryInterface*. Using the C++ *static_cast* operator, which converts an expression to a particular type based solely on the types present in the expression, *TypeSafeQI* provides compile-time error checking that does not permit a *QueryInterface* call for one interface to return a pointer to another.

Although we could (and will in the next chapter) implement *ISum* using any language, such as Java or Visual Basic, let's take this simple interface definition and implement it using a C++ class. Recall the C++ definition of the *ISum* interface generated by MIDL in the component.h file:

```
interface DECLSPEC_UUID("10000001-0000-0000-0000-000000000001")
ISum : public IUnknown
{
public:
```

(continued)

The correct use of *TypeSafeQI* is shown here:

```
ISum* pSum;
hr = pUnknown->TypeSafeQI(ISum, &pSum);
int sum;
pSum->Sum(2, 3, &sum); // Okey-dokey
```

And here is the unsafe code that *TypeSafeQI* is designed to catch:

```
ISum* pSum;
hr = pUnknown->TypeSafeQI(IUnknown, &pSum); // NO WAY
```

TypeSafeQI makes *QueryInterface* not only safer but also nicer since it banishes the ugly *void*** casts. This has the side effect of making it much harder to forget the address-of operator, as this code won't compile either:

```
ISum* pSum;
hr = pUnknown->TypeSafeQI(IUnknown, pSum); // No can do
```

Perhaps an even better version of *TypeSafeQI* is *TypeSaferQI*. This macro relies on the *__uuidof* operator; a Microsoft extension to C++ designed to aid in COM programming. The *__uuidof* operator can be used to retrieve the GUID of a COM interface pointer, as shown in the following code fragment. This technique makes calling *QueryInterface* even easier because you don't need to specify an IID—the correct one is obtained for you.

```
#define TypeSaferQI(ppObject) \
    QueryInterface(__uuidof(*ppObject), (void**)ppObject)
```

The correct use of the *TypeSaferQI* macro is shown here:

```
ISum* pSum;
hr = pUnknown->TypeSaferQI(&pSum);
```

```
virtual HRESULT STDMETHODCALLTYPE Sum(
    /* [in] */ int x,
    /* [in] */ int y,
    /* [retval][out] */ int __RPC_FAR *retval) = 0;
};
```

ISum is defined in C++ as an abstract class because its four methods—three from *IUnknown* plus the *Sum* method declared here—are pure virtual functions, meaning that they are unimplemented. To create a COM class in C++, you would normally define a C++ class that inherits from the interfaces being implemented, as shown in the following code. Notice that the function declarations are no longer declared as *pure* (with the *=0* specifier), which indicates that the *CInsideDCOM* class intends to implement these methods.

```
// g_cComponents keeps track of how many objects are instantiated.
// This value is used to determine when it is safe to unload.
long g_cComponents = 0;

class CInsideDCOM : public ISum
{
public:
    // IUnknown
    ULONG __stdcall AddRef();
    ULONG __stdcall Release();
    HRESULT __stdcall QueryInterface(REFIID riid, void** ppv);

    // ISum
    HRESULT __stdcall Sum(int x, int y, int* retval);

    CInsideDCOM() : m_cRef(1) { g_cComponents++; }
    ~CInsideDCOM() { g_cComponents--; }

private:
    ULONG m_cRef;
};
```

The *AddRef* Method

The *CInsideDCOM* class's implementation of the *AddRef* method is exceedingly simple; its only job is to increment the private variable *m_cRef*. This variable is the actual reference counter for the *ISum* interface. Here is the entire implementation of *AddRef*:

```
ULONG CInsideDCOM::AddRef()
{
    return ++m_cRef;
}
```

The *Release* Method

The component's implementation of *IUnknown::Release* is complicated by the fact that the reference counter may be decremented to 0. A value of *0* indicates that no one is using the object, and therefore we need to destroy this instance of *CInsideDCOM*:

```
ULONG CInsideDCOM::Release()
{
    if(--m_cRef != 0)
        return m_cRef;
    delete this;
    return 0;
}
```

Notice that both *AddRef* and *Release* return the resulting value of the reference counter, which should be used for diagnostic or testing purposes only. If the client needs to know that resources have been freed, an interface with higher-level semantics should be used.

The *QueryInterface* Method:
Preserving the Identity of a COM Object

The implementation of *QueryInterface* is the most interesting of all the *IUnknown* methods. Recall that *QueryInterface* is the method used to retrieve pointers to the other interfaces supported by the object. This technique is sometimes called a sideways cast since the interfaces returned by *QueryInterface* are unrelated by an inheritance hierarchy. The *IUnknown* interface pointer is the most fundamental pointer you can have to an object; it establishes the identity of a COM object. You can always determine whether two pointers are pointing to the same COM object simply by comparing their *IUnknown* pointers; if they both point to the same address, they refer to the same object. This may seem obvious, but understanding the implications of identity in COM will help you understand the entire architecture, which has been built on a few fundamental ideas.

The Symmetric, Reflexive, and Transitive Rules of *QueryInterface*

As a consequence of the need to preserve identity in COM, developers must adhere to several rules regarding their implementations of the *IUnknown* interface. The five specific requirements for implementations of the *IUnknown-::QueryInterface* method are listed on the following page.

■ If a client retrieves an interface pointer from a call to *QueryInterface*, subsequent *QueryInterface* calls for the same interface must return the same pointer value.

■ The set of interfaces accessible on an object through *QueryInterface* must be static, not dynamic. If a call to *QueryInterface* to request a pointer to a specific interface succeeds the first time, it must succeed again, and if it fails the first time, it must fail on all subsequent attempts.

■ *QueryInterface* must be reflexive. If a client holds a pointer to an interface and queries for that same interface, the call must succeed.

■ *Query Interface* must be symmetric. If a client holding a pointer to one interface queries successfully for a second interface, the client must be able to call *QueryInterface* through the second pointer for the first interface.

■ *QueryInterface* must be transitive. If a client holding a pointer to one interface queries successfully for a second interface and through that pointer queries successfully for a third interface, a query for the first interface through the pointer for the third interface must also succeed.

Figure 2-4 shows the effects of the symmetric, reflexive, and transitive rules of *QueryInterface*.

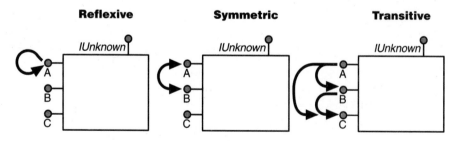

Figure 2-4.
The reflexive, symmetric, and transitive rules of QueryInterface.

Without further ado, here is a typical implementation of *QueryInterface* that meets all five of the requirements stated above:

```
HRESULT CInsideDCOM::QueryInterface(REFIID riid, void** ppv)
{
    if(riid == IID_IUnknown)
        *ppv = (IUnknown*)this;
    else if(riid == IID_ISum)
        *ppv = (ISum*)this;
    else
    {
        *ppv = NULL;
        return E_NOINTERFACE;
    }
    AddRef();
    return S_OK;
}
```

This implementation of *QueryInterface* simply compares the requested IID with every IID that the object supports. Since this object implements only *IUnknown* and *ISum*, only pointers to these interfaces can be returned. Notice that after the *this* pointer has been cast to the requested interface pointer, the *AddRef* method is called. This optimization relieves the client from having to repeatedly call *AddRef* on each interface pointer obtained through *QueryInterface*. The client is required to call *AddRef* for every new copy of an interface pointer on a given object that is not obtained through *QueryInterface*.

It is interesting to note that the C++ comparison operator (= =) is used to compare the IIDs. This comparison is possible because the objbase.h header file overloads the comparison operator to perform the comparison using the *IsEqualGUID* call, as shown here:

```
inline BOOL operator==(const GUID& guidOne, const GUID& guidOther)
{
    return IsEqualGUID(guidOne, guidOther);
}
```

The *ISum::Sum* Method (Finally)

The last remaining method to be implemented is the *Sum* method, the sole method of the *ISum* interface. The implementation of this method should not cause any surprise:

```
HRESULT CInsideDCOM::Sum(int x, int y, int* retval)
{
    *retval = x + y;
    return S_OK;
}
```

CoCreateInstance (Again)

Perhaps you're wondering what really happens when the client calls *CoCreate-Instance*. How does *CoCreateInstance* return that first pointer to an object's *IUnknown* implementation? This is an excellent question, but unfortunately the answer is a bit complicated. *CoCreateInstance* needs only to create an instance of the *CInsideDCOM* class that implements *ISum*. This technique could be as simple as using the C++ *new* operator, and in fact the *new* operator is ultimately used. But here is the place to recall that one of the central tenets of COM is the concept of *location transparency*. Location transparency postulates that clients should be able to reach objects easily, regardless of whether they are contained in in-process, local, or remote components. Assuming that our object is housed in an in-process component, the *new* operator could simply and easily be used to create an instance of the *CInsideDCOM* class. But what if that component was running in a separate process address space or on a remote computer? The *new* operator is obviously not the whole answer.

The *IClassFactory* Interface

> DEFINITION: A *COM class object* is an object that typically has no behavior except to create new instances of some other class. COM class objects normally implement the *IClassFactory* interface and thus are often referred to as *class factories.*

COM's answer to this issue is *IClassFactory*. *IClassFactory* is an interface implemented by class factory objects designed especially to manufacture other COM objects. For this reason, the name *IClassFactory* is a misnomer; a much more descriptive name would be *IObjectFactory*. Be that as it may, every COM class must have an associated class factory (implementing the *IClassFactory* interface), to enable clients to instantiate the class using a function such as *CoCreateInstance*. In fact, *CoCreateInstance* calls *IClassFactory* internally.

In the unknwn.idl file, *IClassFactory* is defined as follows:

```
interface IClassFactory : IUnknown
{
    HRESULT CreateInstance([in, unique] IUnknown* pUnkOuter,
        [in] REFIID riid,
        [out, iid_is(riid)] void** ppvObject);
    HRESULT LockServer([in] BOOL fLock);
}
```

As you can see, *IClassFactory* has two methods: *CreateInstance* and *LockServer*. It is the job of the *CreateInstance* method to actually instantiate a COM object. The client calls the *LockServer* method to keep a component open in memory, thus allowing instances to be created more quickly. Note that most clients do not need to call this function; *LockServer* is provided only for those clients that require special performance in creating multiple instances of their classes.

Here is the C++ class *CFactory*, which implements *IClassFactory* for the purpose of instantiating *CInsideDCOM* objects:

```
class CFactory : public IClassFactory
{
public:
    // IUnknown
    ULONG __stdcall AddRef();
    ULONG __stdcall Release();
    HRESULT __stdcall QueryInterface(REFIID riid, void** ppv);

    // IClassFactory
    HRESULT __stdcall CreateInstance(IUnknown* pUnknownOuter,
        REFIID riid, void** ppv);
    HRESULT __stdcall LockServer(BOOL bLock);

    CFactory() : m_cRef(1) { }
    ~CFactory() { }

private:
    ULONG m_cRef;
};
```

IUnknown needs to be implemented again since all COM objects are required to support this interface. We will not bore you with the implementation of *AddRef* and *Release*, as you can no doubt imagine that these simply increment and decrement the *m_cRef* reference counter. Let's take a moment, however, to look at the implementation of *QueryInterface* for the class factory:

```
HRESULT CFactory::QueryInterface(REFIID riid, void** ppv)
{
    if((riid == IID_IUnknown) || (riid == IID_IClassFactory))
        *ppv = (IClassFactory*)this;
    else
    {
        *ppv = NULL;
        return E_NOINTERFACE;
    }
    AddRef();
    return S_OK;
}
```

Notice that in this case we don't care whether the caller is requesting the *IUnknown* or the *IClassFactory* interface since the same *CFactory* class implements both.

The *CreateInstance* Method

Before we explain the *CreateInstance* code, please answer this question: who calls *IClassFactory::CreateInstance?* The client, of course. When the client calls *CoCreate-Instance* to instantiate an object, COM does some stuff that results in a call to *CreateInstance* in the component. Here is the code for the *IClassFactory::Create-Instance* method:

```
HRESULT CFactory::CreateInstance(IUnknown *pUnknownOuter,
    REFIID riid, void** ppv)
{
    if(pUnknownOuter != NULL)
        return CLASS_E_NOAGGREGATION;

    CInsideDCOM *pInsideDCOM = new CInsideDCOM;
    if(pInsideDCOM == NULL)
        return E_OUTOFMEMORY;

    HRESULT hr = pInsideDCOM->QueryInterface(riid, ppv);
    pInsideDCOM->Release();    // In case QueryInterface fails
    return hr;
}
```

The first parameter to *CreateInstance* tells us whether the client is instantiating the object as part of an aggregate object. This particular component doesn't support aggregation, so for the client that wants the object as part of an aggregate, we return the error *CLASS_E_NOAGGREGATION*. Recall that when the client code presented earlier in this chapter called *CoCreateInstance*, its second parameter specified aggregate information; this is where the value of the *pUnknownOuter* parameter of *IClassFactory::CreateInstance* comes from.

CreateInstance actually manufactures a spanking new *CInsideDCOM* object using the C++ *new* operator. Since each COM class requires its own class factory, *CreateInstance* knows which object to instantiate. Assuming that all is well, we now call *CInsideDCOM::QueryInterface* (not *CFactory::QueryInterface*) to get the interface requested by the client in the fourth parameter of *CoCreateInstance*. In this case, the client has requested the *IUnknown* interface. Recall that inside the *QueryInterface* function, *AddRef* is called to increment the reference counter, so the client doesn't need to call *AddRef* on the interface pointer returned by *CoCreateInstance*.

The call to the *Release* method immediately following the *QueryInterface* call in the code fragment above might seem rather odd. If *QueryInterface* just did us a favor by calling *AddRef*, why should we turn around and call *Release?* The reasoning behind this seemingly inexplicable behavior arises from the problem of what to do if the *QueryInterface* call fails. *QueryInterface* might fail for the very simple reason that the client requested an interface not supported by the object. If that should happen, *AddRef* will not be called, but neither will the *InsideDCOM* object be destroyed. In order to handle this potential catastrophe, the value of the reference counter variable, *m_cRef*, is initialized to *1* by the object's constructor. This setting is artificial because at the time of construction the object does not yet have a client. Instead, the counter is set to *1* so that should the *QueryInterface* call fail, the subsequent *Release* will decrement the reference counter to *0*. Code in the *Release* method, realizing that the object has no remaining clients, will then initiate destruction of the object. Although somewhat confusing, this solution deals cleanly with the problem of a failed *QueryInterface* call with a minimum of overhead. In the more positive case in which *QueryInterface* succeeds, the extra *Release* call does no damage because it is simply undoing the artificial reference count set by the object's constructor.

The *LockServer* Method

The implementation of the *LockServer* method is fairly straightforward. Based on the Boolean parameter *bLock*, this method either increments or decrements a global counter variable named *g_cServerLocks*, as shown here:

```
long g_cServerLocks = 0;

HRESULT CFactory::LockServer(BOOL bLock)
{
    if(bLock)
        g_cServerLocks++;
    else
        g_cServerLocks--;
    return S_OK;
}
```

A client might call *LockServer* if it knew that it wanted to create some objects, use them, free them, and then do it all over again at a later time. Without the ability to call *LockServer*, the class factory's reference counter would go to *0*, and assuming there were no other clients the component would exit and be unloaded. When the client wanted to use the services of the component again later, the component would have to be reloaded. With *LockServer*, the client can force the component to sit tight in memory, waiting to be called. This can result in a performance improvement for clients that create and release multiple objects over a period of time.

Exported DLL Functions

We've almost completed our journey through the code required to build a COM object. Before we go on, you need to make a final decision as to how you want to package this object. Do you want to create an EXE or a DLL component? EXE components require a *main* or *WinMain* function; DLL components require two helper functions: *DllGetClassObject* and *DllCanUnloadNow*. For this first attempt at building a COM-based component, let's create an in-process (DLL) component. (Don't worry about having to implement those two extra functions—it's no big deal.)

The *DllGetClassObject* Function

As you know, each class factory creates only one type of object and a useful component might contain multiple objects. The purpose of *DllGetClassObject* is to direct us to the correct class factory for the type of object we want to create. Since our sample component has only one supported object (*InsideDCOM*), our implementation of *DllGetClassObject* is rather rudimentary:

```
HRESULT __stdcall DllGetClassObject(REFCLSID clsid,
    REFIID riid, void** ppv)
{
    if(clsid != CLSID_InsideDCOM)
        return CLASS_E_CLASSNOTAVAILABLE; // Tough luck!

    CFactory* pFactory = new CFactory;
    if(pFactory == NULL)
        return E_OUTOFMEMORY;

    // riid is probably IID_IClassFactory.
    HRESULT hr = pFactory->QueryInterface(riid, ppv);
    pFactory->Release();    // Just in case QueryInterface fails
    return hr;
}
```

DllGetClassObject first checks to see whether the client has requested the *CLSID_InsideDCOM* COM class. If the client did not, we simply return a *CLASS_E_CLASSNOTAVAILABLE* error. If the client requests a class object supported by this component, *DllGetClassFactory* instantiates a class factory using the C++ *new* operator. After that, *QueryInterface* is called to ask for the *IClassFactory* interface. We did say that manufacturing COM objects is the domain of a class factory. The third parameter is used to return the pointer to our class factory object. Notice once again that the *Release* method is called immediately after the *QueryInterface* call. Remember that this call works to cleanly deallocate the *CFactory* object in case the *QueryInterface* call fails.

You might be wondering why *DllGetClassObject* even bothers with the *IID* parameter of the *IClassFactory* interface. After all, if all objects are instantiated by a class factory, why not simply hard-code *IID_IClassFactory* and rename the *DllGetClassObject* function *DllGetClassFactory?* The answer is that some objects may have special requirements not met by *IClassFactory* and instead will want to implement a custom activation interface. A custom activation interface is useful when a standard implementation of *IClassFactory* just won't do. For example, say that you wanted to support licensing in order to restrict your component to those machines on which it was properly installed. *IClassFactory* does not offer this functionality, but luckily an improved version of the interface, named *IClassFactory2*, does.

In those rare cases in which neither *IClassFactory* nor *IClassFactory2* is sufficient, a custom activation interface may be the only solution. The client will then pass the *IID* parameter of the custom activation interface to *CoGetClassObject*. Keep in mind that if *IClassFactory* or *IClassFactory2* is not supported by a component, clients may no longer instantiate objects using *CoCreateInstance* because *CoCreateInstance* automatically queries for the *IClassFactory* interface. For this reason, the COM specification requires that all classes registered in the system with a CLSID must implement *IClassFactory*. Monikers may also offer a solution where *IClassFactory* is insufficient—for details, see Chapter 7.

In Windows, DLLs are primarily controlled by three functions: *LoadLibrary*, *GetProcAddress*, and *FreeLibrary*. The Win32 API function *LoadLibrary* is used to load a DLL into the caller's address space. *GetProcAddress* is used to retrieve pointers to the DLL's exported functions so that the client can call those functions in the DLL. When a client has finished, the DLL is freed by calling *FreeLibrary*. *FreeLibrary* decrements the internal Windows usage counter and then unloads the library if the counter is *0*.

One of the main reasons for COM's existence is to move to an object-oriented world of components and work with them in a consistent manner. However, it is not possible to entirely shed these ties because underneath the shiny COM veneer is just a plain old DLL. To be able to call the methods of a COM object housed in a DLL, we need their memory address. *IUnknown:: QueryInterface* is designed to give us these pointers, but how do we get that first pointer to *IUnknown?* This is where *DllGetClassObject* comes in. The *DllGetClassObject* function is not a member of any class; it is a fossilized exported function that gives us that first pointer. We don't call *LoadLibrary* or *GetProcAddress*—that's what *CoCreateInstance* is for.

The *DllCanUnloadNow* Function

The last function we need in order to complete the sample component is *DllCanUnloadNow*, shown in the following code. This function is used to determine whether the DLL is in use. If the DLL is not in use, *S_OK* is returned and the caller can safely unload the DLL from memory. Otherwise, *S_FALSE* is returned to indicate that the DLL should not be unloaded.

```
HRESULT __stdcall DllCanUnloadNow()
{
    if(g_cServerLocks == 0 && g_cComponents == 0)
        return S_OK;
    else
        return S_FALSE;
}
```

You do not have to call *DllCanUnloadNow* directly—COM calls it through a call to the *CoFreeUnusedLibraries* function. The *CoUninitialize* function called by clients before exiting calls *CoFreeUnusedLibraries*.

> **NOTE:** Due to the potential for race conditions in multithreaded components (see Chapter 4, "Threading Models and Apartments"), recent implementations of COM do not unload in-process components even if *S_OK* is returned.

CoCreateInstance (The Truth)

With all this discussion, you might be wondering how the *CoCreateInstance* function actually works its magic. *CoCreateInstance* actually calls another function, *CoGetClassObject*, which provides an interface pointer to the requested object associated with a specified CLSID. The following code fragment shows the *CoGetClassObject* function in action. If necessary, *CoGetClassObject* dynamically loads the executable code required to do this, even if that code happens to be on a remote machine. Normally, *CoGetClassObject* is asked to retrieve a pointer to an object's implementation of *IClassFactory*.

```
hr = CoGetClassObject(CLSID_InsideDCOM, CLSCTX_INPROC_SERVER, NULL,
    IID_IClassFactory, (void**)&pClassFactory);
if(FAILED(hr))
    cout << "CoGetClassObject failed." << endl;
```

Retrieving an interface pointer to *IClassFactory* enables *CoCreateInstance* to call *IClassFactory::CreateInstance* to manufacture a COM object, as shown here:

```
hr = pClassFactory->CreateInstance(NULL, IID_IUnknown,
    (void**) &pUnknown);
if(FAILED(hr))
    cout << "pClassFactory->CreateInstance failed." << endl;
```

Once *CoCreateInstance* has finished creating the object using the class factory, the class factory can be released, as shown here:

```
pClassFactory->Release();
```

If you prefer, the call to *CoCreateInstance* in the client can be replaced with equivalent code that uses *CoGetClassObject* directly. Is there a reason for doing this? Absolutely. *CoGetClassObject* provides greater control over how and when objects are instantiated and has lower overhead than multiple calls to *CoCreateInstance*. Since *CoGetClassObject* can be used to return a pointer to an object's *IClassFactory* implementation, clients that want to create several objects of the same COM class should use *CoGetClassObject* followed by *IClass-Factory::CreateInstance* instead of *CoCreateInstance*. The following code replaces *CoCreateInstance* in the client project with equivalent code that uses *CoGet-ClassObject*:

```
IClassFactory* pClassFactory;
CoGetClassObject(CLSID_InsideDCOM, CLSCTX_INPROC_SERVER, NULL,
    IID_IClassFactory, (void**)&pClassFactory);
pClassFactory->CreateInstance(NULL, IID_IUnknown, (void**)&pUnknown);
pClassFactory->Release();
```

In fact, it is even possible to instantiate and access a COM object without using any COM functions. The following C++ code loads an in-process component, obtains a pointer to the *DllGetClassObject* function, and calls *IClass-Factory::CreateInstance*—all without using a single COM API function. (We don't suggest that you actually write code like this, but it can be very helpful to see that what COM is doing for you in *CoCreateInstance* is not all that complex.)

```
IUnknown* pUnknown;
IClassFactory* pClassFactory;

// Load the DLL.
HINSTANCE myDLL = LoadLibrary("C:\\component.dll");

// Declare a pointer to the DllGetClassObject function.
typedef HRESULT (__stdcall *PFNDLLGETCLASSOBJECT)(REFCLSID clsid,
    REFIID riid, void** ppv);

// Get a pointer to the component's DllGetClassObject function.
PFNDLLGETCLASSOBJECT DllGetClassObject =
    (PFNDLLGETCLASSOBJECT)GetProcAddress(myDLL, "DllGetClassObject");

// Call DllGetClassObject to get a pointer to the class factory.
DllGetClassObject(CLSID_InsideDCOM, IID_IClassFactory,
    (void**)&pClassFactory);
```

(continued)

```
// IClassFactory::CreateInstance and IUnknown::Release
pClassFactory->CreateInstance(NULL, IID_IUnknown, (void**)&pUnknown);
pClassFactory->Release();
```

Figure 2-5 puts in perspective the functions and the order in which they are called for an in-process component.

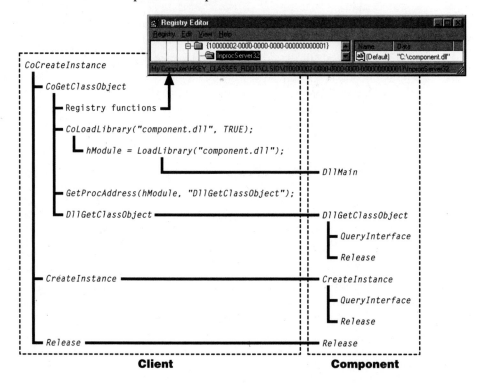

Figure 2-5.
A client calling CoCreateInstance *to instantiate a COM object.*

The Service Control Manager

In reality, *CoGetClassObject* delegates the task of locating and loading the component to the Service Control Manager (SCM, pronounced "scum") implemented by the rpcss.exe process. After the SCM locates and loads the requested component, the COM library and the SCM drop out of the picture, allowing the client and the component to communicate directly. COM does not insert a mediator between in-process components and their clients' that could hurt performance. When an object is invoked on a remote machine, the SCM on the local machine contacts the SCM on the remote machine to request that it locate and load the component. Note that the DCOM SCM is often confused with the Windows NT Service Control Manager used to manage services.

Building the Component Project

Before we build the component, a module definition (DEF) file must be created listing the exported functions, as shown in Listing 2-3.

component.def

```
LIBRARY          component.dll
DESCRIPTION      '(c)1997 Guy Eddon'
EXPORTS

                 DllGetClassObject    @2      PRIVATE
                 DllCanUnloadNow      @3      PRIVATE
```

Listing 2-3.
The component definition file listing the exported functions DllGetClassObject
and DllCanUnloadNow.

Next create a Win32 dynamic-link library (DLL) project in Visual C++ containing the component.cpp and component.def files as well as the component_i.c file generated by MIDL during the build process for the client. The complete component.cpp code is shown in Listing 2-4. Last build the project.

component.cpp

```cpp
#include "component.h" // Generated by MIDL

// {10000002-0000-0000-0000-000000000001}
const CLSID CLSID_InsideDCOM =
{0x10000002,0x0000,0x0000,{0x00,0x00,0x00,0x00,0x00,0x00,0x00,0x01}};

long g_cComponents = 0;
long g_cServerLocks = 0;
HANDLE g_hEvent;

class CInsideDCOM : public ISum
{
public:
    // IUnknown
    ULONG __stdcall AddRef();
    ULONG __stdcall Release();
    HRESULT __stdcall QueryInterface(REFIID riid, void** ppv);
```

Listing 2-4.
The complete component code.

(continued)

component.cpp *continued*

```
    // ISum
    HRESULT __stdcall Sum(int x, int y, int* retval);
    CInsideDCOM() : m_cRef(1) { g_cComponents++; }
    ~CInsideDCOM() { g_cComponents--; }

private:
    ULONG m_cRef;
};

ULONG CInsideDCOM::AddRef()
{
    return ++m_cRef;
}

ULONG CInsideDCOM::Release()
{
    if(--m_cRef != 0)
        return m_cRef;
    delete this;
    return 0;
}

HRESULT CInsideDCOM::QueryInterface(REFIID riid, void** ppv)
{
    if(riid == IID_IUnknown)
        *ppv = (IUnknown*)this;
    else if(riid == IID_ISum)
        *ppv = (ISum*)this;
    else
    {
        *ppv = NULL;
        return E_NOINTERFACE;
    }
    AddRef();
    return S_OK;
}

HRESULT CInsideDCOM::Sum(int x, int y, int* retval)
{
    *retval = x + y;
    return S_OK;
}

class CFactory : public IClassFactory
{
public:
```

```
    // IUnknown
    ULONG __stdcall AddRef();
    ULONG __stdcall Release();
    HRESULT __stdcall QueryInterface(REFIID riid, void** ppv);

    // IClassFactory
    HRESULT __stdcall CreateInstance(IUnknown* pUnknownOuter,
        REFIID riid, void** ppv);
    HRESULT __stdcall LockServer(BOOL bLock);

    CFactory() : m_cRef(1) { }
    ~CFactory() { }

private:
    ULONG m_cRef;
};

ULONG CFactory::AddRef()
{
    return ++m_cRef;
}

ULONG CFactory::Release()
{
    if(--m_cRef != 0)
        return m_cRef;
    delete this;
    return 0;
}

HRESULT CFactory::QueryInterface(REFIID riid, void** ppv)
{
    if((riid == IID_IUnknown) || (riid == IID_IClassFactory))
        *ppv = (IClassFactory *)this;
    else
    {
        *ppv = NULL;
        return E_NOINTERFACE;
    }
    AddRef();
    return S_OK;
}

HRESULT CFactory::CreateInstance(IUnknown *pUnknownOuter,
    REFIID riid, void** ppv)
```

(continued)

component.cpp *continued*

```cpp
{
    if(pUnknownOuter != NULL)
        return CLASS_E_NOAGGREGATION;

    CInsideDCOM *pInsideDCOM = new CInsideDCOM;
    if(pInsideDCOM == NULL)
        return E_OUTOFMEMORY;

    HRESULT hr = pInsideDCOM->QueryInterface(riid, ppv);
    pInsideDCOM->Release();
    return hr;
}


HRESULT CFactory::LockServer(BOOL bLock)
{
    if(bLock)
        g_cServerLocks++;
    else
        g_cServerLocks--;
    return S_OK;
}


HRESULT __stdcall DllCanUnloadNow()
{
    if(g_cServerLocks == 0 && g_cComponents == 0)
        return S_OK;
    else
        return S_FALSE;
}


HRESULT __stdcall DllGetClassObject(REFCLSID clsid, REFIID riid,
    void** ppv)
{
    if(clsid != CLSID_InsideDCOM)
        return CLASS_E_CLASSNOTAVAILABLE;

    CFactory* pFactory = new CFactory;
    if(pFactory == NULL)
        return E_OUTOFMEMORY;

    // riid is probably IID_IClassFactory.
    HRESULT hr = pFactory->QueryInterface(riid, ppv);
    pFactory->Release();
    return hr;
}
```

After the client and component have been built successfully, we are almost ready to run and test the code. First, however, the correct entries must be placed in the Windows registry so that the client will be able to locate the server. The simplest way to arrange for the creation of registry entries is by using a registration (REG) file, as shown in Listing 2-5.

component.reg

```
REGEDIT4

[HKEY_CLASSES_ROOT\CLSID\{10000002-0000-0000-0000-000000000001}]
@="Inside DCOM Sample"

[HKEY_CLASSES_ROOT\CLSID\{10000002-0000-0000-0000-000000000001}\↵
InprocServer32]
@="C:\\component.dll"
```

Listing 2-5.
The component registration file.

The registry file shown here provides the entries necessary to run the client and the component built in this chapter. To add this information to the registry, simply double-click on the registration file or enter a command line such as the following:

C:\WINDOWS>regedit c:\component.reg

Component Self-Registration

Registration files are a useful and relatively easy way to automate the addition of items to the registry. Most commercial software vendors, however, prefer their software packages to have as few unneeded files floating around as possible. Registration files are also not terribly flexible. They do not offer a ready-made solution if an application's setup program decides that due to the configuration of the user's computer, different registry settings should be created. A better way to register a component is to create what is known as a *self-registering component,* which does not need the help of an external registration file to be properly registered. Like mountain climbers who register their projected climbing routes with the local park ranger, self-registering components carry with them all the code required to create the desired registry entries.

At run time, registry entries can be created using the Win32 API functions that manipulate the registry. These functions include *RegCreateKeyEx, RegOpenKeyEx, RegEnumKeyEx, RegSetValueEx, RegCloseKey,* and *RegDeleteKey.*

(These function names are relatively self-explanatory, and therefore will not be described here in detail.) In order to automate the rather dreary process of creating and removing the typically needed registry entries, we have written a module that makes the low-level calls to these registry functions. The registry.cpp file containing the C++ source code can be found on the companion CD. The registry.h file, shown in Listing 2-6, declares the two main functions of the module, *RegisterServer* and *UnregisterServer*. These high-level functions can be called from any component in order to add the standard registry entries.

registry.h

```
// This function will register a component.
HRESULT RegisterServer(const char* szModuleName, REFCLSID clsid,
    const char* szFriendlyName, const char* szVerIndProgID,
    const char* szProgID, const char* szThreadingModel);

// This function will unregister a component.
HRESULT UnregisterServer(REFCLSID clsid, const char* szVerIndProgID,
    const char* szProgID);
```

Listing 2-6.
The registry.h file.

The self-registration mechanism varies slightly from a DLL component to an EXE component. For in-process components, self-registration means that the component needs to export two additional functions, *DllRegisterServer* and *DllUnregisterServer*. A setup program can call these functions to instruct the component to register itself. The RegSvr32 utility that comes with Windows can also be used to call these exported functions, as shown here:

```
C:\WINDOWS\SYSTEM>regsvr32 c:\component.dll
```

When you are working in Visual C++, simply choose Register Control from the Tools menu. This feature uses the RegSvr32 utility to call the *DllRegisterServer* function.

Self-registering local components (EXEs) do not export the *DllRegisterServer* and *DllUnregisterServer* functions but instead examine their command-line parameters for the *−RegServer* or *−UnregServer* flags when they are executed. Some self-registering EXE components automatically reregister themselves each time at startup.

Adding Self-Registering Features to the Component

Several steps are required to replace the registration file used to register the component in the previous section. First include the registry.h file, and then add the following two functions in the component.cpp file, as shown here:

```
// component.cpp
#include "registry.h" // Add this!!!
⋮
// And these...
HRESULT __stdcall DllRegisterServer()
{
    return RegisterServer("component.dll", CLSID_InsideDCOM,
        "Inside DCOM Sample", "Component.InsideDCOM",
        "Component.InsideDCOM.1", NULL);
}

HRESULT __stdcall DllUnregisterServer()
{
    return UnregisterServer(CLSID_InsideDCOM, "Component.InsideDCOM",
        "Component.InsideDCOM.1");
}
```

Next add these new functions at the end of the exported function list in the module definition file, as shown in boldface in Listing 2-7:

component.def

```
LIBRARY          component.dll
DESCRIPTION      '(c)1997 Guy Eddon'
EXPORTS

                 DllGetClassObject    @2    PRIVATE
                 DllCanUnloadNow      @3    PRIVATE
                 DllRegisterServer    @4    PRIVATE    ; Add this.
                 DllUnregisterServer  @5    PRIVATE    ; Add this.
```

Listing 2-7.
The component.def file, showing the additional exported functions
DllRegisterServer *and* DllUnregisterServer.

When you are creating a self-registering component, it is recommended that you indicate this feature by specifying an *OLESelfRegister* value in the version information section of the resource script file. This value would enable potential clients to determine whether a component supports self-registration without first having to load the component and attempt to call *DllRegisterServer* with possible unpleasant side effects if a component does not export this function.

The relevant line is shown in boldface in Listing 2-8. A client program can read the version information resource out of a component using the Win32 API.

component.rc

```
VS_VERSION_INFO VERSIONINFO
 FILEVERSION 1,0,0,1
 PRODUCTVERSION 1,0,0,1
 FILEFLAGSMASK 0x3fL
#ifdef _DEBUG
 FILEFLAGS 0x1L
#else
 FILEFLAGS 0x0L
#endif
 FILEOS 0x10004L
 FILETYPE 0x1L
 FILESUBTYPE 0x0L
BEGIN
    BLOCK "StringFileInfo"
    BEGIN
        BLOCK "000004b0"
        BEGIN
            VALUE "CompanyName", "Microsoft Corporation\0"
            VALUE "FileDescription", "InsideDCOM Component\0"
            VALUE "FileVersion", "1, 0, 0, 1\0"
            VALUE "InternalName", "InsideDCOM\0"
            VALUE "LegalCopyright", "Copyright © 1997\0"
            VALUE "OriginalFilename", "component.dll\0"
            VALUE "ProductName", "Inside DCOM\0"
            VALUE "ProductVersion", "1, 0, 0, 1\0"
            VALUE "OLESelfRegister", ""
        END
    END
    BLOCK "VarFileInfo"
    BEGIN
        VALUE "Translation", 0x0, 1200
    END
END
```

Listing 2-8.
The component resource script file, which can be used to determine whether a component supports self-registration.

Now add the registry.cpp file included on the companion CD and the component.rc file shown in Listing 2-8 to the component's project file, and rebuild. Last choose Register Control from the Tools menu or use RegSvr32 to test the new functionality. You should see the message box shown in Figure 2-6.

Figure 2-6.
The message box displayed when you register a DLL.

Registration Using Context Menus

To make the self-registration of components even easier, use the following registry script. When added to your registry, this script will provide context menus that let you register and unregister components simply by right-clicking on a DLL or an EXE file and selecting Register Component or Unregister Component. For in-process components this script simply launches the RegSvr32 utility.

```
REGEDIT4

[HKEY_CLASSES_ROOT\.dll]
@="dllfile"

[HKEY_CLASSES_ROOT\dllfile\shell\Register Component\command]
@="regsvr32 \"%1\""

[HKEY_CLASSES_ROOT\dllfile\shell\Unregister Component\command]
@="regsvr32 /u \"%1\""

[HKEY_CLASSES_ROOT\.exe]
@="exefile"

[HKEY_CLASSES_ROOT\exefile\shell\Register Component\command]
@="\"%1\" /regserver"

[HKEY_CLASSES_ROOT\exefile\shell\Unregister Component\command]
@="\"%1\" /unregserver"
```

COM Reuse Mechanisms

Containment and aggregation are two mechanisms developed to enable reuse of COM-based components. Since COM is a binary standard, inheritance at a source code level is not possible. Instead, you can have one object reuse another object at run time in order to implement some of its own interfaces. For example, imagine that you have designed a custom interface that inherits from another custom interface designed and implemented by someone else who works in your organization. There are two ways to implement the new interface: either reimplement the entire interface, including the methods belonging to the base interface, or simply delegate those methods to the existing implementation.

Containment

The basic idea of containment, in which one object completely contains another, is shown in Figure 2-7.

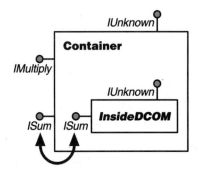

Figure 2-7.
Reusing a COM object through containment.

The technique of containment simply follows through on the idea that any COM object can be a client of another object. Here we see that one object pretends to support an interface when it is really acting only as a mediator by passing along the client's request to a third party. Using multiple inheritance in C++, the container object implements both the *IMultiply* and *ISum* interfaces, as shown in the following class declaration:

```
class CContainer : public IMultiply, public ISum
{
// Methods and data go here...
};
```

The *IMultiply* interface works similarly to the *ISum* interface except that instead of adding two numbers, it returns their product. Using IDL syntax, the *IMultiply* interface is expressed as follows:

```
[ object, uuid(10000011-0000-0000-0000-000000000001) ]
interface IMultiply : IUnknown
{
    HRESULT Multiply(int x, int y, [out, retval] int* retval);
}
```

In the usual fashion, the container object actually implements the *IMultiply* interface using its *Multiply* method. As part of its construction sequence, however, the container object also instantiates the *InsideDCOM* object, as shown in the following code:

```
HRESULT CContainer::Init()
{
    return CoCreateInstance(CLSID_InsideDCOM, NULL, CLSCTX_INPROC_SERVER,
        IID_ISum, (void**)&m_pSum);
}
```

Now when the client calls the *ISum::Sum* method, the container object simply delegates the call to the *InsideDCOM* object, as shown here:

```
HRESULT CContainer::Sum(int x, int y, int* retval)
{
    // Delegate this call to our contained object.
    return m_pSum->Sum(x, y, retval);
}
```

This code demonstrates the simplest kind of containment—it does nothing but delegate to another object. More sophisticated uses of containment might add code before and after delegating the call to the internal object, which might allow the container object to modify the behavior of the internal object in some way. The container object might even decide not to delegate to the internal object under some circumstances. In such cases, the container object is expected to provide the entire behavior necessary to satisfy the client.

Aggregation

Aggregation is a specialized form of containment for which COM provides special support. Instead of requiring an object to provide stub methods that call into the actual object, as was the case with containment, aggregation allows the internal object's interfaces to be exposed as interfaces of the external object. Note that aggregation works only among in-process components. The architecture of an aggregator object and its internal object is shown in Figure 2-8 on the following page.

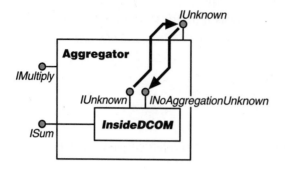

Figure 2-8.
A COM object reused through aggregation.

The aggregating object implements only the *IMultiply* interface, as shown in the following class declaration:

```
class CAggregator : public IMultiply
{
// Methods and data go here...
};
```

During the initialization phase of the aggregator object, the internal object is instantiated, as was done in the containment example. This time, however, the second parameter of *CoCreateInstance* is a pointer to the *IUnknown* interface of the aggregating object, as shown here:

```
HRESULT CAggregator::Init()
{
    return CoCreateInstance(CLSID_InsideDCOM, (IUnknown*)this,
        CLSCTX_INPROC_SERVER, IID_IUnknown, (void**)&m_pUnknownInner);
}
```

This code indicates to the *InsideDCOM* object that it is being instantiated as part of a larger aggregate object.

If the *InsideDCOM* object does not support aggregation, it will return a *CLASS_E_NOAGGREGATION* error, as shown in the code on the facing page. Assuming that *InsideDCOM* does support aggregation, the *IClassFactory::Create-Instance* method will instantiate the object in such a way that it keeps a pointer to its aggregator object's *IUnknown* interface. This step is necessary because the internal object will need to delegate its *IUnknown* calls to its aggregator object. Note that when aggregation is used, the external object must request the internal object's *IUnknown* interface during instantiation because the external object will need to delegate its *QueryInterface* calls to the internal object for the interfaces being aggregated.

```
HRESULT CFactory::CreateInstance(IUnknown *pUnknownOuter,
    REFIID riid, void** ppv)
{
    if(pUnknownOuter != NULL && riid != IID_IUnknown)
        return CLASS_E_NOAGGREGATION;

    CInsideDCOM* pInsideDCOM = new CInsideDCOM(pUnknownOuter);
    if(pInsideDCOM == NULL)
        return E_OUTOFMEMORY;

    // riid is probably IID_IUnknown.
    HRESULT hr = pInsideDCOM->QueryInterface_NoAggregation(riid, ppv);
    pInsideDCOM->Release_NoAggregation();
    return hr;
}
```

In the *CInsideDCOM* class's constructor, the object determines whether it is being created as a stand-alone object or as part of an aggregate object, as shown in the following code. If the pointer to the external object's *IUnknown* interface is *NULL*, the object is being created as a stand-alone object and thus it sets the *m_pUnknownOuter* pointer to its own *IUnknown*. Otherwise, *m_pUnknownOuter* is set to the external object's *IUnknown*.

```
CInsideDCOM::CInsideDCOM(IUnknown* pUnknownOuter) : m_cRef(1)
{
    g_cComponents++;
    if(pUnknownOuter != NULL)
        m_pUnknownOuter = pUnknownOuter;
    else
        m_pUnknownOuter = (IUnknown*)(INoAggregationUnknown*)this;
}
```

Although the aggregating object does not implement the *ISum* interface, it does support this interface in its *IUnknown::QueryInterface* method. Should the client request the *ISum* interface from the aggregating object, the aggregator simply delegates the *IUnknown::QueryInterface* call to the internal object, as shown in boldface in the code on the following page. This technique allows the client to have a direct pointer to the internal object, instead of having to go through a stub function as in the containment example. Of course, in the containment example, predelegation and postdelegation processing were possible—these types of processing are not available with aggregation.

```
HRESULT CAggregator::QueryInterface(REFIID riid, void** ppv)
{
    if(riid == IID_IUnknown)
        *ppv = (IUnknown*)this;
    else if(riid == IID_ISum)
        return m_pUnknownInner->QueryInterface(riid, ppv);
    else if(riid == IID_IMultiply)
        *ppv = (IMultiply*)this;
    else
    {
        *ppv = NULL;
        return E_NOINTERFACE;
    }
    AddRef();
    return S_OK;
}
```

One of the problems with aggregation is that it is easy to break COM's object identity rules. The whole point of aggregation is to make interfaces implemented by some other object part of your object's identity. The trick to pulling this off is never to let the client process know that your component is melding two identities into one. For example, imagine a client that retrieves a pointer to the *IMultiply* interface of the object and then calls *QueryInterface* for the *ISum* interface. The aggregator object delegates the *QueryInterface* call to the internal component and then returns a direct pointer to the *ISum* interface—so far, so good. Using the *ISum* pointer, the client later calls *QueryInterface* again, this time to retrieve the *IMultiply* interface. This call fails because the internal object does not know about the *IMultiply* interface supported by the aggregator object. This failure violates the reflexive rule of *QueryInterface*, which as you remember specifies that if a client holding a pointer to one interface queries successfully for another interface, the client must be able to call *QueryInterface* through the new pointer for the first interface. Thus, the client suddenly finds that what it thought was the single identity of a COM object actually has a split personality.

In order to solve this insidious problem, most objects supporting aggregation end up implementing two sets of *IUnknown* methods. One set of *IUnknown* methods simply delegates to the external object's *IUnknown* interface, sometimes called the controlling *IUnknown*. This delegation enables a client that calls the internal object's *IUnknown::QueryInterface* method looking for an interface implemented by the external object to succeed. This solution ensures that the identity of the COM object is preserved. The implementation of these delegating *IUnknown* methods is shown here:

```
ULONG CInsideDCOM::AddRef()
{
    return m_pUnknownOuter->AddRef();
}

ULONG CInsideDCOM::Release()
{
    return m_pUnknownOuter->Release();
}

HRESULT CInsideDCOM::QueryInterface(REFIID riid, void** ppv)
{
    return m_pUnknownOuter->QueryInterface(riid, ppv);
}
```

The second set of *IUnknown* methods appears more standardized because these methods are used by the external object when it calls *QueryInterface, AddRef,* or *Release* on the internal object. You might expect that with two implementations of *IUnknown* in one object, naming collisions would occur. Since COM is a binary standard, it is concerned not with the name given to an interface, but only with its v-table layout. Therefore, the following new custom interface, *INoAggregationUnknown,* is defined, which happens to have the same v-table structure as the real *IUnknown:*

```
interface INoAggregationUnknown
{
    virtual HRESULT __stdcall QueryInterface_NoAggregation(REFIID riid,
        void** ppv)=0;
    virtual ULONG __stdcall AddRef_NoAggregation()=0;
    virtual ULONG __stdcall Release_NoAggregation()=0;
};
```

This trick enables an aggregatable object to implement two different versions of the *IUnknown* interface: one that delegates to the external object's *IUnknown* interface and one that does the typical work of returning interface pointers and reference counting. When the object is not being aggregated, only the *INoAggregationUnknown* interface is used, as shown here:

```
HRESULT CInsideDCOM::QueryInterface_NoAggregation(REFIID riid, void** ppv)
{
    if(riid == IID_IUnknown)
        *ppv = (INoAggregationUnknown*)this;
    else if(riid == IID_ISum)
        *ppv = (ISum*)this;
    else
    {
```

(continued)

```
            *ppv = NULL;
            return E_NOINTERFACE;
        }
    ((IUnknown*)(*ppv))->AddRef();
    return S_OK;
}

ULONG CInsideDCOM::AddRef_NoAggregation()
{
    return ++m_cRef;
}

ULONG CInsideDCOM::Release_NoAggregation()
{
    if(--m_cRef != 0)
        return m_cRef;
    delete this;
    return 0;
}
```

CHAPTER THREE

Type Libraries and Language Integration

Now that we have built an in-process component in C++ that implements the *ISum* interface and a matching C++ client, what is our next step? Let's find some way of making our component more accessible to a wider variety of developers. Consider this: Who might your customers be if you decided to market this component? Even discounting the fact that a component that can only add two numbers is of limited value, right now only developers with a good grasp of C++ and COM would be interested in spending any money on our component. Perhaps we could broaden our market a bit if we made the component accessible to developers using Microsoft Visual Basic or Java, and maybe we could even make the component easier to use from C++.

In Chapter 2, "*IUnknown* and *IClassFactory*," we built a COM-based component in C++. Recall that COM is a binary standard for component implementation and integration, and therefore the language used to build or call COM objects is irrelevant. Since our component is already built on COM, you might wonder why anything special is required to make it accessible to developers using other languages. Well, to make a component more accessible to developers working in other languages, you need to create a *type library*. For example, Visual Basic and Microsoft Visual J++, by and large, depend on type libraries for their COM integration features.

This chapter begins with a discussion of type libraries. Next we examine how using type libraries can make client-side COM programming in C++ easier. We will also introduce the Active Template Library (ATL), which assists in building COM components in C++. Last we cover COM issues from the perspective of Visual Basic and Visual J++.

Eureka! Type Libraries

A type library is best thought of as a binary version of an Interface Definition Language (IDL) file. It contains a binary description of the interfaces exposed by a component, defining the methods along with their parameters and return types. Many environments support type libraries: Visual Basic, Visual J++, and Microsoft Visual C++ all understand type libraries; so do Delphi, Microsoft Visual FoxPro, and Microsoft Transaction Server. Rumor has it that the next version of Microsoft (Visual) Macro Assembler will support COM via type libraries.

Using Type Libraries

Microsoft has defined the COM interfaces needed to build (*ICreateTypeLib* and *ICreateTypeInfo*) and read (*ITypeLib* and *ITypeInfo*) type libraries. Few programs other than the Microsoft IDL (MIDL) compiler have any need of the interfaces used to build type libraries, but Visual C++, Visual J++, and Visual Basic are all capable of reading type libraries. What is the advantage of describing your interfaces in a type library? Since a type library provides complete information about your interfaces to anyone who is interested, sophisticated modern programming tools can read this information and present it to programmers in an accessible format, making COM programming a breeze.

Visual Basic, for example, has a feature named Auto List Members that displays a drop-down list while you are writing code, as shown in Figure 3-1. The statement builder drop-down list makes code suggestions. To insert an item into your code, simply double-click on it or press the Tab key while the option is selected. With a feature like this, it's no wonder that Visual Basic has become so popular! Visual Basic retrieves all the information it needs to develop the selections presented in the statement builder from the type libraries of available components. Future versions of Visual C++ and Visual J++ might offer a similar feature.

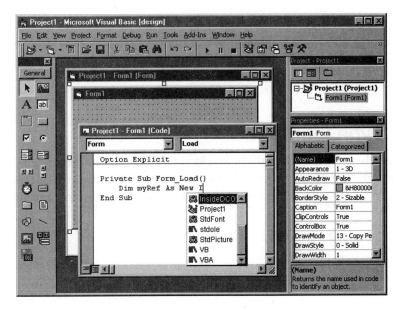

Figure 3-1.
The statement builder feature in Visual Basic.

Creating a Type Library

With a few simple changes, the *ISum* interface definition presented in Chapter 2, "*IUnknown* and *IClassFactory*," can be compiled into a binary type library file by using the MIDL compiler. The improved IDL file that will instruct the MIDL compiler to generate a type library for our component is shown in Listing 3-1; the additions are shown in boldface.

component.idl

```
import "unknwn.idl";

[ object, uuid(10000001-0000-0000-0000-000000000001),
  oleautomation ]
interface ISum : IUnknown
{
    HRESULT Sum(int x, int y, [out, retval] int* retval);
}
```

Listing 3-1. *(continued)*
*The component.idl file from Chapter 2 expanded to include type library
information.*

component.idl *continued*

```
[ uuid(10000003-0000-0000-0000-000000000001),
  helpstring("Inside DCOM Component Type Library"),
  version(1.0) ]
library Component
{
    importlib("stdole32.tlb");
    interface ISum;

    [ uuid(10000002-0000-0000-0000-000000000001) ]
    coclass InsideDCOM
    {
        interface ISum;
    }
};
```

NOTE: The *oleautomation* attribute has been added to the *ISum* definition to indicate that this interface uses only Automation-compatible types. Note that the *ISum* interface is not an Automation interface—it does not inherit from *IDispatch* (the Automation interface). This attribute will come in handy in later exercises.

To instruct MIDL to generate a type library, you must add the *library* keyword to the IDL file. Anything defined in the *library* section of the IDL file is added to the type library. The *library* has a universally unique identifier (UUID) defined for it and contains a *coclass* (COM class) statement that provides a listing of the interfaces supported by a COM class. In this case, the *InsideDCOM* class supports only one interface: *ISum*. The *version* attribute specifies the version number of the type library only; it is not used to specify the COM interface version or the class version. The *helpstring* attribute can be used to describe a type library, coclass, interface, method, or any other element in a type library. This information is often used by applications to provide a user-friendly name for a component. For example, Visual Basic uses these strings in the References dialog box, shown in Figure 3-2, to present the user with a selection of available components. The References dialog box is really used to set a reference to a type library stored inside a component. The type library gives Visual Basic sufficient information to access the component.

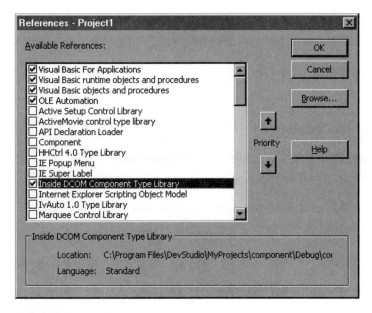

Figure 3-2.
The Visual Basic References dialog box.

Registering the Type Library

Before you can make full use of a type library, its existence must be noted in the registry. Languages such as Visual Basic and Visual J++ scour the registry in search of components containing type libraries. Registering a type library consists basically of inserting the necessary entries under the HKEY_-CLASSES_ROOT\TypeLib and HKEY_CLASSES_ROOT\Interface keys in the registry. The HKEY_CLASSES_ROOT\TypeLib key declares each type library installed on the system. A library identifier (LIBID) consists of a globally unique identifier (GUID) that identifies each registered type library. Every LIBID key in the registry contains several subkeys that specify the version number of the type library, the path to that library, several flags, and an optional path to a directory containing help files with information about the contents of the type library.

As shown in Chapter 2, "*IUnknown* and *IClassFactory*," a registration (.reg) file can be used to create these registry entries. It is preferable to integrate the type library registration step with the component self-registration step, however. Programmatically registering a type library is as easy as calling the *LoadTypeLibEx* function. This call can be used to create all the necessary entries automatically. In addition to filling in a complete registry entry under the TypeLib key, the function adds entries for each of the Automation-compatible interfaces (including dual interfaces) defined in the type library. This information is required to create instances of these interfaces. It is important to note that COM objects are not registered by *LoadTypeLibEx*—that is, the type library registration functions do not write any values into the CLSID key of the object.

The HKEY_CLASSES_ROOT\Interface key contains information about each COM interface available on the system that has an interface identifier (IID). This section begins with *{00000000-0000-0000-C000-000000000046}*, the IID of the *IUnknown* interface, and then proceeds with some very standard COM interfaces, such as *IClassFactory*, *IMalloc*, and *IMarshal*, before heading off into some of the more esoteric COM interfaces, such as *IExternalConnection*, and finally delving into the world of custom interfaces. One IID subkey is required for each new interface your application defines. The Interface key can contain the subkeys listed in the following table.

Subkeys of HKEY_CLASSES_ROOT\ Interface\{*YourIID*}	Description
BaseInterface	Identifies the interface from which the current interface is derived
NumMethods	Specifies the number of methods in the associated interface
ProxyStubClsid32	Identifies the CLSID of the 32-bit proxy/ stub DLL that knows how to marshal this interface
TypeLib	The LIBID associated with the type library in which the interface is described

The following code shows an improved version of the self-registration code that calls *LoadTypeLibEx* to register the component's type library. Notice that the *LoadTypeLibEx* function is called to load the type library from the component.dll file, as shown in boldface. This call assumes that the type library has been embedded in the DLL file, as will be discussed shortly.

```
HRESULT __stdcall DllRegisterServer()
{
    char DllPath[256];
    OLECHAR wDllPath[256];
    GetModuleFileName(g_hInstance, DllPath, 256);
    mbstowcs(wDllPath, DllPath, 256);
    ITypeLib* pTypeLib;
    HRESULT hr = LoadTypeLibEx(wDllPath, REGKIND_REGISTER,
        &pTypeLib);
    if(FAILED(hr))
        return hr;
    pTypeLib->Release();
    return RegisterServer("component.dll", CLSID_InsideDCOM,
        "Inside DCOM Sample", "Component.InsideDCOM",
        "Component.InsideDCOM.1", NULL);
}


HRESULT __stdcall DllUnregisterServer()
{
    HRESULT hr = UnRegisterTypeLib(LIBID_Component, 1, 0, LANG_NEUTRAL,
        SYS_WIN32);
    if(FAILED(hr))
        return hr;
    return UnregisterServer(CLSID_InsideDCOM, "Component.InsideDCOM",
        "Component.InsideDCOM.1");
}
```

Now recompile the updated component.idl file using the MIDL compiler to produce the type library file (component.tlb). Be sure to remove or comment out the *CLSID_InsideDCOM* definition from the client.cpp and component.cpp source files, as shown in the following code. This CLSID is now generated by MIDL, in the component_i.c file linked with those projects.

```
// Remove this stuff.
/*
{10000002-0000-0000-0000-000000000001}
const CLSID CLSID_InsideDCOM =
{0x10000002,0x0000,0x0000,{0x00,0x00,0x00,0x00,0x00,0x00,0x00,0x01}};
*/
```

Embedding the Type Library in the Component

An alternative to leaving a component's type library as a separate .tlb file is to embed the type library in the component as a resource. This technique has the advantage of making your component neater, since the one file includes both the component and the type information that describes how to use that component. To include a type library as a resource in a component, you must first create a resource script (.rc) file, as shown in Listing 3-2:

component.rc

```
1 TYPELIB "component.tlb"
```

Listing 3-2.
A resource script file that includes a type library in a component.

RegTlb: A Utility for Registering Stand-Alone Type Libraries

Calling *LoadTypeLibEx* is programmatically quite easy to do, but it is nonetheless a chore during the development process. To make this task easier, we have created a simple utility named RegTlb that can be used to register any stand-alone type library file. Here's the code for the RegTlb .cpp file:

```
#include <windows.h>
#include <iostream.h>

void main(int argc, char** argv)
{
    if(argc < 2)
    {
        cout << "Usage: regtlb tlbfile.tlb" << endl;
        return;
    }

    CoInitialize(NULL);

    OLECHAR psz[255];
    MultiByteToWideChar(CP_ACP, 0, argv[1], strlen(argv[1]),
        psz, 255);
```

Now simply add the resource script file to the project and rebuild; the resource compiler (rc.exe) will automatically embed the type library into the finished component. Last, register the component by choosing Register Control from the Tools menu in Visual C++. The component should self-register successfully, and you will be able to see several new entries in the aforementioned areas of the registry.

The OLE/COM Object Viewer (oleview.exe) utility that comes with Visual C++ is a good tool to use when you are exploring the registry and type libraries, either as .tlb files or embedded within components. The OLE/COM Object Viewer is a nifty utility that can function as an alternative to the registry editor, since it is designed specifically for viewing the registry information that pertains to COM objects. It can also be used to reverse-engineer type libraries into their original IDL source code.

```
ITypeLib* pTypeLib;
HRESULT hr = LoadTypeLibEx(psz, REGKIND_REGISTER, &pTypeLib);
if(FAILED(hr))
{
    cout << "LoadTypeLibEx failed." << endl;
    return;
}
else
    cout << "Type library registered." << endl;

pTypeLib->Release();

CoUninitialize();
}
```

Once the program has been compiled, simply execute a command-line statement such as *RegTlb mytlb.tlb* and all the necessary registry entries will be created automatically. This technique is similar to the way the RegSvr32 utility works, except that RegSvr32 refuses to register stand-alone type libraries. Improving RegTlb so that it also allows you to unregister type libraries using the *UnRegisterTypeLib* function is left as an exercise for you.

An Easy C++ Client That Utilizes the Type Library

Let's see how the client application we built previously could be simplified using a type library. The easyclient.cpp application shown in Listing 3-3 uses the type library embedded in the component.dll file:

easyclient.cpp

```
#import "C:\Program Files\DevStudio\MyProjects\component\\
Debug\component.dll" no_namespace
#include <iostream.h>

void main()
{
    CoInitialize(NULL);
    ISumPtr myRef(__uuidof(InsideDCOM));
    int result = myRef->Sum(5, 13);
    cout << "5 + 13 = " << result << endl;
    myRef = NULL;
    CoUninitialize();
}
```

Listing 3-3.
A C++ client that uses the type library in component.dll.

The first immediately apparent simplification appears in the layout of the program. From over 30 lines of code without a type library, with a type library we now need only 12 lines of code. More important, the type library has lowered the knowledge barrier required to use this component; the user no longer has to be a C++ or COM expert. How did the type library perform this magic? If you look at the very first line of code in the program, you will see the answer: the *#import* directive. This Microsoft language extension is used to incorporate information from a type library. The *#import* directive instructs the compiler to process the designated type library, converting the contents to C++ code that describes the COM interfaces contained within the type library.

When it encounters the *#import* directive, the C++ compiler generates two header files that reconstruct the type library's contents in C++ source code. The primary header file has the same name as the type library with the .tlh (type library header) extension. This file is similar to the header file produced by the MIDL compiler, as it contains the abstract base class definitions for the interfaces. The secondary header file, also with the same name as the type library but with the .tli (type library implementation) extension, contains the implementations of compiler-generated member functions and is included by using the *#include* directive in the primary (.tlh) header file. Both header files are placed in the compiler's output directory. They are then read and compiled as if the .tlh file were named by using a *#include* directive in the source code.

The most interesting aspect of the contents of these header files is their use of Microsoft's smart pointer template classes. But before we become more deeply engrossed in smart pointers, it is important to have a solid grounding in C++ template classes. If, like us, you struggle to keep up with the latest features of C++, Java, and Visual Basic, you might find the following section useful. If you are already a template guru, just skip to the section on smart pointers.

C++ Templates (A Quick Introduction)

Templates (sometimes called *parameterized types*) in the C++ language are mechanisms for generating code based on a parameter's type. Using templates, you can design a single class that operates on data of many types instead of having to create a separate class for each type. The standard example of a template involves creating a function that compares two values and returns the greater one. In C, you could accomplish this task with a macro, as shown here:

```
#define max(a, b) ((a > b) ? a : b)
```

Although they are valid in C++, macros of this sort are frowned on due to their lack of type checking. For example, the compiler has no objection to code such as this:

```
max(60, 'b'); // Compiler says no problem!
```

Macros can also lead to more insidious bugs like this:

```
int x = 6;
cout << max(++x, 6) << endl; // Displays 8
```

The fact that this code prints the value *8* might seem odd at first, until you mentally expand the macro as the compiler does:

```
cout << ((++x, 6) ? ++x : 6) << endl;
```

Since the preprocessor expands macros by substitution, the variable *x* is incremented twice.

Templates were added to the C++ language to address some of these issues. The template version of the preceding macro is shown here:

```
template <class T>
T max(T a, T b)
{
    return (a > b) ? a : b;
}
```

There are two basic types of templates: *function templates* and *class templates.* A function template defines a function that can accept arguments of any type, as shown in the preceding example. A class template defines an entire class that can be generalized to work with any type. The *template* keyword begins the definition of the template, followed by the type argument enclosed in angle brackets (< and >). The *class* keyword is used to indicate a type argument to a template, even though the actual type argument can be any type—it need not be a class. This keyword is followed by the actual function template definition, with the argument *T* used to represent the type. Think of the argument *T* as a variable representing the type of the actual parameter. This function template can now be used for any of the following types:

```
max(10, 12);            // int
max(10.8, 12.5);        // float
max('a', 'b');          // char
max(true, false);       // bool
```

Because no macro substitution is used, the following code works fine:

```
int x = 6
cout << max(++x, 6) << endl; // Displays 7
```

Type checking is also enforced, making this code illegal:

```
max(60, 'b'); // Compiler says big problem!
```

When a function template is first called for each type, the compiler creates an *instantiation,* or version, of the template function specialized for that type. This instantiation will be called every time the function is used for the type. If you have several identical instantiations, even in different modules, only one copy of the instantiation will end up in the executable file. For example, *max(10, 12)* causes the compiler to generate the following code:

```
int max(int a, int b)
{
    return (a > b) ? a : b;
}
```

And *max('a', 'b')* generates this code:

```
char max(char a, char b)
{
    return (a > b) ? a : b;
}
```

Whereas macros have no overhead because the preprocessor expands them, the overhead of templates can be minimized using the *inline* keyword. The *inline* keyword suggests that the compiler insert a copy of the function body into each place the function is called. Using inline functions can make a program faster because they eliminate the overhead associated with function calls. Inline functions are also subjected to code optimizations not available to normal functions.

Another useful feature of templates is the ability to override a template function in order to define special behavior for a specific type. Say you wanted to compare the lengths of two strings using the *max* function template. The standard version generated by the compiler would compare only the pointer addresses. The following code shows a function that overrides the compiler's default instantiation of the template in order to compare string lengths:

```
template<> char* max(char* a, char* b)
{
    return (strlen(a) > strlen(b)) ? a : b;
}
```

Now you can write code such as this:

```
cout << max("hello", "good-bye") << endl; // Displays good-bye
```

A class template enables you to generalize an entire class so that it can work with any type. For example, a string class might need to work with single-byte characters as well as double-byte Unicode characters. Here is the definition of a rudimentary string template class:

```
template <class T> class String
{
    struct sRep;
    sRep* rep;
public:
    String();
    String(const T*);
    String(const String&);

        ⋮
};
```

This template class could be instantiated for the regular character and a Unicode character, as shown here:

```
String<char> cs;
String<wchar_t> ws;
```

This review of C++ templates should give you enough information to get started with smart pointers. We'll revisit C++ templates in the section "Active Template Library" later in this chapter.

Smart Pointers

A *smart pointer* is an object that looks, acts, and feels like a normal pointer but offers greater functionality. The designers of smart pointers usually have two goals in mind: to make programming safer and to make programming easier. In C++, smart pointers are implemented as template classes that encapsulate a pointer and override standard pointer operators. What do smart pointers have to do with COM? Since COM programming in raw C++ is quite difficult and error prone, smart pointers can be used to improve the programmer's odds of success. Let's look at three aspects of standard smart pointers, with an eye toward how they could improve client-side COM programming:

- Construction and destruction
- Copying and assignment
- Dereferencing

Construction of a smart interface pointer can be as simple as initializing the pointer to *null* or as complex as calling *CoCreateInstance* to retrieve a pointer to the requested interface. Normally, a smart pointer class's constructor is overloaded to support all of these various capabilities. The destructor of a smart interface pointer can automatically call *Release*. A smart pointer can overload the assignment operator (=) so that any attempt to copy the pointer results in an automatic *AddRef* call, relieving the programmer of the burden of reference counting. Last the indirection operator (∗) can be overridden by the smart pointer class to perform some basic error checking, ensuring that the internal "dumb" pointer is not *null* or invalid in some other way.

For the most part, smart pointer classes are implemented as template classes because otherwise they would be useful only with a specific pointer type. For example, you could build a well-designed smart pointer class for *IUnknown* interface pointers, but this class would be of limited value to someone who wanted to access the *ISum* custom interface. Since template classes allow you to create generic wrappers to encapsulate pointers of almost any type and since interface pointers share similar semantics, a template version of the smart pointer class could be built, allowing the smart pointer to be used with any interface pointer type.

Microsoft has defined a set of smart pointer template classes in the header files comdef.h, comutil.h, and comip.h. These template classes are used in the code generated by the compiler in response to the type library specified by the *#import* statement. The fundamental template class defined by Microsoft is *_com_ptr_t*. The *_com_ptr_t* template class is a smart pointer implementation

that encapsulates interface pointers and eliminates the need to call the *AddRef,*
Release, and *QueryInterface* methods of the *IUnknown* interface. In addition, it
wraps the call to *CoCreateInstance* when instantiating a new COM object. The
_COM_SMARTPTR_TYPEDEF macro is used to establish *typedef*s of COM in-
terfaces to be template specializations of the *_com_ptr_t* template class. For
example, the following code:

```
_COM_SMARTPTR_TYPEDEF(ISum, __uuidof(ISum));
```

is expanded by the compiler into:

```
typedef _com_ptr_t<_com_IIID<ISum, __uuidof(ISum)> > ISumPtr;
```

The *ISumPtr* type can then be used in place of the raw interface pointer
ISum*. To instantiate an object, declare a variable of type *ISumPtr* and pass the
COM class's CLSID to the constructor, as shown here:

```
ISumPtr myRef(__uuidof(InsideDCOM));
```

The smart pointer's constructor calls *CoCreateInstance,* followed by *QueryInterface*
for the *ISum* interface. Now *myRef* can be used to call methods of the *ISum*
interface with code nearly identical to that used with dumb pointers:

```
int result = myRef->Sum(5, 13);
```

Notice that the value returned by the function is not an *HRESULT* but
the actual sum previously returned via a pointer in the third parameter. The
compiler notices that the parameter is marked as *[out, retval]* in the type library,
and as shown in the following code, it generates a wrapper function in the .tli
file that provides the real return value:

```
int __inline ISum::Sum ( int x, int y ) {
    int _result;
    HRESULT _hr = raw_Sum(x, y, &_result);
    if (FAILED(_hr)) _com_issue_errorex(_hr, this, __uuidof(this));
    return _result;
}
```

This code ends without calls to *AddRef* or *Release* since the smart pointer
fully automates reference counting. Before calling *CoUninitialize,* however, it
is important to set the smart pointer to *NULL,* as shown in the following code
fragment, in order to force a call to *Release.* After *CoUninitialize,* any attempts
by the smart pointer to call *Release* in the destructor will crash.

```
myRef = NULL;
CoUninitialize();
```

If you decide that you like Microsoft's smart pointer template classes but are not keen to have the C++ compiler generate code based on a type library, you can use the smart pointer classes directly simply by including the comdef.h header file. The client application, shown in Listing 3-4, uses these header files to call the component created in Chapter 2, "*IUnknown* and *IClassFactory*." Be sure to compile and link this file with the component_i.c file generated by the MIDL compiler.

smartpointerclient.cpp

```
#include <comdef.h>
#include <iostream.h>
#include "component.h" // Generated by MIDL

void main()
{
    CoInitialize(NULL);
    _COM_SMARTPTR_TYPEDEF(ISum, IID_ISum);
    ISumPtr myRef(CLSID_InsideDCOM);
    int result;
    myRef->Sum(5, 13, &result);
    cout << "Client: 5 + 13 = " << result << endl;
    myRef = NULL;
    CoUninitialize();
}
```

Listing 3-4.
A C++ client that uses the smart pointer template classes.

Namespaces

By default, the .tlh file generated by the compiler in response to the *#import* directive is enclosed in a namespace with its name lifted from the *library* statement in the original IDL file. A namespace is a declarative region that attaches an additional identifier to any names declared inside it. The additional identifier makes it less likely that a name will conflict with names declared elsewhere in the program. The C++ language provides a single global namespace by default, which can cause problems when global names clash. For example, you might want to import two different type libraries, both of which contain identically named items, into the same C++ source file. Normally, this is not a problem for COM since everything works based on GUIDs. The *#import* directive, however, enables COM objects to appear almost as standard C++ objects, with the GUIDs hidden in the compiler-generated code.

These two C++ header files illustrate the problem:

```
// one.h
class Math { ... };

// two.h
class Math { ... };
```

With these definitions, it is impossible to use both header files in a single program; if you did, the *Math* classes would clash. Namespaces have been introduced into the C++ language to address this problem. It is possible to use the identical names in separate namespaces without conflict even if the names appear in the same translation unit. As long as the names are used in separate namespaces, each name will be unique because of the addition of the namespace identifier.

The C++ *namespace* keyword is used to declare a namespace, as in these examples:

```
// one.h
namespace one
{
    class Math { ... };
}

// two.h
namespace two
{
    class Math { ... };
}
```

Now the *Math* class names will not clash because they have become *one::Math* and *two::Math*.

Declarations made outside all namespaces are still members of the global namespace. You can use the names from a namespace either by an explicit qualification with the namespace name (*one::Math*) or by selecting a namespace using the *using* keyword, as shown here:

```
using namespace two;
Math x();    // Refers to two::Math
```

When the *#import* directive is used, the generated namespace can be suppressed by specifying the *no_namespace* attribute, as shown here:

```
#import "component.dll" no_namespace
```

Be aware that suppressing the namespace may lead to name collisions if you import multiple type libraries from different components. In this example, only one component is used, so specifying the *no_namespace* attribute to avoid dealing with namespaces does not create a problem.

Active Template Library

The *#import* directive and the smart pointer template classes make client-side COM programming significantly easier and more enjoyable. These extensions do not aid in the building of COM components themselves, however. To assist developers building COM components in C++, Microsoft has introduced the Active Template Library (ATL). ATL is a small library composed of C++ template classes that provide support for the most common of COM programming chores, such as implementing the *IUnknown, IClassFactory,* and *IDispatch* interfaces, as well as dealing with component registration issues.

The design of ATL is loosely based on that of the Standard Template Library (STL), originally developed by Hewlett-Packard and now part of the ANSI/ISO standards for C++. As their names imply, both libraries heavily leverage the template functionality found in C++. Template libraries differ from traditional C++ class libraries in several important ways. First, the functionality of a template library is generally accessed by instantiating a class from a template rather than deriving from a base class. Due to this design difference, a class hierarchy does not necessarily define the relationships among the classes in a template library. Second, template libraries are typically supplied in source code form, often contained in header files, with little or no run-time DLL.

The differences between traditional C++ class libraries and template libraries can be illustrated by comparing the Microsoft Foundation Class (MFC) library to ATL. MFC is a heavy-duty library containing over 100,000 lines of code that does everything from supporting database functionality to creating ActiveX controls (with the kitchen sink thrown in for good measure). This versatility makes MFC a great choice for developers working on standard double-clickable Windows-based applications who want as much prefabricated functionality as possible. Nevertheless, the 918-kilobyte (KB) overhead of the mfc42.dll run-time file might prove unacceptable for those working on small and (hopefully) lightweight COM components that may be downloaded over a low bandwidth Internet connection. ATL, on the other hand, has a 20-KB DLL (atl.dll), and even that is optional. Of course, ATL has a much more limited scope than MFC: ATL allows you to easily create COM objects, ActiveX controls, and Automation servers.

The ATL COM AppWizard

To make it easier for you to work with ATL, Microsoft has provided the ATL COM AppWizard in Visual C++, shown in Figure 3-3. This simple wizard asks you to choose one of three types of components: DLL, EXE, or Win32 service. The wizard even allows you to specify that the proxy/stub interface marshaling code should be merged with the main project rather than built as a separate DLL. Based on these few decisions, the wizard generates the source code for a component. For example, if you choose an in-process component, the wizard will generate code for the standard DLL entry points, including *DllMain*, *DllGetClassObject*, *DllCanUnloadNow*, *DllRegisterServer*, and *DllUnregisterServer*.

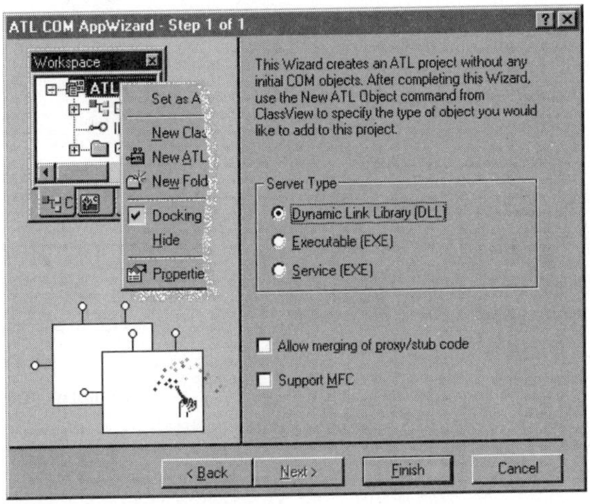

Figure 3-3.
The ATL COM AppWizard, which generates some of the framework code to create a COM component.

The ATL Object Wizard

Although the main housing for a component is quickly generated by the ATL COM AppWizard, no COM objects are implemented as of yet. For this task, Microsoft provides the ATL Object Wizard, shown in Figure 3-4 on the following page. The ATL Object Wizard enables you to add several different types of COM objects to a component, from rudimentary COM objects to objects that can operate within Microsoft Transaction Server. The ATL Object Wizard also supports the creation of several types of ActiveX controls, such as basic controls that work with Microsoft Internet Explorer and full controls that work with almost any container, including Visual Basic.

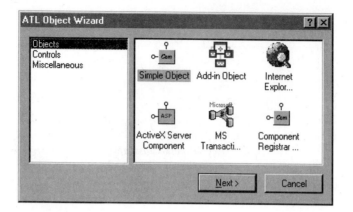

Figure 3-4.
*The ATL Object Wizard, which assists in creating a COM object based
on ATL.*

The simplest type of object, aptly named *simple object,* does not provide
automatic support of any standard COM interfaces besides *IUnknown* and
IClassFactory and thus often makes the best choice when you are implementing custom interfaces. The interfaces implemented automatically for some of
the other available object types are listed in the following table.

Object Type	Implemented Interfaces
Internet Explorer object	*IObjectWithSite*
Microsoft Transaction Server object	*IObjectControl*
Internet Explorer control	*IViewObject*
	IViewObject2
	IViewObjectEx
	IOleWindow
	IOleInPlaceObject
	IOleInPlaceObjectWindowless
	IOleInPlaceActiveObject
	IOleControl
	IOleObject
	IPersistStreamInit

(continued)

Object Type	Implemented Interfaces
Full control	All interfaces implemented for the Internet Explorer control, plus the following:
	IQuickActivate *IPersistStorage* *ISpecifyPropertyPages* *IDataObject* *IProvideClassInfo* *IProvideClassInfo2*
Property page	*IPropertyPage*

Depending on the object type you choose, the ATL Object Wizard presents a set of options, which enable you to select the threading model supported by the object, decide whether a custom interface should include support for *IDispatch*, and specify whether the object supports aggregation. Figure 3-5 shows the most common options presented for a simple object.

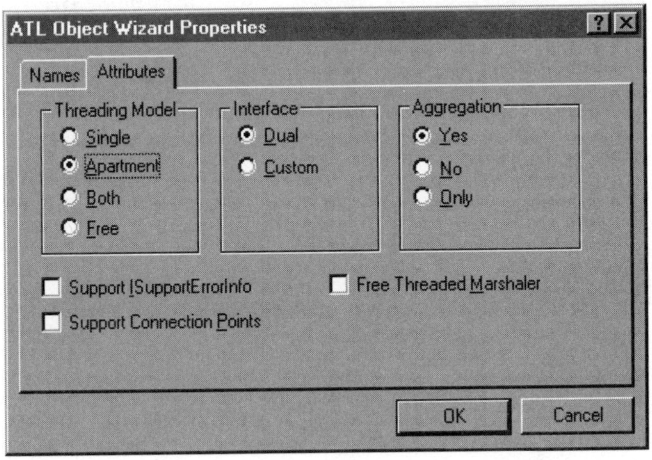

Figure 3-5.
Available options for the simple object in the ATL Object Wizard.

Adding Methods and Properties to an Interface Using ATL

The next step after adding a COM object to an ATL project is to add the desired methods and properties to the interface. The simplest way to add methods and properties to an interface is to use the wizardlike dialog boxes provided by Visual C++. Figure 3-6 on the following page shows the Add Method To Interface dialog box, which lets you do just that.

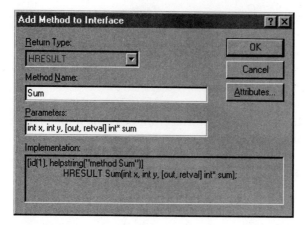

Figure 3-6.
The dialog box used to add a method to an interface.

Once the desired interfaces and methods have been added to an ATL-based component, the implementation work is complete. There is no need to mess with *IUnknown, IClassFactory,* or even registration functions, as all of this default functionality is automatically provided by ATL. The module definition (.def) file containing the DLL exports and the resource script (.rc) file referencing the type library are provided. Even the IDL file is generated and then compiled by MIDL as an automated part of the build process.

Figure 3-7 shows the fundamental ATL classes used to implement a COM object.

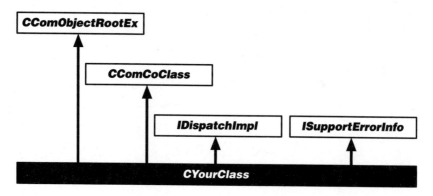

Figure 3-7.
The ATL object model.

CComObjectRootEx is the essential ATL class. It provides the default table-driven *QueryInterface* mechanism and is a required part of every ATL object. The *CComCoClass* class defines the default class factory and aggregation model for an object. For objects supporting a dual interface, *IDispatchImpl* can be used to provide a default implementation of the *IDispatch* interface. The *ISupport-ErrorInfo* interface must be supported if the *IErrorInfo* interface is used to report errors back to the client. This interface can be easily implemented using the *ISupportErrorInfoImpl* template class.

Building a Simple COM Object Using ATL

The following exercise takes you through the steps needed to build a simple COM object using ATL:

1. Open Microsoft Visual C++.

2. Choose File/New and select the Projects tab.

3. Select ATL COM AppWizard, enter the project name *TestATL*, and then click OK.

4. When the ATL COM AppWizard appears, simply click Finish.

5. The wizard will provide some information about what it is about to do. Click OK.

6. Choose Insert/New ATL Object.

7. Select the Simple Object icon, and click Next.

8. In the Short Name text box, type *InsideDCOM*, and in the Interface text box, type *ISum*. Then click OK.

9. Right-click on the *ISum* interface in *ClassView*, and select Add Method.

10. In the Method Name text box, type *Sum*, and in the Parameters text box, type *int x, int y, [out, retval] int* sum*. Then click OK.

11. Now expand the *ISum* interface within the *CInsideDCOM* class in *ClassView*, as shown on the following page, and double-click on the *Sum* method.

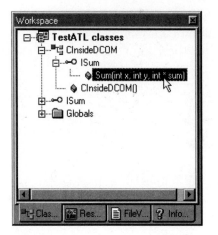

12. Add the following line of code, shown here in boldface:

```
STDMETHODIMP CInsideDCOM::Sum(int x, int y, int * sum)
{
    // TODO: Add your implementation code here
    *sum = x + y;
    return S_OK;
}
```

13. Choose Build/Build TestATL.dll.

You can test this ATL-based component using any language that supports COM. To create a test program in Visual Basic, simply create a Standard EXE project and set a reference to the TestATL 1.0 Type Library in the References dialog box, which can be opened by choosing References from the Project menu. Then type the following code, shown here in boldface, in the *Form_Load* procedure:

```
Private Sub Form_Load()
    Dim x As New InsideDCOM
    MsgBox x.Sum(6, 3)
End Sub
```

COM Programming in Visual Basic

Contrary to popular belief, COM programming can be done quite successfully in Visual Basic. Visual Basic is perhaps best at creating the more complex varieties of COM objects—namely, ActiveX controls and ActiveX documents. Developing such components in raw C++ could become quite an undertaking.

Visual Basic is also surprisingly flexible and easy to use when it comes to providing the fundamental aspects of COM programming.

CoInitialize and *CoUninitialize* are called automatically by Visual Basic with no interventions necessary on the part of the programmer. The *New* keyword in Visual Basic replaces *CoCreateInstance* as the object instantiator. Visual Basic's automatic garbage collection algorithm is used to call *IUnknown::Release* for you on object references that go out of scope. It is also possible to explicitly call *Release* by setting an object reference to *Nothing*, as shown here:

```
Set myRef = Nothing
```

Although a COM class can support multiple interfaces, Visual Basic tries to simplify things by assuming that the programmer wants access to the default interface and therefore automatically calls *QueryInterface* to request that interface. This simplification makes sense, since the majority of classes have a primary interface through which most operations are performed. Unfortunately, in addition to assuming that a programmer wants to access the default interface, Visual Basic also hides the name of the default interface! If you want to access a default interface named *IMyDefault* implemented by a COM class named *MyClass*, the name *MyClass* will be used as an alias for the *IMyDefault* interface. This technique seems to work acceptably when you are accessing a COM object from Visual Basic, but it fails miserably when you are attempting to implement a COM interface in Visual Basic.

Using the *Implements* keyword, a Visual Basic class module can implement any COM interface described in a type library. When the desired interface happens to be the default, writing code that implements the COM class instead of the desired interface can look mighty strange. Perhaps this oddity will be corrected in a future version of Visual Basic. Should a developer need access to the other (nondefault) interfaces supported by an object, a *QueryInterface* call can be executed using the *Set* statement. If needed, the *Set* statement will call the *IUnknown::QueryInterface* method to cast the *rvalue* interface pointer to the type of the *lvalue* reference. For example, the following code snippet shows two references—*MyRef1* and *MyRef2*. *MyRef1* is declared as an *IUnknown* interface pointer; *MyRef2* is a pointer to the *IMyInterface* interface. When *MyRef2* is set to *MyRef1*, a *QueryInterface* call that requests the *IMyInterface* interface pointer from the object pointed to by *MyRef1* takes place.

```
Dim MyRef1 As IUnknown
Set MyRef1 = New MyObject

Dim MyRef2 As IMyInterface
Set MyRef2 = MyRef1 ' QueryInterface executed!
```

In the preceding code, *MyRef1* is declared *As IUnknown*. This declaration might look odd to a Visual Basic programmer, but it is actually much more efficient than declaring references *As Object*. *As Object* actually uses the *IDispatch* (Automation) interface, which is much less efficient than a normal v-table-based interface.

In an IDL file, the default interface is indicated using the *[default]* attribute, shown here in boldface. If no interface in a *coclass* statement is declared as the default, the first interface listed is treated as the default. Here is an IDL file containing multiple interfaces that can be compiled into a type library and used in Visual Basic:

```
import "unknwn.idl";

[ object, uuid(00000000-0000-0000-0000-000000000001) ]
interface IDefaultInterface : IUnknown
{
    HRESULT ThingOne();
}


[ object, uuid(00000000-0000-0000-0000-000000000002) ]
interface ISecondaryInterface : IUnknown
{
    HRESULT ThingTwo();
}


[ uuid(00000000-0000-0000-0000-000000000003) ]
library Component
{
    interface IDefaultInterface;
    interface ISecondaryInterface;

    [ uuid(00000000-0000-0000-0000-000000000004) ]
    coclass TheClass
    {
        [default] interface IDefaultInterface;
        interface ISecondaryInterface;
    }
};
```

The following Visual Basic code uses the previously defined type library, accompanied by C++-style pseudo-code comments that explain what the code is doing in COM terms. Note that the *IDefaultInterface* interface is hidden from the Visual Basic programmer and is instead referred to as *TheClass*.

```
Private Sub Command1_Click()
' IDefaultInterface* myRef1;
```

```
' CoCreateInstance(CLSID_TheClass, NULL, CLSCTX_INPROC_SERVER,
'     IID_IDefaultInterface, (void**)&myRef1);
Dim myRef1 As New Component.TheClass

' ISecondayInterface* myRef2;
Dim myRef2 As Component.ISecondaryInterface

' myRef1->ThingOne();
myRef1.ThingOne

' myRef1->QueryInterface(IID_ISecondaryInterface, (void**)&myRef2);
Set myRef2 = myRef1

' myRef2->ThingTwo();
myRef2.ThingTwo

' myRef1->Release();
Set myRef1 = Nothing

' Garbage collector calls myRef2->Release();
End Sub
```

One solution to the hidden default interface problem in Visual Basic is to make *IUnknown* the default interface of a COM class in the IDL file, as shown in boldface in the following code. This technique tricks Visual Basic into showing all interfaces of a coclass; when Visual Basic thinks it is hiding the default interface from you, it is really hiding only *IUnknown*!

```
[ uuid(00000000-0000-0000-0000-000000000003) ]
library Component
{
    importlib("stdole32.tlb");
    interface IDefaultInterface;
    interface ISecondaryInterface;

    [ uuid(00000000-0000-0000-0000-000000000004) ]
    coclass TheClass
    {
        [default] IUnknown;    // IUnknown will be hidden.
        interface IDefaultInterface;
        interface ISecondaryInterface;
    }
};
```

Pushing the Limits of Visual Basic

It is certainly true that Visual Basic offers developers a mere subset of the total underlying COM functionality. Since Visual Basic programmers don't call

CoCreateInstance, IUnknown::QueryInterface, and the like, they can exercise only a limited degree of control. Perhaps the greatest weakness in its support of COM is Visual Basic's reliance on the registry. When calling *CoCreateInstance,* a C++ programmer may specify an in-process, a local, or a remote component at run time. Visual Basic programs must accept the registry configuration in all such matters. For example, if you want to use DCOM from within a Visual Basic application to call an object on another machine, you need to indicate that desire in the registry using the *RemoteMachineName* value. If the application later wants to connect to another machine, someone must first update the registry.

In order to overcome this limitation of Visual Basic, the *CoCreateInstanceEx* function used by C++ programmers to instantiate an object on a remote machine must somehow be called from Visual Basic. This task is not as difficult as it might sound, since Visual Basic can call nearly all Win32 API functions. Listing 3-5 shows the *CreateObjectEx* function, implemented in Visual Basic, which enables an object to be instantiated on a remote machine using DCOM. This function has been modeled after Visual Basic's own *CreateObject* function, which is used to create objects on a local machine. In the next version of Visual Basic, the *CreateObject* function has been extended to support an optional second parameter that specifies the machine name on which the object should be instantiated.

createobjectex.bas

```
Option Explicit

Private Type GUID
    Data1 As Long
    Data2 As Integer
    Data3 As Integer
    Data4(7) As Byte
End Type

Private Type COSERVERINFO
    dwReserved1 As Long ' DWORD
    pwszName As Long      ' LPWSTR
    pAuthInfo As Long     ' COAUTHINFO*
    dwReserved2 As Long ' DWORD
End Type
```

Listing 3-5. *(continued)*

A Visual Basic function named CreateObjectEx, *which allows the user to create objects locally as well as remotely.*

```
Private Type MULTI_QI
    piid As Long   ' const IID*
    pItf As Object ' IUnknown*
    hr As Long     ' HRESULT
End Type

Enum CLSCTX
    CLSCTX_INPROC_SERVER = 1
    CLSCTX_INPROC_HANDLER = 2
    CLSCTX_LOCAL_SERVER = 4
    CLSCTX_REMOTE_SERVER = 16
    CLSCTX_SERVER = CLSCTX_INPROC_SERVER + CLSCTX_LOCAL_SERVER + ↴
        CLSCTX_REMOTE_SERVER
    CLSCTX_ALL = CLSCTX_INPROC_SERVER + CLSCTX_INPROC_HANDLER + ↴
        CLSCTX_LOCAL_SERVER + CLSCTX_REMOTE_SERVER
End Enum

Private Const GMEM_FIXED = &H0
Private Const IID_IDispatch As String = _
    "{00020400-0000-0000-C000-000000000046}"
Private Declare Function GlobalAlloc Lib "kernel32" _
    (ByVal wFlags As Long, ByVal dwBytes As Long) As Long
Private Declare Function GlobalFree Lib "kernel32" _
    (ByVal hMem As Long) As Long
Private Declare Function IIDFromString Lib "OLE32" _
    (ByVal lpszIID As String, ByVal piid As Long) As Long
Private Declare Function CLSIDFromString Lib "OLE32" _
    (ByVal lpszCLSID As String, pclsid As GUID) As Long
Private Declare Function CLSIDFromProgID Lib "OLE32" _
    (ByVal lpszProgID As String, pclsid As GUID) As Long
Private Declare Function CoCreateInstanceEx Lib "OLE32" _
    (rclsid As GUID, ByVal pUnkOuter As Long, ByVal dwClsContext As Long, _
    pServerInfo As COSERVERINFO, ByVal cmq As Long, _
    rgmqResults As MULTI_QI) As Long
Private Declare Function lstrcpyW Lib "kernel32" _
    (ByVal lpString1 As String, ByVal lpString2 As String) As Long

Public Function CreateObjectEx(ByVal Class As String, _
    Optional ByVal RemoteServerName As String = "") As Object
    Dim rclsid As GUID
    Dim hr As Long
    Dim ServerInfo As COSERVERINFO
    Dim Context As Long
    Dim mqi As MULTI_QI

    mqi.piid = GlobalAlloc(GMEM_FIXED, 16)
```

(continued)

createobjectex.bas *continued*

```
' Convert the string version of IID_IDispatch to a binary IID.
hr = IIDFromString(StrConv(IID_IDispatch, vbUnicode), mqi.piid)
If hr <> 0 Then Err.Raise hr

' Convert the CLSID or ProgID string to a binary CLSID.
If ((Left(Class, 1) = "{") And (Right(Class, 1) = "}") And _
    (Len(Class) = 38)) Then
    ' Create a binary CLSID from string representation.
    hr = CLSIDFromString(StrConv(Class, vbUnicode), rclsid)
    If hr <> 0 Then Err.Raise hr
Else
    ' Create a binary CLSID from a ProgID string.
    hr = CLSIDFromProgID(StrConv(Class, vbUnicode), rclsid)
    If hr <> 0 Then Err.Raise hr
End If

' Set up the class context.
If RemoteServerName = "" Then
    Context = CLSCTX_SERVER
Else
    Context = CLSCTX_REMOTE_SERVER
    Dim MachineArray() As Byte
    ReDim MachineArray(Len(StrConv(RemoteServerName, _
        vbUnicode)) + 1)
    ServerInfo.pwszName = lstrcpyW(MachineArray, _
    StrConv(RemoteServerName, vbUnicode))
End If

' Create the object.
hr = CoCreateInstanceEx(rclsid, 0, Context, ServerInfo, 1, mqi)
If hr <> 0 Then Err.Raise hr
GlobalFree mqi.piid
Set CreateObjectEx = mqi.pItf
End Function
```

To use the *CreateObjectEx* function, simply put the code into any Visual Basic module and then call it. The class can take the form of a programmatic identifier(ProgID) such as *Word.Application* or the equivalent CLSID—in this case, *{000209FE-0000-0000-C000-000000000046}*. Note that if a ProgID is supplied, the local registry is searched for the corresponding CLSID. This function could be enhanced to read the remote computer's registry instead.

The optional *RemoteServerName* parameter references the computer on which the object is to be run. If a remote server name is not provided, the function creates the object on the local machine, analogous to the behavior of the standard *CreateObject* function. The *RemoteServerName* parameter can be set to the computer name of the remote machine, as in *server* (or just *server*), or the Domain Name System (DNS) name, such as *server.com*, *www.microsoft.com*, or *199.34.57.30.*

The following code shows some sample invocations of the *CreateObjectEx* function:

```
Private Sub Form_Click()
    Dim x As Object

    ' Create object based on ProgID.
    Set x = CreateObjectEx("Application.Object", "\\Machine")

    ' Create object based on CLSID.
    Set x = CreateObjectEx("{????????-????-????-????-????????????}", _
        "Machine")

    ' Create object on local machine.
    Set x = CreateObjectEx("Application.Object")
End Sub
```

In addition to creating clients of COM objects in Visual Basic, you can also use Visual Basic to build COM-based components. Visual Basic can produce in-process or local components, as well as components that run remotely using DCOM. No interface definition is required for Visual Basic components, as Visual Basic will deduce the interface automatically. If you want, you can implement a specific interface described in a type library using Visual Basic. This technique is useful when you want to create a component in Visual Basic that will interoperate with some client that demands support for a particular custom interface.

While each class module in Visual Basic defines only one class, a single class can implement multiple interfaces. The public properties, methods, and events of the class module define the default interface of the class. The *Implements* keyword can be used to implement additional interfaces in a class module. For example, a *Math* class might implement several different interfaces, as shown here:

```
Implements IArithmetic
Implements IGeometry

Private Function IArithmetic_Add(x As Integer, y As Integer) As Integer
    ' Code here...
End Function
```

(continued)

109

```
Private Function IArithmetic_Subtract(x As Integer, _
    y As Integer) As Integer
    ' Code here...
End Function

Private Function IGeometry_TriangleArea(base As Integer, _
    height As Integer) As Integer
    ' Code here...
End Function
```

A client program written in C++ would navigate among these interfaces using the *IUnknown::QueryInterface* method; in contrast, a Visual Basic client would use the *Set* keyword to perform the typecast, as described earlier in the section "COM Programming in Visual Basic." Note that the name of each class module becomes the name of the COM class, but the default interface defined by the class module is named using the class name prefixed with an underscore. For example, a Visual Basic class module named *Math* becomes a COM class named *Math* with a default COM interface named *_Math*.

Building a Client in Visual Basic

Now that we have built a COM component containing a type library in C++, we can easily use this component from most other programming environments. Here are the steps required for building a client in Visual Basic:

1. Open Visual Basic.

2. Select the Standard EXE project, and click OK.

3. Choose Project/References, and then check the Inside DCOM Component Type Library Reference check box.

4. Click OK.

5. Place a CommandButton control on Form1.

6. Choose View/Code.

7. From the Object list box, select Command1.

8. Enter the following code shown in boldface:

    ```
    Private Sub Command1_Click()
        Dim myRef As New Component.InsideDCOM
        MsgBox "myRef.Sum(5, 6) returns " & myRef.Sum(5, 6)
    End Sub
    ```

9. Choose Run/Start.

10. Test the component by clicking the Command1 button.

Building a Component in Visual Basic

Since we already have a C++ client that demands that a component support the *ISum* interface, let's use Visual Basic to create a component that implements *ISum* and then call it using the C++ client. To do so, follow these steps:

1. Open Visual Basic.

2. Select the ActiveX DLL project, and click OK.

3. Choose Project/References, and check the Inside DCOM Component Type Library reference check box.

4. Click OK.

5. In the code window, type *Implements InsideDCOM* and press Enter.

6. From the Object list box, select InsideDCOM.

7. In the code window, enter the following code shown in boldface:

```
Private Function InsideDCOM_Sum(ByVal x As Long, _
    ByVal y As Long) As Long
    InsideDCOM_Sum = x + y
End Function
```

8. In the Properties window, set the *Name* property to *VBInsideDCOM*.

9. Choose Project/Project1 Properties.

10. In the Project Name text box, type *VBComponent*.

11. In the Project Description text box, type *The VBInsideDCOM Component*.

12. Select Apartment Threaded in the Threading Model section. This marks your component as ThreadingModel=Apartment in the registry.

13. Click OK to close the Project Properties dialog box.

14. Choose File/Make VBComponent.dll, specify a folder for the DLL, and then click OK.

15. Choose File/Save Project, and accept all the default names.

16. Choose File/Exit.

To test this Visual Basic component from C++, use the easyclient.cpp program in Listing 3-3 on page 88 as a starting point or use the code shown in Listing 3-6 on the following page. Be sure to include the component.h file that was generated by the MIDL compiler in previous exercises so that the compiler can find the *ISum* definition.

vbclient.cpp

```
#import "C:\Program Files\DevStudio\VB\VBComponent.dll" no_namespace
#include <iostream.h>
#include "component.h"      // Generated by MIDL for ISum definition

void main()
{
    int result;

    CoInitialize(NULL);
    _COM_SMARTPTR_TYPEDEF(ISum, __uuidof(ISum));
    ISumPtr myRef(__uuidof(VBInsideDCOM));
    myRef->Sum(5, 13, &result);
    cout << "5 + 13 = " << result << endl;
    myRef = NULL;
    CoUninitialize();
}
```

Listing 3-6.
A C++ client that uses a component created in Visual Basic.

COM Programming in Java

Although one of the major goals of COM is to be programming language independent, COM programming has until recently been almost exclusively the domain of C++. As you know, COM programming in C++ is not for the faint of heart. Many people who actually do COM programming use Visual C++, its wizards, and MFC. Although this makes COM programming significantly easier, it also means you have to wade through thousands of lines of code you didn't write and don't understand. Visual Basic can also be used for COM programming chores by making use of its ability to create ActiveX components, although most developers still don't consider Visual Basic a serious contender in the COM programming arena. Instead, Visual Basic is usually employed as a "glue" language to combine components created in lower-level languages such as C++.

Java is a smart, modern, object-oriented programming language that has received a tremendous amount of industry support. When Microsoft's developers began looking at the Java programming language, they realized that (a) Java was a nice programming language badly in need of some decent development tools and that (b) Java would make a great programming language for building and using COM-based components. Visual J++ is Microsoft's answer to both of these ideas; it is a great Integrated Development Environment (IDE) for Java development and provides Java/COM integration features.

You might be wondering what about Java makes it such a great language for COM programming. The following table shows that although they were developed completely independent of each other, Java and COM are complementary technologies. COM is an architecture for building components; Java is a great programming language in which to build and use those components. You might be surprised to see COM described as simple—the ideas put forth in the COM specification certainly are simple. It's the implementation and use of COM from languages like C++ that make people think COM is complicated. Once you start doing COM programming in Java, you too will agree that COM is simple.

Attribute	Java	COM
Programming language	Yes	No
Language-independent component architecture	No	Yes
Virtual machine	Yes	No
Simple	Yes	Yes
Robust	Yes	Yes
Object-oriented	Yes	Yes
Platform-independent	Yes	Yes
General-purpose	Yes	Yes
Multithreaded	Yes	Yes
Distributed	No*	Yes

* Java 1.1 supports RMI.

It happens often in computing that two diametrically opposed technologies will be forced to coexist. As you will see, Microsoft has integrated COM and Java very cleanly, in a manner that does not conflict with the spirit of Java in any way. The integration of Java and COM has been accomplished without adding any new keywords or constructs to the Java language. Java already has the necessary constructs that allow implementation and use of COM objects. Most of the changes required to support the Java/COM integration model have been made to Microsoft's *Java Virtual Machine* (msjava.dll). A Java Virtual Machine (VM) is a module that translates binary .class files from Java byte code into native op-codes for execution on a particular platform.

The Java Type Library Wizard

To build and use COM objects in Java, Visual J++ includes a Java Type Library Wizard and an ActiveX Wizard for Java. The Java Type Library Wizard, shown in Figure 3-8, goes through the HKEY_CLASSES_ROOT\TypeLib keys in the registry looking for all COM objects with valid type library information. It then displays those entries with the user-friendly name found in the version number key for the type library settings—normally the *helpstring* parameter for the library found in the IDL file.

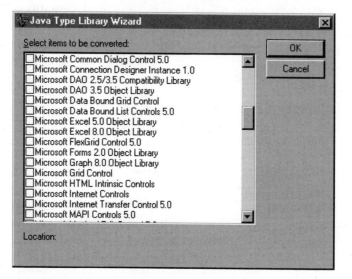

Figure 3-8.
The Java Type Library Wizard, which displays the COM class with type libraries that are listed in the registry.

It is important to understand that the Java/COM integration model is based on type libraries—a Java program can call any COM object for which type library information is available. This type library information might be available as a .tlb file or as a resource within the component. Let's assume that there is a particular component you would like to call from a program written in Java. The first step is to use the Java Type Library Wizard to create Java class wrappers for the COM classes in the component. Simply add a check mark next to the COM components you want to use in the list displayed by the Java Type Library Wizard and click OK. The Java Type Library Wizard then automatically converts the type library information to .class files. (In Java, files with the .java extension are source files and files with the .class extension are compiled binaries in Java byte code.) If you stop to think about it, the Java Type Library Wizard is a rather amazing utility. It takes the type library information contained in a type library and spits out Java .class files; one for each of the classes and interfaces described by the type library. By default, these class files are placed in a new subdirectory with the same name as the type library, in the C:\Windows\Java\TrustLib folder.

You might be wondering exactly how it is that a program crosses the bridge from Java byte code to a COM object. Well, each .class file generated by the Java Type Library Wizard contains a special attribute identifying it as a wrapper for a COM class. When the Microsoft Java VM (msjava.dll) sees this attribute in a class, it translates all Java method invocations in the class into calls to the COM class. So it is actually the Microsoft Java VM that is the bridge between Java and COM. For this reason, Java programs that use COM components will, at least for now, work only on platforms with the Microsoft Java VM.

In addition to the .class files, the Java Type Library Wizard generates a file named summary.txt that contains a summary of the generated .class files. Listing 3-7 shows the summary.txt file produced when the Java Type Library Wizard was run on the Inside DCOM Component Type Library built in Chapter 2, "*IUnknown* and *IClassFactory*."

summary.txt

```
public class component/InsideDCOM extends java.lang.Object
{
}
public interface component/ISum extends com.ms.com.IUnknown
{
    public abstract int Sum(int, int);
}
```

Listing 3-7.
A text file produced when the component created in Chapter 2 is processed by the Java Type Library Wizard to generate Java class wrappers.

Several items are worth noting about the summary.txt file. In the declaration of the class or interface, the *packagename/classname* format is used strictly to provide information about which package the class or interface belongs to. An identifier such as *component/ISum* is not legal in Java. Also notice that only the interface has methods—the class does not. The *InsideDCOM* class extends (Java lingo for "inherits from") *java.lang.Object*, the root of all Java objects, while the *ISum* interface extends *com.ms.com.IUnknown*. At last, our friend *IUnknown*!

Calling a COM Object from Java

When you are using the Java-callable wrappers for COM objects, you must always call methods through an interface, not through the class itself. This technique is identical to the way in which COM objects are always called through an interface in C++. Here is a sample Java program that calls the *InsideDCOM* object, which has been wrapped in Java classes using the Java Type Library Wizard:

```
import component.*;

class TestingTheCOMComponent
{
    public static void main(String str[])
    {
        ISum myRef = (ISum)new InsideDCOM();
        int result = myRef.Sum(5, 4);
        System.out.println("Java client: myRef.Sum(5, 4) returns " +
            result);
    }
}
```

As in the Visual Basic code presented earlier, you won't recognize any COM calls in this code. No *CoInitialize,* no *CoCreateInstance,* and no *IUnknown* calls such as *QueryInterface.* The *import* statement makes the generated Java .class files in the C:\Windows\Java\TrustLib\component folder accessible. Note that this statement is not analogous to the C++ *#import* directive that generates code based on the contents of a type library—although the name of the C++ directive was inspired by the Java statement. In Java, any class can be referenced using its fully qualified name (for example, *java.awt.component*) as long as the class can be found in the class path. The *import* statement simply allows you to refer to the class using its short name (for example, *InsideDCOM*). If the class name is qualified by the package name (*component.InsideDCOM*), the *import* statement may be removed.

Java's *new* keyword instantiates the *InsideDCOM* class. This instantiation leads the Java VM into the InsideDCOM.class file generated by the Java Type Library Wizard, where the Java VM encounters the special attribute, indicating that this is a COM class. The generated .class file also contains the CLSID of the COM class. The Java VM then uses that CLSID to make a call to *CoCreateInstance.* The *IUnknown* pointer returned by *CoCreateInstance* is then cast by the Java code to *ISum,* as shown here:

```
ISum myRef = (ISum)new InsideDCOM();
```

Hidden from view is the call to the *IUnknown::QueryInterface* function that enables clients to choose among an object's supported interfaces. The simple typecast from the *InsideDCOM* class to the *ISum* interface forces the Java VM to call the object's *QueryInterface* function in order to request a pointer to *ISum*. In this manner, a Java program can retrieve an interface pointer for any interface supported by the COM object. Simply casting the object to the appropriate interface will yield correct results.

If the object does not implement the requested interface and the *Query-Interface* call fails, an exception of type *ClassCastException* is thrown when you attempt the cast. To determine whether an object implements the desired interface before casting, the *instanceof* operator may be used, as shown in the following code:

```
InsideDCOM myRef = new InsideDCOM();
if(myRef instanceof ISum)
{
    // Now we know that InsideDCOM implements ISum.
    // It is safe to cast (ISum)myRef.
}
```

Reference counting, another painful COM chore, is handled automatically in Java. As is the case with Microsoft's smart interface pointers in C++, you do not need to call *IUnknown::AddRef* when you are creating a new reference to an object, nor do you need to call *IUnknown::Release* when you've finished using a reference to an object. And as it did for Java's native objects, the garbage collector performs reference counting automatically and calls *Release* on object references that go out of scope. A call to *IUnknown::Release* can be forced by setting an interface reference to *null*, as shown here:

```
myRef = null;
```

Implementing COM Objects in Java

Up to now, we have been examining how to call COM objects built in C++ from Java. It is also possible to implement COM objects in Java. These components can be called from languages such as C++ and Visual Basic as well as from Java itself. Like the rest of the Java/COM integration model, this functionality has been cleanly implemented. Let's assume you want to implement the *Inside-DCOM* object as a COM class in Java, as shown here:

```
public class InsideDCOM
{
    public int Sum(int x, int y)
    {
        return x + y;
    }
}
```

Notice that the class and the *Sum* method are declared as *public* so that they will be accessible from outside the package. No destructor is provided because Java doesn't have destructors.

To make this Java class definition accessible as a COM object, the following steps are required:

1. Create an IDL file describing the interface.

2. Compile the IDL file into a type library file using the MIDL compiler.

3. Generate COM class wrappers based on the type library file.

4. Modify the Java code to implement the interfaces defined in the COM class wrappers.

5. Register the COM object in the registry.

These steps sound fairly involved, and they are. To help automate the process, use the ActiveX Component Wizard for Java.

The ActiveX Component Wizard for Java

The ActiveX Component Wizard will ask you some questions and then will complete steps 1, 2, 3, and 5 in the procedure listed above. You will have to modify the Java code only slightly in order to indicate that the Java class implements a particular COM interface, as shown here:

```
public class InsideDCOM implements ISum
{
    public int Sum(int x, int y)
    {
        return x + y;
    }
}
```

The ActiveX Component Wizard for Java, shown in Figure 3-9, will examine your Java code and generate an IDL file describing its interface. At your request, the wizard will compile the IDL file into a type library and then register the component. The wizard even gives you the option of creating a COM object supporting an *IDispatch* interface or a dual interface (both *IDispatch* and a custom interface).

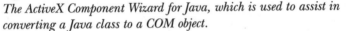

Figure 3-9.
*The ActiveX Component Wizard for Java, which is used to assist in
converting a Java class to a COM object.*

Every Java class automatically implements *IUnknown* and *IDispatch* via the
support in the Java VM. At run time, the Java VM will automatically provide
type information for the *IDispatch* implementation via *IDispatch::GetTypeInfo*
so that clients can avoid the overhead of using *IDispatch::GetIDsOfNames* to
perform late binding. If you selected a dual interface using the ActiveX Component Wizard for Java, the Java VM would also generate a v-table for your
interface. In this way, clients can avoid the overhead of *IDispatch* altogether.

The IDL file generated by the wizard for the *InsideDCOM* Java class shown
above looks like this:

```
[
    uuid(59835a42-fc78-11d0-a6fb-0020aff4591e),
    helpstring("InsideDCOMLib Type Library"),
    version(1.0)
]
library InsideDCOMLib
{
    importlib("stdole32.tlb");

    [
        object,
```

(continued)

119

```
      uuid(59835a41-fc78-11d0-a6fb-0020aff4591e),
      dual,
      pointer_default(unique),
      helpstring("IInsideDCOM Interface")
]
interface IInsideDCOM : IDispatch
{
   [ helpstring("Sum Method") ]
   HRESULT Sum([in] long p1, [in] long p2, [out, retval] long * rtn);

}


[
   uuid(59835a40-fc78-11d0-a6fb-0020aff4591e),
   helpstring("CInsideDCOM Object")
]
coclass CInsideDCOM
{
   interface IInsideDCOM;
};


};
```

Notice that the parameter types used for the methods in the IDL file do not exactly match those used in the Java code. Because COM provides a language-independent binary standard, it needs to play referee among all the different data types used in the various languages.

The following table shows the type mappings between native Java types and IDL types.

IDL Type	Java Type
boolean	*boolean*
char	*char*
double	*double*
int	*int*
float	*float*
long	*long*
short	*short*
unsigned char	*byte*
wchar_t	*short*

(continued)

IDL Type	Java Type
LPSTR	*class java.lang.String*
BSTR	*class java.lang.String*
CURRENCY	*long*
DATE	*double*
SCODE/HRESULT	*int*
VARIANT	*class com.ms.com.Variant*
IDispatch	*class java.lang.Object*
IUnknown	*interface com.ms.com.IUnknown*
SAFEARRAY (<typename>)	*class com.ms.com.SafeArray*
void	*void*

The ActiveX Component Wizard for Java will, if desired, create all the necessary registry entries for a COM component. Here are some of the most interesting registry entries created by the wizard:

```
[HKEY_CLASSES_ROOT\CLSID\{59835a40-fc78-11d0-a6fb-0020aff4591e}]
@="Java Class: InsideDCOM"
"AppID"="{59835a40-fc78-11d0-a6fb-0020aff4591e}"

[HKEY_CLASSES_ROOT\CLSID\{59835a40-fc78-11d0-a6fb-0020aff4591e}\ →
InprocServer32]
@="MSJAVA.DLL"
"ThreadingModel"="Both"
"JavaClass"="InsideDCOM"
```

Notice that the in-process server for the *InsideDCOM* component is listed as msjava.dll—the Microsoft Java VM! Since Java code is compiled into byte code, it can't be called directly from a language such as C++. Instead, the Java VM provides the COM support for your Java programs. COM clients think they are working with msjava.dll, but msjava.dll is actually running your Java code.

Building a Client in Java

To build a COM client in Java, follow these steps:

1. Open Visual J++.

2. Choose the File/New command.

3. Select the Projects tab, and then select Java Project.

4. In the Project name text box, type *TestCOM*, and click OK.

5. Choose Tools/Java Type Library Wizard.

6. Check the Inside DCOM Component Type Library check box, and click OK.

7. Choose Insert/New Class.

8. In the Name text box, type *TestCOM* and click OK.

9. Modify the class template by adding the code shown here in boldface:

```
import component.*;
//
//
// TestCOM
//
//
class TestCOM
{
    public static void main(String str[])
    {
        ISum myRef = (ISum)new InsideDCOM();
        int result = myRef.Sum(5, 4);
        System.out.println(
            "Java client: myRef.Sum(5, 4) returns " +
            result);
    }
}
```

10. Choose Project/Settings, and select the Debug tab.

11. In the Class For Debugging/Executing text box, type *TestCOM*.

12. In the Debug/Execute Project Under section, select the Stand-Alone Interpreter (Applications Only) option and click OK.

13. Choose Build/Build TestCOM.

14. Choose Build/Execute TestCOM.

Building a Component in Java

To build a COM component in Java, follow these steps:

1. Open Visual J++.

2. Choose the File/New command.

3. Select the Projects tab, and then select Java Project.

4. In the Project Name text box, type *JavaSum*, and click OK.

5. Choose Insert/New Class.

6. In the Name text box, type *SumClass*.

7. In the Modifiers section, check the Public check box and then click OK.

8. Modify the class template by adding the code shown here in boldface:

```
//
//
// SumClass
//
//
public class SumClass
{
    public int Sum(int x, int y)
    {
        return x + y;
    }
}
```

9. Choose File/Save.

10. Choose Build/Build JavaSum.

11. Choose Tools/ActiveX Wizard For Java.

12. Read over the wizard's options, click Next, and click Next again. If warnings are displayed indicating that the class file can't be opened, be sure to check that the path to the SumClass.class file is correct.

13. When the wizard asks what type of interface you would like to create, select Dual Interface and click Finish. The wizard will display some instructions for you to follow. Read these over, and then copy all the code in the text box to the clipboard.

14. Click OK to complete the wizard.

15. Modify your code as shown here in boldface and as suggested by the wizard. (The question marks shown for the CLSID are place-holders—the exact CLSID you should use is contained in the code you copied to the clipboard.)

```
import sumclasslib.*;
//
//
// SumClass
```

(continued)

```
//
//
public class SumClass implements sumclasslib.ISumClass
{
    private static final String CLSID =
        "????????-????-????-????-????????????";
    public int Sum(int x, int y)
    {
        return x + y;
    }
}
```

16. Choose Project/Settings, and select the General tab.

17. In the Output Directory text box, type *C:\Windows\Java\Lib*. If your Windows directory has a different name, be sure to use that name.

18. Click OK to close the Project Settings dialog box.

19. Choose Build/Rebuild All.

To test this Visual J++ component from C++, you can use the easyclient.cpp program presented in Listing 3-3 as a starting point or enter the code shown in Listing 3-8.

jclient.cpp

```
#import "C:\Program Files\DevStudio\MyProject\JavaSum\\
SumClasslib.tlb" no_namespace
#include <iostream.h>

void main()
{
    CoInitialize(NULL);
    ISumClassPtr myRef(__uuidof(CSumClass));
    int result = myRef->Sum(5, 13);
    cout << "5 + 13 = " << result << endl;
    myRef = NULL;
    CoUninitialize();
}
```

Listing 3-8.
A C++ client that uses a COM object created in Visual J++.

ActiveX Controls and JavaBeans Integration

JavaBeans is a component model designed for Java. At some point in the future, JavaBeans components might compete with ActiveX controls in the marketplace for reusable components. For Java developers to take advantage of the thousands of commercially available ActiveX controls, Microsoft has extended its Java VM so that ActiveX controls can be hosted in a Java applet. In addition, Microsoft's Java VM enables JavaBeans components to be exposed as ActiveX controls. As compelling JavaBeans components begin to become commercially available, they will immediately be usable by the large number of ActiveX control containers such as Visual Basic, Visual C++, Borland Delphi, and Powersoft PowerBuilder.

Thus, an ActiveX control will appear as a JavaBeans component to a Java programmer, and a JavaBeans component will appear as an ActiveX control to a developer using any of the wide array of development tools that support ActiveX. The Java VM is the bridge that makes this bidirectional support possible. This support enables all developers to work in the environment with which they are most familiar while still retaining the richness of all available components, regardless of which development tools or platforms were used to build the components. Exposing an existing JavaBeans component as an ActiveX control is as simple as running the JavaReg utility to register the control and generate a type library that describes its properties, methods, and events. After you run JavaReg, the JavaBeans component will look and function just like a native ActiveX control in any control container—for example, a Visual Basic application could take advantage of a JavaBeans component turned ActiveX control.

Trusted vs. Untrusted Applets

Since Java applets can be automatically downloaded over the Internet when a user browses a Web site, security is a big concern. To prevent Java applets from potentially damaging the user's system, applets typically run in a *sandbox*. A sandbox is a carefully delimited execution environment that prevents applets from posing a security threat. Local file access, for example, is off limits. COM services are also not available to applets running in the sandbox. Note that the sandbox restriction applies only to applets; standard Java applications do not run in the sandbox and therefore may use COM services. Running applets in the sandbox is a necessity for security reasons, but the restrictions imposed by the sandbox prevent applets from doing many useful and interesting things, such as accessing COM services. To overcome this limitation, the Java VM categorizes applets as either *trusted* or *untrusted*.

Untrusted applets run within the sandbox and cannot use COM services, as is the norm for untrusted applets. All .class files that aren't loaded from the class path—including those downloaded from the Internet—are considered untrusted. Trusted .class files are those that are either loaded from the class path or extracted from a cabinet (.cab) file that has a digital signature. By using .cab files, you can enable Java applets downloaded from the Internet to be considered trusted. Trusted applets run outside of the security sandbox; they can therefore read and write files and use COM services.

Four path-related registry values are relevant to the security of Java applets. These values are stored in the HKEY_LOCAL_MACHINE\SOFT-WARE\Microsoft\Java VM key. The names and typical values are shown here:

```
Classpath = "C:\WINDOWS\java\classes\classes.zip;↴
C:\WINDOWS\java\classes;"
LibsDirectory = "C:\WINDOWS\java\lib"
TrustedClasspath = "C:\WINDOWS\java\trustlib\tclasses.zip"
TrustedLibsDirectory = "C:\WINDOWS\java\trustlib"
```

During development in Visual J++, all .class files are considered trusted, so you don't have to worry about security issues. If you want to distribute a Java applet that uses COM services over the Internet, you will need to ensure that your applet runs outside of the sandbox on the user's machine. To do so, you can create digitally signed .cab files for your Java classes using the cabinet and code signing tools provided in the Cab&Sign folder included with Visual J++. In addition to enabling applets to run outside the sandbox, using .cab files for your classes speeds up downloading and makes installation more secure. Stand-alone Java applications that do not run in a Web browser are automatically executed outside the sandbox and can therefore use COM services.

Threading Models and Apartments

Both COM and its predecessor, OLE, were developed at a time when Microsoft Windows did not support multithreading, and thus, COM initially provided no support for multithreaded components. Later, as threading became ubiquitous in Microsoft Windows, the COM specification was expanded to include threading support. Today COM provides support and interoperability for components that use threads to any extent.

Fundamentally, COM now supports two primary threading models: one for user-driven graphical user interface (GUI) applications and another for worker components that do not display a user interface, both of which utilize the threading infrastructure provided by the operating system. The threading model designed for GUI applications is synchronized with message queues used by windows, which makes it much easier for user-driven applications to work with COM robustly. The threading model designed for worker components, on the other hand, does not use window message queues to deliver COM method calls—this model works well for those components that need the best possible performance and that don't have to worry about synchronizing COM calls with a user interface.

Both models are and will continue to be important. Unfortunately, the details of these threading models and the implications of the various ways in which they may be combined can be overwhelming at first. Luckily, in most cases the details of these threading models are not crucial to the success of a project, and reading this chapter once to obtain an overview of the issues involved will be sufficient. When you are designing a system that will make heavy use of threads, however, you might want to work through this chapter carefully to ensure that you fully understand the implications of your design decisions.

Spinning a Yarn: A Quick Review of Threads

A *thread* is a path of execution through a process. Every process has one or more threads of execution. As part of the Win32 process-creation function *Create-Process*, an initial thread is automatically created. This initial thread begins execution at the *main* function (for console applications) or at the *WinMain* function (for GUI applications). To create additional threads, a process can call the Win32 *CreateThread* function. It is important to realize that the system executes threads only, never processes. Threads enable an application to perform (or appear to perform) several tasks concurrently, which can lead to a higher degree of functionality in an application and improved responsiveness in the user interface. On machines with multiple processors, different threads can execute concurrently on different processors, yielding improved overall performance.

Normal function calls are *synchronous,* meaning that the caller must wait for the function to finish executing before it can proceed, as shown in the following code fragment:

```
// Some code here...
MyFunc();    // Call MyFunc.
// Some more code here...
// Code here executes only when MyFunc has finished.
```

The *CreateThread* function enables asynchronous function calls, meaning that the caller does not have to wait for the called function to finish executing, as shown in this code fragment:

```
// Some code here...
CreateThread(..., MyFunc, ...);    // Call MyFunc.
// Some more code here...
// Code here executes immediately;
// MyFunc is executing concurrently.
```

When a thread eventually finishes executing, the *GetExitCodeThread* function can be called to retrieve the thread's return value. A thread (*MyFunc* in the preceding code) terminates when it returns from the main thread function or when it explicitly calls *ExitThread.* Although not recommended, the Win32 *TerminateThread* function can also be used to kill a misbehaving thread.

All kernel objects, including threads, have an associated usage counter. (Kernel objects are objects owned by the kernel and are used by applications and the system to manage various resources, such as files and threads.) For threads, this usage counter is initially set to *2.* When a thread terminates, its usage counter is implicitly decremented. The thread's creator should also decrement its usage counter by using the Win32 *CloseHandle* function. In this way, the thread object's usage counter will reach *0* and the thread object will automatically be destroyed by the system.

Priority values are assigned to each process and thread. The kernel's thread scheduler uses these values as part of its algorithm to determine the order in which threads should be scheduled for execution. The priority value assigned to a process can be adjusted by calling the *SetPriorityClass* function, whereas a call to *SetThreadPriority* is used to control the priority of a thread. The values of both settings are combined to arrive at the actual priority value of a thread, called the thread's *base priority*. The corresponding *GetPriorityClass* and *GetThreadPriority* functions can be called at any time to obtain the current settings.

One of the biggest problems associated with the safe use of threads is proper synchronization. Any unprotected access to data shared by multiple threads is an access violation waiting to happen. For example, if two threads manipulate an unprotected data structure, the probability of that data becoming corrupted is high. It is easy to envision a scenario in which one thread might begin to read some data only to be preempted by the scheduler. The scheduler might then decide to execute another thread that will begin to modify the data in the shared structure. When execution focus eventually returns to the first thread, the data might no longer be consistent. This scenario will likely end in an error.

This type of synchronization problem is difficult to detect and difficult to correct because it can happen infrequently, seemingly at random, making it very difficult to reproduce the error. Win32 offers several options for thread synchronization: events, critical sections, semaphores, or mutual exclusion (mutex) objects can be used. Since data cannot in itself be protected against concurrent access by different threads, the programmer must write intelligent code that prevents this from happening. The Win32 thread synchronization objects can be used to guarantee that only one thread at a time executes a particular section of crucial code. It is important to note that only data shared by multiple threads are at risk. Automatic variables located on the stack of a particular thread pose no difficulties because they are allocated on a per-thread basis.

Apartments

Over the past decade, Windows has evolved from a cooperatively multitasked 16-bit environment into a preemptively multitasked 32-bit operating system. As Windows has evolved, threads have slowly but surely found their way into nearly all aspects of the operating system, from the C run-time library to the

Microsoft Foundation Class (MFC) library. This transition has at times been painful, but the overarching advantages have far outweighed the temporary inconveniences caused by the integration of threading. And because COM entered the threading game rather late, there has been more than a little consternation on the part of developers as threading support has been added.

Around the time multithreading support was added to COM (in Microsoft Windows NT 3.51), many design decisions made by Microsoft were affected by the amount of thread-unsafe legacy code that existed. Microsoft felt that it was crucial to enable existing thread-unsafe components to interoperate seamlessly with the new multithreaded components. Thus, several levels, called *threading models,* of thread safety were defined.

. The basic unit of thread safety in COM is called an *apartment.* Two types of apartments are defined: *single-threaded apartments* (*STAs*) can have only one thread executing per apartment, and *multithreaded apartments* (*MTAs*) can have more than one thread executing per apartment. In addition to the number of threads executing in an apartment, it is important to note that method calls to objects in an STA are automatically synchronized and dispatched using window message queues, whereas method calls to objects in an MTA are not. The STA and MTA models can be combined in a single process. A process may contain any number of or no STAs, but it can contain at most one MTA.

Immediately to the right of Java Man on the evolutionary time line stands OLE 1, a compound document architecture that originally used Dynamic Data Exchange (DDE) messages for its interprocess communication. Until the advent of the MTA model, COM had not entirely shed its seedy, message-based past. In fact, to this day the STA model notifies an object of method calls by posting messages to a window message queue. That's right, any component supporting the STA model must contain a message loop such as the following or nothing will happen:

```
// Bet you thought you'd never see another one of these!
MSG msg;
while(GetMessage(&msg, NULL, 0, 0))
    DispatchMessage(&msg);
```

Why, you ask in disbelief, does a component architecture with as much finesse as COM rely on message queues? By relying on message queues to dispense method calls, COM effectively has hooks into every object in an STA. In this way, COM can serialize method calls to each STA in order to ensure that thread safety is not compromised. The MTA model does not rely on message queues because COM does not provide thread synchronization for such objects.

In the past, different combinations of STAs and MTAs in a single process have been dubbed single-, apartment-, free-, or mixed-threading models. This terminology should be avoided because it just causes additional confusion. The following table translates these named threading models into the vocabulary of STAs and MTAs. Some documentation might still refer to COM threading models by using these less useful names. A good way to think of these threading models is to remember that they all rely on the basic unit of an apartment. Some of those apartments can have only a single thread (STAs); others support multiple threads (MTAs).

Old-Fashioned Threading Model Terms	Number of STAs	Number of MTAs
Single (legacy)	1	0
Apartment	1 or more	0
Free	0	1
Mixed (both)	1 or more	1

The threading models in COM provide the mechanism for clients and components that use different threading architectures to work together. From the perspective of a client, all objects appear to be using the client's threading model. Likewise, from the perspective of an object, all clients appear to support the object's threading model. Note that not all platforms that support DCOM necessarily support both apartment types. For instance, the implementation of EntireX DCOM on Sun Microsystems' Solaris operating system supports only MTAs because STAs depend on the existence of window message queues, something not available in the Solaris operating system.

Clients and components each have different responsibilities in relation to the threading models. Clients can use the Win32 *CreateThread* function to launch new threads of execution and might want to access COM objects from these new threads. This technique is often used to improve the responsiveness of an application or to enable the application to access several different objects concurrently. Component processes, on the other hand, rarely call the *CreateThread* function, and doing so is strongly discouraged. Instead, a component process simply declares its threading model at start-up and then lets COM handle concurrency.

In any discussion of threading models, distinctions must be made between in-process and local or remote components. We will begin our discussion with local and remote components and then discuss how the in-process model differs. Most of the code samples up to now have been in-process components, so it may be helpful to refer to Chapter 8, "DLL Surrogates and Executable Components," for detailed information about building local components.

The Single-Threaded Apartment Model

The current STA model descended from the original thread-oblivious model used by COM. In the thread-oblivious model, COM objects could be accessed only from a single thread in the process. The STA model evolved to overcome this limitation; it introduced the ability for a single process to contain multiple STAs. Since each STA has one and only one thread associated with it, the ability for multiple STAs to exist in a single process means that several threads can use COM objects concurrently—a big improvement. Under current implementations of COM, legacy components written prior to the advent of the COM threading models actually run in a single STA.

A local component declares its support for the STA model by calling *CoInitialize* or *CoInitializeEx*. The second parameter of *CoInitializeEx* is used to specify whether the component supports the STA (*COINIT_APARTMENT-THREADED*) or the MTA (*COINIT_MULTITHREADED*) model. Thus, *Co-Initialize(NULL)* is equivalent to *CoInitializeEx(NULL, COINIT_APARTMENT-THREADED)*, as shown in the following code fragment. Because these two calls are equivalent, legacy components are considered to support the STA model.

```
// Single-threaded apartment (STA)
// This code is equivalent to CoInitialize(NULL).
CoInitializeEx(NULL, COINIT_APARTMENTTHREADED);
```

The STA owns any COM object instantiated by its thread, and henceforth all method calls on the object will be executed by the thread that created the object. The fact that the same thread that created an object will be used to execute its methods is important to objects that have thread affinity. An object with thread affinity must be executed by a particular thread. For example, the thread local storage (TLS) technique is used by some objects to associate data with a specific thread. An object using TLS expects that the same thread will be used to execute all of its methods. If a different thread executes a method, an attempt to access TLS data will fail. This limitation means that objects running in the MTA cannot use TLS since different threads may be used to execute the method calls.

As in the original thread-oblivious model, method calls on objects running in an STA are dispatched using window message queues. The fact that the

STA model relies on window message queues does not mean that a component is required to display a user interface or even to create a window. The first call to *CoInitialize(Ex)* in a process calls the Win32 function *RegisterClass* to register the *OleMainThreadWndClass* window class. During this and every subsequent call to *CoInitialize(Ex)*, COM automatically calls the Win32 function *CreateWindow* to create a hidden window of the *OleMainThreadWndClass* window class for each STA. The message queue of this hidden window is used to synchronize and dispatch COM method calls on this object. For this reason, the thread associated with an STA must retrieve and dispatch window messages by using *GetMessage* and *DispatchMessage* or similar functions.

This hidden window can be displayed using a utility such as Microsoft Spy++, which comes with Microsoft Visual C++, as shown in Figure 4-1. A method call is received as a message to this hidden window. When the component retrieves the message (*GetMessage*) and then dispatches it (*DispatchMessage*), the hidden window's window procedure will receive the message. This window procedure, implemented as part of COM, will then call the corresponding interface method of the object.

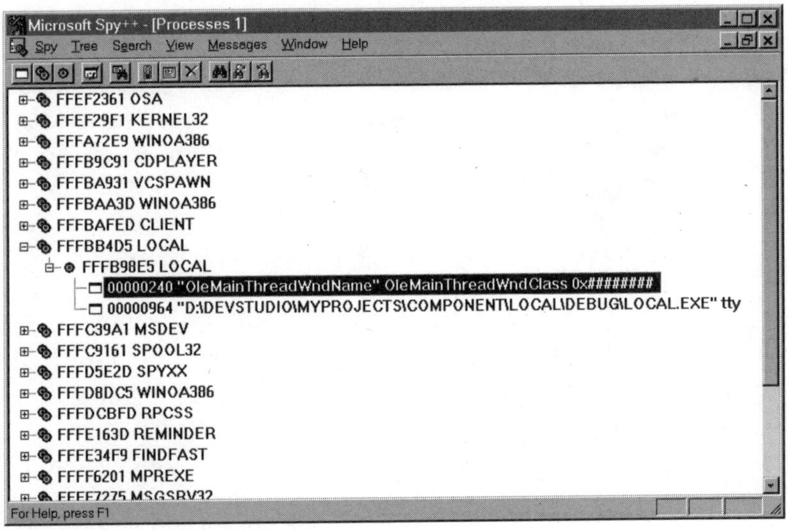

Figure 4-1
The hidden STA window created by COM and displayed using Microsoft Spy++.

This message-queuing architecture solves the problem of multiple clients making concurrent calls to an object running in an STA. Since all the calls are submitted as window messages posted to the message queue, the calls will be serialized automatically. The object will receive method calls when the message loop retrieves and dispatches the messages in the queue. Since COM serializes the calls in this manner, the object's methods do not need to provide synchronization. It is important to note that the dispatched method calls will always be made on the thread that instantiated the object. This is easily verified using the Win32 *GetCurrentThreadId* function to retrieve the thread identifier in each method of an object. The thread identifier will always be the same for objects running in an STA.

Under some circumstances, it is possible for an object to be reentered by the same thread, in a manner similar to the way a window procedure can be reentered. If a method of the object processes window messages, another call to a method might be dispatched. This problem is most easily avoided by not processing window messages during a method call. An object may also be reentered if a method makes an outgoing call using COM and the outgoing method then calls back into the object. COM does not prevent these types of reentrancy; it guarantees only that the calls will not execute concurrently.

The component can optionally implement the *IMessageFilter* interface in each STA to control aspects of the call delivery mechanism employed by COM. The component must inform COM about the object that implements the *IMessageFilter* interface via the *CoRegisterMessageFilter* function. This technique might be used to abort a lengthy method call if the user gets tired of waiting.

The message-based method invocation mechanism of an STA is used even when the client and component are separated by a network. Figure 4-2 shows how the STA model works. Each arrow indicates a separate thread of execution. In the first thread, the client calls the proxy, which in turn calls the *IRpcChannelBuffer::SendReceive* method. Here the second thread is created to actually send the data across the network using an RPC. Meanwhile, the first thread sits in a message loop waiting for a response. Across the network, a server-side thread takes the received data packet and posts a message to the message queue of the hidden window. Omitted from this diagram is the component's *GetMessage/DispatchMessage* loop, which takes messages from the queue and dispatches them back to the window procedure. From within the component's main thread, the window procedure calls the stub's *IRpcStubBuffer:Invoke* method. Last the stub unpacks the parameters and calls the actual method in the COM object. This process of packing parameters for transmission is called *marshaling* and is basically repeated in reverse order once the method has finished executing. For more information about marshaling, see Chapter 9, "Standard and Custom Marshaling."

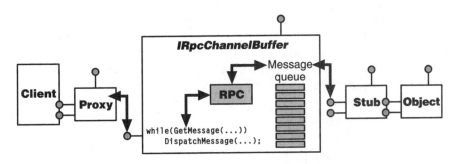

Figure 4-2.
The inner workings of the STA model.

Observe that a total of four threads—two on the client side and two on the server side—are required in order to make the STA model work. An internal optimization of the STA model is possible when the client and the component are both executing on the same machine. In such cases, COM automatically uses only two threads—one thread in the client process and another thread in the component.

The STA Model in Client Applications

Client-side code that uses COM objects creates STAs by using the *CoInitialize-(NULL)* or *CoInitializeEx(NULL, COINIT_APARTMENTTHREADED)* function. Any COM objects created by the client code become members of the STA in which they were instantiated. The client-side application can call the *Create-Thread* function to spawn additional threads, and each thread that wants to access COM objects must declare its apartment type by calling *CoInitialize(Ex)*. The following code fragment shows how a thread in the client process could create an STA and instantiate a COM class:

```
void __stdcall ThreadRoutine(void)
{
    CoInitializeEx(NULL, COINIT_APARTMENTTHREADED);

    IUnknown* pUnknown;
    HRESULT hr = CoCreateInstance(CLSID_InsideDCOM, NULL,
        CLSCTX_INPROC_SERVER, IID_IUnknown, (void**)&pUnknown);

    pUnknown->Release();
    CoUninitialize();
}
```

The *IUnknown* pointer returned by the *CoCreateInstance* call in the preceding code can be used only in this STA. For example, if this pointer were passed through a global variable to the thread of another apartment and then used

135

to call a method, an *RPC_E_WRONG_THREAD* error could result. This error is returned by the interface proxy because the client has attempted to use an interface pointer that was not marshaled for use in a different apartment. Remember, similar to the process-relative file handles returned by the Win32 *CreateFile* function, interface pointers in COM are apartment-relative—that is, they cannot be used by code in another apartment unless special precautions are taken. If COM allowed the sharing of raw interface pointers, it would have no way of guaranteeing the synchronization required by the STA model. Instead, COM provides the *CoMarshalInterThreadInterfaceInStream* and *CoGetInterfaceAndReleaseStream* functions to enable the marshaling of an interface pointer from one apartment to another.

CoMarshalInterThreadInterfaceInStream is called to marshal an interface pointer into a stream object. Imagine that the thread of an STA—let's call it STA1—wanted to pass an interface pointer to the thread of another STA, which we'll call STA3. STA1 would begin by calling *CoMarshalInterThreadInterface-InStream* in order to obtain an apartment-neutral interface representation stored in a stream object. The resultant *IStream* pointer could then be stored in a global variable accessible to STA3. STA3 would pass this *IStream* pointer to the *CoGetInterfaceAndReleaseStream* function to unmarshal the stream and obtain an apartment-relative interface pointer appropriate for use in STA3. Figure 4-3 illustrates this procedure.

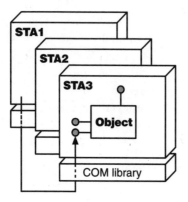
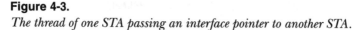

Figure 4-3.
The thread of one STA passing an interface pointer to another STA.

As shown in the following client-side code, the thread in STA1 instantiates a COM object and then calls *CoMarshalInterThreadInterfaceInStream* (shown in boldface) to marshal that interface pointer into an apartment-neutral representation. The resultant *IStream* pointer is then passed as an argument to a newly spawned thread. STA1 can now continue to use its interface pointer, and when it has finished working, it can release the pointer without danger. Notice that the *IStream* pointer is not released in this code; it is released by the receiving thread.

```
// STA1

IMyInterface* pMyInterface;
CoCreateInstance(CLSID_MyCOMClass, NULL, CLSCTX_LOCAL_SERVER,
    IID_IMyInterface, (void**)&pMyInterface);

// Marshal interface pointer to stream.
IStream* pStream;
CoMarshalInterThreadInterfaceInStream(IID_IMyInterface, pMyInterface,
    &pStream);

// Spawn new thread;
// pass pStream to new thread.
DWORD threadId;
CreateThread(NULL, 0, (LPTHREAD_START_ROUTINE)ThreadRoutine,
    pStream, 0, &threadId);

// Do other work...

pMyInterface->Release();
```

The new thread begins execution at the *ThreadRoutine* function. Its only argument is the *IStream* pointer containing the marshaled interface pointer to the object it wants to call, as shown in the following code. This code first creates a new STA, STA3, by calling *CoInitializeEx* and then unmarshals the stream object by calling *CoGetInterfaceAndReleaseStream* (shown in boldface). This has the effect of returning an apartment-relative interface pointer usable by STA3 and automatically releasing the *IStream* pointer. When it has finished using the interface pointer, STA3 must release the pointer.

```
void __stdcall ThreadRoutine(IStream* pStream)
{
    // Create STA3.
    CoInitializeEx(NULL, COINIT_APARTMENTTHREADED);

    // Unmarshal interface pointer from stream.
    IMyInterface* pMyInterface;
    CoGetInterfaceAndReleaseStream(pStream, IID_IMyInterface,
        (void**)&pMyInterface);
```

(continued)

```
    // Do work with pMyInterface...

    pMyInterface->Release();

    CoUninitialize();
}
```

Their long and sophisticated sounding names notwithstanding, *CoMarshalInterThreadInterfaceInStream* and *CoGetInterfaceAndReleaseStream* are basically wrapper functions for *CoMarshalInterface* and *CoUnmarshalInterface*. Interestingly, the *CoMarshalInterThreadInterfaceInStream* function calls *CoMarshalInterface* with the *MSHCTX_INPROC* flag. This flag was added to *CoMarshalInterface* to indicate that the unmarshaling will be performed in another apartment in the same process. The following pseudo-code demonstrates the internals of *CoMarshalInterThreadInterfaceInStream* and *CoGetInterfaceAndReleaseStream:*

```
HRESULT MyMarshalInterThreadInterfaceInStream(REFIID riid, IUnknown*
    pUnknown, IStream** pStream)
{
    CreateStreamOnHGlobal(NULL, TRUE, pStream);
    return CoMarshalInterface(*pStream, riid, pUnknown,
        MSHCTX_INPROC, NULL, MSHLFLAGS_NORMAL);
}

HRESULT MyGetInterfaceAndReleaseStream(IStream* pStream, REFIID riid,
    void** ppv)
{
    HRESULT hr = CoUnmarshalInterface(pStream, riid, ppv);
    pStream->Release();
    return hr;
}
```

The Multithreaded Apartment Model

A local component declares its use of the MTA model by calling *CoInitializeEx-(NULL, COINIT_MULTITHREADED)*. Threads running in the MTA do not need to retrieve or dispatch window messages because COM does not use messages to deliver method calls on objects running in the MTA. Since method calls are made directly through a v-table, COM does not impose any synchronization on objects running in the MTA. Therefore, these objects must provide their own synchronization using critical sections, events, mutexes, semaphores, or other mechanisms, as dictated by their synchronization requirements.

Multiple clients can concurrently execute an object's methods from different threads, and thus threads of an MTA cannot use TLS or have any other thread affinity whatsoever. An object running in the MTA will receive calls through a pool of COM-allocated threads belonging to the object's process. These threads are created by COM at run time and then reused as it sees fit. Since COM automatically spawns threads as necessary to enable concurrent access to the component, it is not advisable to call the Win32 *CreateThread* function. In fact, calling *CreateThread* for the purpose of enabling concurrency in a component process is strongly discouraged since in most cases this will only interfere with COM's threading algorithm. A utility such as Process Viewer (pview.exe), included with Visual C++, can be useful for dynamically spying on the threads created by COM.

Client-side code creates the MTA by calling *CoInitializeEx(NULL, COINIT_ _MULTITHREADED)*, as shown in the following code fragment. Since only one MTA is ever created in a process, only the first thread to call the *CoInitializeEx* function using the *COINIT_MULTITHREADED* flag creates the MTA. Every subsequent thread that calls the *CoInitializeEx* function using this flag joins the existing MTA.

```
// Create the MTA.
CoInitializeEx(NULL, COINIT_MULTITHREADED);
```

> **NOTE:** Some documentation incorrectly states that only the initial thread needs to call *CoInitializeEx* and that all other threads will implicitly join the MTA. While this technique might work in some cases, it is not considered legal COM code and can cause access violations under certain circumstances.

As shown in Figure 4-4 on the following page, interface pointers can be passed directly between threads running in the MTA; they do not need to be marshaled using the *CoMarshalInterThreadInterfaceInStream* and *CoGetInterface-AndReleaseStream* functions. Of course, any attempt to pass an interface pointer from an MTA to an STA must be marshaled using the *CoMarshalInterThread-InterfaceInStream* and *CoGetInterfaceAndReleaseStream* functions. In addition, message filters implementing the *IMessageFilter* interface cannot be used in the MTA model.

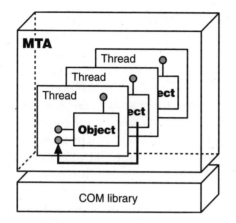

Figure 4-4.
Interface pointers passed directly between threads in an MTA.

Have We Got a Threading Model for You

Which threading model is right for you? Generally speaking, applications that interact with the user should use the STA model, whereas components that run without a significant user interface usually do best with the MTA model. Remember that in the STA model, COM uses window message queues to invoke methods in COM objects. Since any application that displays a window already has a message loop, the STA model is a natural fit. A combination of STAs and an MTA can also be used when both threading models are needed for different purposes in the same application. The following table compares the various aspects of life in an STA and life in an MTA:

Feature	STA	MTA
Synchronization provided by COM	Yes	No
Can have multiple threads in one apartment	No	Yes
Must marshal interface pointers between apartments	Yes	Yes
Must marshal interface pointers between threads in the same apartment	N/A	No
Uses window message queues	Yes	No
Must call *CoInitialize* in every thread that uses COM services	Yes	Yes

If you are designing a new component without a significant user interface, using the MTA model might seem like the obvious choice. The MTA model is faster because COM does not need to synchronize calls into free-threaded objects. When you are using the MTA model, however, it is the responsibility of the object to implement its own synchronization or fall prey to the thread synchronization problems discussed earlier. If you don't feel like dealing with thread synchronization issues, you can tell COM to do the work for you by selecting the STA model. In the STA model, COM synchronizes access to a component at the method level—in other words, COM will ensure that two different threads cannot call into an STA concurrently. It is possible to simulate this behavior in an MTA by using a Win32 mutex object, as shown in the following code. However, instead of building locks around entire methods as the STA does, a component that supports the MTA model will normally use locks only around small portions of the critical code within a method, resulting in improved concurrency.

```
// Create a mutex and store its handle in a global variable.
HANDLE g_hMutex = CreateMutex(NULL, FALSE, NULL);

HRESULT CMyClass::MyMethod(int MyParameters)
{
    // Verify that no other method in the object is being called.
    WaitForSingleObject(g_hMutex, INFINITE);

    // Write your code here...

    // Release the mutex, enabling another method to execute.
    ReleaseMutex(g_hMutex);
    return S_OK;
}

HRESULT CMyClass::MyOtherMethod(int MyParameters)
{
    WaitForSingleObject(g_hMutex, INFINITE);

    // Write your code here...

    ReleaseMutex(g_hMutex);
    return S_OK;
}

// Before exiting, free the mutex.
CloseHandle(g_hMutex);
```

Threading Models for In-Process Components

The *CoInitialize(Ex)* functions provide executable components with the ability to declare their support for a particular threading model. Clients use these functions to create apartments for use in calling components. In-process components work differently than executable components in that they do not call *CoInitialize(Ex)* on start-up because their client will already have initialized COM by the time they are loaded. Instead, in-process components declare their supported threading model using registry settings. In the component's CLSID-\InprocServer32 registry key, the named value *ThreadingModel* can be set to *Apartment, Free,* or *Both* to indicate support for one of those threading models. If no *ThreadingModel* value is specified, the in-process component is assumed to be a thread-oblivious legacy component.

Note that the old-fashioned threading model names are used by the *ThreadingModel* value. The following table translates these names into the modern STA and MTA models.

ThreadingModel Values	Description
[No *ThreadingModel* value]	Thread-oblivious legacy component
Apartment	STA
Free	MTA
Both	Both STA and MTA models

The *RegisterServer* function used in Chapter 2, "*IUnknown* and *IClassFactory*," to perform component self-registration can also be used to set the *ThreadingModel* value in the registry. The last parameter of this function should contain one of the three strings from the preceding table. For example, the following code statement registers a COM class and the last parameter (shown in boldface) specifies that it supports the STA model:

```
RegisterServer("component.dll", CLSID_InsideDCOM, "Inside DCOM Sample",
    "Component.InsideDCOM", "Component.InsideDCOM.1", "Apartment");
```

NOTE: It is legal for different COM classes provided by a single in-process component to have different *ThreadingModel* values—in other words, the *ThreadingModel* value is set on a per-CLSID basis, not per DLL.

Threading Concerns for Visual Basic and Java Components

Components built in Visual Basic can support either the thread-oblivious legacy model or the STA model. Visual Basic will automatically set the *ThreadingModel* registry value to *Apartment* for ActiveX controls or ActiveX DLLs supporting the STA model. Currently, components built in Visual Basic cannot support the MTA model. To specify the threading model used by a Visual Basic application, choose Properties from the Project menu and then make your selection from the Project Properties dialog box, as shown in Figure 4-5.

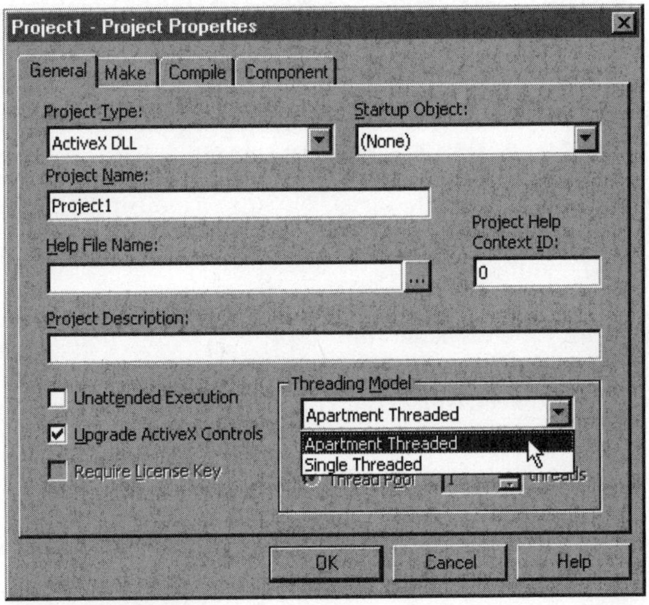

Figure 4-5.
The General tab of the Project Properties dialog box, showing the Threading Model drop-down list.

COM components built in Java are executed by the Microsoft Java VM (msjava.dll). In the registry, components built in Java have the InprocServer32 key set to msjava.dll and the *ThreadingModel* value set to *Both*. Thus, COM components built in Java implicitly support either the STA or MTA model. The *Both* setting for the *ThreadingModel* value is discussed in greater detail in the section "In-Process Objects That Support Both the STA and the MTA Models" later in this chapter.

Apartment Interactions

In this section, we will look at how COM is able to support interoperability among all possible combinations of components, even when those components use different threading models. To recapitulate, here are the basic principles through which components create apartments and declare their supported threading model:

- The client application creates apartments by calling *CoInitializeEx* with the *COINIT_APARTMENTTHREADED* (STA) or *COINIT-_MULTITHREADED* (MTA) flags.

- EXE-based components declare their supported threading model by calling *CoInitializeEx* with the *COINIT_APARTMENTTHREADED* (STA) or *COINIT_MULTITHREADED* (MTA) flags.

- In-process components declare their supported threading model with one of the following registry entries: *Apartment* (STA), *Free* (MTA), or *Both* (STA and MTA).

The interaction of clients and out-of-process components is relatively straightforward even when both parties use different threading models. When a client instantiates an object, COM compares the threading models supported by the client and the component. If the two parties are following the same threading model, in most cases COM has little work to do. Otherwise, COM must interpose itself between the client and the component to ensure that everyone is happy. This is possible because COM is used to deliver the cross-process or cross-machine calls. For example, if an object running in an STA is called concurrently by multiple clients (regardless of their threading model), COM will synchronize access to the object by posting window messages to the component's message queue. The object will receive only one call each time it retrieves and dispatches a COM-related message. While this interference implies some performance penalty, it allows applications supporting different threading models to work together. Thus, all possible combinations of client and out-of-process component interoperability are supported.

Interaction between clients and in-process components that use different threading models is more complex. In the ideal case, in which the client and the in-process component use the same threading model, COM allows direct calls from the client to the in-process code. This access yields the best performance for a given model. However, when the two parties use different threading models, COM must interpose itself between the client and the in-process component. For example, imagine that a client thread running in an MTA loads an in-process component supporting the STA model—COM cannot allow client's calls to proceed directly to the in-process component because the possibility exists for concurrent access. In such cases, COM marshals the interface between the client and the component. In-process components must provide marshaling code for any custom interfaces they implement if they are to support interoperability that requires COM to marshal interface pointers among client apartments.

In-Process Interactions

In-process objects that do not have a *ThreadingModel* value in the registry are considered legacy components written prior to the advent of COM's threading models. Such objects expect to be accessed from one client STA only, the apartment that instantiated the object. COM deals with thread-oblivious objects by creating them in the main STA of the client process. The main STA is a special designation awarded to the first STA created in a process. Calls from all other client apartments, be they STAs or an MTA, are marshaled to the main STA by COM. Only then can a call be executed. Such calls are received by the proxy of one apartment and sent to the stub in the main STA via interapartment marshaling before being delivered to the object. Compared with direct calls, interapartment marshaling is slow, and it is therefore recommended that legacy in-process components be rewritten to support the STA model. Another solution to the performance problem is to access legacy in-process components from the main STA only, as shown in Figure 4-6. Notice that the thread of the main STA can access the legacy component directly.

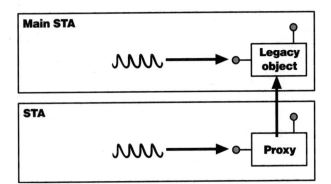

ᔐᕑᕞᕞᕞ = Thread

Figure 4-6.
An STA accessing an in-process object that does not have a specified ThreadingModel *value.*

If you are using legacy in-process objects, it is strongly recommended that you create the main STA in the main thread of the client process because once the main STA terminates, all in-process objects created there are destroyed. Should the client spawn several threads, each of which calls *CoInitialize* or *CoInitializeEx(NULL, COINIT_APARTMENTTHREADED)*, without first creating an STA, one of those threads will randomly become the main STA through which all calls to legacy in-process objects will be marshaled. The danger is that the thread running the main STA might terminate at some point, taking with it all the objects created there. Another difficulty arises when an MTA-based client that does not have an STA instantiates an object from an in-process component that supports the STA model. In such cases, COM dynamically creates the main STA by spawning a new thread and calling *CoInitializeEx(NULL, COINIT_APARTMENTTHREADED)* in that thread. The object is then created in the new host STA, and the interface pointer is marshaled back to the client thread in the MTA.

Making *DllGetClassObject* and *DllCanUnloadNow* Thread-Safe

In-process objects that support the STA model (*ThreadingModel = Apartment*) expect to be accessed by the same client thread that created the object, which is similar to the way thread-oblivious components work. However, objects that support the STA model can be created in multiple STAs of the client process, whereas objects of a legacy component are always created in the main STA. The possibility of multiple threads accessing different objects in the component simultaneously means that a component supporting the STA model must code its *DllGetClassObject* and *DllCanUnloadNow* entry points to allow for the possibility of concurrent access by multiple client STAs.

Let's assume that two different STAs in the client process create instances of the same class simultaneously. It follows that the *DllGetClassObject* function might be called concurrently by two different threads. Fortunately, most typical implementations of *DllGetClassObject*, such as the one shown in the following code, are inherently thread-safe since a new class factory is instantiated for each caller and no global or static data is accessed. If your component is not a typical implementation, the *DllGetClassObject* function must be rewritten to be thread-safe.

```
HRESULT __stdcall DllGetClassObject(REFCLSID clsid, REFIID riid,
    void** ppv)
{
    if(clsid != CLSID_InsideDCOM)
        return CLASS_E_CLASSNOTAVAILABLE;

    CFactory* pFactory = new CFactory;
```

```
    if(pFactory == NULL)
        return E_OUTOFMEMORY;

    HRESULT hr = pFactory->QueryInterface(riid, ppv);
    pFactory->Release();
    return hr;
}
```

DllCanUnloadNow can also be the root cause of a particularly nasty race condition. Since in-process components do not manage their own lifetimes, the *DllCanUnloadNow* function is designed to enable a client to determine whether the DLL can be unloaded. If *DllCanUnloadNow* returns *S_OK*, the DLL can be unloaded; if it returns *S_FALSE*, the DLL should not be unloaded now. The *DllCanUnloadNow* function is called by *CoFreeUnusedLibraries*, a function designed to be invoked by clients in their spare time. Here is a typical implementation of *DllCanUnloadNow*:

```
HRESULT __stdcall DllCanUnloadNow()
{
    if(g_cServerLocks == 0 && g_cComponents == 0)
        return S_OK;
    else
        return S_FALSE;
}
```

Now the client might call the *IUnknown::Release* method, as shown here, decrementing the usage counter to *0* and thus destroying the object (shown in boldface):

```
ULONG CInsideDCOM::Release()
{
    if(--m_cRef != 0)
        return m_cRef;
    delete this;
    return 0;
}
```

As part of its cleanup duties, the destructor decrements the *g_cComponents* global variable, as shown in the code on the following page. If this is the last object that is being destroyed, *g_cComponents* will be decremented to *0*. Now the object is unwittingly in a deadly race to exit the destructor before *DllCanUnload-Now* is called. If another thread in the client process called *CoFreeUnusedLibraries*, the *DllCanUnloadNow* function would return *S_OK*, leading COM to believe that it can unload the DLL. However, unloading the DLL while the destructor's cleanup code is still executing will result in a fault.

```
CInsideDCOM::~CInsideDCOM()
{
    g_cComponents--;
    // Pray nobody calls CoFreeUnusedLibraries now...
    // Some other cleanup code here...
}
```

To mend this race condition, Microsoft has modified the implementation of the *CoFreeUnusedLibraries* function. Instead of immediately unloading a DLL when *DllCanUnloadNow* returns *S_OK*, *CoFreeUnusedLibraries* waits for approximately 10 minutes. If *CoFreeUnusedLibraries* is called again after 10 minutes have elapsed and *DllCanUnloadNow* again returns *S_OK*, then and only then is the DLL unloaded. This heuristic approach, while not foolproof, works very well. After all, how many destructors do you know that take 10 minutes to execute?

In-Process Objects That Support the MTA Model

In-process objects that support the MTA model (*ThreadingModel = Free*) implement their own synchronization and are designed for use from an MTA only. MTA-based client threads that instantiate an object are permitted to use the object directly, resulting in superior performance when compared with the STA model. Initially, it might seem as though any object supporting the MTA model could also be run safely in an STA; unfortunately, this is not the case. Imagine that a client thread belonging to an STA instantiates an object supporting the MTA model. One or more STAs present no threat to the object designed for MTA access because it manages its own synchronization. However, even in this deceptively simple case, COM must still perform thread synchronization.

This time it is not the component but the client that needs protection. Although the component has declared its thread independence, the client has not. Pure clients and components are a rare phenomenon; it is much more common for clients and components to have a two-way conversation using connection points or some other private callback interface. In such cases, an MTA object might feel justified in calling the client back from any thread at any time. In effect, a component supporting the MTA model declares, "You can call me from any thread, so I can call you right back from any other thread." The hapless client, which created the object in an STA, is totally unprepared for this turn of events (pun intended). The possibility of multiple concurrent calls into an STA violates STA rules and would probably result in errors. For this reason, even when an STA calls a component designed for MTA access, COM creates the object in an MTA and marshals all calls into and out of it.

Figure 4-7 shows how an object designed for use from an MTA is created in the MTA even when it is instantiated by an STA-based thread. The result is that MTA-based threads can call directly into the object, while the STA-based thread that instantiated the object must call into the object via a proxy.

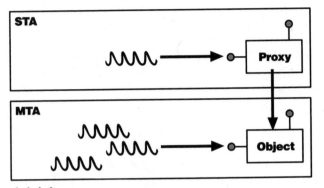

= Thread

Figure 4-7.
When an STA-based thread instantiates an object designed for execution in an MTA, COM creates the MTA if necessary and instantiates the object there.

Perhaps you are wondering how COM can create the object in an MTA if the client instantiates the object from an STA-based thread. If no MTA exists, COM first creates one by spawning a new thread and calling *CoInitializeEx-(NULL, COINIT_MULTITHREADED)*. However, if the MTA already exists in the client process when the MTA-supporting object is instantiated, COM creates the object there. All calls to and from that object are marshaled through the MTA back to the STA-based client thread.

In-Process Objects That Support
Both the STA and the MTA Models

What's a conscientious developer to do when even in-process components designed for MTA access incur the overhead of interapartment marshaling when they are accessed by an STA? Well, in order to avoid the wrath of COM, an in-process component can declare that it supports both the STA and MTA models (*ThreadingModel = Both*). Proxy/stub marshaling DLLs generated by recent versions of the MIDL compiler register themselves using the *Both* value for *ThreadingModel*.

COM permits this type of object to be used directly by client threads running in either an STA or the MTA, resulting in a big performance advantage over MTA-only components loaded into an STA. Like MTA-based objects, an object that supports both the STA and MTA models must provide its own synchronization because it can be accessed concurrently by multiple STA-based and/or MTA-based client threads. An in-process component supporting both the STA and MTA threading models declares to prospective clients, "You can call me from any thread, but I will call you back only on the one thread that received the interface pointer to the callback object." This is a component that would make any developer proud.

Now COM can allow clients to call the component directly from an STA or the MTA. Although a COM class can support both threading models, at run time each object is still instantiated in either an STA or the MTA, not both. If such an object is instantiated by an STA-based thread, it belongs to that STA and all calls by threads in other apartments must still be marshaled, as shown in Figure 4-8. The other possibility is to instantiate the object in the MTA, enabling all threads of the MTA to access the object directly but requiring that STAs access the object through a proxy.

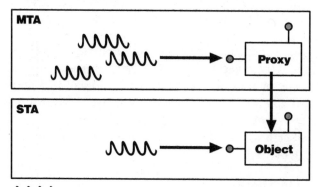

Figure 4-8.
Calls to an in-process object in a different apartment with ThreadingModel = Both *still must be marshaled.*

In-process objects that support both the STA and MTA threading models (*ThreadingModel = Both*) never know whether they'll be created in an STA or in the MTA. However, it might be useful for the object to determine which threading model is in operation at run time. The *isMTA* function, shown in the following code, can be used to obtain this information. The *isMTA* function returns *true* if it is called from the MTA; it returns *false* if the code is running in an STA.

```
bool isMTA()
{
    HRESULT hr = CoInitializeEx(NULL, COINIT_MULTITHREADED);
    CoUninitialize();
    if(hr == S_OK || hr == S_FALSE)
        return true;
    else
        return false;
}
```

Comparing the Threading Models

Although a variety of complex situations can arise when clients and in-process components of different threading models attempt to play together, COM handles all of these situations with aplomb. While COM enables all forms of interoperability using any combination of threading models between clients and components, a performance penalty results when the threading models of the two parties do not match. In most cases, this overhead can be circumvented with a little creative thinking. Imagine a situation in which an MTA accesses a component that supports only the apartment threading model. In this case, COM has little choice but to introduce synchronization into the equation in order to protect the component. If you are aware that the component supports only the apartment threading model, however, it makes sense for the client to create an STA from which to call this component. When an STA calls a component supporting the apartment threading model, little overhead results.

How can the client determine what threading model is supported by a component? For in-process components, you need only examine the object's *ThreadingModel* registry entry in order to obtain this information. For local components, it is not currently possible to determine programmatically what threading model is supported. Of course, if the developer knows in advance what component the client will be calling, the documentation for that component can be consulted. The table on the following page shows the variety of threading models that can be supported by clients and in-process components and describes how COM handles each unique situation.

In-Process Component's *ThreadingModel* Value	Client	Result
None	Main STA	Direct access; object instantiated in the Main STA.
	Any STA	Proxy access; object instantiated in the Main STA.
	MTA	Proxy access; object instantiated in the Main STA. Main STA created by COM if necessary.
Apartment	Main STA	Direct access; object instantiated in the main STA.
	Any STA	Direct access; object instantiated in the calling STA.
	MTA	Proxy access; object instantiated in a new STA created automatically by COM.
Free	Main STA	Proxy access; object instantiated in the MTA. MTA created by COM if necessary.
	Any STA	Proxy access; object instantiated in the MTA. MTA created by COM if necessary.
	MTA	Direct access; object instantiated in the MTA.
Both	Main STA	Direct access; object instantiated in the Main STA.
	Any STA	Direct access; object instantiated in the calling STA.
	MTA	Direct access; object instantiated in the MTA.

Aggregating with the Free-Threaded Marshaler

In-process components that support the STA and MTA models (*ThreadingModel* = *Both*) are designed to handle multiple concurrent access by different client apartments, so it seems as if the client need not marshal its interface pointers between apartments. The client, however, must follow COM's threading rules and always marshal interface pointers between apartments. In such cases, the need for client applications to remain independent of a component's internal threading model comes into conflict with the developer's desire to achieve the best performance. The *free-threaded marshaler* was introduced as an optimization technique designed for just such occasions.

The free-threaded marshaler enables an in-process object to pass a direct pointer into any client apartment. All client threads, regardless of whether they are running in an STA or the MTA, will call the object directly instead of through a proxy. Figure 4-9 shows a client STA (STA1) that instantiates an in-process object supporting both threading models (*ThreadingModel = Both*). STA1 then calls *CoMarshalInterThreadInterfaceInStream* to marshal the interface pointer to another STA (STA2). STA2 now calls the *CoGetInterfaceAndRelease-Stream* function in order to obtain an apartment-relative interface pointer for use in calling the object. Normally, STA2 now has a pointer to a proxy that marshals calls to the thread of STA1 before the object is called. However, if the object uses the free-threaded marshaler, STA2 has a direct pointer to the object. Any threads running in the MTA would also have direct access to the object. In this example, the decision to have STA1 instantiate the object is an arbitrary one. Any apartment in the process could instantiate the object; the result will be identical.

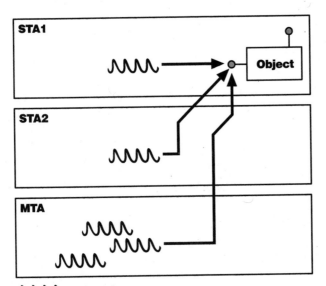

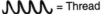 = Thread

Figure 4-9.
An object that uses the free-threaded marshaler allows threads in different apartments but in the same process to access the object without going through a proxy.

The free-threaded marshaler is an object implemented as part of COM and can be created by calling the *CoCreateFreeThreadedMarshaler* function. Unlike a typical stand-alone object, however, the free-threaded marshaler is designed to aggregate with another object. (For information about aggregation, see Chapter 2, "*IUnknown* and *IClassFactory*.") The free-threaded marshaler works by providing an implementation of the *IMarshal* interface that the object will expose as its own, as shown in Figure 4-10. *IMarshal* is COM's custom marshaling interface and is covered in detail in Chapter 9, "Standard and Custom Marshaling."

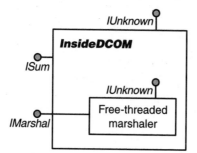

Figure 4-10.
The InsideDCOM *object aggregating the free-threaded marshaler.*

When the client marshals an interface pointer of an object that aggregates with the free-threaded marshaler, the free-threaded marshaler takes the following actions:

1. The free-threaded marshaler checks the *dwDestContext* flag passed to the *CoMarshalInterface* function. This value indicates the type of marshaling that is taking place.

2. If the marshaling type is *MSHCTX_INPROC*, the free-threaded marshaler knows that an interface pointer is being marshaled between apartments in the same process, due to the client's call to *CoMarshalInterThreadInterfaceInStream*. In the *IMarshal::MarshalInterface* method, the free-threaded marshaler simply stores the object's actual interface pointer in the marshaling stream.

3. If the marshaling type is not *MSHCTX_INPROC*, indicating that marshaling is taking place between processes or possibly between computers, the free-threaded marshaler simply delegates the marshaling work to COM's standard marshaler by calling *CoGetStandardMarshal*.

The equivalent pseudo-code for the main portion of the free-threaded marshaler is shown here. (The numbered comments refer to the numbered steps shown on the facing page.)

```
HRESULT FreeThreadedMarshaler::MarshalInterface(IStream* pStream,
    REFIID riid, void* pv, DWORD dwDestContext, void* pvDestContext,
    DWORD dwFlags)
{
    // (1) If interapartment marshaling,...
    if(dwDestContext == MSHCTX_INPROC)
        // (2) simply store the pointer directly in the stream.
        return pStream->Write(this, sizeof(this), 0);

    // (3) Otherwise, delegate the work to the standard marshaler.
    IMarshal* pMarshal = 0;
    CoGetStandardMarshal(riid, pv, dwDestContext, pvDestContext,
        dwFlags, &pMarshal);
    HRESULT hr = pMarshal->MarshalInterface(pStream, riid, pv,
        dwDestContext, pvDestContext, dwFlags);
    pMarshal->Release();
    return hr;
}
```

Using the Free-Threaded Marshaler

If these qualities sound enticing, you probably want to know how to use the free-threaded marshaler. The free-threaded marshaler is usually aggregated in an object's constructor, as shown in boldface here:

```
CInsideDCOM::CInsideDCOM() : m_cRef(1)
{
    InterlockedIncrement(&g_cComponents);
    CoCreateFreeThreadedMarshaler(this, &m_pUnknownFTM);
}
```

In addition to aggregating with the object, the *CoCreateFreeThreadedMarshaler* function also returns a pointer to its *IUnknown* implementation, stored here as *m_pUnknownFTM*. This pointer is required in the object's implementation of *IUnknown::QueryInterface*.

The object's *QueryInterface* method contains code to check for the *IMarshal* interface. COM will automatically call *QueryInterface* to request the *IMarshal* interface whenever an interface pointer on this object is marshaled—for example, when the client calls *CoMarshalInterThreadInterfaceInStream*. Normally, the object returns *E_NOINTERFACE*, causing COM to default to its own standard marshaler. In this case, however, we intercept this request for the *IMarshal* interface and forward it to the free-threaded marshaler. The free-threaded marshaler will return a pointer to its implementation of *IMarshal*, which has the special behavior discussed in the previous section. Here is how the object's implementation of *IUnknown::QueryInterface* should look; the additions are shown in boldface:

```
HRESULT CInsideDCOM::QueryInterface(REFIID riid, void** ppv)
{
    if(riid == IID_IUnknown)
        *ppv = (IUnknown*)this;
    else if(riid == IID_ISum)
        *ppv = (ISum*)this;
    else if(riid == IID_IMarshal)
        return m_pUnknownFTM->QueryInterface(riid, ppv);
    else
    {
        *ppv = NULL;
        return E_NOINTERFACE;
    }
    AddRef();
    return S_OK;
}
```

Before the object is destroyed, the free-threaded marshaler must be released as well. This call is typically made in the object's destructor, as shown here in boldface:

```
CInsideDCOM::~CInsideDCOM()
{
    InterlockedDecrement(&g_cComponents);
    m_pUnknownFTM->Release();
}
```

Using the free-threaded marshaler requires constant vigilance to ensure that COM's threading rules are not broken. Because the free-threaded marshaler enables client apartments to share direct pointers rather than use pointers to proxies, COM's threading rules can be easily forgotten. Imagine an in-process object (OBJ1) that supports both threading models (*ThreadingModel = Both*), uses the free-threaded marshaler, and holds a pointer to some other object (OBJ2). If a client apartment (STA1) marshals an interface pointer to OBJ1, to another apartment (STA2), the free-threaded marshaler will see to it that a direct pointer is passed. Here's the problem: if STA2 calls a method of OBJ1 and the method in turn uses its pointer to call a method of OBJ2, COM's threading rules have been broken. Unless OBJ2 also happens to use the free-threaded marshaler, it cannot be called from STA2 without first being marshaled to that apartment. Attempting to do this might result in random program faults or in the infamous *RPC_E_WRONG_THREAD* error. Figure 4-11 shows that the threads of STA1 and STA2 can access OBJ1 directly but that only the thread of STA1 can access OBJ2.

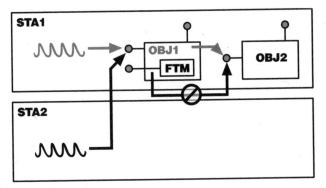

$\Lambda\Lambda\Lambda$ = Thread

Figure 4-11.
COM's threading rules are broken if STA2 calls OBJ1 and then proceeds to call OBJ2 directly.

The problem presented in Figure 4-11 is typical, but it is not easily solved. One possible solution is to call *CoMarshalInterThreadInterfaceInStream* after you instantiate OBJ2. This call would result in a stream-based, apartment-neutral representation of the interface pointer. This stream could later be unmarshaled using the *CoGetInterfaceAndReleaseStream* function to ensure that a valid pointer was used for the calling apartment. The problem with using *CoGetInterfaceAndReleaseStream*, however, is that it unmarshals the interface pointer and frees the stream-based, apartment-neutral representation. This means that the interface pointer can be unmarshaled from the stream only once! All future attempts to use the stream will fail because it has already been released.

IGlobalInterfaceTable to the Rescue

The *IGlobalInterfaceTable* interface is a processwide holding table for interface pointers. Interface pointers can be checked into the Global Interface Table (GIT), where they will be available to any apartment in the process. When a thread requests an interface pointer from the GIT, the interface pointer supplied is guaranteed to be usable by that thread—if necessary, the GIT automatically performs the necessary interapartment marshaling. Because GIT permits an interface pointer to be unmarshaled as many times as desired, it is helpful in solving the problems that might arise through careless use of the free-threaded marshaler.

The *IGlobalInterfaceTable* interface is shown here in IDL notation:

```
interface IGlobalInterfaceTable : IUnknown
{
// Voluntarily check an interface pointer into the GIT.
    HRESULT RegisterInterfaceInGlobal
    (
        [in]  IUnknown *pUnk,
        [in]  REFIID    riid,
        [out] DWORD    *pdwCookie
    );

// Remove an interface pointer from the GIT.
    HRESULT RevokeInterfaceFromGlobal
    (
        [in] DWORD      dwCookie
    );

// Unmarshal an interface pointer from the GIT to the
// caller's apartment.
    HRESULT GetInterfaceFromGlobal
    (
        [in]  DWORD          dwCookie,
        [in]  REFIID         riid,
        [out, iid_is(riid)] void **ppv
    );
};
```

COM provides an implementation of *IGlobalInterfaceTable*, so there is really no need to implement this interface yourself. Calling *CoCreateInstance* with the first parameter set to *CLSID_StdGlobalInterfaceTable* provides access to the standard implementation of the GIT, as shown in the following code. Only one instance of the GIT exists per process, so multiple calls to this function return the same instance.

```
IGlobalInterfaceTable* m_pGIT;
CoCreateInstance(CLSID_StdGlobalInterfaceTable, NULL,
    CLSCTX_INPROC_SERVER, IID_IGlobalInterfaceTable, (void**)&m_pGIT);
```

Now any valid interface pointer can be stored in the GIT by calling the *IGlobalInterfaceTable::RegisterInterfaceInGlobal* method. The *RegisterInterfaceInGlobal* method stores an apartment-neutral object reference in the GIT and returns a processwide cookie value that can be used by any apartment to obtain this interface pointer, as shown here:

```
DWORD m_cookie;
m_pGIT->RegisterInterfaceInGlobal(pMyInterface, IID_IMyInterface,
    &m_cookie);
```

The *IGlobalInterfaceTable::GetInterfaceFromGlobal* method can be called in the thread of another apartment in order to retrieve an apartment-relative interface pointer from a cookie obtained previously, as shown in the following code. The interface pointer must be released later, but any apartment in the process that wants to obtain an interface pointer can reuse the cookie. Thus, the GIT overcomes the limitation of the *CoGetInterfaceAndReleaseStream* function, which permits unmarshaling to occur only once.

```
// Possibly called by a client thread in another apartment
m_pGIT->GetInterfaceFromGlobal(m_cookie, IID_IMyInterface,
    (void**)&pMyInterface);

// Use pMyInterface here.

pMyInterface->Release();
```

Before exiting, you should remove the interface pointer from the GIT by calling *IGlobalInterfaceTable::RevokeInterfaceFromGlobal*, as shown in the following code. There are no restrictions on which threads in the process can call the *RevokeInterfaceFromGlobal* method. This call is typically followed by a call to release COM's implementation of the GIT.

```
m_pGIT->RevokeInterfaceFromGlobal(m_cookie);
m_pGIT->Release();
```

Note that the application is responsible for coordinating access to the GIT in such a way that one thread in the process will not call *RevokeInterfaceFromGlobal* while another is calling *GetInterfaceFromGlobal* for the same cookie.

In addition to solving the problems associated with careless use of the free-threaded marshaler, the GIT represents an easier way for client applications to marshal interface pointers between the threads of different apartments. The GIT can be used to replace calls to the *CoMarshalInterThreadInterfaceInStream* and *CoGetInterfaceAndReleaseStream* functions.

Implementing Multithreaded Local Components

Multithreaded local components can be subject to some unique race conditions. To help avoid these problems, four new helper functions have been added to the COM library to simplify the job of writing robust server code. These helper functions are listed in the table on the following page. COM clients and in-process components typically will not call these new functions; they are designed to help prevent race conditions in server activation when the servers have multiple apartments. However, the functions can be used just as easily with single-threaded components.

COM API	Description
CoResumeClassObjects	Called by a server to inform the Service Control Manager (SCM) about all registered classes; permits activation requests for those class objects
CoSuspendClassObjects	Prevents any new activation requests from the SCM on all class objects registered within the process
CoAddRefServerProcess	Increments a global per-process reference count
CoReleaseServerProcess	Decrements a global per-process reference count

During the start-up and initialization phase of a local component, the *CoRegisterClassObject* function is called once for each CLSID supported by the component. This function tells COM about the component's classes and gives it a pointer to each class's class object. Once it has finished registering all of its class objects, the component is ready for use. For multithreaded components, however, calls might arrive after the first object is registered. This is a problem because, at least theoretically, a client could instantiate an object and perform the final *IUnknown::Release* call before the rest of the component has had a chance to finish initializing. This final *IUnknown::Release* call would decrement the usage reference counter to *0* and initiate a shutdown of the component process.

To avoid this type of activation race condition and simplify the job of the developer, a multithreaded component with more than one class object should use the *REGCLS_SUSPENDED* flag when calling the *CoRegisterClassObject* function, as shown in boldface in the following code. This flag tells COM, "I'm registering a class, but please don't tell anyone else just yet." Now the component has the opportunity to peacefully register the remainder of its class objects, passing the *REGCLS_SUSPENDED* flag with every call to *CoRegisterClassObject*. Once all the classes have been registered with COM and the component is ready to accept client requests, the component calls the *CoResumeClassObjects* function to tell COM that the classes are now available for use. (For information about *REGCLS_MULTIPLEUSE*, see Chapter 8, "DLL Surrogates and Executable Components.")

```
DWORD dwRegister;
IClassFactory *pIFactory = new CFactory();
CoRegisterClassObject(CLSID_InsideDCOM, pIFactory, CLSCTX_LOCAL_SERVER,
    REGCLS_SUSPENDED|REGCLS_MULTIPLEUSE, &dwRegister);
// Register more class objects here.
// Use the REGCLS_SUSPENDED flag with each call.
```

```
// Now tell the SCM about all the call objects in one blow.
CoResumeClassObjects();
```

The *CoResumeClassObjects* function tells COM to inform the SCM (discussed in Chapter 2, "*IUnknown* and *IClassFactory*") about all the registered classes. This technique has several advantages, the most important of which is the fact that no activation or shutdown requests will be received before the component is ready. Aside from solving the aforementioned race condition, this call is also more efficient because COM needs to make only one call to the SCM to tell it about all the class objects instead of working in the piecemeal fashion used when *CoRegisterClassObject* is called without the *REGCLS_SUSPENDED* flag. This technique also reduces the overall start-up and registration time required by the component. One additional function, *CoSuspendClassObjects*, prevents any new activation requests from the SCM on all class objects registered within the process. This function is not usually called directly by local components, but it is nonetheless the complement of *CoResumeClassObjects*. Note also that *CoSuspendClassObjects* does not relieve the component of the need to call *CoRevokeClassObject* for each registered class object.

A similar race condition might occur when a client calls the *CoGetClass-Object* function to obtain a pointer to an object's class factory. This call is often followed by a call to the *IClassFactory::LockServer(TRUE)* method to prevent the component from exiting. However, there is a window of opportunity between the time the class object is obtained and the time the client calls the *LockServer* method, during which another client could connect to the same component. This second client could instantiate an object and then immediately call *IUnknown::Release*, causing the component to shut down and thus leaving the first client with a disconnected *IClassFactory* pointer. To prevent this race condition, COM implicitly calls the *IClassFactory::LockServer(TRUE)* method as part of *CoGetClassObject* and implicitly calls *IClassFactory::LockServer(FALSE)* when the client releases the *IClassFactory* interface pointer. This technique obviates the need for the client process to call the *LockServer* method because COM is handling this step automatically. In fact, the standard proxy for the *IClass-Factory::LockServer* method implemented by ole32.dll simply returns *S_OK* without actually making a remote call.

Local Component Shutdown

To shut down properly, a local component must keep track of how many objects it has instantiated and the number of times its *IClassFactory::LockServer* method has been called. Only when both of these counts, often represented in code as the variables *g_cComponents* and *g_cServerLocks*, reach *0* can the component legally exit. In a thread-oblivious component, the decision to shut down is automatically coordinated with incoming activation requests by virtue of the fact that all incoming requests are serialized by the message queue. Upon receiving a call to the *IUnknown::Release* method for its last object and deciding to shut down, a component revokes its class objects using the *CoRevokeClassObject* function. This function tells COM not to accept any more activation requests. If an activation request does come in after this point, COM recognizes that the class objects are revoked and returns an error to the SCM. The SCM then automatically attempts to launch a new instance of the component process, beginning the entire process anew. At least this is how it works in thread-oblivious components with only one STA.

In a multithreaded component running in the MTA or in a component in which different class objects are registered in multiple STAs, it occasionally happens that during the time the last object in a component is shutting down, another thread in the component will be handing out a new object. If the component proceeds with the shutdown at this critical stage, somewhere there exists a client that thinks it has a valid interface pointer. You can imagine what will happen when the client tries to use that pointer. Thus, the decision to shut down must be coordinated across multiple threads, possibly in different apartments. This technique will ensure that a thread of the component does not decide to shut down while another thread is busy handing out objects. To aid developers in coordinating a component's shutdown across multiple threads, COM provides two reference-counting functions: *CoAddRefServerProcess* and *CoReleaseServerProcess*.

CoAddRefServerProcess increments a processwide reference count; *CoReleaseServerProcess* decrements that reference count. *CoReleaseServerProcess* also has built-in functionality to ensure that when the reference counter reaches *0*, it automatically calls the *CoSuspendClassObjects* function. After the call to *CoSuspendClassObjects*, any incoming activation requests are refused. This technique permits the component to peacefully deregister its class objects from its various threads without worrying that a simultaneous activation request will be accepted. Activation requests received during, as well as after, the shutdown procedure are handled by directing the SCM to launch a new instance of the component process.

CoAddRefServerProcess and *CoReleaseServerProcess* can be used to replace both the global object count (*g_cComponents*) and the global *IClassFactory::LockServer* count (*g_cServerLocks*), in addition to solving the race condition discussed earlier. The simplest way for a local component to make use of these functions is to call *CoAddRefServerProcess* in the constructor of each of its instance objects and to call *CoReleaseServerProcess* in the destructor of each of its instance objects, as shown in the following code. (By *instance objects,* we mean regular COM objects that are not class objects.)

```
CInsideDCOM::CInsideDCOM() : m_cRef(1)
{
    CoAddRefServerProcess();
}


CInsideDCOM::~CInsideDCOM()
{
    if(CoReleaseServerProcess() == 0)
        InitiateComponentShutdown();
}
```

Additionally, *CoAddRefServerProcess* should be called in the *IClassFactory-::LockServer* method when the *bLock* flag is *true,* as shown in the following code. If the *bLock* flag is *false,* the *CoReleaseServerProcess* function should be called.

```
HRESULT CFactory::LockServer(BOOL bLock)
{
    if(bLock)
        CoAddRefServerProcess();
    else
        if(CoReleaseServerProcess() == 0)
            InitiateComponentShutdown();
    return S_OK;
}
```

As you can see in the preceding code, the application should check the value returned by *CoReleaseServerProcess.* A return value of *0* indicates that *CoReleaseServerProcess* has automatically called *CoSuspendClassObjects* and that the component may now initiate shutdown. Typically, this means that the component should signal all of its STAs to exit their message loops and then call *CoRevokeClassObject* and *CoUninitialize.* A component signals an STA to exit its message loop by posting a *WM_QUIT* message to the queue using the Win32 *PostQuitMessage(0)* function, as shown here:

```
void InitiateComponentShutdown()
{
    PostQuitMessage(0);
}
```

If the component supports the MTA, it need only revoke its class objects and then call *CoUninitialize,* since MTA-based code does not use a message loop. Note that unless the *CoAddRefServerProcess* and *CoReleaseServerProcess* functions are used diligently in both the constructors and destructors of instance objects, as well as in the *IClassFactory::LockServer* method, the component process can shut down prematurely. The following code sets an event object in order to prod the MTA-based component to exit:

```
void InitiateComponentShutdown()
{
    SetEvent(g_hEvent);
}
```

The following code shows the complete *main* function of a typical MTA-based component. The *WaitForSingleObject* function, shown in boldface, is waiting for the event to be set. When the *SetEvent* function is called by the shutdown code, it wakes up and executes the remaining steps needed to exit cleanly.

```
void main(int argc, char** argv)
{
    CommandLineParameters(argc, argv);

    CoInitializeEx(NULL, COINIT_MULTITHREADED);
    g_hEvent = CreateEvent(NULL, FALSE, FALSE, NULL);

    DWORD dwRegister;
    IClassFactory *pIFactory = new CFactory();
    CoRegisterClassObject(CLSID_InsideDCOM, pIFactory,
        CLSCTX_LOCAL_SERVER, REGCLS_SUSPENDED|REGCLS_MULTIPLEUSE,
        &dwRegister);
    CoResumeClassObjects();

    WaitForSingleObject(g_hEvent, INFINITE);
    CloseHandle(g_hEvent);

    CoRevokeClassObject(dwRegister);
    pIFactory->Release();
    CoUninitialize();
}
```

The Ten Threading Commandments

As we have seen, apartments are a far-reaching and important concept in COM. Understanding how apartments work and how code running in different apartments interacts is important for every component developer. With single-threaded and multithreaded apartments, COM offers you the best of both worlds: the performance and scalability of the multithreaded apartment, which has no extra overhead for thread switching or synchronization, and the ease of use of the single-threaded apartment, which guarantees that the state of your object will not be trampled by another thread. The following list of COM's threading rules will keep you safe as you travel through the land of COM:

    I. Each STA should have only one thread.

    II. The thread of each STA must retrieve and dispatch window messages.

    III. Always marshal interface pointers between threads running in different apartments.

    IV. Call *CoInitialize(Ex)* in every thread of an executable component that uses COM services in order to declare the apartment type.

    V. Each object is associated with one and only one apartment, but an apartment can contain several objects.

    VI. The main STA is created by the first thread to call *CoInitialize* or *CoInitializeEx(NULL, COINIT_APARTMENTTHREADED)* within a process.

    VII. The main STA should remain alive until the process has completed all COM work.

    VIII. A process can have any number of STAs but at most one MTA.

    IX. Always define the *ThreadingModel* value in the registry for in-process objects.

    X. Build in-process objects that support both the STA and the MTA models (*ThreadingModel = Both*).

PART II

COM FACILITIES

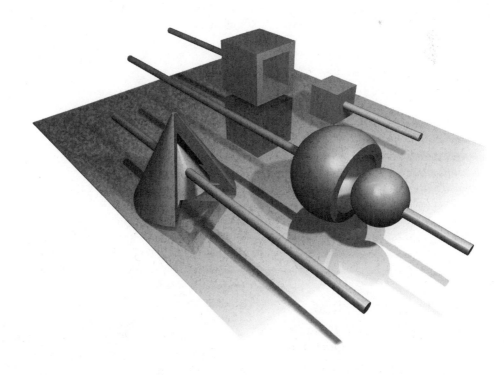

Automation and Component Categories

Automation is the name of a COM facility designed to allow applications to expose their functionality for use by other programs. Full-featured programs such as Microsoft Word expose a hierarchy of objects through Automation. Each object supports specific properties, methods, and events, enabling client programs to take advantage of the rich features offered in such applications by automating their usage. In other words, Automation enables what is normally an end-user application to be controlled by another application programmatically, without any user involvement. Dynamic Data Exchange (DDE), an earlier message-based protocol sometimes used for the same purpose, has been supplanted by Automation. To illustrate the functionality supported by typical applications, the Automation objects exposed by Microsoft Access are shown in Figure 5-1 on the following page.

Imagine developing a business application to perform standard data entry and reporting. Along with the reports that the application produces, it would be nice to have some graphs of the data. Rather than writing the code to produce the graphs yourself, the Automation objects exposed by Microsoft Excel can be used to send the data to Excel and then ask Excel to print some very fancy looking graphs. The user never even has to see Excel being loaded. This type of integration is something that programmers only dreamed of a few years ago.

You might be wondering why a specific facility like Automation is needed to expose the functionality of any application to other programs. After all, isn't that why COM was developed? Using COM, an application can most certainly expose its capabilities via custom interfaces. The problem is that every application might develop its own set of custom interfaces, none of which would work the same way. Switching from one vendor's application to another's would be nearly impossible because all the custom interfaces would be different. COM was designed to prevent exactly this type of limitation. A central tenet of COM is that components implementing the same set of interfaces are polymorphs and can be switched without affecting the client's code.

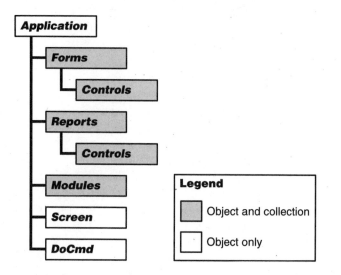

Figure 5-1.
The Automation objects exposed by Microsoft Access.

The *IDispatch* Interface

In order to make things somewhat more systematic, Microsoft proposed that a single standard interface be used by any application wanting to make its functionality available to interested clients. Thus, Microsoft developed the standard *IDispatch* interface, which became known as the Automation facility. *IDispatch*'s primary purpose is to enable what would otherwise be a solely user-driven application to expose its functionality programmatically. *IDispatch* is called a standard interface because Microsoft defined it as part of COM; Microsoft also developed the proxy/stub code (oleaut32.dll) needed to marshal the interface. This proxy/stub code is important because it means that applications implementing the *IDispatch* interface don't have to worry about marshaling.

> NOTE: Although originally the term *Automation* referred exclusively to the *IDispatch* interface, today it is used more generally to mean the programmable aspects of an application.

You might be wondering how it is possible for a single interface to expose the functionality of any application. After all, how could the designers of *IDispatch* imagine every possible object, property, method, and event that an application might want to expose? If this were necessary, the *IDispatch* interface would have to contain hundreds of thousands of methods. In fact, the genius of *IDispatch* is that it was defined using just four methods—*GetTypeInfoCount, GetTypeInfo, Get-IDsOfNames,* and *Invoke.* Here is the *IDispatch* interface defined in IDL notation:

```
interface IDispatch : IUnknown
{
// Do you support type information?
    HRESULT GetTypeInfoCount(
        [out] UINT* pctinfo);

// Gimme a pointer to your object's type information.
    HRESULT GetTypeInfo(
        [in] UINT iTInfo,
        [in] LCID lcid,
        [out] ITypeInfo** ppTInfo);

// Gimme a DISPID of a method or parameters.
    HRESULT GetIDsOfNames(
        [in] REFIID riid,
        [in, size_is(cNames)] LPOLESTR* rgszNames,
        [in] UINT cNames,
        [in] LCID lcid,
        [out, size_is(cNames)] DISPID* rgDispId);

// Call that method.
    HRESULT Invoke(
        [in] DISPID dispIdMember,
        [in] REFIID riid,
        [in] LCID lcid,
        [in] WORD wFlags,
        [in, out] DISPPARAMS* pDispParams,
        [out] VARIANT* pVarResult,
        [out] EXCEPINFO* pExcepInfo,
        [out] UINT* puArgErr);
};
```

IDispatch can be thought of as a kind of surrogate interface. It doesn't really offer any functionality of its own; instead, it acts only as a standard conduit between a client and a component's functionality. Its most important method is *IDispatch::Invoke,* which is called by a client to invoke a particular method in the component. A unique number, called a dispatch identifier (DISPID), identifies each method. The *Invoke* method also takes a pointer to a DISP-PARAMS structure containing the actual parameters to be passed to the method being called. Because the *IDispatch* marshaler knows how to marshal a pointer to the DISPPARAMS structure, it can marshal any Automation-based interface.

Accessing COM Services

Besides its goal of allowing applications to expose their functionality in a standard way, Automation was also developed to enable high-level languages such as Microsoft Visual Basic to access COM services. Before the advent of type libraries, it was difficult for high-level environments to gain access to custom interfaces about which they had no information. On the other hand, support for the standard *IDispatch* interface could be programmed into an environment by its developers. The environment could then work with any component that supported *IDispatch*, regardless of what services the component provided.

Over time, however, it became apparent that even languages like Visual Basic could access COM services directly via custom interfaces as long as some information about the interfaces supported by the component were made available. This requirement was satisfied with the development of type libraries; type libraries have in turn diminished the importance of the *IDispatch* interface. Nevertheless, scripting languages such as VBScript and JScript continue to use Automation, so implementing *IDispatch* remains a requirement in order for components to be accessible from these languages.

Early Binding and Late Binding

IDispatch has some problems that have made it somewhat unpopular with COM developers. The most serious of these problems is the performance of *IDispatch*-based components. Components using *IDispatch* can be accessed in two slightly different ways, known as *early binding* and *late binding*. Originally, *IDispatch* was designed so that every call to *IDispatch::Invoke* to invoke a method was preceded by a call to *IDispatch::GetIDsOfNames*. The client called *GetIDsOfNames* to get the DISPID of a particular method in the component. For example, if a client wanted to call the *Sum* method of an object, it would first call *GetIDsOfNames* to learn the DISPID of that method. This DISPID would then be passed as the first parameter to *IDispatch::Invoke* in order to actually call the *Sum* method. Subsequent calls to the *Sum* method might still call *GetIDsOfNames* to get the DISPID, or the client could cache the DISPID so that later calls to *Sum* could simply be made via a single call to *Invoke*. This original way of using *IDispatch* is known as late binding. The main advantage of this technique is that a type library isn't required. The problem with late binding, however, is that two round-trips to the component are required for at least the first call to each method.

When early binding is used, the compiler consults a component's type library to obtain the necessary DISPIDs so that at run time the client will have to make only a single call to *IDispatch::Invoke*, omitting the call to *IDispatch- ::GetIDsOfNames*. This optimization based on the information from a type library theoretically doubles the execution speed of each Automation-based method call as compared with the late binding technique. However, not even early binding comes close to the performance of accessing an interface directly via its v-table, as is the case with custom interfaces.

Dual Interfaces

More recently, the concept of *dual interfaces* has gained popularity. A COM class that sports a dual interface is indicating its support for clients to access its services either via *IDispatch* or via direct access to its custom interface. In the literature, this access is occasionally referred to as "v-table binding" or even using the rather silly term "very early binding." Like other things in COM, supporting a dual interface sounds more complicated than it is. Figure 5-2 shows the v-table of a pure Automation-based component. The *IDispatch* interface is the only way to access the functionality of the object.

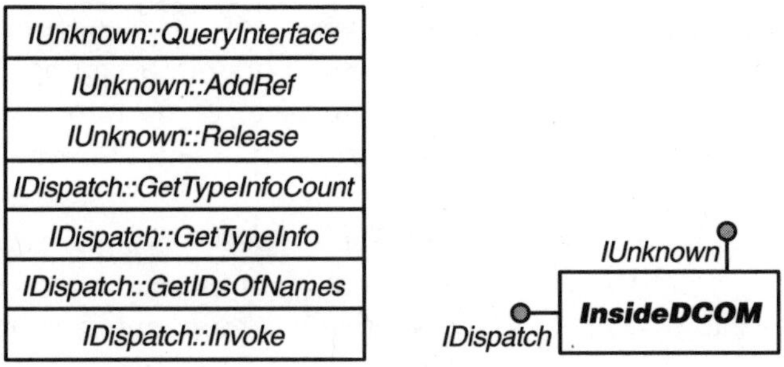

Figure 5-2.
The v-table of a pure Automation-based object.

With a dual interface, the v-table of the interface includes the *IDispatch* members plus any members of the custom interfaces supported by the object. The object shown in Figure 5-3 on the following page supports the *ISum* custom interface in addition to *IDispatch*. The last entry in the object's v-table is the *Sum* method from the *ISum* interface. In this case, a client can choose whether to access the object via Automation or via the custom *ISum* interface.

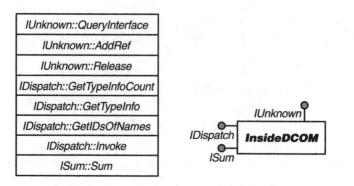

| IUnknown::QueryInterface |
| IUnknown::AddRef |
| IUnknown::Release |
| IDispatch::GetTypeInfoCount |
| IDispatch::GetTypeInfo |
| IDispatch::GetIDsOfNames |
| IDispatch::Invoke |
| ISum::Sum |

Figure 5-3.
An object that supports a dual interface, which includes a custom interface in addition to IDispatch.

Dual interfaces have been strongly hyped, but there are only limited advantages to supporting the *IDispatch* interface. Since high-level environments such as Visual Basic and Microsoft Visual J++ can access custom interfaces directly, why bother with *IDispatch*? Currently, scripting languages such as VBScript and JScript are v-table-challenged. These scripting languages, hosted by the likes of Microsoft Internet Explorer, Microsoft Internet Information Server, Microsoft Developer Studio, and Microsoft Windows Scripting Host, can access components only via the *IDispatch* interface. If you want developers working in a scripting language to access your component, *IDispatch* support is required.

Dual interfaces are one way to provide this support—by supporting a dual interface, you give clients that need to access your component a choice. Visual Basic, for example, always checks to see whether a component supports a dual interface. If it does and if a type library describing the custom interface is available, Visual Basic uses the custom interface, completely bypassing Automation. On the other hand, if no type library is available or if the object supports only *IDispatch*, Visual Basic makes do with that interface.

One danger in using dual interfaces is that they force the designer to concentrate on issues relating to client access from a scripting language—not usually the primary market of a component. Focusing the design of an object on issues of client accessibility from scripting languages that don't have easy access to the *IUnknown::QueryInterface* method can lead the designer to develop an object that has only one interface with many methods. A one-interface-per-object design is not a good choice because you ignore the richness afforded by the *QueryInterface* method. Therefore, instead of using dual interfaces, it is sometimes better to design an object using standard v-table interfaces and then design one additional *IDispatch*-based interface containing many methods specifically for use by scripting languages. The Automation interface might even present a somewhat simplified view of the functionality available in the object to ease its use by scripts.

The Automation Marshaler

While *IDispatch* is not our favorite interface, we do love the marshaler that Microsoft wrote for *IDispatch*. The Automation marshaler (oleaut32.dll) can be used not only for *IDispatch*-based interfaces but also for any interface that restricts itself to Automation-compatible types. These Automation-compatible types for C++ are described in the following table. All Visual Basic types are by definition Automation-compatible. The Java types compatible with Automation are shown in the table on pages 120–121 in Chapter 3, "Type Libraries and Language Integration."

Automation-Compatible Types	Description
boolean	Data item that can have a value of *true* or *false*; size corresponds to *unsigned char*.
unsigned char	8-bit unsigned data item.
double	64-bit IEEE floating-point number.
float	32-bit IEEE floating-point number.
int	Integer whose size is system dependent. On 32-bit platforms, MIDL treats *int* as a 32-bit signed integer.
long	32-bit signed integer.
short	16-bit signed integer.
BSTR	Length-prefixed string.
CY	8-byte fixed-point number. Formerly called *CURRENCY.*
DATE	64-bit floating-point fractional number indicating number of days since December 30, 1899.
SCODE	Built-in error type that corresponds to *HRESULT.*
enum	Signed integer; size is system dependent.
IDispatch ∗	Pointer to *IDispatch* interface (*VT_DISPATCH*).

(continued)

continued

Automation-Compatible Types	Description
*IUnknown**	Pointer to an interface that is not derived from *IDispatch* (*VT_UNKNOWN*). (Any interface can be represented by its *IUnknown* interface.)
SAFEARRAY(TypeName)	Array of *TypeName* that can be any of the above types.
*TypeName**	Pointer to *TypeName* that can be any of the above types.

To use the marshaler, include the *oleautomation* attribute in the IDL file. When *RegisterTypeLib* or *LoadTypeLibEx* is called to register a type library, these functions check the type *library* for the *oleautomation* flag. If the flag is present, they automatically set the ProxyStubClsid32 key in the registry to point to the Automation marshaler. This great feature saves you from always having to build and register a proxy/stub DLL for any custom interfaces. Of course, because the *IDispatch* marshaler is very general, it cannot match the performance of a standard proxy/stub DLL built from the code generated by MIDL. Nevertheless, there are many situations in which the advantages of not having to build and register a proxy/stub DLL may outweigh the slight loss in performance of using the Automation marshaler.

Implementing *IDispatch*

The first step in any COM project is to define the interfaces in an IDL file. Different IDL attributes are required depending on whether you are implementing a pure *IDispatch* interface or a dual interface.

The Pure Automation Interface

Use the *dispinterface* statement shown here when you are designing a pure Automation interface:

```
[ uuid(10000001-0000-0000-0000-000000000001) ]
dispinterface ISum
{
properties:
methods:
    [id(1)] int Sum(int x, int y);
};
```

The *dispinterface* definition is an alternative to the standard *interface* statement, with several interesting aspects. Neither the object nor the *oleautomation* attribute is needed to indicate to MIDL that this is a COM object using only Automation-compatible types—this condition is obvious from the *dispinterface* statement. Notice that the *dispinterface*s statement is not derived from *IUnknown* or *IDispatch*; *dispinterface* implicitly inherit the *IDispatch* interface.

The *Sum* method defined in the *dispinterface* statement returns an integer value rather than an *HRESULT*. Errors that occur during calls to methods in a *dispinterface* are returned by *IDispatch::Invoke*, thus freeing the method to return a real value. The method is assigned a number unique within this *dispinterface*; this is the DISPID. Notice that *dispinterface*s can support properties as well as methods, whereas a standard COM interface supports only methods. This support is for the benefit of high-level languages such as Visual Basic, which are heavily dependent on properties. Of course, all properties are actually implemented by pairs of functions that get and set the value of the property.

The Dual Interface

Keep in mind that using the *dispinterface* statement is not recommended, since doing so restricts clients to using only the *IDispatch* interface when they want to access an object. Marking an object with the *dual* attribute is highly recommended. This technique gives clients a choice of how to access the services of this component, and at the same time it ensures that the object will be accessible to scripting languages such as VBScript. Here is the IDL syntax required to indicate support for both *IDispatch* and a custom interface:

```
[ object, uuid(10000001-0000-0000-0000-000000000001),
  dual ]
interface ISum : IDispatch
{
    [id(3)] HRESULT Sum(int x, int y, [out, retval] int* retval);
}
```

Notice that in the IDL fragment, the syntax seems more standard. Now instead of deriving from *IUnknown*, the *ISum* interface derives from *IDispatch*, which is itself derived from *IUnknown*, so that we still get the *QueryInterface*, *AddRef*, and *Release* methods added to the v-table. The interface header also includes the *dual* attribute to indicate that this is a dual interface. Specifying a dual interface implies that the interface is Automation-compatible, and therefore in the type library generated by MIDL, the interface has both the *TYPEFLAG_FDUAL* and *TYPEFLAG_FOLEAUTOMATION* flags set. Later when a component containing this type library calls *RegisterTypeLib*, this flag is detected and the HKEY_CLASSES_ROOT\Interface\{*YourIID*}\ProxyStubClsid32 registry entry is automatically set to the CLSID of the Automation marshaler (oleaut32.dll).

In the following example, we will create a dual interface by implementing the four *IDispatch* methods. Here is the class declaration for *CInsideDCOM* once it has been modified to implement the *IDispatch* interface:

```
class CInsideDCOM : public ISum
{
public:
    // IUnknown
    ULONG __stdcall AddRef();
    ULONG __stdcall Release();
    HRESULT __stdcall QueryInterface(REFIID iid, void** ppv);

    // IDispatch
    HRESULT __stdcall GetTypeInfoCount(UINT* pCountTypeInfo);
    HRESULT __stdcall GetTypeInfo(UINT iTypeInfo, LCID lcid,
        ITypeInfo** ppITypeInfo);
    HRESULT __stdcall GetIDsOfNames(REFIID riid, LPOLESTR* rgszNames,
        UINT cNames, LCID lcid, DISPID* rgDispId);
    HRESULT __stdcall Invoke(DISPID dispIdMember, REFIID riid,
        LCID lcid, WORD wFlags, DISPPARAMS* pDispParams,
        VARIANT* pVarResult, EXCEPINFO* pExcepInfo,
        UINT* puArgErr);

    // ISum
    HRESULT __stdcall Sum(int x, int y, int* retval);

    CInsideDCOM() : m_cRef(1) { g_cComponents++; }
    ~CInsideDCOM() { g_cComponents--; }
    bool Init(void);

private:
    ULONG m_cRef;
    ITypeInfo* m_pTypeInfo;
};
```

Notice that the class appears to derive only from *ISum* and not from *IDispatch*. In the component.h header file generated by MIDL, the *ISum* class has already been declared as inheriting from *IDispatch*, as shown in boldface in the following code fragment from component.h:

```
// Generated by MIDL
interface DECLSPEC_UUID("10000001-0000-0000-0000-000000000001")
```

```
ISum : public IDispatch
{
public:
    virtual HRESULT STDMETHODCALLTYPE Sum(
        int x,
        int y,
        /* [retval][out] */ int __RPC_FAR *retval) = 0;

};
```

Implementation Techniques

There are three ways to implement the *IDispatch* interface in a COM object: easy, not-so-hard, and hard. The easy way is to call the *CreateStdDispatch* function, which provides a complete default implementation of *IDispatch* for you. The primary drawback of using *CreateStdDispatch* is that it supports only one national language. Even so, *CreateStdDispatch* makes a good choice for components that are not hobbled by this restriction.

The not-so-hard way of supporting *IDispatch* is to implement its four methods but to delegate some of the work to COM functions built especially for the job. This technique is used in the following example, as well as by the majority of components. If you are one of those people who always choose the hard way, you could implement all four *IDispatch* methods without any help from COM. The primary justification for doing this is to optimize performance. However, in cases in which performance is crucial, Automation should not be used at all. Another case requiring a custom implementation of the *IDispatch* interface is when you want to generate new methods at run time. The ActiveX Data Object (ADO) and Remote Data Objects (RDO) components do this when you create a named query. The name of the query automatically becomes a method of the object. This type of specialized functionality requires a specialized implementation of the *IDispatch* interface.

The *IDispatch::GetTypeInfoCount* function is called by the client to determine whether type information is available for the object. If the object provides type information, the integer pointed to by *pCountTypeInfo* should be set to *1*; otherwise, it should be set to *0*. Clients that want to determine whether to use early binding, which requires type information, or late binding when accessing the Automation component can call this function. Here is a typical implementation of *GetTypeInfoCount*:

```
HRESULT CInsideDCOM::GetTypeInfoCount(UINT* pCountTypeInfo)
{
    *pCountTypeInfo = 1;
    return S_OK;
}
```

To implement *IDispatch* using the not-so-hard method shown in this example, type information is essential. The component shown in the following code loads type information from the type library using the *LoadRegTypeLib* function. The *LoadRegTypeLib* function is invoked from the custom *Init* method called during object instantiation. Next the *ITypeLib::GetTypeInfoOfGuid* method is called to retrieve the type information for the *ISum* interface. A pointer to this type information is stored in the member variable *m_pTypeInfo* for use by other methods of the *IDispatch* interface.

```
bool CInsideDCOM::Init(void)
{
    ITypeLib* pTypeLib;
    if(FAILED(LoadRegTypeLib(LIBID_Component, 1, 0, LANG_NEUTRAL,
        &pTypeLib)))
        return false;
    HRESULT hr = pTypeLib->GetTypeInfoOfGuid(IID_ISum, &m_pTypeInfo);
    if(FAILED(hr))
        return false;
    pTypeLib->Release();
    return true;
}
```

After determining that type information is available using the *GetTypeInfoCount* method, a client might call *IDispatch::GetTypeInfo*, as shown in the following code. This method returns a pointer to the type information provided by the object, which can then be used to get the type information for an interface. The first parameter of the *GetTypeInfo* method, *iTypeInfo*, specifies the index number of the interface for which the client is requesting type information. Since this is an *IDispatch* interface, only the index number *0*, which refers to *IDispatch*, is valid. If the client passes any other value, we simply return *DISP_E_BADINDEX*. The second parameter of *GetTypeInfo*, *lcid*, is a locale identifier. This parameter is important because some objects might want to return different type information based on the national language of the user. Since our object does not support localized member names, this parameter is ignored. Before returning, *AddRef* must be called on the type information pointer in accordance with COM's reference counting rules.

```
HRESULT CInsideDCOM::GetTypeInfo(UINT iTypeInfo, LCID lcid,
    ITypeInfo** ppITypeInfo)
{
    *ppITypeInfo = NULL;
    if(iTypeInfo != 0)
        return DISP_E_BADINDEX;
    m_pTypeInfo->AddRef();
```

```
    *ppITypeInfo = m_pTypeInfo;
    return S_OK;
}
```

IDispatch::GetIDsOfNames is called by a client that has a method name—for example, *Sum*—and wants to get the DISPID associated with that method in order to call it via *IDispatch::Invoke*. The first parameter, *riid*, of the *GetIDsOfNames* method is currently unused and must be *IID_NULL*. The second parameter, *rgszNames*, points to an array of names for which the client is requesting DISPIDs. The third parameter, *cNames*, tells the component the number of names in the array, and the fourth parameter, *lcid*, specifies the locale identifier of the caller. Only one method or property can be mapped to a DISPID at a time. The other members of the array can be used to map the parameter names of methods into DISPIDs. This technique can be useful for sophisticated clients such as Visual Basic that enable developers to specify values for named arguments when calling methods.

The last parameter, *rgDispId*, of the *GetIDsOfNames* method is a pointer to an array in which the client wants to receive the requested DISPIDs. The implementation of *IDispatch::GetIDsOfNames* shown in the following code simply delegates to the *DispGetIDsOfNames* helper function, which does the actual work of mapping the requested names to DISPIDs based on the information in the type library. Of course, you could implement this functionality yourself, but with a function as easy to use as *DispGetIDsOfNames*, who would want to?

```
HRESULT CInsideDCOM::GetIDsOfNames(REFIID riid, LPOLESTR* rgszNames,
    UINT cNames, LCID lcid, DISPID* rgDispId)
{
    if(riid != IID_NULL)
        return DISP_E_UNKNOWNINTERFACE;
    return DispGetIDsOfNames(m_pTypeInfo, rgszNames, cNames, rgDispId);
}
```

Last *IDispatch::Invoke* is used when the client is ready to call a method. The first parameter, *dispIdMember*, of the *Invoke* method specifies the DISPID of the member we are invoking. This value can be obtained from a previous call to *IDispatch::GetIDsOfNames*. The second parameter, *riid*, is reserved and must be *IID_NULL*. The third parameter, *lcid*, specifies the locale identifier (LCID) of the client, and once more we will politely ignore this information. The fourth parameter, *wFlags*, can be chosen from the set of flags listed in the table on the following page.

IDispatch::Invoke wFlags	Description
DISPATCH_METHOD	The member is invoked as a method. If a property has the same name, both this flag and the *DISPATCH_PROPERTYGET* flag can be set.
DISPATCH_PROPERTYGET	The member is retrieved as a property or data member.
DISPATCH_PROPERTYPUT	The member is changed as a property or data member.
DISPATCH_PROPERTYPUTREF	The member is changed by a reference assignment rather than by a value assignment. This flag is valid only when the property accepts a reference to an object.

The fifth parameter, *pDispParams*, of *IDispatch::Invoke* is a pointer to a DISPPARAMS structure containing the actual parameters to be passed to this method. The sixth parameter, *pVarResult*, is a pointer to the return value that the client expects to receive after the completion of the method. The last two parameters, *pExcepInfo* and *puArgErr*, are used to return extended error information to the caller.

The following code shows a simple implementation of *IDispatch::Invoke* that defaults to *DispInvoke*, another helper function provided in COM. By deferring to the *ITypeInfo::Invoke* method, *DispInvoke* builds a stack frame, coerces parameters using standard coercion rules, pushes them onto the stack, and then calls the correct member function in the v-table. Keep in mind that the *DispInvoke* helper function can be used only for dual interfaces. Pure *disp-interfaces* do not have method entries in their v-table and thus cannot make use of the services offered by *DispInvoke*.

```
HRESULT CInsideDCOM::Invoke(DISPID dispIdMember, REFIID riid,
    LCID lcid, WORD wFlags, DISPPARAMS* pDispParams,
    VARIANT* pVarResult, EXCEPINFO* pExcepInfo, UINT* puArgErr)
{
    if(riid != IID_NULL)
        return DISP_E_UNKNOWNINTERFACE;
    return DispInvoke(this, m_pTypeInfo, dispIdMember, wFlags,
        pDispParams, pVarResult, pExcepInfo, puArgErr);
}
```

A few minor changes remain to be made to the component's code. The object's *IUnknown::Release* method needs to be modified to release the type information before we exit, as shown here:

```
ULONG CInsideDCOM::Release()
{
    if(--m_cRef != 0)
        return m_cRef;
    m_pTypeInfo->Release();
    delete this;
    return 0;
}
```

The *IUnknown::QueryInterface* function must be improved, as shown in the following code, so that clients requesting the *IDispatch* interface receive a valid pointer instead of being turned away with a *E_NOINTERFACE* return value:

```
HRESULT CInsideDCOM::QueryInterface(REFIID riid, void** ppv)
{
    if(riid == IID_IUnknown)
        *ppv = (IUnknown*)this;
    else if(riid == IID_ISum)
        *ppv = (ISum*)this;
    else if(riid == IID_IDispatch)
        *ppv = (IDispatch*)this;
    else
    {
        *ppv = NULL;
        return E_NOINTERFACE;
    }
    AddRef();
    return S_OK;
}
```

And in the component's *IClassFactory::CreateInstance* method, the *Init* function needs to be called, as shown in the following code, to ensure that the type information is loaded from the type library:

```
HRESULT CFactory::CreateInstance(IUnknown *pUnknownOuter, REFIID iid,
    void** ppv)
{
    if(pUnknownOuter != NULL)
        return CLASS_E_NOAGGREGATION;

    CInsideDCOM *pInsideDCOM = new CInsideDCOM;
    if(pInsideDCOM == NULL)
        return E_OUTOFMEMORY;

    // Call the Init method to load the type information.
    pInsideDCOM->Init();
```

(continued)

```
        HRESULT hr = pInsideDCOM->QueryInterface(iid, ppv);
        pInsideDCOM->Release();
        return hr;
    }
```

After you have made these modifications, rebuild the component. Since the *InsideDCOM* object supports dual interfaces, you can test the component using any of the standard client programs we built in previous chapters. To test the Automation capabilities of the component, a new client must be built that uses the *IDispatch* interface.

Building an Automation Client in C++

Using the *IDispatch* interface from languages such as Visual Basic and VBScript couldn't be easier. These languages automatically make all the necessary calls to the four *IDispatch* methods. Unfortunately, due to the flexibility and power of the *IDispatch* interface, creating Automation clients in C++ is more difficult than calling methods in a custom interface—another reason why Microsoft recommends that COM objects support dual interfaces. The *IDispatch* interface makes the object accessible to scripting languages such as VBScript; a custom interface makes the object easier for C++ developers to use.

Automation clients written in C++ follow a rather predictable series of steps. After initializing COM (*CoInitialize*) and instantiating a class (*CoCreate-Instance*), the client calls *QueryInterface* for the *IDispatch* interface. If successful, the client now has a pointer to the *IDispatch* interface and knows that it is dealing with an Automation object. Now we arrive at the fundamental step of calling the *IDispatch* methods, as shown in the following code. First *IDispatch::Get-IDsOfNames* should be called to retrieve the DISPID of the desired method. Since our example component supports only a single *Sum* method with a DISPID of *1*, we could skip this step, but most clients will not have this luxury. Note that since all COM interfaces use Unicode strings, the string shown in this code fragment is prefixed with the letter *L*, which indicates to the compiler that these are wide characters of the primitive type *wchar_t*. In the system header files, *OLECHAR* is also defined as a *wchar_t*.

```
OLECHAR* name = L"Sum";
DISPID dispid;
pDispatch->GetIDsOfNames(IID_NULL, &name, 1, GetUserDefaultLCID(),
    &dispid);
```

IDispatch::GetIDsOfNames is called using the name of the *Sum* method and returns the DISPID of that method as the last parameter. In this example, the *dispid* variable should have the value *3*, defined for the *Sum* method in the IDL file, upon return from *GetIDsOfNames*. Although our *IDispatch* implementation ignores the locale information passed by *GetIDsOfNames*, it is still polite to provide the user's default LCID, which is retrieved by calling *GetUserDefaultLCID*. If at some point in the future the component is upgraded to support localization, the information provided by the client will be correct.

After retrieving the DISPID, the client calls the specified method using *IDispatch::Invoke*. The hardest part about using the *Invoke* method is packing the DISPPARAMS structure with the required method parameters. The DISPPARAMS structure is defined as follows:

```
typedef struct tagDISPPARAMS {
    // Array of arguments
    [size_is(cArgs)] VARIANTARG* rgvarg;

    // Dispatch IDs of named arguments
    [size_is(cNamedArgs)] DISPID* rgdispidNamedArgs;

    // Number of arguments
    UINT cArgs;

    // Number of named arguments
    UINT cNamedArgs;
} DISPPARAMS;
```

The first member of the DISPPARAMS structure is the actual pointer to an array of method arguments. It is declared as a VARIANT (identical to a VARIANTARG) pointer, which is basically a giant union of all Automation-compatible types. Each VARIANT contains a *vt* member that indicates the data type. This member should be set to the correct *VT_* constant, as shown in the following structure, depending on the type of data stored in the VARIANT:

```
struct VARIANT
{
    VARTYPE vt;
    union
    {
        LONG lVal;              // VT_I4
        BYTE bVal;              // VT_UI1
        SHORT iVal;             // VT_I2
        FLOAT fltVal;           // VT_R4
        DOUBLE dblVal;          // VT_R8
        VARIANT_BOOL boolVal;   // VT_BOOL
        SCODE scode;            // VT_ERROR
        CY cyVal;               // VT_CY
        DATE date;              // VT_DATE
```

(continued)

```
        BSTR bstrVal;               // VT_BSTR
        IUnknown *punkVal;          // VT_UNKNOWN
        IDispatch *pdispVal;        // VT_DISPATCH
        SAFEARRAY *parray;          // VT_ARRAY
        BYTE *pbVal;                // VT_BYREF|VT_UI1
        SHORT *piVal;               // VT_BYREF|VT_I2
        LONG *plVal;                // VT_BYREF|VT_I4
        FLOAT *pfltVal;             // VT_BYREF|VT_R4
        DOUBLE *pdblVal;            // VT_BYREF|VT_R8
        VARIANT_BOOL *pboolVal;     // VT_BYREF|VT_BOOL
        SCODE *pscode;              // VT_BYREF|VT_ERROR
        CY *pcyVal;                 // VT_BYREF|VT_CY
        DATE *pdate;                // VT_BYREF|VT_DATE
        BSTR *pbstrVal;             // VT_BYREF|VT_BSTR
        IUnknown **ppunkVal;        // VT_BYREF|VT_UNKNOWN
        IDispatch **ppdispVal;      // VT_BYREF|VT_DISPATCH
        SAFEARRAY **pparray;        // VT_BYREF|VT_ARRAY
        VARIANT *pvarVal;           // VT_BYREF|VT_VARIANT
        PVOID byref;                // VT_BYREF
        CHAR cVal;                  // VT_I1
        USHORT uiVal;               // VT_UI2
        ULONG ulVal;                // VT_UI4
        INT intVal;                 // VT_INT
        UINT uintVal;               // VT_UINT
        DECIMAL *pdecVal;           // VT_BYREF|VT_DECIMAL
        CHAR *pcVal;                // VT_BYREF|VT_I1
        USHORT *puiVal;             // VT_BYREF|VT_UI2
        ULONG pulVal;               // VT_BYREF|VT_UI4
        INT *pintVal;               // VT_BYREF|VT_INT
        UINT *puintVal;             // VT_BYREF|VT_UINT
    }
};
```

The second and fourth parameters are used for named arguments, and the third parameter specifies the total number of parameters. Thus, in the simplest case—a call to an Automation method with no parameters—the DISPPARAMS structure should be filled out as follows:

```
DISPPARAMS NoParams = { NULL, NULL, 0, 0 };
```

For methods such as *Sum* that expect to receive parameters, the arguments in the array should be arranged from last to first so that *rgvarg[0]* contains the last argument and *rgvars[cArgs−1]* contains the first argument. The following code packs two 4-byte integers into an array of two VARIANTs for the purposes of adding 2 and 7. The *VariantInit* function is called to initialize a new VARIANTARG to *VT_EMPTY*. Note that while the order of the *Sum* method's two parameters doesn't really matter (2 + 7 = 7 + 2), the order of the parameters in the example is 2, 7.

```
VARIANTARG SumArgs[2];

VariantInit(&SumArgs[0]);
SumArgs[0].vt = VT_I4;
SumArgs[0].lVal = 7;

VariantInit(&SumArgs[1]);
SumArgs[1].vt = VT_I4;
SumArgs[1].lVal = 2;
```

Once the VARIANTARG's parameters have been set correctly, a DISP-PARAMS structure must be created that points to the array of parameters. As shown in the following code, here the DISPPARAMS structure is initialized with a pointer to *SumArgs* and the *cArgs* counter is set to *2*, indicating that there are two arguments in the array. Since no named parameters are used, the second and fourth parameters are ignored.

```
DISPPARAMS MyParams = { SumArgs, 0, 2, NULL };
```

Before *IDispatch::Invoke* is called, one final variant must be initialized in which the return value of the *Sum* method will be stored. After all this work, *Invoke* is finally called, as shown here:

```
VARIANT Result;
VariantInit(&Result);

HRESULT hr = pDispatch->Invoke(dispid, IID_NULL, GetUserDefaultLCID(),
    DISPATCH_METHOD, &MyParams, &Result, NULL, NULL);
if(FAILED(hr))
    cout << "pDispatch->Invoke() failed." << endl;

cout << "2 + 7 = " << Result.lVal << endl;
pDispatch->Release();
```

Building an Automation Client in Visual Basic

Working with Automation in C++ can be a somewhat trying experience, but Visual Basic makes it a breeze. In the following code, Visual Basic's *CreateObject* function is used to instantiate the component based on a programmatic identifier. In the registry, under HKEY_CLASSES_ROOT, you can find a ton of semilegible entries known as *programmatic identifiers (ProgIDs),* organized alphabetically. Like a CLSID, a ProgID identifies a class, but with less precision. Since ProgIDs are not guaranteed to be unique, they can be used only where name collisions are manageable—for example, on a single machine. Every ProgID key should have a CLSID subkey containing the CLSID of the object. Given a ProgID, an application can use the *CLSIDFromProgID* function to retrieve the CLSID.

Most ProgIDs come in pairs: the first element is called the version-independent ProgID; it is followed by the standard ProgID. The format of a version-independent ProgID is *Component.Class*; the two elements are separated by a period with no spaces, as in *Word.Document*. The format of the standard ProgID is identical, with the addition of a version number at the end, as in *Word.Document.8*. The version-independent ProgID remains constant across all versions of a class. It is often used with macro languages such as Visual Basic for Applications and refers to the latest installed version of the application's class.

The *RegisterServer* function called in the component's self-registration code creates the ProgID registry entries, as shown in Figure 5-4.

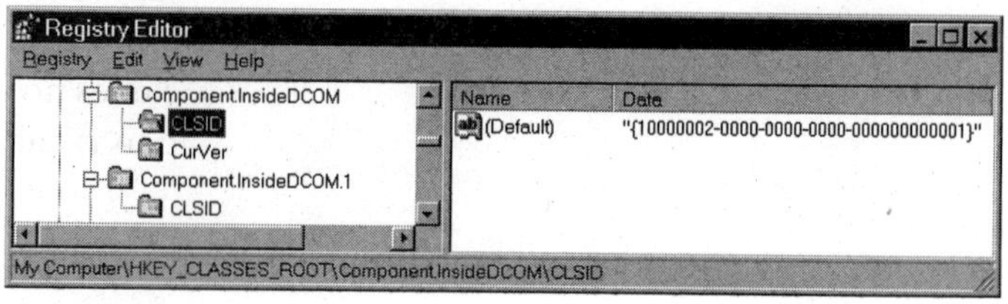

Figure 5-4.
The ProgID registry entries, shown in the Registry Editor.

Without further delay, we present here the entire Visual Basic program that calls the Automation component created earlier in this chapter:

1. In Visual Basic, create a Standard EXE project.

2. Enter the following code on Form1:

```
Private Sub Form_Click()
    Dim myRef As Object
    Set myRef = CreateObject("Component.InsideDCOM")
    Print "Sum(4, 6) = " & myRef.Sum(4, 6)
End Sub
```

3. Run the program, and click on Form1 to test the component.

Because no design-time reference is set to a type library, the *CreateObject* method uses *IDispatch* via the late binding technique, meaning that *IDispatch::GetIDsOfNames* is called before *IDispatch::Invoke*. If you want to use the early binding technique, you must set a reference to the component's type library by choosing References from the Project menu in Visual Basic and selecting the component. Now Visual Basic obtains the DISPIDs for the interface method names at design time by using the information stored in the type library and thus needs to call only *IDispatch::Invoke* at run time.

Some people mistakenly assume that any object instantiated using the *CreateObject* function will always be accessed via the *IDispatch* interface. Although the *CreateObject* function returns an *IDispatch* pointer, this pointer does not necessarily mean that the developer is stuck with that interface. The culprit is Visual Basic's *Object* type, which is the Visual Basic equivalent of an *IDispatch* pointer. Whenever a variable is declared *As Object*, the *IDispatch* interface will be used. To overcome this limitation, simply use the *IDispatch* pointer returned by *CreateObject* and call *IUnknown::QueryInterface* to request some other interface pointer. As we saw in Chapter 3, "Type Libraries and Language Integration," a call to *QueryInterface* from Visual Basic is performed using the *Set* statement to cast one type to another. For example, the following code does not use the *IDispatch* interface at all, even though the *CreateObject* function is called:

```
Dim myRef As InsideDCOM
Set myRef = CreateObject("Component.InsideDCOM")
Print "Sum(4, 6) = " & myRef.Sum(4, 6)
```

The *Set* statement in the preceding code fragment calls *QueryInterface* on the *IDispatch* pointer returned by *CreateObject* to request a pointer to the *ISum* interface. After the *Sum* method is called, Visual Basic calls *ISum::Sum*—not *IDispatch::Invoke*. Since *CreateObject* can be used to instantiate an object that is not accessed through *IDispatch*, perhaps you are wondering what the difference is between the *CreateObject* function and the *New* keyword. The only obvious difference is that the *New* keyword uses the CLSID obtained from the type library, whereas *CreateObject* obtains the CLSID from the registry by calling the *CLSIDFromProgID* function. Here is a code fragment that uses the *New* keyword to access an object via *IDispatch*:

```
Dim myDispatch As Object
Dim myRef As New InsideDCOM

' myRef->QueryInterface(IID_IDispatch, (void**)&myDispatch);
Set myDispatch = myRef

Print "Sum(4, 6) = " & myDispatch.Sum(4, 6)
```

189

NOTE: If you are curious about how Visual Basic's *CreateObject* function is implemented, here is C++ pseudo-code for the call:

```
IDispatch* CreateObject(LPCOLESTR szProgID)
{
    CLSID clsid;
    IDispatch* pDispatch = 0;
    CLSIDFromProgID(szProgID, &clsid);
    CoCreateInstance(clsid, 0, CLSCTX_SERVER, IID_IDispatch,
        (void**)&pDispatch);
    return pDispatch;
}
```

Building an Automation Client in VBScript

COM objects that support the *IDispatch* interface can be automated using VBScript code running inside Internet Explorer. Listing 5-1 shows an HTML document that can be viewed using Internet Explorer in order to test the component.

vbscript.html

```
<HTML>
<HEAD><TITLE>HELLO THERE</TITLE></HEAD>
<BODY>
This is a VBScript sample that uses the Component.InsideDCOM
object.<BR> VBScript will talk only to a component using
IDispatch.<BR>
Here we go: 4 + 5 =
<OBJECT ID="MyComponent"
    CLASSID="CLSID:10000002-0000-0000-0000-000000000001">
</OBJECT>
<SCRIPT LANGUAGE="VBScript">
    Document.Write MyComponent.Sum(4, 5)
</SCRIPT>
</BODY>
</HTML>
```

Listing 5-1.
An HTML document containing VBScript code that uses the InsideDCOM *component.*

The VBScript engine is actually implemented as a COM component, which enables Microsoft to reuse this component in any environment that requires VBScript support. In addition to Internet Explorer, VBScript support is available in Windows Scripting Host, Internet Information Server, and Developer Studio. To test the Automation component from Developer Studio, a special registry entry must be created. Developer Studio is quite careful about loading unknown components. For Developer Studio to work with an Automation component, that component must be marked in the registry as being safe for use by scripting languages, indicating that the component cannot do any damage to the user's data even if it is controlled by a malevolent script.

Because the *ISum* interface of our *InsideDCOM* component cannot do any harm, it is safe to add this setting in the registry. To mark an object as safe for scripting, create an Implemented Categories subkey under the object's CLSID entry, as shown in Figure 5-5. This subkey should contain additional subkeys of the category identifiers (CATIDs) of any categories supported by this component. The available categories are listed in the registry under HKEY_CLASSES-_ROOT\Component Categories. The CATID {7DD95801-9882-11CF-9FA9-00AA006C42C4} indicates that a component is safe for scripting.

Figure 5-5.
An Implemented Categories subkey indicating that a component is safe for scripting.

Once these registry entries have been created, Developer Studio will be willing to work with our Automation component. To create a VBScript macro that can be run inside Developer Studio to test the component, follow these steps:

1. In Developer Studio, choose the Tools/Macro command.

2. In the Macro Name text box, type *TestComponent,* and click Edit.

3. In the Description text box, type *Macro to test InsideDCOM component using IDispatch,* and click OK.

4. Now modify your code as shown here in boldface:

```
'-------------------------------------------------------------
'FILE DESCRIPTION: New Macro File
'-------------------------------------------------------------

Sub TestComponent()
'DESCRIPTION: Macro to test InsideDCOM component using IDispatch
    Dim myRef
    Set MyRef = CreateObject("Component.InsideDCOM")
    MsgBox "Sum(5, 3) = " & myRef.Sum(5, 3)
End Sub
```

5. Choose the File/Save command.

6. Choose the Tools/Macro command again.

7. Click Yes when Developer Studio asks whether you want to reload the macros.

8. Select the *TestComponent* macro and click Run.

Scriptlets: Building COM Objects in HTML

Continuing in the grand tradition of making COM objects accessible to any language, Microsoft enables scripts that are embedded in an HTML file or in a Developer Studio macro to access COM objects. Even more amazing, however, is the capability to actually create COM objects in script code stored in an HTML file. COM objects defined in this way are called *Scriptlets*. Thus, there are now three ways to package a COM object:

- Native code (.dll and .exe files)

- Java classes (.class files)

- Scriptlets (HTML files)

In some respects, Scriptlets may be the most powerful of the three packaging techniques. Scriptlets enable developers to create COM objects using Dynamic HTML and a scripting language. If the HTML document contains user interface elements, it can be treated as an ActiveX control. Otherwise, you can simply work with it as a standard COM object. For example, the following Scriptlet qualifies as a COM object:

```
<HTML>
<SCRIPT LANGUAGE="VBScript">
```

```
Function public_Sum(X, Y)
    public_Sum = X + Y
End Function
</SCRIPT>
</HTML>
```

While this Scriptlet is written in VBScript, Scriptlets do not have to be written in any particular language; any available ActiveX scripting engine will suffice. Scriptlet clients can also be built in any development environment that supports COM. For example, a Scriptlet could be used by another HTML page or from an applet written in Java. For demonstration purposes, let's build a client program in Visual Basic that will call the Scriptlet shown above. Here are the steps to follow:

1. In Visual Basic, open a Standard EXE project.

2. Choose the Project/Components command, check the Microsoft Scriptlet Component (mshtmlwb.dll) option, and click OK. The Scriptlet component installs with Internet Explorer 4.

3. Position a Scriptlet control on the form.

4. Set the *Visible* property to *False* and the *URL* property to the name of a file containing the Scriptlet shown in the preceding code.

5. In the Code window, enter the following code:

```
Private Sub Form_Click()
    MsgBox "Calling scriplet: 6 + 12 = " & Scriptlet1.Sum(6, 12)
```

6. Run the program, and test it by clicking on the form.

Error Handling

Practically all COM methods return an *HRESULT* value. An *HRESULT* is defined simply as a *long* type, meaning that it is a signed 32-bit value. The term *HRESULT* is an anachronism held over from the days when 16-bit operating systems ruled the world and an *HRESULT* was a handle to a result. Today an *HRESULT* is the result value itself. All *HRESULT* values are composed of three parts: the severity, the facility, and the status code. For many *HRESULT* names, these parts are separated by underscores. For example, the *MK_E_MUST-BOTHERUSER* code is a combination of the moniker facility (*MK*), an error severity (*E*), and a status code indicating that user input is required for the operations to succeed (*MUSTBOTHERUSER*). Figure 5-6 on the following page shows how an *HRESULT* is laid out in memory.

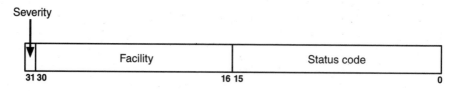

Figure 5-6.

The memory layout of an HRESULT.

The top bit (31) defines the severity code of the *HRESULT* value. The severity code contains *0* for success or *1* for an error. The facility code can be set to one of the facilities shown in the following table:

Facility	Value	Meaning
FACILITY_NULL	*0*	Used for general error codes such as *S_OK*
FACILITY_RPC	*1*	Errors from Remote Procedure Calls (RPCs)
FACILITY_DISPATCH	*2*	Errors from the *IDispatch* interface
FACILITY_STORAGE	*3*	Errors from the *IStorage* or *IStream* interface
FACILITY_ITF	*4*	Error codes defined by custom interfaces
FACILITY_WIN32	*7*	Errors from the Win32 API
FACILITY_WINDOWS	*8*	Errors from standard interfaces
FACILITY_SSPI	*9*	Errors from the Security Support Provider Interface (SSPI)
FACILITY_MSMQ	*14*	Errors from the Microsoft Message Queue Server (MSMQ)
FACILITY_SETUPAPI	*15*	Errors from the Setup API

To ensure that facility codes don't conflict, developers outside Microsoft are not permitted to define new facility codes. In addition, new facility status codes can be defined using only the *FACILITY_ITF* facility code, and then only in the range *0x0200* through *0xFFFF* to avoid conflicting with Microsoft-defined codes in the range *0x0000* through *0x01FF*. It is specifically legal for different interfaces to reuse identical status codes of the *FACILITY_ITF* facility for completely different errors. This reuse is possible because the *HRESULT* values returned by interface methods are considered part of the interface contract and therefore must be interpreted in the context of that interface.

Microsoft provides several helpful macros that can assist developers working directly with *HRESULT* values. The *HRESULT_SEVERITY, HRESULT_FACILITY,* and *HRESULT_CODE* macros can be used to extract the severity, facility, and status codes from an *HRESULT.* The *SUCCEEDED* and *FAILED* macros are often used to test the severity portion of an *HRESULT.* If the top bit of the *HRESULT* is *0,* the *SUCCEEDED* macro returns *true.* The *SUCCEEDED* macro returns *true* for the success (*0*) severity code. For an error (*1*) severity code, the *SUCCEEDED* macro returns *false.* The *FAILED* macro works in the exact opposite manner of the *SUCCEEDED* macro, returning *true* when the top bit of the *HRESULT* is *1.* The *MAKE_HRESULT* macro can be used to compose an *HRESULT* value from severity, facility, and status codes.

All COM and Windows errors as well as the aforementioned macros are defined in the winerror.h system include file. In order to obtain a meaningful string explaining a system error code at run time, the Win32 function *FormatMessage* can be called. The *ErrorMessage* routine shown in the following code is a simple wrapper for *FormatMessage* that can be used for convenience in your own code; it is called with a user-provided string and the *HRESULT.* The companion CD contains a simple utility named Error that can be used to decode *HRESULT* values.

```
void ErrorMessage(char* szMessage, HRESULT hr)
{
    if(HRESULT_FACILITY(hr) == FACILITY_WINDOWS)
        hr = HRESULT_CODE(hr);

    char* szError;
    if(FormatMessage(FORMAT_MESSAGE_ALLOCATE_BUFFER|
        FORMAT_MESSAGE_FROM_SYSTEM, NULL, hr,
        MAKELANGID(LANG_NEUTRAL, SUBLANG_DEFAULT),
        (LPTSTR)&szError, 0, NULL) != 0)
    {
        printf("%s: %s", szMessage, szError);
        LocalFree(szError);
    }
}
```

Rich Error Information

While an *HRESULT* identifies a specific error, its severity, and the facility it originated in, *HRESULT*s do not work very well for applications written in Java or Visual Basic. Both Java and Visual Basic hide *HRESULT* values from the programmer. In Java and Visual Basic, the parameter marked with the *[out, retval]* IDL attributes replaces the *HRESULT* as the method's return value. In these high-level languages, errors are dealt with as exceptions, not return codes.

Therefore, Visual Basic will raise an exception if the *HRESULT* returned by a method indicates an error. This error can be trapped in Visual Basic by using an *On Error Goto MyHandler* statement. Unfortunately, Visual Basic programmers will not have much information to work with when they try to respond to an error message. An *HRESULT* is not a convenient structure for a Visual Basic programmer to deal with. To overcome these limitations and to provide richer error information for components of all languages, the *IErrorInfo, ICreateErrorInfo,* and *ISupportErrorInfo* interfaces were introduced.

Providing Error Information

A component that wants to provide rich error information to its client must implement the *ISupportErrorInfo* interface to indicate this capability. The *ISupportErrorInfo* defines only one method, as shown in the following IDL definition:

```
interface ISupportErrorInfo : IUnknown
{
    HRESULT InterfaceSupportsErrorInfo([in] REFIID riid);
}
```

Both the Visual Basic and Java Virtual Machines (VMs) query for *ISupportErrorInfo* and then call the *ISupportErrorInfo::InterfaceSupportsErrorInfo* method for every custom interface exposed by the component and accessed by the client program. Some C++ client programs, such as those written using MFC, do this as well. Implementing this interface to return *S_OK* or *S_FALSE* whenever a client attempts to determine whether your component offers rich error information for the methods of a specific interface is a simple matter. The following code fragment shows a sample implementation:

```
HRESULT CInsideDCOM::InterfaceSupportsErrorInfo(REFIID riid)
{
    if(riid == IID_ISum)
        return S_OK;
    else
        return S_FALSE;
}
```

During method execution, a component supporting COM's rich error handling mechanism will call the *CreateErrorInfo* function to instantiate a generic error object. The *CreateErrorInfo* function returns an *ICreateErrorInfo* interface pointer. The methods of the *ICreateErrorInfo* interface are used to set the rich error information describing the *HRESULT* value that will be returned by the component. The following code shows the IDL definition of the *ICreateErrorInfo* interface:

```
interface ICreateErrorInfo : IUnknown
{
    HRESULT SetGUID([in] REFGUID rguid);
    HRESULT SetSource([in] LPOLESTR szSource);
    HRESULT SetDescription([in] LPOLESTR szDescription);
    HRESULT SetHelpFile([in] LPOLESTR szHelpFile);
    HRESULT SetHelpContext([in] DWORD dwHelpContext);
}
```

After setting the desired method error information using the *ICreate-ErrorInfo* interface, the component calls the *SetErrorInfo* function. *SetErrorInfo* assigns the error object to the current thread of execution, enabling the client program to retrieve the error information using the *GetErrorInfo* function. The only problem is that *SetErrorInfo* requires an *IErrorInfo* interface pointer and the component currently has an *ICreateErrorInfo* interface pointer. The component can obtain the correct interface pointer for *SetErrorInfo* simply by calling the *QueryInterface* method on the *ICreateErrorInfo* interface pointer to request *IErrorInfo*. Both interfaces are implemented by COM's generic error object. The following code shows a special implementation of the *ISum::Sum* method that returns rich error information if either of the parameters is negative:

```
HRESULT CInsideDCOM::Sum(int x, int y, int* retval)
{
    // If either x or y is negative, return error info.
    if(x < 0 || y < 0)
    {
        // Create generic error object.
        ICreateErrorInfo* pCreateErrorInfo;
        CreateErrorInfo(&pCreateErrorInfo);

        // Set rich error information.
        pCreateErrorInfo->SetDescription(
            L"Negative numbers not allowed.");
        pCreateErrorInfo->SetGUID(IID_ISum);
        pCreateErrorInfo->SetSource(L"Component.InsideDCOM");

        // Exchange ICreateErrorInfo for IErrorInfo.
        IErrorInfo* pErrorInfo;
        pCreateErrorInfo->QueryInterface(IID_IErrorInfo,
            (void**)&pErrorInfo);

        // Make the error information available to the client.
        SetErrorInfo(0, pErrorInfo);
```

(continued)

```
        // Release the interface pointers.
        pErrorInfo->Release();
        pCreateErrorInfo->Release();

        // Return the actual error code.
        return E_INVALIDARG;
    }

    // Business as usual...
    *retval = x + y;
    return S_OK;
}
```

Visual Basic and Java automatically map the rich error information interfaces offered by COM to their language-based exception handling mechanisms. This mapping enables a client program running in Visual Basic to trap a COM error as if it were a regular Visual Basic exception, as shown here:

```
Private Sub Command1_Click()
    On Error GoTo MyHandler
    Dim Test As New Component.InsideDCOM
    Print Test.Sum(4, 3)  ' Everything is OK.
    Print Test.Sum(-1, 5) ' Raises exception.
Exit Sub

MyHandler: ' Exception transfers execution control here.
    MsgBox Err.Description ' Displays: Negative numbers not allowed.
End Sub
```

Obtaining Error Information

A component written in Java can return rich error information by throwing an instance of *ComFailException,* a class provided by the com.ms.com package of the Microsoft Java SDK. For example, the Java component shown here, with the exception in boldface, behaves identically to the C++ component in the preceding section:

```
import insidedcomlib.*;
import com.ms.com.*;

public class InsideDCOM implements insidedcomlib.IInsideDCOM
{
    private static final String CLSID =
        "5ffe7e00-5db6-11d1-a6fc-0000c0cc7be1";

    public int Sum(int x, int y)
    {
        if(x < 0 || y < 0)
            throw new ComFailException(0x80070057,
```

```
            "Negative numbers not allowed.");
        return x + y;
    }
}
```

Client applications that want to obtain rich error information use the methods of the *IErrorInfo* interface. The IDL definition of the *IErrorInfo* interface is shown here:

```
interface IErrorInfo : IUnknown
{
    HRESULT GetGUID([out] GUID * pGUID);
    HRESULT GetSource([out] BSTR * pBstrSource);
    HRESULT GetDescription([out] BSTR * pBstrDescription);
    HRESULT GetHelpFile([out] BSTR * pBstrHelpFile);
    HRESULT GetHelpContext([out] DWORD * pdwHelpContext);
}
```

Before it calls the methods of the *IErrorInfo* interface, the client needs to determine whether the component reporting the error provides rich error information. To do this, the client calls the *QueryInterface* method to request the *ISupportErrorInfo* interface. Assuming this call is successful, the client calls *ISupportErrorInfo::InterfaceSupportsErrorInfo* to verify that rich error information is available for the methods of the interface in question. If this call is successful, the client can call the *GetErrorInfo* function to obtain an *IErrorInfo* pointer to the object containing the rich error information. The methods of the *IErrorInfo* interface shown in the preceding code can now be called to obtain the error information. Later the *IErrorInfo* and *ISupportErrorInfo* interface pointers must be released. The following code fragment shows how a C++ client program can obtain the error information thrown by our sample Java component:

```
hr = pSum->Sum(-2, 3, &sum);
if(SUCCEEDED(hr))
    cout << "Sum = " << sum << endl;
else
{
    ISupportErrorInfo* pSupportErrorInfo;
    if(SUCCEEDED(pSum->QueryInterface(IID_ISupportErrorInfo,
        (void**)&pSupportErrorInfo)))
    {
        if(pSupportErrorInfo->InterfaceSupportsErrorInfo(
            IID_IInsideDCOM) == S_OK)
        {
            IErrorInfo* pErrorInfo;
            GetErrorInfo(0, &pErrorInfo);
```

(continued)

199

```
            BSTR description;
            pErrorInfo->GetDescription(&description);
            wprintf(L"HRESULT = %x, Description: %s\n", hr,
                description);
            SysFreeString(description);

            pErrorInfo->Release();
        }
        pSupportErrorInfo->Release();
    }
}
```

Component Categories

A COM object exposes its functionality through interfaces; a client learns about these interfaces through the *IUnknown::QueryInterface* method. The true purpose of the *QueryInterface* method is twofold. First, it enables clients to determine what interfaces are available. Second, clients use it to retrieve pointers to those interfaces supported by the object. The first job of *QueryInterface*, to determine what interfaces are supported, does not scale well as objects become increasingly complex and begin to support not several but dozens of interfaces. Of course, regardless of the number of interfaces supported by an object, *QueryInterface* is still the method to call when you need an interface pointer.

As objects and their clients become increasingly complex, they require more functionality from one another. Generally speaking, most COM interfaces have between three and seven methods. This is not a rule, however; an interface may have an arbitrary number of methods. But pragmatically, it seems that an interface works best if a programmer can grasp it quickly. This desire for clarity has meant that as COM objects have evolved, they have added functionality by implementing new interfaces rather than extending old ones.

In today's increasingly complex world, most components need to support a gamut of interfaces that work together to accomplish a single task. Visual Basic, for example, requires that an ActiveX control support upwards of a dozen interfaces. Visual Basic displays a list of available ActiveX controls when the user chooses Components from the Project menu, as shown in Figure 5-7. Here's the problem: How can client programs such as Visual Basic determine what objects installed on the user's computer support all the interfaces necessary to qualify as ActiveX controls?

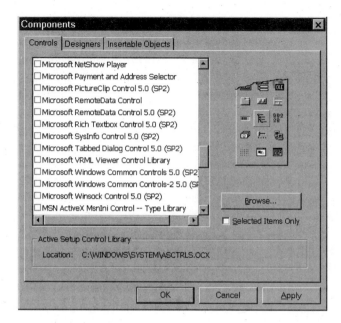

Figure 5-7.
*The Components dialog box in Visual Basic, showing a list of available
ActiveX controls.*

With only the *QueryInterface* mechanism at its disposal, Visual Basic would
need to traverse the HKEY_CLASSES_ROOT\CLSID section of the registry,
instantiate each object, and then call *QueryInterface* a dozen times per object
simply to determine whether the necessary interfaces are available. This technique is not a solution, as it would take an unreasonable amount of time.
Ideally, Visual Basic should be able to determine whether a component will
meet its requirements prior to instantiating the component. This need gave
rise to *component categories.*

Rather than simply identifying a component's functionality by listing the
interfaces it supports, many components belong to a certain type. For example,
controls, documents, scripting engines, and Automation objects are different
types of components. Component categories were devised as an extensible way
to enable clients to quickly identify the group to which a component belongs.
They work by defining registry keys that allow a component to declare its support for one or more categories. A client program can then locate those components supporting a particular category through a quick scan of the registry.
Once located, the desired components can be instantiated and *QueryInterface*
called to obtain interface pointers in the usual way.

Category Identifiers

A category identifier (CATID, identical to a 128-bit GUID) identifies the type of component. For example, any component implementing the CATID {40FC6ED4-2438-11CF-A3DB-080036F12502} is defined as a control, whereas CATID {F0B7A1A1-9847-11CF-8F20-00805F2CD064} is used to identify Active Scripting Engines. By design, component categories are extensible, which means that additional CATIDs can be defined for custom component types. Of course, it is strongly recommended that an existing component category be used if it meets the need. Like the signature of an interface, the semantics of a CATID are immutable. A new component category must be defined instead of expanding the required interfaces for an existing type of component.

The defined CATIDs on an individual machine are stored in the HKEY-_CLASSES_ROOT\Component Categories section of the registry. Stored with each CATID value is a human-readable name that describes the component category. Figure 5-8 shows some of the more standard CATIDs that can be easily located in the registry.

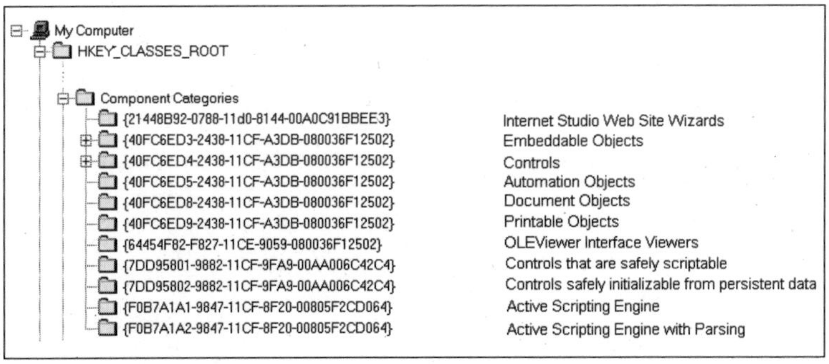

Figure 5-8.
Some standard CATIDs.

An object declares its support for a particular component category via the Implemented Categories key in the registry. A particular object can support multiple component categories by listing all its supported CATIDs in the registry. Component categories can also be a two-way street. Not only can a client search for components that are members of a certain category, but a component can also declare that it requires certain functionality of the client. If a component does not indicate the type of client it is willing to work with, the user might select a component only to discover that it won't work with the user's client. An object declares categories of acceptable clients using the Required

Categories registry key. The Required Categories registry key should be used with restraint because it will severely limit the clients that can access an object.

Figure 5-9 shows a hypothetical registry entry for a COM object. Based on this information, we can deduce that the object is a control that requires a container to support Visual Basic–style data binding. (The labels on the right side of the figure are for descriptive purposes only; they do not actually appear in the registry.)

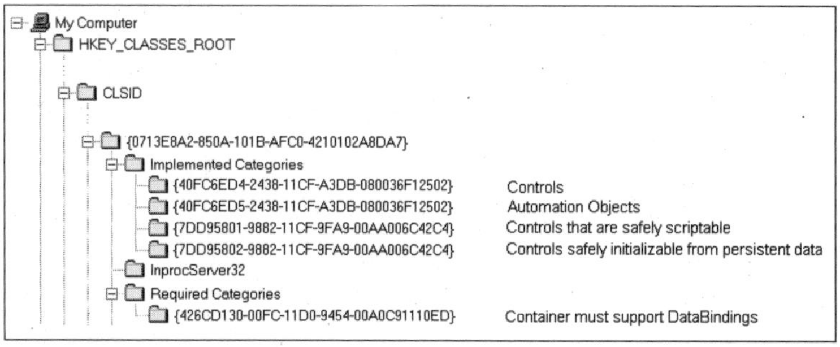

Figure 5-9.
The registry entries for a COM object that uses the Required Categories
subkey to specify required client functionality.

In some cases, it might be useful to associate a CATID with a default object. This technique allows clients to instantiate an object of a particular type without even knowing the object's CLSID! For example, imagine an e-mail application that checks the spelling of a message before it is sent. If the e-mail program does not care what spell checker component it uses, it can simply call *CoCreateInstance* with the CLSID parameter set to the CATID for spell checker components, as shown here:

```
// Instantiate the default object, implementing the
// Spell Checker component category.
CoCreateInstance(CATID_SpellChecker, NULL, CLSCTX_INPROC_SERVER,
    IID_IUnknown, (void**)&pUnknown);

// Now we know that the object must support the
// ISpellChecker interface.
pUnknown->QueryInterface(IID_ISpellChecker, (void**)&pSpell);
```

The default spell checker is located by looking in the HKEY_CLASSES-_ROOT\CLSID section of the registry for the CATID specified. The CATID is defined there using the TreatAs subkey, which references the CLSID of the actual spell checker component, as shown in Figure 5-10 on the following page.

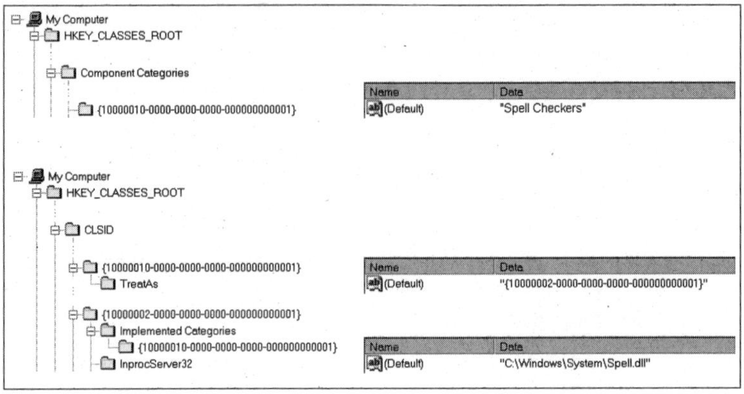

Figure 5-10.
*The default component of a certain category, referenced in the
HKEY_CLASSES_ROOT\CLSID\{ComponentCategoryID}\TreatAs
registry key.*

Using this mechanism can be very helpful when you don't want to tie a
client program with a particular CLSID and at the same time don't want to force
the user to choose from a list of available components. An application can be
designed so that the setup program asks the user to make a selection during
the installation process and then configures that component as the default.

The *ICatRegister* Interface

In contrast to the standard registration of components, in which COM leaves
developers in the lurch by requiring them to write code that manually registers objects, component categories have a lot of built-in functionality. The six
methods of the *ICatRegister* interface help define component categories and
register objects that implement or require them, according to your instructions.
COM provides an object, called the *Component Categories Manager,* which implements this interface. The following code shows the *ICatRegister* interface in IDL
notation:

```
interface ICatRegister : IUnknown
{
// Register a new component category.
HRESULT RegisterCategories(
    [in] ULONG cCategories,
    [in, size_is(cCategories)] CATEGORYINFO rgCategoryInfo[]);

// Remove an existing component category.
HRESULT UnRegisterCategories(
```

```
    [in] ULONG cCategories,
    [in, size_is(cCategories)] CATID rgcatid[]);

// Register a CLSID as implementing a component category.
HRESULT RegisterClassImplCategories(
    [in] REFCLSID rclsid,
    [in] ULONG cCategories,
    [in, size_is(cCategories)] CATID rgcatid[]);

// Remove an implemented component category from the CLSID.
HRESULT UnRegisterClassImplCategories(
    [in] REFCLSID rclsid,
    [in] ULONG cCategories,
    [in, size_is(cCategories)] CATID rgcatid[]);

// Register a CLSID as requiring a component category.
HRESULT RegisterClassReqCategories(
    [in] REFCLSID rclsid,
    [in] ULONG cCategories,
    [in, size_is(cCategories)] CATID rgcatid[]);

// Remove a required component category from the CLSID.
HRESULT UnRegisterClassReqCategories(
    [in] REFCLSID rclsid,
    [in] ULONG cCategories,
    [in, size_is(cCategories)] CATID rgcatid[]);
}
```

To make use of the component category interfaces, the comcat.h file must be included in the source. The following code defines a new CATID, *CATID-_Math,* which is implemented by the *InsideDCOM* class:

```
#include <comcat.h> // For component category stuff

// CATID for the Arithmetic objects category.
CATID CATID_Math =
{0x10000010,0x0000,0x0000,{0x00,0x00,0x00,0x00,0x00,0x00,0x00,0x01}};
```

After calling *CoInitialize,* a client program may instantiate the Component Categories Manager object, which is identified as *CLSID_StdComponentCategoriesMgr* or with the GUID {0002E005-0000-0000-C000-000000000046}. A quick scan of the registry reveals that this class is implemented by the in-process server comcat.dll, which can be found in the Windows\System folder. (In Microsoft Windows NT, this file can be found in the WINNT\System32 folder.) COM's implementation of the component category interfaces is no different from an in-process component you might create. The code on the following page retrieves a pointer to the *ICatRegister* interface.

```
// Instantiate COM's implementation of component categories.
ICatRegister* pCatRegister;
CoCreateInstance(CLSID_StdComponentCategoriesMgr, NULL,
    CLSCTX_INPROC_SERVER, IID_ICatRegister, (void**)&pCatRegister);
```

Next a CATEGORYINFO structure is constructed and the *ICatRegister-::RegisterCategories* method is called to add the necessary entries to the Windows registry. Then the *Release* method is called to free the interface pointer. The following code would normally be executed with other self-registration code in the component:

```
// Set up the CATEGORYINFO structure.
CATEGORYINFO catinfo;
catinfo.catid = CATID_Math;
catinfo.lcid = 0x0409; // English
wcsncpy(catinfo.szDescription, L"Arithmetic Objects", 128);

// Install the component category.
pCatRegister->RegisterCategories(1, &catinfo);

// Release COM's implementation of component categories.
pCatRegister->Release();
```

Should it become necessary to unregister a component category, you can call the *ICatRegister::UnRegisterCategories* method, as shown here:

```
pCatRegister->UnRegisterCategories(1, &CATID_Math);
```

Under most circumstances, however, there will be no need to remove a component category from the registry. Even if a component is unregistered, there might be other components making use of a particular component category.

Perhaps more common than registering or unregistering actual component categories is the task of simply declaring that a particular COM class implements or requires one or more component categories. The following code calls the *ICatRegister::RegisterClassImplCategories* method in order to declare that the *InsideDCOM* class implements the Arithmetic Objects component category. This method adds the Implemented Categories key below the HKEY_CLASSES-_ROOT\CLSID\{*CLSID_InsideDCOM*} entry in the registry. The actual CATIDs supported are inserted below the Implemented Categories key. The following code would probably be executed as part of a component self-registration procedure:

```
CATID rgcatid[1];
rgcatid[0] = CATID_Math;
pCatRegister->RegisterClassImplCategories(CLSID_InsideDCOM, 1, rgcatid);
```

Removing a particular CATID from the registration of a COM class, as shown in the following code, is less commonly performed. During the unregister procedure, most components simply delete all their registry settings, so removing implemented categories specifically is unnecessary. It will, however, do no harm.

```
CATID rgcatid[1];
rgcatid[0] = CATID_Math;
pCatRegister->UnRegisterClassImplCategories(CLSID_InsideDCOM, 1,
    rgcatid);
```

The *ICatInformation* Interface

Clients that want to locate one or more components that implement and/or require certain categories should use the *ICatInformation* interface. Visual Basic, for example, makes use of the *ICatInformation::EnumClassesOfCategories* method to populate the Components dialog box listing the available ActiveX controls. Here is the *ICatInformation* interface in IDL notation:

```
interface ICatInformation : IUnknown
{
// Get an enumerator for the registered categories.
HRESULT EnumCategories(
    [in] LCID lcid,
    [out] IEnumCATEGORYINFO** ppenumCategoryInfo);

// Get the description of a registered component category.
HRESULT GetCategoryDesc(
    [in] REFCATID rcatid,
    [in] LCID lcid,
    [out] LPWSTR* pszDesc);

// Get an enumerator for the classes that support a component category.
HRESULT EnumClassesOfCategories(
    [in] ULONG cImplemented,
    [in,size_is(cImplemented)] CATID rgcatidImpl[],
    [in] ULONG cRequired,
    [in,size_is(cRequired)] CATID rgcatidReq[],
    [out] IEnumCLSID** ppenumClsid);

// Determine whether a class supports a component category.
HRESULT IsClassOfCategories(
    [in] REFCLSID rclsid,
    [in] ULONG cImplemented,
    [in,size_is(cImplemented)] CATID rgcatidImpl[],
```

(continued)

207

```
    [in] ULONG cRequired,
    [in,size_is(cRequired)] CATID rgcatidReq[]);

// Get an enumerator for component categories implemented by a class.
HRESULT EnumImplCategoriesOfClass(
    [in] REFCLSID rclsid,
    [out] IEnumCATID** ppenumCatid);

// Get an enumerator for component categories required by a class.
HRESULT EnumReqCategoriesOfClass(
    [in] REFCLSID rclsid,
    [out] IEnumCATID** ppenumCatid);
}
```

COM's standard implementation of component categories also implements the *ICatInformation* interface. The methods of this interface do not affect the information stored in the registry in any way. Instead, *ICatInformation* can be used to easily retrieve component category information from the registry in a meaningful format. The following code instantiates the *Component Categories Manager* and returns a pointer to the *ICatInformation* interface:

```
// Instantiate COM's implementation of component categories.
// Notice that now we request the ICatInformation interface.
ICatInformation* pCatInformation;
CoCreateInstance(CLSID_StdComponentCategoriesMgr, NULL,
    CLSCTX_INPROC_SERVER, IID_ICatInformation,
    (void**)&pCatInformation);
```

Here the *ICatInformation::EnumClassesOfCategories* method is used to retrieve a pointer to an enumerator that will contain the CLSIDs of those COM classes that implement the Arithmetic Objects component category:

```
// Get an enumerator for the CLSIDs of Arithmetic objects.
IEnumCLSID* pEnumCLSID;
pCatInformation->EnumClassesOfCategories(1, &CATID_Math, 0,
    NULL, &pEnumCLSID);
pCatInformation->Release();
```

Next the code loops through the elements in the enumerator and displays the CLSIDs of all the *Arithmetic* objects, as shown in the following code. At the very least, this display should include the CLSID of the *InsideDCOM* class because it was previously registered as implementing the Arithmetic Objects component category.

```
// Loop through the CLSIDs in the enumeration.
CLSID clsid = CLSID_NULL;
DWORD fetched = 0;
while(true)
```

```
{
    // Get the next CLSID.
    pEnumCLSID->Next(1, &clsid, &fetched);
    if(fetched == 0)
        break;

    // Convert the CLSID to a string.
    char buffer[39];
    OLECHAR ppsz[39];
    StringFromGUID2(clsid, ppsz, 39);
    WideCharToMultiByte(CP_ACP, 0, ppsz, 39, buffer, 39, NULL, NULL);

    // Print the string-form of CLSID.
    cout << "CLSID that supports the Arithmetic Objects component "
         << "category is " << buffer << endl;
}
pEnumCLSID->Release();
```

This code is very similar to that executed by Visual Basic when it is presenting the user with a list of controls. Visual Basic, of course, enumerates classes that implement the Controls component CATID {40FC6ED4-2438-11CF-A3DB-080036F12502}.

Connection Points and Type Information

The *Unknown::QueryInterface* function represents the method by which a client discovers the functionality supported by an object. The more interfaces common to both the client and the object, the more intertwined their relationship becomes. But regardless of the number of interfaces supported by the object, the basic model remains the same: the client calls the methods implemented by the object. The object performs the desired service and then returns the results to the client. This type of relationship is rather one-sided—it always involves the client making requests of the object. So to further broaden the connection between the client and the object, COM supports *connectable objects,* a technology developed to enable an object to "talk back" to its client.

Connectable objects are most often used to notify the client when something interesting happens in its sphere—colloquially known as "firing an event." ActiveX controls are the most famous type of connectable objects that use this technology to raise events in their container. Sometimes connectable objects are used to get further information from the client about the service being requested. At other times, connectable objects might be used to request that the client perform a service for the object—in effect turning the tables on their relationship. Regardless of your reason for using connectable objects, this generic COM service was designed to support two-way communication between a client and an object.

Connectable objects use some rather peculiar terminology, which deserves a moment of attention. An *outgoing interface,* also called a *source interface,* is an interface defined in the object itself but implemented by the client. A *sink* object, residing within the client, is the object that implements the client's outgoing interface. Memorizing these definitions will aid in your understanding of connectable objects. Figure 6-1 on the following page illustrates the layout of these elements.

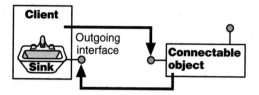

Figure 6-1.
A connectable object using an outgoing interface to "talk back" to the client.

A Simple Version of a Connectable Object

In order to support a generic mechanism for connectable objects, Microsoft designed four interfaces: *IConnectionPointContainer*, *IEnumConnectionPoints*, *IConnectionPoint*, and *IEnumConnections*. Due to their generic design, the connection point interfaces can initially be overwhelming in their complexity. To make this technology more digestible, this section shows you how to build a simple pared-down example of a connectable object. Keep in mind that this simple example is not a full implementation of a connectable object. Later in this chapter, in the section "A Complete Implementation of a Connectable Object," we will develop a full-fledged example.

The simple example of a connectable object implements the two interfaces *IConnectionPoint* and *IConnectionPointContainer*. The two remaining interfaces let you enumerate the available connection points (*IEnumConnectionPoints*) as well as the current connections (*IEnumConnections*). While they are not terribly difficult to implement, enumerators are not all that simple either, and they tend to detract from the discussion of connection points. Therefore, we will wait for the full version of the connection point example to add the enumerators.

The *IOutGoing* Interface

As with most other programming tasks in COM, work with connectable objects often starts in the Interface Definition Language (IDL). First we need to define the outgoing interface that will be implemented by the sink and called by the connectable object. For demonstration purposes, we'll define an outgoing interface, appropriately named *IOutGoing*, shown in IDL notation in the following code. The *GotMessage* method of the *IOutGoing* interface will be used to notify the sink that something has happened in the connectable object.

```
[ object, uuid(10000005-0000-0000-0000-000000000001),
  oleautomation ]
interface IOutGoing : IUnknown
{
    HRESULT GotMessage(int Message);
}
```

Next this interface needs to be added to the *coclass* statement, as shown in the following IDL code. Notice that the *IOutGoing* interface is declared using the *source* attribute, as shown in boldface. In the type library created by the Microsoft IDL (MIDL) compiler, this attribute will indicate that *IOutGoing* is a source of events and that the interface is called rather than implemented by the *InsideDCOM* object. Every *coclass* statement in the IDL file can have a default incoming interface (the standard kind) as well as a default source interface. If the default is not indicated using the *default* attribute, the first outgoing and incoming interfaces are treated as the defaults. This assignment of defaults is important because high-level languages such as Microsoft Visual Basic automatically call *IUnknown::QueryInterface* for the interface marked with the *default* attribute.

```
[ uuid(10000003-0000-0000-0000-000000000001),
  helpstring("Inside DCOM Component Type Library"),
  version(1.0) ]
library Component
{
    importlib("stdole32.tlb");

    interface ISum;
    interface IOutGoing;
    [ uuid(10000002-0000-0000-0000-000000000001) ]
    coclass InsideDCOM
    {
        interface ISum;
        [source] interface IOutGoing;
    }
};
```

NOTE: Actually, the first outgoing and incoming interfaces not marked with the *restricted* IDL attribute are assumed to be the defaults. The *restricted* attribute hides the specified interface from use in languages based on type libraries, such as Visual Basic and Java.

The *IConnectionPoint* Interface

A *connection point* is an object managed by the connectable object that implements the *IConnectionPoint* interface. The main purpose of the *IConnectionPoint* interface is to enable a client to provide a connectable object with a pointer to the client's sink, as shown in Figure 6-2. Each connection point is designed to support exactly one outgoing interface.

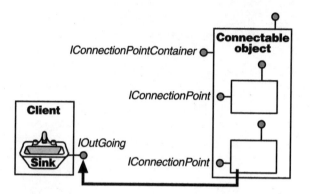

Figure 6-2.
A pointer to the client's sink obtained via the IConnectionPoint *interface.*

Here is the *IConnectionPoint* interface in IDL notation:

```
interface IConnectionPoint : IUnknown
{
// Get the IID of the outgoing interface.
HRESULT GetConnectionInterface
    (
        [out]    IID * piid
    );


// Get the IConnectionPointContainer that we belong to.
    HRESULT GetConnectionPointContainer
        (
        [out]    IConnectionPointContainer ** ppCPC
        );


// Here's a pointer to my sink.
    HRESULT Advise
        (
        [in]     IUnknown * pUnkSink,
        [out]    DWORD *     pdwCookie
        );
```

```
// Don't call us--we'll call you.
   HRESULT Unadvise
   (
       [in]    DWORD dwCookie
   );

// Who else do you talk to?
   HRESULT EnumConnections
   (
       [out]    IEnumConnections ** ppEnum
   );
}
```

Of the five methods of *IConnectionPoint*, we'll initially implement only the two most important ones: *Advise* and *Unadvise*. All the other methods will simply return *E_NOTIMPL* for now. The *IConnectionPoint::Advise* method is called by the client in order to provide the connectable object with a pointer to the sink object. In a certain way, this call can be perceived as a *QueryInterface* call in reverse. *IUnknown::QueryInterface* is the method used by a client to discover the interfaces exposed by an object. *IConnectionPoint::Advise* is called by a client to provide an object with a pointer to its sink. So rather than asking the question, "What interfaces do you support?" asked by *QueryInterface*, the *Advise* method is a statement, telling the object, "Here is a pointer to my sink."

Although the *IConnectionPoint::Advise* method provides the connectable object with a pointer to the client sink's *IUnknown* interface, this pointer alone is not sufficient. In order to be able to call the methods of the client's sink object, we need to obtain a pointer to one of the more interesting interfaces implemented by the sink. Thus, the *IUnknown::QueryInterface* method is the first call made from the connectable object to the client's sink! Last, the *Advise* method must return a unique number to the client that identifies the advisory relationship that has been established. The client retains this number, called a *cookie*, for later use in terminating the connection.

A simple implementation of the *Advise* method looks like this:

```
HRESULT CInsideDCOM::Advise(IUnknown* pUnknown, DWORD* pdwCookie)
{
    *pdwCookie = 1;
    return pUnknown->QueryInterface(IID_IOutGoing,
        (void**)&g_pOutGoing);
}
```

Since this code is prepared to handle only a single connection, the cookie returned to the client is a dummy placeholder. The sink object's *IUnknown::QueryInterface* method is called to obtain a pointer to its *IOutGoing* interface.

This pointer is stored in a global variable for later use. Conveniently, the *IUnknown::AddRef* operation required to increment the reference counter is encapsulated within the *QueryInterface* call.

The *IConnectionPoint::Unadvise* method is used to terminate an advisory relationship that was previously established using the *Advise* method. The cookie argument passed to *Unadvise* identifies which connection should be terminated. In the following implementation, the *Unadvise* method simply releases the interface pointer obtained previously:

```
HRESULT CInsideDCOM::Unadvise(DWORD dwCookie)
{
    g_pOutGoing->Release();
    return NOERROR;
}
```

At this stage, the component has a pointer to the sink object and can call the *GotMessage* method of the *IOutGoing* interface. An interesting question remains, however: How does the client get a pointer to the *IConnectionPoint* interface in the first place? This task is the duty of the *IConnectionPointContainer* interface.

The *IConnectionPointContainer* Interface

The methods of the *IConnectionPoint* interface are used to establish and release connections between a client and a connectable object; the methods of the *IConnectionPointContainer* interface are used to learn about the connection points of a connectable object. When it is implemented by an object, the *IConnectionPointContainer* interface embodies those qualities that make an object "connectable." The two methods of the *IConnectionPointContainer* interface are shown here:

```
interface IConnectionPointContainer : IUnknown
{
// Tell me about your connection points.
    HRESULT EnumConnectionPoints
    (
        [out] IEnumConnectionPoints ** ppEnum
    );

// Do you support this connection point?
    HRESULT FindConnectionPoint
    (
        [in] REFIID riid,
        [out] IConnectionPoint ** ppCP
    );
}
```

Clients that want to enumerate all the outgoing interfaces supported by a connectable object should call *IConnectionPointContainer::EnumConnectionPoints*. *EnumConnectionPoints* retrieves a pointer to an object that supports the *IEnum-ConnectionPoints* enumeration interface. At this stage, we are not supporting enumerator objects, so this method will return *E_NOTIMPL*. Note that returning *E_NOTIMPL* from *IConnectionPointContainer::EnumConnectionPoints* is specifically disallowed by the COM specification because except for type information, there is no way for a client to determine the IIDs of the outgoing interfaces that a connectable object supports.

The *IConnectionPointContainer::FindConnectionPoint* method is the *QueryInterface* of connection points. This method asks the connectable object, "Do you support a particular outgoing interface?" If the connectable object does support the requested interface, it returns a pointer to that outgoing interface's connection point (an object that implements the *IConnectionPoint* interface). *QueryInterface* is actually used to obtain the *IConnectionPoint* interface pointer, as shown in the following implementation of the *IConnectionPointContainer::FindConnectionPoint* method:

```
HRESULT CInsideDCOM::FindConnectionPoint(REFIID riid,
    IConnectionPoint** ppCP)
{
    if(riid == IID_IOutGoing)
        return QueryInterface(IID_IConnectionPoint, (void**)ppCP);
    return E_NOINTERFACE;
}
```

This implementation of *FindConnectionPoint* supports only one outgoing interface, *IOutGoing*. *E_NOINTERFACE* is returned if the client is looking for the connection point of some other outgoing interface. Assuming that the client wants *IOutGoing*, *QueryInterface* is called to obtain a pointer to the connection point and the pointer is returned to the client. This answers the question of how the client obtains the pointer to the *IConnectionPoint* interface. If you are wondering how the *IConnectionPointContainer* interface is obtained, just remember your good friend *QueryInterface*. The *CInsideDCOM* class implements *QueryInterface* in the standard fashion, simply handing out pointers to the *IConnectionPointContainer* interface as requested, as shown in boldface on page 218.

```
HRESULT CInsideDCOM::QueryInterface(REFIID riid, void** ppv)
{
    if(riid == IID_IUnknown)
        *ppv = reinterpret_cast<IUnknown*>(this);
    else if(riid == IID_ISum)
        *ppv = (ISum*)this;
```

(continued)

```
else if(riid == IID_IConnectionPointContainer)
    *ppv = (IConnectionPointContainer*)this;
else if(riid == IID_IConnectionPoint)
    *ppv = (IConnectionPoint*)this;
else
{
    *ppv = NULL;
    return E_NOINTERFACE;
}
AddRef();
return S_OK;
}
```

The *reinterpret_cast* Operator

The *reinterpret_cast* operator is used to coerce the *this* pointer into an *IUnknown* interface pointer. This coercion is required because the *CInsideDCOM* class uses multiple inheritance to implement the *ISum* interface and the *IConnectionPointContainer* interface, as shown here:

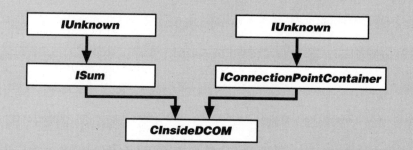

```
class CInsideDCOM : public ISum, IConnectionPointContainer
```

Because *ISum* is derived from *IUnknown* and *IConnectionPoint-Container* is derived from *IUnknown*, we have run into one of the snags of multiple inheritance in C++. Luckily, since all the classes except *CInsideDCOM* are abstract base classes, we don't have to worry about duplicate function implementations. Nevertheless, the code attempting to cast a pointer to *CInsideDCOM* into a pointer to *IUnknown*, a legal operation, runs afoul of the compiler's type checking. The cast is ambiguous because it is not clear whether we want *ISum*'s *IUnknown* or *IConnectionPointContainer*'s *IUnknown*. The truth of the matter is that we couldn't care less, and the *reinterpret_cast* operator enables us to force the compiler to perform the cast.

The final bit of code required in the component is the call to the *IOut-Going::GotMessage* method. To make things interesting, we will call this method whenever the user presses a key on the keyboard. The ASCII key code will be sent as a parameter of *GotMessage* to the client. To make this example even more interesting, we suggest that you use the DCOM Configuration utility (dcom-cnfg.exe) to set up the client and server on different computers and then watch the events fire across the network. For more information about using the DCOM configuration utility, see Chapter 8, "DLL Surrogates and Executable Components." The following code reads keyboard input from the console by using the Win32 function *ReadConsoleInput* (shown in boldface) and then calls the *Got-Message* method in the sink object:

```
// Press any key to fire an event at the client.
HANDLE handles[2] = { g_hEvent, GetStdHandle(STD_INPUT_HANDLE) };

// READY...
while(WaitForMultipleObjects(2, handles, FALSE, INFINITE) -
    WAIT_OBJECT_0 == 1)
{
    INPUT_RECORD ir;
    DWORD read;

// AIM...
    ReadConsoleInput(handles[1], &ir, 1, &read);
    if(ir.EventType == KEY_EVENT && ir.Event.KeyEvent.bKeyDown == TRUE)

// FIRE!!!
        g_pOutGoing->GotMessage(ir.Event.KeyEvent.uChar.AsciiChar);
}
```

Implementing a Sink in C++

In order to test the connectable object, we need to expand the client program built in the previous chapters to include a sink object that will receive and respond to the fired events. The client code is where the *IOutGoing* interface is actually implemented by the *CSink* class, as shown here:

```
class CSink : public IOutGoing
{
public:
    // IUnknown
    ULONG __stdcall AddRef();
    ULONG __stdcall Release();
    HRESULT __stdcall QueryInterface(REFIID riid, void** ppv);
```

(continued)

```
// IOutGoing
HRESULT __stdcall GotMessage(int Message);

CSink() : m_cRef(0) { }
~CSink() { }

private:
    long m_cRef;
};
```

As you can see in the preceding class definition, the *CSink* class implements the *IUnknown* and *IOutGoing* interfaces. We will not bore you with the all-too-standard implementations of *IUnknown::AddRef, Release,* and *QueryInterface.* The *IOutGoing::GotMessage* method, shown here, is more interesting because it is called by the connectable object whenever the user presses a key:

```
HRESULT CSink::GotMessage(int Message)
{
    if(Message == (int)'b' || Message == (int)'B')
        PlaySound("BrockschmidtQuack", NULL, SND_RESOURCE|SND_ASYNC);
    cout << "CSink::GotMessage is " << (char)Message << endl;
    return S_OK;
}
```

NOTE: A quacking sound can be heard whenever the B key is pressed. This sound is borrowed from Kraig Brockschmidt's book, *Inside OLE* (Microsoft Press, 1995).

Setting Up a Connection Point

The main client code starts out in the standard fashion, calling *CoCreateInstance* to instantiate the *InsideDCOM* object, as shown here:

```
// Instantiate the object.
IUnknown* pUnknown;
CoCreateInstance(CLSID_InsideDCOM, NULL, CLSCTX_LOCAL_SERVER,
    IID_IUnknown, (void**)&pUnknown);
```

Next the client calls *IUnknown::QueryInterface* to determine whether *Inside-DCOM* is a connectable object, as shown in the following code. If the object supports the *IConnectionPointContainer* interface, it qualifies as "connectable."

```
// Query for IConnectionPointContainer.
IConnectionPointContainer* pConnectionPointContainer;
hr = pUnknown->QueryInterface(IID_IConnectionPointContainer,
    (void**)&pConnectionPointContainer);
```

The *IConnectionPointContainer::FindConnectionPoint* method is then called to retrieve the connection point for the *IOutGoing* interface, as shown here:

```
// Find the connection point for IOutGoing.
IConnectionPoint* pConnectionPoint;
hr = pConnectionPointContainer->FindConnectionPoint(IID_IOutGoing,
    &pConnectionPoint);
```

Using the pointer obtained from *FindConnectionPoint*, the client calls *IConnectionPoint::Advise* to provide the connectable object with a pointer to the sink object. Of course, the sink object must be instantiated in the client before its pointer can be sent to the component! This task is accomplished using the C++ keyword *new*, as shown here:

```
// Instantiate the sink object.
CSink* mySink = new CSink;

// Give the connectable object a pointer to the sink.
DWORD dwCookie;
pConnectionPoint->Advise((IUnknown*)mySink, &dwCookie);
```

At this stage, there is an advisory relationship between the client's sink object and the connectable object. Whenever the user presses a key from within the component, the sink's *IOutGoing::GotMessage* method is called. When the user tires of this fantastic program and decides to exit, the *IConnectionPoint-::Unadvise* method is called to terminate this connection, as shown here:

```
// Terminate the connection.
pConnectionPoint->Unadvise(dwCookie);
```

This call is followed by several calls to *IUnknown::Release* to free all the pointers used in the course of this exercise, as shown in the following code snippet:

```
// Release everything in sight.
pConnectionPoint->Release();
pConnectionPointContainer->Release();
pUnknown->Release();
```

Figure 6-3 on the following page shows the calls made by the client to the connectable object in order to establish their relationship; the numbered labels indicate the order of the calls.

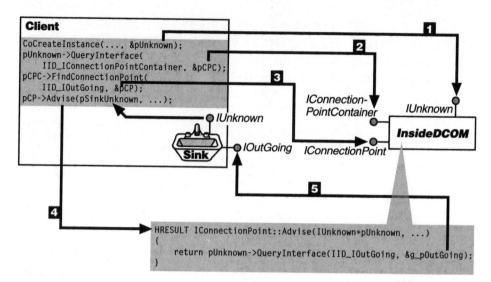

Figure 6-3.
The steps taken so that the InsideDCOM *connectable object can obtain a pointer to its client's sink and fire back events.*

Multicasting with Connection Points

While it is typical, a one-to-one relationship is not the rule between a client and a connectable object. The connection point architecture is generic enough to support a connectable object that fires events at multiple sinks or to support a sink that gets hooked up to several connectable objects. Figure 6-4 illustrates several clients connecting their sinks to a single connectable object.

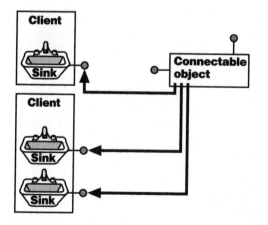

Figure 6-4.
A connectable object firing events to multiple sinks.

Assuming that all the sinks implement the same outgoing interface, the connectable object can sequentially fire the same event at all its client sinks that called *IConnectionPoint::Advise*, simply by iterating through its current connections using the following code:

```
IOutGoing* pOutGoing;
for(int count = 0; count < CCONNMAX; count++)
    if(m_rgpUnknown[count] != NULL)
    {
        pOutGoing = (IOutGoing*)m_rgpUnknown[count];
        pOutGoing->SomethingHappened(WhatHappened);
    }
```

Figure 6-5 shows the inverse of this topology—in this case, a single client application has advised several connectable objects of its sink.

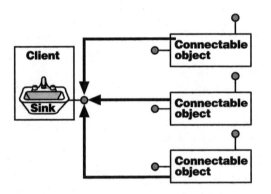

Figure 6-5.
A single sink receiving events fired from multiple connectable objects.

Now the same client sink receives events fired by any of the connectable objects. This setup is most useful when a client wants to listen to several connectable objects at the same time in one sink.

A Visual Basic Sink

To liven things up a bit, let's use Visual Basic to test our simple connectable object. After slogging through the preceding *CSink* code, intercepting events in Visual Basic is almost dishearteningly easy. Simply use the *WithEvents* keyword when you are declaring an object variable, and Visual Basic will dynamically create a sink object that implements the outgoing interfaces supported by the connectable object. Then instantiate the object using the Visual Basic *New* keyword. Now whenever the connectable object calls methods of the outgoing interface, Visual Basic's sink object checks to see whether you have written

223

any code to handle the call. For example, in the following code the standard-looking *myRef_GotMessage* event procedure handles the *InsideDCOM* object's *GotMessage* events:

```
' Declare the object variable.
Dim WithEvents myRef As InsideDCOM

Private Sub Form_Load()
    ' Instantiate the connectable object.
    Set myRef = New InsideDCOM
End Sub

' Catch events here...
Private Sub myRef_GotMessage(ByVal Message As Long)
    Print Chr(Message)
End Sub
```

> **WARNING:** Before you run this sample, be sure to delete the HKEY_CLASSES_ROOT\CLSID\{10000002-0000-0000-0000-0000-00000001}\InProcServer32 subkey from the registry. Visual Basic uses the *CLSCTX_SERVER* flag when calling *CoCreateInstance* to instantiate a component, which means that the in-process flavor of a component, if it exists, will always be chosen over an EXE-based version. The connectable object sample discussed in this chapter is housed in an EXE component.

Although according to the rules and regulations of the COM specification, the connectable object (*InsideDCOM*) written in C++ and described earlier is not legal, the fact that Visual Basic is willing to work with this object gives the connectable object a great deal of credibility. (Either that or it proves that Visual Basic is a most forgiving client.) Perhaps if you have only a relatively basic need for a connectable object, this code is sufficient. Connectable objects were designed for ActiveX controls and thus can sometimes seem unnecessarily complicated if the full power of this paradigm is not required.

Creating Sinks Dynamically

A very interesting question is raised by this simple Visual Basic code: How does Visual Basic's sink object implement the *IOutGoing* custom interface? Notice that in Figure 6-3 on page 222, the sink object exposes the *IOutGoing* interface, which is easy enough to accomplish because the code we wrote in the *CSink* class inherited the interface definition and implemented its methods. Visual Basic, however, has no knowledge of the *IOutGoing* interface, yet it is still able to respond correctly to the *IOutGoing::GotMessage* event. ˙

This fact is as truly amazing as it appears. For Visual Basic to correctly respond to events fired from connectable objects, it must dynamically synthesize a sink object that implements the desired outgoing interface. This means that at run time Visual Basic needs to create a v-table containing entry points for each member function, properly construct a stack frame, and later call the Visual Basic procedure that handles the event (if one exists). Figure 6-6 shows, in numeric order, the steps taken by Visual Basic to perform this miraculous feat. First Visual Basic reads the component's type library to learn about the outgoing (source) interfaces supported by a connectable object. Using this information about the interfaces, their methods, and their arguments, Visual Basic dynamically constructs a v-table for the desired outgoing interface. Now when the connectable object fires an event at Visual Basic, everything works properly. The connectable object is not aware of the extraordinary lengths Visual Basic has gone to in order to make this work.

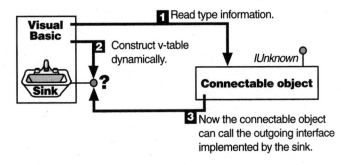

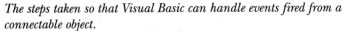

Figure 6-6.
The steps taken so that Visual Basic can handle events fired from a connectable object.

The problem with creating a generic sink, such as that provided by Visual Basic, is that at compile time the methods of the outgoing interfaces supported by the connectable object are unknown. C++ does not prove helpful in solving this problem because a C++ compiler will add only virtual functions that are known about at compile time to a v-table. Dynamically creating a v-table, as Visual Basic does, requires you to drop below the level of functionality offered by virtual functions in C++. Instead, the v-table structure normally generated automatically by the C++ compiler needs to be handcrafted at run time. The sink object can be defined using a structure, which in C++ is equivalent to a class with public members anyway.

In the following declaration, the binary standard that defines all COM objects can be seen. The first entry in the memory structure of an object must always be a pointer to the v-table. Normally, this entry is created automatically and hidden from view by C++ for any class containing virtual functions.

```
// This sink can implement any interface at run time.
// In C++, struct == public class.
struct CStink // Class for the generic sink object
{
    // The first item must be a pointer to the v-table
    // of the sink, declared as a pointer to one or more
    // function pointers.
    // Here we can see the binary standard that defines COM.
    void (__stdcall **pVtbl)();

    // Next comes the object's data.
    long m_cRef; // Reference-counting variable
};
```

Since *IUnknown* is the only interface that a COM object is required to implement, the *IUnknown* interface is the only interface that can be predefined for a truly generic sink object. Because they are no longer members of a C++ class, all three *IUnknown* methods now take a first parameter that points to the current object. This parameter replaces the implicit C++ *this* pointer that is normally available in all nonstatic member functions. Due to the fact that all C++ compilers provide this argument automatically, it has become a de facto part of the binary COM standard. In the following code, the first argument is named *me* to avoid collision with the *this* keyword. Also notice that any access to the member variable *m_cRef* is done through the *me* pointer. A little bit of this type of code can quickly make you appreciate the work normally done automatically by C++.

```
// Nonstatic methods in a class always have an implicit this
// argument that points to the current object.
// Since these methods are not part of a class, we make believe...
// Every method in the interface must pretend to have a this
// argument, as all callers will provide it.
ULONG __stdcall CStink_AddRef(CStink* me)
{
    // me is a stand-in for this, a reserved keyword in C++.
    // Everything must be explicitly accessed through the pointer
    // to the object.
    // Now we can appreciate what C++ does automatically.
    return ++me->m_cRef;
}
```

```
ULONG __stdcall CStink_Release(CStink* me)
{
    if(--me->m_cRef != 0)
        return me->m_cRef;
    delete me; // We can even use delete.
    return 0;
}

HRESULT __stdcall CStink_QueryInterface(CStink* me, REFIID riid,
    void** ppv)
{
    if(riid == IID_IUnknown || riid == IID_IOutGoing)
        *ppv = &me->pVtbl; // Here's a pointer to our interface.
    else
    {
        *ppv = NULL;
        return E_NOINTERFACE;
    }
    CStink_AddRef(me);
    return S_OK;
}
```

When the time comes to instantiate the sink object, the standard C++ *new* operator can be used, as shown in the following code fragment. The result does not qualify as a COM object, however, because it does not yet support the *IUnknown* methods.

```
// Instantiate the object, sort of...
CStink* mySink = new CStink;
```

Memory for a v-table must now be allocated and the individual function pointers initialized. In the following code, the COM memory allocation function *CoTaskMemAlloc* is used. This function automatically gets a pointer to the system's implementation of COM's memory allocation interface *IMalloc* and then allocates memory by calling *IMalloc::Alloc*. The size of the v-table allocated depends on the number of methods in the outgoing interface being implemented. The minimum size is always 12 bytes: 4 bytes for each of the three methods of *IUnknown*. Since the *IOutGoing* interface defines the one additional *GotMessage* method, four v-table entries are required, consuming a grand total of 16 bytes of memory.

```
// 3 methods in IUnknown + number of methods in outgoing interfaces
int num_methods = 4;

// Allocate memory for the v-table, and cast the returned void* to a
// pointer to an array of function pointers.
```

(continued)

227

```
void (__stdcall **IStink)() =
    (void (__stdcall **)())CoTaskMemAlloc(num_methods * sizeof(void*));
    // sizeof(void*) = 4 bytes per pointer.
```

Now each entry in the v-table needs to be initialized so that it points to the correct function, as shown in the following code. Note that the order of these functions is not arbitrary. The order in which an interface's methods appear in the v-table is a defined part of every interface. For *IUnknown*, the order is *QueryInterface*, *AddRef*, and then *Release*.

```
// Initialize the v-table to point to our implementations.
// These three methods always come first (and in this order)!
*(IStink + 0) = (void (__stdcall *)())CStink_QueryInterface;
*(IStink + 1) = (void (__stdcall *)())CStink_AddRef;
*(IStink + 2) = (void (__stdcall *)())CStink_Release;
```

At this stage, the *IUnknown* functionality is in place. Now a truly generic implementation of a sink object, such as that provided by Visual Basic, would get the type information for the connectable object's outgoing interface. Additional functions could then be synthesized once the sink had learned about all the methods (and their associated arguments) of the outgoing interface. How to accomplish this task is a bit beyond the scope of this section, so here we will stick with simply wiring the last v-table entry to point to an implementation of the *IOutGoing::GotMessage* method discussed earlier:

```
// Now add any additional methods to the v-table based on the
// available type information for the outgoing interface.
*(IStink + 3) = (void (__stdcall *)())GotMessage;
// IOutGoing has only one additional method.
```

Last the v-table structure needs to be plugged into the sink object itself, and its reference counter must be initialized, as shown here:

```
// Give the sink a brain.
mySink->pVtbl = IStink;

// Initialize the sink's reference counter.
mySink->m_cRef = 0;
```

Now a pointer to the sink object can be passed to the connectable object using the standard *IConnectionPoint::Advise* method, as shown in the following code. To the connectable object, our handcrafted sink should be indistinguishable from one mass-produced by C++. You can test this theory by running this client with the connectable object built in the section "A Simple Version of a Connectable Object" earlier in this chapter.

```
DWORD dwCookie;
hr = pConnectionPoint->Advise((IUnknown*)mySink, &dwCookie);
```

After *IConnectionPoint::Unadvise* is called to terminate the connection, the v-table we worked so hard to create must be destroyed. Here the *CoTaskMemFree* function, the analogue of *CoTaskMemAlloc*, is called to do the job:

```
// Now free the v-table; the object has probably already
// deleted itself.
CoTaskMemFree(IStink);
```

Implementing unfamiliar outgoing interfaces in a sink is possible only if type information describing the outgoing interface is available. Through type information, Visual Basic can learn about all the attributes, methods, and method arguments for an interface—enough information to correctly generate a sink object that implements the interface and to connect that sink with the connectable object. Without type information, a client that encounters an unfamiliar outgoing interface is completely out of luck. There is simply no information from which to synthesize a sink. In fact, the idea of type information was originally developed in conjunction with connectable objects for the ActiveX Controls specification (then called OLE Controls). For this reason, all the interfaces related to connectable objects are defined in the olectl.h header file. Blessedly, most clients need not be as generic as Visual Basic and thus will know at compile time what outgoing interfaces need to be implemented by their sink.

Visual Basic does have one limitation relating to connection points: it does not support nondefault outgoing interfaces. For example, the following IDL code defines a COM class containing two outgoing interfaces, *IOutGoing* and *INonDefaultOutGoing*, shown here in boldface. Currently, Visual Basic will ignore the *INonDefaultOutGoing* interface, restricting the developer to events of the default outgoing interface:

```
[ uuid(10000003-0000-0000-0000-000000000001) ]
library Component
{
    importlib("stdole32.tlb");

    interface IOutGoing;
    interface INonDefaultOutGoing;

    [ uuid(10000002-0000-0000-0000-000000000001) ]
    coclass InsideDCOM
    {
        [default, source] interface IOutGoing;
        [source] interface INonDefaultOutGoing;
    }
};
```

A Java Sink

A program written in Java can also be used to intercept events fired by a connectable object. Implementing a sink in Java is nearly as simple as doing so in Visual Basic. First use the Java Type Library Wizard to select the Inside DCOM Component Type Library. The Java Type Library Wizard will create a new subdirectory named *component* in the C:\Windows\Java\TrustLib directory and then generate .class file wrappers for the classes and interfaces described in the type library of the component: InsideDCOM.class, ISum.class, and IOutGoing.class.

Implementing the sink in Java is actually quite easy. The *JavaSink* class shown in Listing 6-1 implements the *GotMessage* method of the *IOutGoing* interface. Hooking up the sink to the connectable object is also quite easy using the *ConnectionPointCookie* class provided by Microsoft. The constructor of the *ConnectionPointCookie* class creates a connection between the connectable object and the sink using the interface identifier (IID) of the outgoing interface. Notice the use of the *import* statement to access the classes and interfaces of the *component* package.

JavaSink.java

```java
import component.*;
import com.ms.com.ConnectionPointCookie;

public class JavaSink implements IOutGoing
{
    public void GotMessage(int Message)
    {
        System.out.println((char)Message);
    }
}

class Driver
{
    public static void main(String[] args)
    {
        ISum ref = (ISum)new component.InsideDCOM();
        System.out.println("8 + 9 = " + ref.Sum(8, 9));

        try
        {
```

Listing 6-1.   *(continued)*

A Java client that implements a sink that can handle GotMessage *events fired from the* InsideDCOM *connectable object.*

```
            JavaSink j = new JavaSink();
            ConnectionPointCookie EventCookie = new
                ConnectionPointCookie(ref, j,
                Class.forName("component.IOutGoing"));
            System.out.println("Press Enter to exit.");
            System.in.read();
        }
        catch(Exception e)
        {
        }
    }
}
```

A Complete Implementation of a Connectable Object

Now that we have explored the basic architecture of connection points, it's time to examine a complete implementation of a connectable object, replete with enumerators and full implementations of the *IConnectionPointContainer* and the *IConnectionPoint* interfaces. Let's begin with the main interface exposed by an object that expresses the existence of outgoing interfaces: *IConnectionPoint-Container*. A client that wants to hook up with a connectable object initially queries for the *IConnectionPointContainer* interface. From there, the client can locate individual connection points by calling *IConnectionPointContainer::FindConnectionPoint* or *IConnectionPointContainer::EnumConnectionPoints*. *FindConnectionPoint* takes the IID of the desired outgoing interface and, if successful, returns a pointer to the relevant *IConnectionPoint* interface. *EnumConnectionPoints* is more complicated because it returns a pointer to the *IEnumConnectionPoints* interface.

An implementation of *IConnectionPointContainer::EnumConnectionPoints* might look like this:

```
HRESULT CInsideDCOM::EnumConnectionPoints(
    IEnumConnectionPoints** ppEnum)
{
    CEnumConnectionPoints* pEnum = new CEnumConnectionPoints(
        reinterpret_cast<IUnknown*>(this), (void**)m_rgpConnPt);
    return pEnum->QueryInterface(IID_IEnumConnectionPoints,
        (void**)ppEnum);
}
```

This code instantiates the *CEnumConnectionPoints* class using the *new* operator and then returns a pointer to the *IEnumConnectionPoints* interface exposed by this object. To the constructor of the *CEnumConnectionPoints* class, we pass a pointer to the current object (*this*) for reference counting and an array of connection points that can be enumerated (*m_rgpConnPt*).

The array of connection points is set up during the construction phase of the *CInsideDCOM* object, as shown here:

```
const NUM_CONNECTION_POINTS = 1;

CInsideDCOM::CInsideDCOM() : m_cRef(0)
{
    g_cComponents++;
    m_cRef = 0;
    // Initialize all the connection points to NULL.
    for(int count = 0; count < NUM_CONNECTION_POINTS; count++)
        m_rgpConnPt[count] = NULL;

    // Create our connection point.
    m_rgpConnPt[0] = new CConnectionPoint(this, IID_IOutGoing);
    m_rgpConnPt[0]->AddRef();

    // Additional connection points could be instantiated here.
}
```

In this example, *NUM_CONNECTION_POINTS* equals *1*, indicating that this connectable object supports only one outgoing interface. The code, however, is defined in such a way that it can be easily extended to support connectable objects with multiple outgoing interfaces. Simply set the *NUM_CONNECTION-_POINTS* constant to the number of outgoing interfaces supported by an object, and instantiate the individual connection point objects with the IID of each supported outgoing interface. More sophisticated implementations of the *IConnectionPointContainer::EnumConnectionPoints* method might use a linked list instead of an array to more flexibly support an arbitrary number of connection points.

Enumerators

Enumeration is a common programming task describing the ability of an object to iterate through a sequence of items. An enumerator is a general type of object often used in different areas of COM programming, whenever a set of items lends itself to enumeration. Each enumerator object implements a different interface depending on the type of object it enumerates. For example, COM defines a number of enumerator interfaces including *IEnumUnknown*, *IEnumString*, and *IEnumMoniker*, each of which would be implemented using an enumerator object that enumerated objects of the specified type. However, all of COM's enumerator interfaces have the same four methods: *Next, Skip,*

Reset, and *Clone.* This is not to say that all enumerators are alike; the methods of each enumerator interface generally take parameters of different types since each enumerator is designed to enumerate different kinds of things. Behind the facade of the four *IEnum*XXX methods, the enumerator object can be implemented in whatever way the developer sees fit (through a linked list, an array, and so on). The concept of an enumerator interface can perhaps best be expressed using C++ templates, as shown here:

```
template <class T> class IEnum : public IUnknown
{
public:
    virtual HRESULT Next(ULONG cElement, T* pElement,
        ULONG* pcFetched)=0;
    virtual HRESULT Skip(ULONG cElement)=0;
    virtual HRESULT Reset(void)=0;
    virtual HRESULT Clone(IEnum<T>** ppEnum)=0;
};
```

If you ever find yourself designing a set of custom interfaces in COM, you might need to enumerate objects of a certain type that you have defined. In this case, it is a good idea to design a custom enumerator interface using the same four methods and following the pattern set by standard enumerator interfaces.

The *IEnumConnectionPoints* Enumerator

Here is the IDL definition of the enumerator interface *IEnumConnectionPoints,* which is designed for enumerating connection point objects that implement the *IConnectionPoint* interface:

```
interface IEnumConnectionPoints : IUnknown
{
// Get me the next connection point(s).
    HRESULT Next(
        [in] ULONG cConnections,
        [out, size_is(cConnections), length_is(*pcFetched)]
            IConnectionPoint* ppCP,
        [out] ULONG* pcFetched);

// Skip the next connection point(s).
    HRESULT Skip([in] ULONG cConnections);

// Start at the beginning.
    HRESULT Reset(void);

// Give me a new enumerator object.
    HRESULT Clone([out] IEnumConnectionPoints** ppEnum);
}
```

The *CEnumConnectionPoints* class is publicly derived from *IEnumConnectionPoints* and thus implements the three methods of *IUnknown* plus the four methods of *IEnumConnectionPoints*. The *Next* method, shown in the following code, is the heart of every enumerator. It is called to retrieve one or more consecutive items from the enumeration. The first parameter of the *Next* method is always the number of items to be retrieved. The number of items actually retrieved from the enumerator is returned in the third parameter, a pointer to a long value allocated by the caller. This pointer must point to a valid address unless the client is retrieving only one item, in which case the third parameter may be *NULL*. The second parameter of the enumerator is used to retrieve the desired items from enumeration. In the case of the *IEnumConnectionPoints* interface, the *Next* method retrieves pointers to connection points:

```
HRESULT CEnumConnectionPoints::Next(ULONG cConnections,
    IConnectionPoint** rgpcn, ULONG* pcFetched)
{
    if(rgpcn == NULL)
        return E_POINTER;
    if(pcFetched == NULL && cConnections != 1)
        return E_INVALIDARG;
    if(pcFetched != NULL)
        *pcFetched = 0;

    while(m_iCur < NUM_CONNECTION_POINTS && cConnections > 0)
    {
        *rgpcn = m_rgpCP[m_iCur++];
        if(*rgpcn != NULL)
            (*rgpcn)->AddRef();
        if(pcFetched != NULL)
            (*pcFetched)++;
        cConnections--;
        rgpcn++;
    }
    return S_OK;
}
```

Recall from Chapter 2, "*IUnknown and IClassFactory*," that *IUnknown::AddRef* must be called whenever a method returns an interface pointer. Since the *IEnumConnectionPoints::Next* method hands out pointers to the *IConnectionPoint* interface, it must first call *AddRef*. The caller is responsible for calling *Release* through each pointer enumerated by this method.

The *IEnumXXX::Skip* method instructs the enumerator to skip a specified number of elements. If successful, subsequent calls to *IEnumXXX::Next* will return elements after those that were skipped. In the following implementation of *IEnumConnectionPoints::Skip*, the *m_iCur* member variable is incremented so that it correctly identifies the element following those that were skipped:

```
HRESULT CEnumConnectionPoints::Skip(ULONG cConnections)
{
    if(m_iCur + cConnections >= NUM_CONNECTION_POINTS)
        return S_FALSE;
    m_iCur += cConnections;
    return S_OK;
}
```

The *IEnum*XXX*::Reset* method orders the enumerator to position itself at the first element in the enumeration. It is interesting to note that enumerators are not required to return the same set of elements on each pass through the list, even if *Reset* is not called. For example, an enumerator for a list of files in a directory might continually change in response to changes to the underlying file system. In this sample, the implementation of *IEnumConnectionPoints::Reset* simply sets *m_iCur* to *0*, causing it to refer to the first element in the array:

```
HRESULT CEnumConnectionPoints::Reset()
{
    m_iCur = 0;
    return S_OK;
}
```

The *IEnum*XXX*::Clone* method creates and returns a pointer to an exact copy of the enumerator object, making it possible to record a point in an enumeration sequence, create a clone and work with that enumerator, and later return to the previous element in the first enumerator. In the implementation of the *IEnumConnectionPoints::Clone* method shown in the following code, the *new* operator is used to create a new instance of the *CEnumConnectionPoints* class. In the *CEnumConnectionPoints* constructor, a copy of the array of connection points referenced by *m_rgpCP* is created, and *AddRef* is called on each. The *m_iCur* member variable that references the current element in the enumerator is also copied, ensuring that the new enumerator has the same state as the current enumerator:

```
HRESULT CEnumConnectionPoints::Clone(IEnumConnectionPoints** ppEnum)
{
    if(ppEnum == NULL)
        return E_POINTER;
    *ppEnum = NULL;
```

(continued)

```
// Create the clone.
CEnumConnectionPoints* pNew = new CEnumConnectionPoints(
    m_pUnkRef, (void**)m_rgpCP);
if(pNew == NULL)
    return E_OUTOFMEMORY;

pNew->AddRef();
pNew->m_iCur = m_iCur;
*ppEnum = pNew;
return S_OK;
}
```

The Completed Implementation of *IConnectionPoint*

In the first half of this chapter, we coded a hobbled version of the *IConnection-Point* interface that implemented only the *Advise* and *Unadvise* methods. The time has come to implement the remaining three *IConnectionPoint* methods: *GetConnectionInterface, GetConnectionPointContainer,* and *EnumConnections. IConnectionPoint::GetConnectionInterface* returns the IID of the outgoing interface managed by the connection point. A client might call *GetConnectionInterface* to learn the IID of a connection point retrieved from the *IEnumConnectionPoints* enumerator. One possible implementation of *GetConnectionInterface* is shown here:

```
HRESULT CConnectionPoint::GetConnectionInterface(IID *pIID)
{
    if(pIID == NULL)
        return E_POINTER;
    *pIID = m_iid;
    return S_OK;
}
```

The *IConnectionPoint::GetConnectionPointContainer* method is even simpler. This function returns a pointer to the *IConnectionPointContainer* interface associated with the connection point. It exists to enable a client that happens to have a connection point to work backward to the connection point container. The following implementation of *GetConnectionPointContainer* simply calls *QueryInterface* in order to obtain the pointer. Conveniently, *QueryInterface* automatically calls *AddRef*.

```
HRESULT CConnectionPoint::GetConnectionPointContainer(
    IConnectionPointContainer** ppCPC)
{
    return m_pObj->QueryInterface(IID_IConnectionPointContainer,
        (void**)ppCPC);
}
```

236

The *IConnectionPoint::EnumConnections* method returns a pointer to the *IEnumConnections* interface, enabling a client to enumerate all the connections that exist on a connection point. The following code instantiates the *CEnumConnections* class that implements the *IEnumConnections* enumeration interface:

```
HRESULT CConnectionPoint::EnumConnections(IEnumConnections** ppEnum)
{
    *ppEnum = NULL;
    CONNECTDATA* pCD = new CONNECTDATA[m_cConn];
    for(int count1 = 0, count2 = 0; count1 < CCONNMAX; count1++)
        if(m_rgpUnknown[count1] != NULL)
        {
            pCD[count2].pUnk = (IUnknown*)m_rgpUnknown[count1];
            pCD[count2].dwCookie = m_rgnCookies[count1];
            count2++;
        }
    CEnumConnections* pEnum = new CEnumConnections(this,
        m_cConn, pCD);
    delete [] pCD;
    return pEnum->QueryInterface(IID_IEnumConnections,
        (void**)ppEnum);
}
```

Another Enumerator: *IEnumConnections*

The *IEnumConnections* interface is designed to enable a client to enumerate the known connections of a connection point. This information about each connection is encapsulated in the CONNECTDATA structure defined here:

```
typedef struct tagCONNECTDATA
{
    IUnknown *  pUnk;
    DWORD       dwCookie;
} CONNECTDATA;
```

The CONNECTDATA structure contains the *IUnknown* pointer to the connected sink and also the cookie value that identifies the connection returned by the *IConnectionPoint::Advise* method. The *IEnumConnections* interface defines the same four methods as any other COM enumerator: *Next, Skip, Reset,* and *Clone.* To avoid dragging you through the drudgery of another enumerator, the code for *IEnumConnections* has been omitted here; it can be found on the companion CD.

237

When to Use Connection Points

Connection points were designed as a flexible and extensible technique for enabling two-way communication between an object and its clients. The fundamental design of the connection points architecture was derived from that developed for use by controls destined to work with Visual Basic. As we have seen, Visual Basic has numerous requirements and issues to deal with when it comes to working with events fired by objects. While the connection points architecture was designed to make this feasible for Visual Basic, most applications do not have the stringent requirements of Visual Basic. Aside from the complexity inherent in the connection points model, this model can also be inefficient when used by remote components. To set up a single connection point requires a minimum of four round-trips, as shown in the following list. (It might help to refer back to Figure 6-3 on page 222 as you examine these steps.)

1. The client calls the connectable object's *IUnknown::QueryInterface* method to request a pointer to the *IConnectionPointContainer* interface.

2. The client calls the *IConnectionPointContainer::FindConnectionPoint* method to request a pointer to the *IOutGoing* connection point.

3. The client calls the *IConnectionPoint::Advise* method to provide the connectable object with a pointer to the *IUnknown* interface of its sink object.

4. The connectable object calls the client sink object's *IUnknown::QueryInterface* method to request a pointer to the *IOutGoing* interface.

Now the connectable object can call the methods of the *IOutGoing* interface implemented by the client's sink.

The four calls needed for a client to establish a relationship with a connectable object are not a significant performance problem when you are using in-process components. The connection points architecture was designed primarily for working with in-process components. The ActiveX controls that work with Visual Basic are always implemented as in-process components. When local or remote calls are involved, however, this overhead makes connection points less efficient. Of course, these four calls are required only once to establish the first outgoing method call. Subsequent outgoing calls require no special setup.

Thus, in the process of developing a component, careful consideration needs to be given to the choice of connection points as the vehicle to support two-way communication with clients. If the object will need to work with Visual Basic clients, whether as an ActiveX control or simply as a nonvisual COM object using Visual Basic's *WithEvents* keyword, connection points are required. If the object will need to work with Java clients via the *ConnectionPointCookie* class, connection points are required. If Visual Basic and Java compatibility are not a concern, developing a simple custom protocol through which the client will pass an interface pointer implemented by its sink to the component could work just as well and be far more efficient. Such a protocol might require only one round-trip to set up the two-way communication. As a model for such a design, you might examine the architecture of the standard *IDataObject* and *IAdviseSink* interfaces. Although the *IDataObject* and *IAdviseSink* interfaces were designed before the generic connection points architecture became available, they exemplify a good model on which to base a simpler, custom callback mechanism.

Type Information

The architecture of connection points and type information were developed together, and as we have seen, connection points as implemented by high-level languages such as Visual Basic and Java could not exist without the presence of type information. As we saw in Chapter 3, "Type Libraries and Language Integration," a type library is the binary form of an interface definition. The MIDL compiler, initially designed to generate proxy/stub code in C for programmers using Remote Procedure Calls (RPCs), has been extended by Microsoft to create type library files. MIDL does not contain all the code necessary to create a type library, however. Instead, Microsoft has defined and implemented COM interfaces that can do this job; MIDL is only a consumer of these interfaces. The two primary interfaces that MIDL uses to create type libraries are *ICreateTypeLib* and *ICreateTypeInfo*. Together these interfaces enable MIDL to generate a type library that describes practically any interface you might write in IDL. In addition to the two interfaces used to create type information, the *ITypeLib* and *ITypeInfo* interfaces implemented by COM enable applications to read type information from a type library.

Other programs besides the MIDL compiler use the *ICreateTypeLib* and *ICreateTypeInfo* interfaces. Visual Basic, for example, automatically generates a type library for any ActiveX component. So does Microsoft Visual J++. A Visual Basic or Java program can read the information stored in an existing type library by setting a reference to the TypeLib Information (tlbinf32.dll) component. To better understand the true structure and contents of a type library requires at least a cursory look at these interfaces. In the following section, we will use these interfaces and their associated methods to create a type library that exactly matches the type library produced by the MIDL compiler when it is fed the IDL file shown in Listing 6-2.

mylib.idl

```
import "unknwn.idl";

[ object, uuid(10000001-0000-0000-0000-000000000001),      // (6)
  oleautomation ]                                          // (7)
interface ISum                                             // (5)
    : IUnknown                                             // (12)
{
    HRESULT Sum(int x, int y, [out, retval] int* retval);  // (13)
}
[ uuid(10000003-0000-0000-0000-000000000001),              // (1)
  helpstring("Inside DCOM Component Type Library"),         // (4)
  version(1.0) ]                                            // (3)
library Component                                          // (2)
{
    importlib("stdole32.tlb");                             // (12)

    interface ISum;

    [ uuid(10000002-0000-0000-0000-000000000001) ]         // (9)
    coclass InsideDCOM                                     // (8)
    {
        [default]                                          // (11)
            interface ISum;                                // (10)
    }
};
```

Listing 6-2.
An IDL file containing library information that can be passed to the MIDL compiler to produce a type library.

Creating a Type Library at Run Time

Entering the exclusive world of the type library creation interfaces is possible if you know the magic words. Too many developers treat type libraries as a kind of black box that only the MIDL compiler knows how to create. It is both enlightening and interesting to investigate how MIDL goes about creating this information. *CreateTypeLib2* is the COM function called in order to create a type library and obtain a pointer to COM's implementation of the *ICreateTypeLib2* interface. In the following code fragment, a type library file named mylib.tlb is created:

```
// Create the type library file.
ICreateTypeLib2* pCreateTypeLib2;
CreateTypeLib2(SYS_WIN32, L"C:\\mylib.tlb", &pCreateTypeLib2);
```

With the pointer obtained from *CreateTypeLib2*, any of the *ICreateTypeLib2* methods can be called. The *ICreateTypeLib2::SetGuid* method is used to set the globally unique identifier (GUID) of an element in a type library, as shown in the following code.

N O T E : The numbers in parentheses in the comments in the following code fragments correspond to the numbers in the IDL file shown in Listing 6-2.

```
// (1) Set the library LIBID to
// {10000003-0000-0000-0000-000000000001}.
GUID LIBID_Component =
{0x10000003,0x0000,0x0000,{0x00,0x00,0x00,0x00,0x00,0x00,0x00,0x01}};
pCreateTypeLib2->SetGuid(LIBID_Component);
```

The *ICreateTypeLib2::SetName* method sets the name of our type library to *Component,* as shown in the following code. Note that this is not the name of the type library file but rather the name of the type information stored inside the file.

```
// (2) Set the library name to Component.
pCreateTypeLib2->SetName(L"Component");
```

ICreateTypeLib2::SetVersion is used to set the version numbers for the type description. The following code sets this value to *1.0*:

```
// (3) Set the library version number to 1.0.
pCreateTypeLib2->SetVersion(1, 0);
```

The *helpstring* attribute in the IDL corresponds to the *ICreateTypeLib2::SetDocString* method. The following code sets the *helpstring* attribute to "*Inside DCOM Component Type Library*":

```
// (4) Set helpstring to "Inside DCOM Component Type Library".
pCreateTypeLib2->SetDocString(L"Inside DCOM Component Type Library");
```

Now that the basic attributes of the type library have been configured, the *ICreateTypeLib2::CreateTypeInfo* method can be used to insert additional kinds of fundamental type information into a type library. The more important of these types are described in the table on the following page.

TYPEKIND Value	IDL Keyword	Description
TKIND_ALIAS	*typedef*	A type that is an alias for another type.
TKIND_COCLASS	*coclass*	A set of implemented component object interfaces.
TKIND_DISPATCH	*dispinterface*	A set of methods and properties that are accessible through *IDispatch::Invoke.* By default, dual interfaces return *TKIND_DISPATCH.*
TKIND_ENUM	*enum*	A set of enumerators.
TKIND_INTERFACE	*interface*	A type that has virtual functions, all of which are pure.
TKIND_MODULE	*module*	A module that can have only static functions and data (for example, a DLL).
TKIND_RECORD	*struct*	A structure with no methods.
TKIND_UNION	*union*	A union, all of whose members have an offset of *0.*
TKIND_MAX	*enum*	End of *enum* marker.

The values discussed in this table comprise the nine fundamental elements that can be described in a type library. The following code calls the *CreateTypeInfo* method to create the type information for an interface (*TKIND_INTERFACE*) named *ISum*. If successful, *CreateTypeInfo* returns a pointer to COM's implementation of the *ICreateTypeInfo* interface.

```
// (5) Create the ISum interface.
ICreateTypeInfo* pCreateTypeInfoInterface;
pCreateTypeLib2->CreateTypeInfo(L"ISum", TKIND_INTERFACE,
    &pCreateTypeInfoInterface);
```

Using the methods of *ICreateTypeInfo,* you can set the various attributes of the type information in much the same way as the *ICreateTypeLib2* interface operated on the type library as a whole. Here the *ICreateTypeInfo::SetGuid* method is called to set the GUID of the *ISum* interface:

```
// (6) Set the ISum IID to {10000001-0000-0000-0000-000000000001}.
IID IID_ISum =
{0x10000001,0x0000,0x0000,{0x00,0x00,0x00,0x00,0x00,0x00,0x00,0x01}};
pCreateTypeInfoInterface->SetGuid(IID_ISum);
```

The *ICreateTypeInfo::SetTypeFlags* method enables the configuration of numerous attributes of the type information being created. The following table lists some of the more important flags.

TYPEFLAGS Value	IDL Keyword	Description
TYPEFLAG- _FAPPOBJECT	*appobject*	A type description that describes an application object.
TYPEFLAG- _FCANCREATE	*default* (otherwise, use *noncreatable*)	Instances of this type can be created by *ITypeInfo::CreateInstance*.
TYPEFLAG- _FLICENSED	*licensed*	This type is licensed.
TYPEFLAG- _FHIDDEN	*hidden*	This type should not be displayed to browsers.
TYPEFLAG- _FCONTROL	*control*	This type is a control from which other types will be derived and should not be displayed to users.
TYPEFLAG- _FDUAL	*dual*	The types in this interface derive from *IDispatch* and are fully compatible with Automation.
TYPEFLAG- _FNONEXTENSIBLE	*nonextensible*	This interface cannot add members at run time.
TYPEFLAG- _FOLEAUTOMATION	*oleautomation*	The types used in this interface are fully compatible with Automation and can be displayed in an object browser. Specifying *dual* on an interface sets this flag automatically.
TYPEFLAG- _FRESTRICTED	*restricted*	The item on which this flag is specified is not accessible from high-level languages such as Visual Basic.
TYPEFLAG- _FAGGREGATABLE	*aggregatable*	The class supports aggregation.
TYPEFLAG- _FREPLACEABLE	*replaceable*	The interface is tagged as having default behaviors.

Because the *ISum* interface is fully Automation-compatible, the *TYPE-FLAG_FOLEAUTOMATION* flag is set using the *SetTypeFlags* method, as shown in the code on the following page. This flag has the additional benefit of causing the *LoadTypeLibEx* function to automatically set up type library marshaling for the *ISum* interface when the type library is registered. Type library marshaling is covered in more detail in Chapter 8, "DLL Surrogates and Executable Components."

```
// (7) Set the oleautomation flag.
pCreateTypeInfoInterface->SetTypeFlags(TYPEFLAG_FOLEAUTOMATION);
```

At this stage, the basic structure of the *ISum* interface is specified. Still missing from the type information for *ISum*, however, is the *Sum* method. Before we add this method, let's turn our attention to the COM class *InsideDCOM*. Using the pointer to the *ICreateTypeLib2* interface originally obtained from the call to *CreateTypeLib2*, the following code creates a new piece of type information, this time describing the COM class (*TKIND_COCLASS*) *InsideDCOM*:

```
// (8) Create the coclass InsideDCOM.
ICreateTypeInfo* pCreateTypeInfoCoClass;
pCreateTypeLib2->CreateTypeInfo(L"InsideDCOM", TKIND_COCLASS,
    &pCreateTypeInfoCoClass);
```

Following the familiar pattern, the *ICreateTypeInfo::SetGuid* method is called to set the GUID of the *InsideDCOM* class, as shown here:

```
// (9) Set the InsideDCOM CLSID to
// {10000002-0000-0000-0000-000000000001}.
CLSID CLSID_InsideDCOM =
{0x10000002,0x0000,0x0000,{0x00,0x00,0x00,0x00,0x00,0x00,0x00,0x01}};
pCreateTypeInfoCoClass->SetGuid(CLSID_InsideDCOM);
```

Now the class needs to be marked so that it can be created by clients using the *ITypeInfo::CreateInstance* method. Type libraries generated by MIDL automatically have this flag set, but when you are creating a type description in the manual fashion described here, the *SetTypeFlags* method must be called using the *TYPEFLAG_FCANCREATE* argument, as shown here:

```
// Specify that this coclass can be instantiated.
pCreateTypeInfoCoClass->SetTypeFlags(TYPEFLAG_FCANCREATE);
```

At this stage, the coclass *InsideDCOM* and the interface *ISum* have been defined. Currently, however, no relationship exists between the two. In order to express the fact that the coclass *InsideDCOM* implements the *ISum* interface, we need to insert the type description for *ISum* into that of *InsideDCOM*. The *ICreateTypeInfo::AddImplType* method does exactly this. As its second parameter, *AddImplType* requires a handle that identifies the type description, which is declared as an *HREFTYPE*. To obtain an *HREFTYPE*, you must first call the *ICreateTypeInfo::AddRefTypeInfo* method. This method, however, requires an *ITypeInfo* interface pointer. To obtain a pointer to COM's implementation of the *ITypeInfo* interface for *ISum*, we begin by calling *QueryInterface* to request a pointer to the *ITypeLib* interface. Using the *ITypeLib* interface pointer returned by *QueryInterface*, the following code calls the *ITypeLib::GetTypeInfo-OfGuid* method to obtain the type information describing the *ISum* interface:

```
// Get a pointer to the ITypeLib interface.
ITypeLib* pTypeLib;
pCreateTypeLib2->QueryInterface(IID_ITypeLib, (void**)&pTypeLib);

// Get a pointer to the ITypeInfo interface for ISum.
ITypeInfo* pTypeInfo;
pTypeLib->GetTypeInfoOfGuid(IID_ISum, &pTypeInfo);
```

With the *ITypeInfo* pointer at our disposal, we call the *ICreateTypeInfo-::AddRefTypeInfo* method to obtain the *HREFTYPE*. The *HREFTYPE* handle returned by *AddRefTypeInfo* enables us to call the *ICreateTypeInfo::AddImplType* method to declare that the *InsideDCOM* class implements the *ISum* interface, as shown here:

```
// Trade in the ITypeInfo pointer for an HREFTYPE.
HREFTYPE hRefTypeISum;
pCreateTypeInfoCoClass->AddRefTypeInfo(pTypeInfo, &hRefTypeISum);

// (10) Insert the ISum interface into the InsideDCOM coclass.
pCreateTypeInfoCoClass->AddImplType(0, hRefTypeISum);
```

The *ICreateTypeInfo::SetImplTypeFlags* method sets the attributes for an implemented or inherited interface of a type. This method can be used to set one or more of the flags listed in the following table.

IMPLTYPEFLAG Value	IDL Keyword	Description
IMPLTYPEFLAG-_FDEFAULT	*default*	The interface or *dispinterface* represents the default for the source or sink.
IMPLTYPEFLAG-_FSOURCE	*source*	This member of a coclass is called rather than implemented.
IMPLTYPEFLAG-_FRESTRICTED	*restricted*	This member should not be displayed or be programmable by users.
IMPLTYPEFLAG-_FDEFAULTVTABLE	*defaultvtbl*	Sinks receive events through the v-table.

The following code calls the *SetImplTypeFlags* method to set the default (*IMPLTYPEFLAG_FDEFAULT*) flag for the *ISum* interface in the *InsideDCOM* coclass. This call is important to languages such as Visual Basic that automatically connect the client with the default interface of any object. Note that MIDL automatically sets the default flag for the first unrestricted interface.

```
// (11) Specify ISum as the default interface in
// coclass InsideDCOM.
pCreateTypeInfoCoClass->SetImplTypeFlags(0, IMPLTYPEFLAG_FDEFAULT);
```

The next step in the creation of the type library is to express the fact that the *ISum* interface is derived from *IUnknown*. To do this, we have two choices: either define *IUnknown* using the methods of the *ICreateTypeInfo* interface as we did for *ISum* or load the existing type description of *IUnknown* from the Automation type library (stdole32.tlb) supplied by Microsoft. To make things easier and more standard, we'll opt for the latter. Access to the definition contained in the Automation type library is obtained via the *LoadRegTypeLib* function. The *ITypeLib* pointer returned by *LoadRegTypeLib* is used to call the *ITypeLib::GetTypeInfoOfGuid* method in order to retrieve a pointer to type information for the *IUnknown* interface, as shown here:

```
// Get a pointer to the ITypeLib interface for Automation.
ITypeLib* pTypeLibStdOle;
GUID GUID_STDOLE =
{0x00020430,0x00,0x00,0xC0,0x00,0x00,0x00,0x00,0x00,0x00,0x46};
LoadRegTypeLib(GUID_STDOLE, STDOLE_MAJORVERNUM, STDOLE_MINORVERNUM,
    STDOLE_LCID, &pTypeLibStdOle);

// Get a pointer to the ITypeInfo interface for IUnknown.
ITypeInfo* pTypeInfoUnknown;
pTypeLibStdOle->GetTypeInfoOfGuid(IID_IUnknown, &pTypeInfoUnknown);
```

Now after calling the *ICreateTypeInfo::AddRefTypeInfo* method to retrieve a handle to the type information, the *ICreateTypeInfo::AddImplType* method is called to declare that *ISum* derives from *IUnknown*, as shown here:

```
// (12) Declare that ISum is derived from IUnknown.
HREFTYPE hRefType;
pCreateTypeInfoInterface->AddRefTypeInfo(pTypeInfoUnknown, &hRefType);
pCreateTypeInfoInterface->AddImplType(0, hRefType);
```

The final piece of the type library is the *Sum* method of the *ISum* interface. Using the *ICreateTypeInfo* interface to manually describe methods is not tremendously enjoyable—it requires that you examine and describe every aspect of the method in the most exacting and detailed manner. In the following code, an array of three ELEMDESC structures is defined and initialized. The first two structures are declared as integers (*VT_INT*), and the third is declared as a pointer (*VT_PTR*), with special flags indicating that this is an *[out, retval]* parameter.

```
// Structures for the x, y, and retval parameters of the
// Sum method
TYPEDESC tdescParams = { 0 };
tdescParams.vt = VT_INT;

ELEMDESC myParams[3] = { 0 };
myParams[0].tdesc.vt = VT_INT;                      // x
myParams[0].tdesc.lptdesc = &tdescParams;
myParams[1].tdesc.vt = VT_INT;                      // y
myParams[1].tdesc.lptdesc = &tdescParams;
myParams[2].tdesc.vt = VT_PTR;                      // retval
myParams[2].tdesc.lptdesc = &tdescParams;
myParams[2].paramdesc.wParamFlags = PARAMFLAG_FRETVAL|PARAMFLAG_FOUT;
```

Now a FUNCDESC structure is allocated and initialized with a myriad of settings. The *Sum* method (*INVOKE_FUNC*) is declared as a pure virtual function (*FUNC_PUREVIRTUAL*) using the standard calling convention (*CC_STD-CALL*), which accepts three parameters (*cParams*) and returns an *HRESULT* (*VT_HRESULT*). Last the *ICreateTypeInfo::AddFuncDesc* method is called to add the *Sum* method to the *ISum* interface, as shown here:

```
// Additional data describing the Sum method and its return value
TYPEDESC tdescUser = { 0 };
FUNCDESC FuncDesc = { 0 };
FuncDesc.funckind = FUNC_PUREVIRTUAL;
FuncDesc.invkind = INVOKE_FUNC;
FuncDesc.callconv = CC_STDCALL;
FuncDesc.elemdescFunc.tdesc.vt = VT_HRESULT;
FuncDesc.elemdescFunc.tdesc.lptdesc = &tdescUser;
FuncDesc.cParams = 3;
FuncDesc.lprgelemdescParam = myParams;

// (13) Add the Sum method to the ISum interface.
pCreateTypeInfoInterface->AddFuncDesc(0, &FuncDesc);
```

To attach names to the *Sum* method and its parameters, the *ICreateType-Info::SetFuncAndParamNames* is called with an array of the names to be attached, as shown here:

```
// Set names for the Sum function and its parameters.
OLECHAR* Names[4] = { L"Sum", L"x", L"y", L"retval" };
pCreateTypeInfoInterface->SetFuncAndParamNames(0, Names, 4);
```

247

The *ICreateTypeInfo::LayOut* method is called to assign v-table offsets for virtual functions and instance offsets for per-instance data members, as shown here:

```
// Assign the v-table layout.

pCreateTypeInfoInterface->LayOut();
```

And without a call to the *ICreateTypeLib2::SaveAllChanges* method, all our efforts would have been for naught, since nothing would have been saved on the disk! This call is followed by calls to the *Release* method for all the objects accumulated during this exercise, as shown here:

```
// Save changes.
pCreateTypeLib2->SaveAllChanges();

// Release all references.
pTypeInfoUnknown->Release();
pTypeLibStdOle->Release();
pTypeInfo->Release();
pTypeLib->Release();
pCreateTypeLib2->Release();
pCreateTypeInfoInterface->Release();
pCreateTypeInfoCoClass->Release();
```

Once you have a basic understanding of how to create type libraries using the *ICreateTypeLib* and *ICreateTypeInfo* interfaces, you will have a much better understanding of the information contained in a type library. However, we certainly recommend that you consider using MIDL if your future component development plans call for a type library.

Obtaining Type Information

Up to now, this chapter has examined how type information can be synthesized at run time. By comparison, obtaining access to predefined type information is relatively easy. Normally, a client can find the type library of a COM class simply by looking in the registry. The TypeLib subkey, stored in the registry beneath the CLSID key, is where the type library identifier (LIBID) of the class is stored. With this LIBID, obtaining type information about the class is as simple as calling the *LoadRegTypeLib* function. However, not all objects have a CLSID and the complementary registry entries—for example, subobjects such as connection points do not have a CLSID. To obtain type information about such an object is impossible—unless the object supports the *IProvideClassInfo* interface. Objects that do not have a CLSID but still want to expose type information to their clients normally implement this interface. Adding support for the *IProvideClassInfo* interface is not particularly difficult. The lone method of this interface, *GetClassInfo*, is designed to retrieve type information of the class. Shown here is the *IProvideClassInfo* interface in IDL notation:

```
interface IProvideClassInfo : IUnknown
{
    // Get a pointer to the type information for this CLSID.
    HRESULT GetClassInfo([out] ITypeInfo** ppTI);
}
```

How the *GetClassInfo* method is implemented depends entirely on where the type information for the object is stored. If the type information is created dynamically, the method should simply return a pointer to the *ITypeInfo* interface. If the type information is available in a type library file, simply call *LoadRegTypeLib* and then call *ITypeLib::GetTypeInfoOfGuid*, as shown here:

```
HRESULT CInsideDCOM::GetClassInfo(ITypeInfo** pTypeInfo)
{
    ITypeLib* pTypeLib;
    LoadRegTypeLib(LIBID_Component, 1, 0, LANG_NEUTRAL, &pTypeLib);
    HRESULT hr = pTypeLib->GetTypeInfoOfGuid(CLSID_InsideDCOM,
        pTypeInfo);
    pTypeLib->Release();
    return hr;
}
```

Now the client can simply call *QueryInterface* for the *IProvideClassInfo* interface and follow that with a call to *IProvideClassInfo::GetClassInfo*. This is an equal opportunity interface: every COM object can expose *IProvideClassInfo* regardless of whether it has a CLSID. For objects with a CLSID, the *IProvideClassInfo* interface can represent a convenience for clients. It allows clients to use the standard *QueryInterface* mechanism instead of having to perform a registry lookup in order to locate the LIBID.

As a further improvement, the *IProvideClassInfo2* interface has been introduced; its definition is shown here:

```
interface IProvideClassInfo2 : IProvideClassInfo
{
    // Get the IID of this object's default outgoing interface.
    HRESULT GetGUID(
        [in]  DWORD dwGuidKind,
        [out] GUID * pGUID);
}
```

As you can see, this interface derives from *IProvideClassInfo*, adding only the *GetGUID* method. The *GetGUID* method is designed to make it quick and easy for a client to retrieve an object's default outgoing interface. The *dwGuidKind* parameter can be one of the values in the *GUIDKIND* enumeration. Currently, *GUIDKIND_DEFAULT_SOURCE_DISP_IID* is the only value defined. Using this value, the client requests the IID for the object's default outgoing *dispinterface*. Since the outgoing interfaces shown in this chapter are not based on *IDispatch*, officially we should return an error. But never mind that. Let's see how an implementation of *IProvideClassInfo2::GetGUID* might look:

```
HRESULT CInsideDCOM::GetGUID(DWORD dwGuidKind, GUID* pGUID)
{
    if(pGUID == NULL)
        return E_INVALIDARG;
    *pGUID = IID_IOutGoing;
    return S_OK;
}
```

CHAPTER SEVEN

Monikers and Structured Storage

Naming objects is a crucial aspect of any system. File systems are the most obvious objects for which naming matters, but many other types of objects are affected by naming. Because different developers typically work on different aspects of a system, the naming rules adopted for certain categories of objects can differ radically. COM proposes a standard and extensible way of naming objects throughout the system, called a *moniker*. A moniker is an object that identifies another object. Sometimes known as *intelligent names*, monikers can be used to name and activate other objects in the system.

Like other areas of COM, the COM namespace is rich and complex. Unlike other parts of COM, monikers have been slow to gain acceptance by developers both inside and outside of Microsoft. This situation is changing quickly, however, as monikers are now central to one new area of functionality in Microsoft Windows NT 5.0: the Active Directory. In this chapter, we explain why monikers are so important and show you how to take advantage of this technology in your designs.

Initializing Objects

In earlier chapters, we identified COM classes by their class identifier (CLSID) and instantiated COM objects by using the rather primitive *CoCreateInstance* function. *CoCreateInstance* is typically one of the first functions learned by programmers new to COM, and thus it tends to be overused until they gain experience with and insight into the richness of COM's namespace. *CoCreateInstance* is sometimes seen as the COM analogue of the *new* operator in C++. This parallel is further reinforced by the fact that *CoCreateInstance* is actually called by Visual Basic programs when the *New* keyword is applied to a COM class. Unfortunately, *CoCreateInstance* is a poor substitute for the richness provided by the *new* operator in C++. To demonstrate the limitations of *CoCreateInstance*, assume that you have defined a C++ class that computes prime numbers, as shown here:

```
class prime
{
public:
    prime(int starting_prime) : m_first(starting_number) { }
    int get_next_prime(void);

private:
    int m_first;
};
```

The constructor for this class accepts one argument, whose value becomes the starting prime number. Each call to the *get_next_prime* method returns a subsequent prime number, which implies the following usage:

```
prime* my_prime = new prime(7);      // Calls constructor
cout << my_prime->get_next_prime() << endl; // Displays 11
```

Now imagine that we have decided to turn the C++ prime class into a COM class that implements the *IPrime* interface. The *IPrime* interface, declared in the following code, will define the *GetNextPrime* method:

```
interface IPrime : IUnknown
{
    HRESULT GetNextPrime([out, retval] int* next_prime);
};
```

Noticeably absent from this interface definition is the constructor. Typically, the client program will call *CoCreateInstance* to instantiate the object, automatically invoking the constructor. Unfortunately, *CoCreateInstance* doesn't accept an extra argument for our constructor. As you know, *CoCreateInstance* is a high-level object creation function that is implemented using the *CoGetClassObject* function. The following pseudo-code demonstrates the implementation of *CoCreateInstance*:

```
HRESULT CoCreateInstance(REFCLSID rclsid, IUnknown* pUnkOuter,
    DWORD dwClsContext, REFIID riid, void** ppv)
{
    IClassFactory* pClassFactory;
    CoGetClassObject(rclsid, dwClsContext, NULL,
        IID_IClassFactory, (void**)&pClassFactory);
    pClassFactory->CreateInstance(pUnkOuter, riid, ppv);
    pClassFactory->Release();
}
```

Class Objects

In most contexts, you can substitute the phrase *class factory* with *class object*, but this is not always the case. A class factory is an object that implements the two methods of the *IClassFactory* interface: *CreateInstance* and *LockServer*. This implementation enables *CoCreateInstance* to easily instantiate a COM class. However, notice that the function used by *CoCreateInstance* in the preceding code to obtain a pointer to the *IClassFactory* interface is named *CoGetClassObject*, not *CoGetClassFactory*. In fact, *CoCreateInstance* passes the *IID_IClassFactory* interface identifier to *CoGetClassObject* to ensure that the interface pointer received can be used to call the *IClassFactory::CreateInstance* method.

A class object is a powerful abstraction that can be used to implement a custom activation interface instead of, or in addition to, *IClassFactory*. Therefore, while a class factory (an object that implements *IClassFactory*) can be called a class object, a class object is not necessarily a class factory. Since the *IClassFactory::CreateInstance* method is what really instantiates most COM objects, it, not *CoCreateInstance*, is the true analogue of the *new* operator. The declaration of the *CreateInstance* method in the following code clearly shows that no parameter exists that enables you to pass an argument to a class's constructor. By creating a class object with a custom activation interface (not *IClassFactory*), we effectively redefine (or overload, in C++-speak) COM's *new* operator for a particular COM class.

```
HRESULT IClassFactory::CreateInstance(IUnknown* pUnkOuter,
    REFIID riid, void** ppvObject);
```

Custom Activation Interfaces

Defining a custom activation interface and implementing that interface in a class object would allow us to pass extra arguments for the constructor, as expressed by the *IPrimeFactory* interface shown here:

```
interface IPrimeFactory : IUnknown
{
    HRESULT CreatePrime(
        [in] int starting_prime,
        [out, retval] IPrime** ppPrime);
};
```

A class object implementing the *IPrimeFactory* interface will work as well with the *CoGetClassObject* function called by the client as with the *CoRegisterClassObject* function called by the component. The only requirement of both functions is that the class object implement *IUnknown*, not *IClassFactory*. However, because the *CoCreateInstance* helper function depends on the existence of the *IClassFactory* interface in a class object, it will not work with a class object that does not implement this interface. Thus, a client program will likely access the object by using the *CoGetClassObject* function, as shown here:

```
// Calling CoGetClassObject but requesting IPrimeFactory,
// not IClassFactory
IPrimeFactory* pPrimeFactory;
CoGetClassObject(CLSID_Prime, CLSCTX_SERVER, NULL,
    IID_IPrimeFactory, (void**)&pPrimeFactory);

// Calling the IPrimeFactory::CreatePrime interface and
// passing 7 to the constructor
IPrime* pPrime;
pPrimeFactory->CreatePrime(7, &pPrime);
pPrimeFactory->Release();

// Now we have a Prime object.
int next_prime;
pPrime->GetNextPrime(&next_prime);
cout << next_prime << endl; // Displays 11
```

While this mechanism works well for C++ programs, a Visual Basic application will have a hard time instantiating the *Prime* object because its *New* keyword will result in a call to *CoCreateInstance*. Since *CoCreateInstance* depends on finding an implementation of *IClassFactory*, it will not work with the *Prime* object. While doing so is a theoretical possibility, calling *CoGetClassObject* directly from Visual Basic is not something most Visual Basic programmers would entertain.

Monikers (One More Time)

After following our analysis to this point, you must now have two questions on your mind:

■ Why go to the trouble of creating a class object that implements a custom activation interface if Visual Basic refuses to work with it?

■ How on earth is this related to monikers?

Monikers are COM's answer to the first question, and consequently, they also provide the answer to the second question.

As mentioned, a moniker is an object that names another object. An object might say, "I have been named by a moniker, therefore I am." Names are used throughout Microsoft Windows to identify everything from files to event objects. The difficulty with this approach is that every type of object has its own naming rules. Monikers are designed to enable all objects to deal with naming through a single, standard interface: *IMoniker*. COM provides several implementations of the *IMoniker* interface, described in the following table. Notice that moniker objects are not created by calling *CoCreateInstance* but instead offer their own custom creation function because most monikers require extra information about the object they name.

Moniker Type	Creation Function	Purpose
File moniker	*CreateFileMoniker*	A file moniker acts as a wrapper for the pathname of a file.
Item moniker	*CreateItemMoniker*	An item moniker can be used to identify an object contained in another object.
Pointer moniker	*CreatePointerMoniker*	A pointer moniker identifies an object that can exist only in the active or running state.
Anti-moniker	*CreateAntiMoniker*	An anti-moniker is the inverse of another moniker; when the two are combined, they obliterate each other.
Composite moniker	*CreateGenericComposite*	A composite moniker is composed of other monikers.
Class moniker	*CreateClassMoniker*	A class moniker acts as a wrapper for the CLSID of a COM class.
URL moniker	*CreateURLMoniker*	A URL moniker represents and manages a Uniform Resource Locator (URL).

In many cases, one of the system monikers implemented by COM—or some combination of those monikers—will suffice for the purpose of naming objects. At other times, only a *custom moniker* will do. A custom moniker is an object that implements the *IMoniker* interface. Contrary to popular belief, implementing the *IMoniker* interface is not all that difficult.

The *IMoniker* Interface

The myth that the *IMoniker* interface is difficult to implement probably arises from the number of methods defined in the interface. The *IMoniker* interface itself has 15 methods. To make moniker objects persistent, the *IMoniker* interface is derived from the *IPersistStream* interface (4 methods), which is derived from the *IPersist* interface (1 method), which is in turn derived from the *IUnknown* interface (3 methods). That makes a grand total of 23 methods required to implement a custom moniker. This interface hierarchy is illustrated in Figure 7-1.

Figure 7-1.
The IMoniker *interface hierarchy.*

In practice, not all the methods will be needed by all monikers. Luckily, many of the *IMoniker* methods were designed primarily for file monikers and thus might not be applicable to a custom moniker. In addition, not all monikers need to support persistence, which means that the methods of the *IPersist* and *IPersistStream* interfaces might simply return *E_NOTIMPL*. The system-supplied pointer moniker operates in this fashion.

A warning flag should be raised in your mind whenever several methods of an interface implementation return *E_NOTIMPL*. Either the implementation is incomplete or certain methods of that interface are not applicable. If, as is the case with pointer monikers, certain methods of an interface simply are not relevant to a specific implementation, this might indicate that the interface was not designed properly. Monikers do not take advantage of the richness offered by the *IUnknown::QueryInterface* method to determine what capabilities are offered by a particular implementation. Instead, every implementation of the *IMoniker* interface is forced to provide an implementation of the *IPersistStream* and *IPersist* interfaces, even if those methods do nothing more than return *E_NOTIMPL*. This design flaw is more annoyance than limitation, but it does illustrate the importance of careful interface design.

The following table lists the methods of the *IMoniker* interface.

IMoniker Method	Description
BindToObject	Binds to the object named by the moniker
BindToStorage	Binds to the object's storage
Reduce	Reduces the moniker to its simplest form
ComposeWith	Combines the moniker with another moniker to create a composite moniker (a collection of monikers stored in left-to-right sequence)
Enum	Enumerates component monikers
IsEqual	Compares the moniker with another moniker
Hash	Returns a hash value
IsRunning	Checks whether the object is running
GetTimeOfLastChange	Returns time the object was last changed
Inverse	Returns the inverse of the moniker
CommonPrefixWith	Finds the prefix that the moniker has in common with another moniker
RelativePathTo	Constructs a relative moniker between this moniker and another
GetDisplayName	Returns the display name
ParseDisplayName	Converts a display name to a moniker
IsSystemMoniker	Checks whether the moniker is one of the system-supplied types

Bind Contexts

Roughly half of *IMoniker*'s methods take a pointer to a *bind context* as an argument. A bind context is an object that implements the *IBindCtx* interface and contains information about a moniker *binding operation*. A binding operation consists of the steps needed to connect a moniker with the object that it names. In some situations, a bind context enables certain optimizations to occur during the binding of composite monikers. To create a bind context for use with a moniker, simply call the *CreateBindCtx* function, as shown here:

```
IBindCtx* pBindCtx;
CreateBindCtx(0, &pBindCtx);
```

The real heart of the *IMoniker* interface is the *BindToObject* method. This method enables a moniker to bind to the object it names. A client application might call this method as shown in the code on the following page. Notice the use of the *pBindCtx* parameter passed to the *IMoniker::BindToObject* method.

```
IMyInterface* pMyInterface;
pMoniker->BindToObject(pBindCtx, NULL, IID_IMyInterface,
    (void**)&pMyInterface);
```

Once a moniker is bound to the underlying object it names, a pointer to the requested interface of that object is returned to the client application. The client may now proceed to use the object in the typical fashion by calling any methods of the requested interface. When the client has finished working with the object, the object must be released, as must the bind context and the moniker itself.

To reify monikers without an explicit binding context, Microsoft introduced the helper function *BindMoniker*. The *BindMoniker* function takes an *IMoniker* interface pointer and binds that moniker to the object it names. The bind context required to perform the binding operation is automatically acquired by the *BindMoniker* function. In the following code fragment, *pMoniker* is a pointer to a moniker that is being bound to the underlying object it names. Notice the explicit use of a bind context:

```
IBindCtx* pClassBindCtx;
CreateBindCtx(0, &pClassBindCtx);
pMoniker->BindToObject(pClassBindCtx, NULL, IID_IUnknown,
    (void**)&pUnknown);
pClassBindCtx->Release();
```

The functionally equivalent code shown here uses the *BindMoniker* helper function, but it is significantly easier to read:

```
BindMoniker(pMoniker, 0, IID_IUnknown, (void**)&pUnknown);
```

The *MkParseDisplayName* Function

A string, called a *display name,* can be used to represent most monikers. For example, a file moniker's display name takes the form of a path, such as C:\My Documents\Story.doc, whereas a class moniker supports strings in the form *clsid:10000013-0000-0000-0000-0000000000001.* The *IMoniker::GetDisplayName* method can be used to obtain this string; the *IMoniker::ParseDisplayName* method can convert a string form of a moniker to a moniker object. Both *GetDisplayName* and *ParseDisplayName* are methods of the *IMoniker* interface, which means that you must already have a moniker object of the desired type in order to call either method. This is where the *MkParseDisplayName* function comes in, as declared in the following code:

```
HRESULT MkParseDisplayName(IBindCtx* pbc, LPCWSTR szDisplayName,
    ULONG* pchEaten, IMoniker** ppmk);
```

Technically speaking, *MkParseDisplayName* converts a string to a moniker that identifies the object named by that string. This process is similar to calling the *IMoniker::ParseDisplayName* method, except that it does not require that you have a moniker to begin with—a string is sufficient. The use of a string is possible because DCOM introduced an extensible moniker namespace, and the *MkParseDisplayName* function is the entry point into that namespace. A custom moniker can hook into the namespace and provide any custom naming functionality you want.

MkParseDisplayName accepts two primary string formats. The first format is a file path, such as C:\My Documents\Letter.doc. *MkParseDisplayName* has hard-coded support for file monikers and thus knows that any file path should be converted to a file moniker. The second string format is the more general and thus the more important of the two supported formats. In this format, *MkParseDisplayName* accepts any string in the form *ProgID:ObjectName*, where *ProgID* is a registered program identifier. This architecture allows anyone to write a custom moniker that hooks into COM's namespace simply by virtue of creating a programmatic identifier (Prog ID) entry in the registry.

The following steps are executed whenever *MkParseDisplayName* encounters a string that has the *ProgID:ObjectName* format:

1. The ProgID is converted to a CLSID using the *CLSIDFromProgID* function. The result is the CLSID of the moniker.

2. *CoGetClassObject* is called to instantiate the moniker.

3. *IUnknown::QueryInterface* is called to request the *IParseDisplayName* interface.

4. The *IParseDisplayName::ParseDisplayName* method is called to parse the string passed to *MkParseDisplayName*.

5. Inside the moniker's *IParseDisplayName::ParseDisplayName* method, a moniker that names the object identified by the string is created.

6. The resulting *IMoniker* pointer is returned to the client.

For example, if the string *"Hello:Maya"* is passed to *MkParseDisplayName*, the HKEY_CLASSES_ROOT section of the registry is searched for the ProgID *Hello*. If *Hello* is found, the CLSID subkey below the ProgID is used to locate and load the moniker. The moniker's *IParseDisplayName::ParseDisplayName* method will then be called upon to create a moniker object that names the *Maya* object. Figure 7-2 on the following page shows the registry entries involved in this hypothetical example; the numbered labels simply indicate the order in which the information is obtained from the registry.

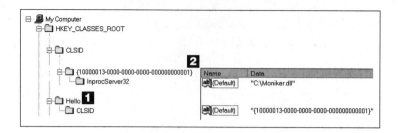

Figure 7-2.
The steps to locate a moniker from a ProgID.

The great thing about *MkParseDisplayName* is that Visual Basic programmers already know and love this function. Well actually, most Visual Basic programmers know the *MkParseDisplayName* function by a different moniker—they call it *GetObject*. Visual Basic's *GetObject* function takes a string and internally calls *MkParseDisplayName* to obtain a moniker. Then *GetObject* calls the *IMoniker::BindToObject* method of the moniker to obtain a pointer to the object requested by the Visual Basic programmer in the string passed to *GetObject*. C++ pseudocode for this portion of Visual Basic's *GetObject* function is shown in the following code. Note that the *GetObject* function has additional functionality, designed primarily for file monikers, which is not discussed here:

```
IUnknown* GetObject(LPCOLESTR szDisplayName)
{
    // Create the bind context.
    IBindCtx* pBindCtx = 0;
    CreateBindCtx(0, &pBindCtx);

    // Call MkParseDisplayName with the user's string.
    ULONG chEaten;
    IMoniker* pMoniker;
    hr = MkParseDisplayName(pBindCtx, szDisplayName, &chEaten,
        &pMoniker);

    // Call IMoniker::BindToObject to get the user's object.
    IUnknown* pUnknown = 0;
    pMoniker->BindToObject(pBindCtx, NULL, IID_IUnknown,
        (void**)&pUnknown);

    // Release stuff.
    pMoniker->Release();
    pBindCtx->Release();
```

```
    // Return a pointer to the class object's IUnknown.
    return pUnknown;
}
```

COM offers C++ programmers a similar helper function named *CoGet-Object*, which, like the *BindMoniker* helper function, obviates the need for an explicit binding context. In fact, all of the preceding code could be reduced to a single call to the *CoGetObject* function, as shown here:

```
IUnknown* GetObject(LPCOLESTR szDisplayName)
{
    // Convert a display name to a moniker,
    // and then bind to the object.
    CoGetObject(szDisplayName, 0, IID_IUnknown, (void**)&pUnknown);

    // Return a pointer to the class object's IUnknown.
    return pUnknown;
}
```

The Class Moniker

Although monikers were originally developed to enable OLE to deal with objects linked to a compound document in a standard way, today monikers are important for different reasons altogether. The class moniker is a system moniker implemented as part of COM, and it represents one of the most important modern implementations of the *IMoniker* interface. The genius of the class moniker is its utter simplicity: a class moniker wraps the CLSID of a COM class. Thus, a class moniker enables a client application, using the standard *IMoniker* interface, to reference any COM class identified by a CLSID. In fact, the class moniker is so simple that in most cases its implementation of the *IMoniker::BindToObject* function simply calls *CoGetClassObject*, as shown here:

```
HRESULT CClassMoniker::BindToObject(IBindCtx *pbc,
    IMoniker *pmkToLeft, REFIID riidResult, void **ppvResult)
{
    BIND_OPTS2 bopts;
    bopts.cbStruct = sizeof(bopts);
    pbc->GetBindOptions(&bopts);
    if(pmkToLeft == NULL)
        return CoGetClassObject(m_clsid, bopts.dwClassContext,
            0, riidResult, ppvResult);

    // Code to deal with moniker to the left...
```

(continued)

```
    // Since a composite moniker is a collection of other
    // monikers stored in left-to-right sequence, there
    // might be a moniker to the left of this class moniker.
}
```

Using the class moniker through *MkParseDisplayName,* you can reference any object based on its CLSID and then activate it by calling the *IMoniker::BindToObject* method. This method can be used instead of the more standard activation sequence of *CoGetClassObject* followed by *IClassFactory::CreateInstance.* The class moniker works for the same reasons as the imaginary *Hello* moniker described earlier; no special support for class monikers is built into the *MkParseDisplayName* function.

When a string in the form *clsid:10000013-0000-0000-0000-000000000001* is passed to the *MkParseDisplayName* function, the *clsid* program identifier is searched for in the registry. Of course, we all know about the HKEY_CLASSES-_ROOT\CLSID section of the registry—after all, this is one of the most important areas in which COM classes are registered. To the *MkParseDisplayName* function, however, HKEY_CLASSES_ROOT\CLSID is just another ProgID in the registry. Once located, it opens the HKEY_CLASSES_ROOT\CLSID\clsid subkey, which contains the actual CLSID of the class moniker.

Using a tool such as the registry editor, this clsid subkey will be visible as the final entry in the HKEY_CLASSES_ROOT\CLSID section of the registry, listed after all of the true class identifiers. The CLSID of the class moniker can be searched for in HKEY_CLASSES_ROOT\CLSID\{0000031A-0000-0000-C000-000000000046}, where the InprocServer32 key has the value ole32.dll, informing us that the class moniker is implemented as part of ole32.dll. This neat setup is what makes class monikers work.

Once a moniker has been returned to the client, it can immediately bind to the underlying object using the *IMoniker::BindToObject* method. The following code uses *MkParseDisplayName* to obtain the moniker and then, by binding the moniker to the named object, obtains a pointer to the *Prime* class object. Using the custom activation interface implemented by the class object, we can create the *Prime* object and then call its *GetNextPrime* method. Last all the interface pointers must be released.

```
// We always need a bind context.
IBindCtx* pBindCtx;
CreateBindCtx(0, &pBindCtx);

// Convert the string to a moniker.
ULONG eaten;
IMoniker* pMoniker;
OLECHAR string[] = L"clsid:10000013-0000-0000-0000-000000000001";
MkParseDisplayName(pBindCtx, string, &eaten, &pMoniker);
```

```
// Bind the moniker to the named object.
IPrimeFactory* pPrimeFactory;
pMoniker->BindToObject(pBindCtx, NULL, IID_IPrimeFactory,
    (void**)&pPrimeFactory);

// Use the custom class object to create a Prime object.
IPrime* pPrime;
pPrimeFactory->CreatePrime(7, &pPrime);

// Now we have a Prime object.
int next_prime;
pPrime->GetNextPrime(&next_prime);
cout << next_prime << endl; // Displays 11

// Release all.
pPrimeFactory->Release();
pPrime->Release();
pBindCtx->Release();
pMoniker->Release();
```

By this time, you are almost certainly wondering what the advantage of using *MkParseDisplayName* and *IMoniker::BindToObject* is, compared with simply calling *CoGetClassObject*. Now that we know about the class moniker as well as how Visual Basic's *GetObject* function works, we can combine this knowledge to make it relatively trivial for an application written in Visual Basic to access the custom activation interface implemented by the *Prime* class object.

The following sample code uses the *GetObject* function to create a class moniker that names the desired class object. Note that Visual Basic can access any custom activation interface so long as it makes use of Automation-compatible types. Interestingly, this restriction means that *IClassFactory* is not accessible to Visual Basic programmers other than through the *New* keyword or the *Create-Object* function, both of which call *CoCreateInstance*.

```
Dim myPrimeFactory As IPrimeFactory
Dim myPrime As IPrime

' Call MkParseDisplayName.
Set myPrimeFactory = _
    GetObject("clsid:10000013-0000-0000-0000-000000000001")

' Call IPrimeFactory::CreatePrime.
Set myPrime = myPrimeFactory.CreatePrime(7)

' Call IPrime::GetNextPrime.
Print myPrime.GetNextPrime  ' Displays 11
```

Managing the Lifetime of an Executable Component: *IExternalConnection*

Actually implementing a custom class object is not difficult. A greater problem is the difficulty of managing the lifetime of an EXE component whose class objects do not support the *IClassFactory* interface. In most cases, components are structured in such a way that a client holding a reference only to a class object is not sufficient to keep the component process running. The following code shows in boldface how the *IUnknown::Release* call destroys the object, thereby invoking the destructor, which sets a global event and finally causes the component to exit:

```
ULONG CPrime::Release()
{
    unsigned cRef = InterlockedDecrement(&m_cRef);
    if(cRef != 0)
        return cRef;
    delete this;
    return 0;
}

CPrime::~CPrime()
{
    if(CoReleaseServerProcess() == 0)
        SetEvent(g_hEvent);
}

void main(int argc, char** argv)
{
    // Initialization and CoRegisterClassObject omitted.

    // Create the event to wait for.
    g_hEvent = CreateEvent(NULL, FALSE, FALSE, NULL);

    // Now wait for SetEvent...
    WaitForSingleObject(g_hEvent, INFINITE);

    // Event set. Exit now.
    CloseHandle(g_hEvent);
    CoRevokeClassObject(dwRegister);
    pPrimeFactory->Release();
    CoUninitialize();
}
```

The difficulty arises when the client releases a pointer to an object but doesn't release a pointer to that object's class object. The client thinks that retaining an open pointer to the class object means that the server will re-main running. At some later point, the client might want to use that class object pointer to create new instances of the actual object. This problem is illustrated in the following code sequence; the release of the *Prime* object is shown in boldface:

```
// Get the PrimeFactory class object.
IPrimeFactory* pPrimeFactory;
CoGetClassObject(CLSID_Prime, CLSCTX_LOCAL_SERVER, NULL,
    IID_IPrimeFactory, (void**)&pPrimeFactory);

// Use the custom class object to create a Prime object.
IPrime* pPrime;
pPrimeFactory->CreatePrime(7, &pPrime);

// Use the Prime object here...
int next_prime;
pPrime->GetNextPrime(&next_prime);

// Release the Prime object.
pPrime->Release();

// Give the component a chance to exit.
Sleep(1000);

// Use pPrimeFactory to create another Prime object.
// Unfortunately, the component has already exited!
pPrimeFactory->CreatePrime(7, &pPrime);
pPrime->GetNextPrime(&next_prime);
```

Typically, COM circumnavigates this problem by automatically calling the *IClassFactory::LockServer(TRUE)* method when the first pointer is marshaled to a client. This call forces the component to keep running until the correspond-ing *IClassFactory::LockServer(FALSE)* call is made, which COM does automatically after the final client disconnects. Notice that COM's solution to this problem relies on the implementation of the *IClassFactory* interface in the class object. Our class object, however, implements the *IPrimeFactory* interface and not *IClassFactory*. Thus, a class object that does not implement the *IClassFactory* interface must correctly manage its own lifetime.

When an executable component calls *CoRegisterClassObject*, COM does not immediately marshal the interface pointer. Instead, COM calls the *IUnknown-::AddRef* method on the class object and then stores the pointer in an internal class object lookup table. Only when a client calls *CoGetClassObject* does COM find the interface pointer in the lookup table and then marshal the interface pointer back to the client, where it is subsequently unmarshaled. Since each marshaling operation represents a new client, you need hooks into this marshaling mechanism only to correctly control the lifetime of an executable component. This is where the *IExternalConnection* interface comes in—offering complete lifetime control in COM. The interface has only two methods, as shown here in IDL notation:

```
interface IExternalConnection : IUnknown
{
    DWORD AddConnection
    (
        [in] DWORD extconn,
        [in] DWORD reserved
    );

    DWORD ReleaseConnection
    (
        [in] DWORD extconn,
        [in] DWORD reserved,
        [in] BOOL  fLastReleaseCloses
    );
}
```

Correctly implementing the *IExternalConnection* interface in a custom class object can prevent the component from exiting prematurely. When an interface pointer is first marshaled from the component to the client, COM calls *IUnknown::QueryInterface* to request the *IExternalConnection* interface from the class object. Most class objects do not implement this interface, and thus COM takes default action. COM's default implementation of *IExternalConnection* first queries for the *IClassFactory* interface and, if found, proceeds to call the *IClassFactory::LockServer* method as discussed earlier in this section.

Responding affirmatively to the *QueryInterface* call with a valid pointer to an implementation of the *IExternalConnection* interface causes COM to make calls to your *IExternalConnection::AddConnection* and *IExternalConnection::ReleaseConnection* methods. COM calls the *AddConnection* method whenever an interface pointer is marshaled to a client; the *ReleaseConnection* method is called when the pointer is released. The *extconn* parameter passed to the *AddConnection* and *ReleaseConnection* methods specifies the type of connection being added or released. The following table lists the valid values for this parameter. Currently, only the *EXTCONN_STRONG* value is used, indicating that the external connection must keep the object alive until all strong external connections are cleared using the *IExternalConnection::ReleaseConnection* method.

Connection Type	Description
EXTCONN_STRONG	Strong connection
EXTCONN_WEAK	Weak connection (table, container)
EXTCONN_CALLABLE	Table vs. callable connection

By implementing *IExternalConnection,* an object can obtain a true count of external connections. In this way, we can ensure that a client retaining only a reference to a class object will be sufficient to keep the component alive. Here is a relatively standard implementation of *IExternalConnection's* two methods:

```
DWORD CPrimeFactory::AddConnection(DWORD extconn,
    DWORD dwreserved)
{
    if(extconn & EXTCONN_STRONG)
        return CoAddRefServerProcess();
    return 0;
}

DWORD CPrimeFactory::ReleaseConnection(DWORD extconn,
    DWORD dwreserved, BOOL fLastReleaseCloses)
{
    if(CoReleaseServerProcess() == 0)
    {
        // No client references exist at all!
        // OK to exit.
        InitiateComponentShutdown();
        return 0;
    }
    return 1;
}
```

Marvelous Moniker: Improving the Class Moniker

The class moniker is powerful in its own right, to the point of offering Visual Basic programmers access to custom activation interfaces implemented by class objects, but it is missing one important piece of functionality: DCOM! As we've seen, the class moniker takes a string in the form *clsid:10000013-0000-0000-0000-000000000001* and converts it to a moniker after performing a lookup in the local registry. The class moniker would be much more powerful if it could be supplied with a string in the form *host:myserver!clsid:10000013-0000-0000-0000-000000000001.* (Note that an exclamation point [!] is typically used to delineate the sections of a composite moniker.) This form would enable us to instantiate a moniker object that named a COM class on another computer. Imagine the power of a Visual Basic program that could pass a magic string to the *GetObject* function that would provide access to any class on any machine!

Although Microsoft does not currently provide this functionality in the system-supplied class moniker, the developers at Microsoft did consider the possibility that other developers might want to extend the class moniker by adding the capability to name classes on other machines. To this end, the class moniker is aware that it might have another moniker to its left. If it is told that such a moniker exists, the class moniker attempts to determine whether the moniker to its left implements the *IClassActivator* interface. The *IClassActivator* interface is a hook that lets you modify the default behavior of the class moniker. Although no implementation of the *IClassActivator* interface currently exists in a system-supplied moniker, it is possible that in the future Microsoft will provide an implementation of this interface. The *IClassActivator* interface is shown here in IDL notation:

```
interface IClassActivator : IUnknown
{
    HRESULT GetClassObject(
        [in] REFCLSID rclsid,
        [in] DWORD dwClassContext,
        [in] LCID locale,
        [in] REFIID riid,
        [out, iid_is(riid)] void **ppv);
}
```

Because this functionality is not currently available in the system, let's implement a custom moniker that provides the functionality needed to redirect the class moniker to another machine. To create a custom moniker, you generally begin with a standard in-process component. The object will be a moniker, so it must implement the *IMoniker* interface, which includes the methods of *IPersistStream* and *IPersist*, as well as *IUnknown*. If the moniker is to be accessible via the *MkParseDisplayName* function, it must have a registered ProgID. Since the desired display name of the moniker is *host:myserver!clsid:????????-????-????-????-????????????*, the registered ProgID must be *host*. Note that ProgIDs are not case sensitive. The registration procedure for this moniker, shown in the following code, creates the correct registry entries:

```
HRESULT __stdcall DllRegisterServer()
{
    // The ProgID host must be registered
    // in order for the moniker to work.
    return RegisterServer("moniker.dll",
```

```
CLSID_MarvelousMoniker, "Marvelous Moniker",
"Host", "Host", NULL);
}
```

With the registration in place, all calls to the *MkParseDisplayName* function that begin with the string *Host* will be directed to the CLSID of the moniker (*CLSID_MarvelousMoniker*). The class object of the moniker is then obtained using *CoGetClassObject*, and *QueryInterface* is called to determine whether the moniker's class object implements the *IParseDisplayName* interface. Thus, the class object of a moniker typically implements only the *IParseDisplayName* activation interface; there is no need to implement *IClassFactory*. The *IParseDisplayName* interface is defined for the specific purpose of enabling *MkParseDisplayName* to load a moniker and request that it parse its own display name, since quite obviously *MkParseDisplayName* is a general function and doesn't have any information about the string format of a specific custom moniker. The *IParseDisplayName* interface is shown here in IDL notation:

```
interface IParseDisplayName : IUnknown
{
    HRESULT ParseDisplayName
    (
        [in, unique] IBindCtx *pbc,
        [in] LPOLESTR pszDisplayName,
        [out] ULONG *pchEaten,
        [out] IMoniker **ppmkOut
    );
}
```

The *IParseDisplayName* interface has only one method: *ParseDisplayName*. The first moniker to be instantiated by *MkParseDisplayName* is handed the entire string provided by the caller. Its job is to digest as much of the string as possible and return a moniker that names the object specified in the string. The following code shows the marvelous moniker's implementation of the *IParseDisplayName::ParseDisplayName* method. This method simply parses the display name into its two components: the host name and the CLSID. These values are stored in the moniker's member variables for later use during the binding operation.

```
HRESULT CClassObject::ParseDisplayName(IBindCtx *pbc,
    LPOLESTR pszDisplayName, ULONG *pchEaten,
    IMoniker **ppmkOut)
{
    // Instantiate the moniker.
    CMarvyMoniker* pCMarvyMoniker = new CMarvyMoniker();
```

(continued)

269

```
        // Parse and check display name;
        // it must have the following format:
        // host:hostname!clsid:????????-????-????-????-????????????
        if(_wcsicmp(wcstok(pszDisplayName, L":"), L"host") == 0)
        {
            pCMarvyMoniker->m_CoServerInfo.pwszName =
                wcscpy(pCMarvyMoniker->m_hostname,
                wcstok(NULL, L"!"));
            if(_wcsicmp(wcstok(NULL, L":"), L"clsid") == 0)
            {
                wchar_t clsid_with_braces[39] = L"{";
                wcscat(wcscat(clsid_with_braces,
                    wcstok(NULL, L"!")), L"}");
                CLSIDFromString(clsid_with_braces,
                    &pCMarvyMoniker->m_clsid);
            }
        }

        // Get IMoniker* to return to caller.
        pCMarvyMoniker->QueryInterface(IID_IMoniker, (void**)ppmkOut);
        pCMarvyMoniker->Release();

        // Indicate that we have digested the entire display name.
        *pchEaten = (ULONG)wcslen(pszDisplayName);
        return S_OK;
}
```

Once the *MkParseDisplayName* function returns, the client holds a valid moniker that names a unique COM class on a particular machine. To use the object named by the moniker, the client will typically bind to the object by calling the *IMoniker::BindToObject* method, as shown here:

```
IPrimeFactory* pPrimeFactory;
pMoniker->BindToObject(pBindCtx, NULL, IID_IPrimeFactory,
    (void**)&pPrimeFactory);
```

Now comes the hard part: the moniker must actually instantiate the COM class on the machine identified by the moniker. Since this moniker is really an extension of the system-supplied class moniker, as part of its implementation of the *IMoniker::BindToObject* method, the marvelous moniker creates a standard class moniker for the specified CLSID by using the *CreateClassMoniker* function. Next the moniker binds to the object by calling the class moniker's implementation of the *IMoniker::BindToObject* method. These steps are shown in the following code:

```
// An AddRef a day keeps the doctor away...
AddRef();

// Create a normal class moniker for this CLSID.
IMoniker* pClassMoniker;
HRESULT hr = CreateClassMoniker(m_clsid, &pClassMoniker);

// Bind to the COM class named by the class moniker;
// tell the class moniker that we are to its left.
hr = pClassMoniker->BindToObject(pbc, (IMoniker*)this,
    riidResult, ppvResult);
pClassMoniker->Release();
```

Typically, the class moniker's implementation of the *IMoniker::BindTo-Object* method simply calls *CoGetClassObject*. However, if the class moniker is aware that there is a moniker to its left, it takes special action. Notice that in the *BindToObject* call in the preceding code the second parameter of the *BindTo-Object* call is a *this* pointer that informs the class moniker that the marvelous moniker is to its left. The following pseudo-code demonstrates the steps executed by the class moniker in its *BindToObject* method; the section dealing with the moniker to its left is shown in boldface:

```
HRESULT CClassMoniker::BindToObject(IBindCtx *pbc,
    IMoniker *pmkToLeft, REFIID riidResult, void **ppvResult)
{
    BIND_OPTS2 bopts;
    bopts.cbStruct = sizeof(bopts);
    pbc->GetBindOptions(&bopts);
    if(pmkToLeft == NULL)
        return CoGetClassObject(m_clsid, bopts.dwClassContext,
            0, riidResult, ppvResult);

    // Code to deal with moniker to the left...
    // Make a recursive call to the BindToObject method
    // of the moniker on the left to obtain a
    // pointer to the IClassActivator interface.
    IClassActivator* pActivate;
    pmkToLeft->BindToObject(pbc, IID_IClassActivator,
        (void**)&pActivate);

    // Call IClassActivator::GetClassObject.
    HRESULT hr = pActivate->GetClassObject(m_clsid,
        bopts.dwClassContext, bopts.locale, riidResult,
        ppvResult);
    pActivate->Release();
    return hr;
}
```

Note that if the class moniker discovers that another moniker is to its left, it will make a recursive call to that moniker's *BindToObject* method. This recursive call has a similar effect to that of *QueryInterface* since the class moniker is attempting to obtain a pointer to our moniker's implementation of the *IClass-Activator* interface. To trap this recursive call from the class moniker and to avoid an endless loop of recursion, the marvelous moniker's implementation of the *BindToObject* method first checks to see whether someone is attempting to obtain a pointer to the *IClassActivator* interface. If so, it simply casts the moniker object to the *IClassActivator* interface and returns *S_OK*. The marvelous moniker's implementation of the *Moniker::BindToObject* method is shown here; the section relevant to the *IClassActivator* interface is in boldface:

```
HRESULT CMarvyMoniker::BindToObject(IBindCtx *pbc, IMoniker
    *pmkToLeft, REFIID riidResult, void **ppvResult)
{
    // This catches the recursive call by the class moniker.
    if(riidResult == IID_IClassActivator)
    {
        *ppvResult = (IClassActivator*)this;
        return S_OK;
    }

    // An AddRef a day keeps the doctor away...
    AddRef();

    // Create a normal class moniker for this CLSID.
    IMoniker* pClassMoniker;
    HRESULT hr = CreateClassMoniker(m_clsid, &pClassMoniker);
    if(FAILED(hr))
        return hr;

    // Bind to the COM class named by the class moniker;
    // tell the moniker that the new moniker is to its left.
    hr = pClassMoniker->BindToObject(pbc, (IMoniker*)this,
        riidResult, ppvResult);
    pClassMoniker->Release();
    return hr;
}
```

Because the marvelous moniker itself implements the *IClassActivator* interface in addition to the *IMoniker* interface, a simple cast in the *BindToObject* method is sufficient. As you saw in the pseudo-code for the class moniker's implementation of the *IMoniker::BindToObject* method above, the class moniker calls the sole method of the *IClassActivator* interface: *GetClassObject*. The purpose of *GetClassObject* is to retrieve the class object of the object the moniker names. This hook method allows us to override the default local behavior of the class moniker and redirect it to bind with a class object on a specific host. The marvelous moniker's implementation of the *IClassActivator::GetClassObject* method simply calls *CoGetClassObject*. However, it uses the COSERVERINFO structure to specify the host name from which the class object is to be retrieved. The implementation of the *GetClassObject* method is shown here:

```
HRESULT CMarvyMoniker::GetClassObject(REFCLSID pClassID,
    DWORD dwClsContext, LCID locale, REFIID riid, void** ppv)
{
    // Call CoGetClassObject using the COSERVERINFO structure
    // that contains the host name from the moniker's display string.
    return CoGetClassObject(pClassID, CLSCTX_SERVER,
        &m_CoServerInfo, riid, ppv);
}
```

The call to the *CoGetClassObject* function in the preceding code obtains and returns the class object from the specified host. The pointer to the remote class object is returned to the class moniker, back to the marvelous moniker, and finally to the client. The client can then proceed to use the class object without regard to the fact that the object was instantiated on a remote machine. Once installed and registered, the marvelous moniker can be used with any language. From C++, simply call the *MkParseDisplayName* function; in Visual Basic, call the *GetObject* function. Shown here is a snippet of Visual Basic code that obtains a class object on any machine:

```
Dim myPrimeFactory As IPrimeFactory
Dim myPrime As IPrime

' Call MkParseDisplayName.
Set myPrimeFactory = GetObject( _
    "host:HostNameHere!clsid:10000013-0000-0000-0000-000000000001")

' Call IPrimeFactory::CreatePrime.
Set myPrime = myPrimeFactory.CreatePrime(7)

Dim Count As Integer
For Count = 0 To 10
    ' Call IPrime::GetNextPrime.
    Print myPrime.GetNextPrime
Next
```

The marvelous moniker also exports a moniker creation function named *CreateMarvelousMoniker*. This function enables a marvelous moniker to be created directly rather than from a display name. The declaration for the *CreateMarvelousMoniker* is shown here:

```
HRESULT CreateMarvelousMoniker(REFCLSID clsid,
    COSERVERINFO* pCoServerInfo, IMoniker** ppMoniker)
```

The Java Moniker

The Microsoft Java Virtual Machine (VM) introduces its own special moniker called the *Java moniker*. Java monikers are identified by a string name in the form *java:myclass.class*, where *java* is a registered ProgID that refers to Microsoft's Java VM. The Java moniker enables an application written in Visual Basic to access Java code by using the syntax *GetObject("java:myclass.class")*. The following Visual Basic code fragment uses the *Date* class implemented as part of the java.util package:

```
Private Sub Command1_Click()
    Dim x As Object
    Set x = GetObject("java:java.util.Date")
    MsgBox x.toString() ' Displays current date and time
End Sub
```

Using the same syntax, it is also possible to access methods of a custom-built Java class. The following code shows the Java class that we exposed as a COM object in Chapter 3, "Type Libraries and Language Integration":

```
//
//
// SumClass
//
//
public class SumClass
{
    public int Sum(int x, int y)
    {
        return x + y;
    }
}
```

In Chapter 3, the *SumClass* class was exposed as a COM object using the ActiveX Wizard for Java to generate Java .class file wrappers and a type library for the COM object. To avoid this drudgery, we could have simply used the Java moniker to access *SumClass*, as shown here:

```
Private Sub Command1_Click()
    Dim x As Object
    Set x = GetObject("java:SumClass")
    MsgBox x.Sum(5, 3)
End Sub
```

> **NOTE:** Unfortunately, Microsoft does not currently provide a mechanism similar to Visual Basic's *GetObject* function for Java. This omission can be overcome by writing an in-process component that reifies moniker display names, which can then be called from Java, or by calling the *MkParseDisplayName* function directly from Java via J/Direct, a Microsoft technology that enables Java applications to call Windows API functions.

The Running Object Table

The *Running Object Table* (*ROT*) is a machinewide table in which objects can register themselves. The ROT enables a moniker to check whether an object is already running at the time the client application calls the *IMoniker::Bind-ToObject* method in order to bind to the object. Thus, the ROT acts mainly as a binding optimization. The ROT is available through the *IRunningObjectTable* interface. The *GetRunningObjectTable* function provides access to COM's implementation of this interface. The *IRunningObjectTable* interface is defined here in IDL notation:

```
interface IRunningObjectTable : IUnknown
{
    // Add an object to the ROT.
    HRESULT Register(
        [in] DWORD grfFlags,
        [in, unique] IUnknown *punkObject,
        [in, unique] IMoniker *pmkObjectName,
        [out] DWORD *pdwRegister);

    // Remove an object from the ROT.
    HRESULT Revoke(
        [in] DWORD dwRegister);

    // Check whether the object named by a moniker is in the ROT.
    HRESULT IsRunning(
        [in, unique] IMoniker *pmkObjectName);
```

(continued)

275

```
    // Get a pointer to the object named by a moniker from the ROT.
    HRESULT GetObject(
        [in, unique] IMoniker *pmkObjectName,
        [out] IUnknown **ppunkObject);

    // Specify the time an object in the ROT was last modified.
    HRESULT NoteChangeTime(
        [in] DWORD dwRegister,
        [in] FILETIME *pfiletime);

    // Get the time an object in the ROT was last modified.
    HRESULT GetTimeOfLastChange(
        [in, unique] IMoniker *pmkObjectName,
        [out] FILETIME *pfiletime);

    // Get an enumerator for all objects in the ROT.
    HRESULT EnumRunning(
        [out] IEnumMoniker **ppenumMoniker);
}
```

A good way to get a feel for the information stored in the ROT is to examine its contents. The ROT makes this easy via the *IRunningObjectTable::EnumRunning* method, which enables an application to simply enumerate all the objects currently registered in the ROT. The *IEnumMoniker* interface returned by the *EnumRunning* method enumerates the registered objects by their monikers. To turn this data into easily browsable information, you can simply call the *IMoniker::GetDisplayName* method on each moniker in the enumerator. The following code snippet is taken from the Running Object Table.cpp sample on the companion CD:

```
// Open the ROT.
IRunningObjectTable* pRunningObjectTable;
GetRunningObjectTable(NULL, &pRunningObjectTable);

// Get an enumerator.
IEnumMoniker* pEnumMoniker;
pRunningObjectTable->EnumRunning(&pEnumMoniker);

IMoniker* pMoniker;
IBindCtx* pBindCtx;
OLECHAR* moniker_name;

// Loop until there are no more monikers.
while(pEnumMoniker->Next(1, &pMoniker, NULL) == S_OK)
{
    // Create a silly bind context.
    CreateBindCtx(0, &pBindCtx);
```

```
    // Get the display name, print it, and free the buffer.
    pMoniker->GetDisplayName(pBindCtx, NULL, &moniker_name);
    wprintf(L"DisplayName is %s\n", moniker_name);
    CoTaskMemFree(moniker_name);

    // Code omitted here that determines the moniker type...

    // Release the moniker and the silly bind context.
    pMoniker->Release();
    pBindCtx->Release();
}

// Free the enumerator and close the ROT.
pEnumMoniker->Release();
pRunningObjectTable->Release();
```

When you are registering an object in the ROT, the *IRunningObjectTable::Register* method requires a flag specifying the type of registration that should occur. This value should be either *0*, indicating a weak registration, or *ROTFLAGS_REGISTRATIONKEEPSALIVE*, which will hold the object in memory even if no other references to the object exist. When an object is registered, the ROT always calls *IUnknown::AddRef* on the object. For a weak registration, the ROT will release the object whenever the last reference to the object is released. For a strong registration, the ROT prevents the object from being destroyed until the object's registration is explicitly revoked. The *ROTFLAGS_ALLOWANYCLIENT* flag can also be used when an object registered in the ROT needs to be accessed by clients running from different security contexts. Without the *ROTFLAGS_ALLOWANYCLIENT* flag, the moniker is registered with a security descriptor that allows only clients from the same security context to access it.

Structured Storage

As software has become increasingly sophisticated, it has also become more demanding of the services offered by the operating system. Operating systems, in turn, have become resource managers attempting to democratically ration the available resources among the various applications vying for them. In the area of persistent storage, most operating systems are willing to provide an application with controlled access to the hard disk. Normally, the application receives a file handle through which it can read from and write to certain areas of the disk. In a typical file system, each file is treated as a raw sequence of bytes, with no meaning other than that given it by the application that created the file. Although the bytes that comprise a file may actually be fragmented into small blocks scattered throughout the drive, the file system is responsible for understanding the layout of the data and presenting the application with a sequential view of it.

Structured storage is a COM service that takes a unique approach to saving data. The idea is to enable an application (or several applications) to save data in a single file in a standardized, structured format. In the past, most sophisticated applications have developed complex proprietary formats for saving the user's data. While workable, this approach is limited in two significant respects. First, only the application itself has any idea what data is stored in a file. Other applications, such as the system shell or other file viewers, have no information about the file other than its name, size, and other file system trivia. Second, using a proprietary format makes it almost impossible for other applications to embed their data within the same file. For instance, a user of a word processor might want to embed a picture produced by a paint utility inside a document. If the user's data is saved in a proprietary format, the word processor will find it difficult to store the embedded data in an organized way. Structured storage is designed to address these limitations by introducing a standard mechanism for applications to use when saving data.

Structured storage is sometimes called "a file system within a file," because it can treat a single file as if it were capable of storing directories and files. A file created using the structured storage service contains one or more *storages*, roughly equivalent to directories, and each storage can contain zero or more *streams*, roughly equivalent to files. A storage can also contain any number of substorages.

The advantages offered by structured storage are numerous. First, instead of developing a proprietary protocol for saving data, an application can use structured storage to develop a more standardized solution. For example, a word processing application might save a document by creating distinct storages and streams for summary information, embedded objects, macros, and the user's data. The storage for embedded objects might contain substorages, one for each application whose data has been embedded in the document. In each of those substorages, one or more streams might exist, each containing the data of a single embedded object. This hypothetical example is illustrated in Figure 7-3.

The structured storage service is accessible through two interfaces: *IStorage* and *IStream*. *IStorage* represents the methods that can be executed on a storage object, and *IStream* represents those methods that can be executed on a stream object. Microsoft has provided implementations of these interfaces as part of the structured storage service. As you will see, the structured storage service is so functional and easy to use there's almost no excuse for not using it to read and write data.

MyFile.doc

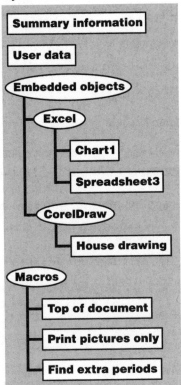

Figure 7-3.
A single file containing different types of data saved in a structured format.

The *IStorage* Interface

Like a directory in the file system, a storage object has a certain number of standard operations that can be performed. To get a general idea of the functionality provided by a storage object, simply consider the standard command-line utilities that are often executed on a directory. These utilities include md (make directory), cd (change directory), deltree (delete a directory tree), xcopy (copy a file or directory), and move (move a file or directory). All of these operations can be executed as methods of the *IStorage* interface and are described in the table on the following page.

IStorage Method	Description
CreateStream	Creates and opens a stream object with the specified name contained in this storage object
OpenStream	Opens an existing stream object within this storage object by using the specified access permissions
CreateStorage	Creates and opens a new storage object within this storage object
OpenStorage	Opens an existing storage object with the specified name according to the specified access mode
CopyTo	Copies the entire contents of this open storage object into another storage object
MoveElementTo	Copies or moves a substorage or stream from this storage object to another storage object
Commit	Reflects changes for a transacted storage object to the parent level
Revert	Discards all changes that have been made to the storage object since the last commit operation
EnumElements	Returns an enumerator object that can be used to enumerate the storage and stream objects contained within this storage object
DestroyElement	Removes the specified storage or stream from this storage object
RenameElement	Renames the specified storage or stream in this storage object
SetElementTimes	Sets the modification, access, and creation times of the indicated storage element, if supported by the underlying file system
SetClass	Assigns the specified CLSID to this storage object
SetStateBits	Stores up to 32 bits of state information in this storage object
Stat	Returns the STATSTG structure for this open storage object

The *StgCreateDocfile* function provided by COM can be used to create a structured storage file containing a root storage. Using the *IStorage* interface pointer returned by the *StgCreateDocfile* function, you could create streams or additional substorages using the methods in the preceding table. The following code fragment creates a structured storage file named TestFile.stg and obtains a pointer to the root storage object's *IStorage* interface:

```
IStorage* pStorage;
hr = StgCreateDocfile(L"TestFile.stg",
    STGM_DIRECT|STGM_CREATE|STGM_READWRITE|STGM_SHARE_EXCLUSIVE,
    NULL, &pStorage);
```

This seemingly simple request to create a new file actually creates on the disk a file that already contains 1.5 kilobytes (KB) of data. This overhead is required by the implementation of the structured storage service.

The *IStream* Interface

Using the *IStorage* interface pointer to create a stream is a straightforward process. The following code fragment creates a stream named *MyDataStream* and retrieves a pointer to the stream object's *IStream* interface:

```
IStream* pStream;
hr = pStorage->CreateStream(L"MyDataStream",
    STGM_DIRECT|STGM_CREATE|STGM_WRITE|STGM_SHARE_EXCLUSIVE,
    0, 0, &pStream);
```

When working with standard files, developers typically use a file handle to execute read and write operations on a file. For structured storage files, the *IStream* interface is used to execute read and write operations on a stream within the file. The *IStream* interface contains methods similar to those that can be executed on a file handle. For example, the *IStream::Write* method is used to write data into a stream, as shown here:

```
ULONG bytes_written;
char data[] = "HELLO THERE!";
pStream->Write(data, strlen(data), &bytes_written);
```

In fact, the *IStream* interface inherits from *ISequentialStream*, which defines the *Read* and *Write* methods, as shown here in IDL notation:

```
interface ISequentialStream : IUnknown
{
    HRESULT Read(
        [out, size_is(cb), length_is(*pcbRead)] void *pv,
        [in] ULONG cb,
        [out] ULONG *pcbRead);

    HRESULT Write(
        [in, size_is(cb)] void const *pv,
        [in] ULONG cb,
        [out] ULONG *pcbWritten);
}
```

Objects that require simple sequential access to a stream will implement the *ISequentialStream* interface. Most applications do not implement *ISequentialStream* as a separate interface, however; instead, they implement the *ISequentialStream- ::Read* and *ISequentialStream::Write* methods as part of an *IStream* interface implementation. This is true of the COM's implementation of these interfaces: calling *QueryInterface* for *ISequentialStream* fails; calling *QueryInterface* for *IStream* succeeds. The following table describes the various methods of the *IStream* interface.

IStream Method	Description
Read	Reads a specified number of bytes from the stream object into memory, starting at the current seek pointer
Write	Writes a specified number of bytes into the stream object, starting at the current seek pointer
Seek	Moves the seek pointer to a new location relative to the beginning of the stream, the end of the stream, or the current seek pointer
SetSize	Changes the size of the stream object
CopyTo	Copies a specified number of bytes from the current seek pointer in one stream to the current seek pointer in another stream
Commit	Ensures that any changes made to a stream object open in transacted mode are reflected in the parent storage object
Revert	Discards all changes that have been made to a transacted stream since the last *IStream::Commit* call
LockRegion	Restricts access to a specified range of bytes in the stream
UnlockRegion	Removes the access restriction on a range of bytes previously restricted using *IStream::LockRegion*
Stat	Retrieves the STATSTG structure for this stream
Clone	Creates a new stream object that references the same bytes as the original stream but provides a separate seek pointer to those bytes

The *IPropertySetStorage* and *IPropertyStorage* Interfaces

The actual data stored by an individual stream might be in a proprietary format, but the fact that the structure of a file saved using the structured storage interfaces is accessible to all applications through a standard protocol is a big advantage. Not only is the data saved in an organized fashion, but also utilities and other applications might be able to obtain information about the data stored in the file. This information access is possible if certain streams in the file are stored in a standardized format. For example, a file might have a summary information stream in the root storage that contains information about the file's contents. Other applications, such as the system shell, might allow the user to execute sophisticated queries based on this information. Perhaps the user could request a list of all documents written by a certain person or containing information about a certain subject.

As part of the structured storage service, Microsoft has defined a property set format that can be used to store summary information in a standard way. This information can then be accessed by anyone who wants it. Windows, for example, displays this information when the user right-clicks on the icon for a file and then chooses Properties from the context menu to display a Properties dialog box, as shown in Figure 7-4. When used to display lists of files in its Web view mode, Microsoft Internet Explorer automatically displays this information for any selected file.

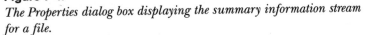

Figure 7-4.
*The Properties dialog box displaying the summary information stream
for a file.*

The *IPropertySetStorage* and *IPropertyStorage* interfaces encapsulate the functionality needed to create property sets, such as the summary information stream described above. The confusing thing about the property storage interfaces is that from the point of view of a structured storage file, a property set is written into a single stream. Therefore, *IPropertySetStream* and *IProperty-Stream* might seem to be more appropriate names for these interfaces. However, the logic behind the *IPropertySetStorage* and *IPropertyStorage* interface names comes from the fact that these interfaces were not designed to be used only by structured storage. Other services might exist that could benefit from these interfaces, and thus conceptually these interfaces abstract the storage of properties.

When you are working with the property set implementation provided by the structured storage service, a pointer to the *IPropertySetStorage* interface is obtained by calling *QueryInterface* on an *IStorage* pointer, as shown here:

```
IPropertySetStorage* pPropertySetStorage;
pStorage->QueryInterface(IID_IPropertySetStorage,
    (void**)&pPropertySetStorage);
```

Every property set is identified by a globally unique identifier (GUID) called a format identifier (FMTID). This identifier allows any application that might come across this property set to quickly determine whether it understands the contents of the property set. The two most widely used FMTIDs are *FMTID_SummaryInformation* and *FMTID_DocSummaryInformation*. The latter is used to store extended summary information for documents created by Microsoft Office applications. When you are creating a new property set, you must define its FMTID. The following code shows how the *IPropertySetStorage* interface can be used to easily create a new property set with the format identifier *FMTID_SummaryInformation*:

```
IPropertyStorage* pPropertyStorage;
pPropertySetStorage->Create(FMTID_SummaryInformation,
    NULL, PROPSETFLAG_ANSI,
    STGM_CREATE|STGM_READWRITE|STGM_SHARE_EXCLUSIVE,
    &pPropertyStorage);
```

The methods of the *IPropertySetStorage* interface are described in the following table.

IPropertySetStorage Methods	Description
Create	Creates a new property set
Open	Opens a previously created property set
Delete	Deletes an existing property set
Enum	Creates and retrieves a pointer to an object that can be used to enumerate property sets

The *IPropertySetStorage::Create* method returns an *IPropertyStorage* interface. The *IPropertyStorage* interface lets you work with an individual property set. The methods of the *IPropertyStorage* interface are described in the following table.

IPropertyStorage Methods	Description
ReadMultiple	Reads property values in a property set
WriteMultiple	Writes property values in a property set
DeleteMultiple	Deletes properties in a property set
ReadPropertyNames	Gets corresponding string names for given property identifiers (PROPIDs)
WritePropertyNames	Creates or changes string names corresponding to given PROPIDs
DeletePropertyNames	Deletes string names for given PROPIDs
SetClass	Assigns a CLSID to the property set
Commit	As in *IStorage::Commit*, flushes or commits changes to the property storage object
Revert	When the property storage is opened in transacted mode, discards all changes since the last commit operation
Enum	Creates and gets a pointer to an enumerator for properties within this property set
Stat	Receives statistics about this property set
SetTimes	Sets modification, creation, and access times for the property set

Two structures are used in defining a property set: PROPSPEC and PROP-VARIANT. The PROPSPEC structure defines the property based on a property identifier (PROPID) or a string name; properties are typically defined by a PROPID. More than a dozen PROPIDs are defined for the summary information property set, defining everything from the document's author to a thumbnail sketch of the document. Of course, an application will work only with the properties it requires.

The value of the property itself is defined in the PROPVARIANT structure. This structure is a variation on a structure used to store variants. For example, to store string data, simply declare the *VT_LPSTR* variant type. The code fragment on the following page stores a single property in a property storage. Notice that in this code fragment, the string *"Anna"* is not saved in Unicode. Although in general all strings used by COM must be in Unicode, string data stored in a property set need not be in Unicode. In fact, for the data stored in a summary information property set to display properly on non-Unicode systems such as Microsoft Windows 95 and Microsoft Windows 98, the string data must specifically not be stored in Unicode.

```
PROPSPEC ps;
ps.ulKind = PRSPEC_PROPID;
ps.propid = PIDSI_AUTHOR;

PROPVARIANT pv;
pv.vt = VT_LPSTR;
pv.pszVal = "Anna";

hr = pPropertyStorage->WriteMultiple(1, &ps, &pv, 0);
```

File System Changes in Windows NT 5.0

In Microsoft Windows NT 5.0, the New Technology File System (NTFS) has been updated so that it now supports native property sets on any file or directory via the *IPropertyStorage* and *IPropertySetStorage* interfaces. These interfaces can be used to attach a property set to flat files (such as a bitmap) in addition to structured storage files. NTFS will store this data on the disk in a special part of the file structure, which will enable applications such as Microsoft Index Server to index and search the contents of native NTFS property sets.

Windows NT 5.0 also provides a new implementation of the *IStorage* and *IStream* interfaces: Native Structured Storage (NSS). NSS is accessed via the *StgCreateStorageEx* and *StgOpenStorageEx* functions. For example, the following code could be used to create an NSS file on an NTFS 5.0 partition:

```
hr = StgCreateStorageEx(L"C:\\TestFile.stg",
    STGM_DIRECT|STGM_CREATE|STGM_READWRITE|STGM_SHARE_EXCLUSIVE,
    STGFMT_NATIVE, 0, 0, 0, IID_IStorage, (void**)&pStorage);
```

REMOTING ARCHITECTURE

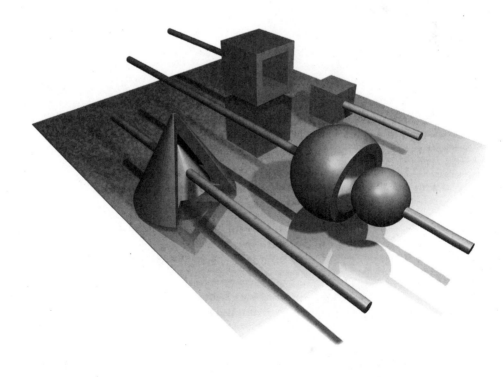

DLL Surrogates and Executable Components

Location transparency, the idea that it doesn't matter whether code is running locally or remotely, in-process or out-of-process, is central to COM. While the concept of location transparency has been part of COM since the beginning of its evolution, its full power has been realized only recently with DCOM. Due to the foresight of COM's designers, the transition from a single machine to a distributed model has been a smooth one.

In previous chapters, we have built and tested in-process components and examined a wide range of COM services available to applications, including connection points, monikers, and structured storage. In this chapter, we will move beyond the in-process model and begin to examine COM's remoting architecture. *Remoting* is the mechanism used to communicate with two types of components: *local* and *remote.* Local components are executable files that run on the same machine as their client but in a separate address space. A remote component executes on a machine separate from that of its client and is a more elusive entity. As you know, in-process components are dynamic-link libraries (DLLs) and local components are executable files (EXEs). Microsoft Windows does not provide a third type of code module, so how do we set about remoting a DLL or an EXE? Well, EXE components don't need much help in this regard because they can simply be launched on a remote computer. As we shall see, however, an EXE is not always the best vehicle for COM objects.

Most COM objects feel much more at home with an in-process component. Why? Since a DLL runs in the process address space of its caller, DLLs usually run faster than equivalent EXE components. In addition, run-time environments such as Microsoft Transaction Server work only with in-process components. But does the much vaunted location transparency apply to in-process components as well as EXE components? In other words, can a DLL be launched and called remotely? Contrary to what logical reasoning might lead you to believe, in-process components can be remoted. Permit us to explain.

DLL Surrogates

DLLs are like children; they need constant attention. A DLL can never run without a parent process nearby to protect it. However, DLL components can be remoted as long as a surrogate is available to provide round-the-clock supervision and security. DCOM provides a default DLL surrogate (dllhost.exe) that will love and protect your in-process components when they are away from home. The file dllhost.exe is an executable component that can be remoted and then instructed to load any in-process component, providing the component with a surrogate parent process and security context. Since an in-process component can be remoted using a DLL surrogate, this is where we will begin our study of COM's remote architecture.

Running In-Process Components Locally

To activate an in-process component in the context of a DLL surrogate, two settings must be configured in the registry. These settings can be made in the component's self-registration code, but for this discussion, we'll add the entries by using the following surrogate.reg file:

```
REGEDIT4

[HKEY_CLASSES_ROOT\CLSID\{10000002-0000-0000-0000-000000000001}]
"AppID"="{10000002-0000-0000-0000-000000000001}"

[HKEY_CLASSES_ROOT\AppID\{10000002-0000-0000-0000-000000000001}]
@="Inside DCOM Sample"
"DllSurrogate"=""
```

The *AppID* value in the class identifier (CLSID) section is used to link clients with the component's entry in the application identifier (AppID) section of the registry. In the AppID section, we have defined the *DllSurrogate* value, which requests that the in-process component be run inside a surrogate and specifies the name of the desired surrogate. Since no surrogate name is provided in this case, the system-supplied surrogate, dllhost.exe, will be used by default.

The AppID Registry Key

An AppID is a 128-bit globally unique identifier (GUID) that groups the configuration and security options for distributed COM objects in one centralized location in the registry: HKEY_CLASSES_ROOT\AppID. To associate a COM class with an AppID, place the named-value of *AppID*, containing the string corresponding to the AppID listed under the AppID subkey, into its CLSID entry in the registry. This mapping is shown in numbered sequence in Figure 8-1.

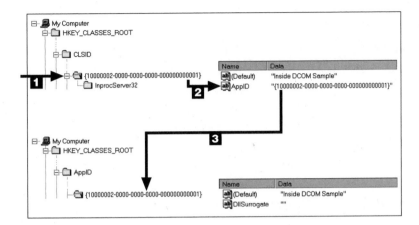

Figure 8-1.
The registry mapping of a CLSID to an AppID.

Note that to simplify the management of common security and configuration settings, distributed COM objects hosted by the same component are grouped together under one AppID. Executables may also be registered under the AppID key in a subkey indicating the module name, such as component.exe. These subkeys contain an AppID value that indicates the AppID associated with the executable and are used to obtain the default access permissions. The following table shows the valid named-values that can be present in an AppID subkey. Note that most of these values can be set via the Distributed COM Configuration utility discussed later in this chapter, in the section "The Distributed COM Configuration Utility."

AppID Named-Values	Description
AccessPermission	Sets the access control list (ACL) that determines default access permissions
ActivateAtStorage	Configures client to activate on same system as persistent storage
AuthenticationLevel	Sets the default authentication level*
DllSurrogate	Names the surrogate process used to load DLLs remotely
LaunchPermission	Sets the ACL that determines who can launch the application

* Microsoft Windows NT 4.0 Service Pack 4 or later

(continued)

continued

AppID Named-Values	Description
LocalService	Configures the component to run as a Microsoft Windows NT Service
RemoteServerName	Names a remote server
RunAs	Sets an application to run only as a given user
ServiceParameters	Sets parameters to be passed to *LocalService* on invocation

Instantiating an In-Process Object in a Surrogate

Well, we're almost there, but we need to change the call to create the object. In the client, you'll first need to adjust the *CoCreateInstance* call to specify that a local component is desired. Yes, that's right—a *local* component. Even though our component is still implemented as an in-process component, we ask *CoCreate-Instance* to instantiate a local component as shown in the following code. With the addition of the AppID and *DllSurrogate* information, this code is now legal.

```
CoCreateInstance(CLSID_InsideDCOM, NULL, CLSCTX_LOCAL_SERVER,
    IID_IUnknown, (void**)&pUnknown);
```

Now it's time to rebuild and run the client. Notice that only messages displayed by the client are visible. Messages from the component are nowhere to be seen because the component is now running in the address space of the dllhost surrogate. The dllhost surrogate doesn't display a user interface, so no output messages from the component appear. You can verify that the surrogate is running by displaying the task list and observing that the dllhost.exe process is running.

NOTE: If it is present, you will need to delete the HKEY_CLASSES-_ROOT\CLSID\{10000002-0000-0000-0000-000000000001}\Local-Server32 registry key in order to run the in-process version of the *InsideDCOM* object within the DLL surrogate.

You might be wondering why someone would want to run an in-process component in a DLL surrogate. Here are several possible benefits:

- Provides fault isolation and the ability to service multiple clients simultaneously

- Enables an in-process component to service remote clients in a distributed environment

- Permits clients to protect themselves from untrusted components while still allowing access to the services provided by the in-process component

- Provides the in-process component with the surrogate's security context

Running Components Remotely

Of course, in most cases an in-process component is run under the guidance of a surrogate in order to enable remote execution. Configuring existing COM components to run remotely does not require that you change one iota of code. To ensure that legacy components, written prior to the availability of DCOM, can still make use of distributed features, all the information necessary to configure how DCOM works can be specified in the registry.

If a client calls *CoCreateInstance* using the flag *CLSCTX_LOCAL_SERVER*, the client is not necessarily restricted to local servers only—it could in fact end up using a remote server. Here's how the process works: Whenever the Service Control Manager (SCM) tries to activate an executable component, it first checks for the *AppID* named-value in HKEY_CLASSES_ROOT\CLSID\\{*Your-CLSID*} key of the registry. If the *AppID* named-value is found, the SCM then looks for the same GUID in the HKEY_CLASSES_ROOT\AppID\\{*YourAppID*} section of the registry, where it might find some of the named-values described in the preceding table that specify how and where the component should be activated. For example, to launch a legacy component on another machine, the *RemoteServerName* value should indicate the name of the desired computer. When requesting an object on a remote machine, the SCM on the local machine contacts the SCM on the remote machine designated by the *RemoteServerName* value to request that the remote SCM locate and load the component on its machine. In this way, DCOM is configured for legacy clients and components.

To configure a surrogate process to run remotely, all the standard registry entries configured via the component's self-registration routine need to be present on the client machine, plus the following entries:

```
REGEDIT4

[HKEY_CLASSES_ROOT\CLSID\{10000002-0000-0000-0000-000000000001}]
"AppID"="{10000002-0000-0000-0000-000000000001}"

[HKEY_CLASSES_ROOT\AppID\{10000002-0000-0000-0000-000000000001}]
@="Inside DCOM Sample"
"RemoteServerName"="Remote_Computer_Name"
```

These entries specify that whenever a client comes looking for the component, the component should actually be run on another machine specified by the *RemoteServerName* value. There is no need to modify that client's call to *CoCreateInstance* to specify *CLSCTX_REMOTE_SERVER* instead of *CLSCTX-_LOCAL_SERVER*. The *RemoteServerName* entry in the registry provides all the information needed for the SCM to know what to do. The remote computer on which the component will actually run must have the registry configured as before, with the *DllSurrogate* value but not the *RemoteServerName* value. Note that if you have both the *DllSurrogate* and *RemoteServerName* entries in the registry, the client's call to *CoCreateInstance* must specify *CLSCTX_REMOTE_SERVER* in order to connect with the component remotely. Otherwise, the client will launch the DLL surrogate locally.

The Distributed COM Configuration Utility

The Distributed COM Configuration utility (dcomcnfg.exe) is designed solely to help configure the registry so that legacy clients and components can participate in a distributed environment. This utility has three pages: Applications, Default Properties, and Default Security. The Applications tab shows a list of executable components and allows the user to configure them for remote execution by selecting a component and clicking the Properties button, as shown in Figure 8-2.

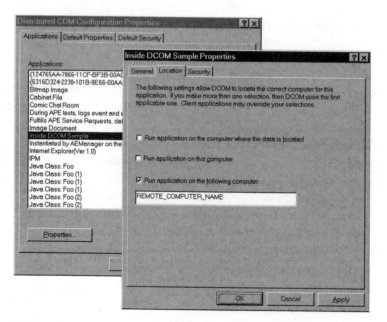

Figure 8-2.
Setting the Inside DCOM Sample properties using dcomcnfg.exe.

The other two tabs are used to control default settings for components. To entirely disable DCOM on the current machine, uncheck the Enable Distributed COM On This Computer option on the Default Properties tab or set the *EnableDCOM* value in the HKEY_LOCAL_MACHINE\SOFTWARE\Microsoft\OLE key of the registry to *N*. Modern components, which were designed for use in a distributed environment, normally offer their own configuration options and thus have no use for the Distributed COM Configuration utility.

> **N O T E :** Every time the Distributed COM Configuration utility runs, it generates AppIDs in the registry for any COM classes that have a CLSID\LocalServer32 key but not an AppID key.

Writing a Custom Surrogate

The default DLL surrogate provided by Microsoft is quite flexible, even enabling multiple in-process components to be loaded into a single surrogate process. Generally speaking, the default surrogate should be more than adequate for most well-behaved in-process components. However, misbehaving components might not run properly in the default surrogate. Any code executed by the component under the assumption that it is running in the process space of its client will fail. Access to global variables and callback functions implemented using function pointers are examples of such assumptions. Running this type of component in a surrogate requires a special surrogate trained to deal with the unique needs of that component. In other words, you need to write a custom surrogate process. Here are some reasons you might decide to do so:

- A custom surrogate can provide special optimizations for a particular component.

- A custom surrogate can be tailored to deal with in-process components that depend on being in the same process as their client.

- A custom surrogate can more flexibly manage the security context for a component.

If the features provided by the default DLL surrogate don't meet your needs, you can build your own custom surrogate by implementing the *ISurrogate* interface in a local component. The definition of the *ISurrogate* interface is shown in IDL notation on the following page.

```
interface ISurrogate : IUnknown
{
    // Load the specified in-process component.
    HRESULT LoadDllServer([in] REFCLSID clsid);

    // Exiting...
    HRESULT FreeSurrogate();
}
```

A Custom DLL Surrogate: *DllNanny*

To further illustrate the concepts discussed in this section, we will present code fragments from a simple DLL surrogate named *DllNanny*. A surrogate process will be launched automatically by the SCM when a client instantiates an in-process object registered for execution within the surrogate. The SCM provides the surrogate with the CLSID of the in-process object as a command-line argument. On start-up, a surrogate process should register its threading model by calling *CoInitialize* or *CoInitializeEx*. Next the wanna-be surrogate should call *CoRegisterSurrogate* to provide COM with a pointer to its *ISurrogate* interface. In the following code fragment from dllnanny.cpp, the surrogate follows this start-up procedure with a call to the *ISurrogate::LoadDllServer* method to indicate the presence of a client activation request. The first (and only) command-line argument provided to the surrogate process on start-up specifies the CLSID for the desired in-process object. This CLSID is converted from a string to a binary CLSID and passed as a parameter to the *LoadDllServer* method.

```
void main(int argc, char** argv)
{
    // Initialize COM and create the multithreaded
    // apartment (MTA).
    CoInitializeEx(NULL, COINIT_MULTITHREADED);

    // Instantiate and register the surrogate.
    CSurrogate surrogate;
    CoRegisterSurrogate(&surrogate);

    // Convert the ASCII string-form CLSID in
    // argv[1] to Unicode.
    OLECHAR wszCLSID[39];
    mbstowcs(wszCLSID, argv[1], 39);

    // Convert the Unicode CLSID to a binary CLSID.
    CLSID clsid;
    CLSIDFromString(wszCLSID, &clsid);

    surrogate.LoadDllServer(clsid);

    // Code omitted...
```

Upon receiving the client request via the *ISurrogate::LoadDllServer* method, the surrogate should instantiate and register a class object. The class factory object registered by the surrogate process is not the actual class factory implemented by the in-process component. Instead, it is a generic class factory implemented by the surrogate process that must support the *IUnknown* and *IClassFactory* interfaces. Although the in-process component is running in the address space of the surrogate, it is effectively out-of-process as far as the client is concerned. To enable remoting, it is also recommended that the surrogate class factory implement the *IMarshal* interface.

Next the implementation of the *ISurrogate::LoadDllServer* method should call the *CoRegisterClassObject* function to register the surrogate class factory for the specified CLSID. All surrogate class factories should be registered using the *REGCLS_SURROGATE* flag when the *CoRegisterClassObject* function is called; *REGCLS_SINGLEUSE* and *REGCLS_MULTIPLEUSE* should not be used for in-process components loaded into surrogates. Here is *DllNanny*'s implementation of the *ISurrogate::LoadDllServer* method:

```
HRESULT CSurrogate::LoadDllServer(REFCLSID rclsid)
{
    // Instantiate the surrogate class factory object.
    m_pcf = new CGenericFactory(rclsid);

    // Register the surrogate class factory object;
    // note the use of the REGCLS_SURROGATE flag.
    return CoRegisterClassObject(rclsid, (IClassFactory*)m_pcf,
        CLSCTX_LOCAL_SERVER, REGCLS_SURROGATE,
        &m_pcf->m_dwRegister);
}
```

When the client calls *CoCreateInstance* to instantiate the desired in-process object as a local server, the surrogate's *IClassFactory::CreateInstance* method is called. The surrogate class factory needs to use the real class factory to create an instance of the desired object. Calling *CoCreateInstance* on the in-process object itself will do the trick. Thus, *DllNanny*'s implementation of the *IClassFactory::CreateInstance* method looks like this:

```
HRESULT CGenericFactory::CreateInstance(IUnknown* pUnknownOuter,
    REFIID riid, void** ppv)
{
    return CoCreateInstance(m_clsid, pUnknownOuter,
        CLSCTX_INPROC_SERVER, riid, ppv);
}
```

During the lifetime of the surrogate process, it is important to periodically call *CoFreeUnusedLibraries*. This function, normally called repeatedly by a low-priority thread, unloads any DLLs that are no longer in use. Later, after all clients have exited and all the in-process components running in the surrogate process have terminated, COM will call the *ISurrogate::FreeSurrogate* method. At that point, the surrogate should revoke all registered class factories using the *CoRevokeClassObject* function and then cause the surrogate process to exit, as shown here:

```
HRESULT CSurrogate::FreeSurrogate()
{
    // Revoke the surrogate class factory.
    HRESULT hr = CoRevokeClassObject(m_pcf->m_dwRegister);

    // Set an event that causes the surrogate to exit.
    SetEvent(g_hEvent);
    return hr;
}
```

The *SetEvent* function signals a global event object created in the surrogate's *main* function, where the *WaitForSingleObject* has been called, as shown in the following code fragment. This call causes the surrogate to wait until it is time to exit. Once the event is signaled, *WaitForSingleObject* returns and the surrogate terminates cleanly.

```
// The main function...

    // Create the event.
    g_hEvent = CreateEvent(NULL, FALSE, FALSE, NULL);

    // Wait for the event to be signaled
    // by ISurrogate::FreeSurrogate.
    WaitForSingleObject(g_hEvent, INFINITE);
    CloseHandle(g_hEvent);

    CoUninitialize();
}
```

Marshaling

In the previous surrogate example, the component has an *ISum* interface with the methods *QueryInterface, AddRef, Release,* and *Sum*. Did you pause to marvel at how the parameters to and from these methods happen to pass successfully between the client and the component? In earlier chapters, we built in-process components, which ran in the address space of the client, obviating the issue of parameter passing. However, in the surrogate process example, our in-process component ran first in the address space of the surrogate process and then on another computer altogether. How did parameter passing work, then? This whole issue of how parameters are passed in DCOM, called *marshaling*, is an area of great concern in DCOM.

In-process components don't have to worry about marshaling since all the action takes place in a single address space. The function parameters are simply pushed onto the stack for a function call and then popped off the stack when executing the function. Executable components, whether running on the same machine as the client or running on a remote computer, need to concern themselves with marshaling. Not that marshaling is a new concern to DCOM, as any component that runs out of process has nearly the same problems to deal with. However, since DCOM adds cross-computer marshaling to the mix, the amount of network bandwidth consumed by marshaling makes this a concern of higher priority. Figure 8-3 illustrates how marshaling is used to send data to and from a component.

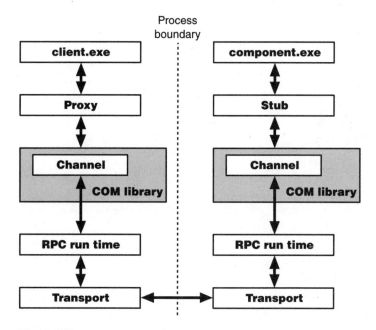

Figure 8-3.
The architecture for cross-computer communication between a client and a component.

To put it more precisely, marshaling is the process of packaging method calls and their parameters into a transmittable packet and then sending that packet to a component. This process can be quite simple or quite complex. For example, marshaling an integer parameter involves simply copying its value into a transmission buffer and sending it off. Marshaling an array of characters, however, is more complicated. How does the marshaler know the size of the array? Even if the entire size of the array can be determined, perhaps only the first several bytes are in use; transmitting the entire array would be a waste of bandwidth. Finally, what if you had a pointer to an element in a doubly linked list? How could the marshaler possibly know how to package this complex data structure for transmission?

In the case of most standard COM interfaces, marshaling is handled by objects instantiated from the system ole32.dll component. The main issue for most developers is what to do about custom interfaces. COM marshaling is too often explained away as some black magic requiring different incantations to work smoothly; here we'll expose it for what it really is. COM offers three basic marshaling options:

- Standard marshaling
- Type library marshaling
- Custom marshaling

These options are discussed in detail in the sections that follow.

Standard Marshaling

Don't confuse the term *standard marshaling* with standard interfaces. Remember, standard interfaces are interfaces defined by Microsoft as part of COM. For most of these interfaces, Microsoft has already built marshaling code. Standard marshaling is used for custom interfaces such as *ISum*. Standard marshaling is easy—it simply requires that you create an IDL file describing your custom interfaces. Then you compile the IDL file using the MIDL compiler to generate the standard marshaling code. The following table lists the files created by the MIDL compiler when it is used to compile COM interface definitions.

Filename	Description
idlname.h	Header file for the interface definitions
*idlname*_i.c	Definitions of the interface identifier (IID) and CLSID constants
*idlname*_p.c	Marshaling code
idlname.tlb	Type library (only if the IDL contains a *library* statement)
dlldata.c	DLL entry points for the marshaling code

By compiling and linking these files, you can produce a *proxy/stub DLL* that will correctly marshal your interfaces. A proxy/stub DLL is a library that can be loaded by both the client and the component in order to properly marshal data back and forth. For COM to automatically load this DLL when it is needed, the proxy/stub DLL must be registered as the *ISum* interface marshaler. Luckily, the DLL built from the code generated by the MIDL compiler exports the *DllRegisterServer* function, which knows how to correctly register the proxy/stub DLL. Simply compile the proxy/stub DLL with the *REGISTER-_PROXY_DLL* symbol defined, and the necessary code will be included in the component. When it is called, the *DllRegisterServer* function will create all the necessary registry entries. Recall that this self-registration feature allows the proxy/ stub component to be registered using the RegSvr32 utility. The advantage of standard marshaling is that you only have to write the IDL—the rest is automatic.

Building a Proxy/Stub DLL for Standard Marshaling

To build a proxy/stub DLL when you are using standard marshaling, follow these steps:

1. Compile your IDL file (component.idl) using MIDL.

2. Open Visual C++, and choose the File/New command.

3. Select the Projects tab, and then select Win32 Dynamic-Link Library.

4. In the Project Name text box, type *ProxyStub*, and then click OK.

5. Choose the Project/Add To Project/Files command.

6. Select the dlldata.c, component_i.c, and component_p.c files generated by MIDL, and click OK.

7. Choose the File/New command, select the Files tab, and then select Text File.

8. In the File Name text box, type *ProxyStub.def*, and then click OK.

9. Enter the following module definition file:

```
; ProxyStub.def
LIBRARY                 proxyStub.dll
DESCRIPTION             'Proxy/Stub DLL'
EXPORTS
    DllGetClassObject   @1 PRIVATE
    DllCanUnloadNow     @2 PRIVATE
    DllRegisterServer   @3 PRIVATE
    DllUnregisterServer @4 PRIVATE
```

10. Choose the File/Save command, and then choose Project/Settings.

11. In the Settings For list box, select All Configurations.

12. Select the C/C++ tab, and in the Category list box, select General.

13. In the Preprocessor Definitions list box, add *REGISTER_PROXY-_DLL* and *_WIN32_DCOM*, separated by commas.

14. Select the Link tab, and in the Category list box, select General.

15. In the Object/Library Modules list box, add *rpcndr.lib*, *rpcns4.lib*, and *rpcrt4.lib*, separated by spaces, and then click OK.

16. Choose the Build/Build ProxyStub.dll command.

17. Assuming all has gone well, choose the Tools/Register Control command.

It is also recommended that self-registering proxy/stub DLLs include a version information resource containing the *OLESelfRegister* value. See Chapter 2, "*IUnknown* and *IClassFactory*," for more details on the *OLESelfRegister* value.

Type Library Marshaling

Type library marshaling uses the Automation (*IDispatch*) marshaler. Normally, components implement the *IDispatch* interface if they want to work with scripting languages such as VBScript or JScript, since these languages require that a component support the *IDispatch* interface. A component implementing the *IDispatch* interface does not need to worry about marshaling since this is a standard interface and COM has a built-in marshaler for *IDispatch* included in oleaut32.dll, available on any 32-bit Windows system.

While the *IDispatch* interface has its uses, it also has its problems, as described in Chapter 5, "Automation and Component Categories." Thus, many components opt for custom interfaces rather than using *IDispatch*. It is possible, however, to make use of the Automation marshaler without implementing the *IDispatch* interface in your component. This option is an intriguing one, possible only if your custom interfaces restrict themselves to Automation-compatible data types. The Automation-compatible data types are listed in the section "The Automation Marshaler," covering the *IDispatch* interface, in Chapter 5. For the Automation marshaler to obtain the information needed to correctly marshal your custom interfaces, you must also register a type library for the component. These interfaces must be declared as Automation-compatible in the IDL file used to build the type library. This specification is made by including the *oleautomation* flag, as shown here:

```
[ object, uuid(10000001-0000-0000-0000-000000000001),
  oleautomation ]
interface ISum : IUnknown
{
    HRESULT Sum(int x, int y, [out, retval] int* retval);
}
```

Note that setting the *oleautomation* flag does not mean that we are using the *IDispatch* interface—only that our interface is compatible with *IDispatch*. Because the Automation marshaler is generic, it is not as efficient as the marshaling code generated by MIDL. Moreover, it imposes a slight performance penalty due to the time consumed by the type library lookup. However, because of the Automation marshaler's great flexibility and ease of use, it is often an excellent choice. As an added benefit, no proxy/stub DLL needs to be built and then registered on each machine—the Automation marshaler is automatically available in Windows. To enable type library marshaling for your components, you simply register each custom interface with the *ProxyStubClsid32* value set to *{00020424-0000-0000-C000-000000000046}*, as shown here:

```
REGEDIT4

[HKEY_CLASSES_ROOT\Interface\→
{10000001-0000-0000-0000-000000000001}\ProxyStubClsid32]
@="{00020424-0000-0000-C000-000000000046}"
```

At run time, the SCM will locate this CLSID and perform a lookup in the HKEY_CLASSES_ROOT\CLSID section of the registry. The Automation marshaler CLSID has the following entries in the registry:

```
HKEY_CLASSES_ROOT\
    CLSID\
        {00020424-0000-0000-C000-000000000046}\
            (Default)="PSAutomation"
            InprocServer32
                (Default)="oleaut32.dll"
                ThreadingModel="Both"
```

Notice that oleaut32.dll is listed as the proxy/stub Automation (*PSAutomation*) component that is implemented in oleaut32.dll. If you decide to use type library marshaling, calling the *LoadTypeLibEx* or *RegTypeLib* function will automatically add the necessary registry entries during self-registration, as shown in the code fragment on the following page. In the previous exercise using the DLL surrogate, marshaling worked correctly because of the *oleautomation* attribute in the IDL file. Just imagine: you have used type library marshaling without even realizing it!

```
ITypeLib* pTypeLib;
HRESULT hr = LoadTypeLibEx(L"mytypelib.tlb", REGKIND_DEFAULT,
    &pTypeLib);
pTypeLib->Release();
```

Custom Marshaling

Custom marshaling affords the developer complete control over the marshaling process. Not surprisingly, it is also the most difficult marshaling technique to implement. Custom marshaling, COM's fundamental marshaling architecture, is the generic mechanism by which one object can specify exactly how it communicates with a proxy in another process. The crux of the custom marshaling architecture is how to take an interface pointer in one process and make it accessible to another process, either on the same machine or remotely. COM's standard marshaling is simply one way to achieve this goal. The standard marshaling architecture is built on top of custom marshaling, and type library marshaling is built on standard marshaling. These relationships are shown in Figure 8-4.

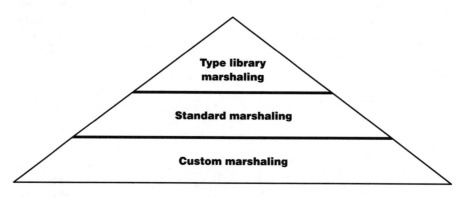

Figure 8-4.
Relationships between the three marshaling options.

Marshaling an interface pointer is far more complex than marshaling simple Remote Procedure Calls (RPCs). In RPCs, marshaling is simply a matter of packaging the parameters of a fixed set of functions in a data packet and then unpacking the data structure on the other side. In COM, each interface specifies a different set of functions that need to be marshaled uniquely. Sometimes the client might not know in advance what interfaces it will be using. Microsoft Visual Basic, for example, can connect to any custom interface you might dream up. How can Visual Basic possibly know how to marshal the parameters to methods in your custom interface? The custom marshaling architecture needs somehow to deal with the very dynamic nature of COM.

While you ponder the possible solutions to this dilemma, we'll cover the executable components on which the detailed discussion of custom marshaling in Chapter 9, "Standard and Custom Marshaling," is based.

Executable Components

Executable components, also known as *out-of-process components,* are executables that house COM objects. They are sometimes called local components because prior to the arrival of DCOM, they ran on the same machine as the client process but not in the client's address space. Today both executable and in-process components (with the help of a surrogate) can run on remote machines in a distributed environment. COM's promise of location transparency means that our client process does not need to be modified, regardless of whether it is the client of an in-process, a local, or a remote component. The code for the component itself needs to undergo some renovation, however, to be able to run as an executable component. In earlier chapters, we have implemented in-process components adhering to the COM specification. Since COM also supports executable components (EXEs), in this section we will examine the process through which an in-process component can be converted to an executable component and then called remotely using DCOM. Figure 8-5 compares a client calling an in-process component to a client calling a local or remote component.

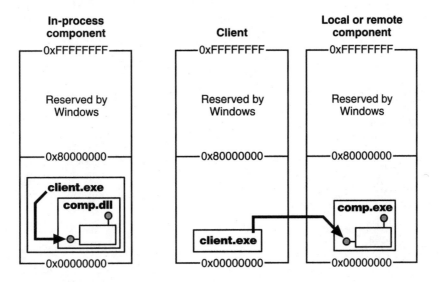

Figure 8-5.
A comparison of the in-memory layout of in-process and executable components, and their clients.

Before you decide to build an executable component, the advantages and disadvantages of using executable components instead of their in-process siblings need to be carefully weighed. As we have seen, it is not necessary to create an executable component in order to take advantage of DCOM. DLL surrogates enable in-process components to run both locally and remotely. Microsoft Transaction Server, the subject of Chapter 13, "Microsoft Transaction Server and COM+," works only with in-process components. In fact, Microsoft Transaction Server can be thought of as the ultimate DLL surrogate.

The two primary advantages of building executable components are that they can run as Windows NT services, as described in Chapter 11, "Security," and that they can be run by the user as double-clickable applications. In both cases, you could still build the desired functionality into an in-process component and then create an executable front to call the component. Another reason some people favor executable components is that because executable components run in a separate address space from the client, they pose less of a security risk to the client. But this security risk can also be addressed through the use of a DLL surrogate. In fact, we wonder whether in the future there will be any need for executable servers that are not surrogates for in-process components.

In some situations, the outgoing parameters of a method call made on an in-process component can work slightly different from a method call made on an executable component. When a method running in an in-process component writes data using pointers provided by the method's *out* parameters, the caller's address space is updated immediately; if the method is running in an out-of-process component, the caller's address space is updated only when the method returns. Normally, this rather subtle difference is of no consequence. However, if a method running in an out-of-process component makes a call back to the caller, the caller might reasonably expect that its variables have been updated by the method. This will not be the case, because the method has not yet returned. The COM specification resolves this issue by specifying that methods should not write data through *out* parameters until just before they return, as is the case automatically with out-of-process components. In this way, this minor variation between the operation of in-process and out-of-process components is better masked.

What about the disadvantages of executable components? The main disadvantage of an executable component is that it runs much slower than an in-process object, due to that fact that cross-process calls need to be made. Of course, an in-process component running in a surrogate or any kind of component running on a remote machine suffers from the same performance impediment, or worse. The following table lists some questions you should ask yourself when you are deciding whether to implement a component of the in-process, in-process running in the default surrogate, or executable variety.

Question	In-Process Component	In-Process Component Running in the Default DLL Surrogate	Executable Component
Do you want instances of the object to be shared by more than one client?	No	Yes	Yes
Do you plan to enter the object in the Running Object Table (ROT)?	No	No	Yes
Does your object need to expose nonremotable interfaces (such as *IViewObject*)?	Yes	No	No
Do you want the object to be insulated from client crashes?	No	Yes	Yes
Do you want to integrate with Microsoft Transaction Server?	Yes	No	No
Do you want the object to have its own security context?	No	Yes	Yes
Does your object require superior performance?	Yes	No	No
Do you intend for the object to be run as a stand-alone application under the direct control of the user?	No	No	Yes
Does your object need to expose internal data structures directly to the client?	Yes	No	No

Building an Executable Component

Fortunately, changing an in-process component into an executable component, or vice versa, is not all that difficult. Nevertheless, if after careful consideration of the alternatives you decide to proceed with an executable component, keep in mind that several aspects of an executable component differ from an in-process component. One of the major differences is that EXEs cannot export functions as DLLs can, which means that the well-known entry points *DllGet-ClassObject*, *DllCanUnloadNow*, *DllRegisterServer*, and *DllUnregisterServer* are specific to in-process components only. An executable component must have a *main* or *WinMain* start-up function where execution begins and must include special code to deal with termination. The remaining concerns with executable components relate to race conditions that can arise in multithreaded EXEs; these concerns are dealt with at length in Chapter 4, "Threading Models and Apartments."

Originally, DLLs worked simply by exporting functions. Other programs could load a DLL and ask for a pointer to a particular function either by name or by number. Whereas in-process components use the *IUnknown::QueryInterface* method to return interface pointers through which calls can be made, COM relies on standard exported functions such as *DllGetClassObject* to retrieve the initial interface pointer. Executable files, unlike DLLs, do not have the capability to easily export functions. An executable file can hand out function pointers only while it is running. COM addresses this difference between DLLs and EXEs by using command-line parameters that are communicated to the EXE on start-up. Thus, the four functions exported by in-process components are replaced with three command-line arguments that can be supplied to executable components. The following table shows the mapping of the exported functions to their equivalent command-line arguments.

Function Exported from an In-Process Component	Equivalent Command-Line Argument Passed to an Executable Component
DllGetClassObject	–Embedding
DllCanUnloadNow	[No equivalent]
DllRegisterServer	–RegServer
DllUnregisterServer	–UnregServer

Note that when an executable is launched in the normal way (in response to the user clicking an icon), no special command-line arguments are passed to the application, which enables an application to determine easily whether it has been launched in response to a client request or by the user. Typical executable components, such as Microsoft Internet Explorer or Microsoft Word, do not show any user interface when they are launched via COM, which allows a client process to request services from these applications without the desktop becoming unnecessarily cluttered. Of course, most executable components also provide methods enabling the client to request that they show themselves to the user.

When you are developing components that will run remotely, displaying a user interface is usually not a good idea. Due to COM's security architecture (covered in Chapter 11, "Security"), most components executing remotely will run in a desktop separate from that displayed on the server. Therefore, ignoring the fact that the user might be a great distance away from the server, the user interface might not even be visible on the server. The following start-up code is typical of that normally executed by executable components in their *main* function:

```
int main(int argc, char** argv)
{
    if(argc > 1)
    {
        char* szToken = strtok(argv[1], "-/");
        if(_stricmp(szToken, "RegServer") == 0)
            return RegisterComponent(...);
        if(_stricmp(szToken, "UnregServer") == 0)
            return UnregisterComponent(...);
        if(_stricmp(szToken, "Embedding") == 0)
        {
            // Launched by COM!
            // Don't show a user interface.
            // Then register a class factory.
        }
    }
    // No COM arguments; run in the normal fashion.
    // Show user interface here.
    return 0;
}
```

This code tests to determine whether more than one command-line argument is present, since the first command-line argument (*argv[0]*) is always the name of the application itself. The *strtok* function is used to find the first dash (–) or slash (/) character in the first command-line argument; either character is a legal prefix to COM's command-line arguments. Next the *_stricmp* function is called to compare lowercase versions of the command-line argument with the three standard strings that may be provided by COM. If *–RegServer* or *–UnregServer* is found, the appropriate registration steps are performed and execution is terminated. That's right—if an executable component is executed using either of the registration commands, the program exits immediately after performing the requested action. This design allows setup programs to launch an executable component and instruct it to register itself, without worrying that it will display a user interface or take some other action.

Note that *CoInitialize* must be called prior to the registration or deregistration routine if type libraries are to be registered using *LoadTypeLibEx* or *RegisterTypeLib* or unregistered using *UnRegisterTypeLib*. Although the samples on the companion CD always refresh their registry settings when they are launched, this is for convenience only and is not generally recommended for production code. Depending on the security environment, a component might not have write access to critical areas of the registry. (See Chapter 11 for more information.)

The actual registration of an executable component is very similar to that of an in-process object. The main difference is that instead of using the Inproc-Server32 subkey, executable components are registered in a LocalServer32 subkey. The same COM class is permitted to be registered in both the Inproc-Server32 and the LocalServer32 subkeys. In such cases, COM will provide the client with whatever form of the object was requested using the class context values (*CLSCTX_LOCAL_SERVER* or *CLSCTX_INPROC_SERVER*). Should the client pass the value *CLSCTX_SERVER* or *CLSCTX_ALL*, COM will default to the most efficient implementation of the COM class, an in-process component. If an in-process implementation is not available, COM will proceed to look for local and then remote components, in that order.

The *RegisterServer* function (provided in the registry.cpp file on the companion CD) automatically checks its first parameter to determine whether an EXE or a DLL component is being registered. For example, if the *RegisterServer* function is called using the name of an executable file, the component is registered in a LocalServer32 subkey. In-process (DLL) components are registered in the InprocServer32 subkey. The following code fragment is taken from the *RegisterServer* function:

```
// Add the component's filename subkey under the CLSID key.
// Is it an EXE?
if(strstr(szModuleName, ".exe") == NULL)
{
    // No; use InprocServer32.
    setKeyAndValue(szKey, "InprocServer32", szModule);
    // More code here...
}
else
    // Yes; use LocalServer32.
    setKeyAndValue(szKey, "LocalServer32", szModule);
```

If the *–Embedding* flag is located in the command line, the component knows that it is being launched in response to a client's activation request. The name of this flag is an anachronism remaining from the linking and embedding days of OLE. The component should respond to the *–Embedding* flag by registering its class factory using the *CoRegisterClassObject* function and take other steps similar to those performed by a DLL when the *DllGetClassObject* function is called. If no COM-related command-line argument is detected, the executable component should assume that it has been launched at the request of the user and should thus behave like a normal application. For EXE components designed to be activated only remotely, the absence of the *–Embedding* flag should also be interpreted as an attempt on the part of the user to launch the application and an appropriate message should be displayed, after which the application should terminate.

Once the processing of command-line parameters is out of the way, executable components need to call *CoInitialize(Ex)*. Recall that in-process components do not normally call *CoInitialize(Ex)* because they are running in the process of their caller, which has already called *CoInitialize(Ex)*. Besides initializing COM, *CoInitializeEx* gives the component an opportunity to specify its supported threading model. In-process components are forced to do this via the *ThreadingModel* value in the registry. An executable component can use the *COINIT_MULTITHREADED* flag of *CoInitializeEx* to declare itself as multi-threaded—or in COM lingo, a free-threaded component—as shown in the following code. (For more information about multithreaded components, refer to Chapter 4, "Threading Models and Apartments.")

```
CoInitializeEx(NULL, COINIT_MULTITHREADED);
```

In place of the *DllGetClassObject* function, an executable component uses the *CoRegisterClassObject* function to inform COM about the objects it supports. Each call to *CoRegisterClassObject* registers one object and its associated class factory. If a component supports multiple objects, it must call *CoRegisterClassObject* once for each object. *CoRegisterClassObject* takes the CLSID of the COM class being registered as its first parameter and a pointer to the object's class factory as its second parameter. Thus, you must first create an instance of the class factory using the C++ *new* operator, as shown here:

```
IClassFactory *pClassFactory = new CFactory();

DWORD dwRegister;
CoRegisterClassObject(CLSID_InsideDCOM, pClassFactory,
    CLSCTX_LOCAL_SERVER, REGCLS_MULTIPLEUSE, &dwRegister);
```

Each class object can specify certain settings via the third and fourth parameters of the *CoRegisterClassObject* function. The third parameter determines whether the class object is visible only to client code running in the process space of the component (*CLSCTX_INPROC_SERVER*) or to clients running in a separate address space on the local machine or a remote machine (*CLSCTX_INPROC_SERVER*). The fourth parameter of the *CoRegisterClassObject* function accepts flags from the *REGCLS* enumeration, as shown here:

```
typedef enum tagREGCLS
{
    REGCLS_SINGLEUSE = 0,
    REGCLS_MULTIPLEUSE = 1,
    REGCLS_MULTI_SEPARATE = 2,
    REGCLS_SUSPENDED = 4,
    REGCLS_SURROGATE = 8
} REGCLS;
```

The *REGCLS_SINGLEUSE* flag is a legacy setting that enables only one client to access the class object. Subsequent client requests cause COM to load a new instance of the entire component. The *REGCLS_MULTIPLEUSE* flag is more commonly used because it enables multiple client applications to connect to a single instance of a class object. In addition, class objects registered with the *REGCLS_MULTIPLEUSE* flag are automatically accessible to code running in the process space of the component itself, regardless of whether the *CLSCTX_INPROC_SERVER* flag was specified in the third parameter of *CoRegisterClassObject*.

The *REGCLS_MULTI_SEPARATE* flag is a variation on the *REGCLS-_MULTIPLEUSE* flag, which restricts client code running in the process of the component from accessing the class object. This flag enables a component to register different class objects for in-process clients (*CLSCTX_INPROC-_SERVER*) and out-of-process clients (*CLSCTX_INPROC_SERVER*). COM specifically allows multiple registrations of the same class object; each registration is independent and returns a unique key via the fifth parameter of the *CoRegisterClassObject* function. A class object registered with the *CLSCTX-_LOCAL_SERVER* class context and *REGCLS_MULTI_SEPARATE* registration flag would exhibit rather odd behavior. Out-of-process clients would share one instance of the component, but client code running in the process of the component would cause COM to launch another instance of the component! The following table describes the behavior exhibited by various combinations of the class context and registration flags.

Class Context Flag	Registration Flag		
	REGCLS-_SINGLEUSE	*REGCLS-_MULTIPLEUSE*	*REGCLS-_MULTI_SEPARATE*
CLSCTX-_INPROC_SERVER	Illegal	In-process	In-process
CLSCTX-_LOCAL_SERVER	Local	In-process or local	Local
CLSCTX-_INPROC_SERVER| *CLSCTX_LOCAL-_SERVER*	Illegal	In-process or local	In-process or local

Of the two remaining class registration flags, *REGCLS_SURROGATE* and *REGCLS_SUSPENDED*, the *REGCLS_SURROGATE* flag was discussed earlier in this chapter in the section "Writing a Custom Surrogate." We will defer a discussion of the *REGCLS_SUSPENDED* flag until later in this section.

At this stage, the executable component is fully operational, but it has a serious problem. Because the program will now continue executing, it will soon reach the end of its *main* function and terminate. Any clients of our component will be justifiably upset if the component simply exits without warning. We must find some way to keep our component alive. In-process components do not have to worry about this problem because they are loaded into the address space of their client and politely wait to be called. When a client has finished using an in-process component, COM calls the exported function *DllCanUnloadNow* before unloading the DLL. Executable components, however, are responsible for managing their own lifetimes. How this issue is addressed depends on whether an executable component is apartment-threaded or free-threaded. Free-threaded components typically address this problem by creating an event object using the Win32 *CreateEvent* function, as shown in the following code. This function call is followed by a call to the Win32 function *WaitForSingleObject*, which waits for the event to be signaled.

```
g_hEvent = CreateEvent(NULL, FALSE, FALSE, NULL);
WaitForSingleObject(g_hEvent, INFINITE);
```

Because the *INFINITE* flag is used in the call to *WaitForSingleObject*, the code will wait forever until the event is signaled, solving the problem of the component exiting prematurely. Now a client can request all the services it wants from the executable component, and only when all clients have finished using the component do we want it to exit. Exiting the component can be accomplished with a slight modification to the final release code in the *IUnknown-::Release* method, as shown here:

```
ULONG CInsideDCOM::Release()
{
    if(--m_cRef != 0)
        return m_cRef;

    // Final release
    SetEvent(g_hEvent);     // ADD THIS!!!
    delete this;
    return 0;
}
```

Notice the addition of the Win32 *SetEvent* call, shown in boldface in the preceding code. When the last client calls *Release* and the object's reference counter is decremented to *0*, only then is the event object signaled. At this stage, the *WaitForSingleObject* call that was on hold in the *main* function returns. Apartment-threaded components typically use the *PostQuitMessage* function to signal their message loop that it is time to exit. After performing a few cleanup steps, the component is permitted to exit. First the component must inform COM that it is no longer offering any objects for use. This notification is sent using the *CoRevokeClassObject* function, the ancillary of *CoRegisterClassObject*, as shown here:

```
CoRevokeClassObject(dwRegister);
```

Once there is no danger of more clients calling to request objects, we release what should be the final class factory pointer. The *Release* method is followed immediately by a call to *CoUninitialize*, as shown here:

```
pClassFactory->Release();
CoUninitialize();
```

When you are building the executable version of the *InsideDCOM* object, be sure to remove the component.def file from the project. This module definition file lists exported functions not present in the executable component. Also be sure that the client's call to *CoCreateInstance* specifies that it wants a local object, as shown here:

```
CoCreateInstance(CLSID_InsideDCOM, NULL, CLSCTX_LOCAL_SERVER,
    IID_IUnknown, (void**)&pUnknown);
```

Here is the entire *main* function needed to turn an in-process pumpkin into an executable horse-drawn carriage:

```
int main(int argc, char** argv)
{
    if(argc > 1)
    {
        char* szToken = strtok(argv[1], "-/");

        // Code to handle other command-line here...

        if(_stricmp(szToken, "Embedding") == 0)
        {
            CoInitializeEx(NULL, COINIT_MULTITHREADED);

            IClassFactory *pClassFactory = new CFactory();

            DWORD dwRegister;
            CoRegisterClassObject(CLSID_InsideDCOM,
                pClassFactory, CLSCTX_LOCAL_SERVER,
                REGCLS_MULTIPLEUSE, &dwRegister);

            g_hEvent = CreateEvent(NULL, FALSE, FALSE, NULL);
            WaitForSingleObject(g_hEvent, INFINITE);

            CoRevokeClassObject(dwRegister);
            pClassFactory->Release();
            CoUninitialize();
            return 0;
        }
    }
    // No COM arguments; exit now.
    return 0;
}
```

Since we are building an executable component, marshaling is a concern. Of the three basic marshaling options (type library, standard, and custom), we strongly recommend either standard marshaling or type library marshaling for most components. To use standard marshaling, simply build and register a proxy/stub DLL from the files generated by the MIDL compiler following the steps described earlier in this chapter, in the section "Standard Marshaling." To use type library marshaling, simply be sure that the interface is marked with the *oleautomation* attribute in the IDL file and that the type library is properly registered, as described in the section "Type Library Marshaling," also earlier in this chapter.

To run an executable component across a network using DCOM, you can either use the Distributed COM Configuration utility or replace the call to *CoCreateInstance* with a call to *CoCreateInstanceEx* in the client.c file, as shown in the following code:

```
COSERVERINFO ServerInfo = { 0, L"Remote_Computer_Name", 0, 0 };
MULTI_QI qi = { &IID_IUnknown, NULL, 0 };
CoCreateInstanceEx(CLSID_InsideDCOM, NULL, CLSCTX_REMOTE_SERVER,
    &ServerInfo, 1, &qi);
pUnknown = qi.pItf;
```

No further work is required if you are using type library marshaling because the Automation marshaler is already available on every machine that supports COM. If, however, you elected to use standard marshaling with a proxy/stub DLL, this DLL must be copied to every machine and properly registered using the RegSvr32 utility, as outlined in the section "Standard Marshaling."

Integrating Marshaling Code with an Executable Component

It is sometimes desirable to avoid distributing and registering a proxy/stub marshaling DLL on every computer that runs either the client application or the component itself. The main reason for wanting to avoid this drudgery is simply to minimize the amount of baggage that must be distributed and installed with an application. Of course, the simplest way to obviate the need for a proxy/stub DLL is to use the type library marshaling facility built into the system. Should this technique prove unacceptable due to performance or other reasons, it is also possible to integrate the proxy/stub code generated by MIDL directly into the client and component executables instead of building a marshaling DLL. This is done by statically linking the proxy/stub code generated by MIDL into the client and component executables.

Be forewarned that integrating proxy/stub code directly with an application is normally frowned upon. For one thing, it means that other client programs will not be able to access the services of the component because they will not have access to the marshaling code. Furthermore, it becomes crucial that the proxy/stub code statically linked into the client and component executables be synchronized. If the component's stub code is updated, the client's proxy code must be updated as well.

If after careful consideration of the alternatives you make the decision to proceed with integrating the proxy/stub code directly with the application's executable file, follow the steps listed below. After following these steps, you will be able to run and test the application. Everything should work as it did before the changes, except that the proxy/stub DLL will no longer be needed.

1. Add the *idlname_*p.c, *idlname_*i.c, and dlldata.c files generated by the MIDL compiler to both the client and component projects.

2. In the main source files of both the client and component, add the following code shown in boldface immediately after the call to *CoInitialize* but replace *IID_ICustom* with the name of the custom interface that the proxy/stub code knows how to marshal. If the proxy/stub code generated by MIDL is used to marshal multiple interfaces, repeat this code once for each custom interface.

```
int main(int argc, char** argv)
{
    CoInitialize(NULL);

    IUnknown* pUnknown;
    DWORD dwUnused;
    DllGetClassObject(IID_ICustom, IID_IUnknown,
        (void**)&pUnknown);
    CoRegisterClassObject(IID_ICustom, pUnknown,
        CLSCTX_INPROC_SERVER, REGCLS_MULTIPLEUSE, &dwUnused);
    CoRegisterPSClsid(IID_ICustom, IID_ICustom);
```

3. Rebuild the client and component.

Normally, COM locates the proxy/stub marshaling code for a custom interface by searching the HKEY_CLASSES_ROOT\Interfaces section of the registry. As a subkey of the desired interface, the ProxyStubClsid32 key will include the CLSID of the in-process component containing the marshaling code. COM uses the *CoGetPSClsid* function to help retrieve this information from the registry. In some cases, however, an application might not want to store this information in the registry. Perhaps a component has been downloaded across a network and due to security settings does not have permission to access the local registry. Or, as in the situation discussed here, the application may already contain the necessary proxy/stub code.

In such cases, the *CoRegisterPSClsid* function used in the preceding code fragment can be called to register the proxy/stub marshaling code for custom interfaces within the context of a running process. The *CoGetPSClsid* function used by COM to locate the marshaling code will return the CLSID of the proxy/stub code registered using the *CoRegisterPSClsid* function. Thus, the *CoRegisterPSClsid* function can be used to perform temporary run-time registration that remains in effect only as long as the process is running, in place of a more permanent registration that would actually be written to the system registry.

Note that in the preceding code, the IID *IID_ICustom* is passed as a CLSID parameter to the *DllGetClassObject, CoRegisterClassObject,* and *CoRegisterPSClsid* functions. By convention, the IID of a custom interface is used as the CLSID of that interface's proxy/stub marshaling code. Since both IIDs and CLSIDs are 128-bit GUIDs, this seemingly odd conversion presents no difficulty to the compiler.

Remote Instantiation

While most DCOM settings can be controlled directly via the registry editor or indirectly by using the Distributed COM Configuration utility, components written today generally do not want to rely on these methods. Instead, the modern application wants precise run-time control over which server it is connected to and over what security settings are involved. To enable this control, the COM library has been extended since the advent of DCOM. Perhaps the most notable of these new functions is *CoCreateInstanceEx*.

The *CoCreateInstanceEx* function creates a single object on a specified machine, be it local or remote. The ability to create an object on a remote machine is an extension of the functionality available in the *CoCreateInstance* function, which creates an object on the local machine only. In addition, rather than requesting a single interface and obtaining a single pointer to that interface, *CoCreateInstanceEx* makes it possible to request multiple interface pointers in a single call. Although *QueryInterface* calls to in-process components are fast, calling *QueryInterface* multiple times to request many different interface pointers from a component that is located on another machine is much less efficient. The *CoCreateInstanceEx* function offers an optimization that enables a developer to obtain multiple interface pointers from an object with a single remote call.

CoCreateInstanceEx lets you specify an array of MULTI_QI structures, each containing a pointer to an IID. The purpose of the MULTI_QI structure is to optimize *QueryInterface* so that fewer round-trips are made between machines. Upon the return of *CoCreateInstanceEx*, each MULTI_QI structure contains (if available) a pointer to the requested interface and the return value of the *QueryInterface* call for that interface. A return value of *E_NOINTERFACE* means that no interface pointers were available; the distinguished error *CO_S_NOTALLINTERFACES* informs you that the object does not implement all of the requested interfaces. The MULTI_QI structure used by *CoCreateInstanceEx* is shown in the following code:

```
typedef struct tagMULTI_QI
{
    const IID* pIID;
```

```
    IUnknown* pItf;
    HRESULT hr;
} MULTI_QI;
```

CoCreateInstanceEx is able to implement this functionality because of the *IMultiQI* interface, shown in IDL notation in the following code. Like the *Co-CreateInstanceEx* function, the *IMultiQI::QueryMultipleInterfaces* method accepts an array of MULTI_QI structures and in a single remote call is able to obtain multiple interface pointers from an object. In fact, COM's internal implementation of the *CoCreateInstanceEx* function actually calls the *QueryMultipleInterfaces* method to provide its functionality.

```
interface IMultiQI : IUnknown
{
    HRESULT QueryMultipleInterfaces(
        [in]      ULONG     cMQIs,
        [in, out] MULTI_QI* pMQIs);
}
```

You do not have to implement the *IMultiQI* interface; together, the proxy and the stub conspire to implement this interface for all objects that use standard marshaling or type library marshaling. Simply call the *IUnknown::Query-Interface* method to request the *IMultiQI* interface, and then use the resultant interface pointer to call the *IMultiQI::QueryMultipleInterfaces* method, as shown in the following code fragment. Note that asking the calling *QueryInterface* to request the *IMultiQI* interface pointer does not execute a round-trip to the server because the in-process proxy implements this interface.

```
MULTI_QI qi[2];
qi[0].pIID = &IID_IHello;
qi[0].pItf = 0;
qi[0].hr = S_OK;
qi[1].pIID = &IID_IGoodbye;
qi[1].pItf = 0;
qi[1].hr = S_OK;

IMultiQI* pMultiQI = 0;
pUnknown->QueryInterface(IID_IMultiQI, (void**)&pMultiQI);
pMultiQI->QueryMultipleInterfaces(2, &qi);
```

The *CoCreateInstanceEx* function also accepts an argument of the type COSERVERINFO, as shown in the code on the following page. *COSERVER-INFO* is used to identify the remote machine on which the object should be instantiated as well as the security provider to be used. The most important field of this structure is the *pwszName* variable that is used to refer to the name of the remote machine. The name used to identify a particular machine depends on the naming scheme of the underlying network transport. By default, all Universal Naming Convention (UNC) paths, such as \\server or server, and Domain Name Service (DNS) names, such as server.com, www.server.com, or 144.19.56.38, are allowed.

```
typedef struct _COSERVERINFO
{
    DWORD dwReserved1;
    LPWSTR pwszName;
    COAUTHINFO* pAuthInfo;
    DWORD dwReserved2;
} COSERVERINFO;
```

Note that *CoCreateInstanceEx* does not search the client's registry for the desired CLSID but instead contacts the SCM residing on the specified remote machine and requests that it search the registry on the server. This technique is advantageous because it means that the CLSID of the remote component does not need to be registered on the client's machine. It also obviates the need for the *RemoteServerName* entry in the AppID section of the registry. Of course, using *CoCreateInstanceEx* doesn't relieve the developer from providing marshaling code for any custom interfaces consumed by the client. The following sample code shows the usage of the *CoCreateInstanceEx* function and can be used to replace calls to *CoCreateInstance* in a client-side application. Notice the use of the *CLSCTX_REMOTE_SERVER* flag.

```
COSERVERINFO ServerInfo = { 0, 0, 0, 0 };
wchar_t* remote_name = L"RemoteServerName";
ServerInfo.pwszName = remote_name;
MULTI_QI qi = { 0, 0, 0 };
qi.pIID = &IID_IUnknown;
CoCreateInstanceEx(CLSID_InsideDCOM, NULL, CLSCTX_REMOTE_SERVER,
    &ServerInfo, 1, &qi);
pUnknown = qi.pItf;
```

Class Emulation

As a particular COM class evolves, it can add support for new interfaces or drop support for older ones. In most cases, it is recommended that a new version of an existing COM class be assigned a new CLSID so that clients can specify which class they want. The older version of the COM class will be used by clients that were released before the new version. For cases in which the new version of a COM class is determined to be fully backward-compatible with the older version, it might make sense for older clients to be routed to the new class. The *CoTreatAsClass* and *CoGetTreatAsClass* functions provide a way for a COM class represented by a CLSID to evolve over time while still supporting older clients. The *CoTreatAsClass* function can be called to insert the TreatAs subkey into the registry entry of a particular CLSID. From then on, any client requests for that CLSID will automatically be routed to the CLSID specified by the TreatAs key in the registry. The *CoGetTreatAsClass* function can be used to learn the current emulation setting of a specific CLSID.

Imagine that the *CLSID_InsideDCOM* class is extended and that the new version has been identified by the class identifier *CLSID_InsideDCOM2*. If the new version of the class is backward-compatible, the *CoTreatAsClass* function can be called to configure class emulation, as shown in the following code fragment:

```
hr = CoTreatAsClass(CLSID_InsideDCOM, CLSID_InsideDCOM2);
```

This code will configure the registry so that the *CLSID_InsideDCOM2* class is used even when clients request the *CLSID_InsideDCOM* class. The actual registry entries in place after the execution of the *CoTreatAsClass* function are shown in Figure 8-6.

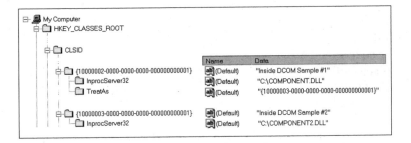

Figure 8-6.
The effect of the CoTreatAsClass *function on the registry.*

The Class Store

The class store is a new feature of Windows NT 5.0 that enables the central deployment and administration of component-based systems. Today COM classes, interfaces, proxy/stub marshaling code, and type libraries must all be registered in the local registry before a typical component can be invoked. Many of the frustrating configuration problems that arise when you are developing and deploying a COM-based system can be traced to incorrect or missing registry entries. For example, if you forget to register a proxy/stub DLL on a particular client, that computer won't be able to access your component. Many of the configuration problems suffered by components can be corrected via good installation, setup, and registration code. One problem remains, however: if you release a new version of a component, that component must be redistributed to all clients.

The class store was designed to enable the central deployment and administration of component-based systems. At its core, the class store is a centralized registry that uses the Active Directory as its store of components and marshaling code. COM activation functions such as *CoCreateInstance(Ex)* and *CoGetClassObject* have been extended to support the class store. Even the Component Categories Manager, described in Chapter 5, "Automation and Component Categories," has been extended to support the class store.

When a client attempts to instantiate an object, COM checks the local registry first. In Windows NT 4.0, registry information is stored on a machine-wide basis in HKEY_LOCAL_MACHINE\Software\Classes. Most programs, however, use the more convenient alias HKEY_CLASSES_ROOT. In Windows NT 5.0, registry information can be stored on a per-user basis in the HKEY_CURRENT_USER\Software\Classes section of the registry. COM checks this area first and then checks HKEY_LOCAL_MACHINE\Software\Classes. If the necessary information is not found in the local registry, COM then proceeds to query the class store for the desired information. If the information is found in the class store, components and marshaling code can be dynamically installed and registered. Because of the built-in class store support throughout most aspects of COM, the class store is more an administrative issue than a programmatic concern to the typical component developer.

Building Singletons in COM

A *singleton* is a useful model for building some types of COM components. A singleton creates only one instance of a COM class and offers that object to all clients. The typical object creates a new class object for each client, and then the client uses the *IClassFactory::CreateInstance* function to instantiate a new object. While this is a good design for most objects, some objects fit better in the singleton model. A component that does not store any information about its clients often fits well into the singleton model. For example, a singleton object might plausibly implement the following interface:

```
interface IPrime : IUnknown
{
    HRESULT IsPrime(long testnumber, [out, retval] boolean* retval);
}
```

The *IPrime* interface does not store a client state between method calls. Implementing the *IPrime* interface in a typical multi-instance component is not difficult, but it does consume unnecessary resources to instantiate a new *Prime* object for each client that connects, when all clients could be sharing a single instance of the object. In theory, the singleton design would enable a prime number component to scale better when accessed by a large number of clients concurrently. While COM does not offer any special APIs or interfaces designed specifically for implementing singletons, building a singleton object does not present any special challenges either. Arguably the simplest way to implement a singleton object is to return the same instance from every call to the *IClass-Factory::CreateInstance* method, as shown here:

```
HRESULT CFactory::CreateInstance(IUnknown* pUnknownOuter,
    REFIID riid, void** ppv)
{
    if(pUnknownOuter != NULL)
        return CLASS_E_NOAGGREGATION;

    static CPrime SingletonPrime;
    return SingletonPrime.QueryInterface(riid, ppv);
}
```

This practical technique works acceptably well, but aesthetically it leaves much to be desired. Returning a pointer to the same object each time the *CreateInstance* method is called seems almost unethical. Whereas the *Create-Instance* method is obviously designed to create a new instance of a class, the *CoGetClassObject* function is designed only to obtain a pointer to a class object, not necessarily to create one. Thus, a second way to design singleton objects in COM is to implement a custom interface directly in the class object. (Custom class objects are discussed in detail in Chapter 7, "Monikers and Structured Storage.")

While this technique is semantically more satisfactory than altering the behavior of the *CreateInstance* method as described above, it is not without its shortcomings. As discussed in Chapter 7, building a custom class object requires that you implement the *IExternalConnection* interface. It also means that *CoCreateInstance* instance will no longer work, which in turn means that client applications written in Visual Basic or Java will not be able to access the singleton object using the *new* operator or Visual Basic's *CreateObject* function. The solution to this problem, at least for Visual Basic clients, is to use the class moniker via the *GetObject* function (also described in Chapter 7).

Whatever mechanism you choose to expose a singleton COM object, be aware that reference counting is normally disabled for such objects—because the final *Release* method should not execute a *delete this* statement! Typically, singleton objects are designed to stay in memory for the lifetime of the process they live in, so reference counting is not terribly important. A common way to implement this type of object is to code the *AddRef* and *Release* methods so that they simply return dummy values, as shown here:

```
ULONG CPrime::AddRef()
{
    return 2;
}

ULONG CPrime::Release()
{
    return 1;
}
```

CHAPTER NINE

Standard and Custom Marshaling

As you know, in-process components (DLLs) always run within the address space of their caller. This fact makes transferring function parameters, whether values or pointers to data, between the client and the component a trivial matter. When you are making out-of-process calls to a local component running on the same machine or to a remote component running on a different machine, things get more complicated. In such cases, all the data that needs to be shared by the client and component must be neatly packaged and transmitted by any means available. This process is called *marshaling*, which according to the closest available dictionary, means to arrange in proper order. Although we have touched on marshaling in earlier chapters, in this chapter we will delve into the details of this most interesting and rather complex COM subject.

Whereas in-process components don't need to worry about marshaling (except in relation to threading—see Chapter 4, "Threading Models and Apartments"), local and remote components must address this important issue. As soon as a method call is executed on an object in another address space, COM needs to get to work organizing the data to be transferred. All of the method's parameters must be packed and transmitted from the sender's to the receiver's address space. For primitive data types such as characters and integers, marshaling does not sound all that difficult. But for more complex types such as structures, strings, linked lists, and interface pointers, marshaling can become exceedingly complex.

The subject of marshaling function parameters, whether integers or linked lists, was thoroughly researched during the development of Remote Procedure Call (RPC) systems. RPCs transmit method parameters using the Network Data Representation (NDR) standard adopted by the Open Software Foundation (OSF). For more information about NDR, see the sidebar "Network Data

Representation" on page 328. Because COM is built on top of Microsoft RPC, it is able to leverage most of the RPC functionality, except in the area of interface pointers. In fact, COM's marshaling architecture is devoted almost exclusively to the problem of how to return an interface pointer from the component to the client.

Marshaling Interface Pointers—An Overview

To perpetuate a bit of a tautology, the purpose of COM's marshaling architecture is to marshal an interface pointer. What does it mean to marshal an interface pointer? To answer this question, we first need to ask a more basic question: What is an interface pointer? As you know, an interface pointer is a pointer to a pointer to a memory-based table, the v-table, which contains the pointers to the virtual functions contained in that interface. For example, the *ISum* interface has four methods, the three methods of *IUnknown* plus the *ISum::Sum* method. The v-table structure at the location specified by an *ISum* interface pointer is shown in Figure 9-1. Although this figure shows a new interface pointer being obtained via the well-known *IUnknown::QueryInterface* method, this is certainly not the only method capable of returning an interface pointer.

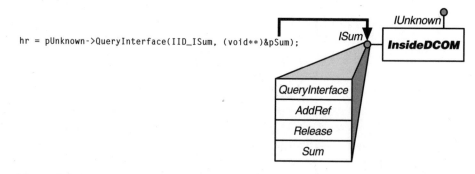

```
hr = pUnknown->QueryInterface(IID_ISum, (void**)&pSum);
```

Figure 9-1.
The layout of a v-table structure.

Now that we have reviewed the concept of an interface pointer, let's return to the broader issue of marshaling. The question remains of how it is possible to take an *ISum* interface pointer and return it to a client in another process, which may or may not be on the same machine. The short answer is that it isn't possible. What constitutes a valid interface pointer in one apartment is complete gibberish in another.

Re-Creating an Interface's V-Table

When a component returns an interface pointer to the client—for example, via *QueryInterface*—that interface pointer must be marshaled. But given that passing an interface pointer from one process to another process is a fruitless pursuit, what's the next best option? To allow the client to think that it is talking directly to the component, for each interface pointer passed to the client we need to re-create that interface's v-table structure in the client's address space. In other words, marshaling an interface pointer means re-creating that interface's v-table in the client's address space.

This v-table is fabricated by loading a proxy DLL into the client's address space. When the client makes a method call on the object, it is really calling the in-process proxy. The proxy then communicates the method request to the component. This architecture, however, requires that the component contain code to listen for the proxy's cries for help. To simplify the job of developing a component, this code is actually encased in another object, called the *stub*, which is loaded into the component's address space. The proxy will direct its SOS calls to this stub, and the stub will make the actual calls into the object.

Interprocess Communications

Within this context, marshaling makes use of a proxy object in the client's address space and a stub object in the component's address space. When the stub receives the request from the proxy, it forwards the call to the actual component. After the method finishes executing, its outgoing parameters and return value are marshaled back to the client in reverse order. This process is illustrated in Figure 9-2.

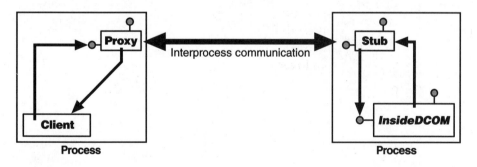

Figure 9-2.
Communication between a client and a component.

The form and format of the interprocess communication used between the proxy and the stub is private to these objects. If the client and the component are running in different processes on one machine, shared memory might be used. If they are running on different machines, a networking interface such as named pipes is required. The format of the interprocess communication between the proxy and the stub is not a defined part of the COM specification. Thus it is left to you, the developer, to decide on the most efficient and appropriate way to implement this communication. The COM specification strongly recommends that when interfaces are being remoted to other machines over a network, the transmitted data should conform to a published standard. The proxy/stub marshaling code generated by the Microsoft IDL (MIDL) compiler, for example, adheres to the NDR format.

Network Data Representation

NDR is a standard originally developed by Apollo Corporation and later adopted by the OSF as part of its Distributed Computing Environment (DCE). Microsoft makes use of NDR in its DCE-compatible RPC implementation and, by consequence, in Distributed COM. The role of NDR is to provide a mapping of Interface Definition Language (IDL) data types onto the streams sent over the wire. NDR supports a multi-canonical format, meaning that there are certain aspects of NDR that support alternative representations. Data properties such as byte order, character sets, and floating-point representation can assume one of several predefined forms. For example, NDR supports ASCII and EBCDIC character sets. This flexibility is accommodated using a "reader makes right" policy. The proxy is allowed to write the data in the best way it sees fit, and the stub (the reader) is expected to be able to read data in any of the NDR flavors. The proxy, however, must inform the stub as to the particular variation of NDR transfer syntax being used. Note that the "reader makes right" strategy was chosen over the alternative approach, "writer makes right," whereby the proxy must determine the transfer syntax supported by the stub before writing the data.

The NDR format label is a 4-byte structure that identifies the particular data formats used to represent primitive values. This NDR format label is itself part of the *Protocol Data Unit* (*PDU*) header. A PDU is a data packet sent by the RPC system; PDUs are described in further detail in Chapter 12, "The Network Protocol." When standard marshaling is used, the format label is set in the *dataRepresentation* field of the RPCOLEMESSAGE structure. The RPCOLEMESSAGE structure and possible values for the *dataRepresentation* field are discussed further in the section "The *IRpcChannelBuffer* Interface" later in this chapter.

The Proxy/Stub DLL

Generally speaking, every custom interface needs a proxy/stub DLL for marshaling purposes. This DLL is loaded into both the client's and the component's address space as required. There is an important reason for building the proxy code as an in-process component rather than just statically linking it into the client code. Imagine that you have written a component that includes a custom interface and that a developer using Microsoft Visual Basic wants to access this component. For Visual Basic to communicate with the component, the proxy needs to be loaded into Visual Basic's address space. If the proxy code is statically linked into one client program, other clients, such as Visual Basic, will be unable to access it. Unless you don't care about this restriction, the proxy code for each custom interface in a local component should be implemented in a DLL. Note that there is no such requirement for stub code. The stub code that communicates with the proxy in the client's address space can be statically linked with the component, but this is generally not as desirable as implementing the stub in a separate DLL.

In previous chapters, we explored the architecture of a local component and dealt with the marshaling issue using either type library or MIDL-generated marshaling code. Recall that type library marshaling relies on the Automation proxy/stub DLL to perform the necessary magic. Using MIDL-generated code is nearly as simple; it requires only that the developer build and register the proxy/stub DLL. Again the marshaling problem is solved. While in most cases one of these two prepackaged solutions will suffice, there are occasions calling for a higher degree of control over the marshaling process. In such cases, you should carefully consider the two fundamental marshaling options offered by COM: *custom marshaling* and *standard marshaling*. In earlier chapters, standard marshaling referred to marshaling code generated by the MIDL compiler, reflecting the fact that the MIDL-generated code actually uses the standard marshaling technique. In this chapter, we discuss standard marshaling without the support of the MIDL compiler, as well as introduce *handler marshaling*—another variation on marshaling.

Will That Be Custom or Standard Marshaling?

Custom marshaling is the fundamental marshaling mechanism in COM. It is also the most difficult way to implement marshaling for an interface. Because most interfaces do not require the fine degree of control offered by custom marshaling, COM provides the standard marshaling mechanism. It is important to realize that standard marshaling is only a specific implementation of the generic custom marshaling architecture, just as type library marshaling is a specific implementation of standard marshaling. Remember that both standard and custom marshaling are appropriate marshaling solutions for custom interfaces such as *ISum*. Standard interfaces such as *IDispatch* already have marshaling code provided by Microsoft. You could replace this code with your own marshaling code, but to do so would be a truly fruitless project.

Before marshaling of interface pointers can be attempted, COM needs to know what type of marshaling is called for. To see how COM makes this determination, let's look at the following code, which shows the tentative first steps taken by a typical client:

```
// client.cpp
// Start your engines.
CoInitializeEx(NULL, COINIT_MULTITHREADED);

// Get a pointer to the object's class factory.
IClassFactory* pClassFactory;
CoGetClassObject(CLSID_InsideDCOM, CLSCTX_LOCAL_SERVER, NULL,
    IID_IClassFactory, (void**)&pClassFactory);
```

CoGetClassObject instructs the Service Control Manager (SCM) to locate the executable component containing the *InsideDCOM* object and launch it. On start-up, a typical executable component performs the following standard steps:

```
// local.cpp
// Start your engines.
CoInitializeEx(NULL, COINIT_MULTITHREADED);

// Instantiate the class factory object.
IClassFactory* pClassFactory = new CFactory();

// Register the object in the global object table.
DWORD dwRegister;
CoRegisterClassObject(CLSID_InsideDCOM, pClassFactory,
    CLSCTX_LOCAL_SERVER, REGCLS_MULTIPLEUSE, &dwRegister);
```

Here the *CFactory* class is instantiated using the C++ *new* operator, and the resulting *IClassFactory* interface pointer is passed to *CoRegisterClassObject*. *CoRegisterClassObject* must somehow take this *IClassFactory* pointer and marshal it to any client process (on any machine) that calls *CoGetClassObject*. Recall that *CoGetClassObject* is used internally by *CoCreateInstance*, the standard object creation function in COM. Inside *CoRegisterClassObject*, COM calls *CoMarshalInterface*, the fundamental interface marshaling function, to do the dirty work of marshaling the *IClassFactory* interface pointer.

The first job of the *CoMarshalInterface* function is to ask the object, "Hey, will that be custom or standard marshaling?" *CoMarshalInterface* is able to determine the object's marshaling preference by calling *IUnknown::QueryInterface* for the *IMarshal* interface. *IMarshal* is the fundamental interface designed to support the custom marshaling of interface pointers. If the object supports the *IMarshal* interface, COM knows that the object has elected to use custom marshaling. Otherwise, if the object does not support *IMarshal*, as shown in the following code, COM assumes that the object wants standard marshaling:

```
HRESULT CFactory::QueryInterface(REFIID riid, void** ppv)
{
    if((riid == IID_IUnknown) || (riid == IID_IClassFactory))
        *ppv = (IClassFactory*)this;
    else
    {
        // IID_IMarshal?! No way!
        *ppv = NULL;
        return E_NOINTERFACE;
    }
    AddRef();
    return S_OK;
}
```

Since *IClassFactory* is a standard interface (defined by Microsoft as part of the COM specification), Microsoft has already provided marshaling code as part of ole32.dll, the systemwide COM DLL. You could override the built-in marshaling to provide custom marshaling code for *IClassFactory*, although the benefits of doing so are dubious. Thus in the class object's *IUnknown::Query-Interface* implementation shown in the preceding code, any request for the *IMarshal* interface returns *E_NOINTERFACE*. Once *CoMarshalInterface* has determined that standard marshaling is in order, it proceeds to marshal the *IClassFactory* interface for us, using the proxy/stub code provided by ole32.dll.

Returning to our examination of the client process, the next step normally executed is shown here in boldface:

```
// client.cpp

// Start your engines.
CoInitializeEx(NULL, COINIT_MULTITHREADED);

// Get a pointer to the object's class factory.
IClassFactory* pClassFactory;
CoGetClassObject(CLSID_InsideDCOM, CLSCTX_LOCAL_SERVER, NULL,
    IID_IClassFactory, (void**)&pClassFactory);

// Instantiate the InsideDCOM object,
// and get a pointer to its IUnknown interface.
IUnknown* pUnknown;
pClassFactory->CreateInstance(NULL, IID_IUnknown, (void**)&pUnknown);
```

The client calls *IClassFactory::CreateInstance* to request that the *InsideDCOM* object be instantiated, and a pointer to *IUnknown* is returned. Inside COM's standard marshaling code for *IClassFactory::CreateInstance*, COM realizes that the *IUnknown* interface pointer about to be returned to the client needs to be marshaled, so the marshaling code for *IClassFactory::CreateInstance* calls *CoMarshalInterface* to marshal the *IUnknown* interface pointer. Note that *CoMarshalInterface* will ask for your *IUnknown* interface pointer several times as part of its standard stub creation and identity testing. Next *CoMarshalInterface* queries the *InsideDCOM* object to determine whether it wants to use standard or custom marshaling.

At this point, thoroughly exhausted by the narrative sequence above, you think, "What the heck, I'll take standard marshaling and call it a day." After all, *IUnknown* is a *very* standard interface, so surely we don't need to provide custom marshaling code for *IUnknown*. It is important to recognize, however, that custom marshaling is done on a per-object basis, not on a per-interface basis like standard marshaling. While COM will be more than happy to provide standard marshaling for *IUnknown*, the *InsideDCOM* object also implements the *ISum* interface, about which COM knows nothing. Thus, we are now at a crucial juncture. We must either respond affirmatively to COM's query for *IMarshal*, opening our minds to the path of custom marshaling, or again respond with *E_NOINTERFACE*, indicating our desire to proceed with standard marshaling.

Standard Marshaling

Standard marshaling is the marshaling mechanism used by MIDL-generated proxy/stub code. However, you can write a proxy/stub DLL without using the MIDL compiler to generate the code. There are many situations in which hand-crafted code might be desirable. For example, suppose you are developing an image-processing component to which clients send a bitmap and a request for a specific type of processing. These bitmaps might be very large and could bog down the network if the client and component are running on different machines. To reduce the amount of network traffic when you are transferring large bitmaps, you could write proxy code that compressed the bitmap before sending it and stub code that decompressed the bitmap before forwarding it to the component. Granted, such compression code could also be built directly into the client and the component, but this technique would place the burden of compression on the clients. Isolating the compression-related code in the proxy and the stub insulates clients and their components from this bandwidth optimization.

When you use standard marshaling, no modifications to the client or component code are required. Instead, a single DLL containing both the proxy and stub code needs to be built and registered. Whenever an interface pointer needs to be marshaled back to a client, COM will load the DLL into the client's and component's address spaces. The proxy object is instantiated in the client's address space; the stub object is instantiated in the component's address space.

In standard marshaling, COM provides a generic proxy and a generic stub that communicate through RPCs. These system-provided proxies and stubs know how to marshal standard COM interfaces. For custom interfaces that these proxies and stubs don't know how to marshal, the standard marshaling architecture enables you to plug in an interface marshaler that does. When loaded, interface proxies are always aggregated with a larger proxy, known as the *proxy manager*, giving clients the illusion that all of the interfaces are exposed from a single COM object. A client holding a pointer to the proxy manager believes that it holds a pointer to the actual object in the component's address space. The proxy manager, sometimes called the standard marshaler, implements *IMarshal*—the fundamental marshaling interface. (A detailed description of the *IMarshal* interface can be found in the section "Can You Say 'Custom Marshaling'?" later in this chapter.)

When a new interface proxy is instantiated, COM passes it a pointer to the proxy manager's implementation of *IUnknown*, to which the interface proxy delegates all *QueryInterface, AddRef,* and *Release* calls. Each interface proxy implements two interfaces of its own: the custom interface it represents and *IRpcProxyBuffer*. The interface proxy exposes its custom interface directly to clients, who obtain access through the *QueryInterface* mechanism. Only COM, however, can call the *IRpcProxyBuffer* interface. This marshaling architecture is shown in Figure 9-3.

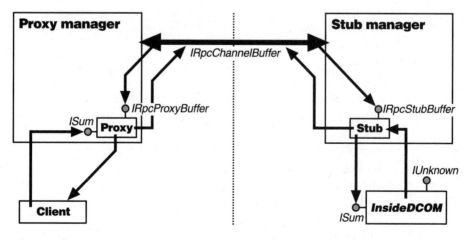

Figure 9-3.
The standard marshaling architecture.

The client calls *QueryInterface* to obtain an *ISum* interface pointer on the proxy object. The interface proxy is part of the greater proxy manager; it communicates with the component through the *IRpcChannelBuffer* interface implemented by COM. On the server side, the channel communicates with the interface stub through the *IRpcStubBuffer* interface, which in turn calls the actual *InsideDCOM* object. Because the stub manager does not need to present a unified identity to any clients, interface stubs are not aggregated with the stub manager. (The stub manager in Figure 9-3 is shown for conceptual purposes and does not actually exist as a separate entity.)

The SCM knows which proxy/stub DLL to load based on the interface identifier (IID) of the interface pointer being returned to the client. In the HKEY_CLASSES_ROOT\Interface section of the registry, the IID must be declared along with the subkey ProxyStubClsid32. This subkey must contain the CLSID of the proxy/stub component for this interface. The SCM then proceeds to the HKEY_CLASSES_ROOT\CLSID section of the registry to locate the CLSID and the InprocServer32 value specifying the name of the proxy/stub DLL to load.

Figure 9-4 illustrates the registry scenario for a proxy/stub DLL set up to marshal an interface—in this case, an interface that uses the Automation (type library) marshaler is shown. (The numbers indicate the order in which the SCM traverses the registry.) Remember that type library marshaling is built on standard marshaling and thus the registry settings follow the same rules.

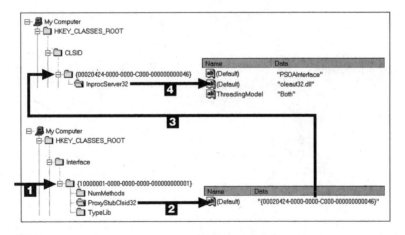

Figure 9-4.
The order in which the SCM scours the registry in search of a proxy/stub DLL for standard marshaling. (In Windows NT, the default value for {00020424-0000-0000-C000-000000000046} is PSOAInterface.)

The Standard Marshaling Interfaces

Standard marshaling involves four COM interfaces: *IPSFactoryBuffer*, *IRpcProxy-Buffer*, *IRpcStubBuffer*, and *IRpcChannelBuffer*. The proxy/stub DLL is itself an in-process component that implements the *IPSFactoryBuffer*, *IRpcProxyBuffer*, and *IRpcStubBuffer* interfaces. The *IRpcChannelBuffer* interface is implemented by COM's standard marshaling mechanism and called by the proxy/stub DLL for interprocess communication. But before we launch into a detailed explanation of these interfaces and the ways in which they are used, take a moment to peruse Figure 9-5.

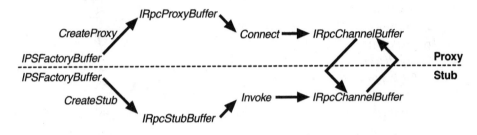

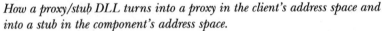

Figure 9-5.
How a proxy/stub DLL turns into a proxy in the client's address space and into a stub in the component's address space.

Figure 9-5 shows how proxy and stub objects start from the same code base and then diverge. In both the client and server address spaces, a proxy or stub object is born at the *IPSFactoryBuffer* interface. Then something dramatic happens. In the client's address space, the *IPSFactoryBuffer::CreateProxy* method is called to create an object that implements the *IRpcProxyBuffer* interface; in the server's address space, the *IPSFactoryBuffer::CreateStub* method is called to instantiate the *IRpcStubBuffer* interface. From there, the proxy calls *IRpcProxyBuffer::Connect* and then communicates with the stub using the *IRpcChannelBuffer* interface. In response to the proxy's request, the stub is awakened using the *IRpcStubBuffer::Invoke* method.

The *IPSFactoryBuffer* Interface

Proxy/stub DLLs that support standard marshaling are themselves COM objects, but their class objects do not need to implement the *IClassFactory* interface. Recall that clients call the *IClassFactory::CreateInstance* method to instantiate objects in a component. A proxy/stub DLL does not instantiate arbitrary COM objects; instead, it is capable only of instantiating either a proxy or a stub object for a particular interface. Thus, instead of supporting *IClassFactory*, the class objects of proxy/stub DLLs implement the *IPSFactoryBuffer* interface.

IPSFactoryBuffer is the interface through which proxies and stubs are created. Every proxy/stub DLL must implement the *IPSFactoryBuffer* interface on the class object accessible through its *DllGetClassObject* entry point. As shown in the following code, the implementation of the *DllGetClassObject* function in a proxy/stub DLL is not substantially different from that of a normal component:

```
HRESULT __stdcall DllGetClassObject(REFCLSID clsid,
    REFIID riid, void** ppv)
{
    // This is a proxy/stub object.
    if(clsid != CLSID_InsideDCOMStdProxy)
        return CLASS_E_CLASSNOTAVAILABLE;

    // Create the PSFactoryBuffer object.
    CFactory* pFactory = new CFactory;
    if(pFactory == NULL)
        return E_OUTOFMEMORY;

    // Calling QueryInterface for IPSFactoryBuffer
    return pFactory->QueryInterface(riid, ppv);
}
```

As described earlier, the SCM consults the registry for the ProxyStubClsid32 subkey of the interface entry in order to get the CLSID of the class that satisfies the interface's marshaling needs. *DllGetClassObject* is then called to request the *IPSFactoryBuffer* interface.

Here is the *IPSFactoryBuffer* interface declared in IDL notation:

```
interface IPSFactoryBuffer : IUnknown
{
    HRESULT CreateProxy
    (
        [in] IUnknown *pUnkOuter,
        [in] REFIID riid,
        [out] IRpcProxyBuffer **ppProxy,
        [out] void **ppv
    );

    HRESULT CreateStub
    (
        [in] REFIID riid,
        [in, unique] IUnknown *pUnkServer,
        [out] IRpcStubBuffer **ppStub
    );
}
```

From this single interface, the gender of a proxy/stub DLL is decided. In the client's address space, *IPSFactoryBuffer::CreateProxy* is called to instantiate the proxy object and, in the component's address space, the same DLL is loaded but *IPSFactoryBuffer::CreateStub* is called. Client-side pseudo-code for the steps executed by the SCM after locating the ProxyStubClsid32 in the registry is shown here:

```
clsid = LookUpInRegistry(riid);
CoGetClassObject(clsid, CLSCTX_INPROC_HANDLER|CLSCTX_INPROC_SERVER,
    NULL, IID_IPSFactoryBuffer, (void**)&pPSFactoryBuffer);
pPSFactoryBuffer->CreateProxy(pUnkOuter, riid, &pRpcProxyBuffer,
    (void**)&ppv);
```

In the component's address space, COM executes the following pseudo-code:

```
clsid = LookUpInRegistry(riid);
CoGetClassObject(clsid, CLSCTX_INPROC_HANDLER|CLSCTX_INPROC_SERVER,
    NULL, IID_IPSFactoryBuffer, (void**)&pPSFactoryBuffer);
pPSFactoryBuffer->CreateStub(riid, pUnkServer, &pRpcStubBuffer);
```

In our proxy/stub DLL, the *CreateProxy* method is written to instantiate a new *CRpcProxyBuffer* object, as shown in the following code. *CRpcProxyBuffer* is the object that actually implements the *IRpcProxyBuffer* interface in the code. *CRpcProxyBuffer* also implements the *ISum* custom interface we are marshaling in this DLL. Next the code calls *QueryInterface* for a pointer to the *ISum* interface. This is the *ISum* interface pointer that will be returned to the client. Now you can see how a v-table is fabricated in the client's address space—a fake object implementing the custom interface is created just so the client has an in-process object on which to call methods. Last the code calls *QueryInterface* for *IRpcProxyBuffer* so that a pointer to the interface proxy can be returned to the proxy manager.

```
HRESULT CFactory::CreateProxy(IUnknown* pUnknownOuter, REFIID riid,
    IRpcProxyBuffer** ppProxy, void** ppv)
{
    // Create the proxy object.
    CRpcProxyBuffer* pRpcProxyBuffer = new CRpcProxyBuffer();

    // Call QueryInterface for IID_ISum.
    HRESULT hr = pRpcProxyBuffer->QueryInterface(riid, ppv);

    // Return a pointer to the IRpcProxyBuffer interface.
    return pRpcProxyBuffer->QueryInterface(
        IID_IRpcProxyBuffer, (void**)ppProxy);
}
```

Meanwhile, as shown in the following code, the *IPSFactoryBuffer::CreateStub* method is implemented to instantiate the *CRpcStubBuffer* class, which implements the *IRpcStubBuffer* interface. The *CreateStub* method receives a pointer to the *InsideDCOM* object for later use by the stub when it needs to call the object. *CreateStub* also provides the IID of the interface we are marshaling—in this case, *IID_ISum*. This IID is passed to the *CRpcStubBuffer*'s constructor for safekeeping by the stub. The *IRpcStubBuffer::Connect* method is then called to provide the interface stub with a pointer to this object. Last the code calls *QueryInterface* for *IRpcStubBuffer* so that a pointer to the interface stub can be returned to the stub manager.

```
HRESULT CFactory::CreateStub(REFIID riid, IUnknown* pUnkServer,
    IRpcStubBuffer** ppStub)
{
    // Create the stub object.
    CRpcStubBuffer* pRpcStubBuffer = new CRpcStubBuffer(riid);

    // Give the stub the pointer to the object.
    pRpcStubBuffer->Connect(pUnkServer);

    // Return a pointer to the IRpcStubBuffer interface.
    return pRpcStubBuffer->QueryInterface(IID_IRpcStubBuffer,
        (void**)ppStub);
}
```

The *IRpcProxyBuffer* Interface

The *IRpcProxyBuffer* interface is the primary interface implemented by an interface proxy. *IRpcProxyBuffer* is the interface through which the proxy manager talks to an interface proxy. When they are created, proxies are aggregated by the proxy manager, to which a pointer is provided by the *IPSFactory::CreateProxy* method. The *IRpcProxyBuffer* is shown here in IDL notation:

```
interface IRpcProxyBuffer : IUnknown
{
    HRESULT Connect
    (
        [in, unique] IRpcChannelBuffer *pRpcChannelBuffer
    );

    void Disconnect
    (
        void
    );
}
```

IRpcProxyBuffer::Connect is obviously the more interesting of these two methods. *Connect* is called by the proxy manager shortly after the interface proxy is created in the *IPSFactoryBuffer::CreateProxy* method. The first (and only) argument for *Connect* is a pointer to an object implementing the *IRpcChannel-Buffer* interface through which the proxy will communicate with the stub. The implementation of *IRpcProxyBuffer::Connect* can be as simple as this:

```
HRESULT CRpcProxyBuffer::Connect(IRpcChannelBuffer* pRpcChannel)
{
    // Store the pointer to the channel.
    m_pRpcChannel = pRpcChannel;

    // AddRef the pointer.
    m_pRpcChannel->AddRef();
    return S_OK;
}
```

This code simply stores the *IRpcChannelBuffer* pointer in a member variable and then calls *AddRef* as dictated by the COM's reference counting rules. This pointer will be used whenever the client calls a method of the object. As we have seen, the client thinks it has a pointer to the object, but in fact it has only a pointer to the proxy. Therefore, all client calls actually end up in the proxy; from there, the request will be forwarded to the stub by using the *IRpcChannelBuffer* pointer.

The *IRpcProxyBuffer::Disconnect* method is called to notify the proxy that it is no longer connected to the stub. At this stage, the RPC channel needs to be released to counteract the *AddRef* method called in *IRpcProxyBuffer::Connect*. A sample implementation of the *Disconnect* method is shown here:

```
void CRpcProxyBuffer::Disconnect()
{
    // Release the channel pointer and set it to NULL.
    m_pRpcChannel->Release();
    m_pRpcChannel = NULL;
}
```

The *IRpcStubBuffer* Interface

As the corollary to *IRpcProxyBuffer*, *IRpcStubBuffer* is the main interface of an interface stub. The stub manager dynamically loads the interface stub into the component's address space and uses the *IRpcStubBuffer* interface to communicate with the stub. The following code shows the *IRpcStubBuffer* in IDL notation:

```
interface IRpcStubBuffer : IUnknown
{
    HRESULT Connect([in] IUnknown *pUnkServer);
```

(continued)

```
            void Disconnect();

            HRESULT Invoke
            (
                [in] RPCOLEMESSAGE *_prpcmsg,
                [in] IRpcChannelBuffer *_pRpcChannelBuffer
            );

            IRpcStubBuffer *IsIIDSupported([in] REFIID riid);

            ULONG CountRefs(void);

            HRESULT DebugServerQueryInterface(void **ppv);

            void DebugServerRelease(void *pv);
        }
```

The *IRpcStubBuffer::Connect* method provides the interface stub with a pointer to the actual object in the component to which the stub is connected. It is to this object that the stub will forward all client requests received from the proxy. To obtain the correct interface pointer for this object, the implementation of *IRpcStubBuffer::Connect* should call *QueryInterface* for the interface we are marshaling—in this case, *ISum*. As shown in the following code, *QueryInterface* takes care of the need to call *AddRef.* The resulting pointer is stored for later use in the *m_pObj* member variable.

```
HRESULT CRpcStubBuffer::Connect(IUnknown* pUnknown)
{
    // Need to keep track of component references for later.
    m_cConnection++;

    // Get a pointer to the interface we are marshaling.
    return pUnknown->QueryInterface(m_iid, (void**)&m_pObj);
}
```

The *IRpcStubBuffer::IsIIDSupported* method is called to determine whether a stub is designed to handle the unmarshaling of a particular interface, as shown in the following code. When COM needs to remote a pointer to a new interface on a given object, the existing stubs are first queried using the *IsIID-Supported* method in an attempt to locate a stub that can handle marshaling for the given interface before COM goes to the trouble of creating a new stub. Most commonly, an interface stub is designed to support only one interface. In such cases, the *IsIIDSupported* method should simply check whether the requested interface is the one the stub was designed to handle. If it is, the method should return *true*; otherwise, the method should return *false.*

```
IRpcStubBuffer* CRpcStubBuffer::IsIIDSupported(REFIID riid)
{
    // Do we support this IID?
    if(riid == m_iid)
        return (IRpcStubBuffer*)true;
    return (IRpcStubBuffer*)false;
}
```

The *IRpcStubBuffer::CountRefs* method returns the total number of references the stub is holding on the component's object, as shown in the following code. The counter value returned should be incremented in every call to *IRpcStubBuffer::Connect* and decremented in *IRpcStubBuffer::Disconnect*.

```
ULONG CRpcStubBuffer::CountRefs()
{
    // Return component connection reference count.
    return m_cConnection;
}
```

IRpcStubBuffer::Disconnect informs the stub that it should disconnect itself from the component's object. The following implementation of *Disconnect* releases the object reference stored in *m_pObj* and then decrements the connection counter *m_cConnection*:

```
void CRpcStubBuffer::Disconnect()
{
    // Release our reference on the object.
    m_pObj->Release();
    m_cConnection--;
}
```

The *DebugServerQueryInterface* and *DebugServerRelease* methods of the *IRpcStubBuffer* interface are designed to support debuggers that provide the ability to step into remote invocations on objects. For our purposes, the implementation shown in the following code is sufficient. (See the COM specification for more information about the recommended implementation of these functions.)

```
HRESULT CRpcStubBuffer::DebugServerQueryInterface(void**)
{
    return E_NOTIMPL;
}

void CRpcStubBuffer::DebugServerRelease(void*)
{
}
```

At this stage, the proxy and stub are fully set up, and we are now prepared for the client to make calls into the component through the marshaling code. To establish communication between the proxy and the stub, COM provides an implementation of the *IRpcChannelBuffer* interface.

The *IRpcChannelBuffer* Interface

At the center of the functionality offered by standard marshaling is COM's implementation of the *IRpcChannelBuffer* interface, through which a proxy invokes a method in its corresponding stub. Conceptually, *IRpcChannelBuffer* implements a channel into which you put data on the client side that magically appears in the component's address space, regardless of the nature of the boundaries separating those two processes. The great thing about *IRpcChannelBuffer* is that it completely handles the transmission of marshaled data between processes, regardless of whether the processes are on the same machine or on different machines connected over a network. (You might take this functionality for granted now, but as you'll see, it's up to the programmer to manage these details with custom marshaling.)

Note that there is no COM function named *CoCreateRpcChannelBuffer*; only through the *IRpcProxyBuffer::Connect* and *IRpcStubBuffer::Invoke* methods do you obtain a pointer to COM's implementation of *IRpcChannelBuffer*. The *IRpcChannelBuffer* interface is internal to and implemented by the RPC infrastructure and is not available outside of standard marshaling.

Here is the *IRpcChannelBuffer* interface in IDL notation:

```
interface IRpcChannelBuffer : IUnknown
{
    // Allocate a transmission buffer.
    HRESULT GetBuffer
    (
        [in] RPCOLEMESSAGE *pMessage,
        [in] REFIID riid
    );

    // Invoke a method and wait for it to return.
    HRESULT SendReceive
    (
        [in,out] RPCOLEMESSAGE *pMessage,
        [out] ULONG *pStatus
    );

    // Free the transmission buffer.
    HRESULT FreeBuffer([in] RPCOLEMESSAGE *pMessage);
```

```
// What is the nature of the boundary between the proxy and stub?
HRESULT GetDestCtx
(
    [out] DWORD *pdwDestContext,
    [out] void **ppvDestContext
);

// Am I connected to the proxy or stub?
HRESULT IsConnected(void);
}
```

The RPCOLEMESSAGE Structure

Of the five *IRpcChannelBuffer* methods, we'll focus initially on *GetBuffer, Send-Receive,* and *FreeBuffer.* Common to these three methods is the RPCOLEMES-SAGE structure—the data structure actually transmitted from the proxy to the stub and back. This data structure is declared as shown here:

```
typedef struct tagRPCOLEMESSAGE
    {
        void            *reserved1;
        RPCOLEDATAREP   dataRepresentation;
        void            *Buffer;
        ULONG           cbBuffer;
        ULONG           iMethod;
        void            *reserved2[5];
        ULONG           rpcFlags;
    } RPCOLEMESSAGE;
```

The most significant field in this structure is the *Buffer* pointer. The proxy packs the parameters of a method into this buffer and then transmits it to the stub. The *cbBuffer* member of the RPCOLEMESSAGE data structure specifies the current size in bytes of the marshaling buffer. Memory is allocated for the *Buffer* pointer by calling the *IRpcChannelBuffer::GetBuffer* method, not by the proxy. The *GetBuffer* method uses the value of the *cbBuffer* field to decide how much memory to allocate for the transmission buffer.

The *dataRepresentation* field of the RPCOLEMESSAGE structure is an unsigned long (4-byte) value defined as the *RPCOLEDATAREP* type. This field contains the NDR format label that identifies the data formats used to represent primitive values. Figure 9-6 on the following page shows the layout of this 4-byte structure.

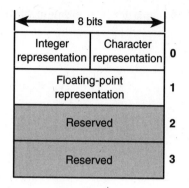

Figure 9-6.
The layout of the RPCOLEMESSAGE dataRepresentation *field.*

The bit flags that can be set in the format label are shown in the following table.

Data Type	Value	Format
Character representation	0	ASCII
	1	EBCDIC
Integer and floating-point byte order	0	Big endian
	1	Little endian
Floating-point representation	0	IEEE
	1	VAX
	2	Cray
	3	IBM

Let's pause now and retrace our steps back to the client to see how all these pieces fit together. To retrieve an interface pointer from the component, the client executes the following code:

```
ISum* pSum;
HRESULT hr = pUnknown->QueryInterface(IID_ISum, (void**)&pSum);
int retval;
hr = pSum->Sum(2, 7, &retval);
```

The *QueryInterface* call actually returns the pointer to the proxy's implementation of *ISum*. When the client calls the *ISum::Sum* method, the proxy's implementation of this method is invoked in the client's address space. At this stage, it is the job of the proxy to pack the necessary method parameters into a buffer for transmission to the stub. Here is the proxy's implementation of the *Sum* method, invoked whenever the client calls *ISum::Sum*:

```
HRESULT CRpcProxyBuffer::Sum(int x, int y, int* retval)
{
    RPCOLEMESSAGE Message = { 0, 0, 0, 0, 0, 0, 0, 0, 0, 0, 0 };
    ULONG status;

    // Specify how much memory to allocate for Message.Buffer.
    Message.cbBuffer = sizeof(int)*2;

    // Allocate the memory for Message.Buffer.
    m_pRpcChannel->GetBuffer(&Message, IID_ISum);

    // Marshal the Sum method's x and y arguments.
    ((int*)Message.Buffer)[0] = x;
    ((int*)Message.Buffer)[1] = y;

    // Set the v-table entry for ISum::Sum.
    Message.iMethod = 3;

    // Send the packet to the stub.
    m_pRpcChannel->SendReceive(&Message, &status);

    // Now the result is available.
    *retval = ((int*)Message.Buffer)[0];

    // Free the memory used for Message.Buffer.
    m_pRpcChannel->FreeBuffer(&Message);
    return S_OK;
}
```

The actual marshaling of method arguments takes place in the *CRpc-ProxyBuffer::Sum* method shown in the preceding code. This surrogate implementation of the *Sum* method declares a variable named *Message* of type RPCOLEMESSAGE. *Message.cbBuffer* is then set to the size of two integers, the total space needed to store the two *in* arguments accepted by the *Sum* method. *IRpcChannelBuffer::GetBuffer* is called to allocate the memory required for the transmission buffer. The following simple code marshals both the *x* and *y* arguments of the *Sum* method into the allocated buffer:

```
// Marshal the Sum method's x and y arguments.
((int*)Message.Buffer)[0] = x;
((int*)Message.Buffer)[1] = y;
```

Before the marshaled data packet can be sent to the proxy, we need to indicate which method of the *ISum* interface is being called. Recall that *ISum* has four methods, the three methods of *IUnknown* plus *ISum::Sum*. The *iMethod* field of the RPCOLEMESSAGE structure is used to specify the desired method. This value is a zero-based number for the desired method's v-table entry in the interface. In the case of *ISum*, the order of the entries in the v-table is *QueryInterface*, *AddRef*, *Release*, and finally *Sum*. Thus, *Sum* exists as method number 3 in a zero-based enumeration of the v-table entries, as shown here:

```
// Set the v-table entry for ISum::Sum.
Message.iMethod = 3;
```

Now we are ready to send the marshaled data packet from the proxy to the stub. The *SendReceive* method is the heart of the *IRpcChannelBuffer* interface. Utilizing the RPC infrastructure, this two-way method transmits the entire RPCOLEMESSAGE structure to the stub. The proxy then goes to sleep while it waits for the actual method to execute and for the return values to be sent back through the RPC channel to the proxy. In the stub, the *IRpcChannelBuffer::Invoke* method is called automatically when data is received in the channel from the proxy as the result of a call to *SendReceive*.

In the *Invoke* method, the stub must first determine which method in the interface is being called. The *iMethod* field of the RPCOLEMESSAGE structure provides this crucial information. Without knowing which method is being called, the stub can have no idea what data to expect from the RPC channel. In the following code, a *switch* statement is used to execute the correct code for the specified method being invoked. In this case, we check only for method number 3—the *Sum* method.

```
HRESULT CRpcStubBuffer::Invoke(RPCOLEMESSAGE* pMessage,
    IRpcChannelBuffer* pRpcChannel)
{
// What method of ISum is the proxy calling?
    switch(pMessage->iMethod)
    {
    case 3: // The proxy is calling ISum::Sum.
        int result;

        // Calling the Sum method!!!
        m_pObj->Sum(((int*)pMessage->Buffer)[0],
            ((int*)pMessage->Buffer)[1], &result);

        // How much memory is needed for the return value?
        pMessage->cbBuffer = sizeof(int);

        // Free the proxy buffer, and allocate a new one.
        pRpcChannel->GetBuffer(pMessage, m_iid);
```

```
      // Pack the return value into the buffer.
      ((int*)pMessage->Buffer)[0] = result;

      // Take it away...
      return NOERROR;

   // case other methods here...
   }
   return E_UNEXPECTED;
}
```

By using the *m_pObj* member variable that points to the actual *Sum* interface in the component, the real *Sum* method can now be called. The two parameters, *x* and *y*, are retrieved from the buffer packed by the proxy. For efficiency's sake, the *Sum* method is passed direct pointers into the message buffer; no copy of the data is made. Now the real *Sum* method executes, adds the two values, and returns the result to the stub. The stub is then responsible for transmitting the method's *out* parameters back to the proxy. First the *cbBuffer* field is set to the size (in bytes) of the memory required for the *out* parameters. Next the *IRpcChannelBuffer::GetBuffer* method must be called to allocate the memory needed to pack the *out* parameters for transmission. Before allocating a reply buffer, the *GetBuffer* method automatically frees the memory buffer allocated for the proxy's buffer. Then the result of the *Sum* method is stored in the transmission buffer. The act of returning from *IRpcStubBuffer::Invoke* returns the RPCOLEMESSAGE structure to the proxy.

In the proxy, the *IRpcChannelBuffer::SendReceive* function now returns, and the RPCOLEMESSAGE structure contains the data returned by the stub. The proxy unpacks the *out* parameters from the buffer and copies them into variables returned to the client, as shown in the following code. Last the *IRpcChannelBuffer::FreeBuffer* method is called to free the buffer containing the marshaled data packet from the stub.

```
// Send the packet to the stub.
m_pRpcChannel->SendReceive(&Message, &status);

// Now the result is available.
*retval = ((int*)Message.Buffer)[0];

// Free the memory used for Message.Buffer.
m_pRpcChannel->FreeBuffer(&Message);
```

The *IRpcChannelBuffer::GetDestCtx* method can be used to obtain the destination context information for this interface. *Destination context* is the term used to describe the barrier between a component and its client. The value returned will be one of the *MSHCTX* enumeration constants described in the

347

following table. This information might be useful to the proxy or the stub in determining how much data to send through the RPC channel.

MSHCTX Enumeration	Description
MSHCTX_LOCAL	The unmarshaling process is local and has shared memory access with the marshaling process.
MSHCTX_NOSHAREDMEM	The unmarshaling process does not have shared memory access with the marshaling process.
MSHCTX_DIFFERENTMACHINE	The unmarshaling process is on a different machine. The marshaling code cannot assume that a particular piece of application code is installed on that machine.
MSHCTX_INPROC	The unmarshaling operation will be performed in another apartment in the same process. If your object supports multiple threads, your custom marshaler can pass a direct pointer instead of creating a proxy object.

IsConnected, the last method of the *IRpcChannelBuffer* interface, can be used to determine whether the RPC channel is still connected to the other side. Interface proxies can use this method as an optimization by which an error can quickly be returned to the client if the proxy is not connected to the stub. This technique saves the time wasted by attempting a call to the *IRpc-ChannelBuffer::SendReceive* method only to receive the *E_RPCFAULT* error.

Registering the Proxy/Stub DLL

Although they are full-fledged COM objects, proxy/stub DLLs are registered a little differently from more standard components. First, a proxy/stub DLL has no need of a programmatic identifier (ProgID) entry in the registry because it is unlikely that any code aside from COM itself will want to instantiate a proxy or a stub object. Second, proxy/stub DLLs must have the special subkey ProxyStubClsid32 for the specified interface in the HKEY_CLASSES-_ROOT\Interface section of the registry.

To handle the unique registry requirements of proxy/stub DLLs, we have added two functions to the psregistry.cpp file: *RegisterProxyStubDLL* and

UnregisterProxyStubDLL. RegisterProxyStubDLL needs to know the IID that the proxy/stub DLL is professing to marshal. A CLSID entry will be added under HKEY_CLASSES_ROOT\CLSID as is done with normal COM objects, and a reference to this CLSID will be placed in the ProxyStubClsid32 subkey. The following code illustrates how a proxy/stub DLL would call the *RegisterProxy-StubDLL* and *UnregisterProxyStubDLL* functions as part of its self-registration procedure:

```
HRESULT __stdcall DllRegisterServer()
{
    return RegisterProxyStubDLL("ProxyStub.dll",
        CLSID_InsideDCOMStdProxy, IID_ISum, "PSSum");
}

HRESULT __stdcall DllUnregisterServer()
{
    return UnregisterProxyStubDLL(CLSID_InsideDCOMStdProxy, IID_ISum);
}
```

Handler Marshaling

Handler marshaling is another variation on marshaling, one closely related to standard marshaling. It can be thought of as a middle ground between regular standard marshaling and full custom marshaling. Handler marshaling is useful for objects that want to perform some of the work in the client's address space, making remote calls only when absolutely necessary. An object might decide to use handler marshaling for a variety of reasons. Sometimes the overhead of a remote call simply overshadows the amount of work the object will perform. For example, making a remote call simply to add two values, as was shown with the *ISum* interface, is terribly inefficient. It would be much more efficient for that call to be implemented within an in-process handler. In other cases, an in-process handler is used because a particular interface is simply not remotable. The *IViewObject* interface used by compound document embedded objects to perform client-side drawing is one example. Since a handle to a device context (*hDC*) used to draw on a window is valid only in a single address space, the remote object cannot use a client's *hDC*. In such cases, the non-remotable methods must be implemented as an in-process handler.

Objects that want to support handler marshaling in their client process implement the *IStdMarshalInfo* interface. The *IStdMarshalInfo* interface is shown on the following page in IDL notation.

349

```
interface IStdMarshalInfo : IUnknown
{
    HRESULT GetClassForHandler
    (
        [in] DWORD dwDestContext,
        [in, unique] void *pvDestContext,
        [out] CLSID *pClsid
    );
}
```

COM automatically calls *QueryInterface* on every object implemented in an executable component for the *IStdMarshalInfo* interface. If the *IStdMarshalInfo* interface is implemented by an object, COM calls the *IStdMarshalInfo::GetClassForHandler* method to retrieve the CLSID of the handler object to be loaded into the client's address space. The InprocHandler32 subkey in the HKEY-_CLASSES_ROOT\CLSID section of the registry references the handler object. COM then loads this in-process component into the client's address space. The following code shows a standard implementation of the *IStdMarshalInfo-::GetClassForHandler* method:

```
const CLSID CLSID_InsideDCOMHandler =
{0x11000006,0x0000,0x0000,{0x00,0x00,0x00,0x00,0x00,0x00,0x00,0x01}};

HRESULT CInsideDCOM::GetClassForHandler(DWORD dwDestContext,
    void* pvDestContext, CLSID* pClsid)
{
    // Load this handler into the client's address space.
    *pClsid = CLSID_InsideDCOMHandler;
    return NOERROR;
}
```

Once the specified handler is loaded into the client's address space, COM proceeds to call the handler's *DllGetClassObject* function, followed by its *IClassFactory::CreateInstance* method. Through this *CreateInstance* method, COM informs the handler that it is being aggregated and passes it a pointer to the controlling *IUnknown* interface implemented by the system identity object, to which the handler should delegate its own implementation of *IUnknown*. During the execution of the *IClassFactory::CreateInstance* method, the handler should create an aggregated standard marshaler (proxy manager) by using the *CoGetStdMarshalEx* function.

NOTE: The *CoGetStdMarshalEx* function is available only in Windows NT 5.0.

When it is called by the handler, the *CoGetStdMarshalEx* function takes a pointer to the controlling *IUnknown* interface provided by the *CreateInstance* method and the *SMEXF_HANDLER* flag, which indicates that the function is being called from the client's address space, as shown in the following code fragment. The other possible flag, *SMEXF_SERVER*, is used when you are calling the *CoGetStdMarshalEx* function from the component's address space in order to create a stub manager.

```
IUnknown* m_pUnknownInner;
CoGetStdMarshalEx(pUnknownOuter, SMEXF_HANDLER, &m_pUnknownInner);
```

The third parameter of the *CoGetStdMarshalEx* function returns a pointer, named *m_pUnknownInner* here, to the *IUnknown* interface implemented by the aggregated marshaler. This pointer can be used to communicate with the interface proxy and by consequence with the actual object in the component's address space.

Recall that the real goal of most handlers is to enable some work to be done in the client's address space while delegating other work to the actual object in the component's address space. With this in mind, a handler's implementation of the *ISum::Sum* method might perform some calculations in-process while delegating others to the *InsideDCOM* object via the *m_pUnknownInner* pointer. This concept is illustrated in the following code, in which the handler's implementation of the *Sum* method adds only numbers smaller than 50. For summations involving values of 50 or higher, the method executes a cross-process or possibly even a cross-machine call to the *Inside-DCOM* object running in the component's address space.

```
HRESULT CInsideDCOM::Sum(int x, int y, int* retval)
{
    if(x > 50 || y > 50)
    {
        // Numbers bigger than 50--better call the object
        ISum* pSum = 0;
        m_pUnknownInner->QueryInterface(IID_ISum, (void**)&pSum);
        HRESULT hr = pSum->Sum(x, y, retval);
        pSum->Release();
        return hr;
    }

    // Numbers smaller than 50--no need to call the object
    *retval = x + y;
    return S_OK;
}
```

Of course, this type of example could have been built using the standard marshaling technique described earlier in this chapter. Notice, however, how much easier it was to use handler marshaling to override certain aspects of standard marshaling. We didn't have to implement or call any of the standard marshaling interfaces, including *IPSFactoryBuffer*, *IRpcProxyBuffer*, *IRpcStubBuffer*, and *IRpcChannelBuffer*.

Custom Marshaling

Custom marshaling is the basic marshaling architecture of COM, on which standard marshaling is built. From the programmer's perspective, custom marshaling is similar to the experience of standard marshaling except that COM will not provide any support for transmitting data between the proxy and the stub. It is the responsibility of the programmer to use whatever form of interprocess communication is deemed best for the job. In this section, we will show you how custom marshaling can be used to handle the marshaling requirements of the *ISum* interface.

The principal goal of the custom marshaling architecture is to marshal an interface pointer. Recall that marshaling an interface pointer simply means re-creating the interface's v-table within the client's address space. A proxy component is needed in order to accomplish this goal. This proxy component is built as a DLL and will be loaded into the client's address space as required. While custom marshaling includes the concept of a proxy DLL in the client's address space, there is no concept of a stub DLL in the component's address space. The code that intercepts the proxy's communiqués can reside directly in the component.

One of the more common occasions for choosing custom marshaling is when an object has one or more clients running on the same machine that want to access the object's state in memory. Let's return to the example of an image-processing component discussed earlier in this chapter. If a client process is running on the same machine as the component, it makes little sense to copy the bitmap from the client to the component's address space. Instead, it is much more efficient to simply allocate shared memory between the two processes. Using custom marshaling gives the developer full control over the marshaling process, and implementing marshaling using shared memory is one possibility. Obviously, this type of custom marshaling is limited to processes running on a single machine.

Another common use of custom marshaling is to obtain marshal-by-value semantics. Some objects, such as monikers, have an immutable state: their internal data never changes. For an object whose state never changes, it doesn't make sense to require the client to make remote method calls to retrieve data. For example, imagine an object that represents a rectangle. If the dimensions and coordinates of the rectangle never change after the object is created, the object is a good candidate for the marshal-by-value optimization. In such cases, the data that defines the object can be transmitted to the proxy using custom marshaling, where the data can be used to create an exact replica of the object. This technique allows the client to make in-process calls to obtain the same information that a remote call would; the client is none the wiser. In still other cases, custom marshaling can be used to batch several client calls and then forward them as a group to the component. This technique can improve performance by cutting down on the number of round-trips made to the component.

When shared memory is used to implement custom marshaling, we still need to consider what happens when the clients and components will not be running on the same machine. In such cases, you can either build the support necessary to remote the interface across a network or delegate to COM's standard marshaler for this task. In fact, it is recommended that implementations of custom marshaling delegate to the standard marshaler destination contexts they do not understand or for which they do not provide special functionality. This information is provided to several methods of the *IMarshal* interface in the form of a flag that indicates whether the client is running in-process, on the same machine, or remotely.

Of course, if you choose standard marshaling for certain destination contexts and custom marshaling for others, all the requirements of standard marshaling must be met as well. This means that a proxy/stub DLL will have to be created and registered in addition to the custom marshaling code discussed here. Remember that MIDL is your friend—you don't have to write proxy/stub DLLs by hand! The *CoGetStandardMarshal* function can be used to return an instance of COM's standard implementation of the *IMarshal* interface. This implementation is the same as the implementation used implicitly when you are not using custom marshaling.

Can You Say "Custom Marshaling"?

Before launching into the code that implements *IMarshal*, the custom marshaling interface, let's review once again the code executed by the prototypical client application:

```
// client.cpp

// Start your engines.
CoInitialize(NULL);
```

(continued)

```
// Get a pointer to the object's class factory.
IClassFactory* pClassFactory;
CoGetClassObject(CLSID_InsideDCOM, CLSCTX_LOCAL_SERVER,
    NULL, IID_IClassFactory, (void**)&pClassFactory);

// Instantiate the InsideDCOM object,
// and get a pointer to its IUnknown interface.
IUnknown* pUnknown;
pClassFactory->CreateInstance(NULL, IID_IUnknown, (void**)&pUnknown);
```

The client calls *IClassFactory::CreateInstance* to request that the *InsideDCOM* object be instantiated, and a pointer to *IUnknown* is returned. Inside COM's standard marshaling code for *IClassFactory::CreateInstance*, COM realizes that the *IUnknown* interface pointer about to be returned to the client needs to be marshaled. So the marshaling code for *IClassFactory::CreateInstance* now calls *CoMarshalInterface* to marshal the *IUnknown* interface pointer. *CoMarshalInterface* now queries the *InsideDCOM* object to determine whether the object wants to use standard or custom marshaling.

Since custom marshaling is performed on a per-object basis, not on a per-interface basis like standard marshaling, we need to respond affirmatively to this query. Recall that although COM will be more than happy to provide standard marshaling for *IUnknown*, the *InsideDCOM* object also implements the *ISum* interface, about which COM knows nothing. We might accept standard marshaling for *IUnknown*, but our code would crash the moment the client requested an *ISum* interface pointer.

The *InsideDCOM* object's implementation of the *IUnknown::QueryInterface* method implementation is shown in the following code; the support for the *IMarshal* interface is indicated in boldface:

```
HRESULT CInsideDCOM::QueryInterface(REFIID riid, void** ppv)
{
    if(riid == IID_IUnknown)
        *ppv = reinterpret_cast<IUnknown*>(this);

    // IMarshal? Absolutely!
    else if(riid == IID_IMarshal)
        *ppv = (IMarshal*)this;

    else if(riid == IID_ISum)
        *ppv = (ISum*)this;
    else
    {
        *ppv = NULL;
```

```
        return E_NOINTERFACE;
    }
    AddRef();
    return S_OK;
}
```

Once a pointer to *IMarshal* is returned by the *QueryInterface* method, the *CoMarshalInterface* function, called by the standard marshaling code for *IClassFactory::CreateInstance*, is now entitled to call any of the six methods in the *IMarshal* interface. These methods are shown here in IDL notation:

```
interface IMarshal : IUnknown
{
    // Component implements this method.
    // Get the CLSID of the proxy object.
    HRESULT GetUnmarshalClass(
        [in] REFIID riid,
        [in, unique] void* pv,
        [in] DWORD dwDestContext,
        [in, unique] void* pvDestContext,
        [in] DWORD dwFlags,
        [out] CLSID *pClsid);

    // Component implements this method.
    // Get the maximum space needed to marshal the interface.
    HRESULT GetMarshalSizeMax(
        [in] REFIID riid,
        [in, unique] void* pv,
        [in] DWORD dwDestContext,
        [in, unique] void* pvDestContext,
        [in] DWORD dwFlags,
        [out] DWORD* pSize);

    // Component implements this method.
    // Marshal that interface and write it to the stream.
    HRESULT MarshalInterface(
        [in, unique] IStream* pStream,
        [in] REFIID riid,
        [in, unique] void* pv,
        [in] DWORD dwDestContext,
        [in, unique] void* pvDestContext,
        [in] DWORD dwFlags);

    // Component implements this method.
    // Tell the proxy that we're going to shut down.
    HRESULT DisconnectObject([in] DWORD dwReserved);
```

(continued)

355

```
// Component implements this method.
// Release the marshaled data in the stream.
HRESULT ReleaseMarshalData([in, unique] IStream* pStream);

// Proxy implements this method.
// Unmarshal that interface from the stream.
HRESULT UnmarshalInterface(
    [in, unique] IStream *pStream,
    [in] REFIID riid,
    [out] void** ppv);
}
```

IMarshal is a peculiar interface because, of its six methods, the first five are called in the component and the remaining method is called in the proxy. Although COM requires that any object returning an interface pointer from *QueryInterface* fully support that interface, in the case of *IMarshal* some of these methods are never called on the component or the proxy. Nevertheless, you must provide dummy implementations of all six *IMarshal* methods in both the component and the proxy. For example, the component provides the following dummy implementation of *IMarshal::UnmarshalInterface*:

```
HRESULT CInsideDCOM::UnmarshalInterface(IStream* pStream,
    REFIID riid, void** ppv)
{
    // This method should be called only in the proxy, not here.
    return E_UNEXPECTED;
}
```

After the object says, "Yes, I perform custom marshaling," the following sequence of steps is executed in the component:

1. *IMarshal::GetUnmarshalClass* is called to obtain the CLSID of the proxy object.

2. *IMarshal::GetMarshalSizeMax* is called to ask what size marshaling packet the interface needs.

3. COM allocates the memory and then creates a pointer to a stream object that refers to the buffer.

4. *IMarshal::MarshalInterface* is called to ask the object to marshal the interface pointer.

At this point, the buffer allocated in step 3 contains all the information necessary to create and initialize the proxy object within the client's address space. This buffer is now communicated back to the client process, where the proxy object is created. Then *IMarshal::UnmarshalInterface* is called in the proxy to initialize the interface proxy. That's it—the whole purpose of the *IMarshal* interface is to give the component a chance to send one measly message back to the proxy!

Now that you have a high-level overview of the process, let's look at custom marshaling in detail.

Pardon Me, What Is the CLSID of Your Proxy Object?

CoMarshalInterface first calls the *IMarshal::GetUnmarshalClass* method to request that the object provide the CLSID of the proxy object. In effect, *GetUnmarshalClass* asks the object, "What is the CLSID of your proxy object?" This value is returned via the pointer to a CLSID in the last parameter of *GetUnmarshalClass*. The purpose of the *IMarshal::GetUnmarshalClass* method is very similar to that of the *IStdMarshalInfo::GetClassForHandler* method used to obtain the CLSID of a handler to be loaded in the client's address space for handler marshaling. An implementation of *IMarshal::GetUnmarshalClass* might look like this:

```
CLSID CLSID_InsideDCOMProxy =
{0x10000004,0x0000,0x0000,{0x00,0x00,0x00,0x00,0x00,0x00,0x00,0x01}};

HRESULT CInsideDCOM::GetUnmarshalClass(REFIID riid, void* pv,
    DWORD dwDestContext, void* pvDestContext, DWORD dwFlags,
    CLSID* pClsid)
{
    // We handle only the local marshaling case.
    if(dwDestContext == MSHCTX_DIFFERENTMACHINE)
    {
        IMarshal* pMarshal;
        // Create a standard marshaler (proxy manager).
        CoGetStandardMarshal(riid, (ISum*)pv, dwDestContext,
            pvDestContext, dwFlags, &pMarshal);

        // Load the interface proxy.
        HRESULT hr = pMarshal->GetUnmarshalClass(riid, pv,
            dwDestContext, pvDestContext, dwFlags, pClsid);
        pMarshal->Release();
        return hr;
    }
    *pClsid = CLSID_InsideDCOMProxy;
    return S_OK;
}
```

COM holds onto this CLSID, which it shortly sends to the client as part of the marshaling packet for use in launching the proxy object in the client's address space. Notice that much of the code in *GetUnmarshalClass* deals with the case of the client running on a different machine. Since this custom marshaling example uses shared memory, we must delegate marshaling to COM's standard marshaler when the client is not running on the local machine. *CoGetStandardMarshal* returns a pointer to COM's implementation of the *IMarshal* interface, from which we call COM's implementation of *IMarshal::GetUnmarshalClass*.

How Big Did You Say Your Interface Is?

Next *CoMarshalInterface* calls *IMarshal::GetMarshalSizeMax*, as shown in the following code. The purpose of *GetMarshalSizeMax* is to ask the object, "What is the maximum space you need in order to marshal your interface?" In this implementation, the object declares that it currently needs a maximum of 255 bytes in order to marshal the desired interface. Notice that once again the code checks to see whether the client is running on the same machine. If it is not, we delegate the call to COM's implementation of *IMarshal::GetMarshalSizeMax*.

```
HRESULT CInsideDCOM::GetMarshalSizeMax(REFIID riid, void* pv,
    DWORD dwDestContext, void* pvDestContext, DWORD dwFlags,
    DWORD* pSize)
{
    // We handle only the local marshaling case.
    if(dwDestContext == MSHCTX_DIFFERENTMACHINE)
    {
        IMarshal* pMarshal;
        CoGetStandardMarshal(riid, (ISum*)pv, dwDestContext,
            pvDestContext, dwFlags, &pMarshal);
        HRESULT hr = pMarshal->GetMarshalSizeMax(riid, pv,
            dwDestContext, pvDestContext, dwFlags, pSize);
        pMarshal->Release();
        return hr;
    }
    *pSize = 255;
    return S_OK;
}
```

To the value returned by the *GetMarshalSizeMax* method, *CoMarshalInterface* adds the space needed for the marshaling data header as well as for the proxy CLSID obtained in the call to *IMarshal::GetUnmarshalClass*. This technique yields the true maximum size in bytes required to marshal the interface, and it is used to allocate a buffer large enough to hold the marshaled interface pointer. This buffer is then turned into a stream object (an object supporting the *IStream* interface) by calling the *CreateStreamOnHGlobal* function. Before it does anything else, *CoMarshalInterface* writes the CLSID of the proxy object into the stream object by calling the *WriteClassStm* function.

Finally, *CoMarshalInterface* is ready to marshal the interface, so it calls *IMarshal::MarshalInterface*. This call says to the component, "Pack up that interface and let's get moving!" It is *MarshalInterface*'s job to marshal the requested interface into the stream object provided as the first parameter. This task is normally accomplished by calling the *IStream::Write* method to serialize the marshaled interface pointer into the stream object.

What Is a Marshaled Interface Pointer?

Perhaps you are wondering what exactly a marshaled interface pointer consists of? A marshaled interface pointer can be whatever you want it to be. Once the *IMarshal* dance is over, you will want the proxy to be able to communicate with the component in order to marshal method calls. That's right, *IMarshal* is designed to marshal interface pointers only. Once the interface pointer is available on the client side, all the work of packing function parameters, sending them to the component, and unpacking them is left to you! You can perform these tasks however you like. For cross-machine calls, you might use sockets or named pipes; for intermachine calls, you might use a file-mapping object for shared memory.

Your implementation of *IMarshal::MarshalInterface* must write to the stream whatever data is needed to initialize the proxy on the receiving side. Such data might include whatever information is needed in order to connect to the object, such as a handle to a window, the name of a named pipe, or an IP address and port number. When implementing custom marshaling to obtain marshal-by-value semantics, the marshaled interface pointer should contain the entire state of the object.

In the following sample code, *MarshalInterface* creates a file-mapping object to share memory between the proxy and the component for the purpose of passing function parameters. Then it creates two event objects that are later used for synchronizing method calls. The names of these Win32 kernel objects are written into the marshaling stream. In other words, a marshaled interface pointer for *ISum* consists of the string *"FileMap,StubEvent,ProxyEvent"*.

```
HRESULT CInsideDCOM::MarshalInterface(IStream* pStream,
    REFIID riid, void* pv, DWORD dwDestContext,
    void* pvDestContext, DWORD dwFlags)
{
    // We handle only the local marshaling case.
    if(dwDestContext == MSHCTX_DIFFERENTMACHINE)
```

(continued)

```
    {
        IMarshal* pMarshal;
        CoGetStandardMarshal(riid, (ISum*)pv, dwDestContext,
            pvDestContext, dwFlags, &pMarshal);
        HRESULT hr = pMarshal->MarshalInterface(pStream,
            riid, pv, dwDestContext, pvDestContext, dwFlags);
        pMarshal->Release();
        return hr;
    }
    ULONG num_written;
    char* szFileMapName = "FileMap";
    char* szStubEventName = "StubEvent";
    char* szProxyEventName = "ProxyEvent";
    char buffer_to_write[255];

    AddRef();

    hFileMap = CreateFileMapping((HANDLE)0xFFFFFFFF, NULL,
        PAGE_READWRITE, 0, 255, szFileMapName);
    hStubEvent = CreateEvent(NULL, FALSE, FALSE, szStubEventName);
    hProxyEvent = CreateEvent(NULL, FALSE, FALSE, szProxyEventName);

    strcpy(buffer_to_write, szFileMapName);
    strcat(buffer_to_write, ",");
    strcat(buffer_to_write, szStubEventName);
    strcat(buffer_to_write, ",");
    strcat(buffer_to_write, szProxyEventName);

    return pStream->Write(buffer_to_write,
        strlen(buffer_to_write)+1, &num_written);
}
```

As with the *IMarshal::GetUnmarshalClass* and *IMarshal::GetMarshalSizeMax* methods shown earlier, the *MarshalInterface* method delegates to COM's standard marshaler if the destination context does not indicate that the client is running on the local machine. The extra *AddRef* thrown into the preceding *MarshalInterface* code is quite necessary. When you use custom marshaling, no stub is available to hold a reference count on the object itself. Without this *AddRef*, the *InsideDCOM* object would simply exit before the client has ever had a chance to call it. In the next section, "Unmarshaling the Interface Pointer," we'll see that the proxy will eventually call *Release*, which will be forwarded to the component in order to undo this *AddRef*.

Remember that *CoMarshalInterface* carefully orchestrates all of these steps. To summarize what we've covered so far, the following pseudo-code shows what COM does in order to ensure that an interface pointer is marshaled properly:

```
// AddRef the incoming pointer to verify that it is safe.
pUnknown->AddRef();

// Do you support custom marshaling?
IMarshal* pMarshal;
HRESULT hr = pUnknown->QueryInterface(IID_IMarshal, (void**)&pMarshal);

// I guess not, so we'll use standard marshaling.
if(hr == E_NOINTERFACE)
    CoGetStandardMarshal(riid, pUnknown, dwDestContext,
        pvDestContext, dwFlags, &pMarshal);

// OK, what's the CLSID of your proxy object?
CLSID clsid;
pMarshal->GetUnmarshalClass(riid, pUnknown, dwDestContext,
    pvDestContext, dwFlags, &clsid);

// How much space do you need?
ULONG packetSize;
pMarshal->GetMarshalSizeMax(riid, pUnknown, dwDestContext,
    pvDestContext, dwFlags, &packetSize);

// Allocate that memory.
HGLOBAL pMem = GlobalAlloc(GHND, packetSize + sizeof(CLSID));

// Turn it into a stream object.
IStream* pStream;
CreateStreamOnHGlobal(pMem, FALSE, &pStream);

// Write the CLSID of the proxy into the stream.
WriteClassStm(pStream, clsid);

// Marshal that interface into the stream.
pMarshal->MarshalInterface(pStream, riid, pUnknown, dwDestContext,
    pvDestContext, dwFlags);

// Release everything in sight.
pStream->Release();
pMarshal->Release();
pUnknown->Release();
```

At this point, the SCM is ready to send the stream object back to the client process. Since the SCM was responsible for launching the component to begin with, it knows exactly what sort of a barrier lies between the client and the component. This barrier is described as one of the marshaling contexts defined by the *MSHCTX* enumeration. (See the section "The RPCOLEMESSAGE Structure" earlier in this chapter.) The mechanism we use to transmit data between the client and the component must depend on the marshaling context. For example, if the client is communicating with the component process on the same machine (*MSHCTX_LOCAL*), a file-mapping object could be used to share memory. If the two processes run on different computers (*MSHCTX_DIFFERENTMACHINE*), a network protocol such as named pipes, sockets, RPC, NetBIOS, or mailslots can be used.

At the end of the marshaling sequence, we're left with a marshaled interface pointer that can either be sent directly to the client or be stored in a table waiting for a client to request it. The flag passed as the last parameter to *CoMarshalInterface* indicates whether the marshaled data is to be transmitted back to the client process—the normal case—or written to a global table called the class table, where multiple clients can retrieve it. This flag can be one of the values from the *MSHLFLAGS* enumeration constants listed in the following table.

MSHLFLAGS Enumeration	Description
MSHLFLAGS_NORMAL	Indicates that unmarshaling is occurring immediately.
MSHLFLAGS_TABLESTRONG	Unmarshaling is not occurring immediately. Keeps object alive; must be explicitly released.
MSHLFLAGS_TABLEWEAK	Unmarshaling is not occurring immediately. Doesn't keep object alive; still must be released.
MSHLFLAGS_NOPING	Turns off DCOM garbage collection by not pinging objects to determine whether they are still alive. (See Chapter 12, "The Network Protocol.") Can be combined with any of the other *MSHLFLAGS* enumeration constants.

The *MSHLFLAGS_NORMAL* flag indicates that the marshaling is occurring immediately, such as when the component returns an interface pointer in response to a client's call to *IUnknown::QueryInterface*. *MSHLFLAGS_TABLE-STRONG* and *MSHLFLAGS_TABLEWEAK*, however, indicate that the unmarshaling isn't happening at the present time. Instead, these flags indicate that the marshaled interface pointer is to be stored in a global table that is accessible to all processes via COM. When a client process wants to connect, the marshaled interface pointer is already there, ready and waiting. For example, table marshaling is used by the *CoRegisterClassObject* function. This function stores a marshaled *IClassFactory* interface pointer in the class table ready for clients to request it via *CoGetClassObject*. Only when the client calls *CoGetClassObject* is the marshaled interface pointer sent to the client for unmarshaling.

If *MSHLFLAGS_TABLESTRONG* is specified, the *IUnknown::AddRef* method is automatically called to ensure that the object remains in memory. In other words, the presence of the marshaled interface pointer in the class table counts as a strong reference to the interface being marshaled, meaning that it is sufficient to keep the object alive. This is the case with *CoRegisterClassObject*. When the *CoRevokeClassObject* function is later called to remove the marshaled interface pointer from the class table, *CoRevokeClassObject* calls the *CoReleaseMarshalData* function to free the stream object containing the marshaled interface pointer. *MSHLFLAGS_TABLEWEAK* indicates that the presence of the marshaled interface pointer in the class table acts as a weak reference to the interface being marshaled, meaning that it is not sufficient to keep the object alive. *MSHLFLAGS_TABLEWEAK* is typically used when you are registering an object in the Running Object Table (ROT). The presence of this flag prevents the object's entry in the ROT from keeping the object alive in the absence of any other connections.

Unmarshaling the Interface Pointer

The purpose of the *IMarshal* interface is to provide a mechanism by which the component can marshal its interface pointer into a stream object that the client can unmarshal. Just as *CoMarshalInterface* directs the marshaling of an interface pointer, *CoUnmarshalInterface* directs the unmarshaling of an interface pointer. Look at the following function declaration for *CoUnmarshalInterface*—you should be able to tell that *QueryInterface* is going to be involved somewhere along the way:

```
STDAPI CoUnmarshalInterface(IStream* pStream, REFIID riid, void** ppv);
```

CoUnmarshalInterface examines the stream object containing the marshaled interface pointer to find the CLSID of the proxy object, which is required to unmarshal the remainder of the stream object. The CLSID is read out of the stream by the *ReadClassStm* function. The SCM then instantiates the proxy object specified by the CLSID by calling *CoCreateInstance* and requesting the *IMarshal* interface. A proxy used for custom marshaling an object must implement the *IMarshal* interface. If standard marshaling is being used, the CLSID in the stream is *CLSID_StdMarshal*, or *{00000017-0000-0000-C000-000000000046}*.

Figure 9-7 shows how the proxy is loaded in the client's address space by the SCM and also shows that the proxy and the object communicate directly via a private protocol of their own choosing.

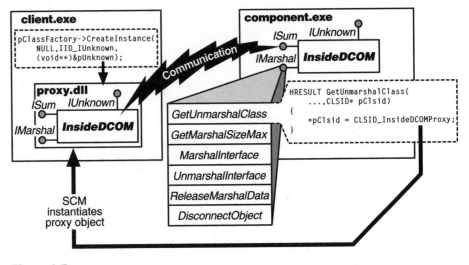

Figure 9-7.
A custom marshaling sample showing the proxy and the actual object communicating.

Here's a quick recap of these events: The client calls *CoCreateInstance* to instantiate the *InsideDCOM* component. Then COM calls *QueryInterface* to determine whether the object supports the *IMarshal* interface and hence custom marshaling. Since this is the case, the *ISum* interface pointer is marshaled into a stream object and returned to the proxy. In the proxy, COM calls the *Co-UnmarshalInterface* function to handle the unmarshaling of the stream object. Once a pointer to the *IMarshal* interface of the proxy object has been retrieved, *CoUnmarshalInterface* calls *IMarshal::UnmarshalInterface*. This method, implemented by the proxy, reads in the marshaling stream using *IStream::Read* and uses the data to establish a connection to the component. Again, any desired communication mechanism can be used (named pipes, sockets, and so on). From this communication, the *UnmarshalInterface* method returns the unmarshaled pointer to the requested interface, usually *IUnknown*. In reality, the unmarshaled pointer is simply a pointer to the proxy's implementation of the requested interface that is now loaded in the client's address space.

Here is the proxy's implementation of *IMarshal::UnmarshalInterface*, which reads the data from the stream previously marshaled by the component in *IMarshal::MarshalInterface*:

```
HRESULT CInsideDCOM::UnmarshalInterface(IStream* pStream,
    REFIID riid, void** ppv)
{
    unsigned long num_read;
    char buffer_to_read[255];
    char* pszFileMapName;
    char* pszStubEventName;
    char* pszProxyEventName;

    pStream->Read((void *)buffer_to_read, 255, &num_read);

    pszFileMapName = strtok(buffer_to_read, ",");
    pszStubEventName = strtok(NULL, ",");
    pszProxyEventName = strtok(NULL, ",");

    hFileMap = OpenFileMapping(FILE_MAP_WRITE, FALSE, pszFileMapName);
    pMem = MapViewOfFile(hFileMap, FILE_MAP_WRITE, 0, 0, 0);

    hStubEvent = OpenEvent(EVENT_MODIFY_STATE, FALSE,
        pszStubEventName);
    hProxyEvent = OpenEvent(EVENT_MODIFY_STATE|SYNCHRONIZE,
        FALSE, pszProxyEventName);

    return QueryInterface(riid, ppv);
}
```

CoUnmarshalInterface also calls *IMarshal::ReleaseMarshalData* to free whatever data might be stored in the marshaling packet. Last *IMarshal::DisconnectObject* is called as a result of code in the component that calls the *CoDisconnectObject* function. *CoDisconnectObject* is a helper function that disconnects all remote client connections that maintain interface pointers to the specified object. First *CoDisconnectObject* queries the object for its *IMarshal* interface pointer; if the object does not support custom marshaling, *CoGetStandardMarshal* is called to obtain a pointer to COM's implementation of *IMarshal.* Next *CoDisconnectObject* uses the *IMarshal* pointer obtained to call the *IMarshal::DisconnectObject* method. It is the job of *DisconnectObject* to notify the proxy that the object itself is exiting and that it should now return the error *CO_E_OBJECTNOTCONNECTED* to client requests. The following pseudo-code summarizes the steps taken in the client process to ensure that unmarshaling is done correctly:

```
// Turn the marshaled interface pointer into a stream object.
IStream* pStream;
CreateStreamOnHGlobal(hMem, FALSE, &pStream);
```

(continued)

```
// Get the CLSID of the proxy object out of the stream.
CLSID clsid;
ReadClassStm(pStream, &clsid);

// Instantiate that proxy object.
IMarshal* pMarshal;
CoCreateInstance(clsid, 0, CLSCTX_INPROC_SERVER, IID_IMarshal,
    (void**)&pMarshal);

// Clone the stream.
IStream* pStreamClone;
pStream->Clone(&pStreamClone);

// Unmarshal your interface.
pMarshal->UnmarshalInterface(pStream, riid, ppv);

// Release any data in the stream.
pMarshal->ReleaseMarshalData(pStreamClone);

// Release anything left.
pStream->Release();
pStreamClone->Release();
pMarshal->Release();

// Free the marshaled memory packet.
GlobalFree(hMem);
```

When the client calls the *ISum::Sum* method, it is actually talking to the in-process proxy object. One of the major reasons for performing custom marshaling is to be able to intelligently cut down on the number of cross-process or cross-machine calls made. For example, rather than making a call to the component every time the client calls *AddRef* or *Release*, the proxy simply keeps a reference count locally. Only when the last *Release* call is made and the reference count returns to *0* does the proxy actually forward the *Release* call to the object.

Here is the proxy's implementation of the *Release* method:

```
ULONG CInsideDCOM::Release()
{
    if(--m_cRef != 0)
        return m_cRef;
    // Notify the component that this is the last Release.
    short method_id = 1; // ISum::Release
    memcpy(pMem, &method_id, sizeof(short));
    SetEvent(hStubEvent);
```

```
        delete this;
        return 0;
}
```

When the reference count returns to *0*, this function copies the value of the *method_id* variable into the file-mapping memory shared by the proxy and the component. It then calls *SetEvent* to notify the component that it is requesting service. The component is waiting for this event in the code shown here:

```
void TalkToProxy()
{
    while(hStubEvent == 0)
        Sleep(0);

    void* pMem = MapViewOfFile(hFileMap, FILE_MAP_WRITE, 0, 0, 0);
    short method_id = 0;

    while(true)
    {
        WaitForSingleObject(hStubEvent, INFINITE);
        memcpy(&method_id, pMem, sizeof(short));
        switch(method_id) // What method did the proxy call?
        {
        case 1:     // IUnknown::Release
            CoDisconnectObject(reinterpret_cast<IUnknown*>(
                g_pInsideDCOM), 0);
            g_pInsideDCOM->Release();
            return;
        case 2:     // ISum::Sum
            SumTransmit s;
            memcpy(&s, (short*)pMem+1, sizeof(SumTransmit));
            g_pInsideDCOM->Sum(s.x, s.y, &s.sum);
            memcpy(pMem, &s, sizeof(s));
            SetEvent(hProxyEvent);
        }
    }
}
```

After the proxy sets the stub event, the component retrieves the first byte, which indicates what method is being called. In this simple case, the component expects to receive only one of two calls from the proxy: *Release* or *Sum*. The component then deciphers the call and forwards it to the actual implementation. The *Sum* method, for example, requires that the component unpack the parameters from the SumTransmit structure and then repack the return value.

The SumTransmit structure is used to transmit the parameters and the return value of the *Sum* method; it is defined here:

```
struct SumTransmit
{
    int x;
    int y;
    int sum;
};
```

As shown in the following proxy code, we wait until the component has finished adding the values and then we retrieve the result for the client. A second event object (*hProxyEvent*) is used to determine when the component has finished processing.

```
HRESULT CInsideDCOM::Sum(int x, int y, int* sum)
{
    SumTransmit s;
    s.x = x;
    s.y = y;
    short method_id = 2; // ISum::Sum

    memcpy(pMem, &method_id, sizeof(short));
    memcpy((short*)pMem+1, &s, sizeof(SumTransmit));

    SetEvent(hStubEvent);
    WaitForSingleObject(hProxyEvent, INFINITE);

    memcpy(&s, pMem, sizeof(s));

    *sum = s.sum;
    return S_OK;
}
```

The custom marshaling mechanism shown in this example depends on shared memory being available between the proxy and the component, something possible only if both the client and the component are running on the same machine. To create a custom marshaling sample that works across machines, a network-capable mechanism would need to be used.

Converting Marshaled Interface Pointers to Strings

In the preceding section, we saw that a marshaled interface pointer could be as simple as the string *"FileMap,StubEvent,ProxyEvent"*. When using custom marshaling, it is up to the developer to decide what constitutes a marshaled interface pointer. Remember that COM's standard marshaling architecture is built on top of custom marshaling and thus the standard marshaler must also decide what constitutes a marshaled interface pointer. It should come as no surprise that interface pointers marshaled by the standard marshaler are stored in a very different format from that of our custom marshaling example. To obtain the marshaled form of an arbitrary interface pointer, regardless of whether it uses custom or standard marshaling, you need only create a stream object and then call the *CoMarshalInterface* function, as shown in the following code fragment:

```
IStream* pStream = 0;
hr = CreateStreamOnHGlobal(0, TRUE, &pStream);
hr = CoMarshalInterface(pStream, riid, pObject,
    MSHCTX_DIFFERENTMACHINE, 0, MSHLFLAGS_NORMAL);
```

Now you can examine the marshaled interface pointer stored in the stream. Of course, the data is stored in a binary format that does not lend itself to casual inspection. One technique often used to view binary data is to convert it to a string that can be displayed. While many algorithms can be used to convert binary data to a string, one of the simplest is to convert each byte of data to two hexadecimal characters. This means that a binary value of 0 is converted to the characters 00, the binary value 78 is converted to the characters 4E, and 255 becomes FF. To automate this conversion, we wrote a function that converts an arbitrary interface pointer to a hexadecimal string using this technique; the code for the function, named *IPToHexString*, is shown here:

```
HRESULT IPToHexString(REFIID riid, IUnknown* pObject, char** output)
{
    HRESULT hr;
    IStream* pStream = 0;
    hr = CreateStreamOnHGlobal(0, TRUE, &pStream);

    hr = CoMarshalInterface(pStream, riid, pObject,
        MSHCTX_DIFFERENTMACHINE, 0, MSHLFLAGS_NORMAL);

    ULONG size;
    hr = CoGetMarshalSizeMax(&size, riid, pObject,
        MSHCTX_DIFFERENTMACHINE, 0, MSHLFLAGS_NORMAL);

    HGLOBAL hg;
    hr = GetHGlobalFromStream(pStream, &hg);
    unsigned char* buffer = (unsigned char*)GlobalLock(hg);
```

(continued)

```
*output = (char*)CoTaskMemAlloc((size * 2) + 1);

char hex[] = { '0', '1', '2', '3', '4', '5', '6', '7',
    '8', '9', 'a', 'b', 'c', 'd', 'e', 'f' };

for(ULONG count = 0; count < size; count++)
{
    (*output)[count*2] = hex[buffer[count] / 16];
    (*output)[(count*2)+1] = hex[buffer[count] -
        (buffer[count] / 16) * 16];
}
(*output)[((count-1)*2)+2] = 0;

GlobalUnlock(hg);
pStream->Release();

return hr;
}
```

Using this function, our eyes are opened to the fascinating world of standard marshaled interface pointers. After converting an interface pointer to a string, you can easily display it using a *printf*-style function. The other day we found a really good one:

4d454f57010000000100001000000000000000000000000100000000000000004
00500004d3b9e044a0500004d3b9e0401000000e5b5f6ff31baf6ff0100000023
0014000700310039003900390002e00330034002e00350038002e00330030005b00310
0330035005d00000000000a00000044004f004d00410049004e005c0047004100
4c0049000000000000004c0100a0346434353466353730313030303030303031

If you are wondering what this data means, don't despair—the exact contents of a standard marshaled interface pointer are covered in Chapter 12, "The Network Protocol." You might be thinking, "Hey, that's pretty neat. But what can I do with a marshaled interface pointer in string form?" The great thing about having a string form of a marshaled interface pointer is the ease with which you can transfer it. For example, you could e-mail the interface pointer shown above to a friend. What could your friend do with a marshaled interface pointer in string form? She could convert the string back to a binary marshaled interface pointer and then unmarshal it—yielding a valid interface pointer to your object. The code needed to convert a hexadecimal stream back to a binary block of memory can be found on the companion CD. Here is the code that unmarshals the interface pointer and provides an actual interface pointer, named *pObject*:

```
IStream* pStream = 0;
hr = CreateStreamOnHGlobal(pointer, TRUE, &pStream);
hr = CoUnmarshalInterface(pStream, riid, pObject);
pStream->Release();
```

This technique for transmitting interface pointers will work regardless of whether you transmit the interface pointer to someone across the hall or across the continent. Of course, the unmarshaled interface pointer is valid only as long as the original object continues running; once the object terminates, the interface pointer is useless. And of course the client machine must have a registered proxy installed that knows how to unmarshal the interface pointer. One interesting idea is to build a custom moniker that uses the string form of a marshaled interface pointer as its display name; this project is left as an exercise for the reader.

CHAPTER TEN

The Interface Definition Language

It is widely acknowledged that the language used to express an idea both limits and shapes what can be expressed. Therefore, while it is true that the infrastructure of COM is entirely divorced from the source-level languages used to access or create components, it is only natural that the available tools and languages heavily influenced COM's design. For COM, this has meant that its design was strongly affected by C++, the most widely used object-oriented programming language; by Microsoft Windows, the platform that gave birth to COM; and by Remote Procedure Call (RPC). RPC made important contributions to the design of COM in several areas. The RPC infrastructure was used to enable COM to work across a network, and the Interface Definition Language (IDL) was adopted and extended for the definition of COM interfaces and classes. You can create components without IDL, and it is possible that tools far better than Microsoft IDL (MIDL) will be developed in the future. Nevertheless, the importance and centrality of IDL to the design of COM should not be underestimated. In this chapter, we will explore IDL and its effect on COM's programming model.

As anyone who has worked on large-scale projects involving network communications is aware, defining the interface between a client and a server and ensuring that both sides correctly adhere to that interface is one of the biggest challenges faced by the developer. The original goal of IDL was to encourage both the client and the server projects to agree upon and specify the communication interfaces and then follow those contracts. To achieve this end, the designers of IDL had several problems to surmount.

Types

IDL has to make up for the shortcomings of the rather weakly typed C programming language on which it is loosely based. For example, the size of the *short*, *int*, and *long* types are implementation-dependent aspects of the C and C++ languages. When using a single compiler on a single computer, you don't need to be overly concerned with internal data formats because data is handled in a consistent manner. However, a distributed environment in which multiple machines with different architectures are involved can become a veritable minefield of inconsistencies. For example, some compilers define the internal representation of an integer as 16 bits while others use 32 bits. If IDL is to define interfaces between programs that are running on different machine architectures, having implementation-dependent data types is unacceptable. For this reason, IDL's designers developed a strongly typed language that concretely defines the size of all base types in IDL. The base types defined by IDL are listed in the following table.

Base Type	Description
boolean	Data item that can have the value *TRUE* or *FALSE*
byte	An 8-bit data item guaranteed to be transmitted without any change
char	An 8-bit unsigned character data item
double	A 64-bit floating-point number
float	A 32-bit floating-point number
handle_t	Primitive handle that can be used for RPC binding or data serializing
hyper	A 64-bit integer that can be declared as either signed or unsigned
int	A 32-bit integer that can be declared as either signed or unsigned
long	A 32-bit integer that can be declared as either signed or unsigned
short	A 16-bit integer that can be declared as either signed or unsigned
small	An 8-bit integer that can be declared as either signed or unsigned
wchar_t	A 16-bit wide-character type

In addition, different machines might be designed around the little endian or big endian architecture that determines the order in which bytes are stored in memory. The little endian architecture used by the Intel platform assigns the least significant byte of data to the lowest memory address and the most significant byte to the highest address. Processors that use the big endian architecture do the opposite. For example, the base-10 value *654* (*0x028E* in base 16) is represented in memory as *0x8E02* by an Intel CPU but as *0x028E* on a Motorola CPU of the big endian variety. IDL uses the Network Data Representation (NDR) transfer format to ensure that network transmissions are independent of the data-type format on any particular computing architecture. See Chapter 9, "Standard and Custom Marshaling," for more information about the NDR transfer syntax.

Directional Attributes

The C and C++ programming languages were designed as general-purpose languages for systems running within a single address space on one computer. Although these languages can be used in the development of distributed systems through the addition of networking libraries such as Windows Sockets, the languages themselves have no special features in this regard. Due to this fundamental assumption on the part of the C programming language, passing parameters to a function is as simple as pushing them onto the stack, jumping to the function address, and then popping the parameters off the stack. With the exception of the function's return value, parameters need not be passed back to the caller when the function returns because the C programming language specifies that parameters are passed by value. This means that a copy of the values is passed to a function, so any changes made to those values within the function are not reflected back to the caller when the function returns. The following code fragment illustrates this situation:

```
void sum(int x, int y, int sum)
{
    sum = x + y
}

void main()
{
    int result = 0;
    sum(5, 3, result);
    printf("5 + 3 = %d\n", result);    // Prints 0
}
```

Pass-by-value functionality in C can be contrasted with languages such as Microsoft Visual Basic and Fortran, which, by default, pass parameters by reference, as shown in the following Visual Basic code. (Java hedges by passing primitive types by value but user-defined types by reference.)

```
Sub Sum(X As Integer, Y As Integer, Sum As Integer)
    Sum = X + Y
End Sub

Sub Form_Load()
Dim Result As Integer
    Sum 5, 3, Result
    Print "5 + 3 = " & Result            ' Prints 8
End Sub
```

Of course, in C you can achieve the pass-by-reference functionality using pointers. When pointers are used, the address of the variable is passed to the function, causing any changes to the address pointed to by the pointer to be immediately visible to the caller, as shown in the following code:

```
void sum(int x, int y, int* sum)
{
    *sum = x + y
}

void main()
{
    int result = 0;
    sum(5, 3, &result);
    printf("5 + 3 = %d\n", &result);    // Prints 8
}
```

When passing parameters by value to a remote function, the system sends the value of the variable across the network to the server. However, several problems exist when you are using pointers to pass data to code in another address space. The most obvious problem is that passing the address of a variable in one address space to a function in another address space will not work. To overcome this situation, the system must send the data that is stored at the location specified by the pointer across the network to the server. Memory will be allocated to store the value in the address space of the server process, and then the address of the newly allocated memory will be passed to the function. All this must be done as transparently as possible.

One of the problems with passing pointers is that C syntax does not indicate whether the function actually modifies the data that a specific function argument points to. For example, a pointer to some data might be passed to a function that will use that data in a read-only manner. In other cases, such as the *sum* function in the preceding code, a pointer is passed to a function for the sole purpose of retrieving data when the function returns. In a third variation on the same theme, a function might both read and write data that is passed via a pointer. C's syntax does not express these variations because it assumes that the caller and the function are both running in the same address space.

For calls between machines, however, this situation is not merely syntactical hairsplitting. It requires that the system pass the data located at the address specified by any pointer parameters to the server when the call is made and then back to the client when the function returns. Since IDL was designed to facilitate the development of distributed systems, one of its goals is to reduce the amount of network traffic generated by remote calls. For this reason, IDL introduces three directional attributes to standard C-style syntax: *[in]*, *[out]*, and *[in, out]*. If no attribute is specified, by default parameters are always passed into the server as part of the request message used to invoke a method, as shown in the following illustration:

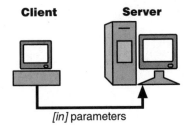

[in] parameters

The *[out]* attribute indicates that data must be sent back to the client in the response message upon completion of the function call. This attribute is meaningful only when applied to a pointer argument since by default function parameters in C and C++ are passed by value. When the call returns, the system allocates memory in the client's address space to store the data returned. The caller is responsible for freeing this memory. The *[out]* attribute makes a good choice when a pointer is passed to a function solely for the purpose of retrieving data, as in the *sum* function shown on the previous page. The process of passing a parameter out is illustrated here:

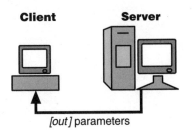

[out] parameters

377

The *[in, out]* attribute indicates that the data at the location specified by a pointer parameter must be passed into the server as part of the request message and then back to the client in the response message. On the server side, the function frees and then reallocates a new buffer, if necessary. On the client side, the system copies the new data returned by the function over the original data, and the client ultimately frees this memory. This technique is used when a function expects to receive meaningful data and the caller expects it to return meaningful data to the same memory address. Since the *[in, out]* attribute transparently models the way normal C code works at the expense of extra network traffic, it should be used only when necessary. The action of a parameter with the *[in, out]* attribute is illustrated here:

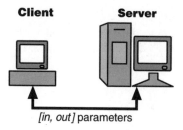

[in, out] parameters

Arrays

The C programming language affords great flexibility when you are dealing with pointers and arrays. In fact, there is almost no difference between pointers and arrays in the C language. This flexibility can translate into great ambiguity in some cases. Consider the following code:

```
int* x;        // A pointer, but to how many integers?
int z;         // One integer
int y[50];     // 50 integers (0 through 49)
x = &z;        // x is a pointer to one integer.
x = (int*)&y;  // x is a pointer to an array of 50 integers.
```

You can see that the intended usage of pointer types defined by C is not always clearly defined; it is unclear from looking at the first line of code whether *x* will point to one integer or to many integers. The truth is that it doesn't matter to C. If a pointer is used to write data past the end of the allocated space, that's the developer's problem. The flexibility of pointers and arrays is the main reason that pointers are considered a dangerous language feature and are not available in higher-level languages such as Java and Visual Basic.

Fixed Arrays

When you make remote calls, it is crucial to know whether an argument points to a single item or to multiple items because all the data at the memory location pointed to by the argument must be transferred to the server. Unless otherwise indicated by the interface definition, a pointer parameter in IDL is assumed to point to a single element of the specified type. By this rule, the *[out]* attribute in the following function declaration is assigned to a parameter that is a pointer to a single integer:

```
HRESULT SquareInteger([in] int myInteger, [out] int* square);
```

When you need an actual array, the number of elements in that array must be clearly defined so that the system knows how much data to transmit over the network. When designing a distributed system, remember that every unnecessary byte sent across the network slows the entire system. The simplest technique for passing an array of elements to a function is known as a fixed array. From the following code fragment, it is easy to see how fixed arrays got their name—the array holds a fixed number of elements that is known at compile time:

```
HRESULT SumOfIntegers1([in] int myIntegers[5], [out] int* sum);
```

At run time, the marshaler for this method will copy the 20 bytes (5 integers multiplied by 4 bytes each) of memory pointed to by *myIntegers* into a transmission buffer. This buffer will then be sent to the server, where the *myIntegers* pointer passed to the *SumOfIntegers1* method will be adjusted to point directly to the buffer received by the server. In theory, fixed arrays are the most efficient means of passing data. In practice, however, it is often difficult to predict in advance exactly how much data needs to be transferred. Choosing too small a size is an obvious problem, while choosing a larger size means that often a largely empty buffer will be sent across the network.

As you might recall from the section "Standard Marshaling" in Chapter 9, for reasons of efficiency, the stub is often able to pass—as a method's parameters—direct pointers into the message buffer obtained from the client. With fixed arrays, this is possible because the data transmitted in the buffer is an exact copy of the data in the client's address space, as shown in Figure 10-1 on the following page.

IDL:
```
HRESULT SumOfIntegers1([in] int myIntegers[5], [out] int* sum);
```

Client:
```
int sum = 0;
int myIntegers[5] = { 0, 1, 2, 3, 4 };
pTest->SumOfIntegers1(myIntegers, &sum);
```

Transmission buffer:

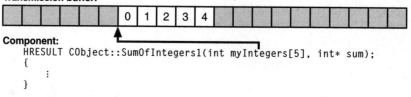

Component:
```
HRESULT CObject::SumOfIntegers1(int myIntegers[5], int* sum);
{
    ⋮
}
```

Figure 10-1.
The marshaled form of a fixed array.

Conformant Arrays

IDL defines several attributes that in turn help define and control the size of arrays and the data transmitted. These attributes are listed in the following table.

Attribute	Description
first_is	Index of the first array element transmitted
last_is	Index of the last array element transmitted
length_is	Total number of array elements transmitted
max_is	Highest valid array index value
min_is	Lowest valid array index value (not supported—always *0*)
size_is	Total number of array elements allocated for the array

To allow the number of elements transmitted to the server to be determined at run time, IDL supports *conformant arrays*. The *size_is* attribute is used to indicate a conformant array. As shown in the following declaration, the caller specifies the actual number of elements in the array at run time. This technique allows the marshaling code to dynamically determine how many elements are in the array and has the added advantage of helping the implementation of this method determine how many numbers to add. As with fixed arrays, the method receives a pointer directly into the transmission buffer received by the server because the total array is always present in the request message sent by the client.

```
HRESULT SumOfIntegers2([in] int cMax, [in, size_is(cMax)] int*
    myIntegers, [out] int* sum);
```

Methods that use conformant arrays can be declared using the preceding pointer notation or with the array notation shown here—they are functionally identical:

```
HRESULT SumOfIntegers2([in] int cMax, [in, size_is(cMax)] int
    myIntegers[], [out] int* sum);
```

Either of these declarations implies that the client will call the *SumOfIntegers2* method, as shown in the following code fragment:

```
int sum = 0;
int myIntegers[] = { 4, 65, 23, -12, 89, -23, 8 };
pTest->SumOfIntegers2(7, myIntegers, &sum);
cout << "Sum = " << sum;
```

Conformant arrays might also be embedded in structures, as shown in the following example. Note that, at most, one conformant array can be nested in a structure and that it must be the last element of the structure.

```
typedef struct tagSUM_STRUCT
{
    int cMax;
    [size_is(cMax)] int* myIntegers;
} SUM_STRUCT;

HRESULT SumOfIntegers3([in] SUM_STRUCT* myIntegers,
    [out] int* sum);
```

The client-side call is shown in the following code:

```
int sum = 0;
int myIntegers[] = { 4, 65, 23, -12, 89, -23, 8 };

SUM_STRUCT x;
x.cMax = 7;
x.myIntegers = myIntegers;
pTest->SumOfIntegers3(&x, &sum);
```

The *max_is* attribute is nearly identical to the *size_is* attribute. The only distinguishing feature is that although the *size_is* attribute specifies the total number of elements in an array, the *max_is* attribute specifies the highest (zero-based) index value into the array. Thus, a *size_is* value of 7 is equivalent to a *max_is* value of 6.

Conformant arrays using the *size_is* or *max_is* attribute work very well for parameters with *[in]* attributes but not as well for parameters with *[out]* or even *[in, out]* attributes. The problem is that the server gets stuck with the number of array elements specified by the caller. Imagine the case of a parameter with an *[out]* attribute. The following method returns a specified number of integers:

```
HRESULT ProduceIntegers1([in] int cMax, [out, size_is(cMax)]
    int* myIntegers);
```

The client must allocate a buffer large enough to hold all the data that the method might return, as shown in the following code fragment:

```
int myIntegers[7];
pTest->ProduceIntegers1(7, myIntegers);
```

This is all well and good as long as the server returns exactly seven integers every time. Since the client is stating the maximum buffer size, the server cannot return more than seven integers; if the server returns less than a full load of integers, network bandwidth will be wasted. As with fixed arrays, conformant arrays are passed directly to the method implementation from the message buffer received in the stub, as shown in Figure 10-2.

```
IDL:
    HRESULT SumOfIntegers2([in] int cMax, [in, size_is(cMax)] int* myIntegers,
        [out] int* sum);

Client:
    int sum = 0;
    int myIntegers[7] = { 0, 1, 2, 3, 4, 5, 6 };
    pTest->SumOfIntegers2(7, myIntegers, &sum);
```

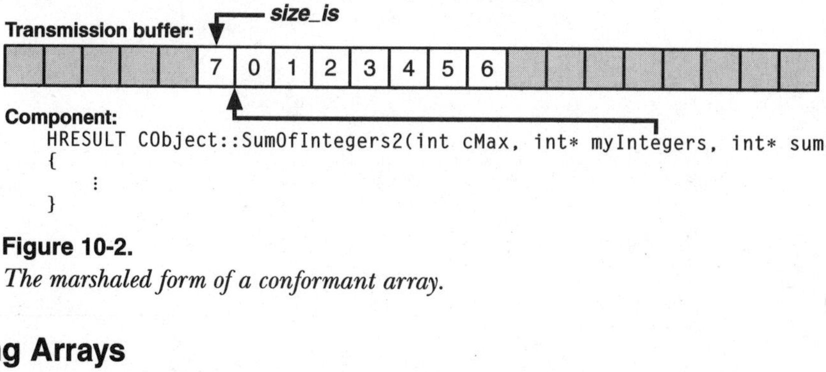

Transmission buffer: ── *size_is*

| | | | | 7 | 0 | 1 | 2 | 3 | 4 | 5 | 6 | | | | | | | |

```
Component:
    HRESULT CObject::SumOfIntegers2(int cMax, int* myIntegers, int* sum);
    {
        ⋮
    }
```

Figure 10-2.
The marshaled form of a conformant array.

Varying Arrays

To deal with the problem of the server returning less than the full number of elements, IDL introduces the concept of *varying arrays*. Like fixed arrays, the bounds of a varying array are decided at compile time, but the range of elements actually transmitted is determined at run time. The *length_is* attribute specifies the number of elements to be transmitted at run time, as shown in the following function declaration:

```
HRESULT ProduceIntegers2([out] int* pcActual,
    [out, length_is(*pcActual)] int myIntegers[4096]);
```

The client-side call is shown here:

```
int how_many_did_we_get = 0;
int myIntegers[4096];
pTest->ProduceIntegers2(&how_many_did_we_get, myIntegers);
cout << how_many_did_we_get << " integers returned.";
```

This mechanism lets the method itself determine how many integers, up to a preset maximum, should be transmitted back to the client in the response message. The first *[out]* parameter, *pcActual,* is also used to tell the client how many elements were returned. This technique ensures that the client code does not walk into part of the uninitialized buffer accidentally. Varying arrays are also useful for methods with *[in, out]* parameters, as shown in the following declaration:

```
HRESULT SendReceiveIntegers([in, out] int* pcActual,
    [in, out, length_is(*pcActual)] int myIntegers[4096]);
```

This method allows the client to send a variable number of elements and then receive a different number of elements back, as shown here:

```
int num_integers = 5;
int myIntegers[4096] = { 0, 1, 2, 3, 4 };
pTest->SendReceiveIntegers(&num_integers, myIntegers);
cout << num_integers << " integers returned";
```

The *first_is* and *last_is* attributes can be used to mark a certain range of elements in the transmission array. Unless otherwise specified with the *first_is* attribute, the zero-index element is always the first element of the array transmitted. Using the *first_is* attribute, the developer can specify a certain element in the array as the starting point for transmission. The *last_is* attribute specifies the index of the last element in the array that is marked for transmission. Like the *max_is* variation on *size_is,* the *last_is* attribute defines an index into the array rather than the count defined by *length_is.* In practice, the *first_is* and *last_is* attributes are rarely used.

When used judiciously, varying arrays have the advantage of reducing network traffic. At the same time, however, varying arrays can hurt performance because the data packet received by the marshaling code is not in the correct format to be handed over to the client or server code. Instead, another block of memory needs to be allocated on the receiving end and the data reconstructed, as shown in Figure 10-3 on the following page.

IDL:
```
HRESULT SumOfIntegers3([in] int cFirst, [in] int cActual,
    [in, first_is(cFirst), length_is(cActual)] int myIntegers[7],
    [out] int* sum);
```

Client:
```
int sum = 0;
int myIntegers[7];
myIntegers[3] = 4; myIntegers[4] = 5; myIntegers[5] = 6;
pTest->SumOfIntegers3(4, 3, myIntegers, &sum);
```

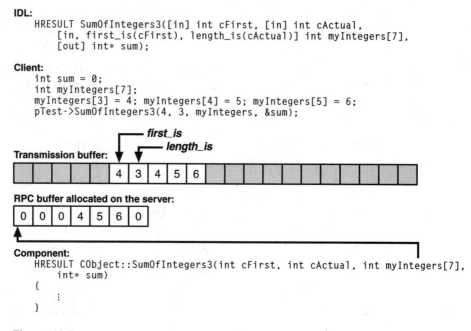

Component:
```
HRESULT CObject::SumOfIntegers3(int cFirst, int cActual, int myIntegers[7],
    int* sum)
{
    ⋮
}
```

Figure 10-3.
The marshaled form of a varying array.

Open Arrays

In practice, varying arrays can be somewhat restrictive because there is always a fixed maximum amount of data that can be transmitted. To combat this problem, IDL offers you the ability to create arrays with attributes of both conformant and varying arrays, known as *open arrays* (sometimes called conformant varying arrays). An open array is recognizable because it uses both the *size_is* attribute of a conformant array and the *length_is* attribute of a varying array. This technique allows the caller to control the size of the buffer but the method itself to control the number of elements transmitted over the wire, as shown in the following code:

```
HRESULT ProduceIntegers3([in] int cMax, [out] int* pcActual,
    [out, size_is(cMax), length_is(*pcActual)] int*
    myIntegers);
```

The client would call the *ProduceIntegers3* method like this:

```
int how_many_did_we_get = 0;
int myIntegers[5];
pTest->ProduceIntegers3(5, &how_many_did_we_get, myIntegers);
cout << how_many_did_we_get << " integers returned.";
```

Generally, conformant arrays are most useful for *[in]* parameters, and open arrays work best for *[out]* and *[in, out]* parameters. Like varying arrays, open arrays require the array to be reconstructed in the second block of memory allocated on the receiving side. The flexibility of varying and open arrays comes with a memory and performance penalty commensurate with the size of the buffer, as shown in Figure 10-4.

IDL:
```
HRESULT SumOfIntegers4([in] int cFirst, [in] int cActual,
    [in] int cMax, [in, first_is(cFirst), length_is(cActual),
    size_is(cMax)] int* myIntegers, [out] int* sum);
```

Client:
```
int sum = 0;
int myIntegers[10];
myIntegers[3] = 4; myIntegers[4] = 5; myIntegers[5] = 6;
pTest->SumOfIntegers4(4, 3, 10, myIntegers, &sum);
```

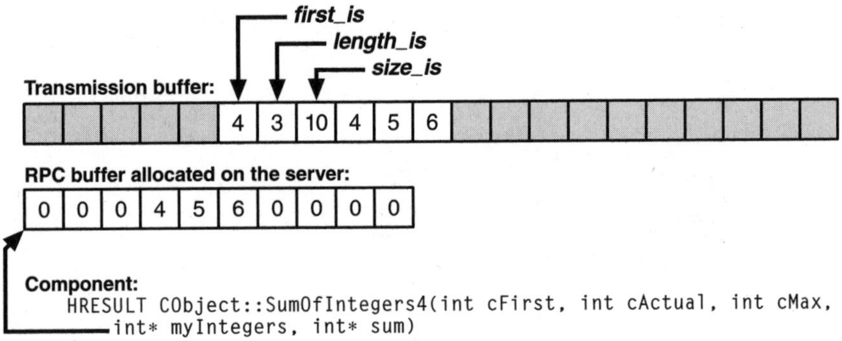

Component:
```
HRESULT CObject::SumOfIntegers4(int cFirst, int cActual, int cMax,
    int* myIntegers, int* sum)
{
    ⋮
}
```

Figure 10-4.
The marshaled form of an open array.

Character Arrays

In C, a string is expressed as an array of characters with a 0 byte indicating the end of the string. Therefore, you can simply pass a string parameter in the same way as in other arrays, as shown here:

```
HRESULT SendString1([in] int cLength, [in, size_is(cLength)]
    wchar_t* myString);
```

The client calls this function as follows:

```
wchar_t wszHello[] = L"Hello COM";
pTest->SendString1(wcslen(wszHello), wszHello);
```

Because passing string parameters is such a frequent occurrence, IDL has special support for this common programming task. As a pure programming convenience, IDL offers the *[string]* attribute to make this job easier. IDL can automate the process of calling the appropriate string length function, based on the knowledge that all C-style strings end with a 0 byte. With the *[string]* attribute, the *SendString2* method declaration looks like this:

```
HRESULT SendString2([in, string] wchar_t* myString);
```

The client calls this function as shown here:

```
wchar_t wszHello[] = L"Hello COM";
pTest->SendString2(wszHello);
```

A potential problem arises when the *[string]* attribute is combined with the *[in, out]* attributes, as shown in the following code:

```
HRESULT SendReceiveString1([in, out, string] wchar_t*
    myString);
```

See whether you can find the error in the following code:

```
// Client-side usage
wchar_t wszHello[256] = L"Hello COM";
pTest->SendReceiveString1(wszHello);
wprintf(L"Received string: %s\n", wszHello);     // ???

// Server-side implementation of the function
HRESULT CObject::SendReceiveString1(wchar_t* myString)
{
    wprintf(L"Received string: %s\n", myString); // Hello, COM.
    wcscpy(myString, L"Nice weather today");     // Uh-oh
    return S_OK;
}
```

This code works fine—as long as the length of the string returned by the *SendReceiveString1* method is smaller than or equal to the length of the string sent. In this sample, however, the method returns a string several characters longer than that sent by the client. This might not seem like a problem since the client has allocated a buffer of 256 characters, which is more than enough to hold a few extra characters. Nevertheless, the *[string]* attribute used by the *SendReceiveString1* method tells the system to compute the length of the client's string and then allocate only the minimum amount of memory needed on the server side. The result is that the implementation on the server side writes past the end of the character array and onto random bits of memory.

This problem can be corrected using the following IDL declaration:

```
HRESULT SendReceiveString2([in] int cMax, [in, out, string,
    size_is(cMax)] wchar_t* myString);
```

The client would now call the function as shown here:

```
wchar_t wszHello[256] = L"Hello COM";
pTest->SendReceiveString2(256, wszHello);
wprintf(L"Received string: %s\n", wszHello);
```

Even this solution is incomplete because the client still must specify the maximum size of the buffer. Yet only inside the method itself can the exact amount of memory necessary for the result be determined. If the client has guessed too small a value, the server is out of luck. To avoid these dire straits, robust COM interfaces usually force the method's implementation to allocate space for the *out* buffer. This dynamically allocated buffer is then returned to the client, where it must later be freed. Thus, the IDL declaration of the method is simplified, as shown here:

```
HRESULT SendReceiveString3([in, out, string] wchar_t**
    myString);
```

But the implementation of the *SendReceiveString3* method is made more complex by the addition of the memory allocation call, as shown in the following example:

```
// Server-side implementation of the function
HRESULT CObject::SendReceiveString3(wchar_t** myString)
{
    wprintf(L"Received string: %s\n", *myString);
    CoTaskMemFree(*myString);
    wchar_t returnString[] = L"Nice weather today";
    *myString = (wchar_t*)CoTaskMemAlloc((wcslen(returnString)+1)*
    sizeof(wchar_t));
    wcscpy(*myString, returnString);
    return S_OK;
}
```

It is now the responsibility of the client-side code to free this memory, as shown here:

```
wchar_t* wszHello = L"Hello COM";
wchar_t* myString = (wchar_t*)CoTaskMemAlloc
    ((wcslen(wszHello)+1)*sizeof(wchar_t));
wcscpy(myString, wszHello);
pSum->SendReceiveString3(&myString);
wprintf(L"Received string: %s\n", myString);
CoTaskMemFree(myString);
```

Multidimensional Arrays

IDL is also prepared to deal with multidimensional arrays. The biggest problem with marshaling multidimensional arrays is their ambiguous nature in C. Let's look at the following declaration:

```
int** test;
```

In C, this declaration can have any one of a number of meanings. Is *test* a pointer to a pointer to an integer? A pointer to a pointer to an array of integers? A pointer to an array of pointers to integers? A pointer to an array of pointers to integer arrays? The intended use of *test* is unclear because as far as C is concerned, it doesn't make any difference. When you are marshaling calls between different address spaces, however, these distinctions become crucial. IDL manages these subtle differences by using a special syntax. The *size_is* and *length_is* attributes can work with a variable number of arguments, each used to indicate the conformance and variance of the one level of indirection.

The simplest case is a pointer to a pointer to a single integer, because if no additional attributes are specified, IDL assumes a pointer to a single element. This situation is illustrated by the following IDL declaration:

```
HRESULT SendInteger([in] int** test);
```

The second possibility is that of a pointer to a pointer to an array of integers. In this case, you can use the following IDL declaration, in which the first level of indirection is omitted and the default value of *1* is used. Note that the *size_is* values are read right to left; the rightmost value affects the rightmost pointer of the parameter.

```
HRESULT SendIntegers([in, size_is(, 2)] int** test);
```

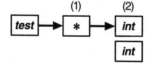

A pointer to an array of pointers to integers is declared using the following IDL syntax:

```
HRESULT SendIntegers([in, size_is(3, )] int** test);
```

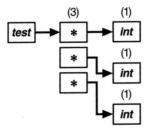

Last a pointer to an array of pointers to integer arrays defines both positions of the *size_is* attribute, as shown here:

```
HRESULT SendIntegers([in, size_is(3, 2)] int** test);
```

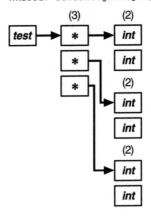

Passing Arrays of User-Defined Types from Visual Basic

From Visual Basic, it is possible to call a method of a COM object that accepts an array of structures. For example, the following interface definition contains a method that accepts an array of MYTYPE structures. The MYTYPE structure is also defined in the interface definition.

```
interface ISum : IUnknown
{
    typedef struct MYTYPE
    {
        short a;
        long b;
    } MYTYPE;

    HRESULT Sum([in] long cMax, [in, size_is(cMax)] MYTYPE*
        myarray);
}
```

If you assume that an arbitrary COM object has implemented the *ISum* interface, calling the *ISum::Sum* method from Visual Basic is not difficult at all. The trick is to pass the array as if you were passing only the first element of that array. For example, if the array is named *myarray*, instead of passing the parameter by using the standard Visual Basic notation *myarray()*, you would use *myarray(0)*, as shown here:

```
Private Sub Command1_Click()
Dim myRef As New InsideDCOM
Dim myarray(3) As MYTYPE
    myarray(0).a = 1
    myarray(0).b = 5
    myarray(1).a = 2
    myarray(1).b = 4
    myarray(2).a = 3
    myarray(2).b = 3
    myRef.Sum 3, myarray(0)      ' myarray(0) makes arrays work!
End Sub
```

Pointers

As you have seen, the flexibility afforded by pointers in the C programming language can inflict pain on the unwary when it comes to making remote calls. In C, pointers can:

- Point to any memory location
- Have the value *0* (*null*)
- Be set to point to a different memory location at any time
- Be aliased

Because IDL must actually transmit the data pointed to by a pointer, it must have a lot of information about what that pointer is pointing to and in what format the data is stored. The designers of IDL were faced with the fundamental choice between modeling the language to work as transparently as possible with C-style pointers, even if the consequence was greater overhead, and exposing the complexity to the developer in the hope of gaining efficiency. In the end, the decision was made to offer several options.

To better accommodate a wide range of programs, IDL offers three pointer types: *full, unique,* and *reference.* These different pointer types are specified in the IDL language with the *ptr, unique,* and *ref* attributes, respectively, and cannot be combined. If you don't specify a pointer type, the pointer type is determined by the *pointer_default* attribute in the interface header. If you don't specify the *pointer_default* attribute, all nonattributed pointers are assumed to be unique pointers. In this section, we'll look at how and when to use the IDL pointer attributes, as well as how to pass COM interface pointers as parameters.

Full Pointers

Full pointers most closely model the attributes of C-style pointers. Although they are rather inefficient, full pointers are useful when you are distributing code that formerly executed within a single process. Full pointers are expensive because they permit aliasing of pointers, which means that full pointers allow more than one pointer to point to the same memory location. For example, imagine a complex memory structure such as a doubly linked list. If you have a pointer to an arbitrary element in the list, several different pointers reference the same memory location, as shown in Figure 10-5.

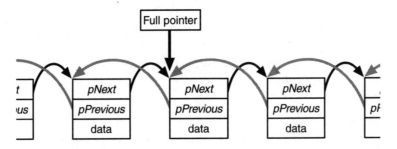

Figure 10-5.
Aliasing with a full pointer.

This situation complicates matters for the marshaling code because it must now manage several pointers to the data. Managing several pointers requires that the system maintain a dictionary of all marshaled pointers. The underlying stub code does this by resolving the various pointers to the addresses and then determining whose copy of the data represents the most recent version. In general, you can avoid the need for full pointers by developing a careful design.

Unique Pointers

With one restriction, a unique pointer is identical to a full pointer. The limitation is that unique pointers cannot cause aliasing of data, meaning that storage referred to by a unique pointer cannot be accessed through any other pointer in the function. If you are certain that a pointer will not be aliased, mark it as a unique pointer in the IDL code. The MIDL compiler is able to generate efficient marshaling code for unique pointers because it can make certain assumptions about ways in which that pointer will be used. Unique pointers have the following characteristics:

- They can point to any memory location.
- They can have the value *0 (null)*.
- They can change from non-*null* to *null* or vice versa during a call.
- Changing from one non-*null* value to another non-*null* value during a call is ignored by IDL.
- They cannot be aliased.

When you pass an uninitialized pointer to a method in order to retrieve an outbound parameter, you must set the pointer to *null*. Uninitialized pointers might work when you make in-process calls, but proxies and stubs assume that all pointers are either initialized with a valid address or are set to *null* at the time the call is made. This requirement is a common source of COM programming errors and can be quite difficult to track down if you don't know about it.

Reference Pointers

From the perspective of IDL, reference pointers are the simplest type of pointer and thus require the least amount of processing by the marshaling code. Reference pointers share the restriction of unique pointers in that they do not permit pointer aliasing. Unlike unique pointers, reference pointers cannot have the value *null*. A reference pointer must always refer to a valid memory address. Reference pointers are mainly used to implement C++-style reference semantics and allow for outgoing parameters. Function return types, however, cannot be reference pointers. To summarize, reference pointers have the following characteristics:

- They can point to any memory location.
- They cannot have the value *0 (null)*.
- They cannot be aliased.
- They cannot be set to point to a different memory location during a call.

Interface Pointers

Although most types of pointers to data can be supported by IDL, pointers to C++ classes or functions are off limits to remote method calls. The only way to access code running in another address space is through an interface pointer. For this reason, occasionally a method of an interface will need to return a pointer to another interface. You might be saying, "Wait a minute, isn't that what *QueryInterface* is for?" Well, *QueryInterface* is useful for retrieving an interface pointer on an object, but sometimes a method needs more information in order to return an interface pointer. In these cases, it makes sense to design a method in a custom interface that will do the job. Many standard COM interfaces have methods that return pointers to other interfaces. If you would like to see some examples of such COM interfaces, look up the definitions of the *IMoniker::BindToObject, IClassFactory::CreateInstance, IClassActivator::GetClass-Object, IStorage::CreateStream, IOleItemContainer::GetObject,* and *ITypeInfo::Create-Instance* methods, to name but a few.

The simplest way to design a method that accepts an interface pointer as a parameter is to prototype the interface pointer argument as *void***, as shown in the following declaration:

```
HRESULT GetInterfacePointer1([out] void** ppObject); // Error
```

The problem with this approach is that the MIDL compiler is unable to generate proxy/stub code for this method because it doesn't know how to marshal a *void*** argument. For this reason, the preceding declaration will result in a compile error reported by the MIDL compiler. For interfaces designed to be implemented by in-process components only, the method declaration can be prefixed with the *[local]* attribute, indicating that no marshaling code needs to be generated by the MIDL compiler, as shown here:

```
[local] HRESULT GetInterfacePointer1([out] void** ppvObject);
```

For interfaces that might be implemented in local or remote components, you need to provide more information regarding the parameter in the IDL file so that the correct proxy/stub code can be generated. Perhaps the simplest way to do this is to specify the *IUnknown* interface, as shown in the following code. This approach is very flexible because all COM interfaces derive from *IUnknown*. However, chances are that the client of this object doesn't want an *IUnknown* pointer, meaning that the client will most likely follow with an immediate *QueryInterface* call for the desired interface. This approach puts an extra burden on the client code and is less efficient because two round-trips must be made to the component in order to retrieve the desired interface pointer.

```
HRESULT GetInterfacePointer2([out] IUnknown** ppvObject);
```

Recall from Chapter 6, "Connection Points and Type Information," that connection points suffer from this problem. The *IConnectionPoint::Advise* method is declared below in IDL notation. Although clients always pass the *IUnknown* pointer of their sink to the *Advise* method, it is a rare object that is interested in the sink for its *IUnknown* interface. Instead, the typical connectable object simply calls *QueryInterface* to request the desired interface.

```
HRESULT Advise
    (
        [in]    IUnknown * pUnkSink,
        [out]   DWORD *    pdwCookie
    );
```

Another approach to this problem is to name the interface being passed, as shown in the following code. Although this tight coupling technique works well initially, it can return to haunt the project at a later date. Problems begin when an improved version of the interface—for example, *IMyCustomInterface2*—is released; the client will first need to obtain a pointer to the *IMyCustomInterface* interface and then call *QueryInterface* to request the *IMyCustomInterface2* interface.

```
HRESULT GetInterfacePointer3([out] IMyCustomInterface**
    ppvObject);
```

By now, you might be wondering how the *IUnknown::QueryInterface* method is defined. After all, *QueryInterface* seems to be able to correctly handle interface pointers for any interface, standard or custom. The definition of the *QueryInterface* method taken from the unknwn.idl file is shown here:

```
HRESULT QueryInterface(
    [in] REFIID riid,
    [out, iid_is(riid)] void **ppvObject);
```

The IDL attribute *iid_is* is designed specifically for methods that have an interface pointer as a parameter and is used to specify the interface identifier (IID) of the interface pointer being transmitted. The *QueryInterface* method obtains this IID from its first parameter. You can follow this design when you create methods that return interface pointers, as shown in the following code. This approach effectively solves the issue of versioning custom interfaces because you always specify the interface pointer being marshaled. Specifying the interface pointer also resolves the need for the client to make an extra *QueryInterface* call to obtain the desired interface.

```
HRESULT GetInterfacePointer4([in] REFIID riid,
    [out, iid_is(riid)] void** ppvObject);
```

The *GetInterfacePointer4* method definition implies the following client-side code:

```
IMyCustomInterface* pCustomInterface;
pObject->GetInterfacePointer4(IID_IMyCustomInterface,
    (void**)pCustomInterface);
```

You can also use the IDL attribute *call_as* to help map a nonremotable method, such as one that uses *void*** as an argument, to a method that can be remoted. For example, without the *call_as* attribute, the method declared here cannot be remoted because it uses a *void*** argument, and thus the method must be defined using the *local* attribute:

```
[local] HRESULT GetInterfacePointer([in] REFIID riid,
    [out] void** ppvObject);
```

With the *call_as* attribute, you can map the *GetInterfacePointer* method to a remotable version of the function, appropriately named *RemoteGetInterfacePointer*, as shown here:

```
[call_as(GetInterfacePointer)] HRESULT
    RemoteGetInterfacePointer([in] REFIID riid,
    [out, iid_is(riid)] IUnknown** ppvObject);
```

The use of the *call_as* attribute to map local-only methods to those that can be remoted requires the developer to write bonding routines that map the local types to the remotable ones. These bonding routines must be compiled and then linked with the proxy/stub code generated by the MIDL compiler. Listing 10-1 shows the binding routines required for the *GetInterfacePointer* method declared above using the *call_as* attribute:

call_as.cpp

```
// Compile and then link this file with the proxy/stub code
// generated by MIDL.
#include "component.h"

HRESULT __stdcall ITest_GetInterfacePointer_Proxy(ITest* Me,
    REFIID riid, void** ppv)
{
    return ITest_RemoteGetInterfacePointer_Proxy(Me, riid,
        (IUnknown**)ppv);
}

HRESULT __stdcall ITest_GetInterfacePointer_Stub(ITest* Me,
    REFIID riid, IUnknown** ppv)
{
    return Me->GetInterfacePointer(riid, (void**)ppv);
}
```

Listing 10-1.
Binding routines used with the GetInterfacePointer *method.*

Interface Design Recommendations

To help you define custom COM interfaces, this section provides several guidelines for improved designs. Although no design guidelines can be considered recipes for creating a useful interface specification, we hope that these suggestions will provide you with ideas. If you have found techniques of your own that have proved successful in COM-based systems, let us know; perhaps we will be able to include them in a future edition of this book.

First study the standard COM interfaces that are defined by Microsoft as part of COM and its fundamental services, such as structured storage, monikers, connection points, type libraries, automation, and apartments. While not always perfect, Microsoft's designs reflect the goals and objectives of COM itself. This knowledge will be invaluable to someone who is defining a set of custom interfaces. In addition to this general recommendation, we offer the following more specific guidelines:

■ **Make interfaces as simple as possible, but no simpler.**   A successful COM interface is one that can be grasped as a whole entity in a single sitting. As a general rule, most COM interfaces have between 5 and 7 methods. Again, this is a very general rule—and very good reasons exist to break it. For example, the *IClassActivator* interface has only 1 method, but the *IMoniker* interface has 15. An interface with too many methods is probably trying to cover too much ground and will result in implementations of the interface that return *E_NOTIMPL* for many methods.

■ **Be exact when you specify semantics.**   Although an interface is a contract, we all know that some contracts are more restrictive than others. When you define a custom interface, it is up to you to specify the exact semantics of the interface. If you explicitly permit some methods to return *E_NOTIMPL*, the resulting interface definition is relatively fluid. Experience has shown us that strict interface definitions that do not permit methods to return *E_NOTIMPL* tend to work better in the long run. This fact raises the issue of *interface factoring*. It is probably better to factor an interface into two or more interfaces instead of designing one interface that permits certain methods to go unimplemented. Factoring allows a more rigid interface definition but doesn't require you to implement undesired functionality.

■ **Avoid the one-interface-per-object design.** Sometimes you might design an object intended solely for use in a single project. "Since this object will be used only by me," you might reason, "it's OK if I design it so that the object has only one interface with 100 methods." (Developers working for large corporations whose main business is *not* software development are especially guilty of this shortsightedness.) This type of one-interface-per-object design is particularly poor because it overlooks a major design goal of COM: the ability of an object to implement multiple interfaces and for the client to use the *QueryInterface* method to navigate among them. Your reasoning might be correct now, but you never know when someone else might want to implement your interface in a different project. Of course, the one-interface-per-object design is a self-fulfilling prophecy; no one in his or her right mind will ever voluntarily implement an interface that has 100 methods.

■ **Evaluate different methods of passing information.** The number of parameters passed with each method of a given interface is another design concern. Although, in most cases, it is obvious what information the method requires to do its job, there are different ways to provide this information. For example, if a method might be called repeatedly, it makes sense for that method to pass the minimum amount of data possible, thus reducing the network bandwidth used when making remote calls. In such cases, it might make sense to define an "initialization" method that is called once with the required information, in advance of the worker method calls. In addition, because all the standard COM interfaces that deal with strings use Unicode characters, we strongly recommend that you do likewise when designing your own interfaces.

■ **Stick to current versioning standards.** When new versions of COM interfaces are created, it has become customary to place a revision number at the end of the interface name. For example, the *IHello* interface would become *IHello2* in a future revision. This numbering technique has made COM the subject of some derision, especially since COM claims to help resolve many of the versioning issues facing applications. The truth of the matter is that COM does help solve these versioning problems by introducing the notion of a *binary contract* (otherwise known as an interface) to which both clients and implementers must adhere. Once it is published, an interface can never be changed because doing so would break the binary compatibility promised by COM. And because COM interfaces are identified by a 128-bit value known as a globally unique identifier (GUID), not by a programmer-friendly name like *IHello2*, when you are programming, it is acceptable and even desirable to refer to the *IHello2* interface as *IHello*. To do this, you need only #*define* the *IID_IHello* symbol to the IID of the new interface. Existing clients will then have code that refers to the old *IHello* interface, and new clients can choose to use the new *IHello* interface via the same name.

CHAPTER ELEVEN

Security

In these paranoid times of globally interconnected computer networks, the issue of security preoccupies individual users as well as large organizations. Computer security describes a diverse body of knowledge. Cryptography, virus detection, authentication, auditing, certificates, permissions, access control, digital signatures, and firewalls are but a few of the topics discussed under the rubric of security. Although the security of computer networks is an important subject, we believe that for most projects, security is more of an administration and deployment issue than a development issue. Security sometimes receives too much attention too early in a project—attention that might be better devoted to other areas of the system. Like a broken clock that tells the correct time twice a day, the most secure systems are those that don't work.

Security Models

It is certainly important for component developers to understand the COM security model since this is one area of COM that can bite you where you least expect it. A few words of caution before we begin: Before you read this chapter, be sure that you are intimately familiar with COM. And after you read this chapter, be sure to read Chapter 13, "Microsoft Transaction Server and COM+," to learn about the role-based security offered by Microsoft Transaction Server. Role-based security simplifies the security and administration issues for most server-side components. In this chapter, we will examine the declarative and programmatic security options that COM offers to system administrators and component developers. You will learn how to protect a component from launch and access by unauthorized clients and how to protect the confidentiality of data transmitted across a network.

The Windows NT Security Model

The security mechanisms in Microsoft Windows NT are designed to enable applications to selectively grant or deny certain users access to specific services.

While any executable code presents a potential security risk, Windows NT mitigates this risk by limiting the access permissions of a given process, depending on the user account it is running under. To this end, Windows NT maintains an *access token* for each user logged on to the system, containing information identifying the user and the user groups to which the user belongs and information about other privileges that might be available. A copy of this access token is later associated with each process launched by that user. The operating system selectively grants or denies access to system services by comparing the access token of the running process with the security information attached to the system object to which access is requested.

Each user and user group is identified in the access token by a unique value called a *security identifier* (*SID*). Every system object—such as a thread, a mutex, a semaphore, an event, or a file—can contain a *security descriptor* that includes the SIDs of the object's owner and of the primary user group to which the owner belongs. Also stored in this security descriptor is the *discretionary access control list* (*DACL*), which controls access permissions, and the *system access control list* (*SACL*), which specifies those operations on the object that should generate audit messages. Both types of *access control lists* (*ACLs*) are really linked lists of *access control entries* (*ACEs*). Each ACE in a DACL either grants or denies a certain permission to a specific user or user group. The system checks each ACE in the DACL until it determines that permission has been granted or denied. Once the determination has been made, the remaining ACEs are not examined, as shown in Figure 11-1.

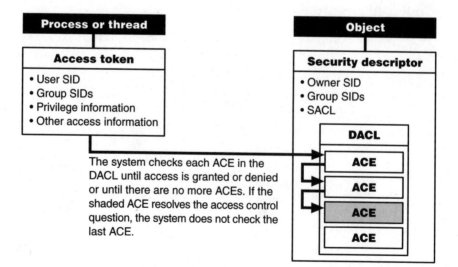

Figure 11-1.
Checking an object's DACL to determine whether the client has the requisite permissions.

The COM Security Model

When you are learning about the COM security model, it is helpful to understand what resources must be secured. Listed here are the primary goals of the COM security model:

- Activation control
- Access control
- Authentication control
- Identity control

Activation control specifies who is permitted to launch components. Once a component has been launched, *access control* is used to control access to the component's objects. In some cases, it might be acceptable for certain users to have access to certain areas of functionality while other services of a component are restricted. For example, perhaps all users connecting over the World Wide Web are permitted to access certain areas of the component's functionality, but other services are reserved for authorized users only. *Authentication control* is used to ensure that a network transmission is authentic and to protect the data from unauthorized viewers. Different authentication levels can be set so that all the data is encrypted before being transmitted. *Identity control* specifies the security credentials under which the component will execute. These credentials can be a specific user account configured for this purpose or the security credentials of the client application.

Security information for COM-based components is configured in two ways: *declarative security* and *programmatic security*. Declarative security settings are configured in the registry external to the component. A system administrator typically configures declarative security. Programmatic security is incorporated into a component by the developer. Activation, access, authentication, and identity security settings for a component can be configured in the declarative manner via the registry, using a utility such as the DCOM Configuration utility (dcomcnfg.exe). Access and authentication security can also be controlled programmatically by using several interfaces and helper functions provided by COM. Activation and identity security cannot be controlled programmatically, because these settings must be specified before a component is launched.

Running the DCOM Configuration Utility on Windows 95/98

By default, Windows 95/98 is set for share-level access control—access control that allows a password to be assigned to each shared resource. Although the DCOM Configuration utility refuses to run in this mode, remote calls can still be executed, albeit without any security. Because the DCOM Configuration utility refuses to run with share-level access control, you must use the registry editor to adjust the registry settings for remote execution of a component. Basically, this amounts to disabling authentication and enabling remote connections. Only in a network with a Windows NT domain controller that can be used to provide pass-through security can COM security be enabled for Windows 95/98 machines. When pass-through security is used, the domain controller provides security information to a system. In a networked environment with a Windows NT domain controller, follow these steps to configure Windows 95/98 for user-level access control:

1. Choose Start/Settings/Control Panel.

2. Open the Network applet in the Control Panel, and select the Access Control tab.

3. Select User-Level Access Control and click OK.

After rebooting, you can run dcomcnfg.exe.

Why Does COM Need a Security Model?

Perhaps you are wondering why COM needs a special security model. Windows NT is a secure operating system platform, so why can't COM-based components simply leverage that security model? The answer is that they can—but they shouldn't. As you know, the design of COM is not tied to the design of Microsoft Windows in any way. In addition to the various flavors of Windows, COM-based components can run on many other operating systems. Most of these operating systems have their own notion of security, and certainly none support the security functions of the Win32 API. In fact, neither Microsoft Windows 95 nor Microsoft Windows 98 supports these security functions. COM requires a security model that can be supported on all platforms on which COM services are available.

COM defines a higher-level security model by abstracting the underlying security mechanisms of both Windows NT and Remote Procedure Calls (RPCs)—which explains why many of the security flags used by COM have been borrowed from the RPC security infrastructure. Aside from platform independence, the COM security model insulates component developers from the Windows NT and RPC security mechanisms so that as these technologies evolve, components will be able to derive benefits from the new security services automatically. This flexible security model is built around the *Security Support Provider Interface* (*SSPI*), a standard API designed to support the security needs of applications running in a distributed environment.

The design of SSPI can be compared with the architecture of *Open Database Connectivity* (*ODBC*). ODBC was designed to insulate database application developers from a specific back-end SQL server by offering numerous ODBC drivers that implement the standard ODBC API for use by client-side developers but that communicate with a specific back-end server using the proprietary interface understood by that server. To support the varying security requirements of different applications, different vendors can implement the SSPI API in a dynamic-link library (DLL) called a *Security Service Provider* (*SSP*). An application written to work with one security provider would require few, or perhaps no, modifications to work with another security provider. All security providers must implement the SSPI, but internally they are free to use different mechanisms to enforce security.

Prior to version 5.0, Windows NT offered only one SSPI-compliant security provider—the Windows *NT LAN Manager Security Support Provider* (*NTLM SSP*). This security package is based on the NTLM authentication protocol. Windows NT 5.0 offers both the NTLM SSP and a new security provider supporting the Kerberos security protocol. Kerberos is the default security provider of the Windows NT 5.0 operating system. Because the details of the NTLM and Kerberos security protocols are beyond the scope of this chapter, we will focus here on the higher-level security model defined by COM.

Declarative Security: The Registry

As it does for many other aspects of COM, the registry contains a great deal of information relating to the COM security model. Many, although not all, of COM's security settings can be controlled by setting various options in the registry. Security settings can also be configured programmatically, but there are decided advantages to using the registry. By manipulating the registry, a knowledgeable system administrator can flexibly configure and customize the security environment. But the best thing about configuring security settings in the registry is that COM will enforce all of these settings automatically. This technique has the effect of reducing the amount of security related code you need to write—a definite plus in our opinion. For example, you could specify that a user named "Mary" or users belonging to the "Accountants" group are not permitted to launch or access a particular component. You need never worry that Mary or Accountants will be able to use the component.

The easiest place to begin exploring the COM security model is with the DCOM Configuration utility. The DCOM Configuration utility is a powerful tool that is used to set component and security settings in the registry. Throughout the first half of this chapter, we will explore the options available with the DCOM Configuration utility and discover where in the registry these settings are stored. Note that there is no security risk associated with storing security information in the registry. Like other parts of the Windows system, the registry is fully securable and permits only privileged users to access and modify sensitive areas. In fact, only administrators are permitted to run the DCOM Configuration utility on Windows NT. Of course, there are also certain disadvantages to using the registry to configure security information, but we'll save these for later in this chapter.

The declarative security information stored in the registry can be neatly divided into two arenas: *default security* and *component security*. Default security specifies the security settings for all components running on the local machine that do not in some way override these default settings. Component security settings can be used to provide special security for a specific component, thereby overriding the default security settings. (Programmatic security, discussed later in this chapter in the section "Programmatic Security," can be used to override both default and component security settings in the registry.) Let's begin by examining the default security settings.

Default Security

Launching the DCOM Configuration utility and selecting the Default Properties tab displays the options shown in Figure 11-2. These options enable the administrator to set the default authentication and impersonation options on a machinewide basis. The Enable Distributed COM On This Computer option is the master switch of DCOM. If this check box is not checked, all remote calls to and from the machine are rejected. When the system is first installed, this option is enabled. The Default Authentication Level setting specifies the base authentication level that will be used on this system, assuming that a component does not override the value programmatically or through other registry settings. When the system is first installed, this setting is configured for connect-level authentication.

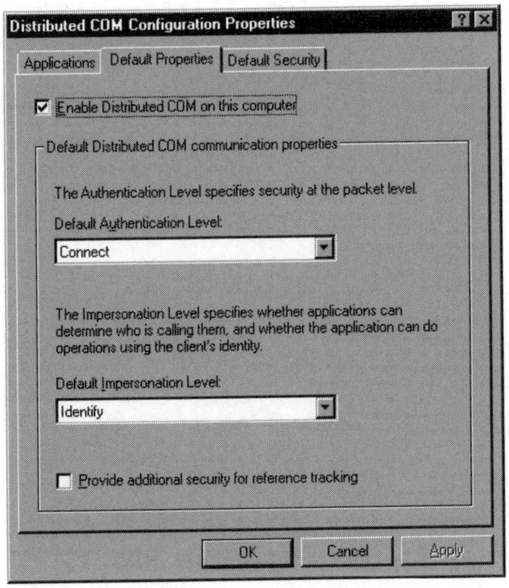

Figure 11-2.
The Default Properties tab of the DCOM Configuration utility.

The possible authentication levels and their attributes are shown in the following table. Although Windows 95 and Windows 98 machines can make calls at any authentication level, they can receive calls made only at the *RPC_C-_AUTHN_LEVEL_NONE* or *RPC_C_AUTHN_LEVEL_CONNECT* levels.

Value	Authentication Level	Flag	Description
0	Default	*RPC_C_AUTHN-_LEVEL_DEFAULT*	Currently maps to connect-level authentication
1	None	*RPC_C_AUTHN-_LEVEL_NONE*	No authentication
2	Connect	*RPC_C_AUTHN-_LEVEL_CONNECT*	Authenticates the client only when the·client first connects to the server
3	Call	*RPC_C_AUTHN-_LEVEL_CALL*	Authenticates the client at the beginning of each remote call
4	Packet	*RPC_C_AUTHN-_LEVEL_PKT*	Authenticates that all of the data received is from the expected client

(continued)

continued

Value	Authentication Level	Flag	Description
5	Packet integrity	*RPC_C_AUTHN-_LEVEL_PKT-_INTEGRITY*	Authenticates all of the data and verifies that it has not been modified when transferred between the client and the server
6	Packet privacy	*RPC_C_AUTHN-_LEVEL_PKT-_PRIVACY*	Authenticates, verifies, and encrypts the arguments passed to every remote call

NOTE: Datagram transports, such as User Datagram Protocol (UDP), default to packet-level authentication if a lower authentication level is requested, which is logical because datagram transports do not maintain a virtual connection between the client and the server. Therefore, each transmitted packet should be authenticated individually.

The Default Impersonation Level setting specifies the base impersonation level that clients running on this system will grant to their servers, again assuming that a component does not override this value. Impersonation levels are used to protect the client from rogue components. From the client's point of view, anonymous-level impersonation is the most secure because the component cannot obtain any information about the client. With each successive impersonation level, a component is granted further liberties with the client's security credentials. When the system is first installed, this setting is configured for identify-level impersonation. The possible impersonation levels and their attributes are shown in the table on the facing page. Note that Windows NT 4.0 supports only the *RPC_C_IMP_LEVEL_IDENTIFY* and *RPC_C_IMP_LEVEL-_IMPERSONATE* impersonation levels; Windows NT 5.0 adds support for the *RPC_C_IMP_LEVEL_DELEGATE* impersonation level.

The Provide Additional Security For Reference Tracking option indicates whether calls to the *IUnknown::AddRef* and *IUnknown::Release* methods are secured. When the system is first installed, this option is turned off. Checking this option causes COM to perform additional callbacks to authenticate distributed reference count calls, ensuring that objects are not released maliciously. This option improves the security of the system but slows execution speed. More information about secure reference counting can be found in Chapter 12, "The Network Protocol."

Value	Impersonation Level	Flag	Description
1	Anonymous	RPC_C_IMP-_LEVEL-_ANONYMOUS	The client is anonymous to the server. The server cannot obtain the client's identification information, and it cannot impersonate the client.*
2	Identify	RPC_C_IMP-_LEVEL_IDENTIFY	The server can obtain the client's identification information. The server can impersonate the client for ACL checking, but it cannot access system objects as the client.
3	Impersonate	RPC_C_IMP-_LEVEL-_IMPERSONATE	The server can impersonate the client's security context while acting on behalf of the client.
4	Delegate	RPC_C_IMP-_LEVEL_DELEGATE	The server can impersonate the client's security context when making outgoing calls to other servers on behalf of the client.**

  * Not currently supported
 ** Supported in Windows NT 5.0 only

Configuring Default Access and Launch Permissions

The DCOM Configuration utility's Default Security tab, shown in Figure 11-3 on the following page, enables the administrator to configure default access and launch permissions on a machinewide basis. These settings are used for components that do not provide their own settings. Clicking the Edit Default button presents a list of users and user groups that can be explicitly allowed or denied permission. When the system is first installed, only administrators, the system account, and the interactive user have access and launch permission. If the default security information is deleted from the registry, only the system account and the interactive user retain permissions. It is generally not recommended to change these values; instead of changing the machinewide default settings that affect all components, it is preferable to adjust the security settings on a component-by-component basis, as described later in this chapter in the section "Configuring Component Security: The AppID Key."

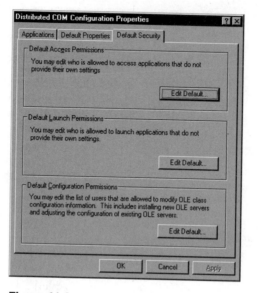

Figure 11-3.
The DCOM Configuration utility's Default Security tab in Windows NT.

The system account is a highly privileged local account used by system processes. It must always have launch and access permissions because the Service Control Manager (SCM; rpcss.exe) runs in this account. If a component does not grant the system account launch permission, the component can never be launched. The requirement that the system account have launch permission explains a common source of confusion regarding the CLSID\LocalServer32 registry key. Component launch always fails if the Local-Service32 registry key contains a Universal Naming Convention (UNC) path in the form *server**share**directory**component.exe*, because although the system account has the right to do most anything on the local machine, it has no network privileges. This means that the SCM cannot launch a local server that resides on a remote machine. Keep in mind that UNC paths fail even if they refer to an executable file that resides on the local machine.

> NOTE: Although it is not generally recommended because it significantly compromises system security, an administrator can make this technique work by setting the HKEY_LOCAL_MACHINE-\SYSTEM\CurrentControlSet\Services\LanmanServer\Parameters-\RestrictNullSessionAccess registry value to *0*.

The Default Configuration Permissions area of the Default Security tab enables the administrator to control the security of the entire HKEY_CLASSES-_ROOT section of the registry. These settings can be used to restrict ordinary users from being able to view or modify the contents of this crucial area in the registry. To view or change the security settings of individual registry keys, use the old Windows NT registry editor (regedt32.exe) instead of the new one (regedit.exe). Note that some legacy components are designed to refresh their registry settings every time they run. (All components written in Visual Basic do this.) Refreshing the registry settings can cause components to fail if you restrict write access to the registry. Therefore, it is recommended that modern components do not refresh their entries in the HKEY_CLASSES_ROOT section of the registry every time they are executed.

In Windows 95 and Windows 98, only the default access permissions are configurable; all the other settings are not applicable due to the limited security available on these platforms. However, an additional option, Enable Remote Connection, is available. The Enable Remote Connection option specifies whether remote clients are permitted to connect to objects running on the local computer. Although Windows 95 and Windows 98 do not support remote launching of components, they do permit connections to running objects. When the system is first installed, however, this option is disabled and must be enabled using the DCOM Configuration utility or another registry editor.

All of the options presented on the Default Properties and Default Security tabs of the DCOM Configuration utility are controlled by registry values stored in the HKEY_LOCAL_MACHINE\SOFTWARE\Microsoft\Ole key. The following table describes the named-values that can be stored in this registry key.

HKEY_LOCAL_MACHINE \SOFTWARE\Microsoft\Ole Values	Description
DefaultLaunchPermission	Defines the default ACL that determines who can launch components
DefaultAccessPermission	Defines the default ACL that determines who can access components
EnableDCOM	Specifies whether DCOM is enabled on this machine
EnableRemoteConnect	Specifies whether objects running on the machine accept remote connections; by default, set to no (N)*
LegacyAuthenticationLevel	Sets the default authentication level

* Windows 95/98 only

(continued)

continued

HKEY_LOCAL_MACHINE \SOFTWARE\Microsoft\Ole Values	Description
LegacyImpersonationLevel	Sets the default impersonation level
LegacySecureReferences	Specifies whether *AddRef* and *Release* method calls are secured
LegacyMutualAuthentication	Specifies whether mutual authentication is enabled**

** Not supported in Windows NT 4.0

Configuring Component Security: The AppID Key

So far, we have explored how the DCOM Configuration utility can be used to set the registry entries that control the default COM security settings. In this section, we will examine the registry settings that control security on a per-component basis. For components with more specialized security requirements, these settings can be used to override the machinewide default settings.

The AppID registry key was designed to group the configuration options for one or more objects housed by a component into one centralized location in the registry. A unique CLSID is assigned to each COM object, but all COM objects housed in one component must map to the same application identifier (AppID). (Chapter 8, "DLL Surrogates and Executable Components," covers the AppID registry key in more detail.) The following table describes the four security-related values that can be stored in an AppID registry entry. These four named-values correspond precisely to the four areas of the COM security model: launch, access, authentication, and identity control.

Security-Related AppID Values	Description
LaunchPermission	Defines the ACL that determines who can launch the component
AccessPermission	Defines the ACL that determines who can access the component
AuthenticationLevel	Sets the authentication level to be used for the component
RunAs	Sets the user account in which the component will execute

When it is first run, the DCOM Configuration utility presents the administrator with a list of components registered on the local machine. To configure the security settings for a particular component, select it from the list and click the Properties button. Then select the Security tab, which lets you specify the launch and access permissions for a specific component. These options affect the *AccessPermission* and *LaunchPermission* values in the component's AppID registry key. Select the Use Default Permissions option to instruct COM to use the machinewide default security settings for this component. Otherwise, click the Edit button to control the specific security for this component, as shown in Figure 11-4.

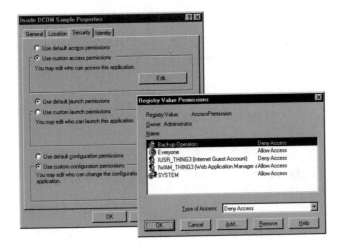

Figure 11-4.
Using the DCOM Configuration utility to set the access permissions for a particular component.

Recall that when the system is first installed, the default launch and access permissions enable only administrators, the system account, and the interactive user to launch and access components. It is not recommended that you change these default settings. However, because remote clients are not likely to be logged on as administrators, you will typically modify the component's launch and access security to grant or deny permissions to everyone, various user groups, or even specific users. This technique is considered preferable to adjusting the machinewide default security settings that affect all components. Granting launch and access permissions to all users (*Everyone*) and setting the authentication level to none (*RPC_C_AUTHN_LEVEL_NONE*) enables anonymous activation and access.

The *IAccessControl* Interface

Although large parts of the COM security model, such as authentication and impersonation, are platform independent through the use of SSPI, until recently access control was performed exclusively using Windows NT DACLs. The Win32 API includes functions that can create and manipulate ACLs. These ACLs can then be serialized into the registry keys that control COM security, allowing you to configure launch and access permissions. However, because ACLs created in Windows NT are obviously not portable (they aren't even supported in Windows 95/98), Microsoft needed a platform-independent solution for the COM security model. That solution was designed in the form of the *IAccessControl* interface, shown here in IDL notation:

```
interface IAccessControl : IUnknown
{
    // Merge the new rights with the existing access rights.
    HRESULT GrantAccessRights([in] PACTRL_ACCESSW pAccessList);

    // Replace the existing access rights with the new rights.
    HRESULT SetAccessRights([in] PACTRL_ACCESSW pAccessList);

    // Set an item's owner or group.
    HRESULT SetOwner(
        [in] PTRUSTEEW pOwner,
        [in] PTRUSTEEW pGroup);

    // Remove explicit entries for the list of trustees.
    HRESULT RevokeAccessRights(
        [in] LPWSTR lpProperty,
        [in] ULONG cTrustees,
        [in, size_is(cTrustees)] TRUSTEEW prgTrustees[]);

    // Get the entire list of access rights.
    HRESULT GetAllAccessRights(
        [in] LPWSTR lpProperty,
        [out] PACTRL_ACCESSW_ALLOCATE_ALL_NODES* ppAccessList,
        [out] PTRUSTEEW* ppOwner,
        [out] PTRUSTEEW* ppGroup);

    // Determine whether a trustee has access rights.
    HRESULT IsAccessAllowed(
        [in] PTRUSTEEW pTrustee,
        [in] LPWSTR lpProperty,
        [in] ACCESS_RIGHTS AccessRights,
        [out] BOOL* pfAccessAllowed);
}
```

Although it is possible to write security code that uses the Win32 API security functions, doing so unnecessarily ties a component to the Windows NT platform. Component developers who want to write portable code that works on Windows NT as well as on other platforms supporting COM should use the *IAccessControl* interface instead. The true goal of the *IAccessControl* interface is to provide programmatic security, but we will first explore its use in creating platform-independent access control information stored in the registry. Although it is normally considered wiser to let the administrator configure the security settings using the DCOM Configuration utility, it might occasionally be advantageous to control the registry settings from within a component. Relying on an administrator to configure critical security settings can sometimes be a mistake. In such cases, configuring the registry-based security settings for a component might be a necessary part of the installation program. Of course, the administrator could later adjust these settings using the DCOM Configuration utility.

The System Implementation of *IAccessControl*

Windows NT, Windows 98, Windows 95, and ports of DCOM to other platforms provide an implementation of the *IAccessControl* interface in the *CLSID_DCOMAccessControl* object. In addition to implementing the *IAccessControl* interface, this system object also implements the *IPersist* and *IPersistStream* interfaces, which allows you to configure an ACL using the methods of the *IAccessControl* interface and then store these settings in a registry key that will be used by COM to determine access and launch permission. The DCOM Configuration utility itself uses the *CLSID_DCOMAccessControl* object to create these registry entries in Windows 95 and Windows 98, where the Win32 API security functions are not available. Future versions of the DCOM Configuration utility in Windows NT will also use this object to persist access control information into the registry.

The ACTRL_ACCESS structure used as a parameter by several methods of the *IAccessControl* interface is somewhat complicated; it has several levels of structures nested within one another, as shown in Figure 11-5 on the following page. Aficionados of the Win32 API security functions will recognize the TRUSTEE structure buried deep within the ACTRL_ACCESS structure. The TRUSTEE structure is borrowed by the *IAccessControl* interface from the security functions of the Win32 API. A trustee identifies a security principal, which can be a user account, a group account, or a logon session. The TRUSTEE structure enables you to use a name (*ptstrName*) or an SID (*pSid*) to identify a trustee. When you are working within the COM security model, it is certainly preferable to identify trustees by name instead of a Windows NT–specific SID.

The Windows NT implementation of the *CLSID_DCOMAccessControl* object automatically performs the task of looking up the SID that corresponds to the trustee name.

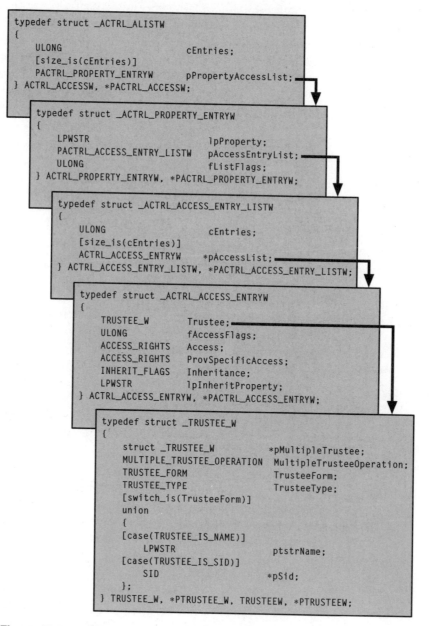

```
typedef struct _ACTRL_ALISTW
{
    ULONG                           cEntries;
    [size_is(cEntries)]
    PACTRL_PROPERTY_ENTRYW          pPropertyAccessList;
} ACTRL_ACCESSW, *PACTRL_ACCESSW;

    typedef struct _ACTRL_PROPERTY_ENTRYW
    {
        LPWSTR                          lpProperty;
        PACTRL_ACCESS_ENTRY_LISTW       pAccessEntryList;
        ULONG                           fListFlags;
    } ACTRL_PROPERTY_ENTRYW, *PACTRL_PROPERTY_ENTRYW;

        typedef struct _ACTRL_ACCESS_ENTRY_LISTW
        {
            ULONG                           cEntries;
            [size_is(cEntries)]
            ACTRL_ACCESS_ENTRYW     *pAccessList;
        } ACTRL_ACCESS_ENTRY_LISTW, *PACTRL_ACCESS_ENTRY_LISTW;

            typedef struct _ACTRL_ACCESS_ENTRYW
            {
                TRUSTEE_W       Trustee;
                ULONG           fAccessFlags;
                ACCESS_RIGHTS   Access;
                ACCESS_RIGHTS   ProvSpecificAccess;
                INHERIT_FLAGS   Inheritance;
                LPWSTR          lpInheritProperty;
            } ACTRL_ACCESS_ENTRYW, *PACTRL_ACCESS_ENTRYW;

                typedef struct _TRUSTEE_W
                {
                    struct _TRUSTEE_W            *pMultipleTrustee;
                    MULTIPLE_TRUSTEE_OPERATION   MultipleTrusteeOperation;
                    TRUSTEE_FORM                 TrusteeForm;
                    TRUSTEE_TYPE                 TrusteeType;
                    [switch_is(TrusteeForm)]
                    union
                    {
                    [case(TRUSTEE_IS_NAME)]
                        LPWSTR                   ptstrName;
                    [case(TRUSTEE_IS_SID)]
                        SID                      *pSid;
                    };
                } TRUSTEE_W, *PTRUSTEE_W, TRUSTEEW, *PTRUSTEEW;
```

Figure 11-5.
The structures nested in the ACTRL_ACCESS structure.

The following sample program shows how to use the *CLSID_DCOMAccess-Control* object to read and display COM security information stored in registry entries in a platform-independent manner. The numbers shown in parentheses here correspond to the numbered elements shown in boldface in the code. The program calls *CoCreateInstance* to instantiate *CLSID_DCOMAccessControl* and obtains a pointer to its *IPersistStream* interface (1). Then the *IPersistStream::Load* method is called to initialize the object with the security information stored in the AppID\AccessPermission registry value of a component (2). Next the program calls the *IUnknown::QueryInterface* method to request a pointer to the *IAccessControl* interface (3) for use in calling the *IAccessControl::GetAllAccessRights* method (4). Not shown in this code is a loop that displays all the trustees enumerated in the ACL obtained from the *GetAllAccessRights* method. Also included on the companion CD is a program, based on a sample from the Microsoft Platform SDK, that shows how to write security settings to the registry using the *CLSID_DCOMAccessControl* implementation of the *IAccessControl* interface.

```c
#define _WIN32_DCOM
#include <windows.h>
#include <stdio.h>
#include <iaccess.h> // For IAccessControl

// Need to define this ourselves!
const IID IID_IAccessControl =
{0xEEDD23E0,0x8410,0x11CE,{0xA1,0xC3,0x08,0x00,0x2B,0x2B,0x8D,0x8F}};

// This is the header stored in the registry.
typedef struct
{
    WORD version;
    WORD pad;
    GUID classid;
} SPermissionHeader;

void main()
{
    HRESULT hr = CoInitialize(NULL);

    // Open the AppID key.
    // Replace the AppID below with an AppID for which you
    // have configured custom access permission.
    HKEY key = 0;
    hr = RegOpenKeyEx(HKEY_CLASSES_ROOT,
        "AppID\\{10000002-0000-0000-0000-000000000001}", 0,
        KEY_READ, &key);
```

(continued)

```
// Read the value from the registry.
DWORD dwSize = 0;
hr = RegQueryValueEx(key, "AccessPermission", NULL, NULL,
    NULL, &dwSize);

void* pMemory = (void*)CoTaskMemAlloc(dwSize);
hr = RegQueryValueEx(key, "AccessPermission", NULL, NULL,
    (unsigned char*)pMemory, &dwSize);

IStream* pStream;
hr = CreateStreamOnHGlobal(pMemory, TRUE, &pStream);

// (1) Create an instance of the
// CLSID_DCOMAccessControl object.
IPersistStream* pPersistStream = NULL;
hr = CoCreateInstance(CLSID_DCOMAccessControl, NULL,
    CLSCTX_INPROC_SERVER, IID_IPersistStream,
    (void**)&pPersistStream);

LARGE_INTEGER size;
size.QuadPart = sizeof(SPermissionHeader);
hr = pStream->Seek(size, STREAM_SEEK_SET, NULL);

// (2) Initialize the CLSID_DCOMAccessControl object with
// the data from the registry.
hr = pPersistStream->Load(pStream);

// (3) Request a pointer to the IAccessControl interface.
IAccessControl* pAccessControl = NULL;
hr = pPersistStream->QueryInterface(IID_IAccessControl,
    (void**)&pAccessControl);

ACTRL_ACCESSW* pAccess = NULL;
TRUSTEEW* pOwner = NULL;
TRUSTEEW* pGroup = NULL;
// (4) Call the IAccessControl::GetAllAccessRights method.
hr = pAccessControl->GetAllAccessRights(NULL, &pAccess,
    &pOwner, &pGroup);

// Program proceeds to enumerate all security principals
// returned by the IAccessControl::GetAllAccessRights method.

// Release everything and bail out.
CoTaskMemFree(pAccess);
CoTaskMemFree(pOwner);
CoTaskMemFree(pGroup);
```

```
    pPersistStream->Release();
    pStream->Release();
    pAccessControl->Release();

    RegCloseKey(key);
    CoUninitialize();
}
```

Configuring Component Identity

The Identity tab of the DCOM Configuration utility for a selected component, shown in Figure 11-6, enables the administrator to determine in which user account the component will execute. The Identity tab provides three possible settings for defining the user account: The Interactive User, The Launching User, and This User. Changes made on the Identity tab affect the *RunAs* value in the component's AppID registry key.

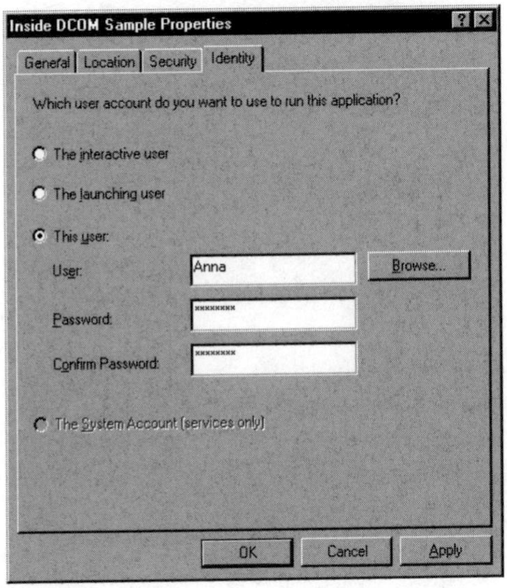

Figure 11-6.
The Identity tab of the DCOM Configuration utility for a selected component.

Run as Launching User

The default identity setting for components—in many ways the least useful setting—is that of the launching user. With this setting, the *RunAs* value is not present in the component's AppID registry key. Running as the launching user means that the component will be executed under the security credentials of the client process, which is somewhat analogous to using impersonation for the lifetime of the component. Since Windows NT 4.0 does not support delegation-level impersonation, components run as the launching user receive somewhat crippled security credentials. For example, remote calls to other machines cannot be made when the component is running under the identity of the launching user; neither can the component access files shared across the net-work. If this access were allowed, impersonation could form an endless chain from one computer to another, allowing a rogue component to assume the client's security credentials and do all sorts of bad things with them. In Windows NT 5.0, delegation-level impersonation is supported when the Kerberos security provider is used. The Kerberos security protocol has many built-in safeguards that limit what can be done with delegation-level impersonation.

Window Stations

Windows NT supports a security environment known as a *window station*. The Windows NT desktop visible on the screen is part of the *interactive window station*. All programs executing in the interactive window station receive the security credentials of the logged-on user. It is possible to create additional, noninteractive window stations for use when you are launching processes under the security credentials of different user accounts. However, processes running in noninteractive window stations are not visible to the user and cannot receive input from the user. This technique is sometimes advantageous in that it decouples a process from the actions of the end user, who might be working on the server machine. Window stations are a limited resource in Windows NT; in its default configuration, only about 15 window stations can be created. For this reason, it is important to be aware of the existence of window stations and their use by COM.

The number of window stations that you are allowed to create can be adjusted by reducing the memory consumed by the desktop heap of each window station. In the HKEY_LOCAL_MACHINE\SYSTEM-\CurrentControlSet\Control\Session Manager\SubSystems registry key, change the Windows named-value *Shared Section = 1024,3072* to *Shared Section = 1024,3072,512*, and then restart the machine. Now Windows NT will be able create approximately 95 noninteractive window stations.

Even if delegation-level impersonation is offered by the underlying security provider, running a component as the launching user is still not recommended because each client that attempts to access the component will force a new window station to be created and a new instance of the component to be loaded. This happens regardless of whether the COM class used the *REGCLS_MULTIPLEUSE* flag when calling the *CoRegisterClassObject* function. Imagine a thousand different users connecting to a component and each one of them causing a new window station and process to be created! Also note that components launched under the identity of the launching user do not have access to the interactive window station visible to the end user.

Run as Interactive User

When it is configured to run as the interactive user, the component will be run under the access token of the end user currently logged on, which means that the component has access to the interactive desktop visible to the user. The problems with configuring a component for execution as the interactive user are threefold. First, a user must be logged on in order for the component to execute. Second, you never know who will log on, and thus the component might have many rights (if the administrator is logged on) or few rights (if a guest is logged on). Third, if the user logs off while the component is running, the component dies. This option is most useful for a system such as a distributed whiteboard-style drawing application that needs to interact with the user, as well as for debugging purposes. It is not recommended for other types of server or middle-tier components. The *RunAs* registry value is set to *Interactive User* for components configured to run under the identity of the end user.

Run as This User

The third identity option is to configure the component for execution under a specific user account. When an attempt is made to launch the component, COM will automatically initiate a system logon using the specified user account by calling the Win32 API function *LogonUser*, followed by a call to the *CreateProcessAsUser* function. As part of the logon procedure, a new, noninteractive window station will be created for use by the component. This setting is often the best option for components that will serve many client programs simultaneously, as all instances of the component will be loaded into one window station. In addition, if the class was registered with the *REGCLS-_MULTIPLEUSE* flag, multiple clients will be able to share access to a single instance of the component.

The *RunAs* value in the component's AppID registry key is set to a string in the form *domain\user*, and the password is stored in a secure part of the registry managed by the Local Security Authority (LSA) subsystem of Windows NT.

The LSA is a protected subsystem used to maintain information about all aspects of local security on a system; only the LSA API functions can be used by an administrator to read and write the secured password information stored in the registry.

Note that components registered to run under a specific account will always fail if you attempt to run them manually under the guise of a different user account. Suffering from an identity crisis, the *CoRegisterClassObject* function will return the error *CO_E_WRONG_SERVER_IDENTITY*. This error occurs because the code calling *CoRegisterClassObject* can't be trusted. Only the securable registry settings that specify which component to run and under what identity can be trusted. This restriction prevents a malicious component from spoofing client programs by masquerading as an upstanding class object with a registered CLSID.

User accounts that are used by COM for logon purposes must be assigned the special right Log On As A Batch Job, or COM will not be able to successfully log in using the account. The DCOM Configuration utility automatically grants this right to any user account specified on the Identity tab. This is possible because the user of the DCOM Configuration utility must be an administrator and therefore has the right to confer special privileges on other users. The User Manager (usrmgr.exe) system utility can also be used to bestow these privileges. From the Policies menu of the User Manager utility, choose User Rights, and then check the Show Advanced User Rights check box, as shown in Figure 11-7. From the Right drop-down list, select Log On As A Batch Job, and then click the Add or Remove button to specify which user accounts will have this right.

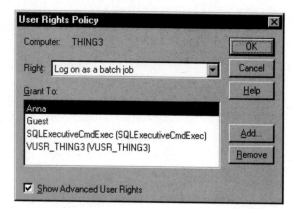

Figure 11-7.
Using the Windows NT User Manager to grant the Log On As A Batch Job right to users.

Note that the identity of components implemented as Windows NT Services is not configured using the DCOM Configuration utility or the *RunAs* registry value. Instead, the *LocalService* value of the AppID registry key names the service, and the identity is configured via the Services applet of the system Control Panel.

Programmatic Security

Configuring security settings in the registry has its advantages: it doesn't require any special work on the part of the component developer, and it allows the administrator great flexibility in configuring the security settings. As you know, component activation security and identity control is always configured via the registry. However, declarative security isn't always the best answer for all security concerns. Certain features of the COM security model can be accessed only via a programming interface. For example, it might sometimes become necessary to temporarily increase the security of sensitive data transmitted across the network. In these cases, taking programmatic control of security settings offers a solution. The best answer for most components is a combined approach, using declarative security for most security jobs and programmatic security for more specialized tasks requiring a finer degree of control than that available via the registry settings.

The *CoInitializeSecurity* Function

COM's security infrastructure is initialized on a per-process basis at start-up. The *CoInitializeSecurity* function sets the default security values for the process. If an application does not call *CoInitializeSecurity*, COM will call the function automatically the first time an interface pointer is marshaled into or out of an apartment in the process. Attempting to call *CoInitializeSecurity* after marshaling takes place will yield the infamous *RPC_E_TOO_LATE* error. Thus, programs that want to call *CoInitializeSecurity* explicitly are advised to do so immediately after calling *CoInitialize(Ex)*. This rule makes it difficult to call *CoInitializeSecurity* from languages such as Visual Basic and Java, in which the virtual machine may call *CoInitializeSecurity* before running any application code. Note that *CoInitializeSecurity* is called only once per process, not in each thread that calls *CoInitialize(Ex)*.

For applications that do not call *CoInitializeSecurity*, COM obtains the security settings from the registry. In this way, legacy components written prior to the advent of COM's security model are not left unsecured. See the section, "Declarative Security: The Registry," earlier in this chapter for more information about how to configure these settings. Although most of the security settings can be configured via the registry, it is often desirable to have programmatic control over the security environment. In this way, a component can override both the default and the component-specific security settings configured in the registry by an administrator. The declaration of the *CoInitializeSecurity* function is shown here:

```
HRESULT __stdcall CoInitializeSecurity(
    PSECURITY_DESCRIPTOR          pSecDesc,
    LONG                          cAuthSvc,
    SOLE_AUTHENTICATION_SERVICE  *asAuthSvc,
    void                         *pReserved1,
    DWORD                         dwAuthnLevel,
    DWORD                         dwImpLevel,
    void                         *pReserved2,
    DWORD                         dwCapabilities,
    void                         *pReserved3 );
```

The following discussion examines these parameters in detail, with the exception of parameters 4, 7, and 9, which are reserved.

The first parameter of *CoInitializeSecurity*, *pSecDesc*, is declared as a *PSECURITY_DESCRIPTOR*, which is simply a pointer to void (*void**). This polymorphic argument defines the component's access permissions in one of three ways. Typically, *pSecDesc* points to a Win32 security descriptor that COM will use to check access permissions on new connections. The *pSecDesc* parameter can also point to a globally unique identifier (GUID) that references an AppID in the registry where declarative security information is stored, or it can point to an implementation of the *IAccessControl* interface. Figure 11-8 shows the three ways the polymorphic *pSecDesc* parameter can be used to perform access control.

If *pSecDesc* points to the GUID of an AppID in the registry, all other parameters of the *CoInitializeSecurity* function are ignored. If the *EOAC_APPID* flag is set in the *dwCapabilities* parameter but the *pSecDesc* parameter is *NULL*, *CoInitializeSecurity* looks for the .exe name of the process in the HKEY_CLASSES_ROOT\AppID section of the registry and uses the AppID stored there. This behavior is identical to the default behavior obtained when you allow COM to call *CoInitializeSecurity* automatically.

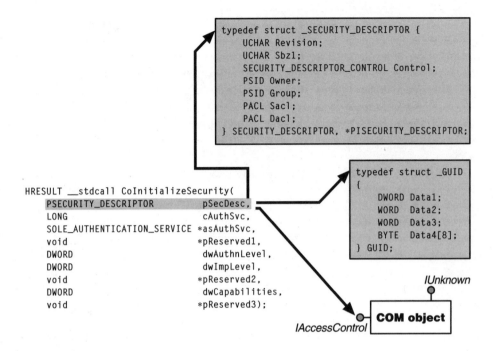

Figure 11-8.
Three different ways to perform access control using the pSecDesc
parameter.

The SOLE_AUTHENTICATION_SERVICE Structure

The second parameter of *CoInitializeSecurity*, *cAuthSvc*, specifies the number of authentication services that are being registered. A value of *0* means that no authentication services are being registered; a value of *−1* instructs COM to choose which authentication services to register. The third parameter, *asAuthSvc*, is a pointer to an array of SOLE_AUTHENTICATION_SERVICE structures, each of which identifies one authentication service. The definition of the SOLE-_AUTHENTICATION_SERVICE structure is shown here:

```
typedef struct tagSOLE_AUTHENTICATION_SERVICE
{
    DWORD dwAuthnSvc; // RPC_C_AUTHN_xxx
    DWORD dwAuthzSvc; // RPC_C_AUTHZ_xxx
    OLECHAR *pPrincipalName;
    HRESULT hr;
} SOLE_AUTHENTICATION_SERVICE;
```

The first field of the SOLE_AUTHENTICATION_SERVICE structure, *dwAuthnSvc*, specifies which authentication service should be used to authenticate the client. This field can be set to one of the constants shown in the following table, which includes some the most useful of the many constants that are available. Note that only the *RPC_C_AUTHN_WINNT* authentication service is supported in Windows NT 4.0. Windows NT 5.0 supports both the NTLM SSP and Kerberos authentications. Additional security providers might be available from third parties.

RPC_C_AUTHN_xxx Flag	Description
RPC_C_AUTHN_NONE	No authentication
RPC_C_AUTHN_DCE_PRIVATE	Distributed Computing Environment (DCE) private key authentication
RPC_C_AUTHN_DCE_PUBLIC	DCE public key authentication
RPC_C_AUTHN_WINNT	NTLM SSP
RPC_C_AUTHN_GSS_KERBEROS	Kerberos authentication

The second field of the SOLE_AUTHENTICATION_SERVICE structure, *dwAuthzSvc*, indicates the authorization service to be used by the server. This field can be set to one of the constants shown in the following table. Note that the *RPC_C_AUTHN_WINNT* authentication service does not utilize the authorization service, and therefore this field must be set to *RPC_C_AUTHZ_NONE* when you are using NTLM SSP authentication.

RPC_C_AUTHZ_xxx Flag	Description
RPC_C_AUTHZ_NONE	Server performs no authorization.
RPC_C_AUTHZ_NAME	Server performs authorization based on the client's principal name.
RPC_C_AUTHZ_DCE	Server performs authorization checking using the client's DCE privilege attribute certificate information, which is sent to the server with each RPC made using the binding handle.

The third field, *pPrincipalName*, defines the principal name to be used with the authentication service. The NTLM SSP and Kerberos authentication packages ignore this parameter, assuming the current user identifier. The last field, *hr*, contains the *HRESULT* value indicating the status of the call to register this authentication service.

Authentication and Impersonation Levels

The fifth parameter of *CoInitializeSecurity*, *dwAuthnLevel*, specifies the default authentication level. This parameter can be set to one of the *RPC_C_AUTHN-_LEVEL_xxx* flags shown in the first of the two tables in the preceding section. The *dwAuthnLevel* setting specified in the client's call to *CoInitializeSecurity* declares the default authentication level the client wants to use for outgoing calls. The *dwAuthnLevel* setting specified in the component's call to *CoInitialize-Security* becomes the minimum level at which client calls will be accepted. In any connection between a particular client and a particular component, COM automatically negotiates the actual authentication level to be the higher of the two settings. In this way, the server does not need to reject client calls because they arrive at an authentication level below the minimum level declared by the component.

If the first parameter passed to *CoInitializeSecurity*, *pSecDesc*, is a valid pointer to a Win32 security descriptor, a GUID, or an implementation of the *IAccessControl* interface, the *dwAuthnLevel* parameter cannot be set to *RPC_C_AUTHN_LEVEL_NONE*. On the other hand, if *pSecDesc* is *NULL*, no ACL checking will be performed, and therefore the *dwAuthnLevel* parameter can be set to *RPC_C_AUTHN_LEVEL_NONE*, indicating that anonymous access is permitted. The sixth parameter of *CoInitializeSecurity*, *dwImpLevel*, specifies the default impersonation level for proxies. This parameter can be set to one of the *RPC_C_IMP_LEVEL_xxx* flags shown in the table on page 407. The *dwImpLevel* setting specified in the client's call to *CoInitializeSecurity* specifies the default impersonation level that the client grants to the component. This value is not used on the server side.

The eighth parameter, *dwCapabilities*, can be used to set additional client-side and server-side capabilities. This value can be composed of a combination of the values from the *EOLE_AUTHENTICATION_CAPABILITIES* enumeration shown in the table on the following page. *CoInitializeSecurity* interprets the data pointed to by the *pSecDesc* parameter, based on the flags set in the *dw-Capabilities* parameter. If *pSecDesc* points to a GUID, the *EOAC_APPID* flag must be set; if *pSecDesc* points to an implementation of the *IAccessControl* interface, the *EOAC_ACCESS_CONTROL* flag must be set. By default, if neither the *EOAC-_APPID* nor the *EOAC_ACCESS_CONTROL* flag is set in the *dwCapabilities* parameter, it is assumed that *pSecDesc* points to a Win32 security descriptor structure. Note that the *EOAC_APPID* and *EOAC_ACCESS_CONTROL* flags are mutually exclusive.

EOLE_AUTHENTICATION_ CAPABILITIES Enumeration	Description
EOAC_NONE	No capability flags.
EOAC_MUTUAL_AUTH	Not used—mutual authentication is determined automatically.
EOAC_CLOAKING	Sets the cloaking capability.
EOAC_SECURE_REFS	Causes COM to perform additional callbacks to authenticate distributed reference count calls, to ensure that objects are not released maliciously.
EOAC_ACCESS_CONTROL	*CoInitializeSecurity* expects *pSecDesc* to point to an implementation of the *IAccessControl* interface. COM will use this pointer to call the *IAccessControl::IsAccessAllowed* method when performing security checks.
EOAC_APPID	*CoInitializeSecurity* expects *pSecDesc* to point to a GUID that is installed in the HKEY_CLASSES_ROOT\AppID section of the registry. *CoInitializeSecurity* uses the security information read from the registry.

The *CoQueryAuthenticationServices* Function

The *CoQueryAuthenticationServices* function retrieves the list of authentication services that were registered when the process called *CoInitializeSecurity*. This information is primarily of interest to custom marshaling code that needs to determine what principal names an application can use. The declaration of the *CoQueryAuthenticationServices* function is shown here:

```
HRESULT __stdcall CoQueryAuthenticationServices(
    DWORD *pcAuthSvc,
    SOLE_AUTHENTICATION_SERVICE** asAuthSvc);
```

Using the *IAccessControl* Interface with *CoInitializeSecurity*

Earlier in this chapter, we explained how to use the *CLSID_DCOMAccessControl* object and its implementation of the *IAccessControl* and *IPersistStream* interfaces to read and write access permissions from the registry. Although it can prove useful in some cases, the *IAccessControl* interface is not designed for this type of administration and configuration code. The *IAccessControl* interface is primarily intended for use by code that needs to perform programmatic access checking. As we know, the first parameter of the *CoInitializeSecurity* function can point to a Win32 security descriptor, to an AppID, or to an implementation of the *IAccessControl* interface. For *CoInitializeSecurity* to accept an *IAccessControl* interface pointer as the first parameter, the *dwCapabilities* parameter must have the *EOAC_ACCESS_CONTROL* flag set. When a pointer to an access control object is passed to *CoInitializeSecurity*, COM calls the object's *IAccessControl::IsAccessAllowed* method to perform access checking at run time. This method determines whether the trustee (user account, group account, or logon session) has access to the object and then simply returns a value of *true* or *false*, indicating that permission is granted or denied.

The system implementation of the *IAccessControl* interface provided by the *CLSID_DCOMAccessControl* object can be used for this purpose. First instantiate the object by calling *CoCreateInstance*, and then request a pointer to the *IAccessControl* interface. Then call any of the first five methods of the *IAccessControl* interface (*GrantAccessRights*, *SetAccessRights*, *SetOwner*, *RevokeAccessRights*, and *GetAllAccessRights*) to configure the process-wide access permissions. Last call the *CoInitializeSecurity* function, passing the *IAccessControl* pointer in the first parameter and the *EOAC_ACCESS_CONTROL* flag in the last parameter. After you call the *CoInitializeSecurity* security function, the access control object can be released using the *IUnknown::Release* method; following COM's reference counting rules, *CoInitializeSecurity* calls the *AddRef* method internally. COM performs all access checking by calling the *IAccessControl::IsAccessAllowed* method. The implementation of this method provided by *CLSID_DCOMAccessControl* will use the access permissions configured in the object to determine whether to grant or deny access to individual trustees.

> **N O T E :** Currently, the *IAccessControl::SetOwner* method is not implemented by the *CLSID_DCOMAccessControl* object.

The following code illustrates these steps by configuring an access control object that grants access to the system account and the Everyone group but denies access to a specific user account. Explicit calls to methods of the *IAccessControl* interface are shown in boldface.

```
// Create a DCOMAccessControl object, and get its IAccessControl
// interface pointer.
IAccessControl* pAccessControl = NULL;
hr = CoCreateInstance(CLSID_DCOMAccessControl, NULL,
    CLSCTX_INPROC_SERVER, IID_IAccessControl,
    (void**)&pAccessControl);

// Set up the property list. We use the NULL property because we
// are trying to adjust the security of the object itself.
ACTRL_ACCESSW access;
```

(continued)

```
ACTRL_PROPERTY_ENTRYW propEntry;
access.cEntries = 1;
access.pPropertyAccessList = &propEntry;

ACTRL_ACCESS_ENTRY_LISTW entryList;
propEntry.lpProperty = NULL;
propEntry.pAccessEntryList = &entryList;
propEntry.fListFlags = 0;

// Set up the ACL for the default property.
ACTRL_ACCESS_ENTRYW entry;
entryList.cEntries = 1;
entryList.pAccessList = &entry;

// Set up the ACE.
entry.fAccessFlags = ACTRL_ACCESS_ALLOWED;
entry.Access = COM_RIGHTS_EXECUTE;
entry.ProvSpecificAccess = 0;
entry.Inheritance = NO_INHERITANCE;
entry.lpInheritProperty = NULL;

// Windows NT requires the system account to have access.
entry.Trustee.pMultipleTrustee = NULL;
entry.Trustee.MultipleTrusteeOperation = NO_MULTIPLE_TRUSTEE;
entry.Trustee.TrusteeForm = TRUSTEE_IS_NAME;
entry.Trustee.TrusteeType = TRUSTEE_IS_USER;
entry.Trustee.ptstrName = L"NT Authority\\System";

// Setting access rights: allow access to
// NT Authority\System.
hr = pAccessControl->SetAccessRights(&access);

// Deny access to an individual user.
entry.fAccessFlags = ACTRL_ACCESS_DENIED;
entry.Trustee.TrusteeType = TRUSTEE_IS_USER;
entry.Trustee.ptstrName = L"Domain\\User";
hr = pAccessControl->GrantAccessRights(&access);

// Grant access to everyone.
entry.fAccessFlags = ACTRL_ACCESS_ALLOWED;
entry.Trustee.TrusteeType = TRUSTEE_IS_GROUP;
entry.Trustee.ptstrName = L"*";
hr = pAccessControl->GrantAccessRights(&access);

// Call CoInitializeSecurity, and pass a pointer to the access
// control object.
```

```
hr = CoInitializeSecurity(pAccessControl, -1, NULL, NULL,
    RPC_C_AUTHN_LEVEL_CONNECT, RPC_C_IMP_LEVEL_IDENTIFY,
    NULL, EOAC_ACCESS_CONTROL, NULL);

// Release the access control object. CoInitializeSecurity holds
// a reference.
pAccessControl->Release();
```

Implementing the *IAccessControl* Interface

Besides using the system-provided *CLSID_DCOMAccessControl* object, *CoInitialize-Security* can be provided with a custom implementation of the *IAccessControl* interface. The first five methods of *IAccessControl* must be implemented so that the caller can configure access permissions. How this access control information is stored internally in the object is entirely implementation-dependent. The last method, *IAccessControl::IsAccessAllowed*, will be called by COM whenever an access check is required to determine whether a client has sufficient rights. Note that implementations of *IAccessControl* must be completely thread-safe because COM can call the access control object on any thread, at any time.

Although time and space do not permit us to provide a more complete implementation of the *IAccessControl* interface, allow us to humbly present *CMyAccessControl*. *CMyAccessControl* is a C++ class that returns *E_NOTIMPL* for all the methods of the *IAccessControl* interface except one: *IsAccessAllowed*. The implementation of the *IAccessControl::IsAccessAllowed* method is shown in the following code. As you can probably guess by looking at the code, each client access causes the method to display a message box asking the user whether permission should be granted or denied. If the user clicks Yes, *IsAccessAllowed* returns *TRUE* in the *pfAccessAllowed* parameter; otherwise, it returns *FALSE*. This security system is ironclad.

```
HRESULT CMyAccessControl::IsAccessAllowed(PTRUSTEEW pTrustee,
    LPWSTR lpProperty, ACCESS_RIGHTS AccessRights,
    BOOL* pfAccessAllowed)
{
    if(MessageBoxW(NULL, pTrustee->ptstrName, L"Grant permission?",
        MB_SERVICE_NOTIFICATION | MB_SETFOREGROUND | MB_YESNO) ==
        IDYES)
        *pfAccessAllowed = TRUE;
    else
        *pfAccessAllowed = FALSE;
    return S_OK;
}
```

Before *CoInitializeSecurity* is called, a static instance of the *CMyAccessControl* object is created. The address of this simple access control object is then passed as the first parameter of *CoInitializeSecurity*, as shown in the following code. COM will later call the *CMyAccessControl::IsAccessAllowed* method to determine whether prospective clients should be granted or denied access.

```
CMyAccessControl ac;
hr = CoInitializeSecurity(&ac, -1, NULL, NULL,
    RPC_C_AUTHN_LEVEL_CONNECT, RPC_C_IMP_LEVEL_IDENTIFY,
    NULL, EOAC_ACCESS_CONTROL, NULL);
```

Activation Credentials: The COAUTHINFO Structure

The security settings discussed to this point have centered on access permissions, which can be configured in the registry or by calling *CoInitializeSecurity*. Recall that launch permissions can be configured only in the registry because the server's SCM will need this information before a component is launched. The client, of course, is running when it issues an activation request using one of COM's instantiation functions, which gives the client the opportunity to specify authentication settings that will be used by the client machine's SCM when making the remote activation request to the server machine's SCM.

Imagine that a component's security settings have been configured in such a way that user X is granted launch permission and both user X and user Y are granted access permission. Now a client process running under the security credentials of user Y wants to launch and access the component. Unfortunately, user Y has not been granted launch permission, and thus the client's call to the *CoCreateInstanceEx* function would fail with the error *E_ACCESSDENIED*. However, if the client process (running under the security credentials of user Y) happens to know the password for user account X, the client can use the security credentials of user account X when making the launch request. This launch request will be successful because the administrator has granted launch permission to user X.

All of COM's instantiation functions, such as *CoCreateInstanceEx* and its friends *CoGetClassObject*, *CoGetInstanceFromFile*, and *CoGetInstanceFromIStorage*, accept an argument of the type COSERVERINFO. This structure contains two interesting fields: the name of the server machine on which the object should be instantiated (this field is covered in the section "Remote Instantiation" in Chapter 8, "DLL Surrogates and Executable Components"), and a pointer to authentication information provided in the form of a COAUTHINFO structure. The COAUTHINFO structure in turn contains a pointer to a COAUTHIDENTITY structure. The definitions of the COSERVERINFO, COAUTHINFO, and COAUTHIDENTITY structures are shown in IDL notation in Figure 11-9.

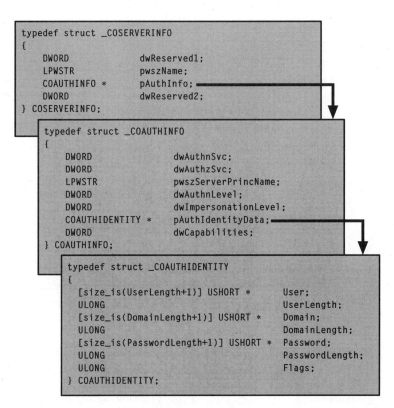

```
typedef struct _COSERVERINFO
{
    DWORD               dwReserved1;
    LPWSTR              pwszName;
    COAUTHINFO *        pAuthInfo;
    DWORD               dwReserved2;
} COSERVERINFO;
```

```
typedef struct _COAUTHINFO
{
    DWORD               dwAuthnSvc;
    DWORD               dwAuthzSvc;
    LPWSTR              pwszServerPrincName;
    DWORD               dwAuthnLevel;
    DWORD               dwImpersonationLevel;
    COAUTHIDENTITY *    pAuthIdentityData;
    DWORD               dwCapabilities;
} COAUTHINFO;
```

```
typedef struct _COAUTHIDENTITY
{
    [size_is(UserLength+1)] USHORT *        User;
    ULONG                                   UserLength;
    [size_is(DomainLength+1)] USHORT *      Domain;
    ULONG                                   DomainLength;
    [size_is(PasswordLength+1)] USHORT *    Password;
    ULONG                                   PasswordLength;
    ULONG                                   Flags;
} COAUTHIDENTITY;
```

Figure 11-9.
The relationship between the COSERVERINFO, COAUTHINFO, and COAUTHIDENTITY structures.

The first two parameters of the COAUTHINFO structure, *dwAuthnSvc* and *dwAuthzSvc*, specify which authentication and authorization services should be used to authenticate the client. Each field can be set to one of the *RPC_C-_AUTHN_xxx* and *RPC_C_AUTHZ_xxx* flags shown in the tables on page 424. The third parameter of the COAUTHINFO structure, *pwszServerPrincName*, points to a string indicating the server principal name to use with the authentication service. If you are using the *RPC_C_AUTHN_WINNT* authentication service, the principal name is ignored.

The fourth and fifth parameters of the COAUTHINFO structure, *dwAuthnLevel* and *dwImpersonationLevel*, specify the authentication and impersonation levels. These fields can be set to one of the progressively higher levels of authentication and impersonation shown in the tables on pages 405–6 and 407. Typically, the impersonation level must be set to at least *RPC_C_IMP_LEVEL-_IMPERSONATE* because the system needs an impersonation token to create a process on behalf of the client. The last parameter of the COAUTHINFO structure, *dwCapabilities*, defines flags that indicate further capabilities of the proxy. Currently, no capability flags are defined.

The sixth parameter of the COAUTHINFO structure, *pAuthIdentityData*, points to a COAUTHIDENTITY structure that establishes the identity of the client. The COAUTHIDENTITY structure allows you to pass a particular user name and password to COM for the purpose of authentication. The *User* field specifies the user name, the *Domain* field specifies the domain or workgroup to which the user belongs, and the *Password* field contains the user's password. The *Flags* field specifies whether the strings are stored in Unicode (*SEC_WIN-NT_AUTH_IDENTITY_UNICODE*) or ASCII (*SEC_WINNT_AUTH_IDENTITY-_ANSI*). Since all COM functions work with Unicode strings, the *Flags* field must be set to *SEC_WINNT_AUTH_IDENTITY_UNICODE*. The corresponding string length fields indicate the string length minus the terminating null character.

When, as is typically the case, the COAUTHINFO pointer in the CO-SERVERINFO structure passed to *CoCreateInstanceEx* and company is set to *NULL,* COM uses the default values for the COAUTHINFO structure shown in the following table.

COAUTHINFO Fields	Default Values
dwAuthnSvc	*RPC_C_AUTHN_WINNT*
dwAuthzSvc	*RPC_C_AUTHZ_NONE*
pwszServerPrincName	*NULL*
dwAuthnLevel	*RPC_C_AUTHN_LEVEL_CONNECT*
dwImpersonationLevel	*RPC_C_IMP_LEVEL_IMPERSONATE*
pAuthIdentityData	*NULL*
dwCapabilities	*RPC_C_QOS_CAPABILITIES_DEFAULT*

The following code fragment shows how a client process can use the CO-AUTHINFO and COAUTHIDENTITY structures to specify its activation credentials when using the *CoCreateInstanceEx* function to instantiate an object on a remote machine:

```
COAUTHIDENTITY AuthIdentity;
AuthIdentity.User = L"User";
AuthIdentity.UserLength = wcslen(L"User");
AuthIdentity.Domain = L"Domain";
AuthIdentity.DomainLength = wcslen(L"Domain");
AuthIdentity.Password = L"Password";
```

```
AuthIdentity.PasswordLength = wcslen(L"Password");
AuthIdentity.Flags = SEC_WINNT_AUTH_IDENTITY_UNICODE;

COAUTHINFO AuthInfo;
AuthInfo.dwAuthnSvc = RPC_C_AUTHN_WINNT;
AuthInfo.dwAuthzSvc = RPC_C_AUTHZ_NONE;
AuthInfo.pwszServerPrincName = NULL;
AuthInfo.dwAuthnLevel = RPC_C_AUTHN_LEVEL_CONNECT;
AuthInfo.dwImpersonationLevel = RPC_C_IMP_LEVEL_IMPERSONATE;
AuthInfo.pAuthIdentityData = &AuthIdentity;
AuthInfo.dwCapabilities = RPC_C_QOS_CAPABILITIES_DEFAULT;

COSERVERINFO ServerInfo;
ServerInfo.dwReserved1 = 0;
ServerInfo.pwszName = L"RemoteServerName";
ServerInfo.pAuthInfo = &AuthInfo;
ServerInfo.dwReserved2 = 0;

MULTI_QI qi;
qi.pIID = &IID_IUnknown;
qi.pItf = NULL;
qi.hr = 0;

HRESULT hr = CoCreateInstanceEx(CLSID_InsideDCOM, NULL,
    CLSCTX_REMOTE_SERVER, &ServerInfo, 1, &qi);
```

The *IServerSecurity* Interface

A server can enforce higher levels of security on a per-method basis using the *IServerSecurity* interface. The *IServerSecurity* interface is used by a component to identify the client and impersonate the client's security credentials. The stub implements the *IServerSecurity* interface, so there is typically no reason to implement this interface unless you are using custom marshaling. The IDL definition of the *IServerSecurity* interface is shown in the code on the following page. Note that implementations of the *IUnknown::QueryInterface* method must never perform access control checking. COM requires an object that supports a particular interface identifier (IID) to always return success when queried for that IID. Besides, checking access permissions in *QueryInterface* does not provide any real security. If client A has a legal *ISum* interface pointer to a component, it can hand that interface pointer to client B without any calls back to the component. Additionally, COM caches interface pointers and does not necessarily call the component's *QueryInterface* method for each client call.

```
interface IServerSecurity : IUnknown
```

```
{
    // Called by the server to find out about the client that
    // has invoked one of its methods
    HRESULT QueryBlanket(
        [out] DWORD    *pAuthnSvc,
        [out] DWORD    *pAuthzSvc,
        [out] OLECHAR **pServerPrincName,
        [out] DWORD    *pAuthnLevel,
        [out] DWORD    *pImpLevel,
        [out] void    **pPrivs,
        [out] DWORD    *pCapabilities);

    // Allows a server to impersonate a client for the duration
    // of a call
    HRESULT ImpersonateClient();

    // Restores the authentication information on a thread to
    // the process's identity
    HRESULT RevertToSelf();

    // Indicates whether the server is currently impersonating
    // the client
    BOOL IsImpersonating();
}
```

To obtain a pointer to the stub's implementation of the *IServerSecurity* interface, the server process calls the function *CoGetCallContext,* as shown in the following code. Note that *CoGetCallContext* can be called only from within a method invoked by a client.

```
HRESULT MyObject::MyMethod()
{
    IServerSecurity* pServerSecurity;
    HRESULT hr = CoGetCallContext(IID_IServerSecurity,
        (void**)&pServerSecurity);

    // Use IServerSecurity interface pointer.

    pServerSecurity->Release();
    return S_OK;
}
```

The *IServerSecurity::QueryBlanket* method is used by the server to find out about the client that has invoked the current method. This technique can be useful for determining the security credentials of the client and then taking special action that depends on the user identity of the client process. The following code fragment uses the *QueryBlanket* method to obtain and display information about the client's security blanket:

```
HRESULT CInsideDCOM::Sum(int x, int y, int* retval)
{
    IServerSecurity* pServerSecurity;
    HRESULT hr = CoGetCallContext(IID_IServerSecurity,
        (void**)&pServerSecurity);

    DWORD AuthnSvc;
    DWORD AuthzSvc;
    OLECHAR* ServerPrincNam;
    DWORD AuthnLevel;
    RPC_AUTHZ_HANDLE Privs;
    DWORD Capabilities;

    hr = pServerSecurity->QueryBlanket(&AuthnSvc, &AuthzSvc,
        &ServerPrincNam, &AuthnLevel, NULL, &Privs, &Capabilities);

    pServerSecurity->Release();

    // Code omitted here that displays the authentication and
    // authorization packages...

    // Display the current principal name.
    wprintf(L"ServerPrincNam %s\n", ServerPrincNam);


    // Code omitted here that displays the
    // authentication level...


    // Display the domain\user information.
    wprintf(L"Privs %s\n", Privs);

    // Free the memory allocated by QueryBlanket.
    CoTaskMemFree(ServerPrincNam);

    *retval = x + y;
    return S_OK;
}
```

Impersonating the Client

Using the *IServerSecurity* interface pointer, the server can call the *IServerSecurity-::ImpersonateClient* method to temporarily assume the security credentials of the client. While impersonating the client's security credentials, the server is limited by the impersonation level granted by the client. For example, if the client has

435

limited the impersonation level to *RPC_C_IMP_LEVEL_IDENTIFY*, the server can impersonate the client only for the purpose of checking permissions using a Win32 API function such as *AccessCheck*. If the client has granted the server *RPC_C_IMP_LEVEL_IMPERSONATE* rights, the server can access system objects such as local files using the credentials of the client. In Windows NT 5.0, which supports the impersonation level *RPC_C_IMP_LEVEL_DELEGATE*, a server with this right could impersonate the client's security credentials when making cross-machine calls.

When the server has finished impersonating the client, it should call the *IServerSecurity::RevertToSelf* method to restore its own security credentials. Regardless of the impersonation level permitted by the client, the impersonation information will last only until the end of the method. If, after impersonating the client, the server has neglected to call the *RevertToSelf* method prior to the completion of the method, COM will restore the server's security credentials automatically.

Using the *IServerSecurity* interface pointer, the server can call any of the four methods of the interface. To make this easier, COM provides several helper functions that call *CoGetCallContext* to obtain the *IServerSecurity* interface pointer, call one of its methods, and then release the interface pointer. The helper functions are listed in the following table, along with their interface method counterparts.

IServerSecurity Method	Equivalent API Function
QueryBlanket	*CoQueryClientBlanket*
ImpersonateClient	*CoImpersonateClient*
RevertToSelf	*CoRevertToSelf*
IsImpersonating	(none)

The *IClientSecurity* Interface

IClientSecurity, the twin of *IServerSecurity*, is an interface used by client processes to adjust security settings on the proxy of a remote object. As with the *IServerSecurity* interface, there is typically no need to implement the *IClientSecurity* interface, since all proxies generated by the MIDL compiler automatically support it, as does the Automation marshaler employed by components using type library marshaling. The *IClientSecurity* interface is shown here in IDL notation:

```
interface IClientSecurity : IUnknown
{
```

```
// Retrieves the current authentication information
HRESULT QueryBlanket(
    [in]  IUnknown *pProxy,
    [out] DWORD    *pAuthnSvc,
    [out] DWORD    *pAuthzSvc,
    [out] OLECHAR  **pServerPrincName,
    [out] DWORD    *pAuthnLevel,
    [out] DWORD    *pImpLevel,
    [out] void     **pAuthInfo,
    [out] DWORD    *pCapabilites);

// Sets the authentication information that will be used
// to make calls on the specified proxy
HRESULT SetBlanket(
    [in] IUnknown *pProxy,
    [in] DWORD    AuthnSvc,
    [in] DWORD    AuthzSvc,
    [in] OLECHAR  *pServerPrincName,
    [in] DWORD    AuthnLevel,
    [in] DWORD    ImpLevel,
    [in] void     *pAuthInfo,
    [in] DWORD    Capabilities);

// Makes a copy of the specified proxy
HRESULT CopyProxy(
    [in]  IUnknown *pProxy,
    [out] IUnknown **ppCopy);
}
```

The methods of the *IClientSecurity* interface can be used to examine (*IClientSecurity::QueryBlanket*) or modify (*IClientSecurity::SetBlanket*) the current security settings for a particular connection to an out-of-process object. One typical use of the *IClientSecurity* interface is for the client process to escalate the authentication level used by a particular interface. Most interfaces of an object are rather pedestrian, but one interface could require the client to submit sensitive data such as the user's credit card information. In this case, it might make sense to establish a default authentication level of *RPC_C_AUTHN_LEVEL_CONNECT* but use the *IClientSecurity::SetBlanket* method to raise that setting to *RPC_C-_AUTHN_LEVEL_PKT_PRIVACY* on the interface dealing with the credit card information. Note that the *IClientSecurity::SetBlanket* method can never set the authentication level lower than was specified by the component in its call to *CoInitializeSecurity*.

The *IClientSecurity::CopyProxy* method is used to make a private copy of the proxy. If you call *IClientSecurity::SetBlanket* on an interface pointer, the security settings will affect all other code in the client process using that interface pointer as well. To limit the scope of the security settings, the client can make a copy of the proxy before adjusting the security blanket. In this way, the client receives a pointer to another proxy through which the object can be invoked. Adjusting the security settings for this proxy does not affect any other code running in the client process.

Obtaining a pointer to the proxy-supplied implementation of the *IClientSecurity* interface is as simple as calling the *IUnknown::QueryInterface* method, as shown in the following code. This interface will always be available for out-of-process objects that employ standard or type library marshaling. If the *IUnknown::QueryInterface* call for *IClientSecurity* fails, the object is either in-process or custom marshaled. Custom marshalers can implement the *IClientSecurity* interface for consistency if necessary.

```
IClientSecurity* pClientSecurity;
HRESULT hr = pUnknown->QueryInterface(IID_IClientSecurity,
    (void**)&pClientSecurity);
if(FAILED(hr))
    cout << "QueryInterface for IClientSecurity failed." << endl;

// Use the IClientSecurity interface pointer.

pClientSecurity->Release();
```

Note that the *IClientSecurity::SetBlanket* method returns an error if you set the *EOAC_SECURE_REFS, EOAC_ACCESS_CONTROL,* or *EOAC_APPID* flags in the *Capabilities* parameter. These settings are valid for use only when you are calling *CoInitializeSecurity*. As with the *IServerSecurity* interface, COM provides several helper functions that assist in calling the methods of the *IClientSecurity* interface. These functions are shown in the following table, along with their equivalent methods.

IClientSecurity Method	Equivalent API Function
QueryBlanket	*CoQueryProxyBlanket*
SetBlanket	*CoSetProxyBlanket*
CopyProxy	*CoCopyProxy*

CHAPTER TWELVE

The Network Protocol

Whereas COM is a specification for building interoperable components, Distributed COM is simply a high-level network protocol designed to enable COM-based components to interoperate across a network. We call DCOM a high-level network protocol because it is built on top of several layers of existing protocols. For example, assume that a computer has an Ethernet network interface card and is using the User Datagram Protocol (UDP). The layering of protocols ranges from the Ethernet frame at the lowest level to DCOM at the highest. Sandwiched in the middle are the Internet Protocol (IP), UDP, and Remote Procedure Calls (RPCs), as shown in Figure 12-1. This is just one of many possible configurations—any available protocols could be substituted below the RPC layer. DCOM automatically chooses the best underlying network protocol based on the protocols available on the client and server machines.

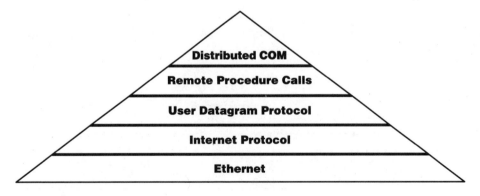

Figure 12-1.
An example of the layering of protocols from the Ethernet frame to DCOM.

It might also be useful to think of a DCOM protocol stack in terms of the Open Systems Interconnection (OSI) seven-layer model. Figure 12-2 shows the OSI seven-layer model juxtaposed with our sample protocol stack. Note that this figure shows how the DCOM protocol stack fits into the OSI seven-layer model on a Microsoft Windows platform. Different operating systems might implement the protocols at different layers.

Application	DCOM/RPC
Presentation	
Session	Winsock driver
Transport	UDP
Network	IP
Data link	Ethernet driver
Physical	Ethernet card

Figure 12-2.
The OSI seven-layer model and the corresponding sample DCOM protocol stack.

The packet sent across the network for each protocol in the protocol stack consists of a header followed by the actual data. Each protocol considers the protocol directly above it in the protocol stack to be part of its data. For example, the IP consists of a header followed by data; this IP data actually consists of the header for UDP followed by UDP's data. Thus, a packet that is transmitted across the network contains the header and data sections of each protocol in the protocol stack. This transmission packet is depicted in Figure 12-3.

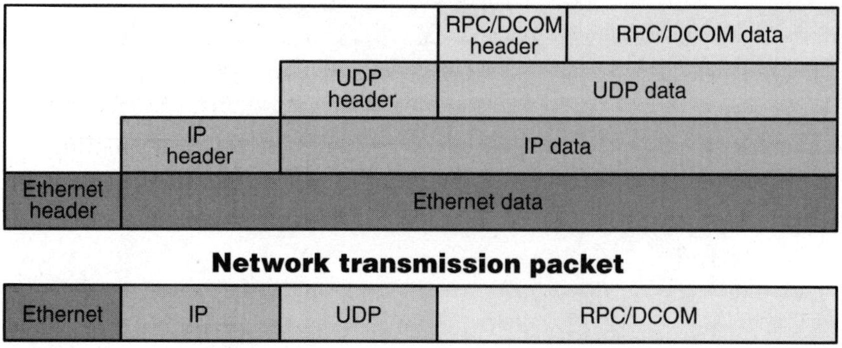

Network transmission packet

Ethernet	IP	UDP	RPC/DCOM

Figure 12-3.
A network transmission packet.

Although it is convenient to think of DCOM as an independent network protocol layered on top of the RPC protocol, that's not really the case. Instead, DCOM is akin to a parasite that piggybacks on its RPC host. DCOM infects the RPC header and data, using the fields of the RPC structures for its own devices. Thus, to better indicate the close relationship between the RPC and the DCOM protocol at the network level, the DCOM network protocol is often called *Object RPC,* or *ORPC.*

Object RPC leverages the functionality of the Open Software Foundation (OSF) Distributed Computing Environment (DCE) RPC network protocol. For example, the authentication, authorization, and message integrity features of the RPC protocol are present in Object RPC. In fact, the major hurdle in porting DCOM to another platform lies in porting the OSF DCE RPC services to that platform. Software AG Americas is working in conjunction with the Microsoft Windows NT development team to port DCOM to multiple platforms. Named EntireX DCOM, this technology is currently available in either release or beta form for the Sun Solaris 2.5 (Sparc), Digital UNIX 4.0 (Alpha), Linux 2.0 (Intel), and IBM OS/390 platforms. Porting is also under way for the release of DCOM on the Hewlett-Packard HP/UX, IBM AIX, SCO UnixWare, IBM OS/400, Digital Open VMS, and Siemens Nixdorf SINIX platforms. For the latest information and release schedules, check Software AG's Web site at http://www.sagus.com.

The Object RPC protocol extends the standard RPC protocol in two specific areas:

- How calls are made on remote objects
- How object references are represented, transmitted, and maintained

Most discourse on COM focuses on the fundamental programming architecture. In other words, you are told what COM function to call in order to perform a specific task. This chapter examines COM from the bottom up. By analyzing the data packets transmitted across a network during the execution of COM-enabled applications, you can learn how COM's remoting architecture works. This knowledge will increase your overall understanding of the COM programming model and can help you design and develop better components.

Spying on the Network Protocol

Because nearly every aspect of the network protocol is hidden from the path of the COM programmer, the most interesting and concrete way to examine the network protocol is to spy on the transmissions between computers during the execution of a DCOM client and component. To do this, a special type of software (and/or hardware) popularly known as a lanalyzer is needed. A variety of third-party tools are available, for every need and budget, that enable the capture and viewing of network traffic. Network Monitor, a Microsoft utility included with Windows NT Server and Microsoft Systems Management Server, represents perhaps the simplest (and cheapest) way to capture meaningful network traffic. Figure 12-4 shows a screen shot of Network Monitor in action.

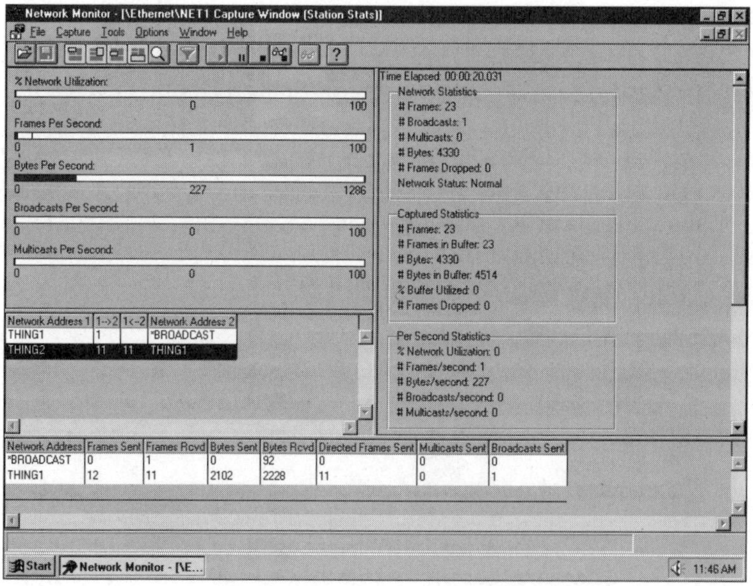

Figure 12-4.
Using Network Monitor to capture network traffic.

Unfortunately, Network Monitor does not currently support the DCOM protocol itself, and thus we are forced to look at DCOM through the eyes of RPC. This affliction does not have to be a permanent one: Network Monitor does have a publicly documented interface for building parser dynamic-link libraries (DLLs) that understand a specific network protocol and interpret the captured data in an intelligent manner. Developing a Network Monitor parser DLL that understands the DCOM network protocol is left as an exercise for the reader.

Running Network Monitor

To turn on Network Monitor's capture facility, simply choose Start from the Capture menu. Then run a DCOM test program to generate the desired network traffic. After the program has completed execution, return to Network Monitor and choose Stop And View from the Capture menu. The network capture facility will be disabled, and the captured packets will be displayed. Network Monitor is quite a clever program in that rather than simply displaying the raw captured packets, it actually understands many standard network protocols and thus presents the captured data in an intelligent and descriptive format. As far as DCOM-related protocols are concerned, Network Monitor can recognize and comprehend Ethernet, IP, UDP, and RPC. To view only the packets captured for certain network protocols, choose Filter from the Display menu.

To analyze the DCOM network protocol, we ran Network Monitor to capture packets as the EXE version of the *InsideDCOM* object executed. The executable we used was the custom marshaling component built in Chapter 9, "Standard and Custom Marshaling." The client ran on one computer, named *Thing1*, and was configured to activate the *InsideDCOM* object on a server named *Thing2*. After calling *CoInitialize*, the client calls *CoCreateInstanceEx* to instantiate the remote object, as shown here:

```
CoInitialize(NULL);

COSERVERINFO ServerInfo = { 0, L"Thing2", 0, 0 };
MULTI_QI qi = { &IID_IUnknown, NULL, 0 };
CoCreateInstanceEx(CLSID_InsideDCOM, NULL, CLSCTX_REMOTE_SERVER,
    &ServerInfo, 1, &qi);
```

The call to *CoCreateInstanceEx* shown in the preceding code results in the Service Control Manager (SCM) on *Thing1* (client) calling the *IRemoteActivation::RemoteActivation* method on the SCM on *Thing2* (server) to activate the *CLSID_InsideDCOM* object and return the interface pointer identifier (IPID) for *IID_IUnknown*. *Thing1* was configured with an IP address of *199.34.58.3*, and *Thing2* was configured with an IP address of *199.34.58.4*. Figure 12-5 on the following page shows how this remote activation translates to the transmission of a network packet as viewed using Network Monitor.

Ethernet
1 Destination address
2 Source address
3 Type (IP)

IP
4 Protocol (UDP)
5 Source address
(*199.34.58.3*)
6 Destination address
(*199.34.58.4*)

UDP
7 Destination port
(*135*; SCM)

RPC header
8 Request PDU
9 Object identifier
A IID_IRemoteActivation
B Interface version (*0.0*)

ORPCTHIS
C Client DCOM version
(*5.1*)
D Causality identifier

Other parameters
E CLSID_InsideDCOM
F RPC_C_IMP_LEVEL-
_IDENTIFY
G IID_IUnknown

```
Ethernet     00000:  00 60 97 8E EB 19 00 60 97 92 D2 6C 08 00 45 00
IP           00010:  00 E8 A6 01 00 00 80 11 91 B7 C7 22 3A 03 C7 22
             00020:  3A 04 04 04 00 87 00 D4 74 D7 04 00 08 00 10 00
UDP          00030:  00 00 00 00 00 00 00 00 00 00 00 00 00 00 00 00
             00040:  00 00 B8 4A 9F 4D 1C 7D CF 11 86 1E 00 20 AF 6E
RPC header   00050:  7C 57 86 C2 37 67 F7 1E D1 11 BC D9 00 60 97 92
             00060:  D2 6C 79 BE 01 34 00 00 00 00 00 00 00 00 00 00
             00070:  FF FF FF FF 68 00 00 00 0A 00 05 00 01 00 00 00
ORPCTHIS     00080:  00 00 00 00 00 00 F1 59 EB 61 FB 1E D1 11 BC D9
             00090:  00 60 97 92 D2 6C 00 00 00 00 02 00 00 10 00 00
Other        000A0:  00 00 00 00 00 00 00 00 00 00 01 00 00 00 00 00
parameters   000B0:  00 00 02 00 00 00 00 00 00 00 01 00 00 00 80 3F
             000C0:  15 00 01 00 00 00 00 00 00 00 00 00 00 00 C0 00
             000D0:  00 00 00 00 00 46 01 00 00 00 01 00 00 00 08 00
             000E0:  64 00 04 00 69 00 01 00 00 00 87 03 B2 D6 99 EE
             000F0:  AC 65 C7 53 81 A4
```

Figure 12-5.
The network packet resulting from an activation request, IRemote-
Activation::RemoteActivation, *as captured by Network Monitor.*

Interpreting Marshaled GUIDs

Globally unique identifiers (GUIDs) that are transmitted over the network must be interpreted in accordance with the IDL definition of a
GUID, shown here:

```
typedef struct _GUID
{
    DWORD Data1;
    WORD  Data2;
    WORD  Data3;
    BYTE  Data4[8];
} GUID;
```

Because the GUIDs are marshaled in little endian format, the original GUID can be reconstructed via a two-step process. First the GUID
found in a captured network packet needs to be formatted to look like
a standard GUID. For example, imagine that you located the GUID *78
56 34 12 34 12 34 12 12 34 12 34 56 78 9A BC* in a network packet. The

The layering of protocols can easily be seen in the network packet depicted in this figure. In the RPC header, we can see that the interface identifier (IID; labeled *A*) is *B8 4A 9F 4D 1C 7D CF 11 86 1E 00 20 AF 6E 7C 57*. In accordance with the rules described in the sidebar below the actual IID is *4D9F4AB8-7D1C-11CF-861E-0020AF6E7C57*, the *IRemoteActivation* interface.

Remote Activation

IRemoteActivation is an RPC interface (not a COM interface) exposed by the SCM on each machine. The SCM process that exists on all Windows machines is named rpcss.exe. The *IRemoteActivation* interface has only one method, *RemoteActivation*, which is designed to activate a COM object on a remote machine. This powerful feature is missing in pure RPC, in which the server must always be running before the client can connect. (Note that due to the lack of security infrastructure on the Microsoft Windows 95 and Microsoft Windows 98 platforms, remote activation will work only on Windows NT.) The IDL definition of the *IRemoteActivation* interface is shown here:

```
[ // No object keyword here. Not a COM interface!
    uuid(4d9f4ab8-7d1c-11cf-861e-0020af6e7c57),
    pointer_default(unique)
]
```

(continued)

following graphic shows this GUID grouped into standard formation:

```
        Data1      Data2 Data3       Data4
    ┌────────┐    ┌───┐┌───┐  ┌────────────────┐
    78563412 - 3412 - 3412 - 1234 - 123456789ABC
```

Better already, isn't it? Now the little endian format needs to be taken into account in order to obtain the actual GUID. The first three elements of the GUID structure (labeled *Data1*, *Data2*, and *Data3* in the structure shown above) need to be reversed on a byte-by-byte basis. The last element of the GUID structure (*Data4*) does not need to be modified because it is already stored as a simple byte array. Thus, after reversing the first three elements of the GUID structure, the completed second step of the process provides the true GUID:

```
12345678-1234-1234-1234-123456789ABC
```

445

```
interface IRemoteActivation
{
    const unsigned long MODE_GET_CLASS_OBJECT = 0xffffffff;

    HRESULT RemoteActivation(
        [in] handle_t                              hRpc,
        [in] ORPCTHIS                              *ORPCthis,
        [out] ORPCTHAT                             *ORPCthat,
        [in] GUID                                  *Clsid,
        [in, string, unique] WCHAR                 *pwszObjectName,
        [in, unique] MInterfacePointer             *pObjectStorage,
        [in] DWORD                                 ClientImpLevel,
        [in] DWORD                                 Mode,
        [in] DWORD                                 Interfaces,
        [in, unique, size_is(Interfaces)] IID      *pIIDs,
        [in] unsigned short                        cRequestedProtseqs,
        [in, size_is(cRequestedProtseqs)]
            unsigned short                         RequestedProtseqs[],
        [out] OXID                                 *pOxid,
        [out] DUALSTRINGARRAY                      **ppdsaOxidBindings,
        [out] IPID                                 *pipidRemUnknown,
        [out] DWORD                                *pAuthnHint,
        [out] COMVERSION                           *pServerVersion,
        [out] HRESULT                              *phr,
        [out, size_is(Interfaces)]
            MInterfacePointer                      **ppInterfaceData,
        [out, size_is(Interfaces)] HRESULT         *pResults
    );
}
```

Through the *IRemoteActivation* interface, the SCM on one machine contacts the SCM on another machine to request that it activate an object. When launching an object on a remote machine, the client machine's SCM calls the *IRemoteActivation::RemoteActivation* method of the server's SCM to request activation of the class object identified by the class identifier (CLSID) in the fourth parameter. The *RemoteActivation* method returns a marshaled interface pointer for the requested object and two special values: the *interface pointer identifier* (*IPID*) and the *object exporter identifier* (*OXID*). The IPID identifies an interface of an object running in a component. The OXID identifies the RPC string binding information needed to connect to the interface specified by an IPID. RPC string bindings are discussed in greater detail in the Appendix.

The SCM resides at well-known *endpoints,* one for each supported network protocol. An endpoint identifies the virtual channel through which you are communicating; it is based on the network protocol in use. For example, when you are using the Transmission Control Protocol (TCP) or UDP, the endpoint will be a port number such as *1066*; if you use named pipes, the endpoint is a pipe name such as *\\pipe\mypipe*. The following table shows the endpoints for the SCM when some of the more popular protocols are used.

Protocol String	Description	Endpoint
ncadg_ip_udp, ip	Connectionless over UDP/IP	*135*
ncacn_ip_tcp	Connection-oriented over TCP/IP	*135*
ncadg_ipx	Connectionless over Interwork Packet Exchange (IPX)	TBD
ncacn_spx	Connection-oriented over Sequenced Packet Exchange (SPX)	TBD
ncacn_nb_nb	Connection-oriented using NetBIOS over NetBEUI	TBD
ncacn_ipx	Connection-oriented over IPX	TBD
ncacn_http	Connection-oriented over Hypertext Transfer Protocol (HTTP)	*593*

Calling All Remote Objects

Method calls made on remote COM objects are considered true DCE RPC invocations in that a standard request *Protocol Data Unit* (*PDU*) is transmitted across the network requesting that a specific method be executed. A PDU is the basic unit of communication between two machines. The request PDU contains all of the *in* parameters that the method expects to receive. When method execution is complete, a response PDU containing the method's *out* parameters is transmitted back to the client. This process sounds rather obvious, but it is quite amazing when you consider how it actually works. A remote COM method call requires two packets to be transmitted across the network: one from the client to the server containing the *in* parameters and the other from the server to the client for the *out* parameters. The 19 defined PDU types and their values are listed in the table on the following page. This table also indicates whether a particular PDU type is specific to a connection-oriented (abbreviated CO here) protocol, a connectionless (CL) protocol, or both.

PDU Type	Protocol(s)	Type Value
request	CO/CL	*0*
ping	CL	*1*
response	CO/CL	*2*
fault	CO/CL	*3*
working	CL	*4*
nocall	CL	*5*
reject	CL	*6*
ack	CL	*7*
cl_cancel	CL	*8*
fack	CL	*9*
cancel_ack	CL	*10*
bind	CO	*11*
bind_ack	CO	*12*
bind_nak	CO	*13*
alter_context	CO	*14*
alter_context_resp	CO	*15*
shutdown	CO	*17*
co_cancel	CO	*18*
orphaned	CO	*19*

A connection-oriented protocol, such as TCP, maintains a virtual connection for the client and server between transmissions and guarantees that messages are delivered in the order in which they were sent. A connectionless protocol, such as UDP, does not maintain a connection between the client and server and does not guarantee that a message from the client will actually be delivered to the server. Furthermore, even if the messages are delivered, they might arrive in a different order from that in which they were sent. By default, DCOM uses the connectionless UDP. A connectionless protocol does not make DCOM unreliable, however, because RPC ensures robustness by using a customized mechanism for message ordering and acknowledgment.

An RPC PDU contains up to three parts, listed here, only the first of which is required:

- A PDU header containing protocol control information.

- A PDU body containing data. For example, the body of a request or response PDU contains data representing the input or output parameters for an operation. This information is stored in Network Data Representation (NDR) format.

- An authentication verifier containing data specific to an authentication protocol. For example, an authentication protocol can ensure the integrity of a packet by including an encrypted checksum in the authentication verifier.

The PDU header used for CL protocols is shown here in IDL notation:

```
typedef struct
{
    unsigned small rpc_vers = 4;  // RPC protocol major version
    unsigned small ptype;         // Packet type
    unsigned small flags1;        // Packet flags
    unsigned small flags2;        // Packet flags
    byte drep[3];                 // Data representation format label
    unsigned small serial_hi;     // High byte of serial number
    GUID object;                  // Object identifier (contains IPID)
    GUID if_id;                   // IID
    GUID act_id;                  // Activity identifier
    unsigned long server_boot;    // Server boot time
    unsigned long if_vers;        // Interface version
    unsigned long seqnum;         // Sequence number
    unsigned short opnum;         // Operation number
    unsigned short ihint;         // Interface hint
    unsigned short ahint;         // Activity hint
    unsigned short len;           // Length of packet body
    unsigned short fragnum;       // Fragment number
    unsigned small auth_proto;    // Authentication protocol ID
    unsigned small serial_lo;     // Low byte of serial number
} dc_rpc_cl_pkt_hdr_t;
```

The packet type field (named *ptype* in this structure) of a PDU identifies the PDU type. (This value will be one of the 19 PDU types defined in the table on page 448.) Object RPC uses the object identifier (OID) field (*object*) of a PDU to store an IPID. An IPID is a GUID that represents an interface of an object hosted by a component. The IID field (*if_id*) must contain the IID of the COM interface. This field is somewhat redundant given that the OID field contains the IPID, which already identifies the interface. However, placing the IID in the *if_id* field allows DCOM to work correctly when it is run on a standard implementation of OSF DCE RPC. On systems such as Windows, the RPC implementation has been optimized to enable method calls to be dispatched solely based on the information contained in the IPID, ignoring the IID. Last the interface version number (*if_vers*) must always be *0.0* because a COM interface can never be modified after it is published. COM interfaces are not versioned; a new interface is defined instead. All of these fields can be found in the RPC header section of the captured network packet, shown in Figure 12-5.

The ORPCTHIS and ORPCTHAT Structures

All COM method invocations are transmitted across the network in a request PDU containing a special first parameter of type ORPCTHIS, which is inserted before all the other inbound parameters of the method. Thus, a COM method defined as *HRESULT Sum(int x, int y, [out, retval] int* result)* is transmitted in a request PDU as *Sum(ORPCTHIS orpcthis, int x, int y)*. The definition of the ORPCTHIS structure is shown here:

```
// Implicit "this" pointer is the first [in] parameter in
// every ORPC call.
typedef struct tagORPCTHIS
{
    COMVERSION      version;      // COM version number (5.2)
    unsigned long   flags;        // ORPCF flags for presence of
                                  // other data
    unsigned long   reserved1;    // Set to 0
    CID             cid;          // Causality ID of caller
    [unique] ORPC_EXTENT_ARRAY *extensions; // Extensions
} ORPCTHIS;
```

The first field of the ORPCTHIS structure specifies the version of the DCOM protocol used to make the method call; currently, this value is set to *5.2*. In Windows 95 and releases of Windows NT 4.0 prior to Service Pack 3, the version is set to *5.1*. In Windows NT 4.0 Service Pack 4, the COM version number is set to *5.3*. Because each remote method call contains an ORPCTHIS structure, the version of DCOM on the client machine is always transmitted to the server. At the server, the client's version of DCOM is compared with the server's, and if the major version numbers don't match, the *RPC_E_VERSION-_MISMATCH* error is returned to the client. It is permissible for the server to have a higher minor version number than the client, however. In such cases, the server must limit its use of the DCOM protocol to match those features available in the client's version.

A *causality identifier* (*CID*) is a GUID used to link together what might be a long chain of method calls. For example, if client A calls component B, and component B, before ever returning to client A, proceeds to call component C, these calls are said to be causally related. Every time a new method call is made (but not during the processing of an existing method), a new CID is generated by the DCOM protocol. The same CID will be propagated in any subsequent calls made by component B on behalf of client A. This is true even if component B uses connection points or some other mechanism to call back into client A. The *extensions* field of the ORPCTHIS structure is designed to enable extra data to be sent with a COM method call. Currently, only two extensions are defined: one for extended error information and the other for debugging control. Custom extensions to the ORPCTHIS structure can also be defined using channel hooks. (See the section "Channel Hooks," later in this chapter.)

In every response PDU for a COM method call, a special outbound parameter of type ORPCTHAT is inserted prior to all other *out* parameters of the method. Thus, a COM method defined as *HRESULT Sum(int x, int y, [out, retval] int* result)* is transmitted in a response PDU as *HRESULT Sum(ORPCTHAT orpcthat, int result)*. The definition of the ORPCTHAT structure is shown here:

```
// Implicit "that" pointer is the first [out] parameter
// on every ORPC call.
typedef struct tagORPCTHAT
{
    unsigned long    flags;         // ORPCF flags for presence
                                    // of other data
    [unique] ORPC_EXTENT_ARRAY *extensions; // Extensions
} ORPCTHAT;
```

Marshaled Interface Pointers

The DCOM network protocol transmits method parameters in the NDR format specified by OSF DCE RPC. NDR specifies exactly how all the primitive data types understood by the Interface Definition Language (IDL) should be marshaled into data packets for network transmission. The only extension made to the NDR standard by DCOM is support for marshaled interface pointers. Use of the *iid_is* IDL keyword (covered in Chapter 10, "The Interface Definition Language") in an interface definition constitutes what can be thought of as a new primitive data type that can be marshaled: an interface pointer. The term *interface pointer* is problematic because it conjures a mental picture of a pointer to a pointer to a v-table structure that contains pointers to functions. But once it is marshaled into a data packet, an interface pointer does not look like that at all. Instead, a marshaled interface pointer is a symbolic representation of access to an object and is therefore called an object reference. The format of a marshaled interface pointer is governed by the MInterfacePointer structure defined on the following page.

```
// Wire representation of a marshaled interface pointer.

typedef struct tagMInterfacePointer
{
    ULONG ulCntData;                        // Size of data
    [size_is(ulCntData)] BYTE abData[]; // Data (OBJREF)
} MInterfacePointer;
```

After the size of the structure is defined by the *ulCntData* field, the *abData* byte array that follows contains the actual object reference in a structure called an OBJREF. An OBJREF is the data type used to represent a reference to an object. The definition of the OBJREF structure is shown in the following code. Notice that OBJREF assumes one of three forms, depending on the type of marshaling being employed: standard, handler, or custom. Chapter 9, "Standard and Custom Marshaling," covers these three types of marshaling in detail.

```
// OBJREF is the format of a marshaled interface pointer.
typedef struct tagOBJREF
{
    unsigned long   signature;          // Must be OBJREF_SIGNATURE
    unsigned long   flags;              // OBJREF flags
    GUID            iid;                // IID

    [switch_is(flags), switch_type(unsigned long)] union {
        [case(OBJREF_STANDARD)] struct {
            STDOBJREF       std;        // Standard OBJREF
            DUALSTRINGARRAY saResAddr;  // Resolver address
        } u_standard;

        [case(OBJREF_HANDLER)] struct {
            STDOBJREF       std;        // Standard objref
            CLSID           clsid;      // CLSID of handler code
            DUALSTRINGARRAY saResAddr;  // Resolver address
        } u_handler;

        [case(OBJREF_CUSTOM)] struct {
            CLSID           clsid;      // CLSID of unmarshaling code
            unsigned long   cbExtension; // Size of extension data
            unsigned long   size;       // Size of data that follows
            [size_is(size), ref] byte *pData; // Extension plus class-
                                              // specific data
        } u_custom;
    } u_objref;
} OBJREF;
```

The OBJREF structure begins with a *signature* field that is defined as the unsigned long hexadecimal value *0x574F454D*. Interestingly, if you arrange this value in little endian format (*4D 45 4F 57*) and then convert each byte to its ASCII equivalent, the resulting characters spell *MEOW*. The great thing about the MEOW structure (a popular nickname for the OBJREF structure) is that when you are scanning through the mountains of packets captured by the Network Monitor utility, it is very easy to tell when you have hit upon an object reference: just say MEOW. Note that regardless of the format of the remainder of the NDR data, the wire representation of a marshaled interface pointer is always stored in little endian form.

A Brief Digression

The MEOW acronym reminds us of a little story. A local business looking for office help put a sign in the window, which read as follows: "HELP WANTED. Must be able to type, must be good with a computer, and must be bilingual. We are an Equal Opportunity Employer." A short time later, a dog trotted up to the window, saw the sign, and went inside. He looked at the receptionist and wagged his tail, and then he walked over to the sign, looked at it, and whined. Getting the idea, the receptionist summoned the office manager. The office manager saw the dog and was surprised, to say the least. But the dog looked determined, so she led him into the office. Inside, the dog jumped up on the chair and stared at the manager. The manager said, "I can't hire you. The sign says you have to be able to type." The dog jumped down, went to the typewriter, and proceeded to type a perfect letter. He pulled out the sheet of paper, trotted over to the manager and gave it to her, and then jumped back on the chair.

The manager was stunned, but then she recovered and said, "The sign says you have to be good with a computer." The dog jogged over to the computer and in no time at all entered and executed a perfect program that worked flawlessly the first time. The manager looked at the dog sadly and said, "You are a very intelligent dog, but I still can't hire you." The dog ran over to a copy of the sign and pointed with his paw to the line that read "Equal Opportunity Employer." The manager brightened visibly: "Yes, but the sign also says that you have to be bilingual." To which the dog replied: "Meow."

Following the MEOW *signature* field is the *flags* field of the OBJREF structure, which identifies the type of object reference. The *flags* field can be set to *OBJREF_STANDARD* (*1*), *OBJREF_HANDLER* (*2*), or *OBJREF_CUSTOM* (*4*) to indicate the type of interface marshaling. The *iid* field is the last omnipresent field of the OBJREF structure; it specifies the IID of the interface being marshaled. Figure 12-6 shows a network packet that was captured as a result of the request PDU shown earlier in this chapter, in the section "The ORPCTHIS and ORPCTHAT Structures." There the *CoCreateInstance* function had been called to request the object's *IUnknown* interface pointer. In this figure, you can see that the response PDU has returned to the client. It contains the marshaled interface pointer (decorated by MEOW and labeled 5) of the object's *IUnknown* interface.

1	Response PDU	6	*flags (OBJREF_STANDARD)*
2	*IID_IRemoteActivation*	7	*iid (IID_IUnknown)*
3	Server DCOM version (*5.2*)	8	*cPublicRefs (5)*
4	*ulCntData (130)*	9	*oxid*
5	MEOW	A	*oid*

B	*ipid*
C	*NumEntries*
D	*SecurityOffset*
E	*TowerId (NCADG_IP_UDP)*
F	*TowerId (NCACN_IP_TCP)*

```
Headers            00000:  00 60 97 92 D2 6C 00 60 97 8E EB 19 08 00 45 00   .`...l.`......E.
                   00010:  02 30 10 01 00 00 80 11 26 70 C7 22 3A 04 C7 22   .0......&p.":.."
                   00020:  3A 03 00 87 04 04 02 1C B8 28 04 02 08 00 10 00   :........(......
                   00030:  00 00 00 00 00 00 00 00 00 00 00 00 00 00 00 00   ................
                   00040:  00 00 38 4A 9F 4D 1C 7D CF 11 86 1E 00 20 AF 6E   ..8J.M.}..... .n
                   00050:  7C 57 86 C2 37 67 F7 1E D1 11 BC D9 00 60 97 92   |W..7g.......`..
                   00060:  D2 6C 79 BE 01 34 00 00 00 00 00 00 00 00 00 00   .ly..4..........
                   00070:  FF FF 6E 00 B0 01 00 00 0A 00 01 00 00 00 00 00   ..n.............
ORPCTHAT           00080:  00 00 3B 01 00 00 38 C2 35 21 28 A0 15 00 69 00   ..;...8.5!(...i.
                   00090:  00 00 69 00 14 00 08 00 31 00 39 00 39 00 2E 00   ..i.....1.9.9...
DUALSTRINGARRAY    000A0:  33 00 34 00 2E 00 35 00 38 00 2E 00 34 00 5B 00   3.4...5.8...4.[.
STRINGBINDING      000B0:  31 00 30 00 36 00 31 00 5D 00 00 00 00 00 0A 00   1.0.6.1.].......
SECURITYBINDING    000C0:  FF FF 41 00 64 00 6D 00 69 00 6E 00 54 00 68 00   ..A.d.m.i.n.T.h.
                   000D0:  69 00 6E 00 67 00 32 00 00 00 0C 00 FF FF 41 00   i.n.g.2.......A.
                   000E0:  64 00 6D 00 69 00 6E 00 54 00 68 00 69 00 6E 00   d.m.i.n.T.h.i.n.
                   000F0:  67 00 32 00 00 00 0C 00 FF FF 41 00 64 00 6D 00   g.2.......A.d.m.
                   00100:  69 00 6E 00 54 00 68 00 69 00 6E 00 67 00 32 00   i.n.T.h.i.n.g.2.
                   00110:  00 00 0C 00 FF FF 41 00 64 00 6D 00 69 00 6E 00   ......A.d.m.i.n.
                   00120:  54 00 68 00 69 00 6E 00 67 00 32 00 00 00 0C 00   T.h.i.n.g.2.....
                   00130:  FF FF 41 00 64 00 6D 00 69 00 6E 00 54 00 68 00   ..A.d.m.i.n.T.h.
                   00140:  69 00 6E 00 67 00 32 00 00 00 0B 00 FF FF 41 00   i.n.g.2......A.
                   00150:  64 00 6D 00 69 00 6E 00 54 00 68 00 69 00 6E 00   d.m.i.n.T.h.i.n.
                   00160:  67 00 32 00 00 00 00 00 54 00 00 00 00 00 2F 00   g.2.....T...../.
                   00170:  00 00 C9 00 00 00 00 00 00 00 02 00 00 00 05 00   ................
                   00180:  02 00 00 00 00 00 01 00 00 00 50 98 15 00 82 00   ..........P.....
MInterfacePointer  00190:  00 00 82 00 00 00 4D 45 4F 57 01 00 00 00 00 00   ......MEOW......
OBJREF             001A0:  00 00 00 00 00 00 C0 00 00 00 00 00 00 46 00 00   .............F..
STDOBJREF          001B0:  00 00 05 00 00 00 3B 01 00 00 38 C2 35 21 44 01   ..;...8.5!D.
                   001C0:  00 00 38 C2 35 21 02 00 00 00 2F 00 00 00 CB 00   ..8.5!..../.....
                   001D0:  00 00 02 00 00 00 1F 00 1B 00 08 00 31 00 39 00   ............1.9.
DUALSTRINGARRAY    001E0:  39 00 2E 00 33 00 34 00 2E 00 35 00 38 00 2E 00   9...3.4...5.8...
STRINGBINDING      001F0:  34 00 00 00 17 00 31 00 39 00 39 00 2E 00 33 00   4.....1.9.9...3.
                   00200:  34 00 2E 00 35 00 38 00 2E 00 34 00 00 00 00 00   4...5.8...4.....
SECURITYBINDING    00210:  0A 00 FF FF 00 00 00 00 00 00 01 00 00 00 00 00   ................
                   00220:  00 00 00 00 00 00 00 00 00 00 04 00 00 00 01 00   ................
                   00230:  00 00 D8 45 F3 82 C9 F0 70 5E C7 53 81 A4         ...E...p^.S..
```

Figure 12-6.

The response PDU captured when IRemoteActivation::RemoteActivation *returns an OBJREF.*

The Standard Object Reference

As you can see in Figure 12-6, the *flags* field of the OBJREF structure indicates that standard marshaling (*OBJREF_STANDARD*) is being used. Based on this field, the remainder of the structure contains a structure of the type STDOBJREF followed by a DUALSTRINGARRAY structure. Here is the definition of the STDOBJREF structure:

```
typedef struct tagSTDOBJREF
{
    unsigned long  flags;        // SORF_ flags
    unsigned long  cPublicRefs;  // Count of references passed
    OXID           oxid;         // OXID of server with this OID
    OID            oid;          // OID of object with this IPID
    IPID           ipid;         // IPID of interface
} STDOBJREF;
```

The first field of the STDOBJREF structure specifies flags relating to the object reference. Although most of the possible settings for the *flags* parameter are reserved for use by the system, the *SORF_NOPING* flag (*0x1000*) can be used to indicate that the object does not need to be pinged. The DCOM network protocol uses pinging to implement a sophisticated garbage collection mechanism that is covered later in this chapter, in the section "DCOM Garbage Collection." The second field of the STDOBJREF structure, *cPublicRefs*, specifies the number of reference counts on the IPID that are being transferred in this object reference. Allocating multiple reference counts on an interface is an optimization used to avoid making remote method calls every time the client calls *IUnknown::AddRef*. This optimization technique is covered later in this chapter, in the section "The *IRemUnknown* Interface."

The third field of the STDOBJREF structure specifies the OXID of the server that owns the object. Although an IPID is used to identify an interface of an object hosted by a component, an IPID alone does not contain enough information to actually carry out a method invocation because the RPC infrastructure uses strings to specify the binding information necessary to carry out a remote call. These strings, called *RPC string bindings* (covered in the Appendix), contain information such as the underlying network protocol and security subsystem that should be used to carry out the call, as well as the network address of the server machine on which the component is running. An *unsigned hyper* (64-bit integer), also called an OXID, is used to represent this connection information. Before making a call, the client translates an OXID into a set of string bindings that the RPC system understands. The details of this translation are covered later in this chapter, in the section "The OXID Resolver."

The fourth field of the STDOBJREF structure specifies the OID of the object that implements the interface being marshaled. OIDs are 64-bit values used as part of the pinging mechanism described later in this chapter, in the section "DCOM Garbage Collection." The final parameter of the STDOBJREF structure is the actual IPID of the interface being marshaled.

The DUALSTRINGARRAY Structure

As part of an object reference, the STDOBJREF structure is followed by the DUALSTRINGARRAY structure. The DUALSTRINGARRAY structure is a container for a large array that contains two parts: STRINGBINDING structures and SECURITYBINDING structures. The definition of the DUALSTRING-ARRAY structure is shown here:

```
// DUALSTRINGARRAYs are the return type for arrays of network
// addresses, arrays of endpoints, and arrays of both used in
// many ORPC interfaces.
typedef struct tagDUALSTRINGARRAY
{
    unsigned short    wNumEntries;     // Number of entries in array
    unsigned short    wSecurityOffset; // Offset of security info

    // The array contains two parts, a set of STRINGBINDINGs
    // and a set of SECURITYBINDINGs. Each set is terminated by
    // an extra 0. The shortest array contains four 0s.

    [size_is(wNumEntries)] unsigned short aStringArray[];
} DUALSTRINGARRAY;
```

The first two fields of the DUALSTRINGARRAY structure simply specify the total number of entries in the array (*wNumEntries*) and the offset at which the STRINGBINDING structures end and the SECURITYBINDING structures begin (*wSecurityOffset*). The array itself is pointed to by the *aStringArray* field.

A STRINGBINDING structure represents the connection information needed to bind to an object. The layout of the STRINGBINDING structure is shown here:

```
// This is the return type for arrays of string bindings or
// protocol sequences (protseqs) used by many ORPC interfaces.

typedef struct tagSTRINGBINDING
{
    unsigned short    wTowerId;      // Cannot be 0
    unsigned short    aNetworkAddr;  // Zero-terminated
} STRINGBINDING;
```

The first field of the STRINGBINDING structure, *wTowerId,* specifies the network protocol that can be used to reach the server via the second parameter, *aNetworkAddr.* The *aNetworkAddr* parameter is a Unicode string specifying the network address of the server. For example, if the *wTowerId* value was set to the tower identifier *NCADG_IP_UDP,* a valid network address for *aNetworkAddr* would be *199.34.58.4.* The following table lists the valid tower identifiers for common protocols that can be used with the *wTowerId* parameter.

Tower Identifier	Value	Description
NCADG_IP_UDP	*0x08*	Connectionless UDP
NCACN_IP_TCP	*0x07*	Connection-oriented TCP
NCADG_IPX	*0x0E*	Connectionless Internetwork Packet Exchange (IPX) Protocol
NCACN_SPX	*0x0C*	Connection-oriented Sequenced Packet Exchange (SPX) Protocol
NCACN_NB_NB	*0x12*	Connection-oriented NetBEUI over NetBIOS
NCACN_NB_IPX	*0x0D*	Connection-oriented NetBIOS over IPX
NCACN_HTTP	*0x1F*	Connection-oriented HTTP

NOTE: The *NCA* prefix for each tower identifier is short for Network Computing Architecture. *CN* stands for a connection-oriented protocol, and *DG* stands for a connectionless, datagram-based protocol.

Each STRINGBINDING structure ends with a null character to indicate the end of the *aNetworkAddr* string. The last STRINGBINDING in a DUAL-STRINGARRAY is indicated by the presence of two extra 0 bytes. After that come the SECURITYBINDING structures. The definition of the SECURITY-BINDING structure is shown here:

```
// This value indicates that the default authorization should be used.
const unsigned short COM_C_AUTHZ_NONE = 0xffff;

typedef struct tagSECURITYBINDING
{
    unsigned short    wAuthnSvc;      // Must not be 0
    unsigned short    wAuthzSvc;      // Must not be 0
    unsigned short    aPrincName;     // NULL terminated
} SECURITYBINDING;
```

The SECURITYBINDING structure contains fields indicating the authentication service, *wAuthnSvc*, and the authorization service, *wAuthzSvc*, to be used. The *wAuthzSvc* field is typically set to *0xFFFF*, which indicates that default authorization should be used.

The *IRemUnknown* Interface

IRemUnknown is a COM interface designed to handle reference counting and interface querying for remote objects. As its name suggests, *IRemUnknown* is the remote version of the holy *IUnknown* interface. Clients use the *IRemUnknown* interface to manipulate reference counts and request new interfaces based on IPIDs held by the client. Following standard reference counting rules in COM, references are kept per interface rather than per object. The definition of the *IRemUnknown* interface is shown in the following IDL notation:

```
// The remote version of IUnknown is used by clients to
// query for new interfaces, get additional references (for
// marshaling), and release outstanding references.
[
    object,
    uuid(00000131-0000-0000-C000-000000000046)
]
interface IRemUnknown : IUnknown
{
    HRESULT RemQueryInterface
    (
        [in] REFIPID        ripid, // Interface to QueryInterface on
        [in] unsigned long  cRefs, // Count of AddRefs requested
        [in] unsigned short cIids, // Count of IIDs that follow
        [in, size_is(cIids)] IID* iids, // IIDs to QueryInterface for
        [out, size_is(,cIids)]
        REMQIRESULT**       ppQIResults // Results returned
    );

    HRESULT RemAddRef
    (
        [in] unsigned short     cInterfaceRefs,
        [in, size_is(cInterfaceRefs)]
        REMINTERFACEREF         InterfaceRefs[],
        [out, size_is(cInterfaceRefs)]
        HRESULT*                pResults
    );

    HRESULT RemRelease
    (
```

```
        [in] unsigned short      cInterfaceRefs,
        [in, size_is(cInterfaceRefs)]
        REMINTERFACEREF          InterfaceRefs[]
    );
}
```

A component developer will never implement the *IRemUnknown* interface, because the OXID object associated with each COM apartment already provides an implementation of this interface. The standard *IUnknown* interface is never remoted in COM. The *IRemUnknown* interface is remoted in its place and results in local calls to *QueryInterface, AddRef,* and *Release* on the server. Client applications can call the *IUnknown::AddRef* method as often as they want. COM will remote calls to *IUnknown::AddRef* only when the first *AddRef* call is made; *IUnknown::Release* is called only for the final *Release.*

The *IRemUnknown::RemQueryInterface* method differs from the *IUnknown-::QueryInterface* method in that it can request several interface pointers in one call. The standard *IUnknown::QueryInterface* method is actually used to carry out this request on the server side. This optimization is designed to reduce the number of round-trips executed. The array of REMQIRESULT structures returned by *RemQueryInterface* contains the *HRESULT* from the *QueryInterface* call executed for each requested interface, as well as the STDOBJREF structure containing the marshaled interface pointer itself. The definition of the REMQIRESULT structure is shown here:

```
typedef struct tagREMQIRESULT
{
    HRESULT      hResult;      // Result of call
    STDOBJREF    std;          // Data for returned interface
} REMQIRESULT;
```

The *IRemUnknown::RemAddRef* and *IRemUnknown::RemRelease* methods are used to increase and decrease the reference count of the object referred to by an IPID. Like *RemQueryInterface, RemAddRef* and *RemRelease* differ from their local counterparts; they can increase and decrease the reference count of multiple interfaces by an arbitrary amount in a single remote call. Imagine a scenario in which an object that received a marshaled interface pointer wants to pass that pointer on to some other object. According to the COM reference counting rules, *AddRef* must be called before this interface pointer can be passed to another object, resulting in two round-trips, one to get the interface pointer and another to increment the reference counter. The caller can optimize this process by requesting multiple references in one call. Thereafter, the interface pointer can be given out multiple times without additional remote calls to increment the reference counter.

The Windows implementation of DCOM typically requests five references when marshaling an interface pointer, which means that the client process receiving the interface pointer can now marshal it to four different apartments in the current process or in other processes. Only when the client attempts to marshal the interface pointer for the fifth time will DCOM make a remote call to the object to request an additional reference. Also, in the interest of performance on the client side, DCOM typically does not immediately translate each call to *IUnknown::AddRef* or *IUnknown::Release* into a remote call to *IRemUnknown::RemAddRef* or *IRemUnknown::RemRelease*. Instead, DCOM defers a remote call to the *RemRelease* method until all interfaces on an object have been released locally. Only then is a single *RemRelease* call made, with instructions to decrement the reference counter for all interfaces by the necessary amount.

It is important to note that in this example scenario, when one component returns the interface pointer of another component to a client process, COM never allows one proxy to communicate with another proxy. For example, if client process A calls object B, which then returns an interface pointer for object C, any subsequent calls made by client A to object C are direct. This happens because the marshaled interface pointer contains information about how to reach the machine on which the actual object instance exists. In order for object B to call object C, object B must keep track of object C's OXID, IP address, IPID, and so on. When object B hands client A a pointer to object C, object B scribbles all that information into a new object reference (OBJREF) for client A. Object B is no longer part of the relationship, thus saving network bandwidth and improving the overall performance.

After calling the *CoCreateInstanceEx* function to instantiate the remote component, our client process possesses an initial *IUnknown* interface pointer. Typically, this call is followed by a call to the *IUnknown::QueryInterface* method to request another interface, as shown in the following code fragment:

```
hr = pUnknown->QueryInterface(IID_ISum, (void**)&pSum);
```

When the client process calls the *IUnknown::QueryInterface* method to request an interface pointer for *ISum*, the proxy manager in the client's address space calls the *IRemUnknown::RemQueryInterface* method on the server. Figure 12-7 shows the network packet transmitted for the *RemQueryInterface* method call. In this packet, we can clearly see that DCOM is requesting a count of five references for the *ISum* interface pointer.

```
Headers    00000:  00 60 97 8E EB 19 00 60 97 92 D2 6C 08 00 45 00
           00010:  00 E8 A8 01 00 00 80 11 8F B7 C7 22 3A 03 C7 22
           00020:  3A 04 04 12 04 25 00 D4 02 48 04 00 08 00 10 00    1  Request PDU
           00030:  00 00 00 00 00 00 2F 00 00 00 C9 00 00 00 00 00
           00040:  00 00 31 01 00 00 00 00 00 00 C0 00 00 00 00 00    2  IID_IRemUnknown
           00050:  00 46 F2 59 EB 61 FB 1E D1 11 BC D9 00 60 97 92
           00060:  D2 6C 00 00 00 00 00 00 00 00 00 00 00 00 03 00
           00070:  FF FF FF FF 68 00 00 00 0A 00 05 00 02 00 00 00
ORPCTHIS   00080:  00 00 00 00 00 00 F1 59 EB 61 FB 1E D1 11 BC D9
           00090:  00 60 97 92 D2 6C 00 00 00 00 02 00 00 00 2F 00    3  IPID
Parameters 000A0:  00 00 CB 00 00 00 02 00 00 00 05 00 00 00 01 00    4  cRefs (5)
           000B0:  00 00 01 00 00 00 01 00 00 10 00 00 00 00 00 00    5  clids (1)
           000C0:  00 00 00 00 00 01 00 00 00 00 00 00 00 00 00 00    6  IID_ISum
           000D0:  00 00 00 00 00 00 00 00 00 00 00 00 00 00 00 00
           000E0:  00 00 04 00 00 00 01 00 00 00 B1 55 95 9C 0C 86
           000F0:  D6 4A 6E 9F 2B 71
```

Figure 12-7.
The request PDU transmitted for the IRemUnknown::Rem-
QueryInterface(IPID, 5, 1, IID_ISum) *call.*

On the server side, the actual *IUnknown::QueryInterface* call is executed in order to request an *ISum* interface pointer from the component. This interface pointer is then returned to the client in the marshaled form of a standard object reference (STDOBJREF). Figure 12-8 shows the response PDU returned to the client.

```
Headers    00000:  00 60 97 92 D2 6C 00 60 97 8E EB 19 08 00 45 00
           00010:  00 C8 12 01 00 00 80 11 25 D8 C7 22 3A 04 C7 22
           00020:  3A 03 04 25 04 12 00 B4 00 0C 04 02 08 00 10 00    1  Response PDU
           00030:  00 00 00 00 00 00 2F 00 00 00 C9 00 00 00 00 00
           00040:  00 00 31 01 00 00 00 00 00 00 C0 00 00 00 00 00    2  IID_IRemUnknown
           00050:  00 46 F2 59 EB 61 FB 1E D1 11 BC D9 00 60 97 92
           00060:  D2 6C 38 C5 01 34 00 00 00 00 00 00 00 00 03 00
           00070:  FF FF 4A 00 48 00 00 00 0A 00 00 00 00 00 00 00
ORPCTHAT   00080:  00 00 10 4B 15 00 01 00 00 00 00 00 00 00 20 02
           00090:  14 00 00 00 00 00 05 00 00 00 2B 01 00 00 38 C2    3  HRESULT
Parameters 000A0:  35 21 44 01 00 00 38 C2 35 21 03 00 00 00 2F 00    4  cPublicRefs (5)
           000B0:  00 00 94 00 00 00 03 00 00 00 00 00 00 00 00 00    5  oxid
           000C0:  00 00 04 00 00 00 01 00 00 00 45 21 81 9C 02 EF    6  oid
           000D0:  58 B7 6E 9F 2B 71                                  7  ipid
```

Figure 12-8.
The response PDU transmitted for the IRemUnknown::RemQueryInterface *call.*

To prevent a malicious application from calling *IRemUnknown::RemRelease* and purposefully trying to force an object to unload while other clients might still be using it, a client can request *private references*. Private references are

461

stored with the client's identity so that one client cannot release the private references of another. However, when you are passing an interface pointer, private references cannot be provided from one object to another. Each client must request and release its own private references by explicitly calling *RemAddRef* and *RemRelease*. The *RemAddRef* and *RemRelease* methods both accept an argument that is an array of REMINTERFACEREF structures. The REMINTERFACE-REF structure is used to specify an IPID and the number of public and private references that are being requested or released by the client. The definition of the REMINTERFACEREF structure is shown here:

```
typedef struct tagREMINTERFACEREF
{
    IPID            ipid;        // IPID to AddRef/Release
    unsigned long   cPublicRefs;
    unsigned long   cPrivateRefs;
} REMINTERFACEREF;
```

The *IRemUnknown2* Interface

The *IRemUnknown2* interface was introduced in version 5.2 of the DCOM protocol. Derived from the *IRemUnknown* interface, *IRemUnknown2* adds the *RemoteQueryInterface2* method, enabling clients to retrieve interface pointers to objects supplying additional data beyond the STDOBJREF in their marshaled interface packets. Like *RemQueryInterface*, this method queries for zero or more interfaces using the interface behind the IPID. Instead of returning the STDOBJREF marshaled interface packet, this method can return any marshaled data packet in the form of a byte array (including a traditional STDOBJREF). The IDL definition of the *IRemUnknown2* interface is shown in the following code:

```
interface IRemUnknown2 : IRemUnknown
{
    HRESULT RemQueryInterface2
    (
        [in] REFIPID                            ripid,
        [in] unsigned short                     cIids,
        [in, size_is(cIids)] IID                *iids,
        [out, size_is(cIids)] HRESULT           *phr,
        [out, size_is(cIids)] MInterfacePointer **ppMIF
    );
}
```

The OXID Resolver

The OXID Resolver is a service that runs on every machine that supports DCOM. The OXID Resolver performs two important duties:

- Stores the RPC string bindings necessary to connect with remote objects and provides them to local clients.

- Sends ping messages to remote objects for which the local machine has clients and receives ping messages for objects running on the local machine. This aspect of the OXID Resolver supports the DCOM garbage collection mechanism.

Similar to the way *CoCreateInstanceEx* incorporates the functionality of *CoGetClassObject* and *IClassFactory::CreateInstance*, the *IRemoteActivation* interface incorporates the functionality of the *IRemUnknown* and the *IOXIDResolver* interfaces so that only one round-trip is needed to activate an object. The OXID Resolver service resides at the same endpoints as the SCM, as described earlier in this chapter, in the section "Remote Activation." Like the *IRemoteActivation* interface, the OXID Resolver service implements an RPC interface (not a COM interface) named *IOXIDResolver*, shown in IDL notation in the following code. Notice that the *object* keyword is conspicuously absent from the interface header, indicating that this is not a COM interface.

```
[ // No object keyword here. Not a COM interface!
    uuid(99fcfec4-5260-101b-bbcb-00aa0021347a),
    pointer_default(unique)
]
interface IOXIDResolver
{
    // Method to get the protocol sequences, string bindings,
    // and machine ID for an object server given its OXID.
    [idempotent] error_status_t ResolveOxid
    (
    [in]        handle_t        hRpc,
    [in]        OXID            *pOxid,
    [in]        unsigned short  cRequestedProtseqs,
    [in,  ref,  size_is(cRequestedProtseqs)]
                unsigned short  arRequestedProtseqs[],
    [out, ref]  DUALSTRINGARRAY **ppdsaOxidBindings,
    [out, ref]  IPID            *pipidRemUnknown,
    [out, ref]  DWORD           *pAuthnHint
    );
```

(continued)

```
// Simple ping is used to ping a set. Client machines use
// this technique to inform the object exporter that it is still
// using the members of the set. Returns S_TRUE if the
// SetId is known by the object exporter, S_FALSE if not.
[idempotent] error_status_t SimplePing
(
[in]  handle_t  hRpc,
[in]  SETID   *pSetId  // Must not be 0
);
// Complex ping is used to create sets of OIDs to ping. The
// whole set can subsequently be pinged using SimplePing,
// thus reducing network traffic.
[idempotent] error_status_t ComplexPing
(
[in]      handle_t      hRpc,
[in, out]  SETID        *pSetId,  // An in value of 0 on first
                                  // call for new set
[in]      unsigned short  SequenceNum,
[in]      unsigned short  cAddToSet,
[in]      unsigned short  cDelFromSet,
[in, unique, size_is(cAddToSet)]  OID AddToSet[],
          // Add these OIDs to the set.
[in, unique, size_is(cDelFromSet)] OID DelFromSet[],
          // Remove these OIDs from the set.
[out]     unsigned short *pPingBackoffFactor
          // 2^factor = multiplier
);
// In some cases, the client might be unsure that a particular
// binding will reach the server--for example, when the
// OXID bindings have more then one TCP/IP binding. This
// call can be used to validate the binding from the client.
   [idempotent] error_status_t ServerAlive
(
[in]      handle_t      hRpc
);
}
```

NOTE: The *idempotent* flag specifies that a method does not modify the state of an object and returns the same results each time it is called. The RPC run-time library can invoke *idempotent* methods multiple times without adverse effects.

When presented with an OXID, it is the job of the OXID Resolver to obtain the associated RPC string binding necessary to connect to the object. This is done on each machine by maintaining a cache of mappings of OXIDs and their associated RPC string bindings. The OXID Resolver maintains each of these cached local tables. When asked by a client to resolve an OXID into the associated string binding, the OXID Resolver first checks its cached local table for the OXID. If the OXID is found, the string binding can be returned immediately. Otherwise, the OXID Resolver contacts the OXID Resolver of the server to request resolution of the OXID into a string binding.

The client machine's OXID Resolver then caches the string binding information provided by the server. This optimization enables the OXID Resolver to quickly resolve that OXID for other clients on the same machine that might want to connect in the future. If the client were to pass the object reference to a process running on a third machine, that computer's OXID Resolver service would not have a cached copy of the OXID's string bindings and thus would be obliged to make a remote call to the server in order to resolve the OXID for itself.

The purpose of the first method, *IOXIDResolver::ResolveOxid*, shown in the preceding code, is to resolve an OXID into the string bindings that are necessary to access an OXID object. The OXID being resolved is passed as the first parameter, *pOxid*, to the *ResolveOxid* method. When calling the *ResolveOxid* method, the client specifies what protocol sequences it is prepared to use when accessing the object, starting with the most preferred. The client passes this information in the *arRequestedProtSeqs* array argument. The OXID Resolver service on the server attempts to resolve the OXID and then returns an array of DUALSTRINGARRAY structures, *ppdsaOxidBindings*, which contains the string binding information—again in decreasing order of preference—that can be used to connect to the specified OXID. The OXID resolution process is described in the following steps:

1. A server process calls *CoRegisterClassObject* to register itself with COM.

2. The OXID Resolver on the server machine caches a reference to the object.

3. A client process calls *CoCreateInstanceEx* and receives an object reference for the object running on the server.

4. The client asks the OXID Resolver (on the client machine) to resolve the OXID for the server object.

5. The client's OXID Resolver calls *IOXIDResolver::ResolveOxid* to request that the server's OXID Resolver return the string bindings for the OXID.

6. The OXID Resolver on the server performs a lookup in its local table and returns the desired string bindings on the client's OXID Resolver.

7. The client's OXID Resolver caches the best string binding in its local table for future use and then returns the string binding for the OXID to the client process.

8. The client binds to the object using the given string binding.

9. The client can now invoke methods on the object.

Because machines can have many network protocols installed, allocating endpoints for each available protocol sequence can be a time-consuming and resource-intensive operation. However, in the standard case, the server registers all available protocol sequences at initialization time. As an optimization, the OXID Resolver can decide to defer protocol registration. To implement lazy protocol registration, the server waits until a client machine calls its *IOXID-Resolver::ResolveOxid* method. Rather than registering all available protocols at initialization time, the implementation of the *ResolveOxid* method registers only those protocols requested by the client at the time of OXID resolution. The network protocols available to DCOM can be found in the HKEY_LOCAL-_MACHINE\SOFTWARE\Microsoft\Rpc registry key under the DCOM Protocols named-value. There you will find the supported protocols listed in order of preference.

In version 5.2 of the DCOM network protocol, the *ResolveOxid2* method was added to the *IOXIDResolver* interface. This method enables a client to determine the version of the DCOM network protocol used by the server, when the server requests OXID resolution. Notice the addition of the last parameter in the IDL definition of the *IOXIDResolver::ResolveOxid2* method, shown here in boldface:

```
[idempotent] error_status_t ResolveOxid2
 (
    [in]        handle_t             hRpc,
    [in]        OXID                 *pOxid,
    [in]        unsigned short       cRequestedProtseqs,
    [in,  ref,  size_is(cRequestedProtseqs)]
                unsigned short       arRequestedProtseqs[],
    [out, ref]  DUALSTRINGARRAY      **ppdsaOxidBindings,
    [out, ref]  IPID                 *pipidRemUnknown,
    [out, ref]  DWORD                *pAuthnHint,
    [out, ref]  COMVERSION           *pComVersion
 );
```

DCOM Garbage Collection

Although a distributed system might offer excellent availability and protection against catastrophic failure, the probability of a failure somewhere in the system is greatly increased due to the higher complexity. From a client's perspective, a failure of either the network or the server will be identified by the failure of a remote method call. In such cases, an *HRESULT* value such as *RPC_S-_SERVER_UNAVAILABLE* or *RPC_S_CALL_FAILED* will be returned.

A more complex situation exists on the server side if a client fails. Depending on the type of server in question, the failure of a client might or might not wreak havoc on the server. For example, a stateless object that always remains running and simply gives out the current time to any client that asks will not be affected by the loss of a client process. However, any object that does maintain state for its clients will obviously be very interested in the death of those clients. Such objects typically have a method, such as *ByeByeNow*, that clients call before exiting. However, if the client process or a portion of the network fails, the client might never have the opportunity to notify the object of its intentions. This failure will leave the server in an unstable state because it is maintaining information for clients that might no longer exist.

RPC deals with this situation by using a logical connection called a *context handle* between the client and the server processes. If the connection between the two processes is broken for any reason, a special function called a *rundown routine* can be invoked on the server side to notify the server that a client connection has been broken. For performance reasons, DCOM does not leverage the functionality of RPC context handles. Instead, the Object RPC protocol defines a pinging mechanism that is used to determine whether a client is still alive. RPC context handles are implemented using a pinging mechanism as well, but due to the special needs of DCOM, they are not suitable. Fundamentally speaking, a pinging mechanism is simple. Every so often, the client sends a ping message to an object saying, "I'm alive, I'm alive!" If the server does not receive a ping message within a specified period of time, the client is assumed to have died and all its references are freed.

This simplistic type of pinging algorithm is not sufficient for DCOM because it leads to too much unnecessary network traffic. In a distributed environment where there might be hundreds, thousands, or hundreds of thousands of clients and components in use, you can easily imagine a scenario in which network capacity is overwhelmed simply by the number of ping messages being transmitted. To reduce the network traffic devoted to ping messages, DCOM relies on the OXID Resolver service running on each machine to detect whether its local clients are alive and then send single ping messages on a per-machine instead of a per-object basis, which means that the client's OXID Resolver sends only one ping message to each computer that is serving its clients.

Even with only one message being sent to each computer, ping messages might still grow quite hefty—the ping data for each OID is 16 bytes. For example, if a client computer held 5000 object references to an object running on another machine, each ping message would be approximately 78 KB! To further reduce the amount of network traffic, DCOM introduces a special mechanism called *delta pinging*. The idea behind delta pinging is that often a server has a relatively stable set of objects that are used by clients. Instead of including data for each individual OID in the ping message, delta pinging stipulates that a set of OIDs can be pinged by a single identifier called a *ping set* that refers to all the OIDs in that set. When delta pinging is employed, the ping message for five OIDs is the same size as a message for one million OIDs.

To establish a ping set, the client calls the *IOXIDResolver::ComplexPing* method. The *AddToSet* parameter of the *ComplexPing* method accepts an array of OIDs that should define the ping set. Once defined, all the OIDs in the set can be pinged simply by calling *IOXIDResolver::SimplePing* and passing it the ping set identifier (SETID) value returned from the *ComplexPing* method. Should it become necessary, the *ComplexPing* method can be called again at any time to add or remove OIDs from the ping set.

In order to clean up after connections that are broken between a client and a server, the pinging mechanism uses a reclaiming process called *garbage collection*. The pinging mechanism activates the garbage collection based on two values—the time that should elapse between each ping message and the number of ping messages that must be missed before the server can consider the client missing in action. The product of these two values determines the maximum amount of time that can elapse without a ping message being received before the server assumes the client is dead. By default, the ping period is set to 120 seconds; three ping messages must be missed before the client can be presumed dead. Currently, these default values are not user-configurable. Thus, 6 minutes (3×120 seconds) must elapse before a client's references are implicitly reclaimed. Whether the server immediately reclaims the object references held by a client once the timeout has occurred is considered an implementation-dependent detail of the DCOM specification. In fact, if the server does not reclaim those references and at a later time begins receiving ping messages from the heretofore-assumed-dead client, it can infer that whatever problem prevented the ping messages from being received has been fixed.

Some stateless objects, such as the time server example discussed at the beginning of this section, have no need for the DCOM garbage collection mechanism. These objects usually run forever and don't really care about a client after a method call has finished executing. For such objects, the pinging mechanism can be switched off by passing the *MSHLFLAGS_NOPING* flag to the *CoGetStandardMarshal* function. The following code fragment (with the relevant code in boldface) shows how to use the *MSHLFLAGS_NOPING* flag in an implementation of the *IClassFactory::CreateInstance* method:

```
IMarshal* pMarshal = NULL;

HRESULT CFactory::CreateInstance(IUnknown *pUnknownOuter,
    REFIID riid, void** ppv)
{
    if(pUnknownOuter != NULL)
        return CLASS_E_NOAGGREGATION;

    CObject *pObject = new CObject;

    if(pObject == NULL)
        return E_OUTOFMEMORY;

    IUnknown* pUnknown;
    pObject->QueryInterface(IID_IUnknown, (void**)&pUnknown);
    CoGetStandardMarshal(riid, pUnknown, 0, NULL,
        MSHLFLAGS_NOPING|MSHLFLAGS_NORMAL, &pMarshal);
    pUnknown->Release();

    // Call QueryInterface, which typically is for
    // IID_IUnknown.
    HRESULT hr = pObject->QueryInterface(riid, ppv);
    pObject->Release();
    return hr;
}
```

Just before exiting, the object should execute the following code to free the standard marshaler:

```
pMarshal->DisconnectObject(0);
pMarshal->Release();
```

Note that objects for which the *MSHLFLAGS_NOPING* flag has been specified will never receive calls to their *IUnknown::Release* methods. Clients can call *Release*, but such calls will not be remoted to the object itself. Due to the highly efficient delta pinging mechanism used by DCOM, turning off the mechanism for an object will not cause a corresponding reduction in network traffic. As long as other objects on the server require ping messages, DCOM must send a ping message to the server machine by calling the *IOXIDResolver::Simple-Ping* method. The only difference is that the object that has specified the

MSHLFLAGS_NOPING flag will not be added to the SETID that is being pinged.

A Remote Method Call

With an understanding of the Object RPC network protocol under our belts, let's examine the data transmitted across the network during an actual remote method invocation. Figure 12-9 shows the request PDU sent when the client process calls the *ISum::Sum* method. Immediately following the ORPCTHIS structure are the *x* and *y* inbound parameters of the *Sum* method. Here the *Sum* method has been called with the values *4* and *9*.

```
00000:  00 60 97 8E EB 19 00 60 97 92 D2 6C 08 00 45 00
00010:  00 A8 AA 01 00 00 80 11 8D F7 C7 22 3A 03 C7 22
00020:  3A 04 04 12 04 25 00 94 9A DD 04 00 08 00 10 00    1 Request PDU
00030:  00 00 03 00 00 00 2F 00 00 00 94 00 00 00 03 00    2 IPID
00040:  00 00 01 00 00 00 10 00 00 00 00 00 00 00 00 00    3 IID_ISum
00050:  00 01 F2 59 EB 61 FB 1E D1 11 BC D9 00 60 97 92
00060:  D2 6C 38 C5 01 34 00 00 00 00 01 00 00 00 03 00
00070:  FF FF 4A 00 28 00 00 00 0A 00 05 00 02 00 00 00    ORPCTHIS
00080:  00 00 00 00 00 00 F1 59 EB 61 FB 1E D1 11 BC D9
00090:  00 60 97 92 D2 6C 00 00 00 00 04 00 00 00 09 00    4 + 9 = ???
000A0:  00 00 04 00 00 00 01 00 00 00 A6 69 F1 50 E2 6B
000B0:  E9 D6 6F 9F 2B 71
```

Figure 12-9.
The request PDU transmitted when the client calls ISum::Sum *with the parameters* 4 *and* 9.

After the *Sum* method executes on the server, the response PDU is generated and sent back to the client. Clearly visible following the ORPCTHAT structure in the response PDU is the outbound value of *13 (4 + 9)*, as shown in Figure 12-10.

```
00000:  00 60 97 92 D2 6C 00 60 97 8E EB 19 08 00 45 00
00010:  00 90 13 01 00 00 80 11 25 10 C7 22 3A 04 C7 22
00020:  3A 03 04 25 04 12 00 7C 76 5F 04 02 08 00 10 00    1 Response PDU
00030:  00 00 03 00 00 00 2F 00 00 00 94 00 00 00 03 00    2 IPID
00040:  00 00 31 01 00 00 00 00 00 00 C0 00 00 00 00 00    3 IID_IRemUnknown
00050:  00 46 F2 59 EB 61 FB 1E D1 11 BC D9 00 60 97 92
00060:  D2 6C 38 C5 01 34 00 00 00 00 01 00 00 00 03 00
00070:  FF FF 4A 00 10 00 00 00 0A 00 00 00 00 00 00 00    ORPCTHAT
00080:  00 00 0D 00 00 00 00 00 00 00 04 00 00 00 01 00    4 + 9 = 13 (0x000D)
00090:  00 00 45 21 81 9C C6 30 FA A9 6F 9F 2B 71
```

Figure 12-10.
The response PDU transmitted when the component returns the value 13 *after executing the* ISum::Sum *method.*

Channel Hooks

Channel is the term given to the logical connection between a client and a component; all communication between the two parties is said to travel through the channel. *Channel hooks* enable a developer to hook into this communication mechanism. Those experienced with the Microsoft Win32 API can compare this capability to that offered by the *SetWindowLong* function. Using this Win32 API function, you can store custom data inside of a window structure held by the Windows operating system. Later you can retrieve data from the window structure with the *GetWindowLong* function. In a similar way, channel hooks allow you to store custom data in the communication channel and then retrieve that data on the other side.

Recall that the last field in the ORPCTHIS and ORPCTHAT structures is an ORPC_EXTENT_ARRAY structure named *extensions*. The *extensions* field of the ORPCTHIS structure can be used to pass additional data in the channel when a method is invoked; the *extensions* field of the ORPCTHAT structure can be used to return additional data in the channel when a method returns. The ORPC_EXTENT_ARRAY itself does not contain the actual extension data. Instead, it simply records the number of *extents* that follow, each stored in an ORPC_EXTENT structure. The memory layout of the ORPC_EXTENT_ARRAY structure is shown here in IDL notation:

```
// Array of extensions
typedef struct tagORPC_EXTENT_ARRAY
{
    unsigned long size;        // Num extents
    unsigned long reserved;    // Must be 0
    [size_is((size+1)&~1,), unique]
        ORPC_EXTENT **extent; // Extents
} ORPC_EXTENT_ARRAY;
```

The actual extent data passed in the channel is stored in an array of ORPC_EXTENT structures. Each extent is identified by a unique GUID. The first field of the ORPC_EXTENT structure is the GUID of the extent data being transmitted. The second field of the ORPC_EXTENT structure declares the size of that data followed by the extent data itself in the final field. The ORPC_EXTENT structure is shown here in IDL notation:

```
// Extension to implicit parameters
typedef struct tagORPC_EXTENT
{
    GUID           id;         // Extension identifier
    unsigned long size;        // Extension size
    [size_is((size+7)&~7)] byte data[]; // Extension data
} ORPC_EXTENT;
```

To make use of channel hooks from an application, you must create a COM object that implements the *IChannelHook* interface. The *IChannelHook* interface consists of six methods, three of which are called in the client process and three that are called in the server process. Two of the three client-side methods of the *IChannelHook* interface are called automatically before a client method call is made, and the third is called immediately on its return. This technique lets you put extent data in the channel to be sent in the ORPCTHIS structure of the request PDU and then retrieve any extent data from the response PDU. On the server side, one method of the *IChannelHook* interface is called just before a method executes and the other two are called immediately before it returns. This technique enables the server process to obtain extent data stored in the request PDU and then store additional extent data to be transmitted in the ORPCTHAT structure of the response PDU. The IDL definition of the *IChannelHook* interface is shown here:

```
interface IChannelHook : IUnknown
{
// How big is your data?
    void ClientGetSize(
        [in]  REFGUID uExtent,
        [in]  REFIID  riid,
        [out] ULONG   *pDataSize );

// Put the data in the channel.
    void ClientFillBuffer(
        [in]       REFGUID uExtent,
        [in]       REFIID  riid,
        [in, out] ULONG    *pDataSize,
        [in]       void    *pDataBuffer );

// Data has arrived from the server.
    void ClientNotify(
        [in] REFGUID uExtent,
        [in] REFIID  riid,
        [in] ULONG   cbDataSize,
        [in] void    *pDataBuffer,
        [in] DWORD   lDataRep,
        [in] HRESULT hrFault );

// Data has arrived from the client.
    void ServerNotify(
        [in] REFGUID uExtent,
        [in] REFIID  riid,
        [in] ULONG   cbDataSize,
```

```
        [in] void    *pDataBuffer,
        [in] DWORD   lDataRep );

// How big is your data?
    void ServerGetSize(
        [in]   REFGUID uExtent,
        [in]   REFIID  riid,
        [in]   HRESULT hrFault,
        [out]  ULONG   *pDataSize );

// Put the data in the channel.
    void ServerFillBuffer(
        [in]      REFGUID uExtent,
        [in]      REFIID  riid,
        [in, out] ULONG   *pDataSize,
        [in]      void    *pDataBuffer,
        [in]      HRESULT hrFault );
};
```

The *riid* parameter of every *IChannelHook* method is actually a structure of type SChannelHookCallInfo passed by value, and not a reference to an IID as the interface definition would have you believe. The SChannelHookCallInfo structure is designed to provide channel hooks with additional information about a method call. For example, the causality identifier (*uCausality*), the server's process identifier (*dwServerPid*), and a pointer to the object (*pObject*) are fields available in this structure. The declaration of the SChannelHook-CallInfo structure is shown here:

```
typedef struct SChannelHookCallInfo
{
    IID             iid;
    DWORD           cbSize;
    GUID            uCausality;
    DWORD           dwServerPid;
    DWORD           iMethod;
    void            *pObject;
} SChannelHookCallInfo;
```

After creating an object that implements the *IChannelHook* interface, you need to inform COM that you intend to hook into its communication channel. The *CoRegisterChannelHook* function is designed for this purpose. It accepts the GUID of the extent and a pointer to the object that implements the *IChannel-Hook* interface, as shown here:

```
WINOLEAPI CoRegisterChannelHook(REFGUID ExtensionUuid,
    IChannelHook* pChannelHook);
```

A Useful Channel Hook: Obtaining the Client's Name

At this stage, you might be wondering why anyone would want to use a channel hook. After all, any data that you might want to pass from client to server and back can be transmitted as one or more parameters of a particular method. This technique is definitely easier than hooking into the communications channel! The advantage of a channel hook, however, is that data being transmitted is not visible in the interface definition. By hooking into the communications channel, you can send additional data with each method call—data that would not be visible to someone examining the interface definition.

One example of when channel hooks might prove useful is in determining the name of the computer on which a particular client is executing. This information can prove quite valuable for a server-based administration application, since COM provides no built-in way to obtain a client's computer name. The simplest solution to this problem is to add one more parameter to every method of the interface implemented by the server process, enabling the client to voluntarily provide its computer name. However, this solution requires that changes be made to the interface definition, thereby requiring that a new IID be defined. This in turn means that the old interface must still be supported for those clients that have not yet been updated to use the new interface. It also indicates that the interface is more obviously designed for remote use; it doesn't make sense to have a computer name parameter if the client and the component are running on the same machine.

Because the data that we want to pass to the server is not related to the primary purpose of that interface, it is bad design to force the two together. A channel hook can solve these problems because it can pass data in the channel outside of the scope of the interface definition. With this goal in mind, you can build a custom channel hook that sends the client's computer name to the server as part of the ORPCTHIS structure in every method invocation. On the server side, the computer name is read from the channel and made available to the component. This makes for a nifty solution to a thorny problem.

The custom channel hook was built as an in-process component to be loaded into the address space of any client or server process simply by calling *CoCreateInstance*. The *DllMain* function that is called on start-up registers the channel hook by calling *CoRegisterChannelHook* and then obtains the computer's name by calling the Win32 *GetComputerName* function, as shown in boldface in the following code:

```
GUID EXTENTID_MyHook = {0x12345678, 0xABCD, 0xABCD, {0x99, 0x99,
0x99, 0x99, 0x99, 0x99, 0x99, 0x99}};
```

```
BOOL WINAPI DllMain(HINSTANCE h, DWORD dwReason, void* pv)
{
    static CChannelHook ChannelHook;
    if(dwReason == DLL_PROCESS_ATTACH)
    {
        if(FAILED(CoRegisterChannelHook(EXTENTID_MyHook,
            &ChannelHook)))
        {
            cout << "CoRegisterChannelHook failed." << endl;
            return FALSE;
        }
        ULONG length = MAX_COMPUTERNAME_LENGTH + 1;
        GetComputerName(g_mhtClientComputerName.computer_name,
            &length);
    }
    return TRUE;
}
```

A structure named MYHOOK_THIS encapsulates the data transmitted, making this channel hook easily extensible. Currently, the MYHOOK_THIS structure simply contains the string name of the computer on which the client is running. That name is obtained in the *DllMain* function shown in the preceding code and stored in *g_mhtClientComputerName,* as shown here:

```
struct MYHOOK_THIS
{
    char computer_name[MAX_COMPUTERNAME_LENGTH + 1];
} g_MYHOOK_THIS, g_mhtClientComputerName;
```

Although hooking into COM's communication channel sounds complex, the code required to implement the *IChannelHook* interface is relatively simple. When COM is assembling the request PDU for a method invocation, the *IChannelHook::ClientGetSize* method is called to determine the size of the data to be transmitted. In the following code, the *pDataSize* value is being set to the size of the MYHOOK_THIS structure:

```
// How big is your data?
void CChannelHook::ClientGetSize(REFGUID uExtent, REFIID riid,
    ULONG* pDataSize)
{
    if(uExtent == EXTENTID_MyHook)
        *pDataSize = sizeof(MYHOOK_THIS);
}
```

The *ClientGetSize* method is followed by a call to the *IChannelHook::ClientFillBuffer* method to request the actual data that you wish to transmit in the communication channel. In the code on the following page, the data pointer is set to the address of the global *g_mhtClientComputerName* variable containing the client's computer name:

```
// Put the data in the channel.
void CChannelHook::ClientFillBuffer(REFGUID uExtent, REFIID riid,
    ULONG* pDataSize, void* pDataBuffer)
{
    if(uExtent == EXTENTID_MyHook)
    {
        MYHOOK_THIS *data = (MYHOOK_THIS*)pDataBuffer;
        *data = g_mhtClientComputerName;
        *pDataSize = sizeof(MYHOOK_THIS);
    }
}
```

COM now has sufficient information to build and transmit the request PDU to the server. The data transmitted in the channel hook will travel coach in the ORPCTHIS structure of the request PDU. Once the server receives the request PDU, the *IChannelHook::ServerNotify* method will be called in the server process, which means that the channel hook needs to be running both on the client and on the server computers to work properly. The *ServerNotify* method tells us that data has arrived from the client. The following code obtains that data from the *pDataBuffer* pointer and temporarily stores it in the G_MYHOOK-_THIS structure for retrieval by the component:

```
// Data has arrived from the client.
void CChannelHook::ServerNotify(REFGUID uExtent, REFIID riid,
    ULONG cbDataSize, void* pDataBuffer, DWORD lDataRep)
{
    if(uExtent == EXTENTID_MyHook &&
        lDataRep == NDR_LOCAL_DATA_REPRESENTATION)
    {
        MYHOOK_THIS* data = (MYHOOK_THIS*)pDataBuffer;
        strcpy(g_MYHOOK_THIS.computer_name, data->computer_name);
    }
}
```

Our channel hook is designed to transmit data from the client to the server, not vice versa, so the *ClientNotify*, *ServerGetSize*, and *ServerFillBuffer* methods of the *IChannelHook* interface are all NO-OPs. Channel hooks that want to return data in the ORPCTHAT structure of a response PDU will need to implement these three methods as well. In order to make the client's computer name available to a component, our channel hook implements a custom interface called *IClientInfo* that offers only one method: *GetClientComputerName*. This method can be called by a server-side component from within a method invoked by the client. The implementation of the *GetClientComputerName* method, shown in the following code, simply retrieves and returns the client's computer name from the G_MYHOOK_THIS structure, where it was stored in the *IChannelHook::ServerNotify* method:

```
HRESULT CClientInfo::GetClientComputerName(BSTR* bstr)
{
    int length = strlen(g_MYHOOK_THIS.computer_name);
    *bstr = SysAllocStringLen(0, length+1);
    strcpy((char*)*bstr, g_MYHOOK_THIS.computer_name);
    return S_OK;
}
```

Using *ClientChannelHook*

To use *ClientChannelHook*, both the client and server processes must load the channel hook by calling *CoCreateInstance*, as shown here:

```
// Load the channel hook.
void* silly;
CoCreateInstance(CLSID_ClientChannelHook, NULL,
    CLSCTX_INPROC_SERVER, IID_IUnknown, &silly);
```

In the client process, the channel hook is instantiated and every remote method call will be sent with the client's computer name in the ORPCTHIS structure of the request PDU. In the server process, the channel hook will retrieve the client's computer name and make it available to the component via the *IClientInfo::GetClientComputerName* method. For example, a method in the component that wants to obtain the client's computer name would instantiate the *ClientChannelHook*, requesting an *IClientInfo* interface pointer. Then the *GetClientComputerName* method would be called to obtain the name of the client's computer from the channel hook. This process is shown in boldface in the following implementation of the *Sum* method:

```
HRESULT CInsideDCOM::Sum(int x, int y, int* retval)
{
    IClientInfo* pClientInfo;
    CoCreateInstance(CLSID_ClientChannelHook, NULL,
        CLSCTX_INPROC_SERVER, IID_IClientInfo,
        (void**)&pClientInfo);

    BSTR bstr = 0;
    pClientInfo->GetClientComputerName(&bstr);
    MessageBox(NULL, (char*)bstr, "GetClientComputerName", MB_OK);
    SysFreeString(bstr);

    *retval = x + y;
    return S_OK;
}
```

There is little overhead associated with the second call to *CoCreateInstance* in the server process because the *ClientChannelHook* is implemented as a singleton object. As described in Chapter 8, "DLL Surrogates and Executable Components," instead of instantiating a new object at each client request, a COM class designed to operate as a singleton always returns a reference to the same object. An easy way to implement a singleton is to declare a static object in the *IClassFactory::CreateInstance* method and then always provide a pointer to that one object, as shown in the following code. Like other singletons, the *ClientChannelHook* object is designed to stay in memory for the lifetime of its container process, so it does not support reference counting.

```
HRESULT CFactory::CreateInstance(IUnknown* pUnknownOuter,
    REFIID riid, void** ppv)
{
    if(pUnknownOuter != NULL)
        return CLASS_E_NOAGGREGATION;

    static CClientInfo ClientInfo;
    return ClientInfo.QueryInterface(riid, ppv);
}
```

CHAPTER THIRTEEN

Microsoft Transaction Server and COM+

In recent years, there has been much talk about migrating enterprise-wide systems from the two-tier paradigm called the client/server model to a three-tier architecture. The surging popularity of the Internet, the advent of the Java programming language, and the network computer have all spurred interest in the concept of three-tier system architecture. In this chapter, we'll take a look at the three-tier solution and examine how Microsoft Transaction Server fits in with this architecture. We'll also introduce an extension to COM called COM+.

Three-Tier Architecture

Many new enterprise information systems are developed to run on Microsoft Windows NT. However, few existing systems are ported from mainframes to Windows NT because in many client/server systems, the user interface and the business logic running on the client are specifically designed to run with the database server on the mainframe. The goal of the three-tier architecture is to separate the business logic from the two-tier system by moving it to a middle tier that runs on Windows NT. The resulting three-tier architecture consists of the client, the business-rules component, and the database server. The ultimate goal is to migrate the database servers as well. When that time comes, your company will unplug its mainframes and build indoor tennis courts in their place.

The Client Tier

The client side of a client/server system typically encompasses the functionality of both the user interface and the business logic that drives the system, leaving only the database on the server side. This design leads to heavyweight client-side applications that tend to be tied to a particular operating system and that can be difficult to deploy and support. In a three-tier architecture, the client is designed to be as lightweight as possible, normally handling only the user interface. Such a client might consist of forms designed in Visual Basic or perhaps only of Hypertext Markup Language (HTML) pages designed to run in a Web browser such as Microsoft Internet Explorer. Developing client-side applications composed solely of HTML pages is alluring to many corporations because of their platform independence and ease of distribution. Developers of applications that require a user interface richer than the one possible purely with HTML might consider including ActiveX controls or Java applets in their Web pages. Like HTML, Java applets are platform-independent, and both Java applets and ActiveX controls offer automated distribution.

The Business-Rules Tier

Whereas the client/server architecture is relatively fixed on deploying the client-side and the server-side components on different computers, the business-rules component of a three-tier design can lead to more flexible solutions. For example, the business-rules component might be implemented as an in-process COM-based component designed to run in the process of the client application on the client side or in the process of a Web server on the server side. Alternatively, the business-rules component might run on a third machine that is separate from both the client and the database server. The particular configuration chosen for a system depends heavily on the network bandwidth available to connect the various machines, as well as the administration and support issues involved in deploying a large distributed system to many client machines.

Where do DCOM and Microsoft Transaction Server (MTS) fit into this picture? Imagine deploying a business-rules component as an EXE-based component. Client applications written in C++, Visual Basic, or Java might use DCOM to connect to the business-rules component, which in turn could use Open Database Connectivity (ODBC) or even OLE DB to connect to a database server, as shown in Figure 13-1.

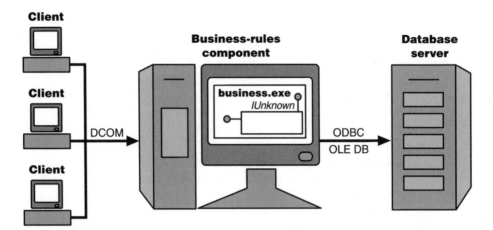

Figure 13-1.
A business-rules component deployed as a middle-tier in a three-tier architecture.

The Database Server Tier

If you want an even lighter weight client—one that does not require any client-side installation and configuration—the Web browser might serve as the client portion, making Hypertext Transfer Protocol (HTTP) the protocol of choice. The Web server can then host MTS components that use ODBC or OLE DB to communicate with a database server, as shown in Figure 13-2.

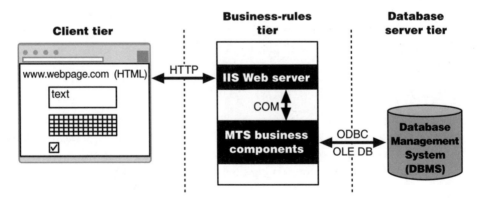

Figure 13-2.
Using a Web browser as a lightweight client in a three-tier architecture.

Three-Tier Architecture Concerns

Figure 13-1 depicts a successful implementation of a three-tier system, but a lot of development effort will be required for you to build the business-rules component. Even if the goals of the business-rules component are relatively modest, you will need to expend a tremendous amount of energy to develop a robust and secure EXE housing for the component. Potential problems abound. With many different clients connecting to the business-rules component simultaneously, you need to ensure that only those clients with the proper authorization are allowed to perform certain privileged operations via the component. Threading will also be a concern as you strive to make the component scalable to a large number of clients. You should anticipate times when too many clients attempt to access a component simultaneously. (A load-balancing feature could be implemented to direct some of the clients to an instance of the business-rules component running on another computer.)

You should also anticipate the potential for client failures in the midst of complex operations involving the database server. The client might have been storing data locally and then updating data on the database server based on some local information. If the client were to fail in the middle of this type of operation, you could not be sure of the integrity of the database without implementing some sort of transaction protocol. Finally, if the internal data structures of the business-rules component were to become corrupted, this corruption would need to be detected before the integrity of the database became compromised. From these hypothetical cases, you can see that a major problem with the three-tier model is that developers are left to implement an enormous amount of functionality in the second tier—functionality that has little to do with the goals of the system itself. Enter MTS.

Microsoft Transaction Server

MTS is a powerful run-time environment designed to host COM-based components and thus make it easier to develop and deploy high-performance, scalable, and robust enterprise, Internet, and intranet applications. MTS defines a set of COM interfaces for developing distributed components and an infrastructure for deploying and administering three-tier solutions. MTS is perhaps one of the least aptly named products to come out of Redmond in recent years. The name leads you to think solely of transactions, but MTS encompasses much more than this. In Chapter 8, "DLL Surrogates and Executable Components," we covered dynamic-link library (DLL) surrogates—processes designed solely to load DLL-based components into the surrogates' address space. In those terms, MTS is the ultimate DLL surrogate. Components are loaded into the MTS surrogate (mtx.exe) process along with the MTS Executive (mtxex.dll), as shown in the following illustration.

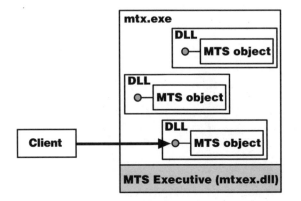

Microsoft's continuing research into component development produced a realization that writing robust server-side systems requires intensive work. Threading and concurrency, security and administration, robustness, and the like are crucial features of any distributed system, and developing software with these features seamlessly integrated requires tremendous effort. This effort is also completely unrelated to the actual processing done by the system. Microsoft SQL Server, for example, is a database server that deals with these issues in addition to its bread-and-butter work of processing SQL queries. Therefore, Microsoft created MTS to help developers who need to build sophisticated three-tier business systems. In some respects, MTS is a server's server. It is designed as a robust run-time environment that deals with most of the issues facing developers of server-side systems and enables them to plug in a COM-based in-process component containing the actual business-related functionality.

Designing Components for MTS

Although any COM-based in-process component qualifies as an MTS component, in-process components not designed specifically for execution within the MTS environment will not be able to take full advantage of the services offered by MTS. It is therefore recommended that developers update components that might benefit from running in the MTS environment. Typically, this update might include components that do not display a user interface or otherwise need to interact with the user. EXE-based components are not supported because they cannot be loaded into the address space of MTS and therefore cannot take advantage of its features. COM components designed to operate within the context of MTS can be built in any language that supports COM. For an in-process component to be hosted by the MTS environment, MTS requires that the component support the following features:

- The component must have a standard class object that implements the *IClassFactory* interface.

- The *IClassFactory::CreateInstance* method of the class object must return a new object every time it is called. Singletons are not the MTS way.

- The component must expose its class object by exporting the standard *DllGetClassObject* function.

- The component must use standard COM reference counting.

- A component running in the MTS process space cannot aggregate with components not running in MTS.

- The component must export the standard *DllRegisterServer* function that registers the programmatic identifier (ProgID), class identifier (CLSID), Interface, and TypeLib in the HKEY_CLASSES_ROOT section of the Microsoft Windows registry.

- The component's interfaces and COM classes must be described in a type library.

- The component must use standard or type library marshaling; custom marshaling is not supported by MTS. In cases in which the component supports both standard and type library marshaling, MTS will use standard marshaling. Even if a component supports the *IMarshal* interface, the methods of the *IMarshal* interface will never be called when the component is running in the MTS environment.

- When you are building a proxy/stub DLL for standard marshaling, the *–Oicf* flag must be used when you are running the MIDL compiler, and the mtxil.lib file must be linked into the resulting proxy/stub DLL.

Although these rules may seem daunting at first, they actually mandate what has become standard COM practice. The more standard your component is, the more likely it is to meet these requirements. For example, components built in Visual Basic and Java automatically meet all these requirements, as do most of the C++ components described in this book. MTS makes certain demands of your components, but it also offers them much in the way of functionality: MTS offers to handle the concurrency requirements of your components, as well as the resource pooling, security, context management, and transaction requirements. For the sake of simplicity and brevity of code, the majority of examples in this chapter are expressed in Visual Basic. Note that all of the features discussed are available to C++ and Java developers.

Threading

It is recommended that components designed for execution in the MTS environment support the single-threaded (STA) or multithreaded (MTA) apartment model. Components supporting the STA model should have their *ThreadingModel* value in the registry set to *Apartment*, and objects running in the MTS environment that support both the MTA and the STA models should have their *ThreadingModel* value set to *Both*. (See Chapter 4, "Threading Models and Apartments.") Legacy single-threaded components do not work well in the MTS environment because all objects in the component must execute in the thread of the main STA. Because such components are not reentrant, execution must be serialized across all objects in the component, limiting their scalability and even making them susceptible to deadlock.

The *–Oicf* MIDL Compiler Option

The *–Oicf* flag must be used to generate proxy/stub DLLs in order for standard marshaling to work with MTS. This flag instructs the MIDL compiler to generate special proxy/stub code that uses a fully interpreted marshaling technique. Typically, the MIDL compiler generates code that marshals some parameters in line in the generated proxy and stub. This inline marshaling results in a larger proxy/stub DLL but offers the best performance. When operating in the fully interpreted mode, instead of generating marshaling code the MIDL compiler generates strings that specify how the data should be marshaled. At run time, the RPC run-time layer interprets the MIDL-generated strings in order to perform the actual marshaling. This option considerably reduces the size of the proxy/stub DLL at the expense of run-time performance. Note that the *–Oicf* option also limits developers to a maximum of 16 parameters per method.

Just-in-Time Activation

From an in-process component's point of view, MTS is a surrogate process with some unique functionality. A client that calls *CoGetClassObject* for a component that is registered with MTS receives a reference to a class object implemented by MTS—not a reference to the component's class object. When the client later calls the *IClassFactory::CreateInstance* method, the class object implemented by MTS does not actually instantiate the object. Only when the client makes a method call into the component does MTS finally instantiate the object by calling the component's *IClassFactory::CreateInstance* method.

In addition to the late instantiation of components, MTS extends the COM model to allow early deactivation of an object. MTS can deactivate a component even while client programs maintain valid references to that component. MTS does this by calling the *IUnknown::Release* method to release all references to the object. This call in turn causes properly built COM objects to be destroyed when their internal reference count reaches 0. If the client requests services from an object that has been deactivated by MTS, that object will be transparently reactivated via the component's *IClassFactory::CreateInstance* method. So while it might appear to a client process that it is using a single COM object from the time of creation until the time it releases the object, the client might in fact be working with many different instances of the same COM class. Objects, unlike cats, really do have nine lives.

The ability for an object running in the MTS environment (called an MTS object) to be activated only only as needed is referred to as *just-in-time activation.* Just-in-time activation is a powerful resource-sharing concept because it enables MTS to share the resources of the server more equitably among the active components. Imagine that a client process spends 10 percent of its time requesting services from a particular object. With the automated deactivation of objects running in MTS, the object will be instantiated only 10 percent of the time instead of 100 percent. This technique can make a particular server machine far more scalable than would be possible if all objects remained active for the entire duration of their clients.

Each object running in the MTS environment is shadowed by a context object that maintains information about the object. The context object implements the *IObjectContext* interface, described later in this chapter, in the section "The *IObjectContext* Interface"; in addition, it stores the identity of the client that instantiated the MTS object, the transactional requirements of the object, and its security properties. As shown in Figure 13-3, when MTS deactivates an object, the context object remains. When the client permanently releases the object, the context object associated with that object is also destroyed.

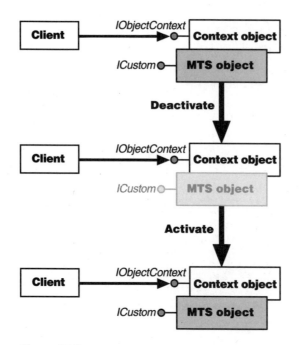

Figure 13-3.
The MTS object is deactivated, but the context object remains.

The *IObjectControl* Interface

Applications that execute code before an object is deactivated and again just before it is activated can implement the *IObjectControl* interface. The *IObjectControl* interface has three methods: *Activate*, *Deactivate*, and *CanBePooled*. The *IObjectControl* interface is shown here in IDL notation:

```
interface IObjectControl : IUnknown
{
    HRESULT Activate(void);
    void Deactivate(void);
    BOOL CanBePooled(void);
}
```

When an object is first instantiated, MTS queries it for the *IObjectControl* interface. If the interface is found, MTS will call the *Activate* method immediately before the object is activated and the *Deactivate* method before it is deactivated, enabling the object to execute any desired code at those specific times in the object's life cycle. After executing the *Deactivate* method, MTS calls the *IObjectControl::CanBePooled* method to determine whether the object is environmentally aware. Such an object returns true from the *CanBePooled* method, thereby informing MTS that this object can be recycled. Objects that support recycling

487

are pooled by MTS for later reuse by the same or another client instead of being destroyed. When some client later attempts to access an object of the COM class, MTS will obtain an object from the pool if one is available. Only when the pool of recyclable objects is empty will MTS use the object's class factory to instantiate a new object.

Giving MTS permission to recycle an object means that you must implement the *IObjectControl::Deactivate* method so that it restores the object to the identical state of an object newly manufactured by the class factory. The decision of whether to support recycling of an object should be based on the expense of creating new objects vs. the cost of holding the resources of that object while it is being stored in the object pool. An object that takes a long time to create and holds many resources when deactivated is a good candidate for recycling. Imagine an object that creates a complex memory structure on start-up. If this type of object supports pooling, it could simply reinitialize the structure in the *Deactivate* event and would thereby increase performance at run time because the structure would not need to be re-created at each activation. For other objects, recycling might not be advantageous, such as for an object that is cheap to create and stores a lot of state for each client. This state is not reusable by other clients, and therefore recycling does not offer any benefits. The following table summarizes the steps taken by MTS when the client calls a method of a deactivated object.

Step	IObjectControl Not Implemented	IObjectControl Implemented
Activate the object.	Call *IClassFactory::CreateInstance* to instantiate the object.	Obtain an object from the pool. If the pool does not contain this type of object, call *IClassFactory::CreateInstance* to instantiate the object. Last, call the *Activate* method.
Execute the method.	Call the method.	Call the method.
Deactivate the object.	Release all references to the object.	Call the *Deactivate* method, and then call the *CanBePooled* method to determine whether pooling is supported. If it is, add the object to the pool; otherwise, release all references to the object.

To implement the *IObjectControl* interface in a Visual Basic component, a reference must be set to the Microsoft Transaction Server Type Library (mtxas.dll). Note that returning *true* from the *IObjectControl::CanBePooled* method doesn't guarantee that the object will be recycled but simply indicates to MTS that the object supports this feature. However, returning *false* from *CanBePooled* does ensure that the object will never be recycled. The current version of MTS does not recycle objects, regardless of the value returned from the *CanBePooled* method. But the functionality is in place for forward compatibility, so implementing the logic today means that it will be in place to work with future versions of MTS.

State

C++ and other object-oriented languages made developers aware of the class vs. object idea for the first time. Subsequently, COM brought the interface vs. implementation issue into the limelight. Now MTS advances the concept of state vs. behavior. In the MTS world, components are seen as code libraries exposing certain interfaces (behaviors). Since the behavior of an object remains consistent throughout its lifetime, MTS can create, destroy, and pool objects at will. Object-oriented fundamentals dictate that an object encapsulates code (behavior) and data (state). The state of an object is volatile, which can limit MTS's ability to create and destroy an object while clients maintain valid references to the object. To overcome this problem, MTS recommends that developers build stateless objects. However, because this is not a realistic solution for many components, MTS defines four specific places in which state can be stored in a controlled manner: the client, the object, the database, and the Shared Property Manager. By defining specific places in which state can be stored and by defining the semantics of its storage and usage in those places, MTS effectively champions the state vs. behavior concept.

Client State Storage

Storing the state of an object in the client application simplifies the implementation of that object because it can basically behave like a stateless object. In this type of system design, the client must pass the object's state with every method of the object. Between method calls, the object itself does not retain this state. This type of design simplifies the implementation of the component, but it can complicate the implementation of the client process. Network bandwidth can be a major bottleneck when you are passing an object's entire state at every method call. Therefore, a stateful client solution is useful only when little state needs to be transmitted or when the client and component are connected via a high-bandwidth network.

Object State Storage

Storing state in the object itself is the typical approach taken for most objects that are not designed specifically for MTS. Objects running in the context of MTS must be careful in their use of the object itself for storing state because when an object is deactivated, that state is lost. Any object that keeps its own state will not be able to take advantage of the resource-sharing, just-in-time activation features of MTS. These types of objects also do not scale well to support a large number of clients. It is therefore recommended that objects being rewritten to take advantage of the MTS environment store their states somewhere else.

Database State Storage

Most business components are designed to store their durable state in a database. (Durable is discussed further on page 498.) Typically, the business component would use the ODBC API or OLE DB interfaces to communicate with a back-end database server such as Microsoft SQL Server. Storing the object's durable state in a database is typically a must. However, the database server is likely to have many clients in contention for its services, and it is important not to overload the server with requests to store temporary data. Additionally, because storing temporal data is not something most SQL servers are designed to do, a component that attempts to work this way will likely suffer a serious performance penalty.

The Shared Property Manager

The Shared Property Manager is an MTS resource dispenser that can be used to store and share state among multiple objects within a server process. The Shared Property Manager is a three-level hierarchy of objects that eliminates naming conflicts by providing shared property groups; the groups contain the actual shared properties. The Shared Property Manager has built-in synchronization that prevents two objects from accessing a shared property simultaneously. If two threads attempted to access a shared property concurrently, the value of the property could be left in an unpredictable state. The three-level hierarchy of Shared Property Manager is shown here.

To access the Shared Property Manager from a component written in Visual Basic, you need to set a reference to the Shared Property Manager Type Library (mtxspm.dll). The *SharedPropertyGroupManager* object needs to be instantiated using *New* (Visual Basic and Java) or *CoCreateInstance* (C++). The *ISharedPropertyGroupManager::CreatePropertyGroup* method is then called to instantiate a property group. Because there is no method of the *ISharedPropertyGroupManager* interface that is designed to open an existing property group, the *CreatePropertyGroup* method takes an outbound boolean parameter that specifies whether the property group existed before the *CreatePropertyGroup* method was called. This existence is determined based on the string name of the property group passed as the first parameter of the *CreatePropertyGroup* method.

The second parameter of the *CreatePropertyGroup* method specifies the lock setting to be employed by the property group object being created. The lock setting can be either *LockSetGet* or *LockMethod*. The *LockSetGet* flag creates a property group that protects the individual properties belonging to the property group during every operation that gets or sets the value of a property. The *LockMethod* flag locks all the properties of the property group while the method of an object that has access to the property group is running, which leads to a higher degree of safety but less concurrency for objects with access to the property group.

Typically, if a method will perform several operations on a shared property, it is best to copy the value of that property to a local variable and then perform the operations using the local memory. Only when the operations have been completed should the value of the shared property be updated. This type of code makes the *LockSetGet* flag sufficient and leads to more efficient execution in the MTS environment. In comparison, when a set of operations is performed directly on a shared property, each individual operation is atomic because of the implicit synchronization provided by the Shared Property Manager but the entire set of operations is not atomic. (Atomic is discussed further on page 498.) Other objects might also be operating on the same properties, leading to corrupted data. With this type of code, it is imperative that the *LockMethod* flag be employed.

The third parameter of the *CreatePropertyGroup* method specifies the release mode of the property group. The valid settings are either *Standard*, indicating that the property group is to be destroyed after all the references to the object have been released, or *Process*, indicating that the property group is not to be released until the process in which it was created has terminated. Note that the values of the lock mode and release settings provided in the second and third parameters of the *CreatePropertyGroup* method are ignored if MTS determines that the property group already exists, and therefore MTS proceeds to open an existing property group. When the *CreatePropertyGroup* method opens an existing property group, the second and third parameters will return the current settings for those values. Although the constants *LockSetGet, LockMethod, Standard,* and *Process* can be passed directly to the *CreatePropertyGroup* method, this method will disable the retrieval of the current settings when it returns. To retrieve these values, it is better to create variables that are passed to the *CreatePropertyGroup* method by reference. The following Visual Basic code fragment creates a property group named *GuyProperties* containing a property named *Hair* with the value *Brown*.

```
Dim spg As SharedPropertyGroup
Dim sp As SharedProperty
Dim fAlreadyExists As Boolean

Dim isolationMode As Long
isolationMode = LockSetGet

Dim releaseMode As Long
releaseMode = Process

Dim spgm As New SharedPropertyGroupManager

Set spg = spgm.CreatePropertyGroup("GuyProperties", isolationMode, _
    releaseMode, fAlreadyExists)

Set sp = spg.CreateProperty("Hair", fAlreadyExists)

sp.Value = "Brown"
```

The *IObjectContext* Interface

The idea that MTS will deactivate a component while clients hold valid references to that component is almost heretical in the world of COM, where *IUnknown* and reference counting rule supreme. MTS is designed to deactivate objects only at certain controlled junctures in the object's lifetime. MTS offers the business component developer a great deal of control over the behavior of MTS via the *IObjectContext* interface, implemented by the context object associated with each object running in the MTS environment. The *IObjectContext* interface is shown here in IDL notation:

```
interface IObjectContext : public IUnknown
{
    HRESULT CreateInstance(
```

```
            [in] REFCLSID rclsid,
            [in] REFIID riid,
            [out, retval, iid_is(riid)] void** ppv);
        HRESULT SetComplete(void);
        HRESULT SetAbort(void);
        HRESULT EnableCommit(void);
        HRESULT DisableCommit(void);
        BOOL IsInTransaction(void);
        BOOL IsSecurityEnabled(void);
        HRESULT IsCallerInRole(
            [in] BSTR bstrRole,
            [out, retval] BOOL* pfIsInRole);
};
```

Although the *IObjectContext* interface is implemented by the context object created by MTS and is automatically associated with every MTS object, there is no need for the component to instantiate an object that implements this interface. Instead, MTS offers the *GetObjectContext* function that returns a pointer to the *IObjectContext* interface implemented by the context object. A component written in Visual Basic, for example, would obtain access to the context object using the following code:

```
Dim oc As ObjectContext
Set oc = GetObjectContext()
```

A C++ programmer obtains access to the *IObjectContext* interface in a similar way, as shown here:

```
#include <mtx.h>

IObjectContext* pObjectContext = NULL;
HRESULT hr = GetObjectContext(&pObjectContext);
```

The following code shows how a Java programmer would obtain access to the *IObjectContext* interface:

```
import com.ms.mtx.*;

IObjectContext pObjectContext = null;
pObjectContext = (IObjectContext)MTx.GetObjectContext();
```

CreateInstance Having obtained a pointer to the context object, you can invoke any methods of the *IObjectContext* interface. The *IObjectContext::Create-Instance* method is designed to enable one MTS object to instantiate another MTS object. The standard *CoCreateInstance* function can be called for the purpose of instantiating an object, but this technique has its limitations. Instead, it is recommended that you use the *IObjectContext::CreateInstance* method for this purpose, as shown in the following code. The advantage of the *CreateInstance* method is that the newly created object will inherit the activity, transaction, and security identities from the creator's context object. For example, assuming that the object's creator is running in a transaction, if the object being created requires a transaction in order to execute, it will run within the scope of the existing transaction. If the new object does not support transactions or require its own transaction, MTS will accommodate it as well.

```
Dim oc As ObjectContext
Set oc = GetObjectContext()

Dim GuysAccount As Bank.Account
Set GuysAccount = oc.CreateInstance("Bank.Account")
```

SetComplete, SetAbort, EnableCommit, and DisableCommit You can also use the *IObjectContext* interface to control when MTS will deactivate an object, by calling the *IObjectContext::SetComplete* method. This method indicates to MTS that the object has successfully completed its work and that its internal representation does not need to be retained for future client calls. If the method is executing within the scope of a transaction, the *SetComplete* method also indicates that the object's transactional updates can be committed. When an object that is the root of a transaction calls *SetComplete*, MTS attempts to commit the transaction on return from the current method.

Similarly, the *IObjectContext::SetAbort* method also tells MTS that the object can be deactivated. However, the *SetAbort* method indicates that an unrecoverable error has occurred, making the object's transactional updates inconsistent and therefore mandating that the transaction be aborted. MTS will also deactivate an object whenever a transaction involving that object is committed or aborted, even if the object did not issue the commit or abort operation itself. These are the only times when MTS will transparently deactivate an object. Of course, when the client releases all references to the object, MTS will permanently destroy the object in accordance with COM's reference counting rules. Remember that objects lose state on transaction boundaries. Use the Shared Property Manager to hold state across transactions, or store the state in a database.

The *EnableCommit* and *DisableCommit* methods of the *IObjectContext* interface are analogues to the *SetComplete* and *SetAbort* methods. The *EnableCommit* method tells MTS that it is safe to commit the transaction in which the object is participating but that the object has not yet finished its work and therefore its internal state must be maintained until the object calls *SetComplete* or *SetAbort* or until the transaction completes. In the meantime, MTS will not deactivate the object. *EnableCommit* is the default state when an object is first activated.

For this reason, you should always call *SetComplete* or *SetAbort* before a method returns, unless you specifically want the object's internal state to be maintained for future client method calls.

The *DisableCommit* method is similar to the *EnableCommit* method in that it forces MTS to maintain its internal state until a later time, at which point either the *SetComplete* or the *SetAbort* method is called. However, the *Disable-Commit* method also informs MTS that the work being performed by the object is currently in an incomplete stage that cannot be committed at the present time. Thus, the *DisableCommit* method is useful for preventing a transaction from committing prematurely between method calls to a stateful object. In this respect, the *DisableCommit* method differs from the *EnableCommit* method, which declares that although the object's work is not necessarily complete, it is safe to commit the object's transactional updates in their present form.

Internally, the *SetComplete/SetAbort* and *EnableCommit/DisableCommit* methods set the *Done* and *Consistent* flags in the context object associated with an MTS object. The *Done* flag specifies whether the object has completed its work so that its state no longer needs to be maintained by MTS. The *Consistent* flag indicates whether the transaction can be committed in its current state. These flags, and hence the methods that set them, have no effect until a method finishes executing and returns to its caller. Thus, any combination of these four methods can be called from within a method, but MTS will act only on the last call that is made before the method returns. The following table lists the effect the four methods have on the internal *Done* and *Consistent* flags maintained by MTS in the context object.

Method	Done	Consistent
SetComplete	True	True
SetAbort	True	False
EnableCommit	False	True
DisableCommit	False	False

Transactions

As you have probably realized by now, MTS is a great DLL surrogate with a myriad of features that can help you develop robust three-tier systems. As mentioned, because of its name, MTS is often thought of as primarily a transaction processor. While transaction processing is one of MTS's more important features, MTS actually enlists the help of the Microsoft Distributed Transaction Coordinator (MS DTC) to perform the actual transaction management.

Microsoft originally designed the OLE Transactions interfaces (*ITransaction, ITransactionDispenser, ITransactionOptions,* and *ITransactionOutcomeEvents*), an object-oriented, two-phase commit protocol based on COM, and then implemented those four interfaces in MS DTC, a transaction manager originally included with Microsoft SQL Server version 6.5. However, Microsoft did not design the transaction management services provided by MS DTC solely for use by Microsoft SQL Server. MS DTC is now included with MTS, and Microsoft is planning on integrating it with future releases of the Windows operating system, where its functionality will be available to a wide variety of applications requiring transaction management services.

In addition to the OLE Transactions specification, MTS also supports the X/Open DTP XA standard. XA is the two-phase commit protocol defined by the X/Open DTP group. XA is natively supported by many UNIX databases, including Informix, Oracle, and DB2. In order for MTS to work with XA-compliant resource managers, the MTS Software Development Kit (SDK) provides a special component that maps OLE Transactions to the XA standard, which makes it relatively straightforward for XA-compliant resource managers to provide resource dispensers that accept OLE Transactions from MTS and then perform the transaction using XA.

A transaction is typically initiated when an application is going to perform some critical operation. First a transaction manager such as MS DTC is notified. The application then enlists the help of various resource managers in performing the desired work. A resource manager is defined as any service supporting the OLE Transactions specification, such as Microsoft SQL Server. Resource managers work in cooperation with MS DTC so that when the client application calls various resource dispensers, it carries with it information identifying the current transaction.

Typically, transaction processing is most often applied to database access because of the crucial nature of the information stored there. However, transaction processing is not limited to the DBMS domain. MTS, for example, also provides two resource dispensers: the ODBC Driver Manager and the Shared Property Manager. A resource dispenser manages nondurable shared state on behalf of MTS objects. Resource dispensers are similar to resource managers, but without the guarantee of durability. The ODBC Driver Manager is a resource dispenser that manages pools of database connections for MTS components. The Shared Property Manager was discussed earlier in this chapter. Add-on resource dispensers can also be developed using the MTS SDK.

A resource manager enlisted to perform work on behalf of the client application also registers itself with the transaction manager. The transaction manager then keeps track of that resource manager through the remainder of the transaction. In transaction processing parlance, a transaction ends when the client application either commits or aborts the transaction. An abort operation causes the transaction manager to notify all resource managers involved in the transaction to roll back any operations performed as part of that transaction. A rollback can be likened to a giant undo operation. If the client application should fail before committing or aborting the transaction, MS DTC will automatically abort the transaction.

If everything goes well and the client application requests that the transaction be committed, MS DTC executes a two-phase commit protocol in order to commit the operations performed in the scope of the transaction. A two-phase commit protocol ensures that transactions that apply to more than one server are completed on all servers or on none at all. The two-phase commit protocol is a result of coordination between MS DTC and supported resource managers. First MS DTC queries each resource manager enlisted in the transaction to determine whether every resource manager agrees to the commit operation. If any one resource manager fails to respond or votes to abort the transaction, MS DTC will notify all the resource managers that the transaction is aborted and their operations must be rolled back. Only if all resource managers agree in the first phase of the protocol will MS DTC broadcast a second commit message, thereby completing the transaction successfully. The two-phase commit process is shown in Figure 13-4.

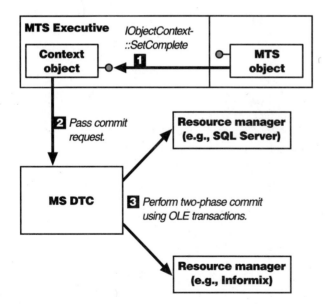

Figure 13-4.
The MS DTC communicating with the resource managers to control a two-phase commit.

The ACID Properties

A client application using transactions in its work must be guaranteed that concurrent transactions are atomic and consistent, that they have proper isolation, and that once committed, the changes are durable. These conditions are sometimes referred to as the *ACID (atomic, consistent, isolated,* and *durable)* properties of transactions. The four ACID properties are described here:

atomic—A transaction is atomic in the sense that all the operations that make up that transaction either succeed or fail as a single unit. Atomicity guarantees that a transaction will never be a partial success when some part of the transaction has failed. If a transaction aborts, all of its effects are undone, which, in turn, guarantees the consistency of the data, as described next.

consistent—A transaction guarantees that the data being operated on by one or more resource managers will remain consistent regardless of the outcome of that transaction. For example, if an SQL query updates two related tables in a database, a transaction can ensure that the data in one table will always refer to a valid item in another table.

isolated—Isolation protects concurrent transactions from seeing each other's partial and uncommitted results. This protection in turn prevents the application from basing another operation on these temporary results. Transactions that concurrently examine the data operated on by code running in another transaction will see the data in either its pretransaction or its post-transaction state; never will transactions see the data in an intermediary state.

durable—Durability ensures that once committed, all updates will persist even in the event of a system failure. Transactional logging even allows you to recover the durable state after disk media failures. If a system failure occurs during a transaction, the transaction will abort and the changes will be rolled back, thereby ensuring consistency.

Configuring Transaction Support in MTS

Each object running in the context of MTS can be set to one of four levels of transaction support. A component can declare that it requires a transaction, requires a new transaction, supports transactions, or does not support transactions. The context objects of components that do not support transactions are created without a transaction, regardless of whether their client is running in the scope of a transaction. Unless the component developer or system administrator specifies otherwise, this setting is the default. Components that do not support transactions cannot take advantage of many features of MTS, including just-in-time activation. Such components are never deactivated while clients hold valid references because MTS does not have enough information about their current state. Thus, the default value is not recommended; it is intended primarily to support components not originally designed for use with MTS.

Most MTS objects are declared as either requiring a transaction or supporting transactions. Objects that support transactions can participate in the outcome of the transaction if their client is running in the scope of a transaction. If the caller is not executing within a transaction, no transaction will be available for the MTS object. Objects declaring that they require a transaction will either inherit the transaction of the caller or, if the caller's transaction is unavailable, have MTS automatically initiate a transaction on their behalf. Objects that require a new transaction never inherit the client's transaction; MTS automatically initiates a fresh transaction regardless of whether the caller has one.

The desired level of transaction support can be set by the developer, using custom attributes defined in a type library or by the system administrator, using the Transaction Server Explorer configuration utility, otherwise known as Microsoft TS Explorer. The mtxattr.h header file defines four custom type library attributes: *TRANSACTION_REQUIRED*, *TRANSACTION_SUPPORTED*, *TRANSACTION_NOT_SUPPORTED*, and *TRANSACTION_REQUIRES_NEW*. These can be easily added to the library portion of a C++ or Java component's IDL file, as shown in boldface in listing 13-1:

component.idl

```
import "unknwn.idl";
#include <MtxAttr.h>

// Interface definition omitted for brevity...

[ uuid(10000003-0000-0000-0000-000000000001),
  helpstring("Inside DCOM Component Type Library"),
  version(1.0),
  TRANSACTION_REQUIRED ]
library Component
{
    importlib("stdole32.tlb");
    interface ISum;

    [ uuid(10000002-0000-0000-0000-000000000001) ]
    coclass InsideDCOM
```

Listing 13-1.   *(continued)*
An IDL file that specifies a component requires a transaction.

component.idl *continued*

```
    {
        interface ISum;
    }
};
```

Later, when you are registering the component with MTS, these custom attributes will be read and the transaction support configured accordingly. Because Visual Basic typically creates the type library automatically, components written in Visual Basic cannot use the custom attributes defined in the mtxattr.h header file. Instead, MTS Explorer must be used to define the level of transaction support offered by a Visual Basic component, as shown in Figure 13-5.

Figure 13-5.
Specifying the level of transaction in the Properties dialog box.

For components that support but do not require a transaction, it might be useful to determine whether the object is currently executing within a transaction scope. The *IObjectContext::IsInTransaction* method can be called by an MTS object to obtain this information. Components that either require or do not support transactions have no use for the *IsInTransaction* method since MTS guarantees their status with regard to transactions.

Client-Controlled vs. Automation Transactions

MTS initiates transactions at certain specific times, as outlined here. *Activation* is a general term used to refer to the first instantiation of an object or its just-in-time activation.

- MTS initiates a new transaction when a component marked as requiring a transaction is activated by a base client or by another MTS object that does not support transactions.

- MTS initiates a new transaction when a component marked as requiring a new transaction is activated, regardless of whether the client has a transaction.

These are the only times and the only ways a transaction can be initiated in the MTS environment. The MTS object ends the transaction by calling either the *IObjectContext::SetComplete* or the *IObjectContext::SetAbort* method. The typical base client process instantiates MTS objects using the *CoCreateInstance* function. This technique does not afford the client application control over the transaction status of an MTS object, however. While there is nothing wrong with this approach per se, it limits the client's ability to combine operations that involve multiple objects in one transaction.

One way to enable the client to exercise greater control over the transactional process is to build a special MTS object declared as requiring a new transaction. This object might simply allow the client to create other MTS objects, which would then inherit the automatic transaction initiated by MTS for the first object. The client could control the outcome of the transaction by calling methods exposed by the first object that simply called *SetComplete* or *SetAbort* to end the automatic transaction. You don't have to build this type of object since MTS offers a built-in object that implements the *ITransactionContext Ex* interface to provide the aforementioned functionality.

Because the *TransactionContextEx* object is declared as requiring a new transaction, MTS is forced to initiate a transaction for it. This enables the base client to instantiate a *TransactionContextEx* object, call its *CreateInstance* method to instantiate other MTS objects, call various methods on those objects, and finally call *Commit* or *Abort* in the *TransactionContextEx* object. The operations performed on the MTS objects instantiated using the *TransactionContextEx* object inherit the automatic transaction initiated by MTS for the *TransactionContextEx* object. Note that this type of control is available only to components that support or require transactions. MTS objects that either do not support transactions or require a new transaction for every operation cannot be grouped into a transaction involving other objects.

The *ITransactionContextEx* Interface

To access the *TransactionContextEx* object from Visual Basic, you must set a reference to the Transaction Context Type Library (txctx.dll). The *ITransactionContextEx* interface is defined in IDL notation on the following page.

```
interface ITransactionContextEx : IUnknown
{
    HRESULT CreateInstance(
        [in] REFCLSID clsid,
        [in] REFIID riid,
        [out, retval, iid_is(riid)] void** pObject);

    HRESULT Commit(void);

    HRESULT Abort(void);
};
```

The *ITransactionContextEx::CreateInstance* method is called by a client to instantiate an MTS object, instead of the *CoCreateInstance* function. In turn, the *ITransactionContextEx::CreateInstance* method instantiates an MTS object by calling the *IObjectContextEx::CreateInstance* method. The client can then call the *ITransactionContextEx::CreateInstance* method again to create additional MTS objects, all of which become parts of the single transaction initiated for the *TransactionContext* object. At some later point, the client might decide to end the entire transaction by calling the *ITransactionContextEx::Commit* or *ITransactionContextEx::Abort* method, which will have the effect of either committing or aborting the operations performed by every MTS object involved in the transaction.

Security

As mentioned at the beginning of this chapter, MTS was designed to relieve developers of the need to code a robust server-side process for every component that runs in the middle tier of a three-tier architecture. To this end, components running in the context of MTS automatically receive help in managing threading, concurrency, scalability, transactions, and security. The MTS security model leverages those of DCOM and Windows NT. However, to simplify security issues for components running in MTS, two types of security are available: declarative and programmatic. Developers can use both declarative and programmatic security when designing an MTS object. Declarative security is security configured with the MTS Explorer, and programmatic security is security defined by interfaces and code that are used to determine proper access to a component. (Note that MTS security, is not supported for middle-tier components running on Microsoft Windows 95 or Microsoft Windows 98.)

The key to understanding the MTS security model is to understand the simple but powerful concept of *roles*. Roles are central to the flexible, declarative security model employed by most MTS objects. A role is a symbolic name that abstracts and identifies a logical group of users, similar to the idea of a user group in Windows NT. During development of an MTS object, roles can be defined and used to perform declarative authorization as well as to program specific security logic that either grants or denies certain permissions. When an MTS object is deployed, the administrator can bind the roles defined in the component to specific users and user groups. For example, an MTS-based accounting package might define roles and permissions for accountants and attorneys. During deployment, the administrator could assign users Fred and Jane to the role of accountants and the entire legal department to the role of attorneys.

To enable the MTS object to determine security levels programmatically, MTS offers the *IObjectContext::IsSecurityEnabled* and *IObjectContext::IsCallerInRole* methods. The *IsCallerInRole* method interrogates the caller to determine whether the user making the call was assigned to a specific role. For example, the accounting package described above might allow certain operations to be performed only by users in the role of accountants. The following code fragment shows in bold how the role of the caller can be checked and the appropriate code executed:

```
Public Function MethodForUseByAccountantsOnly() As Boolean
Dim oc As ObjectContext
Set oc = GetObjectContext()

If oc.IsCallerInRole("Accountants") = True Then
    ' Code here to proceed with operation and return success...
    MethodForUseByAccountantsOnly = True
Else
    ' Code here to deny access and return failure...
    MethodForUseByAccountantsOnly = False
End If
End Function
```

MTS does not support declarative security when running an MTS object in the same process as the base client, and thus this configuration is not recommended. In such cases, the *IsCallerInRole* method always returns *true,* which can lead the component to grant permissions to ineligible users. To overcome this problem, the *IObjectContext::IsSecurityEnabled* method can be called to determine whether role-based security is currently being enforced by MTS. The previous method might be rewritten as follows to call the *IsSecurityEnabled* function:

```
Public Function MethodForUseByAccountantsOnly() As Boolean
Dim oc As ObjectContext
Set oc = GetObjectContext()

If oc.IsSecurityEnabled = False Then
    ' Security is not currently available.
```

(continued)

```
        MethodForUseByAccountantsOnly = False
        Exit Function
End If

If oc.IsCallerInRole("Accountants") = True Then
    ' Code here to proceed with operation and return success...
        MethodForUseByAccountantsOnly = True
Else
    ' Code here to deny access and return failure...
        MethodForUseByAccountantsOnly = False
End If
End Function
```

The *ISecurityProperty* Interface

For those components requiring greater control over the security model than offered by the *IsSecurityEnabled* and *IsCallerInRole* methods of the *IObjectContext* interface, the context object also implements the *ISecurityProperty* interface. An MTS object can use the methods of the *ISecurityProperty* interface to obtain precise information about the identity of its caller stored in the context object. The *ISecurityProperty* interface is defined here in IDL notation:

```
interface ISecurityProperty : IUnknown
{
    HRESULT GetDirectCreatorSID(PSID* pSID);
    HRESULT GetOriginalCreatorSID(PSID* pSID);
    HRESULT GetDirectCallerSID(PSID* pSID);
    HRESULT GetOriginalCallerSID(PSID* pSID);
    HRESULT ReleaseSID(PSID pSID);
};
```

Notice that all the methods of the *ISecurityProperty* interface work with a Windows NT *security identifier* (*SID*), a unique value that identifies a specific user or user group. However, because they specifically identify a unique user, SIDs do not have the flexibility of the role-based security promoted by MTS. After a SID is obtained from a method of the *ISecurityProperty* interface, the MTS object can use this value when calling the security functions of the Microsoft Win32 API. In this way, the richness and complexity of the Windows NT security model is available to components running in the context of MTS. Note that components written in Visual Basic do not have much use for SIDs and are instead provided with the user name identified by the SID.

Figure 13-6 illustrates the *ISecurityProperty* interface. As you can see, a base client (client 1 running as user A) instantiates an MTS object (object X running as user C). The pointer to object X is then passed to another base client process (client 2 running as user B). Client 2 later calls a method of object X, which results in object X instantiating yet another MTS object (object Y running as user D). Last, object X calls a method of object Y.

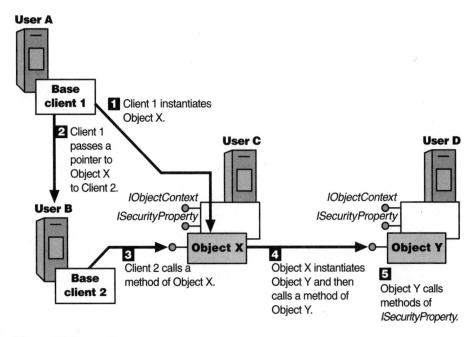

Figure 13-6.
A process demonstrating the use of the ISecurityProperty *interface.*

If the method in object Y now calls the methods of the *ISecurityProperty* interface implemented by its context object, the results are as follows:

- *ISecurityProperty::GetDirectCallerSID* returns user C.

- *ISecurityProperty::GetDirectCreatorSID* returns user C.

- *ISecurityProperty::GetOriginalCallerSID* returns user B.

- *ISecurityProperty::GetOriginalCreatorSID* returns user A.

Note that MTS does not support an impersonation model whereby object X can impersonate user B's security credential when accessing object Y. Instead, security is simplified by the role-based security model. A role can be defined that allows object X to access the services of object Y.

Error Handling

In an ideal world, servers would never fail, and when they did, they would fail in a big way. Believe it or not, it is often better to have a big, dramatic, and immediate system failure than to have a failure go undetected for some time. Undetected failures usually bring the system down eventually, and they might also leave a trail of corrupted data spanning hours or days before bringing down the system or being otherwise detected. To combat this problem, MTS performs extensive checking of internal integrity and consistency to ensure that all components are working properly.

If an error in an internal MTS structure is detected, MTS immediately terminates that process. This failfast technique facilitates fault containment and reduces the likelihood that an error will go undetected, leading to a more reliable and robust system. As part of its error handling mechanism, MTS objects are not permitted to propagate exceptions outside of the object. Unhandled exceptions will be trapped by MTS, and the process will be terminated because it is assumed that an unhandled exception has left the object in an indeterminate and possibly unsafe state.

MTS does not typically modify the *HRESULT* value returned from a method of an MTS object. One exception to this rule is when either the *S_OK* or the *S_FALSE* value is returned to the caller. In such a case, MTS might modify the value returned to the client into an MTS error code. For example, if a method of an object calls *SetComplete* to commit a transaction but for some reason the transaction cannot be committed by MS DTC and must be aborted, the *HRESULT* of the method will be converted to *CONTEXT_E_ABORTED* and all of the method's outbound parameters will be set to *null*.

Registering Components with MTS

To register a component for execution with MTS, launch MTS Explorer and create a new package. An MTS package defines a group of components identified by a globally unique identifier (GUID) that will be launched in a single server process. MTS Explorer will prompt you for the name of the package and the Windows NT security account under which the package will execute. You can specify the interactive user or a particular user account under which the package should always execute. You can also specify whether the package of components will run in a server process (called a *server package*—the default) or in a client process (called a *library package*). MTS components that run directly in the client process are not recommended because they lose the component tracking, role-based security, and process isolation features of MTS.

After you've created a package, you can add in-process components. MTS Explorer allows the administrator to choose from components already listed in the registry or from components that are simply present in the directory structure. When an unregistered component is selected, MTS Explorer loads it and then calls its *DllRegisterServer* function to invoke its self-registration routine. At this stage, you can set the transactional attribute of the component.

When a component is registered within the MTS environment, its Inproc-Server32 key is cleared and a LocalServer32 key is created. The LocalServer32 key points to the MTS surrogate and passes the package identifier as a command-line parameter, as shown in the following example:

```
C:\WINNT\SYSTEM32\mtx.exe /p:{C300DE46-56AD-11D1-A6FC-0000C0CC7BE1}
```

New roles are also defined within an MTS package. A role can be mapped to one or more users and/or user groups, and that role can then be added to a component within the package. Security configured with the MTS Explorer define the declarative security model of MTS components and packages. Note that a Visual Basic or VBScript program can automate the configuration of all these settings through the Automation interface exposed by MTS.

OLE, Network OLE, COM, ActiveX, DCOM,...COM+

COM+ encompasses an evolutionary set of enhancements to COM that make it easier to develop COM-based components. While the fundamental ideas of COM have been the picture of parsimony, both the use and the implementation of COM objects in programming languages such as C++ have been downright painful. Just as MTS makes it easier to write server-side components, COM+ offers features that make it easier to build standard components, including those destined to run in MTS. The improvements of COM+ over COM lie in two major areas: it provides additional services, and it provides default implementations of standard COM services. A few of the new services Microsoft is planning to implement in COM+ include transactions, interception, inheritance, data binding, automatic persistence, dynamic load balancing, and a simplified security model. Some of these areas overlap functionality offered today by MTS. Eventually, many of the services found today in MTS will be rolled into COM+.

Two of the more useful features are *interception* and *inheritance.* Interception is an interesting service that grew out of research into a technology called *HookOLE.* HookOLE, which never graduated from the alpha stage, could be used to trap COM method calls for the purpose of debugging or modifying the behavior of a COM object, similar to the idea of hooking a window procedure. Interception is a more general implementation of this extensibility mechanism, whereby components can hook into COM method calls, allowing them to provide additional services or supplant a method call with another implementation altogether. Extensions to COM+ could be built as special components called interceptors that would be able to trap events related to object instantiation, method calls, errors, and object destruction.

507

COM has often been criticized in the trade press for its lack of inheritance support. Although COM has always supported a variety of reuse mechanisms such as aggregation and containment, inheritance was not among them. COM+ will address this weakness by supporting true implementation inheritance for in-process components. This support will be particularly useful for developing standard frameworks such as the Microsoft Foundation Class (MFC) library that could provide functionality inherited by a client process. Perhaps someday the MFC will be implemented as an in-process COM+ component, which may mean we will finally be able to stop wading through trillions of lines of MFC source code!

The COM+ Run Time

COM+ will also improve on COM by providing default implementations of standard COM interfaces such as *IUnknown, IClassFactory, IDispatch, IConnection-PointContainer, IConnectionPoint, IProvideClassInfo*, and *IProvideErrorInfo*. Remember our friends *DllGetClassObject, DllCanUnloadNow, DllRegisterServer*, and *DllUnregisterServer*? COM+ gives you these as well. Even COM-style reference counting is a thing of the past. Of course, reference counting still exists, but COM+ will handle it for you. All this is possible without sacrificing interoperability between COM+ and existing COM objects because at its core COM+ is COM.

Perhaps you are thinking that implementing *IUnknown, IClassFactory*, and even *IDispatch* isn't so difficult when you understand the concepts and some sample code is available. True, but remember the implementation of *IConnection-PointContainer* and *IConnectionPoint* covered in Chapter 6, "Connection Points and Type Information." You'd have to be a braver programmer than either of us to volunteer to implement this pair of interfaces. We hope that by providing one implementation of standard COM interfaces, COM+ will bring a certain degree of uniformity to COM-based components. Imagine a developer who implements *IConnectionPointContainer* without a complete understanding of the semantics of that interface. Such a flawed implementation would definitely cause problems for a client program written in Visual Basic or Java. By writing a run-time DLL for COM+ that provides standard implementations of these interfaces used by all components, COM+ hopes to overcome these types of difficulties. Of course, developers will always be able to override the COM+ run time by providing their own implementations of these standard interfaces.

COM developers tend to spend too much of their time writing housekeeping code. It has been estimated that as much as 30 percent of the effort of building a COM-based component is expended on writing housekeeping code. COM+ handles this chore automatically, leaving the developer freer to concentrate on the business problem at hand. The developers of COM+ hope that this will bring the ideas originating in COM to an even wider audience, which is important if COM is to fulfill its goal of becoming the component object technology through which future services will be offered. Already, most new operating system services are offered through COM—Internet Explorer, OLE Transactions, DirectX, OLE DB, Active Directory Services Interface (ADSI), MTS, ActiveX Data Objects (ADO), ActiveX scripting, ActiveX controls, and ActiveX documents, to name but a few.

Writing COM objects in C++ may be difficult today, but writing COM objects in Visual Basic and Java couldn't be much easier. These languages already provide default implementations of the standard COM interfaces. Bet you've never seen a Visual Basic programmer struggling over the implementation of *IDispatch*! COM+ will aim to offer C++ developers some of the features that Visual Basic and Java programmers have enjoyed for some time. Visual Basic and Java programmers will probably not notice any major changes when COM+ becomes available. The changes will be primarily internal, as the developers of Visual Basic and the Java VM at Microsoft will be able to replace their hard-written code with standard COM+ implementations. COM+ will be advantageous for all developers because many interoperability issues facing today's component developer should disappear once standard COM+ run-time services are used in all development environments.

COM+ is also being designed to address cracks that have appeared in the language-neutral position held by its predecessor. Recall that COM claims to be a language-independent binary standard for components. Today, however, there are many issues relating to interoperability between C++, Java, Visual Basic, VBScript, and so on. Each of these languages has certain peculiarities regarding the way it uses and builds COM-based components. For example, a component built in C++ will not be accessible to a VBScript developer unless that component implements the *IDispatch* interface, because VBScript does not currently support custom v-table interfaces. COM+ will provide services that make a component written in any language automatically accessible to all other languages supporting COM+. In the case of the C++ component that does not implement *IDispatch*, COM+ will transparently implement *IDispatch* for the component and then map Automation-based calls from the VBScript program to the v-table methods of the C++ component.

Another major problem facing developers attempting to reuse COM-based components built in different languages is the different set of types supported by each language. For example, a Visual Basic *Integer* is identical to a C++ *short*, and a C++ *int* is identical to a Visual Basic *Long*. While COM might claim to be language-neutral, it doesn't fully deliver unless a standard set of types, and their memory representation, on which all languages can agree is defined. Automation, a fundamental COM service (covered in Chapter 5,

"Automation and Component Categories") takes a stab at defining a common set of types. COM+ adopts and extends the Automation types, making them a formal part of the COM+ specification that all COM+ compliant languages will need to support. The COM+ data types are shown in the following table.

COM+ Type	Size (Bits)
BOOLEAN	8
BSTR	32
BYTE	8
char	16
ClassRef (any class type)	32
COM interface pointer	32
const (any native type)	
CURRENCY	64
DATE	64
double	64
float	32
HRESULT	32
int	32
Java array (any native type)	
long	64
pointer (any native type)	32
reference counted object reference	32
SAFEARRAY	
short	16
sized array	32
unsigned char	8
unsigned int	32
unsigned long	64
unsigned short	16
GUID	128
VARIANT	128
void	0

Whereas COM functionality has been built into Java and Visual Basic in a relatively clean fashion without the addition of special language keywords,

COM+ functionality is offered to C++ programmers in the form of a bastardized programming language we like to call COM++. While some developers might scoff at the idea of modifying a standardized programming language, programming languages are not quite as sacrosanct as they once were. Portability was once considered the major advantage of a standardized programming language. However, once you stir in the Win32 API, MFC, or Active Template Library (ATL), few programs are even the slightest bit portable. If there is no longer a point to being a language purist, there is no reason we should not embrace the language modifications made in COM++ as pragmatic solutions for building components. The following code is a sample component, similar to one you might be writing in the COM++ programming language just a short time from now. Notice that *IUnknown*, *IClassFactory*, and *DllGetClassObject* are nowhere to be found.

```
#import "ISum.tlb"

coclass CSum : implements ISum
{
attributes:
    transaction = "supported";
    threading = "rental";
    state = "stateless";

    HRESULT Sum(int x, int y, int* retval)
    {
        *retval = x + y;
        return S_OK;
    }
};
```

Remote Procedure Calls

Microsoft's Remote Procedure Call (RPC) service constituted the first complete implementation of distributed processing available on the Microsoft Windows platform. Using RPC, an application could, for the first time, call a function that would execute on another computer connected over a network. This appendix describes a computation-intensive application that uses RPC to compute prime numbers; the calculations required to compute prime numbers are distributed across a network of computers. Understanding this example will bring you to the root of the client/server technology and shed light on the transition from RPC to DCOM.

Applications that use RPC are usually divided into two parts: a client and a server. The client always makes requests of the server; the server's only purpose is to provide the client with whatever information it requests. Such servers are usually classified by the type of resource they offer. For instance, we are all familiar with file servers, print servers, and communications servers. In Windows, it is now possible for a server to share not only its peripherals—such as hard disk space, printers, and modems—but also its computational horsepower.

The advent of RPC within the distributed computing environment enabled work to be distributed throughout the system, thus gaining the advantages of connectivity and efficiency. Using RPC, idle computers on the network became *compute servers*. Compute servers do not have to be locked in a room with the file server because any computer running Windows that is on the network can be considered a compute server. By developing RPC, Microsoft addressed the complexity and reliability problems perceived in client/server architecture as opposed to the centralized system heaven.

The Design and Purpose of RPC

RPC was designed to alleviate the difficulties commonly associated with building distributed applications. These difficulties consist of all the possible errors that can occur in applications that communicate over a network. When an application sends a message to another application, such as a Dynamic Data Exchange (DDE) message, the sending application can be reasonably sure that the other application will receive it. However, even with DDE, a lot of programming effort is focused on error handling. What if an application engaged in the conversation does not follow the DDE protocol properly? What if it crashes? What if it sends garbage? These types of problems tend to increase exponentially when you are communicating over a network. As anyone who has ever done low-level network programming knows, the number of errors that can occur is mind-boggling. Someone can trip over the network cable, the server can crash, or an application can fail to acknowledge a message. When you're working with network communications, the following rule of thumb still applies: If it can go wrong, it will.

RPC addresses these problems by providing a high-level procedural interface to the network. Until recently, all distributed computing has been centered on the problem of I/O. Centralized systems, however, were not built on the basis of I/O but rather on a procedural foundation. RPC resolved this discrepancy by providing a facility to build distributed systems based on the procedural model of its centralized ancestors. The goal of RPC in action is to be as unobtrusive as possible. The RPC model attempts to adhere closely to the Local Procedure Call (LPC) model. When RPC is implemented correctly, a programmer would not know whether a function executed remotely or locally. This transparency is made possible by a special language originally designed for RPC and later commandeered by COM, the Interface Definition Language (IDL).

Interface Definition Language

In RPC, as in COM, IDL defines the interface between the client and the server, which lends a unique vantage point to IDL in that all communications between the client and the server pass through its interface. Many programmers have worked on a project involving communications in which different applications were written by different teams. The problem is to define a common interface to which both sides will adhere. Each side usually ends up blaming the other for not following the specifications. With IDL, however, this process is automated. When the interface has been defined with IDL, both sides must adhere to it or they will not be able to compile their programs.

Here's how IDL works. You specify the name, version, and universally unique identifier (UUID) of the interface in the definition file. The UUID is a special number that ensures that RPCs are made to the correct server. Also included in the interface definition are special prototypes for all the exported functions that the client might call. All this data is saved in a file that ends with an .idl extension. An interface definition file is somewhat analogous to a module definition file (.def) used for a dynamically-linked library (DLL). The Microsoft IDL (MIDL) compiler is used to compile the source IDL file.

Technically speaking, MIDL is a translator and not a compiler—it does not produce machine code but instead translates IDL code into C. The C code generated by MIDL forms the remote procedure stubs in both the client and the server. Thus, the master IDL file produces code that is compiled and linked by both sides of the distributed application. If one side does not follow the specified interface, the compile and the link will fail. You might find it interesting to examine the code produced by the MIDL compiler to see what the compiler is actually doing in there. In addition to the IDL file, the Application Configuration File (ACF) is an optional file that the MIDL compiler uses when translating the IDL file. In the ACF file, a programmer can declare the type of binding handles used, as well as server optional parameters.

Binding

A programmer uses the IDL to define the interface between the client and the server. The client connects to the server via a *binding* mechanism. A binding is the logical connection between the client and the server. Binding is a type of linking used for RPCs. Of the two standard types of linking, static and dynamic, binding is most similar to the latter. When a programmer uses dynamic linking, the address of the function called is resolved at run time. Using the binding mechanism in RPC is somewhat different from dynamic linking in that the procedure being called is located on a different computer. Therefore, no correct address for the function can ever be determined by the client because the function called is in the server's address space. Only the server knows the actual address of the function called by the client. Thus, the client never actually calls the remote procedure but rather asks the server to do so on the client's behalf. If you keep in mind that all communication is inherently I/O, it becomes obvious that it is impossible for the client to actually execute a jump to an address located on the server.

Types of Binding

There are two types of binding available to RPC applications: *manual* and *automatic*. The manual binding method is more complex than automatic binding, and it requires the programmer to create and maintain the binding manually. This method, however, affords the programmer more control of the binding and the RPCs made. And since RPC applications are inherently complex, the manual binding method will probably be used for most RPC applications.

When programmers use automatic binding, the MIDL compiler generates all the code to create and maintain the binding. This code generation makes the programmer's job much easier, but the cost is less control. Automatic binding is usually restricted to general applications that do not care which server they bind to. For example, an application that wants to get the time from a remote server is a good candidate for automatic binding.

The RPC Charade

When the client calls the remote procedure, the code usually looks exactly the same as if it were written for an LPC. What happens, however, is radically different. When the RPC is executed, the client jumps to the client stub generated by the MIDL compiler. The stub packages all the function parameters into a complex data structure in Network Data Representation (NDR) format. This structure is transmitted over the network to the server, where it is unpacked by the server stub and delivered to the remote procedure as regular function parameters. Because the client stub has the same name as the remote procedure, this whole procedure is transparent to the programmer. All things considered, RPC is a powerful tool for communication and distribution.

Handles

Two main types of handles are managed by an RPC application: *binding handles* and *context handles*. Binding handles contain information about the binding between the client and server; context handles maintain state information.

Binding Handles

A client initiates the binding process by calling several RPC run-time functions. If everything goes smoothly (a valid server is found), the client receives a binding handle. A binding handle is an opaque data structure that is used by the client when it makes RPCs and is always the first parameter passed to a remote procedure. There are two methods of passing binding handles in an RPC application: *implicit* and *explicit*.

Implicit binding handles are easier to use than explicit binding handles because the code to pass implicit binding handles is generated by the MIDL compiler. When programmers use implicit binding handles, the binding handle is declared as a global variable so that the C code generated by the MIDL compiler can package it for transmission to the remote procedure's stub. All binding handles are eventually converted to explicit binding handles; the only difference is that the programmer is not concerned with the details.

Explicit binding handles are passed explicitly by the programmer as the first parameter to every RPC made, affording the programmer more control at the cost of extra complexity. With explicit binding handles, a programmer can manage simultaneous connections to multiple servers. The RPC application presented later in this appendix uses explicit binding handles. Microsoft RPC also allows programmers to define their own structures for use as binding handles. These handles can associate data unique to each binding for the application's use, similar to the ability to store application-defined data in a window handle.

Context Handles

Context handles are special handles created and returned by the server. Context handles store information about the state of a particular server. In our example RPC application, context handles are used to determine when a client goes off line. If a client terminates, a special callback function known as a context handle *rundown routine* is executed on the server to notify the server that the client has terminated. The server can determine which client terminated by using the value stored in the context handle passed to the rundown routine.

Subtle Differences Between RPC and LPC

Although RPC adheres closely to the LPC model, there are some subtle differences. The main differences involve passing variables.

Global Variables

Because the client and the server are two different executable programs, they cannot share global variables. If a remote procedure attempts to access one of the client's global variables, the linker will report an unresolved external. The solution is to pass the global variable as a function parameter to the remote procedure.

Passing Pointers

Under the LPC model, the most efficient way to pass a string is often to pass a pointer to that string. Passing a pointer is efficient because the function called can use the pointer to access the string directly. Using RPC, however, it is impossible to pass a pointer. When you pass a pointer to a remote procedure, that pointer is valid only on the client. If the server were to receive that pointer and attempt to access the string with it, a general protection fault would probably result because the pointer contained a valid memory address for the client but not the server. To avoid this problem, when the client passes a pointer, the client stub generated by the MIDL compiler actually transmits the entire string to the server stub. The server stub then copies the string into memory allocated on the server. Last the server stub assigns the pointer a new value that points to the correct memory location of the string on the server. Most C programmers know that the most efficient way to pass information is via a pointer. With RPC this is not true, however, because no matter what method of passing you choose, the data eventually will be passed verbatim over the network. Thus, all distributed RPC applications must be designed to minimize the amount of network traffic they generate. To accomplish this optimization, RPC applications can transmit three basic categories of pointers: *reference, unique,* and *full.*

Reference Pointers

Reference pointers are the most efficient but allow you the least power in manipulating the pointer. A reference pointer is similar to a reference in C++. A reference pointer is not *NULL*—it points to valid data, and it does not change its value. It is like a constant pointer to a specific address in memory. In addition, a reference is not allowed to cause aliasing, which means that a reference pointer is the only way to access the block of memory it is pointing to. Using a reference pointer allows the compiler to perform significant optimizations on the data transfer and on the pointer emulation mechanism.

Unique Pointers

Unique pointers are less efficient than reference pointers but allow you more flexibility. A unique pointer can be *NULL*, and it can change its memory address on the fly. Also, a unique pointer cannot be aliased.

Full Pointers

A full pointer is the least efficient of the three pointer types, but it does allow you the most flexibility in specifying what your pointer can do. A full pointer can be *NULL*, and it can change its memory address. In addition, a full pointer can be aliased. A full pointer by any other name is still a valid pointer. Using a full pointer does not allow the compiler to make any assumptions about the pointer and about memory referenced by this pointer. The memory can be accessed at any time and by any pointer. Full pointers are most useful for distributing existing code using RPC. This way, you can get your application up and running in the shortest time possible and then go back later and improve it. Unfortunately, Microsoft RPC does not support full pointers.

The case of the string pointer was simple enough, but let's consider what happens if you attempt to pass a pointer to a doubly linked list to a remote procedure. In such cases, the code generated by the MIDL compiler is insufficient; it cannot know the exact structure of your linked list. Microsoft RPC provides the solution to this problem in the form of user-defined marshaling and unmarshaling routines. In these cases, the programmer supplies special callback functions executed by the client and server stubs that transfer all or part of the special memory structure into a standard array, which MIDL can transmit to and from the server. On the server, the unmarshaling routine is called to convert the array back to the structure expected by the remote procedure.

Multithreading and Structured Exception Handling

Windows includes support for multithreading, which gives an application the capability to create multiple threads of execution in one process via the *Create-Thread* function. Combining multithreading with RPC results in a particularly potent mixture. Multithreading gives RPC servers the ability to support multiple clients and allows clients to make RPCs to multiple servers while performing some computations locally.

Multithreading is a double-edged sword. Although it makes many things possible with RPC, it can cause some subtle problems related to concurrency. Use of global variables from a thread is problematic; the variables must be embedded within a critical section, as mentioned in Chapter 4, "Threading Models and Apartments." Otherwise, another thread might be able to access it simultaneously, causing the variable to become corrupted. Such subtle bugs can be very difficult to find because they are hard to reproduce. An application might work most of the time, but occasionally there could be an unexplained problem. Therefore, it is important to minimize the number of global variables used and to embed code that accesses global variables within critical sections.

Structured Exception Handling (SEH) is a sophisticated type of error handling available in Windows. SEH is intended to simplify the enormous task of error handling in this complex operating system. SEH is implemented via three C keywords: *try, except,* and *finally*. These keywords are usually embedded in a set of high-level macros, as is the case with RPC. With RPC, exception handling is not an option; it is a must. Exception handling with RPC provides a high-level error handling mechanism to make the awesome task of network error handling manageable.

The Prime Application

The RPC Prime application uses most of the RPC features described so far in this appendix to compute prime numbers. Prime number computation might not seem to be the pinnacle of all applications, but it's an excellent vehicle for demonstrating the power of RPC. In this example, the prime number computations are widgets for any computationally intensive operation you might need to perform.

The client side of the Prime application has been designed so that it can operate whether or not a Prime server is available. When executed, the application creates a thread for each designated Prime server. Each thread then attempts to bind to its designated Prime server. The client sends work to all available Prime servers with which it bound successfully. Each thread that was unsuccessful in its attempt to bind to the server waits a predetermined period of time before trying to rebind. In addition, the client creates one local thread that computes prime numbers on the client's computer. The source code for the Prime client is contained in the primec.c source file on the companion CD.

To ensure that work is not replicated between the threads, the client keeps one global variable, *NextNumber*, that contains the value of the next number to be tested for prime status. Each thread increments this number within the context of a critical section to ensure that no other thread is accessing it simultaneously. When the increment is complete, the thread copies the number to a local variable, *temp*, and exits the critical section. The *temp* variable can now be used safely because it is local to the thread, so no other thread can modify it. The *NextNumber* variable can now be accessed by another thread that will access the already incremented value of *NextNumber*, ensuring that no two threads will compute the same number. This technique is referred to as the divide-and-conquer method and is shown in the following code:

```
EnterCriticalSection(&GlobalCriticalSection);
if((temp = ++NextNumber) >= ULONG_MAX)
    break;
LeaveCriticalSection(&GlobalCriticalSection);
```

The client has several options that can be set. Type *PRIMEC /?* at a command prompt for a list of these features. The client is executed by typing this command:

```
PRIMEC -N \\FIRST_SERVER_NAME;\\SECOND_SERVER_NAME;...
```

Client Initialization

After parsing the command-line arguments, the client calls the *RpcStringBindingCompose* function, shown in the following code, to create a *string binding* for each server it intends to bind with. A string binding is a string of characters that defines all the attributes for the binding between the client and the server:

```
status = RpcStringBindingCompose(pszUuid,
    pszProtocolSequence, pszNetworkAddress[i],
    pszEndpoint[i], pszOptions, &pszStringBinding[i]);
```

The *RpcStringBindingCompose* function is a convenience function that combines all the pieces of a string binding together and returns the combined string in a character array allocated by the function. This memory is later freed by a call to the *RpcStringFree* function.

As you can see from the preceding example, a string binding consists of the UUID, protocol sequence, network address, endpoint, and options. The user, through the use of command-line arguments, can modify all the parameters used to create the string binding. The UUID specifies an optional number used for identification purposes. This UUID allows clients and servers to distinguish different objects from one another. In this example, the field is set to *NULL* by default. The protocol sequence specifies the low-level network protocol to be used for the network communication. There are several network protocols currently supported. This example uses the named pipes (*ncacn_np*) protocol native to Microsoft Windows NT. The currently supported network protocols are as follows:

Protocol Sequence	Description
ncacn_np	Named pipes
ncacn_ip_tcp	Internet address
ncacn_dnet_nsp	DECNet phase IV
ncacn_osi_dna	DECNet phase V
ncadg_ip_udp	Internet address
ncacn_nb	NetBIOS
ncacn_nb_nb	NetBEUI
ncacn_spx	SPX
ncacn_mq	Microsoft Message Queue Server
ncacn_http	Microsoft IIS as HTTP proxy
ncacn_at_dsp	AppleTalk DSP
ncacn_vns_spp	Vines SPP transport
ncadg_ipx	IPX
ncalrpc	Local RPC

The network address is the address of the server with which the client wants to bind. When the named pipes protocol sequence is used, the network address is described in the form *servername*, where *servername* is the name of the server computer. The type of valid network address is dependent on the protocol sequence used. Different protocol sequences have different methods of defining network addresses.

The endpoint used to create the binding specifies the network endpoint at which the server application is listening. The endpoint is like a street address to a particular server application, and the network address is more like knowing the city in which your server lives. Similarly, to a network address the type of endpoint used reflects the protocol sequence being used. When the named pipes protocol sequence is used, the valid endpoint specifies the pipe that the server is listening to. A valid endpoint for the named pipes protocol sequence is as follows: *pipe\pipename*, where *pipename* is an application-defined name for the pipe used for low-level network communications between the client and the server.

The goal of RPC is to provide a high-level interface to networks, allowing an RPC to travel transparently over any type of available transport. The *options* parameter is a miscellaneous string to be used for whatever special settings are appropriate for a particular protocol sequence. In the case of the named pipes protocol sequence, the only available option is *security = true*. This setting turns on the security mechanisms for the RPC. For other network protocols, valid options will vary.

The *RpcStringBindingCompose* function is used to combine the parts of a string that bind together. The purpose of binding a string is to specify all the parameters for the protocol sequence (network protocol) used. The client then transforms each string binding into the actual binary binding using the *RpcBindingFromStringBinding* function, as shown here:

```
status = RpcBindingFromStringBinding(pszStringBinding[i],
    &BindingHandle[i]);
```

You can now think of the binding as a magic cookie, or handle, with which you can make RPCs. Next the client creates a thread to manage each server using the *CreateThread* function, as shown here:

```
hthread_remote[count - 1] = CreateThread(NULL, 0,
    (LPTHREAD_START_ROUTINE)thread_remote, (LPVOID)count, 0,
    &lpIDThread[count - 1]);
```

Each thread is passed a number that designates a server that the thread is responsible for. In addition, the client initializes a critical section object for use later, when accessing global variables from the threads, as shown in the following example:

```
InitializeCriticalSection(&GlobalCriticalSection);
```

The client calls the *GetComputerName* function so that it can pass the returned string to the server. The server uses this string for display purposes so that the user can see which client is making RPCs, as shown here:

```
GetComputerName(computer_name_buffer,
    &Max_ComputerName_Length);
```

After the client has obtained a valid binding to each server, it attempts to initialize these servers on a logical level. To do so, it calls a special remote procedure available on each Prime server: *InitializePrimeServer*. This function is designed to notify the server that a client is planning to make requests. As you can see in the following example, the *InitializePrimeServer* function accepts a binding handle, context handle, and the name of the computer retrieved by the *GetComputerName* function:

```
RpcTryExcept
    {
    PrimeServerHandle[iserver] = InitializePrimeServer(
        BindingHandle[iserver],
        &phContext[iserver], computer_name_buffer);
    IsActiveServer[iserver] = TRUE;
    }
RpcExcept(1)
    {
    value = TRUE;
    IsActiveServer[iserver] = FALSE;
    }
RpcEndExcept
```

Client Computation

After the client initialization is completed, prime number computation begins. The *thread_local* function computes prime numbers locally on the client computer via the *IsPrime* function, as shown here:

```
if(IsPrime(temp - 1) != 0)
```

The *thread_remote* function makes an RPC to determine whether a number is prime by using the *RemoteIsPrime* function. In this case, because *RemoteIsPrime* is an RPC, it is embedded in an exception handler, as shown on the following page.

```
RpcTryExcept
    {
    if(RemoteIsPrime(BindingHandle[count-1],
        PrimeServerHandle[count-1], temp - 1) != 0)
        {
        /* Code displays prime number. */
        }
    }
RpcExcept(1)
    {
    /* If exception occurred, respond gracefully. */
    }
RpcEndExcept
```

If an exception occurs, the client attempts to recognize the error and provides an error message on the console display. If the exception that occurred indicates that the server is off line, the client thread waits a specified period of time before attempting to rebind to that server. When the client terminates normally, via the Esc key, a special RPC, *TerminatePrimeServer*, is made to notify the server of the client's plans to exit, as shown in the following code. The server can then take action to free memory and update its display to reflect the new status.

```
TerminatePrimeServer(BindingHandle[iserver],
    PrimeServerHandle[iserver]);
```

The Prime Server

The Prime server has an important, if unrewarding, job. It must register its interface and listen for client requests. The source code for the Prime server module is located in the files primes.c and primep.c on the companion CD. The *RpcServerUseProtseqEp* function notifies the RPC run-time module to register a protocol sequence, an endpoint, and a security attribute on which to accept RPCs. This call designates the station the server listens to so that it can hear the client's cries for help, as shown in the following code:

```
status = RpcServerUseProtseqEp(pszProtocolSequence,
    cMaxCalls, pszEndpoint, pszSecurity);
```

The *RpcServerRegisterIf* function registers the server's interface. It accepts the handle to the interface being registered and two optional management parameters (not used in this example). This interface is defined in the Prime IDL file as shown here:

```
status = RpcServerRegisterIf(prime_v1_0_s_ifspec, NULL,
    NULL);
```

The last RPC run-time function called by the Prime server begins listening for client requests. In this example, the *RpcServerListen* function never returns:

```
status = RpcServerListen(cMinCalls, cMaxCalls, fDontWait);
```

Until a client initiates an RPC, the server can do nothing. To avoid this waste of resources, we create a special thread for the server to perform maintenance tasks even when the server is not in use. This thread is created with the *CREATE_SUSPENDED* flag so that it can be subsequently modified with the *THREAD_PRIORITY_LOWEST* flag. This technique ensures that the maintenance thread consumes the least amount of CPU cycles possible when it is restarted using the *ResumeThread* function. In the following example, the maintenance thread provides some prime number statistics and checks to see whether the Esc key was pressed:

```
hthread_server = CreateThread(NULL, 0,
    (LPTHREAD_START_ROUTINE)thread_server, NULL,
    CREATE_SUSPENDED, &lpIDThread);
SetThreadPriority(hthread_server, THREAD_PRIORITY_LOWEST);
ResumeThread(hthread_server);
```

Context Rundown

The Prime server also includes a special context rundown routine, which can be seen in the primep.c file on the companion CD. As you might recall, the client calls the *TerminatePrimeServer* function when the user presses the Esc key. What happens if the client terminates abnormally? Perhaps the client crashed, the power went out, or the computer failed. In any case, the server must be fault-tolerant and not allow such a possibility to impair its performance for other clients that might still be on line. Whatever the *TerminatePrimeServer* function would have done, the server needs to do. The designers of RPC took this situation into account and came up with the special rundown facility. This rundown is a user-defined function that is called automatically by the RPC at run time whenever the client terminates. If the client terminates normally by calling the *TerminatePrimeServer* function, the rundown routine is skipped. However, if the client terminates abnormally, the rundown routine is called to perform the necessary cleanup.

The Prime interface definition file specifies this interface between the client and the server. The prime interface is defined in the prime.idl file. The UUID, version number, and pointer type used are defined in the following code for the interface header. Following that is the actual interface definition consisting of the function prototypes with special IDL flags.

```
[ uuid (906B0CE0-C70B-1067-B317-00DD010662DA),
  version(1.0),
  pointer_default(unique) ]
interface prime
    {
    /* Function definitions */
    }
```

Debugging RPC Applications

Debugging distributed RPC applications is slightly different from debugging conventional applications because of the added factor of the network. For this reason, it is best to separate the server initialization code from the remote procedures themselves. The separation is done in the Prime RPC application using the primes.c and primep.c source files. These files are linked to produce the server application, but during the debugging stage, their separation can be invaluable. By dividing the server application into two parts, you give yourself the option of linking the remote procedures directly with the client application to produce one standard application. In this manner, you can test the application as a whole without worrying about the network. Once your program works properly, you can divide it into a client and server to test the distribution factor.

The Advantage of Distributed Prime Calculations

After all the effort we have made to compute prime numbers, it's a shame there isn't more of a market for them. By now, we could probably package and sell them by the metric ton. What advantage is there to computing prime numbers in a distributed manner across a network, compared to the conventional way on one computer? The Prime application provides some simple timer routines to let you know how long the computations are taking. The following table should give you an idea of the practicality of RPCs. Here you can see that when the number of computations is relatively small (1 to 1000), distributing an application can cause the performance to worsen because the overhead of RPC is quite large. Although RPC makes programming of a distributed application much easier, the application is relatively slow. But under some circumstances, much better performance can be achieved using RPC. If the number of calculations required becomes very large (10,000,000 and up), the overhead of RPC becomes insignificant. When we clocked these times, the improvement with the distributed prime computations approached an order of 3.5 times faster with four computers than with only one. A well-written application would make RPCs only when the possible gain outweighed the overhead.

Range	1 Computer (sec.)	4 Computers (sec.)	Ratio
1–1000	35	40	0.88
100,000–101,000	40	42	0.95
1,000,000–1,001,000	100	61	1.64
10,000,000–10,001,000	581	170	3.42

Bibliography

Specifications

Component Object Model Specification, version 0.9, October 1995. Microsoft Corporation, http://www.microsoft.com/oledev/olecom/title.htm.

DCE 1.1: Remote Procedure Call Open Group CAE Specification, Document Number C706, August 1997. The Open Group, http://www.opengroup.org/pubs/catalog/c706.htm.

DCE 1.2.2: Introduction to OSF DCE, Open Group Product Documentation, F201, November 1997. The Open Group, http://www.opengroup.org/pubs/catalog/f201.htm.

Distributed Component Object Model Protocol, version 1.0, January 1998. Microsoft Corporation, http://www.microsoft.com/oledev/olecom/draft-brown-dcom-v1-spec-02.txt.

Books

Born, Guenter. *Inside the Registry for Microsoft Windows 95.* Redmond, Wash.: Microsoft Press, 1997.

Box, Don. *Essential COM.* Reading, Mass.: Addison-Wesley, 1998.

Brockschmidt, Kraig. *Inside OLE.* 2d ed. Redmond, Wash.: Microsoft Press, 1995.

Chan, Patrick, and Rosanna Lee. *The Java Class Libraries,* 2 vols. 2d ed. Reading, Mass.: Addison-Wesley, 1998.

Chappell, David. *Understanding ActiveX and OLE.* Redmond, Wash.: Microsoft Press, 1996.

Custer, Helen. *Inside the Windows NT File System.* Redmond, Wash.: Microsoft Press, 1994.

———. *Inside Windows NT.* Redmond, Wash.: Microsoft Press, 1993.

Davis, Ralph. *Windows NT Network Programming.* Reading, Mass.: Addison-Wesley, 1994.

Denning, Adam. *ActiveX Controls Inside Out.* 2d ed. Redmond, Wash.: Microsoft Press, 1997.

Eddon, Guy. *RPC for NT*. Lawrence, Kans.: R&D Publications, 1994.

Eddon, Guy, and Henry Eddon. *Active Visual Basic 5.0*. Redmond, Wash.: Microsoft Press, 1997.

Ellis, Margaret A., and Bjarne Stroustrup. *The Annotated C++ Reference Manual*. Reading, Mass.: Addison-Wesley, 1990.

Flanagan, David. *Java in a Nutshell*. 2d ed. Sebastopol, Calif.: O'Reilly, 1997.

Gamma, Erich, et al. *Design Patterns*. Reading, Mass.: Addison-Wesley, 1995.

Grimes, Richard. *Professional DCOM Programming*. Birmingham, UK.: WROX Press, 1997.

Kernighan, Brian W., and Dennis M. Ritchie. *The C Programming Language*. 2d ed. Englewood Cliffs, N.J.: Prentice Hall, 1988.

Knuth, Donald. *The Art of Computer Programming*. Vol. 1, *Fundamental Algorithms*. 3d ed. Reading, Mass.: Addison-Wesley, 1997.

Meyers, Scott. *Effective C++: 50 Specific Ways to Improve Your Programs and Designs*. 2d ed. Reading, Mass.: Addison-Wesley, 1998.

————. *More Effective C++: 35 New Ways to Improve Your Programs and Designs*. Reading, Mass.: Addison-Wesley, 1996.

Microsoft Corporation. *Automation Programmer's Reference*. Redmond, Wash.: Microsoft Press, 1997.

————. *OLE 2 Programmer's Reference*, 2 vols. Redmond, Wash.: Microsoft Press, 1994.

Richter, Jeffrey. *Advanced Windows*. 3d ed. Redmond, Wash.: Microsoft Press, 1997.

Rogerson, Dale. *Inside COM*. Redmond, Wash.: Microsoft Press, 1997.

Stroustrup, Bjarne. *The C++ Programming Language*. 3d ed. Reading, Mass.: Addison-Wesley, 1997.

————. *The Design and Evolution of C++*. Reading, Mass.: Addison-Wesley, 1994.

Tanenbaum, Andrew S. *Computer Networks*. 3d ed. Upper Saddle River, N.J.: Prentice Hall PTR, 1996.

————. *Distributed Operating Systems*. Englewood Cliffs, N.J.: Prentice Hall, 1995.

————. *Modern Operating Systems*. Englewood Cliffs, N.J.: Prentice Hall, 1992.

INDEX

Numbers in italics refer to figures, tables, or charts.

Guy Eddon

Although he maintains his original ambition to become a world-famous cello player, Guy has taken a sabbatical to learn about the wonderful world of software development. His first real project was a game, Danny's Rooms, written for the autistic son of his cello teacher. In 1992, Danny's Rooms won an award from the Johns Hopkins National Search for Computing to Assist Persons with Disabilities and was featured on the National Public Radio program *All Things Considered*. Guy's first article, about OS/2, was published in *Windows Developer's Journal*. He has also written for *Microsoft Systems Journal*, *Microsoft Interactive Developer*, and *IEEE Proceedings*. *RPC for NT*, his first book, was published in 1994 by R&D Publications and has since been translated into Japanese. In 1997, he coauthored *Active Visual Basic 5.0* with Henry Eddon for Microsoft Press. At different times, Guy has flown small airplanes, fermented grapes into wine, gone scuba diving, and traded securities. He recently bought his first car, a signal red 1972 Porsche 914. Guy also teaches Visual Basic, Java, and Win32 programming courses for Learning Tree International.

Henry Eddon

Henry's involvement with computers dates back to the IBM 1132 series at Haifa University. There he created the first computerized student admissions record, written in Fortran IV. He later graduated from Columbia University in Mathematics and moved from a Commodore SuperPET to a HERO 1 robot and later to an original IBM PC. In 1984, Henry and an ophthalmologist friend started AMOS, an insurance billing and patient appointment–scheduling program that achieved speed by bypassing MS-DOS to access video memory directly. Henry has earned a Master Mechanic license from the NIASE, written a 6800 Motorola assembler to enable programming of the HERO 1 robot in assembly language instead of machine code, and earned Certified Computing Professional status from the Institute for Certification of Computing Professionals. He is employed in the information services division of United Parcel Service and enjoys Dilbert cartoons.

The manuscript for this book was prepared and submitted to Microsoft Press in electronic form. Text files were prepared using Microsoft Word 97. Pages were composed by Microsoft Press using Adobe PageMaker 6.5 for Windows, with text in New Baskerville and display type in Helvetica bold. Composed pages were delivered to the printer as electronic pre-press files.

Cover Graphic Designer
Tim Girvin Design, Inc.

Cover Illustrator
Glenn Mitsui

Interior Graphic Designer
Pam Hidaka

Interior Graphic Artist
Michael Victor

Principal Compositor
Paul Vautier

Copy Editor/Principal Proofreader
Richard Carey

Indexer
Julie Kawabata

Strategic thinking
about applications for
Windows
and the Internet.

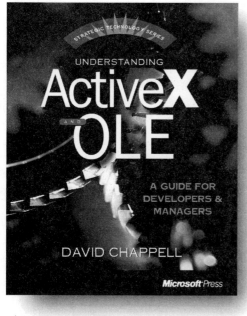

U.S.A.   **$22.95**
U.K.   £20.99
Canada $30.95
ISBN 1-57231-216-5

It's your job to make strategic development and design decisions about new applications, Windows®, the Internet, and how they all interact. To do your job even better, get UNDERSTANDING ACTIVEX™ AND OLE. It's a conceptual, language-independent technical introduction to all of the powerful ActiveX technologies—the Component Object Model (COM), ActiveX Controls, OLE technology, Internet applications, and more. With UNDERSTANDING ACTIVEX AND OLE, you'll gain a firm conceptual grounding without extraneous details or implementation specifics. You'll see the strategic significance of COM as the foundation for Microsoft's object technology. And you'll get a clear introduction to subjects such as the relationship among OLE, ActiveX, and COM; sharing files among objects with Structured Storage; using monikers to identify objects; and far more. This book is for every programming professional, whether you work in C++, Java, Visual Basic®, Visual Basic Script, or other environments. And it's equally useful for managers. In short, UNDERSTANDING ACTIVEX AND OLE is the efficient way to quickly get up to speed on a fundamental business technology.

IMPORTANT—READ CAREFULLY BEFORE OPENING SOFTWARE PACKET(S). By opening the sealed packet(s) containing the software, you indicate your acceptance of the following Microsoft License Agreement.

MICROSOFT LICENSE AGREEMENT

(Book Companion CD)

This is a legal agreement between you (either an individual or an entity) and Microsoft Corporation. By opening the sealed software packet(s) you are agreeing to be bound by the terms of this agreement. If you do not agree to the terms of this agreement, promptly return the unopened software packet(s) and any accompanying written materials to the place you obtained them for a full refund.

MICROSOFT SOFTWARE LICENSE

1. GRANT OF LICENSE. Microsoft grants to you the right to use one copy of the Microsoft software program included with this book (the "SOFTWARE") on a single terminal connected to a single computer. The SOFTWARE is in "use" on a computer when it is loaded into the temporary memory (i.e., RAM) or installed into the permanent memory (e.g., hard disk, CD-ROM, or other storage device) of that computer. You may not network the SOFTWARE or otherwise use it on more than one computer or computer terminal at the same time.

2. COPYRIGHT. The SOFTWARE is owned by Microsoft or its suppliers and is protected by United States copyright laws and international treaty provisions. Therefore, you must treat the SOFTWARE like any other copyrighted material (e.g., a book or musical recording) except that you may either (a) make one copy of the SOFTWARE solely for backup or archival purposes, or (b) transfer the SOFTWARE to a single hard disk provided you keep the original solely for backup or archival purposes. You may not copy the written materials accompanying the SOFTWARE.

3. OTHER RESTRICTIONS. You may not rent or lease the SOFTWARE, but you may transfer the SOFTWARE and accompanying written materials on a permanent basis provided you retain no copies and the recipient agrees to the terms of this Agreement. You may not reverse engineer, decompile, or disassemble the SOFTWARE. If the SOFTWARE is an update or has been updated, any transfer must include the most recent update and all prior versions.

4. DUAL MEDIA SOFTWARE. If the SOFTWARE package contains more than one kind of disk (3.5", 5.25", and CD-ROM), then you may use only the disks appropriate for your single-user computer. You may not use the other disks on another computer or loan, rent, lease, or transfer them to another user except as part of the permanent transfer (as provided above) of all SOFTWARE and written materials.

5. SAMPLE CODE. If the SOFTWARE includes Sample Code, then Microsoft grants you a royalty-free right to reproduce and distribute the sample code of the SOFTWARE provided that you: (a) distribute the sample code only in conjunction with and as a part of your software product; (b) do not use Microsoft's or its authors' names, logos, or trademarks to market your software product; (c) include the copyright notice that appears on the SOFTWARE on your product label and as a part of the sign-on message for your software product; and (d) agree to indemnify, hold harmless, and defend Microsoft and its authors from and against any claims or lawsuits, including attorneys' fees, that arise or result from the use or distribution of your software product.

DISCLAIMER OF WARRANTY

THE SOFTWARE (INCLUDING INSTRUCTIONS FOR ITS USE) IS PROVIDED "AS IS" WITHOUT WARRANTY OF ANY KIND. MICROSOFT FURTHER DISCLAIMS ALL IMPLIED WARRANTIES INCLUDING WITHOUT LIMITATION ANY IMPLIED WARRANTIES OF MERCHANTABILITY OR OF FITNESS FOR A PARTICULAR PURPOSE. THE ENTIRE RISK ARISING OUT OF THE USE OR PERFORMANCE OF THE SOFTWARE AND DOCUMENTATION REMAINS WITH YOU.

IN NO EVENT SHALL MICROSOFT, ITS AUTHORS, OR ANYONE ELSE INVOLVED IN THE CREATION, PRODUCTION, OR DELIVERY OF THE SOFTWARE BE LIABLE FOR ANY DAMAGES WHATSOEVER (INCLUDING, WITHOUT LIMITATION, DAMAGES FOR LOSS OF BUSINESS PROFITS, BUSINESS INTERRUPTION, LOSS OF BUSINESS INFORMATION, OR OTHER PECUNIARY LOSS) ARISING OUT OF THE USE OF OR INABILITY TO USE THE SOFTWARE OR DOCUMENTATION, EVEN IF MICROSOFT HAS BEEN ADVISED OF THE POSSIBILITY OF SUCH DAMAGES. BECAUSE SOME STATES/COUNTRIES DO NOT ALLOW THE EXCLUSION OR LIMITATION OF LIABILITY FOR CONSEQUENTIAL OR INCIDENTAL DAMAGES, THE ABOVE LIMITATION MAY NOT APPLY TO YOU.

U.S. GOVERNMENT RESTRICTED RIGHTS

The SOFTWARE and documentation are provided with RESTRICTED RIGHTS. Use, duplication, or disclosure by the Government is subject to restrictions as set forth in subparagraph (c)(1)(ii) of The Rights in Technical Data and Computer Software clause at DFARS 252.227-7013 or subparagraphs (c)(1) and (2) of the Commercial Computer Software — Restricted Rights 48 CFR 52.227-19, as applicable. Manufacturer is Microsoft Corporation, One Microsoft Way, Redmond, WA 98052-6399.

If you acquired this product in the United States, this Agreement is governed by the laws of the State of Washington.

Should you have any questions concerning this Agreement, or if you desire to contact Microsoft Press for any reason, please write: Microsoft Press, One Microsoft Way, Redmond, WA 98052-6399.

Register Today!

Return this
Inside Distributed COM
registration card for
a Microsoft Press® catalog

U.S. and Canada addresses only. Fill in information below and mail postage-free. Please mail only the bottom half of this page.

1-57231-849-X   *INSIDE DISTRIBUTED COM*   *Owner Registration Card*

_____

NAME

_____

INSTITUTION OR COMPANY NAME

_____

ADDRESS

_____

_____

CITY   STATE   ZIP

Microsoft® Press
Quality Computer Books

**For a free catalog of
Microsoft Press® products, call
1-800-MSPRESS**